Microsoft®

Microsoft®

OFFICE
2003 EDITIONS

The Microsoft Office Team

Resource Kit

PUBLISHED BY
Microsoft Press
A Division of Microsoft Corporation
One Microsoft Way
Redmond, Washington 98052-6399

Library of Congress Cataloging-in-Publication Data.
    Microsoft Office 2003 Editions Resource Kit / The Microsoft Office Team.
        p. cm.
    Includes index.
    ISBN 0-7356-1880-1
    1. Microsoft Office. 2. Business--Computer programs. I. Microsoft Office Team.

    HF5548.4.M525M52495   2003
    005.369--dc21   2003050972

Printed and bound in the United States of America.

1 2 3 4 5 6 7 8 9   QWT   8 7 6 5 4 3

Distributed in Canada by H.B. Fenn and Company Ltd.

A CIP catalogue record for this book is available from the British Library.

Microsoft Press books are available through booksellers and distributors worldwide. For further information about international editions, contact your local Microsoft Corporation office or contact Microsoft Press International directly at fax (425) 936-7329. Visit our Web site at www.microsoft.com/mspress. Send comments to *rkinput@microsoft.com*.

Acquisitions Editor: Martin DelRe
Project Editor: Maureen Williams Zimmerman

Body Part No. X09-71479

Contents at a Glance

iv   Contents

Contents

4	**Customizing Office 2003**	**37**

Part 4   Worldwide Deployment

13   Preparing for an Office Multilingual Deployment   301

Upgrading an Input Method Editor installation 367

Resources and related information. 368

Office 2003 MUI Pack Languages and Corresponding Locale Identifiers 368

15   Sample Office 2003 Multilingual Deployments   371

Deploy Office with One MUI Pack 372

Deploy Office with Multiple MUI Packs. 375

Deploy Different Language Configurations
to Different Groups of Office Users. 378

Choose the number of installation points to use 379

Create a transform for different groups of users 379

Modify Setup.ini to chain the MUI Packs 381

Deploying to your users 383

16   Maintaining an Office 2003 Multilingual Installation   385

Updating Language Settings in Office 386

Changing the installation language 386

Enabling additional editing languages 387

Resources and related information. 388

Removing Office Multilingual Resource Files 389

Sharing Multilingual Files Between Different Versions of Office 389

Sharing Office files across language versions 389

Sharing Access database files across language versions 390

Sharing Excel workbooks across language versions 393

Sharing FrontPage files across language versions 394

Exchanging Outlook messages across language versions. 396

Sharing Publisher files across language versions. 402

Sharing Word documents across language versions. 402

Resources and related information. 405

Distributing Multilingual User Interface Pack Updates. 405

17   Unicode Support in Office 2003 Editions   407

Unicode Support and Multilingual Office Documents 408

Understanding Unicode 408

Unicode Support in Outlook 2003 410

Resources and related information. 411

Printing and Displaying Unicode Text in Office 411

Compressing Office Files That Contain Unicode Text 412

Copying Multilingual Text in Different Formats in Office. 412

Multilingual text formatted as RTF, HTML, or Unicode. 412

Multilingual code page–based single-byte text 413

Troubleshooting Corrupt Office Text Results with Older Multilingual Files 413

Part 8   Appendixes

A   Toolbox   557

Acknowledgements

This book and its online version on the World Wide Web were produced by members of the Office Product Unit of Microsoft Corporation.

Project Lead

Randy Holbrook

Writers

Tami Amador, Michael L. Cook, Jennifer M. Hendrix, Samantha J.W. Robertson, Stacia Snapp

Lead Editor

Stanley K. McKenzie

Copy Editors

Ramona Gault, Olwen Moery, Diana Rain

Contributing Editor

Caroline Briggs

Program Managers

Paul C. Barr, C. Scott Walker

Designer

Kristin Lynn Bergsma

Production

Donalee Edwards, Kevin McDowell

Toolbox Contributors

Jay Alabraba, Jesse Bedford, Jim Bennett, Terri Cheff-Goldade, Vladimir Chepurnoi, Gordon Church, Derek Cicerone, Dan Costenaro, Lutz Gerhard, Kevin Grace, Steve Greenberg, Bill Hunter, Christophe Loisey, Rachel Miller, Stephan Mueller, Nithya Ramkumar, Janny Wong Rivers, Jon Sheppard, Vivek Srinivasan, Teruhisa Takeuchi, Ambrose Treacy, Brian Trenbeath, Sairaj Uddin, Jixin Wu

Part 1

Getting Started

Chapter 1

Office 2003 and the Office Resource Kit

The *Microsoft® Office 2003 Editions Resource Kit* is designed for administrators, information technology (IT) professionals, and support technicians who deploy and maintain Microsoft Office 2003 in their organizations. The Office Resource Kit features a collection of tools designed specifically to support the Microsoft Office System, as well as comprehensive chapters on such areas as deployment, security, messaging, and worldwide support.

For this latest edition, the Office Resource Kit tools have been updated to help you configure and manage the new features added to Office 2003 applications. Included also is information about settings for the new products to join the Microsoft Office System, Microsoft Office OneNote™ 2003 and Microsoft Office InfoPath™ 2003.

The *Microsoft Office 2003 Editions Resource Kit* is available both on the Web and as a book published by Microsoft Press®. The Web site includes all of the information provided with the book, plus new information about software updates, emerging technologies, and software management issues. The printed book is available through your local bookseller, online bookstores, or directly from the Microsoft Press Web site at *http://www.microsoft.com/mspress/*. Included with the book is a CD that contains Office Resource Kit tools, reference information, and supplementary documents.

Office 2003 Resource Kit Tools

For Microsoft Office 2003, the Microsoft Office 2003 Editions Resource Kit tools have been updated to help provide you with increased control over how you customize, configure, and deploy Office within your organization. If you have the Office 2003 Resource Kit CD, you can install the tools, samples, and support documents through one integrated Setup program.

A significant part of the Office Resource Kit is the ongoing support provided on the Office Resource Kit Web site. The Web site includes all of the information provided with the book, plus additional tools and articles on software updates, emerging technologies, and management strategies. Current versions of all tools and support files are provided in the Office 2003 Resource Kit Toolbox, along with links to administrative update files for any Office 2003 service releases offered at a later date.

Office 2003 Resource Kit Toolbox

The following table summarizes the tools that are installed when you run the Office Resource Kit Setup program. For information about specific tools, see Appendix A, "Toolbox," and the companion CD.

Tool name	Description
Answer Wizard Builder	Enables you to build your own Answer Wizard content that contains information specific to your organization.
CMW File Viewer	Enables you to view the changes that a configuration maintenance file (CMW file) makes to a user's computer.
Custom Installation Wizard	Allows you to create a unique Windows Installer transform (MST file) for every installation scenario you need, without altering the original Windows Installer package (MSI file).
Custom Maintenance Wizard	Enables you to change settings, installation states, and other options after Office has been initially deployed.
Customizable Alerts	Contains the Errormsg.xls workbook, which consists of lists of error messages for Office 2003 applications.
International Information	Contains updated reference files that provide information about international versions of Office 2003.
MST File Viewer	Enables you to view customizations that a transform (MST file) makes to a user's computer.
Office Information	Contains a variety of support files such as the product file list, comprehensive registry key list, and security certificates.

Tool name	Description
Office Profile Wizard	Helps you to create and save a default user profile, including standard locations for files and templates.
Office Removal Wizard	Lets you maintain a fine level of control over which files are removed from a user's system.
OPS File Viewer	Displays the contents of an Office profile settings file (OPS file) created by the Profile Wizard in a readable text format in Microsoft Notepad.
Package Definition Files	Files used by Microsoft Systems Management Server to install Office remotely.

Supplementary tools and information

The Office 2003 Resource Kit also includes a number of supplemental tools and support files that are copied to your computer during installation, but which must be installed separately before use. These tools are also available separately from the Toolbox on the Office Resource Kit companion CD. The following table summarizes the available tools.

Document file name	Description
HTML Help Workshop	Version 1.3 of the HTML Help Workshop can be used to create Help topics that provide information and assistance specific to your organization. To install, run Htmlhelp.exe from the \Program Files\ORKTools\ORK11\TOOLS\HTML Help Workshop folder on your computer.
Office Converter Pack	A collection of converters designed to help you migrate files from third-party products and earlier versions of Microsoft Office. To install, run Oconvpck.exe from the \Program Files\ORKTools\ORK11\TOOLS\Office Converter Pack folder on your computer.
Outlook Administrator Pack	Enables administrators to modify the default settings of the Microsoft Office Outlook® 2003 security features. To install, run Admpack.exe from the \Program Files\ORKTools\ORK11\TOOLS\Outlook Administrator Pack folder on your computer.
Office policy templates	Office policy templates (ADM files) are designed for use with the Microsoft Windows® Group Policy snap-in. They are installed in the \windows\inf directory on your computer.

Other Microsoft administration tools

Some of the services that were previously provided by Office Resource Kit tools are now available from other Microsoft sources.

Tool	Description
Microsoft Internet Explorer Administration Kit	The current version of the Internet Explorer Administration Kit is available for download from the Internet Explorer Web site at *http://www.microsoft.com/windows/ieak/*.
Group Policy snap-in	The Windows Group Policy snap-in provides full support for Office policy templates (ADM files). It is included with all versions of Microsoft Windows from Windows 2000 on. The Group Policy snap-in replaces the System Policy Editor provided with previous editions of the Office Resource Kit.

Office 2003 Resource Kit Documentation

The information in the *Microsoft Office 2003 Editions Resource Kit* has been updated to cover the latest changes in tools, deployment strategies, and administration techniques. You'll find broad coverage of new features, such as the many enhancements to Microsoft Office Outlook 2003, along with details on the more subtle changes that can affect your customizations. The information on security has been expanded to describe how you can help improve the reliability and protection of your systems, while the new Appendix B, "Office 2003 Resource Kit Reference" gives you quick access to information on settings, properties, and options.

A key part of the Office Resource Kit is the ongoing support provided on the Office Resource Kit Web site at *http://www.microsoft.com/office/ork/2003*. The Web site includes all of the information provided with the book, plus articles on software updates, deployment and support strategies, and emerging issues. Current versions of all tools and support files are provided in the Office Resource Kit Toolbox on the Web site, along with administrative update files for current and past versions of Office products.

If you've used previous versions of the Office Resource Kit, you'll find that the latest edition follows a familiar format, while calling out the new features and techniques for your attention. Documentation for the Microsoft Office 2003 Editions Resource Kit is organized into seven parts and two appendixes.

Part 1: Getting Started

Getting Started summarizes the tools, documentation, and other resources provided with the Office 2003 Resource Kit. You'll find tips on installing the Office Resource Kit, along with tables listing the tools and supplemental information. The section on documentation highlights some of the major changes in deployment, messaging, and other key areas of the product. Information about system requirements for the Office 2003 System is included, as well as addresses of articles on Microsoft licensing programs.

Security is a major theme in the Office 2003 Resource Kit, and you'll find new chapters that summarize the technical information and strategies designed to help you manage the security of your Office 2003 System. A final section catalogs other resources on the Microsoft Web site for administrators and information technology (IT) professionals who support Microsoft Office in their organizations.

Part 2: Deployment

The deployment chapters provide the core information you need to get Office 2003 up and running across your organization. This part includes broad coverage of the updated deployment tools, along with information about platform issues, customization, and distribution. You'll find tips and strategies for deploying Office in small or medium-sized organizations, as well as expanded information about Microsoft Windows technologies such as Group Policy.

New to the Office 2003 Resource Kit is the option to deploy from a copy of the compressed Office CD image and take advantage of a local installation source. When you install from a compressed CD image on the network, Setup automatically creates a cache of installation files on the local computer. The local cache provides improved resiliency for users to repair, reinstall, or update Office after the initial deployment. Full support and information is still provided for creating an uncompressed administrative installation point using the **/a** option.

After you create an installation source on the network (either an administrative installation point or a compressed image of the Office 2003 CD), you can make extensive customizations before you install Office on users' computers. The deployment chapters guide you through the customization process, and show you how you can control many aspects of the installation process itself, including how much users interact with Setup and whether Setup creates a local cache of installation files.

Part 3: Messaging

Microsoft Outlook has been extensively redesigned for Office 2003, and the Office Resource Kit provides information to help you configure and take advantage of the new features. The following list summarizes some of the key enhancements:

- Cached Exchange Mode is a new option that configures Outlook to use a local copy of users' mailboxes, allowing users more reliable access to their Outlook data whether they are connected to a network or working offline.

- A new Junk E-mail Filter replaces the rules used in previous versions of Outlook to filter mail. Messages that are caught by the filter are moved to the Junk E-mail folder where they can be viewed or deleted later.

- Outlook 2003 supports cryptographic features—such as digital signing and message encryption—to help provide security-enhanced e-mail messaging over the Internet or local intranet. You can customize features in your Outlook 2003 deployment to set cryptographic options appropriate for your organization.

- Information Rights Management (IRM), another new feature, helps users prevent sensitive e-mail messages and other Office 2003 content, such as documents and worksheets, from being forwarded, edited, or copied and pasted by unauthorized people.

- In Outlook 2003, Unicode® support has been expanded throughout the product. You can specify several options for managing how users experience Unicode in Outlook 2003, including specifying the format of automatically created PST files in Outlook.

- Through the use of a new feature called RPC over HTTP, you can configure user accounts in Outlook 2003 to connect to Microsoft Exchange Server 2003 over the Internet without the need to use virtual private network (VPN) connections.

Part 4: Worldwide Deployment

Microsoft Office 2003 provides tools that simplify deploying and supporting Office across language boundaries—including the Microsoft Office 2003 Multilingual User Interface (MUI) Pack, which gives organizations the option to configure the Office user interface in multiple languages. Deploying Microsoft Office 2003 with the MUI Pack is typically a straightforward process. You can easily include one or more MUI Packs with your Office deployment by using several methods, including chaining packages to the installation.

Outlook 2003 supports Unicode and provides full support for multilingual data. If you work in a multinational organization or share messages and items with people who use Outlook on systems that run in other languages, you can take advantage of Unicode to work with messages and items that are composed in different languages.

There are a variety of ways to deploy Microsoft Office 2003 in a multilingual environment. The Office Resource Kit describes several deployment scenarios, with step-by-step examples of how to customize and install Office in those situations. If your organization's deployment needs do not follow one of these examples exactly, you can often adapt the examples to customize your own multilingual deployment.

Part 5: Maintenance

After Microsoft Office 2003 has been deployed, you can modify users' configurations, lock down a particular configuration, or deploy service releases and product updates. The Office Resource Kit guides you through these processes by describing how to use the Custom Maintenance Wizard and other tools provided in the Office 2003 Resource Kit, as well as tools such as Group Policy provided with the Microsoft Windows operating system.

In a Microsoft Windows-based network, Group Policy settings help administrators control how users work with Microsoft Office 2003. Chapters in the Maintenance part explain how you can set policies to define and maintain a particular Office 2003 configuration on users' computers.

Other maintenance tasks discussed in the Office Resource Kit include using the automatic and manual Detect and Repair feature, managing crash reports with Windows Corporate Error Reporting, and distributing Office 2003 product updates.

Part 6: Collaboration Resources

Key among new collaboration resources is Information Rights Management (IRM), a feature of Microsoft Office 2003 designed to enhance collaboration methods and help restrict unauthorized access to the content of Microsoft Office Word 2003, Microsoft Office Excel 2003, Microsoft Office PowerPoint® 2003, and Outlook 2003 files. IRM uses encryption, permissions, licenses, Microsoft Active Directory® directory service, license revocation, and Microsoft Windows Rights Management Services for Windows Server 2003 (RMS) or Passport to help provide a rights-managed method of content collaboration among a well-defined and carefully managed group of individuals.

Also included in the Collaboration part is a summary of Microsoft Windows SharePoint™ Services 2.0, which can be used with Office 2003 to help users work together and share information. SharePoint sites provide a central repository for documents, information, and ideas, and they allow users to work interactively with these items and with each other.

Additional information about collaboration and Web services for Office 2003 is available on the Office Resource Kit Web site.

Part 7: Security

Security has been a major focus in the development of Office 2003, and this part addresses many of the security issues an administrator should consider when deploying or maintaining an Office configuration in an organization. You'll find information on security strategy planning and suggested ways you can help to limit exposure to attacks. Guidance is also provided on how to help manage the security of a deployed installation through security-related policies.

Examples and scenarios are designed to help you avoid many of the administrative and user-level security vulnerabilities that can be exposed by improper configuration of settings and user methods. A section on macro security provides a summary of many of the vulnerabilities that can be exposed by custom solutions your users may create to work with the Office 2003 System.

Appendixes

The Office 2003 Resource Kit tools have been updated to help you customize, configure, and deploy the Office 2003 System within your organization. With the *Microsoft Office 2003 Editions Resource Kit* companion CD, you can install the core tools and support documents through one integrated Setup program. The tools are also available for download from the Toolbox on the Office 2003 Resource Kit Web site.

Appendix B, "Office 2003 Resource Kit Reference" provides detailed information about the mechanics of the installation and maintenance processes. You can use Appendix B to look up definitions for Setup command-line options, properties, and settings. Appendix B also provides information about text files and tools used both during and after installation.

Documentation conventions in the Office Resource Kit

The following terms and text formats are used in the Office Resource Kit.

Convention	Meaning
Bold	Indicates the actual properties, commands, words, or characters that you type, view, or click in the user interface.
Italic	In procedures, command lines, or syntax, italic characters indicate a placeholder for information or parameters that you must provide. For example, if the procedure asks you to type a file name, you type the actual name of a file.
Path\File name	Indicates a Windows file system path or registry key—for example, the file Templates\Normal.dot. Unless otherwise indicated, you can use a mixture of uppercase and lowercase characters when you type paths and file names.
Monospace	Represents examples of code text.

Office 2003 Licensing and System Requirements

The Microsoft Office System is available in a range of editions, as well as individual programs, designed to let you build the right collection of applications to fit the needs of your organization. Complete information on the different editions of Microsoft Office is available on the Microsoft Office Web site at *http://www.microsoft.com/office/*.

Volume licensing programs

To acquire Microsoft Office, most organizations take advantage of Microsoft's volume licensing programs. Volume licensing offers low administration cost, easy license management, and great opportunities for keeping your software current through the Microsoft Software Assurance program. By acquiring a 2003 license, you are granted permission to legally copy and redistribute a particular edition of Microsoft Office within your organization.

Volume license customers can bypass the mandatory activation process by using the Volume License Key (VLK) assigned to their organization. Using a VLK means that individual users in a large organization can install Office without having to enter a product key (which is available only on the back of a retail CD case) and without having to activate the product.

Licensees are eligible for a range of extra services, upgrades, and other benefits, depending upon the terms of their agreements. Different licensing programs are available, based upon your requirements and the size of your organization. For more information, see the Microsoft Licensing Web site at *http://www.microsoft.com /licensing/* or contact your software reseller.

> **Note**   The Microsoft Office 2003 Resource Kit tools have been primarily designed to serve the deployment scenarios found in organizations using volume licensing programs. For this reason, you cannot use Microsoft Office 2003 Resource Kit tools, such as the Custom Installation Wizard, with a 2003 retail edition of Microsoft Office, nor can you run Setup in administrative mode to create an administrative installation point with retail packaged products. In addition, all retail editions require product activation and do not include the bypass capability supported by licensed editions.

Microsoft Office as a client on Windows Terminal Services

The terminal services technology of Microsoft Windows 2000 Server and Microsoft Windows Server™ 2003 can deliver the Windows desktop, as well as Microsoft Office 2003, to virtually any desktop computing device, including those that cannot run Windows. When a user runs Office 2003 through Windows Terminal Services, all of the application execution takes place on the server—only the keyboard, mouse, and display information are transmitted over the network to the client computer.

If you elect to deploy Office 2003 as a client on a Windows Terminal Services–enabled computer, you will need to acquire one license for each client computer that makes use of the Microsoft Office System. For more information about Office 2003 licensing on Windows Terminal Services, see the Microsoft Terminal Services License Basics white paper available from the Microsoft Licensing Web site at *http: //www.microsoft.com/licensing/downloads/terminal_services.doc*.

Office 2003 system requirements

All Microsoft Office editions in the 2003 release have approximately the same minimum system requirements.

Item	Minimum requirements
Processor	Pentium 233 MHz or higher processor; Pentium III recommended.
Operating system	Microsoft Windows 2000 Service Pack 3 or later, or Windows XP or later (recommended).
Memory	64 MB RAM (minimum);128 MB RAM (recommended).

Item	Minimum requirements
Monitor	Super VGA (800 x 600) or higher resolution with 256 colors.
Disk drive	CD-ROM drive.
Pointing device	Microsoft Mouse, Microsoft IntelliMouse®, or compatible pointing device.

Disk space requirements   Hard disk space usage varies depending on the configuration; custom installation choices may require more or less hard disk space. The following table lists the disk space requirements for standard configurations of the products.

Office Professional with InfoPath (includes Publisher)	450 MB
Office Professional (includes Publisher)	420 MB
Office Basic	220 MB
Office Small Business	380 MB
Office Standard	260 MB
Office Personal (Japanese only on Japanese operating system)	380 MB
Word	150 MB
Excel	150 MB
Outlook	150 MB
PowerPoint	150 MB
Access	180 MB
OneNote	100 MB
InfoPath	100 MB
Publisher	250 MB
FrontPage	180 MB

A local installation source requires approximately 2 GB of hard disk space during the installation; the local installation source that remains on users' computers requires as much as 240 MB of hard disk space beyond that required for Office.

> **Note**   None of the Microsoft Office editions in the 2003 release run on the Microsoft Windows Millennium Edition, Windows 98, or Windows NT® operating systems. If any client computers are currently running one of these operating systems, you must upgrade the operating system before installing Microsoft Office.

Additional requirements

Certain programs in the Microsoft Office System require additional items or services:

- Speech recognition requires a Pentium II 400 MHz or higher processor.

- Microsoft Office InfoPath™ 2003 requires Microsoft Internet Explorer 6.0 or later. If your organization is running Windows 2000 Service Pack 3, you must upgrade to Internet Explorer 6.0 before users can start InfoPath. For more information, see the Microsoft Internet Explorer Web site at *http://www.microsoft.com/windows/ie/default.asp*.

- Handwritten notes in Microsoft Office OneNote 2003 require Tablet PC pen input for capturing digital ink. Digital ink enables features such as numbering handwritten notes, converting handwritten notes to text, and searching handwritten notes.

- Advanced collaboration features in Microsoft Office Outlook 2003 may require Microsoft Exchange Server 2003.

- Internet functionality requires separate dial-up or broadband Internet access.

- Microsoft Office PowerPoint 2003 broadcasts require a Windows Media Encoder–compatible video camera for broadcasts including video; Microsoft Exchange 2000 Chat Service to enable chats during live broadcasts; and Microsoft Windows Media Server to enable multicasts of live broadcasts to more than 10 audience members.

- Microsoft Office Access 2003 requires the Microsoft Jet 4.0 Service Pack 7 update. This service pack includes an updated sandbox mode that allows Microsoft Office Access 2003 to block potentially unsafe expressions. Some features in Office Access 2003 will not function properly if you do not install Microsoft Jet 4.0 Service Pack 7. To download the latest version of Jet 4.0, see the Microsoft Windows Update Web site at *http://www.microsoft.com/windows/ie/default.asp/*.

IT Resources on the Web

Microsoft provides a number of Web sites that feature information and tools designed to meet the needs of administrators and information technology (IT) professionals. The following sites might be of special interest to those of you who deploy and support Microsoft Office 2003.

Microsoft Office home page

The Microsoft Office home page at *http://www.microsoft.com/office/* provides overview information about the Microsoft Office System of products. The site includes feature guides, evaluation information, deployment support, and links to a wide range of resources designed to help you get the most out of your products. You can click **Site Map** on the home page to view a list of sites related to specific Office products.

Microsoft Office Online

The Microsoft Office Online Web site at *http://www.microsoft.com/office/* serves as a gateway to a number of specialized sites that support and enhance the Microsoft Office System of products. The site includes Template Gallery, Design Gallery Live, Office Assistance Center, Office eServices, and Office Update, as well as links to related sites covering platform, developer, and international issues.

Office Resource Kit

The Office Resource Kit Web site at *http://www.microsoft.com/office/ork* provides the complete set of content and tools featured in the Microsoft Office 2003 Resource Kit. The site is updated frequently to keep you current on service releases, security issues, and strategies and tactics for deployment. Links to previous resource kits for Office XP, Office 2000, and Office 97/98 are included at the bottom of the left pane of the site's home page.

Microsoft TechNet

Microsoft TechNet, *http://www.microsoft.com/technet*, is a broad-based information and community resource for administrators and IT professionals. TechNet contains a wealth of information about planning, evaluating, deploying, maintaining, and supporting a range of IT products and systems.

Microsoft Product Support Services

The Microsoft Product Support Services site at *http://support.microsoft.com/* provides links to such resources as the searchable Knowledge Base, the Download Center, and the Customer Support site. You'll also find links to support phone numbers, online support requests, and worldwide support resources.

MSDN Office Developer Center

The Office Developer Web site on MSDN (*http://msdn.microsoft.com/office*) features articles, tools, and tips for creating programmable solutions using Office 2003. Topics include such areas as data access, automation, and developing applications with Office components and Microsoft Visual Basic® for Applications (VBA).

Microsoft Windows

The Microsoft Windows site at *http://www.microsoft.com/windows* provides links to information about both current and past versions of Windows products. You can browse links in the left pane of the home page to access the Windows Update center, technology sites such as Microsoft Internet Explorer, and other resources such as MSDN and TechNet.

Office Sites Worldwide

International customers can visit the Office Sites Worldwide page at *http://www.microsoft.com/office/worldwide.asp* to find links to localized Microsoft Office Web sites around the world.

Chapter 2

Office 2003 Security

Security threats delivered through the Internet and e-mail messages have forced many businesses to change the way they deploy and configure Microsoft® Office. To help address these threats, Microsoft has conducted a major review of code in Office and new security-related features both in the user interface and behind the scenes. The *Microsoft Office 2003 Editions Resource Kit* includes features to help reduce possible security vulnerabilities. Along with these features are suggestions and recommendations for how to address specific types of security threats and possible exposure to future attacks.

Security and Office 2003

The new security part of the *Microsoft Office 2003 Editions Resource Kit* covers a range of security-related concepts and features of Microsoft Office 2003. To help address growing concern about the security of information and systems, several new features were included in Office 2003 for administrators and users.

Some of the new improvements include the following:

- Revised macro security

    While the previous macro security method helped to address many security-related issues, a few subtle improvements have been made to how documents, attachments, and linked references are opened.

    However, this may cause some minor problems for some users when attachments to some files no longer open or are disabled. Administrators can revise some of these features and how they work through policy settings or from within the Custom Installation Wizard on the **Specify Security Settings** page.

    For more information on the effects of these improvements on users—as well as how the administrator can configure security settings in the Custom Installation Wizard—see "Macro Security Levels in Office 2003" in Chapter 23, "Office 2003 Security Environment."

- Revised Trusted Publishers store management

    When administrators accept certificates of trusts from external vendors, they can now more easily roll out those certificates to others by using the Active Directory® directory service. Active Directory makes it easy for administrators to do several tasks that were previously difficult to perform. Reliance on this feature of Microsoft Windows–based servers is more important than with previous releases, and several new features of Office require the use of Active Directory in order to work properly.

    This feature has a different user interface for Windows® 2000 than under Windows XP. See the **Tools | Macro | Security | Trusted Publishers** tab for more information. It is now also possible to remove an installed and trusted certificate of trust if you no longer require it or suspect it was compromised.

    For more information on managing the Trusted Publishers store, see "Working with Trusted Trust Publishers" in Chapter 23, "Office 2003 Security Environment."

- Revised Microsoft ActiveX® controls

    The concern about how ActiveX controls start and run on users' computers is more important than ever. A new paradigm was developed that allows administrators more control over how these types of programs are opened and run. In essence, the new paradigm defends against unknown or ill-defined controls that may possess security flaws; it allows you to set the degree of risk you are willing to accept from an unknown ActiveX control when it starts.

Even with this improved paradigm, an ActiveX control only makes use of possible security-related options if the one who creates the control decides to use the options. For more information on ActiveX controls as they relate to security, see "ActiveX Controls and Office Security" in Chapter 23, "Office 2003 Security Environment."

- New encryption types

   Added to Office 2003 are new encryption types and the ability to set all Office applications to use a specific encryption type as their default. This does not mean that every document will have encryption when it is saved; it only means that if a password is set to encrypt the document, the user does not have to select an encryption type to use.

   For more information on configuring Office 2003 for encryption, see "Important Aspects of Password and Encryption Protection" in Chapter 23, "Office 2003 Security Environment."

- Revised core Office programming objects

   Due to the security review of all Office applications, the core objects were updated in an endeavor to help eliminate the classic buffer overflow attack to any data entry points. Along with this review, programmers worked to implement improved programming methods—such as those that relate to handling user IDs and passwords stored within code.

   For more information on Office code objects as related to security, see "Important Aspects of Password and Encryption Protection" in Chapter 23, "Office 2003 Security Environment."

Security and Outlook 2003

The security-related features in Microsoft Office Outlook® 2003 help to minimize the risks posed to your organization from viruses that spread through e-mail messages.

If you use Microsoft Exchange Server for your messaging server, you can use the Outlook Security Template to modify these security settings to help meet the needs of your organization. Publishing a Security Form with settings configured by using the Security Template helps to give your organization further protection, even if you do not modify the existing security features. For example, by using the Security Template to publish the Security Form with the default list of Level 1 blocked file attachment types, users in your organization cannot remove file types from the list on their local computers.

You can also make changes to Outlook security settings, such as trusting COM add-ins or adding to the list of file types that are blocked in e-mail messages. Because Outlook 2003 is designed to help limit the spread of e-mail viruses in an organization, be aware that any changes you make to relax this security—such as removing file types from the list of blocked attachments, or demoting Level 1 restricted file types to Level 2—make it more likely that viruses can invade your e-mail system.

Resources and related information

For more information about configuring security options by using the Security Template, see Chapter 12, "Customizing Outlook 2003 to Help Prevent Viruses."

Part 2

Deployment

Chapter 3

Preparing to Deploy Office 2003

The Microsoft® Office 2003 Setup program uses Windows Installer technology, just as Office 2000 and Office XP did. Because no system file updates or computer restarts are required, however, installing the Office 2003 client is even more straightforward and efficient than installing previous versions.

New to Office 2003 is the option to deploy from a copy of the Office 2003 CD and allow Setup to create a local installation source on users' computers. The local installation source provides improved resiliency for users to repair, reinstall, or update Office later on. Alternatively, you can run Setup with the /a option to create an uncompressed administrative installation point.

Setup Sequence of Events

The basic installation process for Microsoft Office 2003 is the same as it is for Microsoft Office XP and Microsoft Office 2000. The Office Setup program calls Windows Installer to install Office 2003 and related packages. Setup coordinates the installation process from beginning to end, terminating when the last chained package is installed. Because no system file updates or computer restarts are required, installing the Office 2003 client is even more straightforward and efficient than installing previous versions.

The files listed in the following table are often used during an Office 2003 installation.

File	Description
Setup.exe	Office Setup program.
Setup.ini	Setup settings file. Located in the Files\Setup folder.
Ose.exe	Office Source Engine installed by Setup.exe. Copies installation files from the source to a local installation source.
Msiexec.exe	Windows Installer. Called by Setup.exe to install Office.
MSI file	Windows Installer package. Used by Windows Installer to install Office.
MST file	Windows Installer transform. Used by Windows Installer to customize Office.
LogFile_Taskn.txt	Setup log file. Separate log file generated by Setup for each task.

You run Setup by running or double-clicking **setup.exe** on the Office 2003 CD or at the root of the installation image. If Office 2003 is not installed on the computer, you can also run Setup by inserting the Office 2003 CD or by typing the following command line:

```
setup.exe [display settings] [logging settings] [options]
```

Note   Microsoft Office Professional Edition 2003 includes Microsoft Office InfoPath™ 2003. InfoPath 2003 requires Internet Explorer version 6.0. Internet Explorer version 6.0 is included in Microsoft Windows® XP but if your organization is running Windows 2000 Service Pack 3, you must upgrade to Internet Explorer 6.0 before users can use InfoPath. For more information on how to obtain and install Internet Explorer 6.0, see the Microsoft Internet Explorer Web site at *http://www.microsoft.com/windows/ie/default.asp*.

Starting the installation process

At the start of the installation process, Setup performs the following tasks:

1. Reads the Setup settings file (Setup.ini) and assembles the appropriate command line to pass to Windows Installer.

    Setup.exe manages the installation based on the information contained in Setup.ini. You can customize Setup.ini or create your own custom INI file to control many aspects of the installation process.

2. Installs the Office Source Engine (Ose.exe) to copy required installation files to the local hard drive. This step occurs only when you are installing from the Office 2003 CD or a compressed CD image on the network.

3. Calls Windows Installer (Msiexec.exe).

When Setup runs in administrative mode (/**a**), Windows Installer creates an administrative installation point from which users install Office over the network. Setup also calls Windows Installer to install Office and any chained packages on users' computers. In maintenance mode, Setup calls Windows Installer to update, repair, or reinstall features after Office is installed.

Caching installation files on the local computer

When you install Office from the Office 2003 CD or an image of the CD, Setup installs a system service named Office Source Engine (Ose.exe) to copy required installation files to the local computer. After it reads the Setup settings file, Setup.exe determines which drive on the local computer has the most space, verifies that the user has administrative privileges, and then installs Office Source Engine to the following folder:

    <Drive with most space>\MsoCache\Downloadcode

> **Note**   If the MsoCache folder already exists on the computer—for example, if the user has previously installed an Office 2003 product—then Setup uses that location for caching new installation files.

Office Source Engine copies a single cabinet (CAB) file to the local computer and extracts the files in a hidden folder. This initial CAB file includes the following files:

- Office package (MSI file)
- Files to support upgrades from previous versions (Offcln.exe, Oclncore.opc, Oclncust.opc, and Oclnintl.opc)
- Error reporting tools (Dw.exe and Dwintl.dll)
- Setup Help

If there is sufficient disk space, Office Source Engine continues running in the background and caches the entire installation source. You can also customize Setup to cache only the CAB files required for the features being installed.

After Office 2003 is installed, users can install features on demand or run Setup in maintenance mode to add new features. If Windows Installer cannot find the files it needs in the local installation source, Office Source Engine runs again and copies additional CAB files from the original source to the local installation source. (You can specify additional backup sources in an MST file or CMW file or by setting the **SOURCELIST** property.) Then Windows Installer resumes the maintenance process. In this case, the user might be prompted for the source.

The installation source files (CAB files) require as much as 240 MB of hard disk space beyond what is required for Office 2003. Setup can be configured to delete the cache after installation, or users with limited disk space can delete the cache after Office is installed. However, keeping the local source makes repairing and updating Office 2003 more efficient: required installation files are always available, and users do not need to connect to the network or find the Office 2003 CD to repair broken features, install features on first use, or apply updates.

Because Setup works only with CAB files when it creates a local installation source, it requires a compressed source. When you run Setup with **/a** to create an administrative installation point, Setup extracts the compressed CAB files on the network share. When users install Office, Windows Installer copies extracted files directly from the network source. Setup does not install Office Source Engine or cache installation files on users' computers; instead, Windows Installer uses the administrative installation point as the source.

Corporate customers can take advantage of the local installation source when they deploy Office from a CD or compressed CD image on the network. (Note that retail editions of Office 2003 do not support this option.) For more information about installing from a CD image and customizing local installation source settings, see "Taking Advantage of a Local Installation Source" later in this chapter.

Passing command-line options and properties to Windows Installer

Setup uses command-line options and properties to control the installation process. Most global command-line options, such as **/qb**, are passed to Windows Installer for all the tasks that Setup handles. Others, such as **LOCALCACHEDRIVE**, affect the behavior of Setup.exe itself. Some command-line options, such as **PIDKEY** or **INSTALLLOCATION**, are passed only during the call to install the Office 2003 package.

The default values for Setup properties are defined in the package (MSI file), but you can customize an Office installation by specifying new values. For example, you can use the **INSTALLLOCATION** property to define the default installation path for Office.

In general, Setup properties are passed only during the call to install the Office package. To pass a property to a package other than Office 2003 (that is, a chained package), you must specify the property in the relevant section of the Setup settings file and not on the command line. For example, you can customize Setup to install Office 2003 with a full user interface, but install Microsoft Office 2003 Multilingual User Interface Packs with only progress indicators by setting the **DISPLAY** property to **Basic** in the [ChainedInstall_*n*] section of Setup.ini.

Setup.exe recognizes all the command-line options and properties from Microsoft Office XP. (The properties that controlled the System Files Update and Internet Explorer installation for computers running Microsoft Windows NT® 4.0 or Windows 98 are ignored.) In addition, Office 2003 Setup recognizes new properties that control the creation of the local installation source during installations from a compressed CD image.

For definitions and examples of all the Setup options and properties used during an Office installation, see "Setup Command-line Options" and "Setup Properties" in Appendix B, "Office 2003 Resource Kit Reference."

For a detailed description of each section of Setup.ini, see "Setup Settings File" in Appendix B, "Office 2003 Resource Kit Reference."

Calling Windows Installer to install Office and chained packages

Setup.exe calls Windows Installer to install Office and any chained packages. Windows Installer (which includes Msiexec.exe) installs Office 2003 by using a dynamic-link library (Msi.dll) to read the Windows Installer package (MSI file), apply any specified Windows Installer transform (MST file), incorporate command-line options supplied by Setup.exe, and install programs and files on users' computers.

> **Important**   Do not run Msiexec.exe directly. Instead, always run Setup.exe to install Office and related packages. Running Setup.exe ensures that all system verifications are performed.

When a user selects a feature to install during Office Setup, Windows Installer identifies a corresponding set of components to copy to the computer. Each component consists of a unique set of files, programs, dynamic-link libraries (DLLs), and registry entries that work together as a unit.

Windows Installer uses two types of files to install Office 2003 and related products: packages (MSI files) and transforms (MST files). A Windows Installer package is a relational database that contains all the information necessary to install a product. The MSI file associates components with features. It also contains information about the installation process itself, such as installation sequence, destination folder paths, system dependencies, installation options, and properties that control the installation process.

A Windows Installer transform is a file that contains information about changes to components, features, and Setup properties in an associated package (MSI file). A transform is based on a particular package and contains the modifications to apply to that package during installation. When you use the Custom Installation Wizard to create a transform, the wizard compares the original MSI file and the MSI file with all your customizations incorporated. The differences are recorded in an MST file; the original package is never altered.

Office 2003 requires Windows Installer version 2.0 or later. Both Microsoft Windows 2000 Service Pack 3 and Windows XP include Windows Installer 2.0, which offers the following advantages over previous versions:

- Allows users to rely interchangeably on a compressed source (Office 2003 CD) and an uncompressed source (Office 2003 administrative installation point).

> **Note** In order for users to switch between compressed and uncompressed sources, you must set the **MSINODISABLEMEDIA** property to **1** when you create an administrative installation point or before users install Office 2003.

- Patches already installed features more efficiently, usually without requiring the original source.
- Replaces unversioned files more selectively.

For more information about Windows Installer, including Help and other documentation, search the MSDN Library at *http://msdn.microsoft.com/library /default.asp* for Windows Installer.

The Office Professional 2003 package (Pro11.msi) includes all the core applications and shared features included in the product. The core package also includes Input Method Editors (IMEs) for Korean, Japanese, Simplified Chinese, and Traditional Chinese. After Office is installed, Windows Installer continues to use the original package to add or remove features or to replace missing or damaged files. When you set Office features to be installed on first use, Windows Installer uses the package to copy the files from the source the first time the user activates a feature.

For more information about the available editions of Office 2003 and related products, see "Office 2003 Licensing and System Requirements" in Chapter 1, "Office 2003 and the Office Resource Kit."

Installing Office

Setup calls Windows Installer to install the core Office 2003 package by using the following command line:

```
msiexec [display settings] [logging settings] [options] /i <pro11.msi>
```

The name and location of the package are specified in the [MSI] section of Setup.ini; the path defaults to the location of Setup.exe. You can specify a transform to apply other property-value pairs on the command line or in the Setup settings file. During the calls, Setup passes command-line options and properties to Windows Installer.

> **Note**   No portion of the Office 2003 installation requires that users restart their computers to complete the installation. In some cases, however, Windows might prompt the user to restart the computer to replace files in use. To suppress these requested reboots, use the **/noreboot** command-line option (equivalent to setting the Windows Installer **REBOOT** property to **REALLYSUPPRESS**).

Installing chained packages

Office 2003 Setup can also handle installation of multiple chained packages, which are listed in the [ChainedInstall_1] to [ChainedInstall_*n*] sections of the Setup settings file. The following example shows the syntax used in Setup.ini:

```
[ChainedInstall_1]
PATH=\\server\share\<LCID>\Mui.msi
MST=Custom.mst
DISPLAY=Basic
CMDLINE=SOURCELIST=\\server2\share\<LCID>
```

When the core Office 2003 installation is complete, Setup.exe makes a series of calls to Windows Installer to install each chained package.

For example, you can include Multilingual User Interface Packs (MUI Packs) on the same administrative image as Office 2003 and chain them to the Office installation. (The Office 2003 Multilingual User Interface Pack Setup program is named MuiSetup.exe to allow you to use the same administrative installation point.) To chain individual MUI Packs directly to your Office 2003 installation, add the Mui.msi files to the [ChainedInstall_*n*] sections of the Setup settings file. Setup.exe writes tasks to the registry for each chained package and installs them after the Office installation completes.

For more information about chaining additional packages and setting properties for chained installations, see "Deploying Office and Other Products Together" in Chapter 5, "Installing Office 2003."

> **Note**   By using the Custom Installation Wizard, you can create a transform that specifies additional programs—for example, the Profile Wizard (Prfl-wiz.exe)—to run at the end of the Office 2003 installation. These programs are started by the core Office 2003 installation before Setup.exe calls Msiexec.exe to install any chained packages. You cannot use the Add Installations and Run Programs page of the wizard to chain additional Windows Installer packages to the core Office installation.

Generating log files

Both Office 2003 Setup and Windows Installer generate log files during the installation process. Windows Installer allows you to set a number of logging options that apply to each package that it installs during Office 2003 Setup. Note that any logging options you set apply to all log files created by Windows Installer during the Office 2003 installation.

You can also specify the name and path for log files. By default, Setup creates log files in the %Temp% folder on each user's computer. Setup and Windows Installer create log files for each package that is installed, append the task number to each log file name, and store log files in the same location. For example, %Temp%\<SetupLogFile>_Task(0001).txt is the name of the Setup log file for the first package installed by Setup. Setup.exe controls the sequential numbering of the log files using the settings in the [Logging] section of the Setup settings file.

For more information about customizing logging options and log files, see "Customizing How Setup Runs" in Chapter 4, "Customizing Office 2003."

Taking Advantage of a Local Installation Source

When users install Microsoft Office 2003 from the CD or from a compressed CD image on the network, Setup uses a system service named Office Source Engine (Ose.exe) to copy required installation files to a hidden folder on the local computer. Windows Installer uses this local installation source to install Office, and the local source remains available for repairing, reinstalling, or updating Office later on. Users can install features on demand or run Setup in maintenance mode to add new features.

Setup creates a local installation source by default in Office 2003, but only when you install Office from the CD or a compressed CD image. If sufficient hard disk space exists on the local computer, Setup caches the entire installation source by default. Maintaining this local installation source after Office 2003 is installed offers a number of benefits to users in large organizations:

- Traveling users, or users with slow or intermittent network connections, can install features on demand or run Setup in maintenance mode to add new features without requiring a source on the network.

- When Office is updated, administrators can distribute smaller client patches and users can apply them even when they do not have access to the original source.

- Because Setup caches the compressed cabinet (CAB) files, the local installation source requires considerably less hard disk space than a copy of the entire uncompressed administrative image.

When you run Setup with the **/a** option to create an administrative installation point, Setup extracts the compressed CAB files on the network share, and Setup can no longer create the local installation source. However, installing Office from a compressed CD image offers almost all of the same deployment options as an administrative installation point:

- You can create a transform and modify Setup.ini to customize Office, and you can create multiple configurations from the same compressed CD image.

- You can set features to be installed on demand; however, you cannot run Office applications over the network.

- You can chain additional packages to the Office installation, including stand-alone products such as Microsoft Office FrontPage® 2003 and Microsoft Office Publisher 2003. Chained packages that support creation of a local installation source inherit the local installation source settings specified for the core Office package.

- You can use deployment tools such as Microsoft Systems Management Server to install Office on users' computers.

> **Note**   The creation and maintenance of the local installation source is managed entirely by Office Setup and the Office Source Engine (Ose.exe), and not by Windows Installer.

For more information about how Setup handles creation of the local installation source, see "Setup Sequence of Events."

Creating a compressed CD image on the network

Office 2003 source files are compressed in cabinet (CAB) files to fit on the Office 2003 CD. You copy the compressed CAB files to a network share before customizing the CD image. In this scenario, you do not run Setup to create an administrative installation point; instead, you copy the compressed files directly to the network share.

Unlike the process of running Setup with the /**a** option—which expands the compressed files on the administrative installation point—the files in the CD image remain compressed. Nor does copying the CD enter the product key or accept the end-user license agreement (EULA) automatically on behalf of all users who install Office 2003 from this network share. You must set properties to handle these aspects of the installation.

To create a CD image on a network share

1. Insert the Office 2003 CD into your CD-ROM drive.

2. In Windows Explorer, select all the folders on the CD.
   Be sure to display all hidden files so that you see the entire contents of the Office 2003 CD.

3. Copy the CD contents to a network share.
   The complete CD image for Microsoft Office 2003 Professional requires approximately 250 MB of space.

Setting local installation source options

Because Setup creates the local installation source by default, you do not need to set any additional options. Setup creates the local installation source in the following hidden folder on users' computers:

<drive with most space>\Msocache\Downloadcode

In Office 2003, Setup caches the entire source by default; if the user's computer has insufficient disk space, Setup caches installation file for only the selected features. Setup retains the local installation source after the installation is complete. You can modify how Setup handles the local installation source by setting the following properties in the [Cache] section of Setup.ini:

- **LOCALCACHEDRIVE**   Specify a different drive for the local installation source. By default, Setup searches for the drive with the most space or uses an existing MsoCache folder if one exists.

- **DELETEABLECACHE**   Give users the option to delete the local installation source at the end of Setup.

- **CDCACHE**   Enable or disable creation of a local installation source. You can set this property to cache the entire source, to cache installation files for only selected features, or to run the installation directly from the source and bypass creation of a local installation source entirely.

Note that when you force creation of a local installation source, the installation fails if the local computer lacks sufficient disk space. The default setting (**CDCACHE=auto**) allows Setup to fall back on options to cache installation files for only selected features or to install from the network source when the user's computer has insufficient disk space; however, this scenario may result in inconsistent local installation source configurations across an organization.

> **Note**   Because Setup creates the local installation source before applying a transform (MST file), you should set local installation source properties in the Setup settings file, and not on the Modify Setup Properties page of the Custom Installation Wizard.

For more information about the [CACHE] section of Setup.ini, see "Setup Settings File" in Appendix B, "Office 2003 Resource Kit Reference."

Customizing the compressed CD image

After you copy the contents of the Office 2003 CD to a network share, the process of customizing an Office CD image is similar to the process of customizing an administrative installation point. You can edit the Setup.ini file and use the Custom Installation Wizard to create a transform (MST file) as long as you point to the MSI file on the compressed image. You can also customize files that reside outside the Office 2003 CAB files, such as the OPC file used by Setup or the Removal Wizard to remove previous versions.

Unlike deploying from administrative installation point, however, you must accept the EULA and enter a valid Volume License Key before users can install Office from the compressed CD image. New functionality has been added to the Custom Installation Wizard to handle these settings and to hide those pages from users during interactive Setup.

To customize the Office 2003 CD image

1. Start the Custom Installation Wizard and open the MSI file on the CD image.

2. On the **Configure Local Installation Source** page, select the option **Configure local installation source**.

3. In the **Product Key** box, enter a valid 25-character Volume License Key.

4. Select the **I accept the terms in the License Agreement** check box.

5. Make any additional customizations you want, and save the MST file.

6. Have users run Setup from the network share with your transform.

    or

    Copy the entire compressed image onto a CD and distribute copies to users. The volume label of the CDs you create must match the volume label of the Office 2003 CD for Setup to run properly from the custom CDs. The CDs that you create can be used in the same way as the original Office CD, except that Setup runs with your modifications.

Important   You must obtain the proper user licenses before copying, modifying, or distributing a customized version of the Office 2003 CD. For more information about volume licensing programs, contact your software reseller or see the Microsoft Licensing Web site at *http://www.microsoft.com/licensing/default.asp*.

Users do not need administrator rights to install new features from the local installation source. However, installing features on demand directly from the Office 2003 CD requires administrator rights each time a feature is installed. This scenario is the only exception to persistent administrator rights after an initial installation with elevated privileges. For this reason, users who rely on an Office CD as an alternate source must be administrators of their computers.

Caution   Setting the Windows Installer policy **Enable user to use media source while elevated** allows a user without administrator rights to run programs from any CD. The installation runs with elevated privileges, and the user has unlimited access to system files and the registry. Setting this policy leaves the computer highly vulnerable, potentially allowing an attacker to run malicious code on the computer. Using this policy to elevate the installation of features on demand from an Office CD is not recommended.

Creating an Administrative Installation Point

One method of deploying a customized version of the Microsoft Office 2003 client to a large number of users is to create an administrative installation point on a network server and to run Setup from there. This method—the same method used with Office 2000 and Office XP—allows you to do the following:

- Manage one set of Office files from a central location.

- Create a standard Office configuration for a group of users.

- Take advantage of flexible installation options.
  For example, you can set Office features to be installed on first use or to run from the network. You can use other deployment tools, such as Microsoft Systems Management Server or Group Policy software installation, to install Office from an administrative installation point.

- Manage updates of Office by patching a single administrative image.

On the Resource Kit CD   Only editions of Office 2003 acquired through a Volume License agreement or other non-retail channel allow you to create an administrative installation point. You cannot run Setup.exe in administrative mode (**/a**) with an Office 2003 retail edition.

Running Setup to create an administrative image

To distribute Office from a network server, you must first install Office on an administrative installation point by running Setup.exe with the **/a** command-line option. Then you can customize your Office configuration before running Setup on users' computers.

To create an administrative installation point for Office

1. Create a share on a network server for the administrative installation point.
   The network share must have at least 550 megabytes (MB) of available hard disk space.

2. On a computer that has write access to the share, connect to the server share.
   The computer must be running a supported operating system: Microsoft Windows 2000 Service Pack 3 or Windows XP or later.

3. On the **Start** menu, click **Run**, and then click **Browse**.

4. On the Office 2003 CD, double-click **setup.exe** and add **/a** to the command line.

5. Enter the organization name that you want to define for all users who install Office from this administrative installation point.

6. Enter the server and share you created as the installation location.

7. Enter the 25-character Volume License Key and click **Next**.
   You must enter a valid Volume License Key when you create the administrative installation point; users who install Office 2003 from this administrative image do not need to enter the product key when they install Office 2003 or start an Office 2003 application for the first time.

8. Accept the end-user license agreement and click **Install**.
   By accepting the agreement here, you are accepting on behalf of all users who install Office from this administrative installation point.

   Setup copies the files from the Office 2003 CD to the administrative installation point, extracts the compressed cabinet (CAB) files, and creates a hierarchy of folders in the root folder of the share.

> **Note**   When you install Office 2003 and you set features to run from the network (**Run from Network** or **Run All from Network**), you must create your administrative installation point in a subfolder on the share; for example, \\server\share\admin_install_point\setup.exe. If Setup.exe is stored at the root of the share, Office 2003 features do not run properly.

The following table identifies the location of key files on the Office 2003 administrative image.

File	Location
Setup.exe	Root of the administrative image
Setup.ini	Files\Setup
Office 2003 package (MSI file)	Root of the administrative image
OPC files used to clean up previous versions	Files\Program Files\MSOffice\Office11

Setup also modifies the Windows Installer package for Office, identifying it as an administrative installation package and setting the **ProductID** and **COMPANYNAME** properties accordingly. After you create the administrative installation point, you make the share available to users by providing them with read access.

When users run Setup to install Office, any Office features that are installed to run from the network use this administrative installation point as the source of Office files, and Office runs the features over the network from this server. Similarly, for features that are set to be installed on first use, Office copies files from this server when needed. If you install features in one of these two states, then you must keep this network server available to users. You can copy the administrative image to one or more backup servers to help ensure that users always have access to the source.

When users install Office from the administrative installation point, Setup uses the organization name that you specify as the default. With the Office 2003 Custom Installation Wizard, you can create a Windows Installer transform (MST file) that modifies the organization name during installation. This flexibility allows you to create different organization names for different groups of users in your organization.

You can specify the organization name on the **Specify Default Path and Organization** page of the wizard, or set the **COMPANYNAME** property on the **Modify Setup Properties** page. In most cases, you can change the organization name by resetting **COMPANYNAME** on the Setup command line or in the Setup settings file (Setup.ini). For more information about how Setup determines which organization name to use, see **COMPANYNAME** in "Setup Properties" in Appendix B, "Office 2003 Resource Kit Reference."

> **Note**   The Office 2003 Resource Kit includes the Custom Installation Wizard as part of the core tool set. The Custom Installation Wizard is installed by default when you run the Office 2003 Resource Kit Setup program. For more information about the wizard, see "Custom Installation Wizard" in Appendix A, "Toolbox."

Copying the administrative image to alternate servers

To help improve source resiliency, you can replicate the administrative installation point to multiple backup servers from which users can install Office—and to which Windows Installer can connect to repair Office features or to install on demand. When you create and identify alternate administrative installation points, users can rely on any one of the installation servers as a source. Windows Installer automatically enumerates the servers on the list until it finds an available one.

As long as you use relative paths for any customizations that include paths, you can copy the complete folder hierarchy and files from one administrative installation point to another server. If you copy the folders, then each new administrative image that you create has the same default organization name and **ProductID** specified during the administrative Setup.

You list the paths to the servers that contain replicated administrative installation points on the **Identify Additional Servers** page of the Custom Installation Wizard. You can also identify additional installation servers by setting the **SOURCELIST** property on the **Modify Setup Properties** page of the Custom Installation Wizard, in the [Options] section of Setup.ini, or on the command line.

Copying the administrative image onto a CD

If you support users who cannot install or run Microsoft Office over the network, you can copy the entire Office 2003 administrative installation point (including custom Setup.ini or MST files) onto CDs and distribute them to users. For example, if your network is decentralized and some groups work over slow links, you can send a CD to each hub. When traveling users who have limited or inconsistent access to the network need access to the original source to repair Office or to install new features, you can ensure that the source is available by providing custom copies of the Office 2003 administrative image on CD.

In this scenario, the custom CD functions as an interchangeable equivalent to the administrative installation point on the network. Users are not prompted to enter a product key or accept the end-user license agreement when they install Office from your custom CD, because you entered that information for them when you created the original administrative installation point.

When you run Setup with the **/a** option to create an administrative installation point, however, Windows Installer automatically sets the **DISABLEMEDIA** property to 1. This property prevents users who install from the administrative image from using any physical media, including your custom CD, as an alternate source.

To allow users to rely on a CD as an alternate resiliency source, set the **MSIN-ODISABLEMEDIA** property to 1 on the command line or in Setup.ini when you create the administrative installation point. **MSINODISABLEMEDIA** prevents Windows Installer from setting the **DISABLEMEDIA** property. For example:

```
setup.exe /a MSINODISABLEMEDIA=1
```

Important   You must obtain the proper user licenses before copying, modifying, or distributing a customized version of the Office 2003 CD. For more information about volume licensing programs, contact your software reseller or see the Microsoft Licensing Web site at *http://www.microsoft.com/licensing/default.asp*.

Storing additional files on the administrative image

The administrative installation point is a logical place to store custom files that you create, including transforms (MST files), custom Setup settings files (INI files), and batch files or shortcuts to Setup.exe. If you are customizing user settings, you can store the Profile Wizard and Office profile settings files (OPS files) in the same location. If you are planning a staged deployment and you use the Custom Maintenance Wizard to create a configuration maintenance file (CMW file) to distribute after your initial deployment, you can store the CMW file on the administrative installation point, too.

If you are chaining additional packages to the Office 2003 installation, storing them on the administrative installation point simplifies file management and replication of the administrative image. For more information about chaining additional packages to the Office installation, see "Deploying Office and Other Products Together" in Chapter 5, "Installing Office 2003."

Note   If you are staging deployment of Office 2003 and related applications, you can deploy both the core Office 2003 package and another stand-alone package, such as Microsoft Office InfoPath 2003 or Microsoft Office FrontPage 2003, from the same installation image. When both packages use the same name for the Setup settings file, however, the second Setup.ini file overwrites any existing Setup.ini file on the same image. To avoid this problem, give each Setup.ini file a unique name. When you run Setup, use the **/settings** option to specify the correct Setup.ini file. Alternatively, you can rename Setup.exe to match the INI file: for example, ProSetup.exe with ProSetup.ini and FPSetup.exe with FPSetup.ini.

Specifying an installation point on a Web server

Office 2003 Setup does not support installing from an installation point on a Web server. For security reasons, Microsoft no longer recommends installing any Windows Installer package (MSI file), including Office applications, from an HTTP source. For this reason, you cannot use the **/webinstall** command-line option to specify an Office 2003 administrative installation point on a Web server. However, you can still use a hyperlink on a Web page to point to an administrative installation point that is hosted on a file server (for example, a UNC path).

Chapter 4

Customizing Office 2003

After you create an installation source on the network—either an administrative installation point or a compressed image of the Microsoft® Office 2003 CD—you can make extensive customizations before you install Office on users' computers. You can control many aspects of the installation process itself, including how much users interact with Setup and whether Setup creates a local installation source. You can also determine which Office features are available and specify default settings for most options.

Methods of Customizing Office

After you create an administrative installation point or compressed CD image for the Microsoft Office 2003 client, you can make extensive customizations before installing Office on users' computers. You can also customize many aspects of the installation process itself, including the following:

- Customize the way Setup runs, including display and logging options.

- Determine which Office applications and features are installed.

- Specify default settings for Office applications.

- Add files or shortcuts to an Office installation.

- Determine which previous versions of Office are removed when Office 2003 is installed.

- Distribute a default Microsoft Office Outlook® 2003 profile.

- Chain additional packages, such as Microsoft Office 2003 Multilingual User Interface Packs (MUI Packs), to the Office installation.

Many of the customizations you make to an Office installation can be accomplished by one of several methods:

- Specifying options on the command line.

- Customizing the Setup.ini file.

- Creating a transform (MST file) with the Custom Installation Wizard.

- Creating an Office profile settings file (OPS file) with the Profile Wizard.

- Running the Removal Wizard during or after the Office installation.

The following table shows packages (MSI files) related to Office that you can customize, and it provides recommended methods for different types of customizations.

Customization	MSI file	Command line	INI file	MST file	OPS file	Removal Wizard
Setup process (display, logging, installation location, organization name, and so on)	Pro11.msi	x	x	x		
Local installation source (compressed CD image only)	Pro11.msi	x	x			
Office features, added files, and shortcuts	Pro11.msi			x		

Customization	MSI file	Command line	INI file	MST file	OPS file	Removal Wizard
Security settings	Pro11.msi			X	X	
Outlook settings	Pro11.msi			x	x	x
Other user settings	Pro11.msi			x	x	
Removal options	Pro11.msi			x		x
Language settings	LCID\Mui.msi			x		
Chained packages	*Chained*.msi		x			

On the Resource Kit CD   The Office 2003 Resource Kit core tool set includes the Custom Installation Wizard, Profile Wizard, and Removal Wizard. These tools are installed by default when you run the Office Resource Kit Setup program. For more information, see Appendix A, "Toolbox."

Working with Setup properties

Setup properties control many aspects of the installation process, including the following:

- Display settings, logging options, and other properties used by Setup to manage the installation process.

- Properties that customize button labels and descriptive text in the Setup user interface.

- Properties that control how Office features are installed.

- Properties that determine how Outlook is installed with Office.

The default values for Setup properties are defined in the Windows Installer package (MSI file). You can specify new values on the command line, in Setup.ini, or on the **Modify Setup Properties** page of the Custom Installation Wizard. During the installation, Setup passes all Setup property values to Windows Installer.

Most properties are passed only during the call to install Office 2003. However, global display settings are passed to every installation included with Office. For example, when you specify **/qb** on the command line, or when you set **Display=basic** in the [Display] section of Setup.ini, Setup displays simple progress indicators and error messages throughout the entire installation. To install a chained package with a full user interface, you must set **Display=full** in the [ChainedInstall_*n*] section of Setup.ini.

For definitions and examples of all the properties that you can use with Office 2003 Setup, see "Setup Properties" in Appendix B, "Office 2003 Resource Kit Reference."

Specifying options on the command line

When you run Setup, you can use command-line options to change some of the parameters that Setup uses to install Office. By using command-line options, you can do the following:

- Identify the package (MSI file) and transform (MST file) to use.

- Specify a custom Setup settings file (INI file) to use.

- Direct Setup to run in quiet mode.

- Set Windows Installer logging options.

- Change default values of Setup properties.

For example, you can enter the following options on the command line:

```
setup.exe /qb+ /l* %temp%\office11.txt COMPANYNAME="Northwind Traders"
```

This command line customizes Setup in the following ways:

- Setup does not prompt the user for information, but displays progress indicators and a completion message when it installs Office (**/qb+**).

- Windows Installer logs all information and any error messages (**/l***) for Setup.exe to the file C:\Documents and Settings*<Username>*\Local Settings\Temp\Office11.txt on the user's computer.

- Setup sets the default organization name to Northwind Traders.

- Because no custom INI or MST file is specified, Setup installs the same Office features that it would if the user clicked **Typical Install** in the Setup user interface.

For definitions and examples of all the options that you can use with Office 2003 Setup, see "Setup Command-line Options" in Appendix B, "Office 2003 Resource Kit Reference."

When to use command-line options

The Setup command line is most useful when you have few customizations to make, or when you want to create several different installations quickly. You can use one custom INI file or apply the same MST file to install a basic Office 2003 configuration to everyone, but define different command lines for targeted groups of users.

For example, you can have your Engineering and Accounting departments install the same set of Office 2003 features and settings, but specify unique organization names. On the installation image, you create two shortcuts that have the following command lines:

```
setup.exe /q /settings Custom.ini COMPANYNAME="Engineering Department"

setup.exe /q /settings Custom.ini COMPANYNAME="Accounting Department"
```

Command-line options are also useful if you use Microsoft Systems Management Server or another systems management tool to create multiple deployment packages, each of which requires a different command line.

> **Tip** Any settings that you can specify on the command line can also be added to Setup.ini—including the command line itself. For extensive or complex command-line customizations, use Setup.ini to make the installation process easier to track and troubleshoot.

How to distribute command-line options

When users double-click **setup.exe** on the installation image, Setup runs with no command-line options. To apply your custom command-line options, users must click **Run** on the Microsoft Windows® **Start** menu and enter the path to Setup.exe, along with your command-line options.

To simplify this process, you can create a Windows batch file that runs Setup.exe with your command-line options. Or, you can create a Windows shortcut and add your custom options to the command-line box. Users double-click the batch file or shortcut to run the Setup command line that you have defined. You can store the batch file or shortcut in the root folder of the installation image.

If you run Setup from a network logon script or through a systems management tool (such as Systems Management Server), you can add your custom options to the Setup command line in the script or deployment package.

Customizing the Setup settings file

Before applying the values specified on the command line, Setup reads the properties specified in the Setup settings file (Setup.ini), where you can set all the properties that you can on the command line. For example, you can:

- Identify the MSI and MST files to use in the [MSI] and [MST] sections.

- Direct Setup to run in quiet mode in the [Display] section.

- Set logging options for Windows Installer and Office 2003 Setup in the [Logging] section.

- Change the default values of Setup properties in the [Options] section.

- Chain multiple Windows Installer packages, including MUI Packs, to your core Office installation in the [ChainedInstall_*n*] sections. (You cannot specify chained packages on the command line.)

- Customize the way Setup creates a local installation source on users' computers when you install Office from a compressed CD image.

In most sections of Setup.ini, including the [Options] section, you use the syntax **property=value** to specify custom property values. In the [ChainedInstall_*n*] sections, you can set the **Display** and **MST** values with this syntax; however, you must use the **Cmdline** property to add other options to the command line that Setup passes to Windows Installer for a chained package.

For more information about each section of Setup.ini, see "Setup Settings File" in Appendix B, "Office 2003 Resource Kit Reference."

When to use a custom INI file

Because the Setup settings file organizes Setup options in an easy-to-read format, it is more convenient to use than long or complex command lines. If you use Setup.ini to set most Setup properties, then you can reserve the command line for specific and targeted modifications, or changes that you need to make late in the deployment process.

If you are installing Office from a compressed CD image and you want to customize the way Setup creates the local installation source on users' computers, you set properties in the [Cache] section of Setup.ini. Because Setup creates the local installation source before a transform is applied, you cannot set most local installation source options in a transform.

If you want to chain MUI Packs from the Office 2003 Multilingual User Interface Pack or chain other Windows Installer packages to your core Office 2003 installation, then you must enter the Mui.msi files by adding the name and path in the [ChainedInstall_*n*] section of Setup.ini.

Other scenarios in which the Setup settings file is the preferred customization method to use include the following:

- You want users to run Setup.exe directly from the installation image, instead of creating a batch file or shortcut to install a customized version of the Office 2003 client.

- You want to override global display settings (that is, the display settings specified for Office 2003) and set unique display settings for chained packages.

- You want to set additional options for a chained package, such as specifying a transform to apply.

How to distribute a custom INI file

When you edit the default Setup settings file (Setup.ini), users can run Setup without using command-line options to install Office with your customizations.

To create multiple custom installations that use different Setup options, you can create several custom INI files that have different names and store them in the root folder of the installation image. Users specify the name of a settings file by using the /**settings** Setup command-line option. You can simplify this process by creating a batch file or Windows shortcut that contains the appropriate /**settings** command-line option.

> Note   If your custom INI file is stored in any location other than the folder that contains Setup.exe, you must include the relative or absolute path with the /settings option. For example:
>
> ```
> Setup.exe /settings \\server\share\files\setup\offl1eng.ini
> ```

If you run Setup from a network logon script or through a systems management tool (such as Systems Management Server), then you must edit the Setup command line in the script or deployment package to refer to the appropriate settings file by using the /**settings** option.

You can create multiple custom INI files for different groups of users. For example, you might want to deploy the French and Spanish Multilingual User Interface Packs with Office to your Accounting department, but give users in your Engineering department their choice of languages in the MUI Pack Wizard. In this case, you can create two custom INI files: one that chains the French and Spanish Mui.msi packages, and another that chains the Muiwiz.msi package. Users in each department run Setup by using one of the following command lines:

```
setup.exe /settings offl1act.ini
```

```
setup.exe /settings offl1eng.ini
```

> Note   When you create a custom INI file, you can also specify options on the Setup command line. If you specify a command-line option that conflicts with a value in the INI file, Setup uses the command-line option.

Creating a transform by using the Custom Installation Wizard

When you install Office 2003 from an administrative installation point or compressed CD image, you can customize the Office configuration that is installed on users' computers by applying a Windows Installer transform (MST file). Many of the customizations that you make in Setup.ini or on the command line can also be made in a transform, but some tasks are better handled in a transform. For example, a transform is typically used to set default installation states for Office features or to specify default application settings.

You create a Windows Installer transform by using the Office Custom Installation Wizard. The transform contains the changes that you want to make to the Windows Installer package (MSI file). When you apply the transform during the installation, your modifications become the default settings for anyone who runs Setup from your installation image. If you run Setup in quiet mode (with no user interaction), your selections define precisely how Office is installed on users' computers.

> **On the Resource Kit CD**   The Office 2003 Resource Kit core tool set includes the Custom Installation Wizard, which is installed by default when you run the Office Resource Kit Setup program. For more information, see "Custom Installation Wizard" in Appendix A, "Toolbox."

For information about how to set options on each page of the Custom Installation Wizard, see the Custom Installation Wizard Help on the companion CD.

When to use a transform

A Windows Installer transform is most useful when you want to make extensive customizations, particularly customizations that you cannot readily make by using the Setup command line or Setup settings file. By creating multiple transforms, you can also install different Office configurations to different groups of users from the same installation image.

When you create a transform, the Custom Installation Wizard allows you to do the following:

■ Define the path where Office is installed on users' computers.

■ Accept the end-user license agreement (EULA) and enter a product key on behalf of users who are installing from a compressed CD image.

■ Define the default installation state for Office 2003 applications and features.
   For example, you can install Microsoft Office Word 2003 on the local computer, but set Microsoft Office PowerPoint® 2003 to be installed on demand or run from the network. You can also hide and lock features so that users cannot make changes after Office is installed.

■ Add your own files and registry entries to Setup so that they are installed with Office.

- Modify Office application shortcuts, specifying where they are installed and customizing their properties.

- Define a list of servers for Office to use if the primary installation source is unavailable.

- Specify other products to install or programs to run on users' computers after Setup is completed.

- Configure Microsoft Outlook.
    For example, specify a default user profile.

- Specify which previous versions of Office are removed.

You can also create transforms for chained Windows Installer packages, including the MUI Packs.

> **Note**   Office 2003 Setup automatically matches MUI Pack feature installation states to the corresponding features in the core English version of Office. If you specify different installation states for MUI Pack features in a transform, you must set the **NOFEATURESTATEMIGRATION** property to override the default matching behavior.

How to apply a transform during Office installation

For users to install Office with your customizations, you must specify the name and path to the transform by setting the **TRANSFORMS** property on the command line or by adding an entry to the [MST] section of the Setup settings file.

For example, to direct Setup to use the transform Custom.mst (stored in the same folder as Setup.exe), you use the following Setup command line:

```
setup.exe TRANSFORMS=custom.mst
```

> **Note**   If you misspell the **TRANSFORMS** option on the command line as **TRANSFORM** (singular), then Setup returns an error and your transform is not applied.

This step is equivalent to adding the following entry to the [MST] section of Setup.ini:

```
MST1=Custom.mst
```

You can specify a transform for chained packages, too, in the appropriate ChainedInstall_*n* section of Setup.ini. (Note that the property used to specify a transform for a chained package in Setup.ini differs from the property used for the core Office package.) For example:

```
[ChainedInstall_1]
MST=French.mst
```

If you create unique transforms for different groups of users, you must specify—on the command line or in Setup.ini—which transform to use. For example, users in your Accounting department might need all the add-ins included with Microsoft Office Excel 2003, and users in the Engineering department might need a custom set of Microsoft Office Access 2003 features. In this scenario, you can create different transforms that specify different installation states for Excel and Access features, and then create two shortcuts on the installation image by using the following command lines:

```
setup.exe TRANSFORMS=off11eng.mst
setup.exe TRANSFORMS=off11act.mst
```

> **Note**   You can apply a transform only when Office is initially installed. To make changes to an Office configuration after Office is installed, you must use the Custom Maintenance Wizard. For more information, see "Updating Feature Installation States and Application Settings" in Chapter 18, "Updating Users' Office 2003 Configurations."

Resolving conflicting Setup options

Office 2003 offers many ways to customize an Office installation, and using a combination of methods can result in conflicting settings. If you specify different values for the same Setup options on the Setup command line, in the Setup settings file, and in a transform, then Setup uses the following rules to determine which value to use:

- If you set an option in the Custom Installation Wizard that corresponds to a Setup property, the wizard automatically sets the corresponding property in the MST file. For example, when you customize removal behavior on the **Remove Previous Versions** page, then the Custom Installation Wizard sets the **SKIPREMOVEPREVIOUSDIALOG** property to **True**.

- If you modify a Setup property on the **Modify Setup Properties** page of the Custom Installation Wizard, this setting overrides any corresponding options that you set on previous pages of the wizard. Your modified Setup property is written to the MST file.

- If you set options (including Setup properties) in the Setup settings file that conflict with options in the transform, then the values in the INI file take precedence over the transform.

■ If you set options on the command line, those settings take precedence over any conflicting values in either the INI file or the transform.

> **Note**   The **COMPANYNAME** property is an exception to the normal precedence of settings. If you supply an organization name when you create an administrative installation point and then specify a new default organization name on the **Specify Default Path and Organization** page of the Custom Installation Wizard, that setting takes precedence over any other **COMPANYNAME** setting you specify later in the wizard, in Setup.ini, or on the command-line.

Resources and Related Information

For more information about creating an Office profile settings file (OPS file) with the Profile Wizard, see "Customizing User-defined Settings" later in this chapter.

For more information about using the Removal Wizard during or after the Office installation, see "Customizing Removal Behavior" later in this chapter.

Customizing How Setup Runs

You can always run Setup interactively to install Microsoft Office 2003—or allow users to run Setup interactively. However, by using command-line options or setting values for Setup properties in the Setup settings file (Setup.ini) or in a transform (MST file), you can customize the way Setup installs Office 2003 throughout your organization.

You set most properties that control the behavior of Setup in one of three locations, listed in order of precedence:

■ On the command line

■ In the Setup settings file (Setup.ini)

■ On the **Modify Setup Properties** page of the Custom Installation Wizard, which stores your settings in a transform (MST file)

Note that settings specified on the **Modify Setup Properties** page override most corresponding settings specified on previous pages of the wizard.

Customize display settings

When you distribute Office 2003 throughout an organization, you can determine how much of the Setup user interface is displayed to users. You can allow users to interact fully with Setup and make choices that differ from the defaults you specify, or you can run Setup silently so that your configuration of Office is installed with no opportunities to make changes. You can even set different display settings for different portions of the installation process.

You set display options on the command line by using the **/q** switch or by setting the **Display** property in Setup.ini. The following display settings are available:

- **none**   No user interface is displayed; Office is installed silently.
- **basic**   Only simple progress indicators, error messages, and a completion message are displayed.
- **reduced**   Full progress indicators and error messages are displayed, but Setup collects no information from the user.
- **full**   All dialog boxes and messages are displayed to the user, and the user can enter information during the Setup process.

> **Note**   Display settings like **/q**option are passed globally to every installation. For example, if you set the display level on the command line or in the [Display] section of Setup.ini, the primary Office 2003 installation and any chained packages are installed with the same level of user interface, unless you set a different display setting for a chained package.

Install Office quietly

By default, Setup installs Office 2003 with a full user interface and displays a completion notice at the end of the installation. When you run Office 2003 Setup silently or with only a basic user interface, you can determine whether users see a completion message when the installation is finished by using the following command-line options:

- When you install Office with a basic user interface (**/qb**), Setup displays the completion message by default. To suppress the completion message and display only progress indicators, append a minus sign to the command-line option (**/qb-**). When you install Office silently, Setup does not display a completion message by default. To force the display of the completion message, append a plus sign to the command-line option (**/qb+**).

In many large organizations it is more efficient to install Office without any user interaction. In this case, the recommended setting is **/qb-**, which installs Office as follows:

- Progress indicators are displayed during the installation.
- Error messages and other modal dialog boxes are not displayed.

- Setup does not display a completion notice when the installation is finished.

- Setup automatically restarts the computer, if necessary, unless the Windows Installer **REBOOT** property is set to override default behavior.

When you run Office 2003 Setup with a basic or reduced display, users can still click the **Cancel** button to stop the installation process. However, if you set the **NOCANCEL** property to **1**, then the **Cancel** button is displayed but is unavailable. Users know that the installation is occurring and they know when it is complete, but they cannot interrupt the process.

You can install Office 2003 with no user interface whatsoever by using the **/qn** option or by setting the **Display** option to **none** in Setup.ini. If you are using a deployment tool such as Microsoft Systems Management Server to run the installation when users are not logged on, then you must use this display setting.

Set unique display settings for other packages

In some circumstances, you might want to specify different display options for different packages installed with Office 2003. You must use Setup.ini to override global display settings set on the command line or in the [Display] section of Setup.ini.

For example, if you install Office 2003 quietly, but you want users to select Microsoft Office 2003 Multilingual User Interface Packs (MUI Packs) in the MUI Pack Wizard, you can specify a full user interface for the chained Muiwiz.msi package in the appropriate section of Setup.ini. For example:

```
[ChainedInstall_1]
Path="\\server\share\admin_install_point\Muiwiz.msi"
Display=full
```

> **Note**   If you specify a display setting on the command line, that setting overrides display settings specified in any section of Setup.ini.

Customize the Setup user interface

When you run Office 2003 Setup with a full user interface, you can customize some of the text and buttons that users see by setting properties on the command line, in Setup.ini, or on the **Modify Setup Properties** page of the Custom Installation Wizard.

Customize installation type descriptions

If a user selects the **Custom Install** option, Setup prompts for the installation location and then displays a list of Office applications or a hierarchy of Office features so that the user can select an installation state for each one. You can change descriptive text for the **Custom Install** option. For example, if you have omitted

Microsoft Office Access 2003 from the installation, but you want to tell users how to install it for themselves, specify the following:

```
CUSTOMINSTALLDESCRIPTION="By default Access is not installed. Click Custom Install
to install Access on your computer."
```

You can also customize the button labels and descriptive text for the **Upgrade**, **Typical Install**, **Minimal Install**, and **Run from Network Install** installation options. Each of the following properties is described in detail in Appendix B, "Office 2003 Resource Kit Reference":

- **COMPLETEINSTALLDESCRIPTION**
- **CUSTOMINSTALLDESCRIPTION**
- **CUSTOMTEXT**
- **MINIMUMINSTALLDESCRIPTION**
- **MINIMUMTEXT**
- **RUNFROMSOURCEINSTALLDESCRIPTION**
- **RUNFROMSOURCETEXT**
- **TYPICALINSTALLDESCRIPTION**
- **TYPICALTEXT**
- **UPGRADEINSTALLDESCRIPTION**
- **UPGRADETEXT**

Note   Although you can customize the text that describes the **Complete Install** option, you cannot change the radio button label for this installation option.

Customize Add/Remove Programs

You can customize what users see in **Add/Remove Programs** (**Control Panel**) when they run Office 2003 Setup in maintenance mode. For example, to help prevent users from changing an installed Office configuration, you can set the **ARPNO-MODIFY** property in a transform. When users run Office 2003 Setup in maintenance mode, the **Change** button in **Add/Remove Programs** is unavailable.

Note   In Microsoft Windows XP or later, users without administrative privileges are prevented from changing or removing programs listed in **Add/Remove Programs**.

For more information about customizing **Add/Remove Programs**, look up properties that begin with **ARP** in "Setup Properties" in Appendix B, "Office 2003 Resource Kit Reference."

Customize logging options

Both Office 2003 Setup and Windows Installer generate log files during the installation process. You cannot set options for the Setup log file; however, Windows Installer allows you to set a number of logging options that apply to each package that it installs during Office 2003 Setup. Note that any logging options you set apply to all log files created by Windows Installer during the Office 2003 installation; you cannot specify unique logging options for a chained package.

Set logging options in Setup.ini

You can set Windows Installer logging options by specifying values in the [Logging] section of the Setup settings file. In Setup.ini, you specify the logging options by setting the **Type** option, and you determine a name for the log files by setting the **Template** option. The following example shows the syntax used in Setup.ini:

```
[Logging]
Type=<options>
Path=<path>
Template=<file name>.txt
```

You must include the .txt file extension when you specify a Setup log file name. Appending an asterisk (*) to the file name results in a unique log file for each installation performed by Setup.exe. The same log file name is used for each Windows Installer log file, with the incremented task number appended to the base file name. For example:

```
[Logging]
Type=v*
Path=%Temp%
Template=OfficeSetup(*).txt
```

These values create the following verbose log files during the installation process and store them in the %Temp% folder on each user's computer. (%Temp% is the default location for log files.) This example assumes that a log file with the same base name and numbered 0002 already exists in the folder.

Log file	Description
OfficeSetup(0003).txt	Setup.exe log file
OfficeSetup(0003)_Task(0001).txt	Office 2003 log file
OfficeSetup(0003)_Task(0002).txt	Log file for first chained package

> **Note**   Verbose logging is useful to diagnose installation problems during the testing phase or after a failed installation; however, verbose logging can produce very large log files.

Set logging options on the command line

You can set the same logging options on the command line by using **/l***option*. For example:

```
/lv* 'Office Setup(*).txt"
```

This example creates a log file in the default %Temp% folder, automatically increments the number in the file name, and instructs Windows Installer to use verbose logging with all logging parameters.

> **Note**   If your custom log file name includes spaces, you must enclose it in quotation marks on the command line.

The logging options you use with **/l** determine what information is written to the log file. For a description of logging options, see **/l** in "Setup Command-line Options" in Appendix B, "Office 2003 Resource Kit Reference."

Specify a new installation location

By default, Setup installs Office 2003 in the Program Files\Microsoft Office\Office11 folder on each user's computer. You can change this location by specifying a different path for the **INSTALLLOCATION** property on the command line or in the Setup settings file.

In the Office Custom Installation Wizard, you can specify a default value for the installation location on the **Specify Default Path and Organization** page. You can also specify the location by setting the **INSTALLLOCATION** property on the **Modify Setup Properties** page of the wizard.

> **Note**   Like Office 2000 and Office XP, Office 2003 is always installed in a version-specific folder. If you choose to retain a previous version of Office on the computer, you can specify the same custom location. Setup installs Office 2003 in a version-specific subfolder of that location so that previous files are not overwritten.

Manage the local installation source

When Office is installed from the Office 2003 CD or a compressed CD image, Setup automatically copies required installation files to a hidden folder on the local computer. Windows Installer uses this local installation source to install Office, and the local source remains available for repairing, reinstalling, or updating Office later on. Users can install features on demand or run Setup in maintenance mode to add new features even when they do not have access to the original source.

You can customize how Setup handles the creation of the local installation source by modifying properties in the [Cache] section of Setup.ini:

- **LOCALCACHEDRIVE** Specify a different drive for the local installation source.

- **CDCACHE** Enable or disable local caching.

- **DELETEABLECACHE** Give users the option to delete the local installation source at the end of Setup.

For more information about setting these properties, see [CACHE] in "Setup Settings File" in Appendix B, "Office 2003 Resource Kit Reference."

To take advantage of a local installation source, users must install Office from a CD or compressed CD image on the network. To facilitate this deployment option, the Custom Installation Wizard contains a new page for handling the end-user license agreement (EULA) and Volume License Key (**PIDKEY**). For more information, see "Taking Advantage of a Local Installation Source" in Chapter 3, "Preparing to Deploy Office 2003."

Handle Setup problems

Office 2003 Setup helps you manage Setup problems in the following ways:

- Customize the error messages that users see when they run Setup with a full or reduced user interface.

  For example, you can add text to the error message box that refers users to an internal support group. Specify a string value for the **SUPPORTERROR-STRING** property on the command line, in Setup.ini, or in a transform.

- Collect data about Setup failures.

  In Office 2003, Setup Error Reporting is a subset of Corporate Error Reporting. By default, Setup Error Reporting (Dw.exe) is turned off when you create an administrative installation point. However, you can turn it back on by setting the **SETUPDW** property to **True**.

  When you redirect error reporting to an internal location, information from Setup failures is recorded there, too. In order to take advantage of this functionality, you must configure Corporate Error Reporting policies before you deploy Office. For more information, see "Reporting Office 2003 Application Crashes" in Chapter 19, Maintaining Office 2003 Installations."

Related links

For a detailed description of each section of Setup.ini, see "Setup Settings File" in Appendix B, "Office 2003 Resource Kit Reference."

For definitions and examples of the Setup properties and command-line options that you can use during an Office installation, see "Setup Command-line Options" and "Setup Properties" in Appendix B, "Office 2003 Resource Kit Reference."

For additional information about Windows Installer properties and command-line options, see the Platform SDK on the MSDN Web site at *http://msdn.microsoft.com /library/en-us/msi/setup/roadmap_to_windows_installer_documentation.asp.*

Customizing Office Features and Shortcuts

When you install Microsoft Office 2003 from an administrative installation point or compressed CD image, you can determine which applications and features are installed on users' computers, including how and when features are installed. You can also customize the way that Setup creates shortcuts for Office 2003 applications and even add your own custom files to the Office installation.

Selecting Office features

When running Office Setup interactively, users can choose which Office applications and features are installed by selecting options from the feature tree that Setup displays. Office features can be installed in any of the following states:

- Copied to the local hard disk.

- Run from the network server (administrative installation point only).

- Installed on first use, which means that Setup does not install the feature until the first time it is used.

- Not installed, but accessible to users through **Add/Remove Programs** or the command line.

- Not installed, not displayed during Setup, and not accessible to users after Office is installed.

By using the Office Custom Installation Wizard, you can make these choices for users ahead of time. When users run Setup interactively, the installation states that you specify in the transform (MST file) appear as the default selections. When you run Setup quietly, your choices determine how the features are installed.

On the Resource Kit CD   The Office 2003 Resource Kit includes the Custom Installation Wizard, which is installed by default when you run the Office Resource Kit Setup program. For more information, see "Custom Installation Wizard" in Appendix A, "Toolbox."

Set the installation state for features

The **Set Feature Installation States** page of the Custom Installation Wizard displays the same feature tree that users see when they select the **Customize** option during Setup. The feature tree is a hierarchy. Parent features contain child features, and child features can contain subordinate child features. For example, the Microsoft Word for Windows feature includes the child feature **Help**. The Help feature includes the child feature **Help for WordPerfect Users**.

When you click a feature in the feature tree, you can select one of the following installation states:

- **Run from My Computer**   Setup copies files and writes registry entries and shortcuts associated with the feature to the user's hard disk, and the application or feature runs locally.

- **Run all from My Computer**   Same as **Run from My Computer**, except that all child features belonging to the feature are also set to this state.

- **Run from Network**   Setup leaves components for the feature on the administrative installation point, and the feature is run from there. The **Run from Network** option is available only when users install from an uncompressed administrative image.

- **Run all from Network**   Same as **Run from Network**, except that all child features belonging to the feature are also set to this state.

  Note that some child features do not support **Run from Network**; these child features are installed on the local computer.

- **Installed on First Use**   Setup leaves components for the feature and all its child features on the administrative installation point until the user first attempts to use the feature, at which time the components are automatically copied to the local hard disk.

  If the user installed from a compressed CD image with the local installation source enabled, then the components are installed from the local source.

  Note that some child features do not support **Installed on First Use**; these features are set to **Not Available**.

- **Not Available**   The components for the feature, and all of the child features belonging to the feature, are not installed on the computer. Users can change this installation state during Setup or later in maintenance mode.

- **Not Available, Hidden, Locked**   The components for the feature are not installed and the feature does not appear in the feature tree during Setup—nor can users install it by changing the state of the parent feature or by calling Windows Installer directly from the command line.

Not all installation states are available for every feature. For example, if a feature contains a component that cannot be run over the network, then **Run from Network** is not included in the list of available installation states.

When you change the installation state of a feature, Windows Installer may automatically change the installation state of a parent or child feature to match. If you set the **Help** feature to **Installed on First Use**, for example, but set the child feature **Help for WordPerfect Users** to **Run from My Computer**, then Setup installs the entire **Help** feature on the local hard disk.

> **Tip** If you run the Custom Installation Wizard (Custwiz.exe) with the **/x** command-line option, the wizard displays the feature tree fully expanded on the **Set Feature Installation States** page.

Hide or lock features during Setup

In addition to setting the installation state, you can right-click any feature on the **Set Feature Installation States** page and click **Hide** to hide the feature from the user. Setup does not display hidden features in the feature tree when users run Setup interactively; instead, the feature is installed behind the scenes according to the installation state that you have specified. When you hide a feature, all of the child features belonging to the feature are also hidden.

The best use of the **Hide** setting is to simplify the feature tree for users. For example, you might hide the **Office Tools** branch of the feature tree so that users do not have to decide which tools they need. Only the tools that you select are installed.

> **Note** When you edit the transform in the Custom Installation Wizard, you can reverse the **Hide** setting by right-clicking the feature and clicking **Unhide**. However, you cannot use the Custom Maintenance Wizard to expose a hidden feature after Office is installed.

Even if you set a feature to **Not Available** and hide it in the feature tree, users can still change the setting and install the feature by installing the parent feature or by running Office 2003 Setup in maintenance mode. For example, if you set the **Help for WordPerfect Users** feature to **Not Available** and hide it, users can still install it by setting the parent **Help** feature to **Run All from My Computer**.

If you want to help prevent users from installing hidden features, choose the **Not Available, Hidden, Locked** installation state. In this case, the feature or application is not installed and is not available in maintenance mode. Users cannot install it by changing the state of the parent feature or by calling Windows Installer directly from the command line. The only way to reverse the **Not Available, Hidden, Locked** installation state after Office 2003 is installed is to use the Custom Maintenance Wizard.

> **On the Resource Kit CD**   The Office 2003 Resource Kit includes the Custom Maintenance Wizard, which is installed by default when you run the Office Resource Kit Setup program. For more information, see "Custom Maintenance Wizard" in Appendix A, "Toolbox."

When users install Office, Setup does not display the feature tree by default. Clicking the **Custom Install** option displays a top-level list of Office applications. Users can select the check box next to an application to install a typical set of features. When you set an Office application to **Not Available, Hidden, Locked**, the check box on this page remains visible but appears grayed out—users cannot select the application. To hide this page during Setup altogether, set the **SKIPCHECKBOX-DIALOG** property to **1**.

For more information about changing feature installation states after Office 2003 is installed, see "Updating Feature Installation States and Application Settings" in Chapter 18, "Updating Users' Office 2003 Configurations."

Disable installation states that rely on a network connection

Installing features on demand or running features over the network is not always efficient. Both of these installation states require a fast connection and reliable access to the administrative installation point on the network—which laptop users in the field might not always have.

The Custom Installation Wizard for Office 2003 includes two options on the **Set Feature Installation States** page that disable these installation states and help ensure that users do not reset features to these states during Setup or in maintenance mode:

- **Disable Run from Network**   When you select a feature in the feature tree and then select this check box, users are prevented from setting the feature to run from the network. The installation state does not appear in the list of options during initial Setup or in maintenance mode.

- **Disable Installed on First Use**   When you select a feature in the feature tree and then select this check box, users are prevented from setting the feature to be installed on first use. The installation state does not appear in the list of options during initial Setup or in maintenance mode.

Child features do not inherit these settings from parent features automatically. You must select each feature in the tree and set **Disable Run from Network** or **Disable Installed on First Use** for only that feature. You can also select a feature and click **Apply to Branch** to apply either of these settings to a feature and all of its subordinate features.

> **Note** The **Disable Run from Network** and **Disable Installed on First Use** settings remain in effect for as long as Office is installed on the user's computer. You cannot reverse these settings by using the Custom Maintenance Wizard.

Modify intelligent Setup behavior

To make an Office 2003 installation more efficient, Setup automatically sets default feature installation states in the following circumstances:

- When you upgrade to Office 2003, Setup detects and matches feature installation states from the previous version.

    For example, if Microsoft Word 2002 is installed to run from the network, Setup installs Microsoft Office Word 2003 to run from the network. If Microsoft PowerPoint 2002 is set to **Not Available**, Setup does not install Microsoft Office PowerPoint 2003.

- When you install MUI Packs from the Microsoft Office 2003 Multilingual User Interface Pack, Setup matches the feature installation states specified for the core version of Office.

    For example, if the core English version of Microsoft Office Access 2003 is set to be installed on demand, then Setup automatically sets international versions of Access 2003 features to **Installed on First Use**.

- When you install Office under Microsoft Windows Terminal Services, Setup applies the most efficient installation state for each feature.

    For example, because the speech recognition feature does not run efficiently over most networks and might not be supported by all clients, Windows Terminal Services automatically changes the feature installation state from **Installed on First Use** to **Not Available**.

This intelligent Setup behavior works to your advantage in most situations. However, you can override Setup and specify your own default feature installation states in a transform by using one of the following two settings:

■ **NOFEATURESTATEMIGRATION** property

Setting this property to **1** for the Office 2003 package overrides intelligent Setup behavior for the entire package. Note that this property has no effect on Windows Terminal Services logic; you must override optional Windows Terminal Services installation states on a per-feature basis.

■ **Do Not Migrate Previous Installation State** check box on the **Set Feature Installation States** page of the Custom Installation Wizard

Selecting an Office 2003 feature in the feature tree and then selecting this check box overrides intelligent Setup behavior and enforces the installation state you set in the transform. (If you have already set the property **NOFEATURESTATEMIGRATION** for the entire package, then selecting this check box for a given feature has no effect.) Note that this check box has no effect on default feature installation state matching for MUI Pack features.

The following table summarizes the results of setting the property **NOFEATURESTATEMIGRATION** for an Office 2003 package or selecting the **Do Not Migrate Previous Installation State** check box for a feature.

Package	Property set to True	Check box selected
Office	Default feature installation state migration is disabled for all of Office.	Does not apply the installation state from a previous version to the selected feature.
MUI Pack	Default feature installation state matching is disabled for the entire package.	Has no effect on default feature installation state matching.
Proofing Tools	Default feature installation state matching is disabled for the entire package.	Has no effect on default feature installation state matching.

Although the **NOFEATURESTATEMIGRATION** property has no effect on Windows Terminal Services logic, you can override default Windows Terminal Services settings for some features by selecting the **Do Not Migrate Previous Installation State** check box. For example, if your network and clients support the speech recognition feature, you can set that feature to **Run from My Computer** and select the **Do Not Migrate Previous Installation State** check box to enforce your setting. However, you cannot override all of the installation states set by default under Windows Terminal Services. For example, Windows Terminal Services does not allow any feature to be set to **Installed on First Use**.

Microsoft Access 2000 and Office 2003

When you upgrade from Microsoft Office 2000 to Office 2003, you might choose to keep Access 2000 installed on users' computers. In this scenario, if you set Access 2003 to **Not Available** and install Office quietly, then Windows Installer removes the MDB file extension registration, and Access 2000 no longer recognizes the databases. Selecting the **Do Not Migrate Previous Installation State** check box for Microsoft Access does not prevent this problem.

To help ensure that Access 2000 users can continue to use their MDB files after the upgrade, you can take one of two steps:

- Set Microsoft Office Access 2003 to **Not Available, Hidden, and Locked** in the transform.
  or

- Set the **NOFEATURESTATEMIGRATION** property to **True** for the entire Office package.

Adding files to the installation

In addition to selecting which Office files are installed, Setup allows you to add your own files to the Office installation. You can deploy corporate templates, images, custom applications, or other files along with Office. On the **Add/Remove Files** page of the Office Custom Installation Wizard, click **Add** to add a new file to the installation.

After you select one or more files to add, enter the destination path for the file or files in the File Destination Path dialog box. You can enter an absolute path on the user's computer, or you can select a path from the list. If you select a path, you can add a subfolder to it by appending a backslash (\) followed by the subfolder name. When you click **OK**, the wizard adds the file to the transform. Setup installs the file on the user's computer, in the folder you specified, when the user installs Office.

Note   Files that you add to the installation on this page are not removed if the user subsequently modifies the file or removes, repairs, or reinstalls Office.

After you add the file, you can add a shortcut for the file on the Add, Modify, or Remove Shortcuts page of the wizard. On that page, click **Add**; the file you added appears in the Target box. Because the file is copied into the transform, you must update the transform if the file changes later on.

To update the installation with modified files

1. On the **Open the MST File** page, enter the name of the Windows Installer transform (MST file).

2. On the **Select the MST File to Save** page, enter the name of the MST file again.

3. On the **Add/Remove Files** page, select the file that has changed, and then click **Remove**.

4. Click **Add**, and then enter the information for your modified file.

The Custom Installation Wizard also allows you to specify files to remove from users' computers when Office is installed. For example, you can have Setup delete custom templates designed for Word 2002 or Word 2000 when you upgrade to Word 2003. Click the **Remove Files** tab to list files to remove.

For more information about adding or removing files by using a transform, see the Help for the **Add/Remove Files** page in the Custom Installation Wizard.

Customizing Office shortcuts

By using the Custom Installation Wizard, you can customize the shortcuts that Setup creates for Microsoft Office applications and files. You can control what shortcuts are installed, and you can also specify which folder a shortcut is stored in and what command-line options to use with a shortcut.

On the **Add, Modify, or Remove Shortcuts** page, the Custom Installation Wizard displays shortcuts for all the features that you selected on the **Set Feature Installation States** page.

An additional tab displays shortcuts for Office 2003 features that you did not set to be installed. Use the **Not Installed** tab to customize shortcuts for applications that you plan to install later.

For example, if you omitted Access 2003 from your initial installation, you can use the Custom Maintenance Wizard to install Access later. However, because the Custom Maintenance Wizard does not allow you to customize the way shortcuts are installed, you must customize Access shortcuts ahead of time in the transform.

> **Note**   Shortcuts for Office 2003 applications are stored in a new sub-folder: Start\Programs\Microsoft Office. Shortcuts to Office tools are stored in a subfolder in the same location: Start\Programs\Microsoft Office\Microsoft Office Tools. If you upgrade to Office 2003 but retain some applications from a previous version, the shortcuts for the applications you have chosen to keep, and those for any shared components, remain in their original location: Start\Programs and Start\Programs\Microsoft Office Tools. Shortcuts to the new versions of the applications and tools appear in the new location.

Modify an existing shortcut

On the **Add, Modify, or Remove Shortcuts** page, you modify any existing shortcut by selecting the shortcut and clicking **Modify**. In the **Add/Modify Shortcut Entry** dialog box, you can make the following changes:

- Change the target application associated with a shortcut.
- Change the location in which the shortcut (LNK file) is created.
- Rename a shortcut.
- Change the starting folder for the application—that is, the folder in which the application starts when the user clicks the shortcut.
- Specify a keyboard shortcut for a shortcut.
- Change the icon associated with a shortcut.

For more information about modifying shortcuts by using a transform, see the Help for the **Add, Modify, or Remove Shortcuts** page in the Custom Installation Wizard.

Add or remove shortcuts

You can click **Add** to add a new shortcut for any file being installed by Setup. This step allows you to create duplicate shortcuts for the most frequently used Office applications on the user's computer. It also allows you to create shortcuts for custom files or applications that you add to the installation.

To remove a shortcut from the list, select the shortcut and click **Remove**.

Create Windows Installer shortcuts

Windows Installer shortcuts support automatic repair of Office features and allow you to advertise Office applications. Advertised applications are installed the first time a user clicks the shortcut or opens a file associated with the application.

In some circumstances, you might not want Setup to create Windows Installer shortcuts. For example, if you are deploying to roaming users who sometimes log on to computers that do not support Windows Installer shortcuts, you can circumvent the default behavior by clearing the **Create Windows Installer shortcuts if supported** check box on the **Add, Modify, or Remove Shortcuts** page.

Migrate or clean up custom shortcuts from previous versions

Office users can create shortcuts with custom names or command-line options. For example, a custom shortcut might open a particular document whenever Word is started. In versions of Office prior to Office XP, these shortcuts were left behind and broken when users upgraded to a new version of Office. When you upgrade to Office 2003, however, Setup automatically migrates custom shortcuts to point to the corresponding Office 2003 application.

For example, if a user has created a shortcut to Word 2002 on the desktop, Setup replaces it with a shortcut to Word 2003. If you associated a custom command line with the shortcut, Setup preserves that, as well.

> **Note**   Custom shortcuts for previous versions of Access are not updated to point to Access 2003 when you upgrade.

How Setup handles custom shortcut migration

Setup handles shortcut migration for each application separately. If you upgrade most of your applications to Office 2003 but retain Microsoft Excel 2002, for example, then all your shortcuts point to the correct versions—Office 2003 applications and Excel 2002.

If you install more than one version of the same application on your computer—for example, both Excel 2002 and Microsoft Office Excel 2003—then Setup updates all custom shortcuts to point to the Office 2003 application. In this multiple-version scenario, you might later uninstall Office 2003; however, your custom shortcuts are not migrated back to the previous version.

If you are installing Office 2003 in a multiple-version environment, and you do not want to update custom shortcuts to point to the new version, you can prevent Setup from upgrading existing custom shortcuts. Set the **DISABLESCMIGRATION** property to **True** in a transform or on the command line.

Setup handles migration of custom shortcuts in the following circumstances:

- When Office 2003 is first installed.

- When an advertised Office 2003 application is installed.

- When the installation state of an installed application is changed to **Not Available**.

Setup searches the following locations for custom shortcuts:

- Desktop
- **Start** menu, including the **Programs** and **Microsoft Office Tools** submenus
- **Quick Launch** toolbar

> **Note**   The Office Shortcut Bar has been removed from Office 2003 and none of the Office Shortcut Bar shortcuts from previous versions migrate to Office 2003.

You can specify additional custom shortcuts in other locations by editing the Oclncust.opc file in the Office folder. These shortcuts are migrated when Office is installed. In the OPC file, custom shortcuts are specified by using the following syntax:

```
SHORTCUT=OPC directory token or drive letter and colon\subdirectory
\target file name | feature | version | component | command line
```

To remove a custom shortcut during the installation, you must specify only the target file name. Setup matches the target file name with any shortcut, regardless of the actual shortcut name (LNK file). For example, to remove any custom shortcut to Word in the Office subfolder of the StartMenu\Programs folder, add the following line to the Oclncust.opc file:

```
SHORTCUT=SYSMENUPROGRAMSDIR\Office\winword.exe
```

However, if you want Setup to automatically migrate this custom shortcut to point to Word 2003, add the following line instead:

```
SHORTCUT=SYSMENUPROGRAMSDIR\Office\winword.exe|WORDFiles||Global_Word_Core
```

> **Note**   When a custom Windows Installer shortcut that includes command-line options migrates to Office 2003, the new shortcut becomes a normal Windows shortcut. The new shortcut no longer supports install-on-demand functionality, but users can modify the command line after the upgrade.

For more information about editing the OPC files used by Setup and the Removal Wizard to clean up previous versions, see "OPC File Syntax" in Appendix B, "Office 2003 Resource Kit Reference."

How Setup cleans up custom shortcuts

Office 2003 removes custom shortcuts to Office 2003 applications more efficiently than versions prior to Office XP. For example, if a user copies a shortcut to Excel 2003 onto the desktop and then removes Excel 2003 from the computer, Setup automatically removes that shortcut.

In addition to the default locations that Setup checks for custom shortcuts to remove, you can direct Setup to search additional folders for outdated custom shortcuts by setting the **CIWEXTRASHORTCUTDIRS** property in a transform or on the command line. You specify additional locations by using a list delimited by semicolons.

For example, to direct Setup to clean up custom shortcuts in the Startup and Favorites\My Office folders, specify the following:

```
CIWEXTRASHORTCUTDIRS=<StartMenu\Programs\Startup>; <Favorites>\My Office
```

When you specify additional folders, you can use any of the following folder keywords, appending other path information to them:

- `<Desktop>`

- `<StartMenu>`

- `<StartMenu\Programs>`

- `<StartMenu\Programs\Startup>`

- `<ProgramFiles\Microsoft Office>`

- `<ApplicationData>`

- `<Favorites>`

- `<NetHood>`

You can also specify additional locations by using a full path, such as C:\Office\My Office. Wildcards—both asterisks (*) and question marks (?)—are supported. For example, the following setting causes Setup to search the Start Menu\Programs folder for all folders that include Office in the name:

```
CIWEXTRASHORTCUTDIRS=<StartMenu\Programs\*Office*>
```

Customizing User-defined Settings

Microsoft Office 2003 applications are highly customizable. Users can change how Office 2003 functions by setting options or adding custom templates or tools. For example, a sales department can create a custom template for invoices or a custom dictionary with industry-specific terms. Users can change everything from the screen resolution to the default file format for saving documents. Most of these user-defined settings are recorded as values in the Microsoft Windows registry.

As an administrator, you can customize user-defined settings and distribute a standard Microsoft Office 2003 configuration to all the users in your organization by using the Profile Wizard to capture settings an Office profile settings file (OPS file). When you add the OPS file to a transform (MST file), your customized settings are included when Office 2003 is installed on client computers.

The Custom Installation Wizard also allows you to customize user-defined settings directly in the transform. You can set user options and add or modify registry entries. You can even add the Profile Wizard to a transform and run it separately to distribute new default settings. When Office is installed, your customizations modify values in the Windows registry, and your settings appear as the defaults on users' computers.

Methods of customizing user settings

The method you choose to customize user-defined settings depends on the following:

- How extensively you want to configure Office 2003.

  You can create a custom configuration for all of Office 2003 or preset just a few key options.

- How complex your deployment scenarios are.

  You can distribute the same custom settings to all the users in your organization, or you can configure Office 2003 applications differently to meet the needs of different groups of users.

- How and when you deploy Office 2003 applications.

  If you are staging your Office 2003 deployment, you can customize only the applications that you are installing at a given time. Or, if you have already deployed Office, you can distribute a standard configuration to all Office 2003 users.

- Whether you want to enforce your custom settings.

  Settings that you distribute through a transform (MST file) or Office profile settings file (OPS file) appear to users as the default settings—but users can choose different options for themselves. By contrast, using Office 2003 policies ensures that your settings are always applied.

The following table lists typical scenarios for customizing user settings and the recommended methods and tools to use in each case.

Scenario	Method	Tool
Distribute a standard default Office 2003 configuration.	Add an OPS file to a transform.	Profile Wizard and Custom Installation Wizard (**Customize Default Application Settings** page)
Set just a few options or adjust your Office 2003 configuration without recreating the OPS file.	Add user settings to a transform.	Custom Installation Wizard (**Change Office User Settings** page)
Set default security levels.	Specify security settings in a transform.	Custom Installation Wizard (**Specify Office Security Settings** page)
Distribute a default Microsoft Office Outlook 2003 profile.	Specify Outlook settings in a transform.	Custom Installation Wizard (**Outlook: Customize Default Profile** page)
Specify settings that are not captured in an OPS file.	Add registry values to a transform.	Custom Installation Wizard (**Add/Remove Registry Entries** page)
Distribute a default Office 2003 configuration but store one or more OPS files separately from the MST file.	Run the Profile Wizard during Setup.	Profile Wizard and Custom Installation Wizard (**Add Installations and Run Programs** page)

Scenario	Method	Tool
Preserve users' custom settings from a previous version instead of specifying new default settings.	Allow Setup to migrate settings from a previous version of Office.	Default Setup behavior
Set unique options for Microsoft Office 2003 Multilingual User Interface Packs or other chained packages.	Specify settings in the transform applied to the chained package.	Custom Installation Wizard and Setup settings file (Setup.ini)
Distribute a default Office 2003 configuration that overrides individual users' settings.	Run the Profile Wizard as a stand-alone tool after Office is installed.	Profile Wizard
Modify user settings after Office is installed.	Distribute a configuration maintenance file (CMW file) after Office is installed.	Custom Maintenance Wizard
Prevent users from modifying the options you set.	Set Office policies.	Group Policy snap-in

Resolving conflicting settings

Most customized user options correspond to entries in the Windows registry. If you define conflicting values for the same setting, Windows Installer must determine which value to use. In most cases, a setting applied later in the installation process overwrites any settings applied earlier.

Settings for user options are applied in the following order:

1. Settings in an OPS file included in a transform.

2. Settings specified in a transform.

   These settings can be entered on the **Change Office User Settings**, **Specify Office Security Settings**, or **Outlook: Customize Default Settings** pages of the Custom Installation Wizard.

3. Registry values specified in a transform.

4. Settings applied by running the Profile Wizard during Setup.

5. Settings that migrate from a previous version of Office.

6. Settings applied by using the Profile Wizard or Custom Maintenance Wizard after Office is installed.

   This precedence assumes that users have already started each Office 2003 application and any migrated settings have already been applied.

7. Settings managed through policies.

Using the Profile Wizard

The Profile Wizard saves and restores user-defined settings in Office 2003 applications. Most user-defined settings can be stored in an Office user profile. When you run the Office Profile Wizard to save a user profile, you create an Office profile settings file (OPS file). Setup uses the OPS file to apply default settings when Office 2003 is installed.

For Office 2003, the Profile Wizard allows you to save settings for only a selected application or group of applications. This feature is particularly useful when you are staging your Office 2003 deployment; you can limit the settings saved in the OPS file to only the applications that you are deploying at a given time.

By design, the Profile Wizard excludes some settings, including user-specific information such as the user name and the Most Recently Used file list (**File** menu). Nor does the Profile Wizard capture all Outlook 2003 settings. For a list of the settings not captured by the Profile Wizard, see "Office Profile Wizard" in Appendix B, "Office 2003 Resource Kit Reference."

> **On the Resource Kit CD**   The Office 2003 Resource Kit includes the Office Profile Wizard, which is installed by default when you run the Office Resource Kit Setup program. For more information, see "Office Profile Wizard" in Appendix A, "Toolbox."

Add an OPS file to a transform

Adding an OPS file to a transform is a convenient way to deploy a collection of custom settings throughout your organization. Settings contained in the OPS file are implemented when users install Office, and those settings apply to every user who logs on using that computer. However, any other method of customizing user options—including specifying user settings elsewhere in the transform or choosing to migrate settings from a previous version of Office—overwrites default settings in the OPS file.

To customize default options for users by using an OPS file, follow these general steps:

1. Use the Profile Wizard to create an OPS file that contains your default settings for Office application options.

2. Use the Custom Installation Wizard to create a transform (MST file) that contains the OPS file.

3. Install Office 2003 on users' computers with your transform.

Create an OPS file

Before you create an OPS file, you must start each Office application on a test computer and set all the options you want to customize. You can set most options by using the Options command (**Tools** menu). To customize toolbars and menus, use the Customize command (**Tools** menu). After you have customized the Office applications, run the Profile Wizard to save the settings to an OPS file.

To save settings to an OPS file

1. Start the Profile Wizard.

2. On the **Save or Restore Settings** page, select **Save the settings from this machine**, and enter the name and path for the OPS file.

3. Select the check boxes next to the Office 2003 applications you want to include in your OPS file, and then click **Finish**.

    The Profile Wizard saves the Office application settings on your computer to the OPS file.

> **Note**   If an OPS file contains settings for an application that is not installed on a user's computer, those settings are still written to the registry.

Create a transform that contains the OPS file

You use the Custom Installation Wizard to create a transform that includes the OPS file.

To create a custom transform that contains the OPS file

1. Start the Custom Installation Wizard.

2. On the **Customize Default Application Settings** page, select **Get values from an existing settings profile**, and enter the file name and path of the OPS file you created.

    The Custom Installation Wizard creates a transform that contains your OPS file and any other customizations you have made.

> **On the Resource Kit CD**   The Office 2003 Resource Kit includes the Custom Installation Wizard, which is installed by default when you run the Office Resource Kit Setup program. For more information, see "Custom Installation Wizard" in Appendix A, "Toolbox."

Determine whether Setup migrates settings

By default, if a previous version of Office is installed on a user's computer, Windows Installer copies the previous application settings for that version to Office 2003. Migrated settings are applied the first time each user starts an Office application, and the user's migrated settings overwrite any duplicate settings contained in an OPS file or added to the transform.

On the **Customize Default Application Settings** page of the Custom Installation Wizard you can modify this Setup behavior. If you are not including an OPS file in the installation, the wizard selects the **Migrate user settings** check box by default. When users install Office 2003 with your transform, Setup migrates relevant settings from a previous version. If you add an OPS file to the transform, the wizard clears the **Migrate user settings** check box and uses the values in your OPS file instead.

> **Note** If you add an OPS file to the transform and also select the **Migrate user settings** check box, the settings from your OPS file are applied during the initial installation. However, the first time a user starts an Office application, Windows Installer migrates settings from a previous version of Office and overwrites any corresponding settings previously applied.

Run the Profile Wizard during Setup

Adding an OPS file to the MST file increases the size of the transform and also requires that you recreate the transform whenever you modify the OPS file. Alternatively, you can store the OPS file on a network server and direct Setup to run the Profile Wizard with that OPS file during the Office 2003 installation.

Running the Profile Wizard during Setup applies a standard default Office 2003 configuration to users' computers. However, because the OPS file is stored separately, you can modify the configuration without changing the transform. You can also create different OPS files for different groups of users.

When you run the Profile Wizard separately, you can choose whether to apply the settings in the OPS file once per user (the recommended option) or once per computer. You can also specify whether user-defined options are returned to their original default settings before your customized settings are applied; this step ensures that all users begin with exactly the same Office 2003 configuration.

When you add Proflwiz.exe to a transform, the Profile Wizard runs after Office is installed, so settings from this OPS file overwrite any duplicate settings specified in the transform, including the following:

- Settings specified in an OPS file added to a transform
- Settings specified on the **Change Office User Settings** page
- Microsoft Outlook e-mail options specified on the **Outlook: Customize Default Settings** page
- Security levels specified on the **Specify Office Security Settings** page
- Registry entries added on the **Add/Remove Registry Entries** page

To run the Profile Wizard during Setup

1. Copy the Profile Wizard executable file (Proflwiz.exe) and your customized OPS file to the Office administrative installation point.

   You can place the files in the same folder as Office Setup.exe, or you can create a subfolder for them.

2. Start the Custom Installation Wizard.

3. On the **Add Installations and Run Programs** page, click **Add**.

4. In the **Target** box, type the file name and path to Proflwiz.exe, or click **Browse** to select the file.

5. In the **Arguments** box, add command-line options directing the Profile Wizard to apply the OPS file to the user's computer, and then click **OK**.

6. Choose **Run this program once per machine** to apply your default settings the first time a user logs on.

   or

   Choose **Run this program once per user** to apply your default settings to every user of the computer. Note that this option requires a connection to the network every time a new user logs on.

For example, to run the Profile Wizard from the Profile subfolder on the Office administrative installation point, enter the following in the **Target** box:
\\server\share\admin_install_point\profile\proflwiz.exe
Then add the following command-line options to the **Arguments** box:
profile\newprofile.ops /r /q
These arguments run the Profile Wizard quietly (**/q**), reset all options to their original default settings (**/r**), and apply settings from the file Newprofile.ops (**profile\newprofile.ops**).

For more information about using the Profile Wizard, including command-line options that customize the way the wizard runs, see "Office Profile Wizard" in Appendix B, "Office 2003 Resource Kit Reference."

Run the Profile Wizard after Office is installed

You can run the Profile Wizard as a stand-alone tool after you deploy Office 2003. This method allows you to distribute a standard user profile that overwrites any other settings distributed through a transform, migrated during Setup, or set by users. Running the Profile Wizard separately also allows you to customize the process more precisely and include only the particular applications settings you want to manage.

To customize the performance of the Profile Wizard, you edit the INI file (Opw11adm.ini). Open the file in Notepad or another text editor, and then add or delete references to settings that you want to include or exclude. You can include or exclude registry settings or Application Data folders, template files, and so on. You can also run the Profile Wizard from the command line with no loss in functionality. Every option available in the wizard has a corresponding command-line switch.

> **Tip**   You do not need to edit the Profile Wizard INI file to include or exclude Office applications. On the **Save or Restore Settings** page of the wizard, select the check boxes next to the applications for which you want to save settings.

For more information about customizing the Profile Wizard, editing the Profile Wizard INI file, or specifying command-line options for the Profile Wizard, see "Office Profile Wizard" in Appendix B, "Office 2003 Resource Kit Reference."

For more information about using the Profile Wizard to update user settings after Office is deployed, see "Updating Feature Installation States and Application Settings" in Chapter 18, "Updating Users' Office 2003 Configurations."

Specifying user settings in a transform

If you do not want to distribute an entire Office 2003 configuration, you can customize selected user-defined options in a transform.

Add user settings to a transform

Most of the options captured by the Profile Wizard can also be set on the **Change Office User Settings** page of the Custom Installation Wizard. This method is useful for presetting just a few key options, or for modifying a standard configuration without recreating the OPS file.

When users install Office with your transform, the settings you specify are applied to every user of the computer. However, only settings that differ from existing default settings are applied. Options that you set on this page of the wizard overwrite corresponding settings in an OPS file added to the transform.

Specify Outlook settings in a transform

Many Outlook options appear on the **Change Office User Settings** page, and you customize them the same way you customize options for any other Office 2003 application. However, several important Outlook settings appear on their own pages of the Custom Installation Wizard.

Outlook profile information

You cannot define an Outlook profile by running the Profile Wizard, adding registry entries, or setting Office policies. Instead, you must create or modify an Outlook profile on the **Outlook: Customize Default Profile** page of the Custom Installation Wizard. These settings are not overwritten by any other method of customizing user options.

Outlook account information

When you add or modify an Outlook profile, you can also configure e-mail account information. For example, on the **Outlook: Specify Exchange Settings** page, you can configure an Exchange connection and specify whether users work with a local copy of their Exchange mail box (Cached Exchange Mode feature). On the **Outlook: Add Accounts** page, you can include more e-mail accounts in the user's Outlook profile.

Outlook e-mail settings

You specify default settings for the following options or items on the **Outlook: Customize Default Settings** page of the wizard:

- Whether to convert the personal address book (PAB file) to an Outlook Address Book

- Default e-mail editor

- Default e-mail format

For more information about customizing Outlook, see "Customizing Outlook Features and Installation with the Custom Installation Wizard" in Chapter 7, "Deploying Outlook 2003."

Specify security settings in a transform

You can customize Office 2003 security settings in a transform or OPS file, but some security settings are implemented differently than other user-defined settings.

Security levels

Security levels—**High**, **Medium**, or **Low**—apply to each Office 2003 application. However, the default security level can be set in one of two areas of the Windows registry:

- HKEY_CURRENT_USER\Software\Microsoft\Office\11.0\<Application>\Security
  The **Level** value in this subkey is the security setting captured by the Profile Wizard when you create an OPS file or when you customize the setting on the **Specify Security Settings** page of the Custom Installation Wizard. It is applied once for each user of the computer.

■ HKEY_LOCAL_MACHINE\Software\Microsoft\Office\11.0\<Application>\Security

The **Level** value in this subkey is the security setting that applies to the local computer. This setting takes precedence over the per-user setting, regardless of how the per-user setting is customized. You can customize this setting on the **Change Office User Settings** page or the **Add/Remove Registry Entries** page of the Custom Installation Wizard.

For example, on the **Specify Security Settings** page, you can set the default security level for Microsoft Office Word 2003 to **Medium**. This step sets the **Level** value in the Security subkeys in the HKEY_CURRENT_USER branch to **2**. However, on the **Change Office User Settings** page, you can also set the **Level** value in the Security subkey in the HKEY_LOCAL_MACHINE branch to **3**. In this scenario, Word is installed on the computer with the default security level set to **High** for all users.

You can also set security levels by using policies—a policy that applies to the security level in the HKEY_CURRENT_USER branch or another policy that applies to the HKEY_LOCAL_MACHINE branch. In this case, the security level set by policy for the local computer takes precedence over the policy set for the current user.

Trusted publishers

On the **Specify Security Settings** page of the Custom Installation Wizard, you can manage the list that identifies trusted sources for digitally signed macros, add-ins, ActiveX® controls, and other executable code used by Office applications. You can add Microsoft digital certificates (CER files) to help ensure that all add-ins and templates are installed with Office 2003. On the same page of the wizard, you can determine whether unsigned, and therefore potentially unsafe, ActiveX controls can initialize using persisted data.

For more information about configuring security settings for Office 2003 applications, see the Help for the **Specify Office Security Settings** page in the Custom Installation Wizard.

Add registry values to a transform

Because most Office options correspond to entries in the Windows registry, you can customize those options by adding or modifying registry values in a transform. Setup applies your new default options when users install Office. Depending on which branch of the registry you customize, your settings are applied once per user (HKEY_CURRENT_USER) or once per computer (HKEY_LOCAL_MACHINE).

In addition, you can add registry settings to customize some options that cannot be set directly in the Office 2003 user interface and are not captured by the Profile Wizard in an OPS file. For example, you can include custom applications in Office Setup that require custom Windows registry settings.

After Office Setup is complete, Windows Installer copies the registry entries that you added to the transform to users' computers. Options that you set by adding or modifying registry entries override duplicate values that you set on other pages of the Custom Installation Wizard, including the following:

- Settings specified in an OPS file added to a transform

- Settings specified on the **Change Office User Settings** page

- Options on the **Outlook: Customize Default Settings** page

- Settings configured on the **Specify Office Security Settings** page

Add registry entries to a transform

You add or modify registry entries on the **Add Registry Entries** page of the Custom Installation Wizard. You need to know the complete path for each registry entry, as well as the value name and the data type for that entry.

To add Windows registry entries to a transform

1. Start the Custom Installation Wizard.

2. On the **Add Registry Entries** page, click **Add**.

3. In the **Root** box, select the portion of the registry you want to modify.

4. In the **Data type** box, enter a data type for the new entry.

5. In the remaining boxes, enter the full path for the registry entry you want to add, enter the value name and data, and click **OK**.

   For more information about these values, see the Help for the **Add/Remove Registry Entries** page in the Custom Installation Wizard.

Import a registry file into a transform

To add multiple registry entries to a transform, you can create a registry (.reg) file, and then use the **Add Registry Entries** page of the Custom Installation Wizard to import the registry file.

A registry file is a text file that contains a copy of a section of the Windows registry. If your computer already has the registry entries you want to copy to users' computers, then creating a registry file is an efficient way of distributing those entries.

To create a registry file

1. On the computer that has the registry entries you want to add to the installation, click **Run** on the **Start** menu and type **regedit**.

2. In the Registry Editor, select the portion of the registry tree that you want to copy.

3. On the **Registry** menu, click **Export Registry File**, and follow the instructions to export the selected portion of the registry tree to a registry file.

To import a registry file to a transform

1. Start the Custom Installation Wizard.

2. On the **Add Registry Entries** page, click **Import**.

3. Select the registry file you created, and click **Open**.

   The wizard adds the registry entries from the registry file to the list on the **Add Registry Entries** page. If the wizard encounters an entry in the registry file that is a duplicate of an entry already in the list, and the two entries contain different value data, then the wizard prompts you to select the entry you want to keep.

Specify settings for chained packages

You can specify default settings for packages that you chain to your Office 2003 installation. If you create a transform for a chained package, you can include an OPS file or set options on other pages of the Custom Installation Wizard that apply only to the chained package. Because Windows Installer installs chained packages after Office 2003 is installed, any conflicting settings in the chained package overwrite options set during the Office 2003 portion of the installation.

For example, you can set the default installation language to French in a transform applied to the Office 2003 installation. You can also chain the German Multilingual User Interface Pack (MUI Pack) and apply a transform that sets the default language to German. In this scenario, Office 2003 installs with French as the default language; but the default language changes to German when the MUI Pack is installed.

For more information about chaining packages to the Office 2003 installation, see "Deploying Office and Other Products Together" in Chapter 5, "Installing Office 2003."

Modify settings by using the Custom Maintenance Wizard

You can apply a transform only during your initial installation of Office 2003. If you want to make changes after Office 2003 is installed, you can use the Custom Maintenance Wizard to modify almost everything that you can set in the Custom Installation Wizard—including default user settings, security levels, Outlook settings, and registry entries.

The user interface of both wizards is very similar. For example, you specify new default settings on the **Change Office User Settings** page of the Custom Maintenance Wizard. However, you cannot use the Custom Maintenance Wizard to distribute a new OPS file; you must run the Profile Wizard separately.

For more information about updating user-defined settings after Office is installed, see "Updating Feature Installation States and Application Settings" in Chapter 18, "Updating Users' Office 2003 Configurations." For more information about using the Custom Maintenance Wizard, see the Custom Installation Wizard Help on the companion CD.

> **On the Resource Kit CD**   The Office 2003 Resource Kit includes the Custom Maintenance Wizard, which is installed by default when you run the Office Resource Kit Setup program. For more information, see "Custom Maintenance Wizard" in Appendix A, "Toolbox."

Modify settings by using Office policies

When you install Office, you can modify registry values by using Office Group Policy settings. Policy settings take effect when the user logs on to the network, and they override any duplicate values set during installation. Unlike default application settings set by means of an OPS file, policies are not optional; if a user changes a setting set by policy, Windows reinstates the policy setting the next time the user logs on.

For more information about setting Office 2003 policies, see "Managing Users' Configurations by Policy" in Chapter 18, "Updating Users' Office 2003 Configurations."

Customizing Removal Behavior

When you upgrade to Microsoft Office 2003, the Removal Wizard (Offcln.exe) removes unnecessary or obsolete components from previously installed versions of Office and related applications. The wizard components run behind the scenes during Setup, but you can also run the Removal Wizard on its own.

Both the wizard and the Office Setup program use the same logic and the same text file (OPC file) to detect and remove unneeded or obsolete files and settings from users' computers. You can determine which previous versions of Office applications are removed by setting options in a transform (MST file). You can also customize the OPC file so that only the files and components that you specify are removed.

> **On the Resource Kit CD**   The Office 2003 Resource Kit includes the same stand-alone Removal Wizard (Offcln.exe) that is included with Office 2003. The Removal Wizard is installed by default when you run the Office Resource Kit Setup program. For more information, see "Office Removal Wizard" in Appendix A, "Toolbox."

Removal Wizard components (which are used by both the wizard and Setup) include the following files:

- **Offcln.exe**   Provides the user interface that lets you run the wizard as a stand-alone utility; located in the \Files\Pfiles\MSOffice\Office11 folder on the installation image. The wizard is also available in the Office 2003 Resource Kit.

- **Oclean.dll**   Used by the stand-alone Removal Wizard and Setup to carry out instructions in the OPC files and clean up the user's hard disk.

- **Oclncore.opc**   Global OPC file for Office 2003; located in the \Files\Pfiles\MSOffice\Office11 folder on the installation image. This file specifies files, registry entries, INI file settings, and shortcuts associated with all components in the core English version of Office 2003.

- **Oclnintl.opc**   Satellite OPC file for each language version of Office 2003; located in the LCID subfolders. Specifies language-specific components, including files, registry entries, INI file settings, and shortcuts.

- **Oclncust.opc**   Template file for adding additional content to be deleted by the Removal Wizard, including all content that was commented out in previous versions of the wizard; located in the \Files\Pfiles\MSOffice\Office11 folder on the installation image. Modify this file if you want to delete additional files or registry keys.

Removing previous versions during Setup

When users install Office 2003, Setup detects files, settings, and shortcuts from previously installed versions of Office and removes them. When you run Setup in quiet mode (**/q**), default Setup behavior removes all previous versions of Office applications that are also included in the version of Office 2003 that you are installing.

For example, if you are installing the stand-alone version of Microsoft Office Word 2003 over Microsoft Office XP Professional, only Word 2002 is removed by default during the update process. If you run Setup with a full user interface, users can choose which previous-version applications to remove.

> **Note**   The Setup user interface allows users to keep or remove all previous versions of a particular application. However, you can use the Custom Installation Wizard or stand-alone Removal Wizard to select particular versions to keep or remove. For example, you can keep Word 2000 but remove Word 97.

Setup can detect and remove the following versions of Office and Office-related products:

- Microsoft Office 95, Office 97, Office 2000, Office XP (including stand-alone applications)

- Microsoft Outlook 97, Outlook 98, Outlook 2000, Outlook 2002 (does not include Outlook Express)

- Microsoft FrontPage® 1.1, FrontPage 97, FrontPage 98, FrontPage 2000, FrontPage 2002

- Microsoft Publisher 95, Publisher 97, Publisher 98, Publisher 2000, Publisher 2002

- Microsoft Office 2000 and Office XP Multilingual User Interface Packs (MUI Packs)

    MUI Packs are removed by default only if all other Office 2000 or Office XP applications are also being removed. If you are installing MUI Packs or Proofing Tool Kits separately, then Offcln.exe does not run.

- Obsolete files, including orphaned files, registry settings, **Start** menu shortcuts, and INI file settings used by any previously installed edition of Office applications

Note   Setup does not remove documents or other user files from the user's hard disk.

In addition, Setup detects the following products to avoid deleting shared files that overlap with Office:

- Microsoft Project 95, Project 98, Project 2000, Project 2002

- Microsoft PhotoDraw® 1, PhotoDraw 2

- Hagaki 1, Hagaki 2, Hagaki 3, Hagaki 4, Hagaki 5

- Team Manager 97

- Bookshelf® 1 (Office 97)

Note   Because Setup recognizes components at the application level, the removal process detects and removes stand-alone versions of applications such as Word and Microsoft Excel. If all the core applications are removed, Setup also removes shared components such as Office Binder and Equation Editor.

Setup also detects the following as candidates for removal:

- Incompletely installed or uninstalled components that leave unusable files on the hard disk

- Files that begin with a tilde (~)

Finally, Setup detects and can remove temporary files, which are defined as files found in any of the following folders:

- Microsoft Windows temporary folder (Windows\Temp or Windows\Tmp)

- Folders identified by the environment variable %TEMP% or %TMP%

- Other temporary folders (*drive*:\Temp or *drive*:\Tmp); Setup searches every drive on the computer.

Setup removes files according to instructions contained in the global OPC file (Oclncore.opc) plus any language-specific OPC files (Oclnintl.opc) that you add to the LCID subfolders on your installation image.

For example, a user might have a French version of Microsoft Word and an English version of Microsoft Excel. The global OPC file cleans up all components included in the core English version of Office. If you add the Oclnintl.opc file to the 1036 subfolder, then Setup also removes components unique to the French version of Office.

Removing Small Business Tools

Office 2003 does not include the Microsoft Small Business Tools programs (Small Business Customer Manager, Business Planner, Direct Mail Manager, and Financial Manager) that were part of Microsoft Office 2000 Premium Edition. If you are upgrading from Office 2000, Small Business Tools components are not removed by default.

If you want Office 2003 Setup to remove Small Business Tools during the installation, set the following properties on the command line, in Setup.ini, or in a transform:

- **OPCREMOVESBT2000**   Setting this property to **1** allows Office 2003 Setup to remove Small Business Tools from users' computers.

- **OPCREMOVESBTTEXT**   Setting this property to a string value—for example, **"&Small Business Tools"**—adds a check box to the **Remove Previous Versions** page of Setup so that users can choose to remove Small Business Tools the same way they remove any other previous-version Office application.

Customizing the removal process

There are several ways that you can specify how the Setup program for Office or the Removal Wizard cleans up users' computers:

- In the Custom Installation Wizard, specify which Office components to remove on the **Remove Previous Versions** page.

■ Customize the OPC file used by Setup to include or exclude additional files or registry entries during the removal process. When users run Setup, your custom removal routine runs automatically.

■ Create your own OPC file and run the Removal Wizard with a command-line option that specifies your custom OPC file.

On the Resource Kit CD   The Office 2003 Resource Kit includes the Custom Installation Wizard, which is installed by default when you run the Office Resource Kit Setup program. For more information, see "Custom Installation Wizard" in Appendix A, "Toolbox."

Customize removal behavior in a transform

You can use the Custom Installation Wizard to customize removal behavior during Office 2003 Setup. On the **Remove Previous Versions** page of the wizard, you specify exactly which previous versions of each application are removed from users' computers. In this case, Setup does not display the **Remove Previous Versions** page to users during the installation—the instructions in the transform are carried out regardless of the display setting.

Note   When you remove previous applications during Setup, the Removal Wizard always runs in safe mode.

Customize the OPC file used by Setup

Setup follows the instructions in the global OPC file and any language-specific OPC files to determine which components to remove. The OPC files identify files, registry entries, INI file entries, and **Start** menu items that were installed or modified by previously installed versions of Office and Office-related products. The OPC file also contains rules that describe which of these files or entries to remove, where they are located, and under what conditions they can be deleted.

By editing the default OPC file or by creating a custom OPC file, you can specify which components to remove from the users' computers. You can also use the OPC file to remove non-Office components, such as custom applications. To add components to the removal list, customize the Oclncust.opc file. To exclude components from removal, you must edit the default Oclncore.opc file.

For more information about customizing the OPC files, see "OPC File Syntax" in the Appendix B, "Office 2003 Resource Kit Reference."

Run the Removal Wizard separately

After Setup removes files and settings from previously installed versions of Office or Office components, other unneeded files might remain on users' computers. For example, font files and dynamic-link libraries (DLLs) might not be removed. You can run the Removal Wizard as a stand-alone utility to remove all Office-related files from users' computers.

Situations in which it makes sense to run the Removal Wizard as a stand-alone utility include the following:

- Before you upgrade to Office 2003, to clean up existing Office-related files.

- When you stage your upgrade to Office 2003 applications.

    For example, if you upgrade to Word 2003 before upgrading to the rest of Office 2003, you can remove previously installed versions of only Word.

- When upgrading to Office 2003 replaces the need for a custom application on users' computers. You can use the wizard to remove the custom application.

> **Note** You must have administrator rights to run the Removal Wizard. If a user does not have administrator rights, you must log on as an administrator and run the wizard with the proper permissions.

You can run the Removal Wizard in one of three modes, depending on the degree to which you want to clean up users' hard disks:

- **Aggressive mode** Removes all Office-related components, including components shared by more than one Office application. Before installing Office 2003, you might run the wizard in aggressive mode for users who are upgrading from a variety of Office versions. In aggressive mode, the wizard marks all items listed in the OPC file for removal.

- **Safe mode** Removes only components that are no longer needed. Components deleted in safe mode are not being used by any application. In safe mode, the wizard marks items listed in the OPC file for removal only if it does not detect a corresponding application.

- **Safe mode with user discretion** Runs in safe mode but allows users to select which detected applications to keep and which to delete.

> **Caution** Never run the Removal Wizard in aggressive mode after you install Office 2003. The wizard might remove shared components that are needed by other applications installed on the computer.

The final page of the Removal Wizard lists all files scheduled for removal. This list is accurate for all Office applications from Microsoft Office 97 or earlier. However, because the Removal Wizard relies on Windows Installer to manage removal of files associated with a particular application, the list might be incomplete for Office 2000 and Office XP. This behavior results in a cleaner and safer removal of Office files, even though the list in the Removal Wizard might be incomplete.

Using command-line options with the Removal Wizard

Creating a custom OPC file and running the Removal Wizard with command-line options gives you the greatest amount of flexibility. To run the Removal Wizard with command-line options, click **Run** on the **Start** menu, and then type **Offcln.exe** followed by the command-line options you want.

Removal Wizard command-line options use the following syntax:

```
Offcln.exe [/a | /s [/q[/r]] [/l][!][logfile]] [directory]
```

These command-line options are defined in the following table.

Option	Definition
/a	Indicates aggressive mode; the Removal Wizard removes files associated with all previously installed versions of Office and Office-related applications. When you use this command-line option, the wizard does not allow you to select which files to keep.
/s	Indicates safe mode; the Removal Wizard removes only those files for which it does not detect an associated application. When you use this command-line option, the wizard does not allow you to select which files to keep.
/q	Indicates quiet mode; the Removal Wizard runs without prompting the user for information or displaying progress indicators. The wizard does not restart the user's computer; therefore, changes might not be completed until the user restarts the computer.
/r	Used with the **/q** option to restart the computer automatically if necessary. The user has no opportunity to save files before the computer restarts.
/llogfile	Generates a log with the file name *logfile*. If no log file name is specified, the Removal Wizard creates a default log file, Offcln11.log, in the current folder of the wizard.
/l!logfile	Generates a log file in the same manner as **/l**, but the Removal Wizard does not perform the removal process. This option is useful to test the Removal Wizard before running it to remove files.
directory	Specifies the folder that contains the files used by the Removal Wizard: Ocln-core.opc, Oclncust.opc, and <LCID>\Oclnintl.opc files. By default, the Removal Wizard searches the same folder that contains Offcln.exe.

For example, you can enter the following command line:

```
Offcln.exe /a /q /r /l
```

This command line does the following on users' computers:

- Removes all files from previously installed versions of Office (/**a**)
- Runs the Removal Wizard without user intervention (/**q**)
- Restarts the computer automatically if needed (/**r**)
- Creates the default log file (/**l**)

> **Tip**   The Removal Wizard returns a value to indicate whether the wizard ran with any errors. If you create a batch file to run the wizard, you can include code that captures this value. The wizard returns **0** to indicate that no errors occurred; any other value indicates errors.

Running the Removal Wizard with a custom OPC file

When you run the Removal Wizard separately, you can create a custom OPC file that controls the removal process. For example, suppose you want to remove an internal company tool that is being replaced by Office 2003 functionality. The internal tool, Chart.exe, resides on users' computers in the folder C:\Program Files\Internal\Chart. In addition, the folder contains support files—Chartsub.dll, Chartprt.dat, and Readme.txt. The following procedure shows you how to modify the OPC file to accomplish all these aims.

To modify the Oclncust.opc for a custom removal routine

1. Create a backup copy of the default Oclncust.opc file.

2. Open Oclncust.opc in a text editor.

3. Add the following lines:
   > **[SAFE] "Internal charting tool"**
   > **C:\program files\internal\chart\chart.exe**
   > **C:\program files\internal\chart\chartsub.dll**
   > **C:\program files\internal\chart\chartprt.dat**
   > **C:\program files\internal\chart\readme.txt**

   These entries direct the wizard to always delete files in the [SAFE] section and specify the name and location of the files to delete.

4. Save and close Oclncust.opc.

> **Tip**   Test your customized OPC file on a computer by using the /**l!***logfile* command-line option. This step generates a log of the files that will be deleted by your customized OPC file without actually removing any files.

Chapter 5

Installing Office 2003

After you run Setup to create an administrative installation point or you copy the Microsoft® Office 2003 CD to create a compressed installation image, you can install Office on users' computers in one of several ways. Users can run Setup from the administrative installation point or the compressed CD image, or you can use other distribution tools that capture or reference the installation source.

Installing Office with Elevated Privileges

In the Microsoft Windows® environments that support Microsoft Office 2003, different groups of users have different levels of rights and permissions. In these environments, default users have limited access to system areas of the computer. Because Office 2003 Setup writes to system areas of the Windows registry, a user must have administrator rights to the local computer to install Office 2003.

Users without administrator rights cannot install Office 2003. To install Office on computers where users lack administrator rights, you must run Setup with elevated privileges. After Office is installed, users without administrator rights can run all installed features, including installing features on demand, provided the initial installation was performed in an elevated context.

In organizations where users are not the administrators of their computers, there are three methods of elevating the Office installation:

- Log on to the computer as an administrator and install Office 2003.

- Assign, publish, or advertise Office applications.

  You can use Group Policy software installation and management to assign or publish Office 2003. You can also log on to the computer as an administrator and run Setup with the **/jm** command-line option to advertise Office.

- Use a software management tool, such as Microsoft Systems Management Server, in an administrative context.

Because all of the core Office 2003 products are installed as Windows Installer packages, any of the preceding methods grants users elevated privileges and allows them to install Office and any chained packages. When the initial installation is performed with elevated privileges, all subsequent installations—including install on demand and automatic repair of features—are also automatically elevated.

Caution   Setting the Windows Installer policy **Always install with elevated privileges** allows a user without administrator rights to the computer to install any Windows Installer package. The installation runs with elevated privileges, and the user has unlimited access to system files and the registry. Setting this policy leaves the computer highly vulnerable, potentially allowing an attacker to run malicious code on the computer. Using this policy to elevate an Office 2003 installation is not recommended.

Logging on as an administrator

If you log on to a computer with an account that has administrator rights, you automatically install Office 2003 and Office 2003 MUI Packs with elevated privileges. However, this method requires that all users have administrator rights when they run Office Setup or that an administrator visits every computer.

You can give users a temporary administrator name and password and have them use the **Run as** command to install Office 2003 or MUI Packs in an elevated context. If you create a shortcut to Setup.exe, you can include command-line options to customize the installation. To help maintain a high level of security in this scenario, you can write a script that contains administrator credentials and calls the **Run as** command. For more information, type **runas \?** at the command prompt.

Assigning, publishing, or advertising Office

You can also elevate the Office installation by using Group Policy software installation to assign or publish Office 2003 and MUI Packs. Alternatively, if you are not using Windows software installation and maintenance, you can advertise Office 2003 by logging on as an administrator and then running Setup with the **/jm** option. If you also include a Windows Installer transform (MST file) to customize the installation, use the **/t** command-line option to specify the MST file. For example:

```
setup.exe /jm pro11.msi /t office.mst
```

When you advertise Office 2003 in this way, Windows Installer shortcuts for each application appear on the **Start** menu, and a minimal set of core Office files and components is installed on the computer. When a user clicks a shortcut or opens a file associated with an Office application, Windows Installer runs with elevated privileges to install the application, regardless of how the user logged on. After Office is advertised, users can also run Setup from an administrative installation point and install Office with elevated privileges.

Like Office XP, the language packs in the Microsoft Office 2003 Multilingual User Interface Pack are Windows Installer packages, and you can advertise them to grant users elevated privileges when installing them. You must be logged on as an administrator when you advertise a package.

Resources and related information

For security reasons, applying an update (MSP file) to an Office 2003 installation always requires elevated privileges even if the original installation was performed with elevated privileges. For more information, see "Distributing Office 2003 Product Updates" in Chapter 18, "Updating Users' Office 2003 Configurations."

By using a Systems Management Server script, you can install Office in an elevated context. For more information, see the Microsoft Systems Management Server Web site at *http://www.microsoft.com/smserver/default.asp.*

Running Setup from an Installation Image

After you create an administrative installation point or compressed CD image on the network and you customize Microsoft Office 2003, you can distribute Office from this source in a number of ways. Users can run Setup.exe using the command-line options, Setup settings file, or transform that you specify. You can copy the image onto a CD and distribute the physical media to users. Or you can use other deployment tools, such as Microsoft Systems Management Server or hard disk imaging, to deploy a customized configuration of Office from the source.

The tools and procedures for customizing Office are largely the same whether you are deploying from an administrative image or a compressed CD image. After Office is deployed to users, however, each type of installation image offers some unique advantages.

For example, installing Office from a compressed CD image allows Setup to create a local installation source on users' computers, which offers the following benefits after the initial deployment:

- Users have a reliable resiliency source on the local computer for operations such as installing features on demand, repairing, reinstalling, and updating Office.

- Administrators can copy the compressed CD image onto physical media to distribute to users who do not have network access. They do not need to customize both an administrative image and a CD image.

- Administrators can distribute binary (client) patches to update Office installations and leave the original installation image on the network at a baseline level.

In some organizations, however, installing from an administrative image may be more efficient. For example:

- Organizations that use custom tools that bypass Office Setup or that rely on the Windows Installer source list should deploy from an administrative image. When users install from a compressed image, creation and maintenance of the local installation source is managed entirely by Setup and the Office Source Engine (Ose.exe)—and not by Windows Installer.

- Organizations that use Group Policy software installation, advertise Office applications, or run any Office applications from the network must install from an administrative image. A compressed CD image does not support these installation options.

- Users with limited hard disk space may not be able to install Office with a local installation source. Setup requires as much as 2 GB of free hard disk space during the installation or the process may fail. After the installation, the local installation source requires approximately 240 MB of hard disk space in addition to what is required by Office.

For more information about creating a local installation source on users' computers, see "Taking Advantage of a Local Installation Source" in Chapter 3, "Preparing to Deploy Office 2003."

For more information about deploying from an administrative image, see "Creating an Administrative Installation Point" in Chapter 3, "Preparing to Deploy Office 2003."

Interactive Setup

When users double-click **setup.exe** on the installation image, Setup runs with no command-line options. To apply your customizations, users must run Setup.exe with the appropriate command-line options. For example, the command line can include the **/settings** option to specify a custom Setup settings file or the **TRANS-FORMS** property to specify a transform (MST file).

To help ensure that Office 2003 is installed with the correct customizations, you can create and distribute a batch file that runs Setup.exe with your command-line options. Or you can create a Microsoft Windows shortcut and add options to the command-line box. In many organizations, the most efficient method is to create a logon script that runs Office Setup.

Unless you choose to install Office 2003 in quiet mode, the Setup user interface guides users through the following steps to install Office on their computers:

1. Enter user information.

2. Select installation type and location.

3. Select installation options for Office features.

4. Select previous versions of Office to keep.

5. Choose whether to keep the local installation source (only when deploying from a compressed CD image).

Most of the customizations that you specify on the command line, in the Setup settings file, or in a transform appear as defaults in the Setup interface; however, users can modify your choices when they run Setup interactively. To help prevent users from changing the configuration during the installation, run Setup in quiet mode.

For more information about command-line options that you can use to customize the Office 2003 installation, see "Setup Command-line Options" in Appendix B, "Office 2003 Resource Kit Reference."

For information about installing Office 2003 quietly, see "Customizing How Setup Runs" in Chapter 4, "Customizing Office 2003."

Enter user information

User information appears on users' computers in the **About** box (**Help** menu) in Office applications. When a user installs Office from an administrative installation point, Setup uses the organization name you specify without prompting the user.

Because you must enter the 25-character Volume License Key when you create an administrative installation point, users are not prompted for a product key when they run Setup from an administrative image, nor are they required to activate the product. In addition, the referral code field is not displayed when users run Setup to install Office 2003.

If you deploy Office from a compressed CD image, you can use new functionality in the Custom Installation Wizard to create a transform in which you enter a Volume License Key on behalf of users. When you apply the transform, Setup does not prompt users for a product key. For more information, see the Help for the **Configure Local Installation Source** page in the Custom Installation Wizard.

Accept end-user license agreement

When users install Office 2003 from the CD, Setup displays an end-user license agreement page. When users install Office from the administrative installation point, however, the license agreement that you accepted when you created the administrative installation point applies, and users do not see this page of Setup.

If you deploy Office from a compressed CD image, new functionality in the Custom Installation Wizard also allows you to accept the EULA on behalf of users. When you apply the transform, users do not see this page of Setup. For more information, see the Help for the **Configure Local Installation Source** page in the Custom Installation Wizard.

Select installation type and location

After they enter the required user information, users select the type of installation to perform and the location to install Office on the next page in Setup.

Installation type

Users can select one of the following installation types:

- **Upgrade** Automatically upgrades to Office 2003 and skips the remaining pages of Setup. This option removes all previous versions of Office applications and installs Office 2003 features based on the user's current configuration. This option is available only if a previous version of Office is installed on the computer.

- **Typical Install** Automatically installs the most frequently used Office features in the default installation location and skips the remaining pages of Setup.

- **Minimum Install**   Installs only required components of Office 2003. Additional components are configured for installation on first use and will require a connection to the installation source. This option is designed for installing on computers with limited hard disk space or when installing over limited bandwidth.

- **Custom Install**   Allows the user to configure all aspects of the Office installation on the remaining pages of Setup.

- **Complete Install**   Installs all Office features locally on the user's computer. This option requires the most disk space but ensures that users do not need access to the Office 2003 CD or an administrative installation point to install additional components later.

- **Run from Network**   Installs all Office features to run over the network; only components that must be installed locally are copied to the user's computer. This option requires access to the network to run any Office application.

> Note   When you deploy Office from a CD or compressed CD image, the **Run from Network** installation type is not available.

By using the Custom Installation Wizard, you can create a Windows Installer transform (MST file) that specifies the default features installed by Setup when the user clicks **Upgrade** or **Typical Install**. You can also change the button labels and descriptive text on this page by setting the following properties:

- **UPGRADETEXT**
- **UPGRADEINSTALLDESCRIPTIOND**
- **TYPICALTEXT**
- **TYPICALINSTALLDESCRIPTION**
- **CUSTOMTEXT**
- **CUSTOMINSTALLDESCRIPTION**
- **COMPLETEINSTALLDESCRIPTION**
- **MINIMUMTEXT**
- **MINIMUMINSTALLDESCRIPTION**
- **RUNFROMSOURCETEXT**
- **RUNFROMSOURCEINSTALLDESCRIPTION**

For more information about properties you can set to customize the Setup user interface, see "Setup Properties" in Appendix B, "Office 2003 Resource Kit Reference."

For more information about customizing the Setup behavior, see "Customizing How Setup Runs" in Chapter 4.

Installation location

Users can also enter the path to the installation location they want. The default location is Program Files\Microsoft Office\Office11.

You can specify a custom default value for the installation location on the **Specify Default Path and Organization** page of the Custom Installation Wizard. You can also specify the location by setting the **INSTALLLOCATION** property on the command line, in the Setup settings file, or on the **Modify Setup Properties** page of the Custom Installation Wizard.

Select installation options for Office features

When users choose the **Custom** installation mode, Setup displays a list of all the applications included in the edition of Office that they are installing. Users select the check boxes next to the applications they want, and Setup installs a typical set of features for each one.

Alternatively, users can select **Choose advanced customization of applications** to further customize their Office 2003 configuration. In this case, Setup displays the Office feature tree and allows users to set an installation state for each feature. The installation states you specify in a transform are set by default, but users can modify them. Features that you have hidden or locked or installation states that you have disabled are not displayed.

The following feature installation states are normally available to users during Setup:

- **Run from My Computer** Setup copies files and writes registry entries and shortcuts associated with the feature to the user's hard disk, and the application or feature runs locally.

- **Run all from My Computer** Same as **Run from My Computer**, except that all child features belonging to the feature are also set to this state.

- **Run from Network** Setup leaves components for the feature on the administrative installation point, and the feature is run from there. Available only when you are deploying from an administrative image.

- **Run all from Network** Same as **Run from Network**, except that all child features belonging to the feature are also set to this state. Available only when you are deploying from an administrative image.

- **Installed on First Use** Setup leaves components for the feature and all its child features on the administrative installation point until the user attempts to use the feature for the first time, at which time the components are automatically copied to the local hard disk.

- **Not Available**   The components for the feature, and all of the child features belonging to this feature, are not installed on the computer.

For more information about customizing what users see in the feature tree, see "Customizing Office Features and Shortcuts" in Chapter 4, "Customizing Office 2003."

For more information about setting installation states in a transform, see the Help for the **Set Feature Installation States** page in the Custom Installation Wizard.

Select previous versions of Office to keep

If the user is upgrading from a previous version of Office, Setup displays a list of all the Office applications currently installed—applications that Setup removes when it installs Office 2003. Users can choose to keep all or some previous-version applications on the computer.

Because Office 2003 is always installed in a version-specific folder, users can choose to keep previous versions without overwriting any files. However, Setup does redefine system settings, such as file types and shortcuts, to point to the Office 2003 applications.

On the **Remove Previous Versions** page of the Custom Installation Wizard, you can specify custom default settings for this Setup page. The wizard also includes an option to remove obsolete files, shortcuts, and registry settings left over from previous versions. When you customize removal options in the Custom Installation Wizard, the **SKIPREMOVEPREVIOUSDIALOG** property is automatically set to **1**, which hides this page from users during interactive Setup.

Note   You cannot install more than one version of Microsoft Outlook® on the same computer. If you are installing Microsoft Office Outlook 2003, then you must remove all previous versions of Outlook.

Delete the local installation source

When you install Office from a compressed CD image, Setup displays an additional page. On this page, users are given the options to check the Web for Office product updates and to delete the local installation source. To help ensure that users retain the local installation source, set the **PURGE** property to **0** in the [CACHE] section of Setup.ini. When the **PURGE** property is set to **0**, users do not see this page of Setup.

Advertising Office

Advertising is a quick and efficient means of making Office 2003 available to users without actually installing it until they need it. If you want users to install the Office 2003 package on demand, you must create an administrative installation point. You cannot advertise Office applications from a compressed CD image.

After you create the administrative image, you log on as an administrator and run Setup with the **/jm** option. If you also include a Windows Installer transform (MST file) to customize the installation, you use the **/t** command-line option to specify the MST file. For example:

```
setup.exe /jm pro11.msi /t office.mst
```

> **Note**   When you use the **/t** command-line option to specify a transform, you must insert a space between the option and the transform name to help ensure that the transform is correctly applied.

When you advertise Office 2003 in this way, Windows Installer shortcuts for each application appear on the **Start** menu, and a minimal set of core Office files and components is installed on the computer. When a user clicks a shortcut or opens a file associated with an Office application, Windows Installer installs the feature or application from the administrative installation point. After Office is advertised, users can also run Setup directly from an administrative installation point to install Office. Because Office was advertised by an administrator, Windows Installer handles elevation of privileges for users.

Like core Office 2003, the language packs in the Microsoft Office 2003 Multilingual User Interface Pack are Windows Installer packages, and can also be advertised on users' computers. For more information, see "Customizing and Installing Office 2003 MUI Packs" in Chapter 14, "Deploying Office 2003 Multilingual Resources."

Resources and related information

If you have an Active Directory® directory service structure set up in your organization, you can use Group Policy software installation to deploy and manage Office. Because Group Policy bypasses Office Setup and deploys the MSI file directly, however, you cannot take advantage of a local installation source when you deploy from a compressed image. For more information, see "Using Group Policy to Deploy Office" later in this chapter.

If you use Microsoft Systems Management Server to distribute Office 2003 to users' computers, you also begin by creating an Office 2003 administrative installation point or compressed CD image on the network. For more information, see "Using Microsoft Systems Management Server to Deploy Office" later in this chapter.

When you create a hard disk image, you first create an administrative installation point or compressed CD image for Office 2003 and then you customize the installation image. For more information, see the next section, "Creating a Hard Disk Image."

Creating a Hard Disk Image

Some organizations deploy a complete user system at one time, including Microsoft Windows software, device drivers, Microsoft Office 2003 applications, and custom settings. In this scenario, you install the entire system onto a test computer, and then you create an image of the hard disk to copy to users' computers.

Installing Office with a complete user system is almost as fast as installing Office by itself. It is a particularly efficient way to configure new computers or to restore a computer to its original state. When you distribute the hard disk image to users, everything on the computer is replaced by your custom configuration, so users must back up any documents or other files they want to keep.

To create the hard disk image, you begin by running Office 2003 Setup with the **/a** option to create an administrative installation point. If you are including Microsoft Office 2003 Multilingual User Interface Packs in your installation, run MuiSetup.exe with the **/a** option and install the MUI Packs on the same administrative installation point.

Alternatively, if you want to take advantage of new Setup functionality and create a local installation source on users' computers, you can create a compressed CD image by copying the contents of the Office CD and MUI Pack CDs to a network share. You customize the compressed image the same way you customize an administrative image. For more information, see "Taking Advantage of a Local Installation Source" in Chapter 3, "Preparing to Deploy Office 2003."

Customize user settings

If your hard disk image includes custom settings captured in an Office profile settings file (OPS file), then you must first install Office 2003 and the MUI Packs from the installation image to a separate test computer. After you configure the settings you want, run the Profile Wizard to capture them in the OPS file.

To customize users settings on the Office 2003 image by using an OPS file

1. Install Office from the installation image to a test computer.

2. On the test computer, run the Office applications and modify application settings, and then close all the Office applications.

3. Start the Profile Wizard.

4. On the **Save or Restore Settings page**, click **Save the settings from this machine**.

5. Enter the file name and path for the OPS file, and click **Finish**.

6. When you create the transform, enter the file name and path of the OPS file on the **Customize Default User Settings** page of the Custom Installation Wizard.

Note that you do not run the Profile Wizard on the computer you intend to image. If you start any Office applications on that computer, then user- and computer-specific settings are included in the hard disk image.

Customize Office on the installation image

You can use the Custom Installation Wizard to create a transform and you can modify the Setup settings file (Setup.ini), just as you do when you customize Office 2003 in any other network installation scenario. In addition, you must take several steps to exclude user-specific information from the hard disk image.

To customize Office 2003 for a hard disk image

1. Start the Custom Installation Wizard.

2. On the **Customize Default User Settings** page, specify the name and path of any Office profile settings file (OPS file) you have created.

3. On the **Set Feature Installation States** page, set installation states for each Office application.

4. On the **Modify Setup Properties** page, set the **NOUSERNAME** property to **True**.

   This property prevents Setup from defining a user name during installation and allows users to enter their own user names the first time they run an Office application.

5. If you are installing Microsoft Office Outlook 2003, choose to create a new Outlook profile on the **Outlook: Customize Default Profile** page, and configure the profile on subsequent pages of the wizard.

6. Make any additional customizations and save the transform.

7. Open the Setup settings file (Setup.ini) and specify the transform you created, along with any other modifications you want to make.

   For example, add MUI Packs to the [ChainedInstall_*n*] sections of Setup.ini. If you are installing from a compressed CD image, customize local installation source options in the [Cache] section.

Install Office on a clean test computer

The next step is to install Office 2003 from the installation image to a clean client computer—one that already has the Windows configuration you want and one that has never had Office 2003 or any previous version of Office installed. This installation becomes the model for your hard disk image.

After you have installed and configured all the system software on the test computer, run Office Setup to install Office from the installation image.

To install Office on the test computer

1. Install Office from the administrative installation point or compressed CD image.

2. If you created a custom INI file, specify it by using the **/settings** command-line option.

3. If you have not already done so, set the **NOUSERNAME** property on the command line; for example:

```
\\server\share\admin_install_point\setup.exe NOUSERNAME=True
```

4. Unless you want all users who receive the hard disk image to use your installation image as a source for installing, repairing, or removing Office features, reset the source list to point to the Office CD or another network share.

> **Caution**   To help prevent user-specific information from appearing on the hard disk image, do not start any Office applications on the test computer. After you install Office on the test computer, you can make additional modifications to the configuration. However, starting an Office application writes user-specific information to the Windows registry, which is then duplicated to all users.

Distribute the hard disk image

After you test the hard disk image to make sure that Office 2003 applications are installed and configured correctly, you can use any one of a number of tools to replicate the hard disk image. The Windows operating system includes several new or improved technologies for automating the installation of the Windows client and Office on users' computers through hard disk imaging.

System Preparation Tool

The Microsoft Windows System Preparation Tool (SysPrep.exe), which is included with Windows 2000 or later, prepares the hard disk on the test computer for duplicating and for customizing client installations with computer-specific information such as user name, computer name, and domain membership. Once the hard disk is prepared, administrators can quickly and efficiently deploy Windows and Office throughout their organization by using a disk-imaging tool to replicate the image to client computers.

For more information about SysPrep.exe, see the white paper "Automating Windows 2000 Deployments with Sysprep" on the Windows 2000 Web site at *http://www.microsoft.com/windows2000/techinfo/planning/incremental/sysprep11.asp*.

To download the most up-to-date version of SysPrep.exe, see Windows 2000 System Preparation Tool on the Windows 2000 Web site at *http://www.microsoft.com /windows2000/downloads/tools/sysprep/default.asp*.

Remote Installation Services

Remote Installation Services (RIS), which ships with Windows 2000 or later, installs an administrator-configured image of the Windows client remotely on users' computers. You can include Office 2003 in the RIS image. After using RIS to install Windows on a test computer, you customize and install Office 2003 on the same test computer. Then you run the Remote Installation Preparation Wizard (RIPrep.exe) to create an image of the hard disk on the RIS server. When clients connect to the RIS server remotely, they install both the Windows client and Office 2003 with your configuration settings.

RIS allows you to set up new computers and new users without on-site technical support and to recover more quickly from computer failures. Unlike SysPrep, however, RIS requires relies heavily on network resources, including network capacity and the Active Directory directory service.

For a detailed outline of the steps necessary to install, configure, and use Remote Installation Services (RIS), see the Step-by-Step Guide to Remote OS Installation on the Microsoft Windows 2000 Web site at *http://www.microsoft.com/windows2000/techinfo /planning/management/remotesteps.asp*.

To find out how to create an installation image by using the Remote Installation Preparation Wizard, search for **Creating an installation image** in the Windows 2000 Server Help page on the Microsoft Windows 2000 Web site at *http: //www.microsoft.com/windows2000/en/server/help/default.asp?url=/windows2000 /en/server/help/*.

Using Group Policy to Deploy Office

The Microsoft Windows 2000 or later operating system includes tools that allow administrators to install and maintain software applications based on Group Policy. Using Group Policy software installation features, you can assign or publish Microsoft Office 2003 and Microsoft Office 2003 Multilingual User Interface Packs (MUI Packs) to all the users or computers in a designated group.

For large or complex organizations, Microsoft Systems Management Server offers more sophisticated functionality, including inventory, scheduling, and reporting features. However, using Group Policy to deploy Office 2003 can be a good choice in the following settings:

- Small- or medium-sized organizations that have already deployed and configured the Active Directory® directory service.

- Organizations or departments that comprise a single geographic area.

- Organizations with consistent hardware and software configurations on both clients and servers.

If you are managing large numbers of clients in a complex or rapidly changing environment, consider using Microsoft Systems Management Server to install and maintain Office 2003. For more information, see "Using Microsoft Systems Management Server to Deploy Office" later in this chapter.

> **Note**   Because Group Policy bypasses Office Setup.exe and Setup.ini, you cannot use Group Policy to deploy Office from a compressed CD image, nor can you take advantage of new Setup functionality to create a local installation source on users' computers.

Active Directory and Group Policy

In a Windows-based network, Active Directory provides a framework for centralized administration of users and computers. Active Directory makes it possible to manage all users, computers, and software on the network through administrator-defined policies, known as Group Policy in Windows 2000 or later.

A collection of Group Policy settings is contained in a Group Policy object (GPO), and the GPO is associated with an Active Directory container. The Group Policy object can be applied at any level of the Active Directory hierarchy. You can set policies that apply to an entire site, a domain, or an individual organizational unit.

The deployment and management tools designed for Office 2003—including the Custom Installation Wizard and Office 2003 policy template files (ADM files)—work with Group Policy software installation. By using all aspects of Group Policy, you can make a unique configuration of Office available to all users or computers in a given GPO, and then rely on Windows to maintain users' software configurations automatically.

Deploying the Office package

There are three ways to install and manage Office 2003 applications by policy:

- Assign Office to computers.
- Assign Office to users.
- Publish Office to users.

Assigning Office to computers

Assigning Office to computers is the simplest way to use Group Policy to manage a package as large and complex as Office 2003. With this method, Office is installed on the computer the next time the computer starts and is available to all users of the computer.

Assigned applications are resilient. If a user removes an Office application from the computer, Windows automatically reinstalls it the next time the computer starts. Users can repair Office applications on the computer, but only an administrator can remove applications.

Assigning Office to users

When you assign Office to users, information about the software is advertised on users' computers in the Windows registry and on the **Start** menu or Windows desktop the next time the users log on. When a user clicks an Office application shortcut, Windows Installer retrieves the package from the administrative installation point, installs the application on the user's computer, and starts the application. If you choose to activate installation by file extension, clicking an Office item (such as a Microsoft Office Word 2003 document or a Microsoft Office Excel 2003 worksheet) automatically installs the corresponding application in the same way.

After an assigned user installs Office, the applications are not necessarily available to subsequent users of the computer. Instead, each assigned user's Office configuration follows the user from computer to computer.

Applications assigned to users are also resilient. If a user removes an assigned Office application from the computer, Windows automatically restores the registry information and Windows Installer shortcuts the next time the user logs on.

Avoiding installation conflicts

Do not assign Office to both a user and a computer. When assigned to a computer, Office applications are installed locally (based on settings in the transform). When assigned to a user, Office applications are advertised on the computer, but are not installed until the user activates them—one Windows Installer shortcut at a time.

Assigning Office to both users and computers can create conflicts in which Office applications appear to be installed locally but are actually only advertised.

In addition, if you assign Office to both users and computers and also apply different transforms, Windows automatically uninstalls and reinstalls Office every time the computer starts or the user logs on.

Publishing Office to users

When you publish Office to users, no information about the software is present in the registry or on the **Start** menu. However, users can click **Add/Remove Programs** in Control Panel and view a list of all software published to them.

If a user selects Office from this list, **Add/Remove Programs** retrieves information about the Office installation location from Active Directory, and Windows Installer installs the package on the computer and applies any transform that you have associated with the Office package.

If you plan to have users run Office Setup themselves (for example, if your organization routinely makes a variety of software applications available to users from an installation location on the network), consider publishing Office to users. In this case, users in the designated group can install Office from **Add/Remove Programs** anytime they choose.

Unlike assigned applications, published applications are not automatically reinstalled. If a user removes Office after installing it from **Add/Remove Programs**, the shortcuts and registry information are not automatically reapplied on the computer. However, the next time the user logs on to the network, Office is republished in **Add/Remove Programs**.

> **Note**   You cannot publish Office to a computer.

Applying a transform to the Office package

You control which Office applications and features are available to users by applying a transform (MST file) when you assign or publish the Office package (MSI file). Note that you can apply only one transform to a given installation of the Office 2003 package.

Transforms are applied when Office is assigned or published. You cannot reapply a transform after Office is installed. If you need to modify a managed Office installation, you must remove and then reinstall Office with a new transform.

> **On the Resource Kit CD**   The Office 2003 Resource Kit includes the Custom Installation Wizard and Custom Maintenance Wizard, which are installed when you run the Office Resource Kit Setup program. For more information, see "Custom Installation Wizard" and "Custom Maintenance Wizard" in Appendix A "Toolbox."

Resources and related information

For a general introduction to the new management services in Windows 2000 or later, see the documentation on the Management Services page of the Microsoft Windows 2000 Web site at *http://www.microsoft.com/windows2000/technologies /management/default.asp.*

For a comparison of application deployment features in Systems Management Server 2.0 and Windows 2000 or later, see Application Deployment Using Microsoft Management Technologies on the Windows 2000 Web site at *http://www.microsoft.com /windows2000/techinfo/howitworks/management/apdplymgt.asp.*

The Windows 2000 Technical Library on the World Wide Web contains detailed step-by-step guides for using the new installation tools and technologies, including the following:

- Step-by-Step Guide to Understanding the Group Policy Feature Set, *http: //www.microsoft.com/windows2000/techinfo/planning/management /groupsteps.asp*

- Step-by-Step Guide to Software Installation and Maintenance, *http: //www.microsoft.com/windows2000/techinfo/planning/management /swinstall.asp*

    This guide includes examples of several Office installation scenarios.

Using Microsoft Systems Management Server to Deploy Office

Microsoft Systems Management Server (SMS) is a software distribution tool designed for medium- and large-sized organizations that manage large numbers of clients in a complex and rapidly changing business environment. Unlike Group Policy, SMS does not require that you have an Active Directory® directory service structure set up, and you can use SMS to deploy software applications to a mixture of Microsoft Windows clients.

When you use SMS to install and maintain Microsoft Office 2003 and Microsoft Office 2003 Multilingual User Interface Packs (MUI Packs), you can help to set a precise control over the deployment process. For example, by using SMS you can query client computers for software requirements before you install Office, and you can target the installation only to computers that meet your criteria.

Systems Management Server features span the full range of deployment tasks, including the following:

- Creating an inventory of hardware and software already deployed across the organization.

- Deploying Office 2003 with or without MUI Packs to a large number of clients or across multiple sites.

- Scheduling and tracking the status of application deployment.

- Pushing, or forcing, installation of Office 2003 on client computers.

- Deploying to users who do not have administrative rights on the local computer.

- Reporting and troubleshooting installation processes.

Note   You must have Systems Management Server 2.0 with Service Pack 2 to deploy Office 2003.

If your organization has deployed Systems Management Server 2.0 with Service Pack 2 and you plan to use it to install Office 2003, you can install the package definition files (PDF files) from the Office 2003 Resource Kit. PDF files contain the information required for Systems Management Server to create a software distribution package. The PDF files for Office 2003 have been consolidated into two files: Office11.sms (for all Office editions) and MUI11.sms (for Office MUI Packs).

On the Resource Kit CD   The Office 2003 PDF files are available in the Office Resource Kit Toolbox. For more information, see "Package Definition Files" In Appendix A, "Toolbox."

In a small- or medium-sized organization, Group Policy may be the preferred tool for managing software deployment, particularly if you have already deployed the Active Directory directory service and you have clients with consistent software and hardware configurations. For more information about using Group Policy to deploy Office 2003, see "Using Group Policy to Deploy Office" earlier in this chapter.

For a comparison of application software deployment features in Systems Management Server 2.0 and Windows 2000, see Application Deployment Using Microsoft Management Technologies on the Windows 2000 Web site at *http://www.microsoft.com/ windows2000/techinfo/howitworks/management/apdplymgt.asp.*

For more information about using Systems Management Server to deploy Office, see Using SMS 2.0 to Deploy Microsoft Office XP on the TechNet Web site at *http://www.microsoft.com/technet/treeview/default.asp?url=/technet/prodtechnol /sms/deploy/depopt/smsoffxp.asp.* Note that this white paper references Office XP. Procedures specific to SMS 2.0 have not changed for Office 2003; however, some Office XP requirements are no longer relevant for Office 2003. For example, the system file update for Office XP is no longer required for Office 2003.

For more information about Systems Management Server 2.0, including information about upgrading to the latest version, see the Systems Management Server Web site at *http://www.microsoft.com/smserver/.*

Deploying Office and Other Products Together

The Microsoft Office 2003 Setup program supports the chaining of additional packages (MSI files) or executable programs to the core Office 2003 installation. Chaining allows you to deploy Office 2003 and related applications in one seamless process. After the core Office installation is complete, Setup calls Windows Installer or the specified executable program to install any number of chained programs in the order that you specify in the Setup settings file (Setup.ini). You customize chained installations by setting properties in Setup.ini or by creating a transform.

You can chain packages to the core Office installation whether you deploy from an administration installation point or from a compressed CD image. In either case, you specify the chained installation in Setup.ini and customize the installation by setting properties or by creating transform. If you are installing from a compressed image with the local installation source option enabled and the chained package supports it, Setup includes the chained installation in the local installation source. (To determine whether a package supports creation of a local installation source, Setup looks for a file named ProductName.xml in the Files\Setup folder on the installation image.)

Chaining is an efficient way to deploy Office-related products that are not included in the core Office 2003 package, such as Microsoft Office FrontPage® 2003, Microsoft Office OneNote™ 2003, or Microsoft Office Project Professional 2003. You can also deploy Microsoft Office 2003 Multilingual User Interface Packs (MUI Packs) with Office by chaining individual Mui.msi files. If you install Office from a compressed CD image and create a local installation source on users' computers, you can use chaining as part of your update strategy: install the original release version of Office on new clients and chain a set of client patches to the core installation.

Specifying chained installations in Setup.ini

Setup reads the Setup.ini file at the start of the installation process and writes a set of tasks to the Windows registry to install each product listed in the [ChainedInstall_1] through [ChainedInstall_n] sections. By default, Setup passes to Windows Installer the command-line options and properties defined for the core Office 2003 package to each chained installation; however, you can set unique properties for a chained installation in Setup.ini by using the following syntax:

```
[ChainedInstall_1]
TaskType=msi
Path=\\server\share\admin_install_point\[MSI file]
Display=None
MST=[MST file]
Cmdline=property=value
```

For more information about the [ChainedInstall_n] section of Setup.ini, see "Setup Settings File" in Appendix B, "Office 2003 Resource Kit Reference."

Customize chained packages

In most sections of Setup.ini, including the [Options] section, you use the syntax *property=value* to specify custom property values. In the [ChainedInstall_*n*] sections, you can set the **Display** and **MST** values with this syntax, along with several additional options that customize the installation process. However, you must use the **Cmdline** option to add other properties to the command line that Setup passes to Windows Installer for the chained installation.

You can set the following options for chained installations in Setup.ini:

- **TaskName=*task_name***   Assigns a friendly name to the installation. Setup uses this name in the Setup log file. Optional.

- **TaskType=*task_type***   Identifies whether the chained installation is an MSI file or an executable file (such as an EXE file or a BAT file). Required.

- **Path=*path***   Specifies the relative or full path to the MSI file or executable file. Required.

- **Display=*setting***   Specifies a user interface display setting for the chained installation.

  Use a **basic** setting to display only progress indicators; use **none** for a completely silent installation. For more information about display settings, see the [Display] section in "Setup Settings File" in Appendix B, "Office 2003 Resource Kit Reference."

> **Note**   By default, chained installations inherit the display setting specified for the core Office package. Use this setting to override the default setting.

- **MST=*MSTfile***   Specifies the path and file name of a transform (MST file) to apply to the chained package (MSI file). Optional.

> **Note**   You can specify only one transform with the MST option; to specify multiple transforms, add the **TRANSFORMS** property to the **Cmdline** entry.

- **Cmdline=*options***   Specifies other *property=value* pairs or command-line options that Setup passes to Windows Installer or an executable program during the call to install the chained package or program.

- **IgnoreReturnValue=[0 | 1]**   To continue installing successive chained installations even if this installation fails, set this property to **1**. The default setting is **0**.

> **Note**   If you inadvertently enter an incorrect name or path for the MSI file, then Setup halts the installation process and neither the chained installation nor any subsequent chained installations are installed. This occurs even if **IgnoreReturnValue** is set to **1**.

- **Reboot=[0 | 1]**   To restart the computer after an installation completes, set this option to **1**; Setup restarts and then resumes the installation process.

Requirements and limitations to deploying chained installations

The Setup program for Office 2003 is designed to support chaining of other Windows Installer packages and simple executable programs (EXE files). This chaining functionality makes it more efficient to deploy MUI Packs from the Multilingual User Interface Pack at the same time you deploy Office. However, chaining is not the best method to use in all circumstances, as described in the following sections.

Adding programs through the Custom Installation Wizard

The Custom Installation Wizard allows you to add installations and run programs during the Office 2003 installation. For example, you can run the Profile Wizard (Proflwiz.exe) to distribute custom settings at the end of the Office 2003 installation. However, you cannot use the **Add Installations and Run Programs** page of the Custom Installation Wizard to chain additional Windows Installer packages. If Windows Installer tries to start the installation of a second package before it has completed the installation of the core Office package, the entire installation process stops.

> **On the Resource Kit CD**   The Office 2003 Resource Kit includes the Customization Installation Wizard and the Profile Wizard, which are installed by default when you run the Office Resource Kit Setup program. For more information, see "Custom Installation Wizard" or "Office Profile Wizard" in Appendix A, "Toolbox."

Using Group Policy software installation

Group Policy software installation works directly with the MSI file and bypasses Office 2003 Setup and the Setup.ini file when assigning or publishing packages. For this reason, you cannot use Setup.exe to chain Office 2003 installations when you assign or publish packages. Instead, Microsoft Windows deploys Office 2003, the

Office 2003 Multilingual User Interface Pack, and other Office-related packages separately and in random order. Because Office 2003 must be installed first, before a MUI Pack installation can succeed, you cannot use chaining with Group Policy software installation to combine these installations.

Restarting the computer after a chained installation

Office 2003 Setup does not support computer restarts forced by chained installations themselves. In other words, Setup does not allow you to chain a package or program that must restart the computer to complete its installation because restarting interrupts the Office 2003 Setup.exe thread and stops the installation process. To avoid this problem, Office Setup sets the Windows Installer **REBOOT** property to **REALLYSUPPRESS** by default for all but the last chained installation.

You can, however, direct Setup.exe to restart the computer to complete a chained installation without interrupting the installation process. Setting the **Reboot** option to **1** in the [ChainedInstall_*n*] section of Setup.ini adds a task to the registry that directs Setup to restart the computer and then resume the Office 2003 installation, including any additional chained installations.

> **Note**   The Reboot option in the [ChainedInstall_*n*] section of Setup.ini takes the value **1** or **0**. It is not the same as the Windows Installer **REBOOT** property, which takes the value **FORCE**, **SUPPRESS**, or **REALLYSUPPRESS**. For more information about the Windows Installer property, look up **REBOOT** in "Setup Properties" in Appendix B, "Office 2003 Resource Kit Reference."

Elevating installation of a chained package

If you chain a package that requires elevated privileges to install, you must take the same steps to elevate the installation that you do for Office 2003. Setup.exe does not automatically install a chained package with administrator privileges when the Office 2003 installation is elevated. However, several of the methods that you use to elevate the Office 2003 installation also elevate any chained installations:

- If you use the **/jm** option to advertise Office 2003, then every installation listed in Setup.ini is also advertised and therefore elevated.

- If you use a tool such as Microsoft Systems Management Server to install Office.

- If you log on as an administrator when you begin the Office 2003 installation and do not log off or restart before it completes, then chained installations run with elevated privileges.

For more information about elevating the Office 2003 installation for users who are not administrators, see "Installing Office with Elevated Privileges" earlier in this chapter.

Chaining MUI Packs

Chaining is particularly useful for adding individual MUI Packs to the core Office 2003 installation. Each MUI Pack in the Office 2003 Multilingual User Interface Pack is installed as a separate Windows Installer package (Mui.msi). To create an administrative installation point for all the MUI Packs on a particular CD, you run MuiSetup.exe with the **/a** option from the root of the MUI Pack CD. You can also install individual MUI Packs by running Setup.exe **/a** from the appropriate LCID folder. Alternatively, you can copy the contents of the MUI Pack CD to a compressed CD image.

You can install MUI Packs on the same installation image as Office 2003 or create a separate one. The folder structure for each MUI Pack is parallel:

\\server\share\admin_install_point\<LCID>\Mui.msi

After you install the MUI Packs on the administrative installation point or compressed CD image, you edit the Office 2003 Setup.ini file to chain them to the core Office 2003 installation. You can set a new display setting, specify a transform to apply, and set other properties that apply only to the MUI Pack installation. If you are installing from a compressed image, Setup automatically includes the MUI Packs in the local installation source.

To chain MUI Packs to the Office 2003 installation

1. Open the Setup settings file (Setup.ini) in a text editor such as Wordpad.

2. Create a [ChainedInstall_1] section and specify the name and path of the MUI Pack you want to chain.

3. Specify a unique display setting or transform to apply to the MUI Pack installation by setting the **Display** or **MST** property.

    For example, even if you are installing Office 2003 with a full user interface, you can specify **basic** to install the MUI Pack quietly.

4. Specify additional options by using the **Cmdline** property.

    For example, set the **NOFEATURESTATEMIGRATION** property to **True** to cancel the custom action that matches installation states for MUI Pack feature states to corresponding Office feature installation states.

The following example adds the French Multilingual User Interface Pack (MUI Pack) to the Office 2003 installation. The package is installed silently (regardless of the display setting specified for the Office installation), the customizations in the transform French.mst are applied, feature installation state matching is turned off for the MUI Pack, and an alternate source is identified for when the primary installation image is unavailable.

Example:

```
[ChainedInstall_1]
TaskType=msi
Path=\\server\share\admin_install_point\1036\Mui.msi
Display=None
MST=French.mst
Cmdline=NOFEATURESTATEMIGRATION=True SOURCELIST=\\server2\share
admin_install_point\1036
```

Deploying to Roaming Users

Traveling users (sometimes referred to as roaming users) move between different computers on a network. By using Microsoft Office 2003, roaming users can move between computers without changing the way they work. Their application settings and working files travel with them, along with any system preferences.

Roaming user profiles make it possible for users to travel from one computer to another on the network. Microsoft Windows 2000 Professional and Windows XP Professional both support roaming user profiles, as do Windows 2000 Server, Windows Server 2003, and third-party servers. Office 2003 takes advantage of the operating system's features to make Office settings travel with users.

When you turn on roaming user profiles, users can switch between computers as long as they log on to the same network and retrieve their user information from that network. This flexibility helps you make the most of your computer resources.

Preparing Office for roaming users

Users are able to travel easily from computer to computer when their documents and application preferences travel with them. This convenience requires that you configure the Microsoft Office 2003 installation and the operating system to support users who travel.

Operating system recommendations

Roaming works best when users travel between client computers that use the same version of the same operating system:

- Use a consistent version of the operating system.
      For example, Windows 2000 to Windows 2000, Windows XP Professional to Windows XP Professional, and so on.
- Use a consistent operating system language.

Office installation recommendations

Roaming users rely on user profiles to transfer their individual settings. However, roaming is more successful when the computers to which they travel have Office installed in a consistent way:

- Use the same version of Office.

  Ensure that the same language version and release version of Microsoft Office are installed on all computers that users roam between.

- Install Office using the same installation method on each computer.

  Install Office as either per-user or per-computer, but do not use a combination of these. To save both hard disk space and download time, install Office on a per-computer basis on every computer. This method ensures that the installation information is shared by all users of that computer, so it does not need to be stored separately for each user.

- Install Office to the same drive and folder on each computer.

  If users travel from a computer that has Office installed on drive C to a computer that has Office installed on drive D, or if users travel from a computer that has Office installed in C:\Program Files\Microsoft Office to a computer that has Office installed in C:\Program Files\Office, their shortcuts and customized settings might not work correctly.

- Install Office from an administrative installation point, and not from a compressed CD image.

- Install Office applications to run from the network.

  If you install the Office applications on the network, these applications are always available to roaming users, as long as your network is running. With the applications on the network, you also cut down on the number of files and other objects that must be copied to each hard disk when users travel to a new computer.

- Install crucial Office applications to run from the local hard disk.

  You can install the Office applications that users need most to run from the local hard disk. For example, if everyone uses Microsoft Office Word 2003 on a daily basis to work on reports, memos, and other documents, you can help to ensure that their work is not interrupted by server problems by installing Word 2003 on the local hard disk.

User information recommendations

Creating a standard Office configuration for all users and storing user information on a server ensures that roaming users have access to their application settings, files, and folders from any computer on the network:

- Store user information on the network.

  When you configure a user profile for use by a roaming user, it is copied to the network and then downloaded when the user travels to a new computer. To make roaming even easier, you can also store other information, such as your users' My Documents or Personal folders, on a server so that users can open those documents from any computer they are using.

> **Tip**   If you store user information on a file server, rather than your Primary Domain Controller (PDC), you can balance the load on your servers more efficiently. For more information about load balancing, see your network documentation.

- Create a default Office user profile.

     You can use the Office 2003 Profile Wizard to save a set of Office options called an Office user profile. You can start all of your users with the same configuration by creating and deploying a default Office user profile when you deploy Office 2003.

- Set policies.

     You can help to protect or enforce important settings through policies. For example, if you want all users to save files in a particular format, you can set the file type to use through a policy.

> **Tip**   Make sure that user profiles and policies give users the required permissions to install the applications they need when they travel to a new computer. For example, you can advertise Office, which allows any user to install Office 2003 features as if the user were an administrator for that computer.

Resources and related information

You can use the Profile Wizard to create an Office profile and give your roaming users a standard environment to start from. For more information about using the Office Profile Wizard, see "Customizing User-defined Settings" in Chapter 4, "Customizing Office 2003."

You can set policies to help control which options are available to your roaming users. For more information about policies, see "Managing Users' Configurations by Policy" in Chapter 18, "Updating Users' Office 2003 Configurations."

Roaming users rely on roaming user profiles to track their user information. For more information about roaming user profiles in Windows 2000 or later, look up **User profiles** in the Windows 2000 Server documentation.

Customizing Office for roaming users

You can get the optimal performance out of Office 2003 for your roaming users by customizing certain Office installation settings, and by configuring user profiles so that user data is available from any computer on the network.

Customizing the Office installation

There are several settings that you can change in the Custom Installation Wizard to make it easier to set up Office 2003 for roaming users. For example, setting Office applications to run from the network eliminates the need for Windows to copy Office applications to a user's computer the first time the user logs on to that computer.

To customize the Office 2003 installation for roaming users

1. Start the Custom Installation Wizard.

2. On the **Specify Default Path and Organization** page, verify that <Program Files>\Microsoft Office appears in the **Default installation path** box.

3. On the **Set Feature Installation States** page, set the installation state for Microsoft Office to **Run from Network**.

   To set a critical or frequently used application to run from the local hard disk, set the installation state for the application to **Run from My Computer**.

4. On the **Customize Default Application Settings** page, click **Get values from an existing settings profile** and then type the path to your Office profile settings file (OPS file).

5. On the **Modify Setup Properties** page, set the property **TRANSFORMSAT-SOURCE** to **True** to apply MST files from the root of the administrative installation point, instead of caching them on the local computer.

6. Make any other customizations in the wizard, and then click **Finish**.

Managing user profiles

Users who roam from one computer to another on the network rely on roaming user profiles to track their user information, and on servers to make sure that the user profile information travels with them. To support roaming users, you must set up both client and server computers with roaming user profiles (profiles that travel with the user account). Roaming user profiles are stored on the server and automatically downloaded to the client computer when users log on.

With roaming user profiles, roaming users can log on to any computer on the network and download their user profile information. When users change any of their settings, the profile is automatically updated on the server when they log off, and their new information is automatically updated, too.

> **Note**   During Setup, Windows Installer lets you set Office applications to **Installed on First Use**. This installation option works on a per-computer basis rather than on a per-user basis, so Windows Installer cannot track which applications your users have installed as they travel between computers. Your users' application settings travel, but not the specific applications that have been installed on a particular computer. When users log on to the new computer and attempt to open an application, they might have to wait while the application is installed.

Microsoft Office 2003 helps roaming users by storing all application data (such as user information, working files, and settings and preferences) in the Application Data folder for easy retrieval by the profile. All files that reside in the Application Data folder are available to the user from any computer in the network. The Application Data folder is located under %SystemRoot%\Documents and Settings\%Username%.

> **Note**   Microsoft Office Outlook 2003 stores some files in folder locations that do not roam with users. In addition, in certain configurations Outlook must open files that it cannot access from a network share. For more information, see "Configuring Outlook for Roaming Users" in Chapter 8, "Special Deployment Scenarios for Outlook 2003."

Special considerations for international travelers

Because operating systems differ in their support of some languages, users who are traveling internationally can take their roaming user profiles to another computer only when both the source and destination computers use the same code page.

Within the limitations of multilingual support in various operating systems, you can make accommodations for users who travel internationally. Windows 2000 Professional or later with support for multiple languages allows users to take roaming user profiles from one computer to another. However, users can only roam between computers that have Multilingual User Interface Packs (MUI Packs) installed or between computers that have localized versions of the operating system installed. They cannot roam from a computer with a MUI Pack to a computer with a localized version of the operating system.

For example, if you do not want to use the English version of the operating system in foreign subsidiaries, you can install Windows 2000 Professional configured with the MUI Pack. Roaming users can set the locale of their operating system, travel to any other computer running Windows 2000 Professional, and take their roaming user profiles with them.

However, if international users need the Office MUI Pack to display the user interface and online Help in another language, you must install the Office MUI Pack on computers that will be used by roaming users. Just as with Office, set the MUI Pack to be installed on a per-computer basis, and install it on the same drive (such as drive C or D) throughout your organization.

> **Tip**   When roaming users log on to the network, their roaming user profiles are downloaded to their new location. For users who travel abroad, it might be more efficient to set them up to use a local server at their destination rather than downloading large amounts of data from their original domain.

Resources and related information

If all roaming users have the Office Multilingual User Interface Pack, they can use the Office MUI Pack to run the user interface and online Help in any supported language. For more information about the plug-in language capability of Office, see "Overview of Office 2003 Multilingual Resources" in Chapter 13, "Preparing for an Office Multilingual Deployment."

Office does not automatically uninstall Office MUI Pack files. If a roaming user leaves behind a set of languages, you might want to delete the associated language files. For more information, see "Removing Office Multilingual Resource Files" in Chapter 16, "Maintaining an Office 2003 Multilingual Installation."

Deploying Office 2003 in a Windows Terminal Services Environment

Unlike with previous versions of Microsoft Office, installing Microsoft Office 2003 to a Terminal Services–enabled computer is not much different than installing Office to a non-Terminal Services–enabled computer. Before installing Office in this environment, however, the administrator needs to perform some tasks relating to how Terminal Services was installed.

Installing Office 2003 on a Terminal Services–enabled computer

Before you install Office to a computer that is enabled with Terminal Services, it is very important that you check to make sure that specific operating modes of Terminal Services were enabled when Terminal Services Setup was run, including the following:

- The installation of Terminal Services must have been installed to use **Application Server mode**.

- Terminal Services must be enabled and running on the server before installation of Office 2003 begins.

- For Microsoft Windows 2000 servers, **Windows 2000 compatibility mode** should be selected to retain a locked-down installation.

- Once you have checked for these modes, you are ready to install Office 2003.

To install Office 2003 on a Terminal Services–enabled server

1. Open Control Panel.

2. Run the **Add/Remove Programs** utility.

3. Click **Add New Programs** (left-hand pane).

4. Click **CD or Floppy**.

5. Insert the Office 2003 CD into the CD-ROM drive, and then click **Next**.
   If needed, browse for the Office 2003 Setup program (Setup.exe) and select it, then click **OK**.

   or

   If you are installing from an administrative installation point, browse to that location, select **setup.exe**, and then click **OK**. In the resulting **Run Installation Programs** dialog, add any command-line customizations you require (unless already specified in the Setup settings file (Setup.ini) stored in the administrative installation point).

6. Click **Finish**.

Customizing Office 2003 for a Terminal Services installation

Customizing Office 2003 for a Terminal Services–enabled installation is possible, but you need to first understand the differences between how Office runs with a Terminal Services–enabled operating system versus one that is not enabled as such.

By default, almost all features in Office 2003 are enabled and installed as part of the installation. This helps reduce the number of subsequent application or feature installations an administrator might need to perform for users. Because Office, by default, is installed in a locked-down configuration, users cannot perform installations (like adding a feature), because they cannot write to the registry or application and system folders. Therefore, it is recommended to install all the applications and available features to minimize the need for further installations by the administrator.

As part of an installation to a Terminal Services–enabled system, some specific features are disabled by default because of their high bandwidth requirements for network and dial-up users. For instance, animations, sounds, and high-resolution graphics are disabled; or, in the case of high-resolution graphics, substituted with lower-resolution graphics.

To determine which settings are enabled or disabled, you can attempt to install Office to a properly configured Terminal Services–enabled server and examine the feature installation options during the installation. This will give you a baseline of what features are installed. Then, if you need to install many Terminal Services–enabled systems, you can create a transform using the Custom Installation Wizard and set the appropriate settings you want to use.

> **Note**   Any features you set to **Install on Demand** will be ignored and installed as **Run from My Computer**. Also, by default, installations to Terminal Services–enabled systems will always install the low-resolution graphics for splash screens.

Though you can create a transform for use with deployment of Office 2003, the majority of settings configured for installation are by default optimized for a Terminal Services-enabled system. Also, since most installations of this type are performed in a server farm or within a controlled environment, the creation and use of transforms is not as necessary as with distributed-client system scenarios.

When creating transforms for use with Terminal Services–enabled systems, it is highly recommended that you not enable features that are disabled or set to **Not Available**. If you expect to deploy Office 2003 to more than two or three Terminal Services-enabled systems, creating a transform is worthwhile, especially if there are several customizations. See Chapter 4, "Customizing Office 2003" for more information about creating transforms for use with Office.

Part 3

Messaging

Chapter 6

Planning an Outlook 2003 Deployment

A close review of your organization's messaging needs will help you plan the optimal Microsoft® Office Outlook® 2003 deployment. Among the configuration and installation choices you will make are deciding which e-mail messaging server to use with Outlook, and timing your Outlook deployment to suit your organization's needs.

Overview of an Outlook Deployment

Every organization's messaging environment is unique. For example, one organization might be upgrading to the Microsoft Office Outlook 2003 messaging and collaboration client, while another might be installing Outlook for the first time; one needs services for roaming users, another needs support for different languages. A close review of your organization's messaging needs will help you plan the optimal Outlook 2003 deployment.

Determining your organization's needs

Your organization's messaging environment will help shape your Outlook 2003 deployment. Factors to consider include whether you are upgrading Outlook, installing the application for the first time, planning for roaming or remote users, or choosing a combination of these and other factors.

Upgrade or initial installation

If you are upgrading to Outlook 2003 from an earlier version of Outlook, consider whether you will migrate previous settings, modify user profiles, and use new customization options. The Custom Installation Wizard provides options for migrating users' current settings and for making other customizations, such as defining new Microsoft Exchange servers or customizing new features.

If you are deploying Outlook on client computers for the first time, each user will need an Outlook profile to store information about e-mail messaging server connections and other important Outlook settings. You can define profile settings for your users by using the Custom Installation Wizard.

If you need to migrate data from another messaging application, importers are provided in Outlook (for example, for Eudora Lite) that might be helpful.

Collaboration Data Objects dependencies

If you use Collaboration Data Objects, this feature must be installed to run locally, not on demand. Use the **Set Feature Installation States** page in the Custom Installation Wizard to specify the installation state as **Run from My Computer**.

Remote and roaming users

Special customizations are required for deploying Outlook to remote users or roaming users, and for setting up Outlook for multiple users on the same computer.

When you are deploying to remote users, ensure that features are not set to install over the network as they are needed, since users may be using slow access lines. Use the **Set Feature Installation States** page in the Custom Installation Wizard to specify the installation state for Outlook features as **Run from My Computer**. For features that you are not deploying and you do not wish to be available, you can set the feature state to **Not Available, Hidden, Locked**.

You may also want to configure features such as Remote Procedure Call (RPC) over HTTP and Cached Exchange Mode for remote users, to enhance their experience when they use Outlook 2003 over slower or less reliable connections. With RPC over HTTP, you can configure connections that help users connect more securely to Exchange servers in your organization without using a Virtual Private Network (VPN) connection. Cached Exchange Mode is a new feature that configures Outlook to use a local copy of users' mailboxes, allowing users more reliable access to their Outlook data whether they are connected to a network or working offline.

Roaming users should have the same messaging environment on each computer to which they roam. This includes the type and version of the operating system, version of Outlook, and the Outlook installation location on the computer.

For multiple users sharing the same computer, use Microsoft Windows® logon features on the computer's operating system to manage user logon verification. Also, make sure that each user runs the same version of Outlook so that conflicts do not arise among shared files. Conflicts can happen when one version of Outlook attempts to write a file to a file folder location that is shared by other versions of Outlook used on the same computer.

Multilingual requirements

Microsoft Office 2003 provides broad support for deploying in international or multilingual environments. Office products such as the Office 2003 Multilingual User Interface Pack and Microsoft Office 2003 Proofing Tools help multilingual groups work with and edit files in a variety of languages and provide support for localized Help and user interfaces.

Outlook 2003 now supports Unicode® throughout the product to help multilingual organizations seamlessly exchange messages and other information in a multilingual environment.

Outlook 2003 and Terminal Services

With Microsoft Terminal Services, you install a single copy of Microsoft Office Outlook 2003 on a Terminal Services computer. Then, instead of running Outlook locally, multiple users connect to the server and run Outlook from there.

To achieve the optimal results when you use Outlook with Terminal Services, pay close attention to how you customize your Outlook configuration. Note that Outlook may be part of an environment that includes other applications provided on the same Terminal Services computer.

Client and messaging server platforms

Some features of Outlook 2003 (for example, Cached Exchange Mode) require Microsoft Exchange Server as a messaging platform. While Outlook 2003 works well with earlier versions of Exchange, some features of Outlook 2003 require specific versions of Exchange. Because of this and other enhanced integration with Exchange throughout Outlook 2003, you may gain the greatest benefit by combining Outlook 2003 with the latest version of Exchange.

Deployment customization decisions for Outlook 2003 depend on which version of Exchange Server you are using. If you currently use Exchange Server as your messaging server and have not upgraded to Exchange 2000 or later, consider coordinating your Exchange Server upgrade with your deployment timing for Outlook 2003.

Choosing when and how to install Outlook 2003

You have options for when and how you install Outlook 2003. For example, consider whether it would be best for your organization to:

- Install or upgrade Outlook in stages (for different groups of users) or at one time.
- Install Outlook as a stand-alone application.
- Install Outlook before, with, or after Office 2003.

Each organization has a different environment and might make different choices about timing Outlook 2003 upgrades. For example, you might have a messaging group that is responsible for upgrading Outlook and a separate group that plans deployment for other Office applications. In this case, it might be easier to upgrade Outlook separately from the rest of Office, rather than attempting to coordinate deployment between the two groups.

> **Note** Outlook 2003 cannot coexist with previous versions of Outlook. If you choose to keep previous versions, do not install Outlook 2003.

Customizing Outlook settings and profiles

You can customize your Outlook installation to handle Outlook user settings and profiles in several ways. For instance, you can:

- Capture Outlook settings in an Office profile settings file (OPS file), then include the OPS file in a transform (MST file) that is applied during Setup.
- Specify Outlook user settings in the Custom Installation Wizard.
- Specify options for managing new and existing Outlook profiles in the Custom Installation Wizard.

For example, you can allow Outlook users to migrate their current profiles and settings while defining default profiles and settings for new Outlook users. Or, you can modify existing profiles as well as establish new default profiles for new Outlook users.

After you customize Outlook using these options, you save your choices—along with other installation preferences—in a transform (MST file) that is applied during Setup. Later, you can update settings and profile information by using the Custom Maintenance Wizard.

Migrating data

In your Outlook deployment, you might choose to migrate data from other mail clients to Outlook.

If your organization currently uses a different mail client, you might need to migrate data from that program to Outlook 2003. If you need to migrate data from another messaging application, importers are provided in the product (for example, for Eudora Lite) that might be helpful in your situation.

Limiting viruses and junk e-mail messages for your users

Outlook 2003 comes with features designed to help minimize the spread of viruses. You can use the Outlook Security Template to configure these security settings to support the needs of your organization. For example, you can modify the list of file types that are blocked in e-mail messages.

You can also configure Outlook 2003 to display users' Hypertext Markup Language (HTML) e-mail messages in plain text to limit the exposure to potential viruses and scripts that might be contained in those messages.

Outlook 2003 has several features to help users avoid receiving junk e-mail messages. Outlook 2003 includes a new Junk E-mail Filter for users that replaces the rules used in previous versions of Outlook to filter mail. Messages that are caught by the filter are moved to the Junk E-mail folder where they can be viewed or deleted later. In addition, Outlook 2003 reduces the likelihood that users will become targets for future junk e-mail by blocking (by default) automatic picture-downloads from external servers. Junk e-mail senders can include a "Web beacon" in HTML e-mail messages that includes external content. When users open or view the e-mail, their e-mail address is verified as being valid which increases the likelihood that they will receive more junk e-mail messages.

Configuring cryptographic features

Outlook 2003 provides cryptographic features for sending and receiving security-enhanced e-mail messages over the Internet or local intranet. You can customize features in your Outlook 2003 deployment to set cryptographic options appropriate for your organization. New buttons in the user interface make it easy for users who have cryptographic capabilities enabled on their computers to quickly sign and encrypt their e-mail messages.

You can also implement additional features to help enhance security in e-mail messaging. For example, you can provide security labels that match your organization's security policy. An Internal Use Only label might be implemented as a security label to apply to e-mail messages that should not be sent or forwarded outside of your company.

Restricting permission on e-mail messages

Information Rights Management (IRM), a new feature in Office 2003, helps users prevent sensitive e-mail messages and other Office 2003 content, such as documents and worksheets, from being forwarded, edited, or copied by unauthorized people. In Outlook 2003, users can use IRM to mark e-mail messages with "Do not forward," which automatically restricts permission for recipients to forward, print, or copy the message. In addition, you can define customized Office-wide IRM permission policies for your organization's needs and deploy the new permission policies for users to use with e-mail messages or other Office documents.

Resources and related information

You can configure a number of options when deploying Outlook 2003. For more information about Outlook configuration choices, see "Options for Installing Outlook 2003" in Chapter 7, "Deploying Outlook 2003."

The Office Custom Installation Wizard provides a straightforward way to configure and install Outlook 2003. For more information about Outlook configuration choices, see "Customizing Outlook Features and Installation with the Custom Installation Wizard" in Chapter 7, "Deploying Outlook 2003."

You can stage your Outlook 2003 deployment to install Outlook with Office, before Office, or after Office, depending on the needs of your organization. For more information about staging an Outlook deployment, see "Determining When to Install Outlook" in the next section of this chapter.

Careful planning can help your upgrade to a new release of Outlook go smoothly. For more information about planning an Outlook upgrade, see "Planning an Upgrade to Outlook 2003" in Chapter 9, "Upgrading to Outlook 2003."

Planning and implementing an appropriate security plan for your organization is key to a successful Outlook installation. For more information about security in Outlook 2003, see Chapter 11, "Administering Cryptography in Outlook 2003."

Determining When to Install Outlook

You can install Microsoft Office Outlook 2003 before, with, or after an installation of other Microsoft Office 2003 applications, and you can deploy Outlook to different groups of users at different times. Each installation staging strategy has its own requirements, as well as advantages and disadvantages.

Installing Outlook with Office

You can install Outlook 2003 as a part of your overall upgrade to Office 2003. Outlook is included in most editions of the Microsoft Office System of products.

Installing Outlook with Office is recommended because it is the simplest installation strategy—you avoid the extra steps involved in creating separate application deployments.

Installing Outlook before Office

Choosing to install Outlook 2003 before you deploy other Office 2003 applications might be preferred in the following circumstances:

- When you want to test custom solutions that rely on previous versions of Office applications (such as Microsoft Office Word 2003 or Microsoft Office Excel 2003) before you install the current version.

- When your messaging support group has the resources to install Outlook now, but the desktop applications support group must wait to install the rest of Office.

> **Note**   Outlook 2003 cannot coexist with previous versions of Outlook. If you choose to keep previous versions, do not install Outlook 2003.

If you choose to install Outlook 2003 before you install Office 2003, you can do so by:

- Installing the stand-alone version of Outlook from its own administrative installation point.

  Later, you can create a separate administrative installation point for Office and direct users to upgrade to Office from there.

- Installing the stand-alone version of Outlook from the same administrative installation point from which you plan to deploy Office.

  With this method, you might need to rename the Setup program files for Office or Outlook to prevent the files from being overwritten.

- Running Office Setup to install only Outlook.

  Later, you can run the Custom Maintenance Wizard to install the rest of Office.

Advantages to installing before Office

If you deploy Outlook 2003 promptly, users can begin using new features without waiting for testing or technical support to become available for a complete upgrade to Office.

Disadvantages to installing before Office

Installing Outlook before you install the rest of Office has several disadvantages:

- When you deploy the other Office applications later on, you must customize the installation process in order to preserve your original Outlook settings.

- You cannot use the WordMail editor in Outlook 2003 until Word 2003 has also been installed.

- If you use separate administrative installation points for Outlook and Office, you must also allow for more hard disk space, because the files common to all of Office are duplicated on the server.

- If you use the same administrative installation point for Outlook and Office, you must take extra steps to manage multiple versions of the Setup files or to modify installation options.

Installing Outlook after Office

You can wait to install Outlook until after you have installed Office 2003. For example, if any of the following scenarios describes your organization, you might consider delaying your deployment of Outlook:

- You plan to coordinate your Outlook deployment with a future upgrade of Microsoft Exchange Server.

- You want to convert Lotus Notes to a Microsoft Exchange Server solution before you upgrade to Outlook.

- Your desktop support group has the resources to upgrade to Office now, but the messaging support group must wait to deploy Outlook.

If you choose to install Outlook after you have installed Office 2003, you can do so by:

- Installing the stand-alone version of Outlook from a separate administrative installation point.

- Installing the stand-alone version of Outlook from the same administrative installation point from which you installed Office.

  With this method, you must rename the Setup program files (for Office or Outlook) to prevent the original files from being overwritten.

- Running Office Setup to install Office but exclude Outlook.

  Later, you can use the Custom Maintenance Wizard to install Outlook.

Advantages to installing after Office

In many organizations, it makes sense to coordinate an Outlook deployment with an upgrade of a mail server, rather than with an upgrade of other desktop applications.

Disadvantages to installing after Office

When you install Office without Outlook, you must explicitly change default Setup settings in the Custom Installation Wizard so that previous versions of Outlook are not removed from users' computers.

Regardless of when or how you install Outlook separately from Office, you must take extra steps to manage duplicate files, multiple versions of the Setup files, or customizations to the installation process.

Staging an Outlook deployment

Some groups in your organization might be ready to upgrade to Outlook immediately, while other groups might need more time to prepare or find additional resources. A situation like this, or one of the following conditions, might be best managed by a staged deployment of Outlook:

- Your normal policy is to stage upgrades to help ensure a smooth rollout of new software throughout your organization.

- You have remote systems support groups (for example, in regional sales offices) that require relative autonomy in scheduling upgrades for their areas.

- Some groups want to wait until after a project deadline before making changes to their local computers.

- You have limited resources for staging and upgrading systems throughout your organization.

Advantages to staging a deployment

Staging your Outlook deployment gives you more flexibility in managing your upgrading resources. In addition, pilot users immediately become familiar with the new features and productivity enhancements of Outlook 2003.

Having users on different versions of Outlook within an organization does not pose any significant technical problems. Outlook 2003 users can communicate seamlessly with users of Outlook 2002 and Office XP.

Disadvantages to staging a deployment

You must take into account the logistics of scheduling and managing a staged deployment. Your organization might also encounter extra overhead to support users on different versions of the same product.

Resources and related information

Specific procedures can help you successfully deploy Outlook before or after you install Office. For more information about implementing a staged deployment of Outlook, see "Installing Outlook 2003 Before Office 2003" and "Installing Outlook 2003 After Office 2003" in Chapter 8, "Special Deployment Scenarios for Outlook 2003."

Microsoft Exchange Server Support for Outlook 2003

Microsoft Office Outlook 2003 works well with a variety of e-mail servers, but you can take advantage of a richer feature set by using Outlook with the latest version of Microsoft Exchange Server. Some Outlook 2003 features require certain Exchange versions (and, in some cases, specific Exchange configurations running on certain versions of Microsoft Windows), while other features simply work better with newer versions of Exchange.

Several features of Outlook 2003 work best with Microsoft Exchange Server 2003 or later, especially for mobile users accessing their mailboxes over slower connections. This is apparent for the new remote procedure call (RPC) over HTTP feature, which enables users to log on to Exchange servers behind the corporate firewall without needing to use a virtual private network connection. Furthermore, the exchange of information between the Outlook client and Exchange Server is more efficient with Exchange Server 2003 because of the new data compression and partial-item update features. Also, on slow connections using the Headers Only mode in Outlook, an expanded plain text header preview now gives users more information to help them decide whether to download the full item or not. Finally, transactions between Outlook and Exchange Server are now more robust for the following reasons:

- Scenarios that previously caused synchronizations to fail are now managed so the synchronization can continue.

- Updates are checkpointed. This means that if a download of new information is interrupted—for example, by a connection failure—Outlook can resume the update at the point where the failure occurred, instead of starting over from the beginning.

These enhancements work together to help ensure that Outlook users accessing Exchange servers remotely over slower connections have a better user experience.

Outlook 2003 and e-mail protocols and servers

Outlook 2003 can be used with a wide variety of e-mail servers and services. The primary e-mail servers and services supported by Outlook include:

- The Simple Mail Transfer Protocol (SMTP)

- The Post Office Protocol version 3 (POP3)

- The Internet Mail Access Protocol version 4 (IMAP4)

- The Messaging Application Programming Interface (MAPI), which includes Microsoft Exchange Server and Lotus Domino/Notes Server

Outlook can also be used with a number of other messaging and information sources, including Hewlett-Packard OpenMail and Banyan Intelligent Messaging. Use of these additional service providers is made possible by the way that Outlook uses the MAPI extensibility interface.

If users want to use the Contacts, Tasks, and Calendar features in a stand-alone configuration, they can also use Outlook without an e-mail server.

The following sections list the new features supported only when Outlook 2003 is used with Exchange 2003 or later. They also list the features that work better when Outlook 2003 is used with Exchange 2003 or later.

Outlook 2003 features supported only with Exchange Server 2003 or later

Using Outlook 2003 with an Exchange Server 2003 or later messaging server has a number of advantages. For example, the following Outlook features work only with Exchange Server 2003 or later:

- Cached Exchange Mode using Download Headers
  Cached Exchange Mode automatically downloads only headers when a user's connection mode is perceived by the user's operating system to be "slow."

- Cached Exchange Mode using Download Headers and then Full Items
  With this option, all item headers are downloaded first, followed by item bodies and other detailed information. Users can choose to see specific items right away (headers as well as item bodies and attachments) by clicking item headers.

- RPC over HTTP connection support

    You can configure user accounts to connect to an Exchange server over the Internet. This feature allows users security-enhanced access to their Exchange Server accounts from the Internet when they are traveling or are working outside their organization's firewall.

- Kerberos authentication

    Outlook can use Kerberos authentication with Exchange 2003. The Kerberos network security protocol uses cryptography to help provide mutual authentication for a network connection between a client and a server (or between two servers).

- Performance tracking support

    Outlook 2003 provides information about client processing that Exchange can use to help track down networking or server problems. For more information, see Exchange Server 2003 documentation.

Outlook 2003 enhancements that work better with Exchange Server 2003 or later

Exchange Server 2003 and later versions of Exchange Server provide support for new features in Outlook 2003, but Outlook 2003 also simply works better with Exchange 2003 or later in several ways—most notably for synchronization processing, user synchronization status reports, and junk e-mail filtering.

Synchronization processing between Outlook and Exchange has been enhanced in a number of ways. For example, data exchanged between the Outlook 2003 client and Exchange 2003 servers is now compressed, and the data buffer size is larger. In addition, the buffers themselves are now "packed," so more compressed data is included in each buffer. With these improvements, more data can be transferred with fewer server calls. This is especially beneficial when users are synchronizing across networks that charge by the byte of data that is transmitted. When large information sets are being downloaded—for example, when users update mailboxes after being on vacation—cost can be significantly lowered, and the transaction shortened, with these improvements.

Another improvement that users will notice is better status information about Cached Exchange Mode synchronization with the Exchange 2003 server. With Exchange 2003, the Outlook status bar shows detailed information about synchronization such as:

- How many bytes have yet to be downloaded for the current folder.

- How many items have yet to be downloaded in the current folder.

- Approximately how long it will be until the current folder is synchronized.

- Folder status such as "Up to Date" and "Last updated at <date and time>."

In addition, the Headers Only mode in Outlook 2003—when used with Exchange 2003—provides a 256-byte plain text preview that includes part of the message body, rather than showing just the message header information. This message preview can help remote users to make better decisions about whether to download a whole message—which, for example, might include a large attachment.

Finally, using Outlook 2003 with Exchange Server 2003 or later helps to provide a better experience for users in filtering junk e-mail. The new Junk E-mail Filter provides some support for Outlook 2003 users with Cached Exchange Mode on versions of Exchange Server earlier than Exchange Server 2003. However, with Exchange Server 2003, the experience is much improved and Exchange Online users can also benefit from junk e-mail filtering. With Exchange Server 2003 Service Pack 1, even more junk e-mail filtering support is provided. To learn more about how junk e-mail filtering is supported with different versions of Exchange Server, see "Helping Users Avoid Junk E-Mail Messages in Outlook 2003" in Chapter 7, "Deploying Outlook 2003."

Resources and related information

You can configure Microsoft Exchange Server settings for Outlook profiles as part of your Outlook 2003 deployment. For more information about using the Custom Installation Wizard to customize Outlook profiles, see "Customizing Outlook Features and Installation with the Custom Installation Wizard" in Chapter 7, "Deploying Outlook 2003."

Using Outlook 2003 to Help Protect Messages

You have two main options for helping to protect messages in Microsoft Office Outlook 2003 from unauthorized use, tampering, or change: 1) Information Rights Management (IRM), and 2) cryptographic messaging using the S/MIME standard. While both of these options can help protect messages your users send and receive, they work differently and are each best suited for different scenarios.

S/MIME is a standard for sending digitally signed and encrypted e-mail messages. Using S/MIME in Outlook 2003 is the preferred way to:

- Sign a message to prove the identity of the sender.

  S/MIME is the only option Microsoft Office 2003 supports for digital signatures. Technically, an IRM message is a lot like a signed message because it cannot be tampered with. But IRM protection is more limited because there are no authorities that will attest to the identities of the senders, and the Outlook 2003 user interface does not show information about the identity of the sender.

- Help ensure that Internet e-mail messages are not vulnerable to attackers "sniffing" the wire.

  The focus here is on the Internet, as that is where point-to-point encryption is most valuable and where interoperability standards are most important.

The biggest value for using S/MIME is when users are sending and receiving e-mail messages outside of corporate boundaries, where they are not protected by the corporate firewall.

Another feature that can help to protect messages in Outlook is IRM. IRM gives organizations and information workers greater control over sensitive information. IRM is the preferred way to help to:

- Protect messages containing sensitive information by restricting the ability to forward or copy the message.

   The reasons to use IRM have little to do with whether an unauthorized person outside the organization—for example, a hacker on the Internet—will intercept the communication. Instead, IRM is best put to use when the sender is concerned that the intended recipient will share the information inappropriately with others.

- Prevent people from using out-of-date information by enforcing message expiration.

   With IRM, expiration dates on messages are enforced (unlike expiration dates set on messages without IRM).

The biggest value for IRM is within the corporation, where employees need to share information while maintaining some control over who has access to this information—especially to help ensure that this information does not leak outside the corporate firewall.

Resources and related information

You can set several options when you deploy Information Rights Management in an organization. For more information about understanding and customizing IRM in Office 2003, see Chapter 20, "Information Rights Management." To learn about the options you have for deploying IRM with Outlook 2003, see "Configuring Information Rights Management for Messaging in Outlook 2003" in Chapter 7, "Deploying Outlook 2003."

Cryptography in Outlook 2003 can be configured to suit the specific needs of your organization. For more information about customizing and managing cryptographic messaging, see Chapter 11, "Administering Cryptography in Outlook 2003."

Unicode Enhancements in Outlook 2003

Microsoft Office Outlook 2003 supports Unicode and provides full support for multilingual data. If your users work in a multinational organization or share messages and items with people who use Outlook on systems that run in other languages, they can take advantage of Unicode support in Outlook. In addition, a new file format for Outlook files that supports Unicode can store more data than file formats from earlier versions of Outlook.

Using Unicode mode in Outlook

Previous versions of Outlook provided support for multilingual Unicode data in the body of e-mail messages. However, Outlook data—such as the To and Subject lines of messages and the **ContactName** and **BusinessTelephoneNumber** properties of contact items—was limited to characters defined by your system code page. Outlook 2003 no longer has this limitation, provided Outlook is running in Unicode mode with Microsoft Exchange Server as the messaging server.

Outlook 2003 can run in one of two mailbox modes with an Exchange messaging server: Unicode or non-Unicode. Unicode mode is recommended and is the default mode if the configurations of the user's profile, Exchange server, and administrator settings allow it. The mode is automatically determined by Outlook based on these settings, and it cannot be changed manually by the user. An administrator can deploy settings that can change the default behavior or limit the ability of users to use Unicode.

POP3 accounts can also support multilingual Unicode data in Outlook 2003, provided that items are delivered to a Personal Folders file (PST file) that can support multilingual Unicode data. By default, new POP3 profiles that deliver to a new PST file created in Outlook 2003 support multilingual Unicode data.

Note   Other accounts, such as IMAP and HTTP, do not support Unicode.

Running Outlook in Unicode mode enables users to work with messages and items that are composed in different languages, but if you prefer, you can configure Outlook so that your users run in non-Unicode mode with Exchange server accounts.

Caution   Switching between Unicode mode and non-Unicode mode can cause data loss or make text unreadable. For this reason, users who begin using Outlook in Unicode mode should continue to use Unicode mode.

How Unicode works better for users in multilingual environments

Non-Unicode systems typically use a code page based environment, in which each script has its own table of characters. Items based on the code page of one operating system rarely map well to the code page of another operating system. In some cases, the items cannot contain text that uses characters from more than one script.

Running Outlook in Unicode mode with Exchange Server also helps ensure that, by default, Offline Folder files (OST files) and Personal Folders files (PST files) used in the Outlook profile are able to store multilingual Unicode data. In addition, Unicode files in Outlook provide greater storage capacity for items and folders.

A new Outlook file format supports Unicode

In Outlook 2003, an enhanced file format for PST and OST files offers greater storage capacity for items and folders, and supports multilingual Unicode data. An Outlook file with this format is not compatible with previous versions of Outlook and cannot be opened in a previous version of Outlook.

Outlook automatically determines the format in which PST and OST files are created based on the version of Microsoft Exchange Server, administrator settings, and formats of the data files that are configured for the profile.

If settings for Outlook or other characteristics of a user's Outlook profile do not allow a file to be created in the new format, Outlook creates the file in the format that is compatible with previous versions of Outlook. The earlier file format (called Microsoft Outlook 97-2002 Personal Folder File) does not support Unicode and offers the same storage capacity that was available in previous versions of Outlook.

Resources and related information

For more information on configuring Unicode settings for Outlook as part of your Outlook 2003 deployment, see "Configuring Unicode Options for Outlook 2003" in Chapter 7, "Deploying Outlook 2003."

Using the Unicode character encoding standard enables almost all written languages in the world to be represented by using a single character set. In Microsoft Windows operating systems, the two standard systems of storing text—code pages and Unicode—coexist. But Unicode-based systems are replacing code page based systems. For more information about using Unicode with Microsoft Office 2003, see "Unicode Support and Multilingual Office Documents" in Chapter 17, "Unicode Support in Office 2003."

Chapter 7

Deploying Outlook 2003

Tools provided with Microsoft® Office 2003 allow you to control how Microsoft Office Outlook® 2003 is installed for your users. By using the Custom Installation Wizard, you can customize your Outlook deployment to include new or modified default Outlook profiles as well as other settings. In addition, you can create or modify profiles by using the Outlook profile file (PRF file).

Options for Installing Outlook 2003

Microsoft Office Outlook 2003, like other Microsoft Office 2003 applications, takes advantage of the Office Custom Installation Wizard to help configure how Outlook 2003 is installed on users' computers. The Custom Installation Wizard allows you to include custom settings and profile configurations for Outlook 2003 in a transform (MST file) that is applied when Outlook is installed from an administrative installation point.

> **Note**   If you install Outlook 2003 on a per-user basis, the **Start** menu will still display the Outlook shortcut icon for all users. Users without privileges to use Outlook will receive an error message indicating that "this product is not installed."

Outlook features that can be customized with the Custom Installation Wizard

Outlook 2003 uses the same installation tools as your other Microsoft Office 2003 applications, including the Custom Installation Wizard. When you customize an Outlook 2003 installation with the wizard, you can do the following:

- Specify installation states for the Outlook features.
- Specify Outlook user settings.
- Specify how to set user profile information—create a profile, modify a profile, or use an existing Outlook profile file (PRF file)—or choose to use existing profile settings.
- Configure profile and account information, including Microsoft Exchange server connections.
- Remove existing information services.
- Optionally export your profile settings to a PRF file (for advanced scenarios).
- Configure Send/Receive settings for Microsoft Exchange accounts.
- Customize other settings to apply during the installation process.

> **Note**   To function correctly, Outlook 2003 requires that Internet Explorer 5.01 or later is installed on the client computers.

After your initial installation, you can use the Office Custom Maintenance Wizard to modify and deploy customizations for your installation.

On the Resource Kit CD   The Office 2003 Resource Kit core tool set includes the Custom Installation Wizard, Office Profile Wizard, and Custom Maintenance Wizard. You use these tools to customize Office application deployments. These tools are installed by default when you run the Office Resource Kit Setup program. For more information, see Appendix A, "Toolbox."

Specifying installation states for Outlook features

As with the other Office 2003 applications, you can specify how and when specific features of Outlook 2003—or all of Outlook—is installed. You can use the **Set Feature Installation States** page in the Custom Installation Wizard to set feature installation states for Outlook.

For example, for the feature **Microsoft Outlook for Windows**, you might set the feature installation state to **Run all from My Computer**. In this case, all Outlook features are installed on the user's local hard disk. Or you might choose to set some features to be installed locally (with **Run from My Computer**), and others to install when the user first gains access to the feature (**Installed on First Use**). Another common option (**Not Available, Hidden, Locked**) is to set some features to not be installed, and to not even appear in the feature tree if users change the installation state of the parent feature.

Specifying Outlook user settings

There are two ways to customize Outlook user settings for your installation:

- You can specify default Office settings for users by using the Office Profile Wizard. In this case, you install Office on a test computer and customize Office with the defaults you select, including Outlook options, and capture those settings in an Office profile settings file (OPS file). Then you include the OPS file in a transform on the **Customized Default Application Settings** page in the Custom Installation Wizard.

Note   While using the Office Profile Wizard is an efficient way to save most Outlook settings, not all options are captured by the wizard. For more information about settings that are not captured by the Office Profile Wizard, see "Locating and Configuring Outlook Settings" in Chapter 10, "Maintaining Outlook 2003."

- You can also customize Outlook user settings individually on the **Change Office User Settings** page in the Custom Installation Wizard.

This requires stepping through the options tree and setting each option individually. This option might be more time-consuming than capturing settings with the Office Profile Wizard, especially if you have a large number of user settings to specify.

> **Note**   Several Outlook settings that would otherwise have been included on the **Change Office User Settings** page are customized instead on the **Change Outlook: Change Default Settings** page. These options are:
>
> ■ Migration option: Choosing to convert Personal Address Books to Outlook Address Books.
>
> ■ Default settings for e-mail defaults: Specifying defaults for the Outlook e-mail editor and for the default format of e-mail messages.

One approach for specifying user settings is to customize an Outlook installation on a test computer and capture the settings with the Office Profile Wizard. Then specify the OPS file in the Custom Installation Wizard to establish a basic installation configuration. Finally, adjust additional settings by using the **Change Office User Settings** page in the Custom Installation Wizard.

If you have just a few Outlook user settings to specify and you are not already using the Office Profile Wizard to capture other Office settings, it may be more efficient to find and set the user options in the Custom Installation Wizard without using an OPS file.

Customizing Outlook profiles

The Outlook pages in the Custom Installation Wizard provide options for creating Outlook profiles or modifying the settings in existing Outlook profiles. For example, you can keep all existing Outlook user profiles and specify a default configuration for new Outlook user profiles.

Your options for configuring profiles include:

■ Specifying Exchange server connections.

■ Defining account information, such as adding POP3 or LDAP accounts.

Once you have configured user profiles to meet your organization's needs, you can also save the profile configuration information in an Outlook profile file (PRF file). For more information about using Outlook profile files, see "Customizing Outlook Profiles by Using PRF Files" later in this chapter.

Resources and related information

Detailed information about using the Office Profile Wizard to save user options is available. For more information about the Office Profile Wizard and OPS files, see "Methods of Customizing Office" in Chapter 4, "Customizing Office 2003."

Outlook settings and profile information can be viewed and modified in different ways, depending on the specific type of setting or option. For more information about Outlook settings, see "Locating and Configuring Outlook Settings" in Chapter 10, "Maintaining Outlook 2003."

Customizing Outlook Features and Installation with the Custom Installation Wizard

Like the rest of Microsoft Office 2003, a Microsoft Office Outlook 2003 installation is highly customizable. By using the Office Custom Installation Wizard, you can specify which features you want installed, whether they should run from the local hard disk or the network, how to customize profiles, and so forth.

Specify installation states for Outlook 2003 features

You can specify installation states for many features in Outlook 2003 when you customize your Office 2003 installation.

To set installation states for Outlook 2003 features

1. Start the Custom Installation Wizard.

2. On the **Set Feature Installation States** page, click the plus sign (+) next to **Microsoft Outlook for Windows** to expand the feature tree.

3. Click the down arrow next to the feature you want to set, and then select the installation state to use for that feature.

    For example, you might not want users to install Collaboration Data Objects, if your organization does not use this feature. In this case, you click the down arrow, then choose **Not Available, Hidden, Locked** in the menu. After deployment, users will not be able to see Collaboration Data Objects as an Outlook feature that they could install.

Specify user settings

If you have specified settings by using the Office Profile Wizard and have saved those settings in an Office profile settings file (OPS file), you can provide the OPS file name on the **Customize Default Application Settings** page of the Custom Installation Wizard. You can also specify user settings on the **Change Office User Settings** page. These settings will override choices that are specified in the OPS file.

If you want current user settings to migrate for all users, select the check box next to **Migrate user settings** on the **Customize Default Application Settings** page in the Custom Installation Wizard. If you choose to migrate user settings, other customizations to user settings that you specify—including those in an OPS file or selections you make on the **Change Office User Settings** page—will not override existing user settings.

> **Caution**   User options that are configured by using the **Change Office User Settings** page become the default settings for users (if you are not migrating user settings). If you want to lock down user settings, you must use Group Policy. For more information about using Group Policy to lock down user settings in Office, see "Managing Users' Configurations by Policy" in Chapter 18, "Updating Users' Office 2003 Configurations."

Customize Outlook profile creation and modification

Outlook 2003 uses profiles to store information about users' e-mail servers, where their Outlook information is stored (on the server or in a local file), and other options.

Configuring how Outlook handles creating default profiles

If you do not configure default profiles for your users, when users install Outlook 2003 on a clean computer, the Outlook Profile Wizard assists them in creating a profile the first time they start Outlook. If a user is upgrading from a previous version of Outlook or Microsoft Exchange Client, Outlook 2003 (by default) detects the existing profile on the user's computer and uses that profile instead of creating a new one.

Outlook profile configurations affect how e-mail messages are sent and received. Because profiles are so important, the process to create profiles can be automated—saving users from having to create profiles through the Outlook Profile Wizard. You can use the Office Custom Installation Wizard to create profiles automatically for your users when Outlook starts up for the first time (overriding their existing default profiles), or to modify existing profiles.

After your initial Outlook deployment, you can modify how Outlook manages profile creation by using the Custom Maintenance Wizard to update the original profile configuration information you specified in your transform.

Configuring how Outlook handles existing and new profiles

The Outlook pages in the Custom Installation Wizard provide options for creating Outlook profiles or modifying the settings in existing Outlook profiles. Your options for how to handle Outlook profile settings are shown on the **Customize Default Profile** page:

- **Use existing profiles**   If an Outlook profile exists, Outlook uses that profile. If an Outlook profile is not found, the Outlook Profile Wizard takes the user through creating a profile.
- **Modify Profile**   Users who have an Outlook profile have their profiles migrated to Outlook 2003 (a typical scenario). Settings you define in the Custom Installation Wizard automatically create new default user profiles for users who have no profile when Outlook first runs.

- **New Profile**   Current Outlook users will get new profiles (a less common scenario). This option creates a new default user profile for all users. Existing profiles remain on the user's computer but are not the default profiles used by Outlook.

- **Apply PRF**   Imports the options you save in an Outlook profile file (PRF file). To import these settings the next time you run the Custom Installation Wizard, enter the file name here.

Note that with both the **Modify Profile** and **New Profile** options, you can define new Exchange Server connections for new and existing users.

Defining and customizing an Outlook profile file (PRF file)

A simple way to create a PRF file that is compatible with Outlook 2003 is to step through the Custom Installation Wizard to specify Outlook profile settings. Then, when prompted, export the settings to a PRF file.

You can modify this PRF file in a text editor to include other customizations. For example, you may have profile customizations in a PRF file from an earlier version of Outlook that you want to incorporate in your Outlook 2003 deployment. Manually editing the Outlook 2003 profile file gives you maximum flexibility for customizing your Outlook profile settings.

Now you can use the PRF file to define Outlook user profile options. For example, in the Custom Installation Wizard on the **Customize Default Profile** page, select **Apply PRF** and enter the name of the file.

For more information about creating and using PRF files, see "Customizing Outlook Profiles by Using PRF Files" later in this chapter.

To choose how to customize Outlook profiles in the Custom Installation Wizard

1. In the Custom Installation Wizard, on the **Outlook: Customize Default Profile** page, click the option for how you choose to customize your users' profile information—**Modify Profile**, **New Profile**, or **Apply PRF**.

   Note that if you select **Modify Profile** or **New Profile**, you are prompted to specify user profile settings in subsequent pages of the wizard. If you choose **Apply PRF**, the settings in your PRF file establish the profile customizations for the transform.

2. If you select **Modify Profile**, Outlook uses the default name for Outlook profiles, Microsoft Outlook, to save the profile information for users without an existing profile.

3. If you select **New Profile**, enter a profile name for saving the new user profile information.

4. If you select **Apply PRF**, enter (or browse to) the name of the PRF file to use.

> **Note**   If you use **New Profile** to create new Outlook profiles or if you change an existing Exchange server account by using **Modify Profile**, a new OST file is created. This can be problematic if you plan to deploy with the Cached Exchange Mode feature turned on. For more information about best practices for setting up Cached Exchange Mode for groups of users, see "Setting Up Outlook 2003 Cached Exchange Mode Accounts" later in this chapter.

Configure Exchange settings for user profiles

You have several options for configuring Microsoft Exchange Server connections for users (including not configuring connection information). You can make configuration changes for new Exchange users and for existing users.

■ For users who do not have an Exchange Server connection configured, you can specify a user name and server name, as well as offline settings.

■ For users with an existing Exchange Server connection, you can keep that connection or replace the current Exchange Server configuration with a new one.

To specify Exchange settings for Outlook user profiles in the Custom Installation Wizard

1. In the Custom Installation Wizard, on the **Outlook: Specify Exchange Settings** page, click **Configure an Exchange Server connection**.
   Note that if you chose **New Profile** on the previous page, this configuration will apply to all Outlook users.

2. Use the default %UserName% variable setting for the user's logon name.
   You can choose to use another system variable name if, for example, you have a separate user name for Outlook access. Use **=%UserName%** to help prevent prompting for ambiguous user names. For more information about preventing prompts to resolve user names when Outlook starts up, see "Ensuring a Quiet Installation and Startup for Outlook" in Chapter 8, "Special Deployment Scenarios for Outlook 2003."

3. Enter the name of an Exchange server on your network.
   This will be replaced with the specific Exchange server for each individual user when Outlook first starts.

4. Specify a default download mode for Cached Exchange Mode.

5. Click on **More Settings** to configure offline and RPC over HTTP settings, then click **OK**.

6. Select **Overwrite existing Exchange settings if an Exchange connection exists** to use the Exchange Server connection you have defined for all users.

    This only applies when modifying a profile. If you are defining new default profiles, the one you define will be used for all users.

7. Click **Next**.

For more information about configuring Cached Exchange Mode for your deployment, see "Setting Up Outlook 2003 Cached Exchange Mode Accounts" later in this chapter.

For more information about configuring RPC over HTTP for your deployment, see "Configuring Outlook 2003 for RPC over HTTP" in Chapter 8, "Special Deployment Scenarios for Outlook 2003."

Add and customize accounts for Outlook user profiles

You can add account definitions to Outlook user profiles. For example, you might create a POP3 e-mail account or configure an Internet Directory Service (LDAP) to add to user profiles.

To add and customize Outlook accounts

1. In the Custom Installation Wizard, on the **Outlook: Add Accounts** page, select **Customize additional Outlook profile and account information**.

2. To create a new account for user profiles, click **Add**.

3. Select an account from the list, and then click **Next**.

4. Follow the directions shown to configure the account.

    The additional information required varies depending on the account type that you choose.

5. When you click **Finish**, the account appears in the table on the **Outlook: Add Accounts** page.

    When an account is added, the column **If Account Exists** is populated with one of two values—**Do Not Replace** or **Replace**. This applies only when you have chosen to modify user profiles (**Modify Profiles**).

6. To modify an account you have created, click on the account name in the list and then click **Modify**.

7. To delete an account you have created, click on the account name in the list and then click **Delete**.

8. In the **Deliver new mail to the following location field**, the value **<default>** is displayed.

With this option, new mail is delivered to a user's existing default mail delivery location. For new users, **<default>** means that mail is delivered to the server. To change the location for new mail delivery, click the drop-down arrow and click a new location.

Note that if you have not added any accounts to the profile, no additional locations are displayed in the drop-down list.

9. When you are finished adding and modifying accounts, click **Next**.

Add and customize Send/Receive groups for Exchange users

You can create Send/Receive groups for Exchange users and specify the characteristics you want for each group—for example, how often to execute a Send/Receive, which folders to include in a Send/Receive, whether to download full details for the Offline Address Book, and so on.

To add and customize Send/Receive groups for Exchange users

1. In the Custom Installation Wizard, on the **Outlook: Specify Send/Receive Groups (Exchange Only)** page, select **Configure Send/Receive Settings**.

2. To create a new Send/Receive group, click **New** and enter a name in the **New Group Name** box.

3. To configure an existing Send/Receive group, select the group in the list and click **Modify**.

4. Specify options for a Send/Receive group, such as the folders to include in the group when Outlook executes a Send/Receive.

5. Click **OK** to return to the main Send/Receive configuration page in the wizard.

6. Specify settings for a Send/Receive group, such as how often to execute Send/Receive for this group.

7. Specify options for downloading the Exchange Address Book for this Send/Receive group.

8. Click **Next** to configure more options in the Custom Installation Wizard.

Remove extra mail accounts and export user profile settings

If you are modifying user profiles, you can choose to remove extra mail accounts for Lotus cc: Mail or Microsoft Mail from your users' profiles.

To remove extra mail accounts

■   In the Custom Installation Wizard, on the **Outlook: Remove Accounts and Export Settings** page, click the check boxes to select the accounts you want to remove from user profiles.

On this page of the wizard, you can also choose to save to a PRF file the current Outlook user profile settings that you have configured in the previous four pages in the Custom Installation Wizard. This is optional and does not affect your user profile customizations.

> **Note** Any changes you make after exporting the current settings will not be updated in the exported PRF file.

To save Outlook user profile settings to a PRF file

1. In the Custom Installation Wizard, on the **Outlook: Remove Accounts and Export Settings** page, click **Export Profile Settings** button.

2. Enter (or browse to) the file name and location for the PRF file and click **Save**. Later, you can manually edit this file (for example, using Notepad) to make changes not available through the Custom Installation Wizard. To include your updates, you must import the revised PRF file by using **Apply PRF** on the **Outlook: Customize Default Profile** page.

3. Click **Next**.

> **Note** This process is a fast way of creating a PRF file for use in your deployment. Create your preliminary configuration by specifying Outlook options in the Custom Installation Wizard, then export the settings. After saving the file, open it with a text editor and make any additional changes you choose. For more information about working with PRF files, see "Customizing Outlook Profiles by Using PRF Files" later in this chapter.

Customize default migration and e-mail settings

In addition to configuring Outlook user profile information, you can specify whether to migrate users' Personal Address Books. You can also specify default e-mail settings—the default settings for the editor Outlook will use in composing messages and for the message format in which Outlook will send messages.

To set Outlook migration option and default settings

1. In the Custom Installation Wizard, on the **Outlook: Customize Default Settings** page, you can select the check box to have users' Personal Address Books converted to Outlook Address Books when Outlook first runs.

2. Next, choose default settings options. Set the Outlook default e-mail editor by clicking the drop-down arrow and choosing an option.

3. Set the Outlook default e-mail format by clicking the drop-down arrow and choosing an option.

4. Click **Next** to continue setting options for your Office transform.

> **Note**   If you selected **Migrate user settings** on the **Customize Default Application Settings** page, then users' current settings will override what you specify on this page. If you did not select **Migrate user settings**, your selections here will override users' current settings.

Specify registry key settings

If there are registry key settings that you want to include in your Outlook deployment, you can specify them on the **Add/Remove Registry Entries** page of the Custom Installation Wizard.

For example, you might want to reset folder names for all users when you deploy Outlook to synchronize users' folder names to the User Interface Language of their version of Outlook. This could be useful, for example, if a corporate-wide process has initialized new mailboxes before new users have started Outlook for the first time. In this case, the mailboxes will end up with default folders in the language of the server. (Note that users can, instead, specify the **/resetfoldernames** option on the Outlook.exe command line to synchronize the folder names on their computers.)

To reset folder names when deploying Outlook

1. In the Custom Installation Wizard, go to the **Add/Remove Registry Entries** page.

2. Click **Add** to add a registry entry for **ResetFolderNames**.

3. On the **Add/Modify Registry Entry** page, select or type the following:

    - Under **Root:**, select **HKEY_CURRENT_USER**.

    - Under **Data type:**, select **Dword**.

    - In the **Key:** field, type **Software/Microsoft/Office/10.0/Outlook/Setup**.

    - In the **Value name:** field, type **ResetFolderNames**.

    - In the **Value data:** field, type **1**.
        Any non-zero value will cause Outlook to synchronize the user's folder names to the User Interface Language of Outlook.

4. Click **OK** to save the entry.

Resources and related information

The Custom Installation Wizard offers a wide range of configuration options for defining and modifying user profiles. For more information about creating and using PRF files, see "Customizing Outlook Profiles by Using PRF Files" in the next section.

If your organization uses Exchange 2003 or later, you can deploy Outlook 2003 with Cached Exchange Mode. It is important to use a systematic rollout strategy when deploying Cached Exchange Mode so the Exchange server can smoothly manage updating users' local computers with copies of their mailboxes. For more information, see "Setting Up Outlook 2003 Cached Exchange Mode Accounts" later in this chapter.

Outlook 2003 includes new features that you can configure to best suit your organization's needs. For more information, see "Configuring User Interface Options in Outlook 2003" later in this chapter.

You have a number of options for configuring Send/Receive groups for Exchange users. For more information, see "Configuring Exchange Server Send/Receive Settings in Outlook 2003" later in this chapter.

Customizing Outlook Profiles by Using PRF Files

The Microsoft Outlook profile file (PRF file) allows you to quickly create MAPI profiles for Microsoft Office Outlook 2003 users. The PRF file is a text file with syntax that Microsoft Outlook uses to generate a profile. By using a PRF file, you can set up new profiles for users or modify existing profiles without affecting other aspects of your Outlook (or Microsoft Office) installation. You can also manually edit a PRF file to customize Outlook to include services that are not included in the Custom Installation Wizard user interface.

PRF file features in Outlook 2003

As in earlier versions of Outlook, you can continue to use the PRF file to provide options for specifying additional services, as well as verification for account settings.

The Outlook 2003 PRF file format is the same as the Outlook 2002 PRF file format. This file format combines the features included in two previous PRF file formats (used with Outlook 2000 and earlier). One format was designed for the Outlook tool Newprof.exe. The second format worked with the Modprof.exe tool for Outlook 2000.

Note   The Outlook tools Newprof.exe and Modprof.exe are no longer required. The tools will not work with Outlook 2003 or Outlook 2002. You can use the Custom Installation Wizard to quickly modify profile settings and create a new PRF file that includes those settings.

Outlook 2003 continues to provide the following PRF file processing:

- Outlook 2003 PRF files are executable, so you can update profiles by double-clicking the file name to run the file directly.

- When Outlook processes the PRF file, Outlook verifies that services that should be unique are not added more than once, and that services that cannot be duplicated have unique account names.

Most MAPI services and accounts can be added only once to a profile. The exceptions to this rule include mail server and directory service providers for POP, IMAP, PST (personal store folder), and LDAP.

Using Outlook 98 and Outlook 2000 PRF files

You may already have a PRF file from an earlier version of Outlook (before Outlook 2002) that you want to update and use with Outlook 2003. If you have a PRF file from Outlook 98 or Outlook 2000 that includes Corporate or Workgroup settings only, you can import the file into the Custom Installation Wizard to specify profile settings for your transform.

If your earlier PRF file specifies Internet Only settings, create a new PRF file using the Custom Installation Wizard, then export the settings to a PRF file. The new PRF file can now be used to configure profile settings in your transform or used to customize Outlook profiles through other methods (such as starting the file directly on a user's computer).

Creating and updating PRF files

To create an Outlook 2003 PRF file, you can configure profile settings in the Custom Installation Wizard, and then export the settings to a PRF file. This process creates a new Outlook 2003 PRF file with your specifications.

You can also specify profile settings by editing an existing PRF file manually using a text editor. This existing PRF file might be one that you created by using the Custom Installation Wizard, or a PRF file from a previous version of Outlook.

Creating PRF files in the Custom Installation Wizard

A straightforward way to create a PRF file with Outlook 2003 profile settings is to customize the settings in the Custom Installation Wizard, and then export the settings to a PRF file.

To create a PRF file in the Custom Installation Wizard

1. In the Custom Installation Wizard, on the **Outlook: Customize Default User Profile** page, select how you want to customize profiles for your users.

   To specify settings to be included in a PRF file, choose **Modify Profile** or **New Profile**, then click **Next**.

2. On the next three pages, customize profile information such as configuring Microsoft Exchange server connections and adding accounts.

3. On the **Outlook: Remove Accounts and Export Settings** page, click **Export Profile Settings**, then when prompted, enter (or browse to) a file name and location.

Manually editing PRF files

If your organization requires special modifications to Outlook profiles—for example, if you want to add a new service that is not included in the Custom Installation Wizard—you can edit the PRF file. Use a text editor such as Notepad to edit your older PRF file or a new PRF file created with the Custom Installation Wizard. Make your changes or additions, and then save the file.

The main functional areas in the Outlook 2003 PRF file include:

■ A section specifying actions to take, such as creating new profiles, modifying existing profiles, overwriting existing profiles, and so on.

■ Sections with organization-specific customizations, including server names, configurations to deploy, and so on.

■ Sections that map information specified in earlier parts of the file to registry key settings.

The PRF file includes detailed comments for each section, describing existing settings and options for modifying the file with your updates. The file includes seven sections:

■ Section 1: Profile defaults.

■ Section 2: A list of MAPI services to be added to the profile.

■ Section 3: A list of Internet accounts to be created.

■ Section 4: Default values for each service.

■ Section 5: Settings values for each Internet account.

■ Section 6: Mapping for profile properties.

■ Section 7: Mapping for Internet account properties.

To allow each service definition to be customized individually, default variables and values in Section 4 can be duplicated under the separate headings (Service1, Service2, and so on) for each service in the profile. Section 6 also groups variables under each service definition, so, for example, some services can be defined as unique (UniqueService is Yes) while others are not (UniqueService is No).

You typically do not modify existing entries in sections 6 and 7. These sections define mappings for information that is defined elsewhere in the file to registry key settings. However, if you define new services in the PRF file, you must add the appropriate mappings for those services to sections 6 and 7.

The following table lists accounts that are unique, and how Outlook determines if a new account of the same type can be added. Keep this information in mind when you add providers in the PRF file. Outlook verifies that unique services are not added more than once, and that other services do not collide (for example, that all POP accounts have unique names).

Account	Unique account?	Method for determining collisions when adding new account
POP	No	Account name
IMAP	No	Account name
Hotmail®/HTTP	No	Account name
PST	No	Full path to PST (including file name)
Outlook Address Book	Yes	Existence of account
Personal Address Book	Yes	Existence of account
LDAP	No	Account name
Exchange	Yes	Existence of provider

Applying Outlook user profiles by using a PRF file

You can apply a PRF file in several ways to update Outlook 2003 profiles:

- Import the PRF file in the Custom Installation Wizard or Custom Maintenance Wizard to specify profile settings in a transform, and then include the transform when you deploy or update Outlook.

- Specify the PRF file as a command-line option for Outlook.exe to import a PRF file without prompting the user. For example:

```
outlook.exe /importprf \\server1\share\outlook.prf
```

- Specify the PRF file as a command-line option for Outlook.exe but prompt the user before importing the PRF file. For example:

```
outlook.exe /promptimportprf \\localfolder\outlook.prf
```

- Launch the PRF file directly on users' computers by having users double-click the file.

- Set a registry key to trigger Outlook to import the PRF file when Outlook starts up and include the registry key in your transform.

  In the HKEY_CURRENT_USER\Software\Microsoft\Office\11.0\Outlook\Setup subkey, set the data of the **ImportPRF value** to a string value that specifies the name and path of the PRF file. For example, set **ImportPRF** to **\\server1\share\outlook.prf**.

Resources and related information

For more information about customizing Outlook profiles by using the Custom Installation Wizard, see "Customizing Outlook Features and Installation with the Custom Installation Wizard" earlier in this chapter.

Setting Up Outlook 2003 Cached Exchange Mode Accounts

When Microsoft Office Outlook 2003 is configured for Cached Exchange Mode, the user enjoys a better online and offline messaging experience because a copy of the user's mailbox is stored on the local computer. The guidelines and procedures in this section will help make the process of configuring Outlook for Cached Exchange Mode go more smoothly.

> **Note**   This feature can only be configured for Microsoft Exchange Server e-mail accounts. While Cached Exchange Mode is supported on Microsoft Exchange Server 5.5 and later, users will have the best supported experience using Cached Exchange Mode with Exchange Server 2003 or later.

When an Outlook account is configured to use Cached Exchange Mode, Outlook works from a local copy of a user's Exchange mailbox stored in an Offline Folder file (OST file) on the user's computer, along with the Offline Address Book (OAB). The cached mailbox and OAB are updated periodically from the Exchange server.

When a user starts Outlook for the first time with Cached Exchange Mode configured, Outlook creates a local copy of the user's mailbox by creating an OST file (unless one already exists), synchronizing the OST with the user's mailbox on the Exchange server, and creating an OAB. (If a user is already configured for offline use with an OST and an OAB, Outlook can typically download just the new information from the server, not the whole mailbox and OAB.)

How Cached Exchange Mode can help improve the Outlook user experience

The primary benefits of using Cached Exchange Mode are the following:

- Shielding the user from troublesome network and server connection issues
- Facilitating switching back and forth from online to offline for mobile users

By caching the user's mailbox and the OAB locally, Outlook no longer depends on on-going network connectivity for access to user information. In addition, users' mailboxes are kept up to date, so if a user disconnects from the network—for example, by removing a laptop from a docking station—the latest information is automatically available offline.

In addition to improving the user experience by using local copies of mail-boxes, Cached Exchange Mode optimizes the type and amount of data sent over a connection with the server. For example, if **On Slow Connections Download Headers Only** is configured, Outlook will automatically change the type and amount of data sent over the connection.

Note   Outlook determines a user's connection speed by checking the network adapter speed on the user's computer, as supplied by the operating system. Reported network adapter speeds of 128 KB or lower are defined as slow connections. There may be circumstances when the network adapter speed does not accurately reflect data throughput for users. More information about adjusting the behavior of Outlook in these scenarios is provided in this chapter in the section "Managing Outlook behavior for perceived slow connections."

By offering different levels of optimization, Outlook can adapt to changing connection environments, such as disconnecting from a corporate local area network (LAN), going offline, and then reestablishing a connection to the server via a slower dial-up connection. As your Exchange server connection type changes—LAN, wireless, cellular, General Packet Radio Service (GPRS), offline—transitions are seamless and never require changing settings or restarting Outlook.

For example, a user may have a laptop computer at work with a connection—by means of a network cable—to a corporate LAN. In this scenario, the user has access to headers and full items, including attachments. He also has quick access and updates to the computer running Exchange Server. If he disconnects his laptop from the LAN, Outlook switches to **Trying to connect** mode. He can continue to work uninterrupted with his data in Outlook. If he has wireless access, Outlook can reestablish a connection to the server and then switch back to **Connected** mode. If the user later connects to the Exchange server by using dial-up access, Outlook recognizes that the connection is slow and automatically optimizes for that connection by downloading only headers and not updating the Offline Address Book. In addition, Outlook 2003 includes new optimizations to reduce the amount of data sent over the connection. Users do not need to change any settings or restart Outlook during this scenario.

Outlook features that can reduce the effectiveness of Cached Exchange Mode

Some Outlook features reduce the effectiveness of Cached Exchange Mode because they require network access or bypass Cached Exchange Mode functionality and cause bad behavior. The primary benefit of using Cached Exchange Mode is being shielded from network and server connection issues. Features that rely on network access can cause delays in Outlook responsiveness that users would not otherwise experience when using Cached Exchange Mode.

The following features rely on network access and can therefore cause delays in Outlook unless users have fast connections to Exchange data:

- Delegate access

- Opening another user's calendar or folder

- Using a public folder that has not been cached

In addition, some aspects of certain Outlook features also require network access to retrieve necessary information—such as looking up free/busy information—which can cause a delayed response even when users have fast connections to Exchange data. The delays can occur unpredictably, rather than only when the feature is accessed by the user.

It is recommended that you disable or do not implement the following features—or combination of features—if you deploy Cached Exchange Mode:

- **Instant Messaging integration**   If users right-click on the Person Names Smart Tag in an e-mail message header, Outlook checks for free/busy status for that person. You can disable Instant Messaging integration by using Group Policy. For more information, see "Configuring User Interface Options in Outlook 2003" later in this chapter.

- **The "toast" alert feature together with digital signatures on e-mail messages**   To verify a digital signature, Outlook must check a network server. By default, Outlook displays a "toast" message that contains a portion of an e-mail message when new messages arrive in a user's Inbox. If the user clicks on the toast message to open a signed e-mail message, Outlook checks (using network access) for a valid signature on the message.

- **Multiple Address Book containers**   Typically, the Address Book contains the Global Address List (GAL) and user Contacts folders. Some organizations configure subsets of the GAL, which are displayed in the Address Book. These subset address books can also be included in the list that defines the search order for address books. If subset address books are included in the search order list, Outlook might need to access the network to check these address books each time a name is resolved in an e-mail message a user is composing.

- **Custom properties on the General tab in Properties dialog box for users**   When you double-click a user name (for example, on the To line of an e-mail message), the **Properties** dialog box appears by default. This dialog box can be configured to include custom properties unique to an organization—such as a user's cost center. If you add properties to this dialog box, however, it is recommended that you not add them to the **General** tab. Out-look must make a remote procedure call (RPC) to the server to retrieve custom properties; because the **General** tab is shown by default when the **Properties** dialog box is accessed, an RPC would be performed each time the user accessed the **Properties** dialog box. As a result, a user running Outlook in Cached Exchange Mode might experience noticeable delays when accessing this dialog box. To help avoid such delays, you should create a new tab on the **Properties** dialog for custom properties, or include custom properties on the **Phone/Notes** tab.

Another way in which the benefits of using Cached Exchange Mode can be reduced is by installing certain Outlook add-ins. Some add-ins can bypass the expected functionality of Headers Mode (Download Headers Only) in Cached Exchange Mode by accessing Outlook data by using the object model. For example, if you use Microsoft ActiveSync® technology to synchronize a handheld computer, full Outlook items will be downloaded, not just headers, even over a slow connec-tion. In addition, the update process will be slower than if you downloaded the items in Outlook because one-off applications use a less efficient type of synchronization.

Synchronization, disk space, and performance considerations

There are a number of issues to be aware of when you are configuring and deploy-ing Cached Exchange Mode. The way the feature works in Outlook to maintain an up-to-date local copy of a user's Exchange mailbox and other information can affect or interact with other Outlook features and behavior. In some scenarios, you might choose to take steps to improve how Cached Exchange Mode works together with—or in parallel with—other Outlook features, for your whole organization or for a certain group of users (for example, users who travel frequently).

Send/Receive synchronization considerations

Cached Exchange Mode works independently from existing Outlook Send/Receive actions to synchronize users' OST and OAB files with Exchange Server data. Send/Receive settings still—by default—update users' Outlook data in the same manner that Send/Receive works in older versions of Outlook. Users who are accustomed to synchronizing Outlook data by pressing F9 or clicking **Send/Receive** may not real-ize that manual synchronization is not necessary to keep Outlook data current with Cached Exchange Mode. In fact, if a number of users repeatedly execute unneces-sary Send/Receive requests to Exchange Server, Exchange Server and network per-formance may be affected.

To minimize additional network traffic and server usage, you might want to inform users that manual Send/Receive actions are unnecessary in Cached Exchange Mode. This might be especially helpful for certain groups of Outlook users—for example, users who typically used Outlook in offline mode with earlier Outlook versions and used Send/Receive to synchronize their data regularly or just before disconnecting from the network. This type of data synchronization now occurs automatically with Cached Exchange Mode.

Another option to manage the issue of unnecessary Send/Receive activity is to disable the Send/Receive option for users. However, this might be unadvisable in some scenarios when disabling the feature creates problems for users—such as when you upgrade current Outlook users with POP accounts and existing customized Send/Receive groups to Outlook 2003. In this situation, disabling Send/Receive removes the capability to download POP e-mail messages.

Offline Address Book (OAB) considerations

In addition to using a local copy of the user's mailbox, Cached Exchange Mode also allows Outlook to access the local Offline Address Book for needed user information instead of requesting the data from Exchange Server. Local access to user data greatly reduces the need for Outlook to make remote procedure calls (RPCs) to Exchange Server, shielding the user from much of the network access required in Exchange online mode or in previous versions of Outlook.

To be shielded from as many unnecessary server calls as possible, users should have the Full Details OAB available on their computers. Once users have a reasonably current OAB downloaded to (or installed on) their computers, only incremental updates to the OAB are needed to continue to help protect users from otherwise unnecessary server calls to retrieve user data. Outlook in Cached Exchange Mode synchronizes the user's OAB with updates from the Exchange Server copy of the OAB every 24 hours. You can help to control how often users download OAB updates by limiting how often you update the Exchange Server copy of the OAB. If there is no new data to synchronize when Outlook checks, the user's OAB is not updated.

> **Note**   Although users with a No Details OAB can use Outlook with Cached Exchange Mode, it is recommended to ensure that users have a Full Details OAB installed on their computers. In addition, it is recommended that users use the Unicode® OAB. The ANSI OAB files do not include certain properties that are included in the Unicode OAB files. Outlook must make server calls to retrieve any required user properties that are not available in the local OAB, which can result in significant network access time when users do not have a Full Details OAB in Unicode format.

Offline File Folders (OSTs) considerations

When deploying Cached Exchange Mode for Outlook, be aware that users' OST files can increase in size by 50 percent to 80 percent over the size of the mailbox reported in Exchange Server. The format Outlook uses to store data locally for Cached Exchange Mode is less efficient than the server data file format, resulting in more disk space used when mailboxes are downloaded to provide a local copy for Cached Exchange Mode.

When Cached Exchange Mode first creates a local copy of a user's mailbox, the user's current OST file—if one exists—is simply updated. When users have relatively small mailboxes (for example, less than 500 megabytes (MB) of Exchange Server data), this works fine. However, for users with larger mailboxes, you should ensure that users have Unicode-formatted OST files—the new file format in Outlook 2003—before deploying Cached Exchange Mode. Unicode OST files can store up to 20 gigabytes (GB) of data, instead of the limit of 2 GB on non-Unicode (ANSI) Outlook files.

By creating Unicode OST files, you can help avoid error messages for users that result when Outlook runs out of OST file space when attempting to create a local copy of the user's mailbox for Cached Exchange Mode. Outlook with Cached Exchange Mode also works better when there is plenty of free space in the user's OST file—for example, when only 5 percent to 10 percent of a 20 GB OST file is used.

Also be sure that users' OST files are located in a folder with sufficient disk space to accommodate users' mailboxes. For example, if users' hard drives are partitioned to use a smaller drive for system programs (the system drive is the default location for the folder that contains the OST file), you should specify a folder on another drive with more disk space as the location of users' OST files. For more information about deploying OST files in a location other than the default location, see the section in this chapter "Cached Exchange Mode deployment settings."

Managing performance issues

There are many factors that influence a user's perception of Cached Exchange Mode performance, including how much hard disk space and how fast a CPU the user has on his computer, and what level of performance the user is accustomed to when using Outlook. For example, offline users might experience Cached Exchange Mode as providing a better user experience, while users who formerly accessed Exchange in online mode might perceive Outlook performance as having decreased (depending on other factors as well).

One factor that can contribute to reduced performance is a large OST file. If the user's OST file grows too large (for example, larger than 1 GB), Outlook with Cached Exchange Mode performance degrades. To improve response time in Outlook, users should either reduce the size of their mailbox (for example, by archiving older files) or turn off Cached Exchange Mode. To help prevent the problem of overly large OST files, you can set a limit on the mailbox size in Exchange Server. You might also choose to turn off synchronizing users' Public Folder Favorites if you previously enabled the option in your deployment of Cached Exchange Mode.

Public Folder Favorites considerations

Cached Exchange Mode can be configured to download and synchronize the public folders included in users' Favorites folders for Outlook Public Folders. By default, Public Folder Favorites are not synchronized. However, if your organization uses public folders extensively, you may want to turn on this option. You can configure an option to download Public Folder Favorites in the Custom Installation Wizard when you customize your Cached Exchange Mode deployment.

However, if users' Public Folder Favorites folders include large public folders, their OST files can become large also, which can adversely affect Outlook performance in Cached Exchange Mode. Before you configure Cached Exchange Mode to turn on this option, ensure that users are selective about the public folders that are included in their Public Folder Favorites, and also ensure that users' OST files are large enough—and are in folders with enough disk space—to accommodate the additional storage requirements for the public folder downloads.

Managing Outlook behavior for perceived slow connections

Outlook is configured to automatically determine a user's connection speed by checking the network adapter speed on the user's computer, as supplied by the operating system. If the reported network adapter speed is 128 KB or lower, the connection is defined as a slow connection.

When Outlook detects a slow connection to a user's Exchange server, Outlook reduces the amount of less-critical information that is synchronized with the Exchange server to help users have a better experience. On slow connections, Outlook automatically makes the following changes to synchronization behavior:

- Switches to downloading headers only.

- Does not automatically download the Offline Address Book or OAB updates.

- Downloads the body of an item and any associated attachments only when requested by the user.

Outlook will, however, continue to automatically synchronize with personal digital assistants (PDAs) and some client-side rules may run.

> **Note** Synchronizing PDAs while using Cached Exchange Mode is not recommended. When you synchronize a handheld computer—for example, by using ActiveSync—full items will be downloaded in Outlook and the synchronization process used is less efficient than with regular Outlook synchronization to users' computers.

This more efficient mode of synchronization is designed for Outlook users with dial-up connections or cellular wireless with GPRS connections to minimize network traffic when there is a slow or expensive connection.

However, there may be circumstances when the network adapter speed does not accurately reflect data throughput for users. For example, suppose a user's computer is on a local area network for fast access to local file servers. The network adapter speed is reported as "fast" because the user is connected to a local area network (LAN). However, the user's access to other locations on an organization's network—including the Exchange server—might use a slow link, such as an ISDN connection. For a scenario like this—where users' actual data throughput is slow although their network adapters report a fast connection—you might want to configure an option to change or lock down the behavior of Outlook—for example, by disabling automatic switching to downloading only headers and configuring Outlook to download only headers. Similarly, there might be connections that Outlook has determined are "slow" in which users actually have high data throughput. In this scenario, you might also turn off automatic switching to downloading only headers.

The setting you configure to change the behavior of Outlook for reported connection speed is the **On slow connections, download only headers** check box. You can configure this option in the Custom Installation Wizard or lock down the option by using Group Policy. For more information about customizing this setting, along with other settings for Cached Exchange Mode deployment, see the section "Cached Exchange Mode deployment settings" later in this chapter.

Staging a Cached Exchange Mode deployment

If you plan to upgrade a large group of users to Outlook 2003 with Cached Exchange Mode enabled, you should stage the rollout over time so that your organization's Exchange servers can manage the requirements of creating or updating users' OST files.

Caution   If most users are updated to use Cached Exchange Mode at once and then start Outlook around the same time (for example, on a Monday morning after a weekend upgrade), the Exchange servers will experience significant performance problems. Under some circumstances, the performance issues in this scenario can be mitigated—for example, if most of the users in your organization have relatively current OST files. But in general, staging deployment of Cached Exchange Mode over a period of time is recommended.

The following scenarios include examples of how you could deploy Cached Exchange Mode to avoid a large initial performance impact on the Exchange servers and—in some cases—minimize the time users spend waiting for the initial synchronization:

- Retain Outlook OST files while deploying Cached Exchange Mode.

  Since existing OST files are merely updated with the latest mailbox information when Outlook with Cached Exchange Mode starts for the first time, retaining these files when you deploy Cached Exchange Mode can help reduce the load on your organization's Exchange servers. Users who already have OST files will have less to synchronize with the server. This scenario works best when most users already have OST files that have been synchronized with Exchange Server relatively recently.

  To retain OST files while deploying Outlook with Cached Exchange Mode, do not specify a new Exchange server when customizing Outlook profile information in the Custom Installation Wizard. Or alternatively, when you customize Outlook profiles, clear the **Replace existing accounts** check box.

  (If you specify an Exchange server when you configure and deploy Outlook, Outlook replaces the Exchange service provider in the MAPI profile, which removes the profile's entry for existing OST files.)

- Provide "seed" OST files to remote users, and then deploy Cached Exchange Mode after users have installed the OST files you provide.

  If most users in your organization do not currently have OST files, you can deploy Outlook 2003 with Cached Exchange Mode disabled. Then before the date on which you plan to deploy Cached Exchange Mode, you provide "seed" OST files to each user with a snapshot of the user's mailbox—for example, by providing or mailing to the user a CD that contains the file, along with installation instructions. You may also want to provide a recent version of your organization's Office Address Book (OAB) with Full Details. When users confirm that they have installed the files, then configure and deploy Cached Exchange Mode.

  When you update your Outlook deployment to use Cached Exchange Mode later—for example, by distributing a configuration maintenance file created using the Custom Installation Wizard—the Exchange server will update users' existing OST files and there will be much less data to synchronize than would be the case if a new OST and OAB were created for each user.

  Creating individual CDs for each user's OST file can be time consuming, so this procedure might be most useful for select groups of remote users who would otherwise spend a lot of time waiting for the initial mailbox and OAB synchronization, perhaps at high cost depending on their remote connection scenario.

- Deploy Outlook 2003 with Cached Exchange Mode to groups of users at a time.

  By upgrading groups of users to Cached Exchange Mode over a period of time, you can balance the workload on your Exchange servers and the local area network. The network traffic and server-intensive work of populating OST files with users' mailbox items and downloading the OAB is mitigated by rolling out the new feature in stages. The way that you create and deploy to groups of users depends on your organization's usual deployment methods. For example, you might create groups of users in Microsoft Systems Management Server (SMS), to which you would deploy—to each group, over a period of time—an SMS package that updates Outlook to use Cached Exchange Mode. To balance the load as much as possible, choose groups of users whose accounts are spread across groups of Exchange servers.

Cached Exchange Mode deployment settings

To deploy Outlook 2003 with Cached Exchange Mode, you enable the option in the Custom Installation Wizard, and then choose from several options for Cached Exchange Mode download settings (for example, **Download only headers**). After you configure the desired options, you save the settings with other configurations in the transform that you use to deploy Office or Outlook 2003 to your users.

If users in your organization do not already have OST files, you might choose to configure a default OST file location for Cached Exchange Mode (and offline use). If you do not specify a different OST location, Outlook will automatically create an OST in the default location when users start Outlook in Cached Exchange Mode.

To configure Cached Exchange Mode settings in the Custom Installation Wizard

1. In the Custom Installation Wizard, on the **Outlook: Specify Exchange Settings** page, click **Configure an Exchange Server connection**.

    Note that you must choose **Modify Profile** or **New Profile** on the **Outlook: Customize Default Profile** page in order to configure Exchange Server settings in the wizard.

2. To specify a new location for users' OST files, click **More Settings**, and then click **Enable offline use.** Enter a folder path in the **Directory path to store the Offline Address Book files** box, and then click **OK**.

3. To specify default download behavior for Cached Exchange Mode, on the **Outlook: Specify Exchange Settings** page, click **Configure Cached Exchange Mode**.

4. Select the **Use Cached Exchange Mode** check box to turn on Cached Exchange Mode for users. If you do not select the check box, Cached Exchange Mode will be disabled for users by default.

5. If you selected to turn on Cached Exchange Mode in step 3, choose a default download option:

    ■ **Download only headers**   Users see header information and the beginning of the message or item body (a 256 KB plain-text buffer of information). Full items are downloaded only when users click the InfoBar to request a full-item download.

- **Download headers followed by the full item**   All headers are down-loaded first, and then full items are downloaded. The download order might not be chronological. Outlook downloads headers and then full items in the folder the user is currently accessing, and then downloads headers (followed by full items) in folders the user has recently viewed.

- **Download full items**   Full items are downloaded. The download order may not be chronological. Outlook downloads full items in the folder the user is currently accessing, and then downloads full items in folders the user has recently viewed.

6. To turn off Headers Only mode, clear the **On slow connections, download only headers** check box.

    Downloading only headers is the default behavior when users are on slow connections. However, there are scenarios in which Outlook perceives that users are on slow connections when users' data throughput is fast, or vice versa. In these situations, you may want to set or clear this option.

7. Choose to have Public Folder Favorites downloaded as part of Cached Exchange Mode synchronizations to users' OST files.

    By default, Public Folder Favorites are not downloaded. Downloading Public Folder Favorites might cause users' OST files—if they use non-Unicode OSTs—to grow past the 2 GB size limit, resulting in errors when Outlook synchronizes. Also, synchronizing Public Folder Favorites causes extra network traffic that might be unwelcome for users on slow connections.

> **Note**   If you specify a new Exchange server under **Configure an Exchange Server connection**, a new OST file will be created automatically for your users.

Deploying Cached Exchange Mode for users with existing OST files

If your organization includes users who already have OST files, there are several issues to consider when you deploy Cached Exchange Mode to these users:

- **Users with large Exchange mailboxes**   If users with existing OST files have large Exchange mailboxes, they may experience errors when Outlook attempts to synchronize their mailboxes to their OST files. To help prevent this, you can first set a policy requiring new Outlook files to be Unicode-formatted, since Outlook Unicode files do not have the 2 GB size limit that Outlook ANSI files do. Then, when Outlook is deployed with Cached Exchange Mode, Outlook will create a new Unicode OST file for users that currently have ANSI OST files. Users' existing OST (and OAB) files are not removed.

- **Users without a Full Details Offline Address Book (OAB)**   For users who have not downloaded a Full Details Offline Address Book (OAB), a Full Details OAB will be downloaded when Cached Exchange Mode synchronizes for the first time. Existing OAB files—including files for a No Details OAB—are not removed. Depending on several factors—including the version of Exchange Server you are using, your Exchange server Unicode settings, and the Outlook client Unicode settings—the new OAB files might be Unicode. If Unicode OAB files are created, and users have ANSI OAB files (with Full Details or No Details), the ANSI OAB files are not removed.

If your Exchange Server version and settings support Unicode, you can require that new Outlook files be Unicode.

To specify Unicode for new Outlook files

1. In Group Policy, load the Outlook 2003 template (Outlk11.adm).

2. Under **User Configuration\Administrative Templates\Microsoft Office Outlook 2003\Miscellaneous**, double-click Preferred PST Mode (Unicode/ANSI).

3. Select **Enabled** to enable configuring the policy.

4. In the drop-down list under **Choose a default format for new PSTs**, select **Enforce Unicode PST**, and then click **OK**.

Using policy to enforce Cached Exchange Mode settings

By using Group Policy, You can help prevent users from enabling Cached Exchange Mode in Outlook, or enforce download options for Cached Exchange Mode—for example, you can specify that users cannot set **Download Only Headers**.

If you prefer to specify default settings for Cached Exchange Mode instead of locking down the options, use the Custom Installation Wizard and specify settings on the **Change Office User Settings** page. The Cached Exchange Mode settings are in the same location in the **Microsoft Office Outlook 2003** tree on this page as they are in the **Microsoft Office Outlook 2003 tree** in Group Policy.

To lock down Cached Exchange Mode options in Group Policy

1. In Group Policy, load the Outlook 2003 template (Outlk11.adm).

2. To require Cached Exchange Mode for users, under **User Configuration\Administrative Templates\Microsoft Office Outlook 2003\Cached Exchange Mode**, double-click **Disable Cached Exchange Mode on new profiles**.

3. Click the **Enabled** radio button to enable configuring the policy.

4. Clear the **Check to disable Cached Exchange Mode on new profiles** check box.

5. Click **OK**.

6. To specify that new user profiles will use Cached Exchange Mode and to select the download mode for new user profiles, double-click **Cached Exchange Mode (File | Cached Exchange Mode)**.

7. Click the **Enabled** radio button to enable configuring download options for Cached Exchange Mode in new Outlook user profiles.

8. In the **Select Cached Exchange Mode for new profiles** drop-down list, select a download option. For example, select **Download Full Items**.

9. Click **OK**.

10. To disallow setting the option to **Download Full Items** for existing user profiles with Cached Exchange Mode configured, double-click **Disallow Download Full Items (File | Cached Exchange Mode)**.

    Or you can enforce other download settings by using one of the following policies instead:

    ■ Disallow Download Headers then Full Items (File | Cached Exchange Mode)

    ■ Disallow Download Headers (File | Cached Exchange Mode)

11. Click the **Enabled** radio button to enable configuring the policy.

12. Select the check box in the policy.

13. Click **OK**.

> **Note**   Outlook is configured to optimize timing for synchronization with Exchange servers. However, there may be circumstances when you need to modify the default synchronization values.
>
> For example, you can specify the default times between synchronizations with the Exchange servers when data changes on an Exchange server—in which case those changes will be downloaded—or when data changes on the client computer—in which case those changes will be uploaded. You can configure these options as defaults by using the **Change Office User Settings** page in the Custom Installation Wizard or lock down the settings by using Group Policy. These synchronization settings are available under the same location as the other Cached Exchange Mode settings (for example, in Group Policy, go to **User Configuration\Administrative Templates\Microsoft Office Outlook 2003\Cached Exchange Mode**).

Configuring Information Rights Management for Messaging in Outlook 2003

Information Rights Management (IRM), a new feature in Microsoft Office 2003, can help prevent sensitive information from being distributed to or read by people who do not have permission to access the content. In Microsoft Office Outlook 2003, users can create and send e-mail messages with restricted permission to help prevent messages from being forwarded, printed, or copied and pasted. Microsoft Office 2003 documents, workbooks, and presentations that are attached to messages with restricted permission are automatically restricted as well.

> **Note**   The ability to create content or e-mail messages with restricted permission using Information Rights Management is available only with the Microsoft Office Professional Edition 2003 version of the following applications: Microsoft Office Word 2003, Microsoft Office Excel 2003, Microsoft Office PowerPoint® 2003, and Outlook 2003. IRM is also available in the stand-alone version of those applications. Users who have Microsoft Office Standard Edition 2003 installed can read and use content and e-mail messages with restricted content but cannot create new content or e-mail messages with restricted permission. If users reply to or forward messages with restricted permission (assuming their permission to reply or forward is not restricted), the reply or forwarded message will not have restricted permission.

Administrators can configure several options for IRM in e-mail messaging, including the following:

- **Disable IRM**   To disable IRM in Outlook, you use a policy that disables IRM for all Office applications. You cannot disable IRM for only one Office application.

- **Download permissions when downloading a message**   This option allows users to download e-mail messages while connected to the network, and later work with e-mail messages that have restricted permission without requiring network connectivity when the messages and documents are opened. IRM licenses are cached on the user's computer when the messages are downloaded. This option is enabled by default.

> **Note**   When Outlook is used with Cached Exchange Mode, users can download permissions with messages only when the full message is downloaded to the user's computer.

■ **Help enforce message expiration**   When you specify the number of days before a message expires with IRM enabled, the message cannot be accessed after the expiration period.

There are also Office-wide IRM settings that you can configure, such as the following:

■ Specify a custom URL or e-mail address for users to request additional IRM permissions.

■ Specify how groups can be used with IRM permissions.

> **Note**   You can customize your Office IRM deployment to select how users validate licenses and to include custom rights templates (collections of selected IRM permissions). To learn more about deploying IRM in Office, see "Customizing Information Rights Management and Installing Client Software" in Chapter 20, "Information Rights Management."

Deploying IRM user settings

Default Outlook or Office IRM settings can be configured on the **Change Office User Settings** page in the Custom Installation Wizard, or you can lock down the settings by using Group Policy with either the Office (Office11.adm) or Outlook (Outlk11.adm) ADM template. The IRM settings are located in parallel locations in each tool under the Microsoft Office Outlook 2003 or Microsoft Office 2003 tree. Setting message expiration is in a separate area (see the procedure for locking down Outlook IRM settings).

To disable IRM for Office and configure other Office IRM settings for users

1. In Group Policy, in the Office 2003 policy template (Office11.adm), under **User configuration\Administrative templates\Microsoft Office 2003**, double-click **Manage Restricted Permissions**.

2. Double-click **Disable Information Rights Management User Interface**.

3. Select the **Enabled** radio button to enable configuring the settings.

4. To disable IRM, select the **Check to enforce setting on; uncheck to enforce setting off** check box.

5. Click **OK**.

6. Configure other IRM settings to enforce for users.

You can also configure Outlook-specific settings, including automatic license caching for IRM and an e-mail message expiration period.

To disable automatic license caching (permission download) for Outlook IRM

1. In the Group Policy snap-in, in the Outlook 2003 policy template (Outlk11.adm), navigate to **User configuration\Administrative templates \Microsoft Office Outlook 2003\Miscellaneous**.

2. To disable downloading permissions when e-mail messages are downloaded, double-click **Do not download permission for e-mail during offline Exchange folder sync**.

3. Select the **Check to disable download of permission** check box.

4. Click **OK**.

If users add restricted permission to an e-mail message, the message expiration period is enforced. Users will see the e-mail message in their Outlook folder with a strike-through line—the same appearance for expired messages as when message expiration is not enforced—but they will not be able to access the message. You can lock down the number of days before messages expire for all Outlook e-mail messages.

To configure e-mail message expiration settings

1. In Group Policy, in the Outlook 2003 policy template (Outlk11.adm), navigate to **Tools | Options\Preferences\E-mail options\Advanced E-mail options**.

2. Double-click **When sending a message**.

3. Select the **Enabled** option button to enable configuring the settings.

4. In the box following **Messages expire after (days)**, enter a number of days.

5. Click **OK**.

Resources and related information

To learn more about how Information Rights Management in Office 2003 is implemented, see "Overview of Information Rights Management" in Chapter 20, "Information Rights Management."

You can configure and deploy new Information Rights Management settings and other updates to Outlook 2003 after initial installation. For more information about updating an Outlook installation, see "Updating Outlook 2003 by Using the Custom Maintenance Wizard" in Chapter 10, "Maintaining Outlook 2003."

Configuring Unicode Options for Outlook 2003

Microsoft Office Outlook 2003 can now provide full Unicode support. Using Outlook in Unicode mode is especially advantageous for organizations with multilingual needs and—because Outlook Unicode-formatted files are much bigger than non-Unicode files—for users who need very large Outlook files.

Taking advantage of Unicode support in Outlook depends on users' Microsoft Exchange Server version and other criteria that are checked when users run Outlook. If the criteria for using Unicode are met and users are running in Unicode mode, Unicode is used throughout Outlook when used with Exchange Server (for e-mail messages, the Address Book, and so forth).

To determine whether to use Unicode mode or non-Unicode (ANSI) mode, Outlook evaluates a set of requirements and options. One requirement for Unicode mode is that users must have Exchange 2000 or later accounts. Outlook also checks the formats—Unicode or ANSI—of users' Offline Store (OST) files and the default archive file. Finally, Outlook checks the format of users' PST files that are used as a delivery location (if any).

> **Caution**   Switching between Unicode mode and non-Unicode mode (ANSI) can cause data loss in multilingual text fields or prevent text from being readable. For this reason, users who begin using Outlook in Unicode mode should continue to use Unicode mode.

If you want users in your organization to use Unicode for Outlook, you can use several methods to deploy Outlook so users can run in Unicode mode. One deployment option is to encourage Unicode usage by establishing an environment in which, for most users, the criteria that Outlook checks to allow Unicode mode are met. Unicode is used by default if the criteria are met, unless you set options to use ANSI. Another option is to require Unicode for Outlook usage (when supported by an appropriate Exchange Server version) by setting options that create new Unicode user files automatically, if that is necessary for Outlook to run in Unicode mode. Or you can use a combination of these approaches.

Coordinating Cached Exchange Mode and Unicode deployment

If you plan to deploy Cached Exchange Mode with Outlook 2003, you may want to configure and deploy options for migrating users to Unicode mode first. Cached Exchange Mode synchronizes users' OST and Offline Address Book (OAB) files with Exchange Server data. When you deploy Unicode options to users, synchronizing OST and OAB files might also be required.

For example, Outlook files are synchronized with Exchange Server in the following Unicode deployment scenarios:

- When you deploy a new offline Outlook profile—for example, to move current offline users to Unicode mode—Outlook synchronizes OST and OAB files, after creating the new files for users as part of the new profile.

- When Outlook users are moved to an Exchange 2003 server with a Unicode OAB, the new OAB is downloaded.

In scenarios like these, you may want to wait to deploy Cached Exchange Mode until after you have deployed Unicode options for your organization. This will help minimize the load on your Exchange servers and the time users spend downloading data to their computers.

Facilitating usage of Unicode mode by Outlook

Using Unicode for messaging and other Outlook features has benefits that you may want your users to be able to take advantage of, without mandating that everyone migrate to Unicode mode directly when Outlook 2003 is installed. To facilitate greater usage of Unicode mode, you can help provide a messaging environment configured to help Outlook be able to run in Unicode mode.

Since Outlook uses Unicode mode by default if all criteria it looks for are met, take steps to make sure that the requirements are met, such as the following:

1. By using the Custom Installation Wizard, create a new Outlook profile to deploy to users. By default, a new offline profile creates a new OST file for users and a new default archive file, both of which will use the new Unicode file format.

2. Ensure that in the new Outlook profile, users' Exchange accounts are on Exchange Server 2000 or later.

3. Deploy Outlook to your users.
   You can deploy Outlook using your organization's standard Office deployment method.

It is straightforward to create and customize a new Outlook profile by using the Custom Installation Wizard.

To create new Outlook offline profiles for users

1. In the Custom Installation Wizard, on the **Outlook: Customize Default Profile** page, click **New Profile**.

2. In the **Profile name** box, type a name for the new Outlook profile, and then click **Next**.

3. On the **Outlook: Specify Exchange Settings** page, click the **Configure an Exchange server connection** radio button.

4. In the **User Name** box, leave the default user name system variable or enter a different variable.

5. In the **Exchange Server** box, enter the name of an Exchange server. (The Exchange server name will be replaced with the correct Exchange server when the user starts Outlook for the first time after upgrading.)
   Note that the Exchange server with the user account must be running Exchange 2000 or later for Outlook to run in Unicode mode.

6. Click **More Settings**.

7. On the **Microsoft Exchange Server** page, select the **Enable offline use** check box to deploy a new OST file, and then click **OK**.

8. Click **Next**.

After completing your customizations for Outlook in the Custom Installation Wizard, you click **Finish** to create a transform (MST file), and then deploy Outlook to your organization with this transform. For example, you might use Microsoft Systems Management Services (SMS) or Group Policy software installation to deploy Office software. Other options include having users run an Outlook Setup command line from the administrative installation point or creating a custom CD and providing it to your users.

> **Tip**   Unicode format is used for new PST files by default. You can also set a policy to enforce Unicode format for new PST files. In Group Policy, using the Outlook ADM file (Outlk11.adm), go to **User Configuration\Administrative Templates\Microsoft Office Outlook 2003\Miscellaneous\PST Settings** and double-click **Preferred PST Mode (Unicode/ANSI)**. Click the **Enabled** radio button to enable configuring the policy, and then in the **Choose a default format for new PSTs** drop-down list, select **Enforce Unicode PST**.

Enforcing Unicode mode for Outlook users

There may be scenarios in which it is important that all users in an organization are migrated to use Unicode mode in Outlook when Outlook 2003 is installed, without modifying all users' profiles. You can enforce migrating users to Unicode by making sure that the criteria that Outlook uses for determining if users run in Outlook mode are met, or that Outlook takes steps to help ensure that Unicode file formats are used in users' profiles by creating and synchronizing new Outlook files if necessary.

The first criterion for using Unicode mode is that users must use Outlook with Exchange Server 2000 or later.

Next, Outlook checks the format of a user's OST file to determine if the file format is Unicode or non-Unicode (ANSI). If the format of the OST file is ANSI, Outlook will run in ANSI mode. However, you can set a policy so that when Outlook checks the file format, if a user has an ANSI OST file, a new Unicode OST file is automatically created and synchronized with Exchange Server. You can define the policy so that users are prompted with a dialog box that notifies them that their new OST file is about to be synchronized with the Exchange server, so users can confirm to proceed with the update at that time. Or you can require that new OST files be created without providing users the option to defer the action.

Outlook next checks the file format for the user's default archive file (if one exists). You can set a policy that will automatically create a new Unicode default archive file as well. (Users can still access ANSI archive files.) Unlike the policy that manages new Unicode OST files, you cannot provide the option for users to defer creation of a new default archive file.

Finally, if a user's mail delivery location is a PST file, Outlook checks the delivery PST file to determine if the file format is Unicode. However, you cannot require a new Unicode PST file to be created to replace the existing PST file if Outlook determines that a user has an ANSI PST file. In this scenario—where Outlook delivers to ANSI PST files and you want to require Unicode mode for users—you can instead create and deploy new profiles to users with the delivery location set to new PST files, which will be Unicode by default.

Pointing Outlook to use a new delivery PST file automatically—without users themselves specifying the change—might lead users to believe that their existing mail has vanished. Older mail is still in the original PST file, but that file is no longer in the user's profile and is therefore not accessible by default. Users would need to manually add the older PST file back to their profile to access the information. Because the PST file being removed from the user profile can be perceived as data loss by users —though the data still exists, it is not where users can readily see and access it—the option to automatically switch to a new Unicode PST is not provided.

You may want to carefully time the implementation of the policies that might create and populate new Unicode files. When Outlook creates and synchronizes new Unicode OSTs and default archive files, users must wait for server data to be downloaded. You should also make sure that users have synchronized with Exchange Server prior to the new policies taking effect. Any local changes that have not been synchronized—such as e-mail messages in a user's Outbox or updates to Contacts information—will be lost.

To enforce Unicode mode in Outlook

1. In Group Policy, load the Outlook 2003 template (Outlk11.adm).

2. Under **User Configuration\Administrative Templates\Microsoft Office Outlook 2003**, click **Exchange Settings**.

3. Double-click **Exchange Unicode Mode—Ignore Archive format**.

4. Click the **Enabled** radio button to enable configuring the policy.

5. Select the **Ignore existing format of the Archive PST** check box, and then click **OK**.

6. Double-click **Exchange Unicode Mode—Ignore OST format**.

7. Click the **Enabled** radio button to enable configuring the policy.

8. In the **Choose whether existing OST format determines mailbox mode** drop-down list, select **Create new OST if format doesn't match mode**.

    or

    To prompt users with a dialog allowing them to defer creating a new OST, select **Prompt to create new OST if format doesn't match mode**.

9. Click **OK**.

After completing your customizations for Outlook in the Custom Installation Wizard, you click **Finish** to create a transform (MST file), and then deploy Outlook to your organization.

Using Unicode format for Outlook messages dragged to the desktop

When you use the Microsoft Windows drag-and-drop feature to drag an Outlook item to the Windows desktop, the format of the file that is automatically created is ANSI by default. You can configure a default option by using the Custom Installation Wizard to use Unicode for the message format instead of ANSI.

To use Unicode format for message files that are dragged to the desktop from Outlook

1. In the Custom Installation Wizard, on the **Change Office User Settings** page, click the plus sign (+) next to **Microsoft Office Outlook 2003**.

2. Under **Tools | Options\Other\Advanced**, double-click **MSG Unicode format when dragging to file system**.

3. Click the **Apply Changes** radio button.

4. Select the **Check to set messages as Unicode format. Uncheck for ANSI.** check box.

5. Click **OK**.

> **Note** If you drag an Outlook item into the body of a message that you are composing when using Microsoft Office Word 2003 as your e-mail editor, the format of the item will be ANSI regardless of the setting specified in the **MSG Unicode format when dragging to file system** policy. However, if you drag the item to the **Attachments** box in the message instead, the file format policy will be followed.

Resources and related information

■ To learn more about the benefits of Unicode support in Outlook 2003, see "Unicode Enhancements in Outlook 2003" in Chapter 6, "Planning an Outlook 2003 Deployment."

■ You can configure a number of options for your Outlook deployment. To learn more about customizing your Outlook 2003 deployment, see "Customizing Outlook Features and Installation with the Custom Installation Wizard" earlier in this chapter.

Configuring Encoding Options in Outlook 2003

Microsoft Office Outlook 2003 can automatically select an optimal encoding for outgoing e-mail messages. This feature increases the likelihood that when you send a message with Outlook, users receiving the message will see all the characters rendered properly, even if the users run older e-mail programs. Automatic messaging encoding results in less configuration work for administrators and a better experience for users.

Outlook scans the entire text of the outgoing message to determine a minimal popular encoding for the message. Outlook selects an encoding that is capable of representing all of the characters and that is optimized so that the majority of the receiving e-mail programs can interpret and render the content properly.

This table shows a few examples of how this works.

If the message contains these characters:	Outlook selects this encoding:
English (ASCII) text (A-Z, a-z)	US-ASCII
German (Latin 1) text (A-Z, a-z and Umlauts)	Western European (ISO)
Greek text (A-Z, a-z and Greek characters)	Greek (ISO)
Japanese text (A-Z, a-z, Hiragana, Katakana, Kanji)	Japanese (JIS)
Multilingual text (different scripts)	Unicode® (UTF-8)

This works for users sending Internet mail through the POP/SMTP or IMAP transport, or for messages sent through Microsoft Exchange Server 5.5 SP 1 or later.

Note   To use the automatic message encoding feature, users sending the message must have Microsoft Internet Explorer 5.5 or later installed.

With earlier versions of Outlook, users had to manually overwrite format encoding to choose the most appropriate encoding for an individual message, but this is no longer necessary.

Disabling automatic encoding for outbound messages

By default, Outlook automatically selects the type of encoding that will be used for outbound messages once Internet Explorer 5.5 or later is installed. You can disable Auto-Select outbound message encoding with a registry key. For the following sub-key, set **Autodetect_CodePageOut** to **0**:

HKEY_CURRENT_USER\Software\Microsoft\Office\11.0\Outlook\Options \MSHTML\International

The value is a **DWORD** data type.

If the registry subkey is not found, if there is no value set for the registry sub-key, or if the value is set to **1**, Auto-Select is enabled.

You can enforce this setting by using Group Policy with the Outlook ADM file. In the Group Policy snap-in, the policy for disabling automatic message encoding is located in User Configuration\Administrative Templates\Microsoft Office Outlook 2003\Tools | Options\Mail Format\International Options. Double-click **Encoding for outgoing messages**, then select **Disable** to prevent Outlook from automatically encoding messages.

You can also set automatic encoding for outbound messages in the user interface.

To set automatic message encoding through the user interface

1. On the **Tools menu, click Options**, then click the **Mail Format** tab.

2. In the **Message format** section, click **International Options**, then select **Auto-Select encoding for outgoing messages**.

Setting default encoding for outbound messages

You can set a registry key to establish a default encoding for outbound e-mail mes-sages. This encoding is used for all outbound messages if Auto-Select encoding is not enabled. This encoding is also used as the preferred encoding if the Auto-Select encoding algorithm finds multiple suitable encodings for the message. By default, Outlook sets preferred encoding to a popular Internet encoding corresponding to the active Microsoft Windows® code page of the user's computer. For example, Out-look specifies Western European (ISO) when running on Western European Latin1 Windows code page 1252.

For example, to set the default code page to be used for message encoding to "Western European (ISO)," you would set **Default_CodePageOut** to **00006faf** in the following registry subkey:

HKEY_CURRENT_USER\Software\Microsoft\Office\11.0\Outlook\Options \MSHTML\International\

This value is a **DWORD** data type. (See the table in the next section for a list of encodings and corresponding code pages.)

You can enforce a specific encoding by using Group Policy with the Outlook adm file. In the Group Policy snap-in, the policy for configuring encoding for all out-going messages is located in User Configuration\Administrative Templates\Microsoft

Office Outlook 2003\Tools | Options\Mail Format\International Options. Double-click **Encoding for outgoing messages**, then select **Enabled** to allow configuring the policy. Choose an encoding from the **Use this encoding for outgoing messages:** drop-down list, then click **OK**.

To set a specific encoding value through the user interface

1. Click **Tools**, click **Options**, then click the **Mail Format** tab.

2. In the **Message format** section, click **International Options**.

3. In the drop-down list for **Preferred encoding for outgoing messages**, select the encoding that you prefer.

Outlook encoding support

Outlook supports the encodings listed in the table below when sending and receiving e-mail messages.

> **Note**   For automatic encoding selection in Outlook to work properly, you must make sure that appropriate international support (NLS files and fonts) is installed on users' computers. For more information about enabling international support, see "Preparing Users' Computers for Multilingual Capabilities in Office" in Chapter 13, "Preparing for an Office Multilingual Deployment."

By default, automatic encoding selection in Outlook considers for detection all encodings marked "Yes" in the table below. All encodings in the list below are valid values to set as the "Preferred encoding for outgoing messages" by using the registry subkey Default_CodePageOut, described above.

Name	Character set	Code page	Auto-Select?
Arabic (ISO)	ISO-8859-6	28596	
Arabic (Windows)	Windows-1256	1256	Yes
Baltic (ISO)	ISO-8859-4	28594	
Baltic (Windows)	Windows-1257	1257	Yes
Central European (ISO)	ISO-8859-2	28592	Yes
Central European (Windows)	Windows-1250	1250	
Chinese Simplified (GB2312)	GB2312	936	Yes
Chinese Simplified (HZ)	HZ-GB-2312	52936	
Chinese Traditional (Big5)	Big5	950	Yes

Name	Character set	Code page	Auto-Select?
Cyrillic (ISO)	ISO-8859-5	28595	
Cyrillic (KOI8-R)	KOI8-R	20866	Yes
Cyrillic (KOI8-U)	KOI8-U	21866	
Cyrillic (Windows)	Windows-1251	1251	Yes
Greek (ISO)	ISO-8859-7	28597	Yes
Greek (Windows)	Windows-1253	1253	
Hebrew (ISO-Logical)	ISO-8859-8-I	38598	
Hebrew (Windows)	Windows-1255	1255	Yes
Japanese (EUC)	EUC-JP	51932	
Japanese (JIS)	ISO-2022-JP	50220	Yes
Japanese (JIS-Allow 1 byte Kana)	ISO-2022-JP	50221	
Japanese (Shift-JIS)	Shift-JIS	932	
Korean	KS_C_5601-1987	949	Yes
Korean (EUC)	EUC-KR	51949	
Latin 3 (ISO)	ISO-8859-3	28593	
Latin 9 (ISO)	ISO-8859-15	28605	
Thai (Windows)	Windows-874	874	Yes
Turkish (ISO)	ISO-8859-9	28599	Yes
Turkish (Windows)	Windows-1254	1254	
Unicode (UTF-7)	UTF-7	65000	
Unicode (UTF-8)	UTF-8	65001	Yes
US-ASCII	US-ASCII	20127	Yes
Vietnamese (Windows)	Windows-1258	1258	Yes
Western European (ISO)	ISO-8859-1	28591	Yes
Western European (Windows)	Windows-1252	1252	

Resources and related information

Outlook 2003 provides Unicode support throughout the product. For more information about how you can define Outlook user profiles to use Unicode, see "Configuring Unicode Options for Outlook 2003" earlier in this chapter.

Helping Users Avoid Junk E-Mail Messages in Outlook 2003

Microsoft Office Outlook 2003 provides two new features that can help users avoid receiving and reading junk e-mail messages—the new Junk E-mail Filter and the disabling of automatic content download from external servers:

- A new filtering manager helps users avoid reading junk e-mail messages. The filter is on by default and the protection level is set to Low, which is designed to catch the most obvious junk e-mail messages. The filter replaces the rules for processing junk e-mail messages in previous versions of Outlook.

- Outlook 2003 helps reduce the risk of Web beacons activating in e-mail messages by automatically blocking download of pictures, sounds, and other content from external servers in e-mail messages. Automatic content download is disabled by default.

You can configure settings to deploy these features to meet the needs of your organization. For example, you can configure the Junk E-mail Filter to be more aggressive, though it might catch more legitimate messages as well.

Configuring the Junk E-mail Filter

There are two parts to the Junk E-mail Filter:

- Three Junk E-mail Filter lists—Safe Senders, Safe Recipients, and Blocked Senders.

- State-of-the-art technology developed by Microsoft Research. This technology evaluates whether an unread message should be treated as junk e-mail based on several factors, including the message content and whether the sender is included in Junk E-mail Filter lists.

All settings for the Junk E-mail Filter are stored in each user's Outlook profile. You can override the profile settings by using policies for all options except the Junk E-mail Filter lists. However, you can create and deploy initial lists of Safe Senders, Safe Recipients, and Blocked Senders for your users.

The Junk E-mail Filter is provided for a subset of Outlook account types. The filter works best when used with Microsoft Exchange Server 2003 and later accounts, as described in detail below.

When Outlook users are upgraded to Outlook 2003 with the new Junk E-mail Filter, the old junk e-mail rules are removed and the rules information is not migrated.

Supported account types

Outlook 2003 supports junk e-mail filtering for the following account types:

- Microsoft Exchange Server e-mail accounts in Cached Exchange Mode

- Microsoft Exchange Server e-mail accounts when mail is delivered to a Personal Folders file (PST file)

- HTTP accounts

- POP accounts

- MSN® Hotmail accounts

- IMAP accounts

The following account types are not supported for junk e-mail filtering:

- Microsoft Exchange Server e-mail accounts in Online (MDB) mode

- Third-party MAPI providers

In scenarios in which POP e-mail messages are downloaded into an Exchange Online (MDB) mailbox, Outlook blocks junk e-mail messages for the user's POP e-mail but does not block Exchange Online junk e-mail messages.

Support in different versions of Exchange Server

Junk E-mail Filter behavior varies depending on the Exchange Server version you use for messaging. Later versions of Exchange Server support more filtering options than earlier versions do.

The following list details Junk E-mail Filter behavior with different versions of Exchange Server.

- **Versions earlier than Exchange Server 2003** If users use Cached Exchange Mode or download to a Personal Folders file (PST file): Users can create and use the Junk E-mail Filter lists, which are available from any computer that users use.

- If users work online: The Junk E-mail Filter is not available.

- **Exchange Server 2003** If users use Cached Exchange Mode or download to a Personal Folders file (PST file): The Junk E-mail Filter lists that are available from any computer are also used by the server to evaluate mail. This means that if a sender is on a user's Blocked Senders list, mail is moved to the Junk E-mail folder on the server and is not evaluated by Outlook 2003. In addition, Outlook 2003 uses the Microsoft Research technology to evaluate e-mail messages.

- If users work online: The Junk E-mail Filter lists that are available from any computer are also used by the server to evaluate mail. This means that if a sender is on a user's Blocked Senders list, mail is moved to the Junk E-mail folder on the server and is not evaluated by Outlook 2003.

- **Exchange Server 2003 Service Pack 1** If users use Cached Exchange Mode or download to a Personal Folders file (PST file): The Junk E-mail Filter lists that are available from any computer are also used by the server to evaluate mail. This means that if a sender is on a user's Blocked Senders list, mail is moved to the Junk E-mail folder on the server and is not evaluated by Outlook 2003. In addition, Outlook 2003 uses the Microsoft Research technology to evaluate e-mail messages. A third party add-in junk e-mail filter can be added to the Exchange server to help provide additional filtering capability.

■   If users work online: The Junk E-mail Filter lists that are available from any computer are also used by the server to evaluate mail. This means that if a sender is on a user's Blocked Senders list, mail will be moved to the Junk E-mail folder on the server and not evaluated by Outlook 2003. A third party add-in junk e-mail filter can be added to the Exchange server to help provide additional filtering capability.

Upgrading from a previous installation of Outlook

When users' older version of Outlook is upgraded to Outlook 2003, the rules that previously handled junk e-mail messages are removed. The existing rules and files used by the old filter are not migrated. The existing rules are handled as follows:

■   **Rules created by the old filter**   With the old rules filter for junk e-mail messages, users could create up to three client-side rules for their mailbox—**Adult Content Rule, Junk E-mail Rule**, and **Exception List**.

■   Outlook removes these rules from the user's mailbox when Outlook 2003 is started for the first time on the user's computer. This means that Outlook 2003 always disables the old junk e-mail filter.

■   **Files that contain the Adult Senders list and the Blocked Senders list** These text files are left on the user's computer, but are no longer used by Outlook.

Configuring the Junk E-mail Filter user interface

You can specify several options to configure how the Junk E-mail Filter works for your users, including the following:

■   Set the Junk E-mail Filter protection level.

■   Permanently delete suspected junk e-mail messages or move them to the Junk E-mail folder.

■   Trust e-mail messages from users' Contacts.

The default values for the Junk E-mail Filter are designed to help provide a good experience for users. However, you can configure these settings to different defaults when deploying Outlook to your organization, as well as set other options or policies, such as defining an alternative URL for the location of filter updates.

Default values for the Junk E-mail Filter settings are:

■   Junk E-mail: Set to LOW

■   Permanently delete: Set to OFF

■   Trust my Contacts: Set to ON

These options can be set as registry keys to specify default values for users or enforced by policy.

To enforce Outlook Junk E-mail Filter user interface options for users

1. In Group Policy, load the Outlook 2003 template (Outlk11.adm).

2. Under **User Configuration\Administrative Templates\Microsoft Office Outlook 2003\Tools | Options\Preferences**, click **Junk Mail**.

3. Double-click **Junk E-mail protection level**.

4. Click the **Enabled** radio button to enable configuring the policy.

5. In the **Select level** drop-down list, select a protection level to enforce.

6. Click **OK**.

7. Set other policies, such as specifying to permanently delete junk e-mail messages.

Creating and deploying the Junk E-mail Filter lists

You can deploy default Junk E-mail Filter lists to your users. The Junk E-mail Filter uses these lists as follows:

- **Safe Senders list**   E-mail messages received from the e-mail addresses in the list or from any e-mail address that includes a domain name in the list will never be treated as junk e-mail.

- **Safe Recipients list**   E-mail messages sent to the e-mail addresses in the list or from any e-mail address that includes a domain name in the list will never be treated as junk e-mail.

- **Blocked Senders list**   E-mail messages received from the e-mail addresses in the list or from any e-mail address that includes a domain name in the list are always treated as junk e-mail.

If a domain name or e-mail address is on both the Blocked Senders list and the Safe Senders list, the Safe Senders list takes precedent over the Blocked Senders list to reduce the possibility of mail that users want mistakenly being marked as junk e-mail messages. The lists are stored on the server and so are available if users roam.

To deploy the Junk E-mail Filter lists, you create the lists on a test computer, and then distribute the lists to your users. The lists you provide are default lists; they cannot be locked down by policy.

The steps to create and deploy these lists are as follows:

1. On a test computer, install Outlook 2003.

2. Start Outlook and enter the desired entries for each Junk E-mail Filters list: Safe Senders, Safe Recipients, and Blocked Senders.

3. Export each list to a separate text file.

4. In the Custom Installation Wizard, on the **Add/Remove Files** page, include the three text files.

5. Also in the Custom Installation Wizard, on the **Change Office User Settings** page, configure Junk E-mail Filter settings to turn on importing the filter list files and to specify the location of the files.

6. After saving your customizations, deploy the transform (MST file) to users.

    Start by installing Outlook on a test computer and creating the lists.

To create default Junk E-mail Filter lists to deploy to users

1. In Outlook 2003, on the **Tools** menu, click **Options**.

2. On the **Preferences** tab, click **Junk E-mail Options**.

3. On the **Safe Senders** tab, click **Add**.

4. Enter an e-mail address or domain name. For example:
    someone@exchange.example.com

5. Click **OK**.

6. To add more e-mail addresses or domain names, repeat steps 3 through 5.

7. Click **Export to file**.

8. Enter a unique file name for the Safe Senders list, and then click **OK**.

9. Repeat steps 3 through 8 with the **Safe Recipients** tab and the **Blocked Senders** tab to create Safe Recipients and Blocked Senders lists. Be sure to specify a unique file name for each of the three lists.

    Next you configure your Outlook deployment so that the lists are distributed to users and imported when they start Outlook 2003 for the first time.

To customize Outlook deployment to install Junk E-mail Filter lists for users

1. In the Custom Installation Wizard, on the **Add/Remove Files** page, click **Add**.

2. In the **Add Files to MST** dialog box, select the three Junk E-mail Filter files that you created in the previous procedure.
Hold down the CONTROL or SHIFT key to select multiple files.

3. Click **Add**.

4. In the **Destination path on the user's computer** drop-down list, select the location where the files will be installed for users.

5. Click **OK**.

6. On the **Change Office User Settings** page, under **Microsoft Office Outlook 2003\Tools | Options\Preferences**, click **Junk Mail**.

7. Double-click **Junk Mail Import List** and ensure that the check box is cleared so that the Junk E-mail Filter lists will be imported for users.

8. To overwrite existing Junk E-mail Filter lists with new lists, double-click **Overwrite or Append Junk Mail Import List**.

9. Click **Apply Changes**.

10. Select the **Check to overwrite list. Uncheck to append.** check box.

11. Click **OK**.

12. To specify a path to each Junk E-mail Filter list, double-click the settings corresponding to each list (for example, **Specify path to Trusted Senders list**) and enter a path and file name in the box (for example, in the **Specify path to Trusted Senders list** box).

13. Click OK (or click Next setting to specify the path for another Junk E-mail Filter list).

After completing your customizations for Outlook in the Custom Installation Wizard, click **Finish** to create a transform (MST file), and then deploy Outlook to your organization.

You can later update an existing Outlook 2003 installation to update the Junk E-mail Filter lists or to deploy the filter separately from your deployment of Outlook. To update current Outlook 2003 installations, use the Custom Maintenance Wizard to include the files and trigger an import for users (as described with the Custom Installation Wizard in the preceding procedure).

Configuring automatic\ picture download

To help protect users' privacy and to combat Web beacons—functionality embedded within items to detect when recipients have viewed an item—Outlook 2003 is configured by default to not automatically download pictures or other content from external servers on the Internet. You can configure options to change how automatic picture download works for your users by default, or lock down (enforce) settings for this feature by using Group Policy.

Messages in HTML format often include pictures or sounds, and sometimes these pictures or sounds are not included in the message itself, but are instead downloaded from a Web server when the e-mail message is opened or previewed. This is typically done by legitimate senders to avoid sending extra large messages.

However, junk e-mail senders can use a link to content on external servers to include a Web beacon in e-mail messages, which notifies the Web server when users read or preview the message. The Web beacon notification validates the user's e-mail address to the junk e-mail sender, which can result in more junk e-mail being sent to the user.

This feature to not automatically download pictures or other content can also help users to avoid viewing potentially offensive material (for external content linked to the message), and if they are on a low bandwidth connection, to decide whether an image warrants the time and bandwidth to download it. Users can view the blocked pictures or content in a message by clicking the InfoBar under the message header or right-clicking the blocked image.

By default, Outlook does not download pictures or other content automatically except when the external content comes from a Web site in the Trusted Sites zone. You can change this behavior so that content from any of the zones (Trusted Sites, Local Intranet, and Internet) will be downloaded automatically or blocked automatically.

You can also set other options to manage automatic content downloading, such as locking down the feature so that users cannot allow automatic content download for any content.

Automatic content download settings can be configured by default for users, or locked down by policy. To deploy default settings for users, go to the **Change Office User Settings** page in the Custom Installation Wizard. The settings to customize automatic content download behavior are in the same location in the **Microsoft Office Outlook 2003** tree in the Custom Installation Wizard as they are in the **Microsoft Office Outlook 2003** tree in the ADM template viewed in Group Policy.

To configure options for automatic picture download behavior in Outlook

1. In Group Policy, load the Outlook 2003 template (Outlk11.adm).

2. Under **User Configuration\Administrative Templates\Microsoft Office Outlook 2003\Tools | Options\Security**, click **HTML Mail External Content Settings**.

3. To change a policy for the automatic picture download feature, double-click an item in the **Setting** column.

   For example, to lock down disabling automatic content downloading from all sites, double-click **Block all external content**.

4. Click the **Enabled** radio button to enable configuring the policy.

5. Select the check box in the policy, and then click **OK**.

Resources and related information

■ You can configure a number of options for your Outlook deployment. To learn more about customizing your Outlook 2003 deployment, see "Customizing Outlook Features and Installation with the Custom Installation Wizard" earlier in this chapter.

You can use the Custom Maintenance Wizard to update your Outlook installation. For more information, see "Updating Outlook 2003 by Using the Custom Maintenance Wizard" in Chapter 10, "Maintaining Outlook 2003."

Configuring User Interface Options in Outlook 2003

You can deploy a variety of end-user interface options in Microsoft Office Outlook 2003, including configuring whether default Search Folders are created, what kinds of messages users will see by default in the notification area at the far right of the taskbar, and so on. You customize default settings for these options by using one of the following options:

- Set options on the **Change Office User Settings** page in the Custom Installation Wizard.

- Configure registry keys to deploy by using the **Add/Remove Registry Entries** page in the Custom Installation Wizard.

- Configure settings in Outlook on a test computer, and then capture the settings by using the Office Profile Wizard.

For some settings, you can use more than one of the above options. In addition, some configurations can be enforced ("locked down") by using Group Policy.

This section describes setting options for Search Folders, Navigation Pane module display order, Instant Messaging integration, notification area message display, and location of the Date Picker in Calendar. Additional Outlook user interface options are covered in other chapters (see "Resources and related information" at the end of this section).

> **Note** The Favorites menu is no longer available in Outlook, so the registry key to disable the menu has been removed and is no longer available in the Outlook policy template (Outlk11.adm).

Configuring Search Folder options

Outlook folders are where items are stored—such as new e-mail messages (Inbox folder), sent e-mail messages (Sent Items), or e-mail messages you want to save. In contrast, messages are not stored in Search Folders. Search Folders are virtual folders that contain views of all e-mail items matching specific search criteria.

Search Folders display the results of previously defined search queries of your Outlook folders. The e-mail messages remain stored in one or more Outlook folders. Each Search Folder is a saved search that is kept up to date, monitoring all Outlook folders for new items that match the criteria of the Search Folder.

When you create a Search Folder, you have a number of default Search Folder options to choose from, such as "Mail with attachments" or "Mail from specific people." you can also create custom Search Folders.

You can configure how long Search Folders remain active for Cached Exchange Mode accounts and for online Exchange accounts. You can specify the number of days after which Search Folders become dormant—that is, items listed in the Search Folder are no longer up to date with current searches of Outlook folders. A dormant Search Folder appears in italics in a user's Navigation Pane. When a user visits a dormant Search Folder, the view is refreshed and the elapsed time count begins again.

The period of time that you specify with this setting begins the last time that a user clicked the Search Folder. You can specify a different number of days for users in Exchange online mode and in Cached Exchange Mode. Separate counts are maintained for each Search Folder for each mode. The default value is 60 days. If you specify zero days, Search Folders in Exchange online mode are always dormant.

You can also disable the Search Folders user interface altogether.

You set default values for these options in the Custom Installation Wizard. You cannot lock down the settings with Group Policy.

To configure default Search Folder options

1. In the Custom Installation Wizard, on the **Change Office User Settings** page, click the plus sign (+) next to **Microsoft Office Outlook 2003**.

2. Click **Search Folders**.

3. Double-click **Default Search Folders at startup**.

4. Click the **Apply Changes** radio button.

5. To disable creating default Search Folders when users start Outlook 2003, select the **Do not create Search Folders at startup** check box.

6. Click **OK**.

7. Double-click **Keep Search Folders Exchange online**.

8. Click the **Apply Changes** radio button.

9. Specify a number of days in the **Specify days to keep folders alive in Exchange online mode** box.

10. Click **OK**.

11. Double-click **Keep Search Folders offline**.

12. Click the **Apply Changes** radio button.

13. Specify a number of days in the **Specify days to keep folders alive in offline or cached mode** box.

14. Click **OK**.

> **Note**   If users use Search Folders with Exchange online (using a mailbox on the Exchange server) rather than with Cached Exchange Mode, the number of users that can be supported by the Exchange server may be decreased.

Configuring Instant Messaging integration

Instant Messaging is a feature of Microsoft Windows Messenger, Microsoft MSN Messenger, and the Microsoft Exchange Instant Messaging Service. With Instant Messaging, users can communicate with each other in real time.

When a user opens a message in Outlook or when it is viewed in the Reading Pane, the person names smart tag is displayed beside the sender's name. This smart tag also appears in other places in Outlook, including in Contacts (when users rest the pointer on an e-mail address) and in new meeting requests (when users rest the pointer on an attendee's name). Users can right-click the smart tag to see a menu of information and options, such as the person's free/busy status.

You can deploy settings to disable Instant Messaging in Office or configure other options for Instant Messaging functionality. Or you can deploy preferences for these options by using the **Change Office User Settings** page in the Custom Installation Wizard.

To configure Instant Messaging options

1. In Group Policy, load the Office 2003 template (Office11.adm).

2. To disable Instant Messaging, under **User Configuration\Administrative Templates\Microsoft Office 2003\Instant Messaging Integration**, double-click **Display the Online Status item in the person names Smart Tag menu**.

3. Click the **Enabled** radio button to enable configuring the policy.

4. Select the **Check to disable Online Status** check box, and then click **OK**.

5. To configure online status lookup for people who are not in users' Online Contacts lists, double-click **Allow IM status queries for people not on the Messenger contact list**.

6. Select the **Enabled** radio button to enable configuring the policy.

7. In the **Select** drop-down list, choose a group of users for whom Instant Messenger status will be checked (for example, **Query Messenger contact list only**), and then click **OK**.

8. To configure how often free/busy information is updated, double-click **Set refresh time for Calendar information in the person names Smart Tag**.

9. Select the **Enabled** radio button to enable configuring the policy.

10. In the **Set time in minutes (Default 15min)** box, specify a number of minutes, and then click **OK**.

11. To configure how much Microsoft Active Directory® directory service information is displayed for a person in the person names smart tag, configure other Instant Messaging policies such as **Display the Manager item in the person names Smart Tag menu**.

The Instant Messaging policies deployed with earlier versions of Outlook are removed. The two policies are:

- HKEY_LOCAL_MACHINE\Software\Policies\Microsoft\Office\10.0\Outlook \IM\InstallURL

- HKEY_LOCAL_MACHINE\Software\Policies\Microsoft\Office\10.0\Outlook \IM\ForceDisableIM

Configuring Navigation Pane module display order

You can configure the modules in the Navigation Pane (such as Calendar, Mail, and so on) to appear in a specific order. Setting the display order is most easily accomplished by using the Office Profile Wizard to capture the desired arrangement; however, you can instead use registry keys to specify the order and other options that determine how modules are displayed.

On the Resource Kit CD   You can install the Office Profile Wizard from the Microsoft Office 2003 Editions Resource Kit. To access the toolbox that includes this tool, see the "Office Profile Wizard" on the companion CD.

The Navigation Pane options cannot be locked down by policy. Users can change the display order by clicking **Options** on the **Tools** menu, and then, on the **Other** tab, clicking **Navigation Pane Options**.

The following table lists the registry settings that you can configure for your custom installation. You add these value entries in the following subkey:

HKEY_CURRENT_USER\Software\Microsoft\Office\11.0\Outlook\NavigationPane

Value name	Value data (Data type)	Default value	Description
NumBigModules	REG_SZ	3	Controls how many large buttons (each representing a Navigation Pane module) appear on the Navigation Pane. The maximum number that you can specify to be displayed is **8**.
ModuleOrder	REG_SZ	1,2,3,4,5,6,7,8	Determines the order in which the modules are displayed on the Navigation Pane. The data is an ordered list of indexes, where each position represents a Navigation Pane module, and the number in that position determines where the matching module appears.
			The index positions match this list: Mail, Calendar, Contacts, Tasks, Notes, Folder List, Shortcuts, Journal.
			For example, if the user switches Mail to be the third module showing, and Contacts to be the first, the registry value has this data: **3,2,1,4,5,6,7,8**
ModuleVisible	REG_SZ	1,1,1,1,1,1,1,0	Determines whether a module is visible on the Navigation Pane. (This does not affect the order of items listed in the **Go** menu.) The values match the positions used in the module ordering list. For example, the first position determines whether Mail is shown.
			By default, the Journal is not shown in the Navigation Pane. You can choose to not display other modules as well. For example, to not display Contacts, Tasks, Notes, and Shortcuts, set this data: **1,1,0,0,0,1,0,0**

Configuring Outlook messages in the notification area

As users work in Outlook, messages appear in the notification area with information about network and Exchange server availability. You can configure how and when these messages are displayed in the notification area by default.

The types of warnings are:

- **Network warnings**   For example: "Network problems are preventing connection to the Microsoft Exchange Server servername."

- **Exchange Server warnings**   For example: "Outlook is trying to retrieve data from the Microsoft Exchange Server computer."

- **Network connectivity changes**   For example: "Connection to the local area network has been restored."

- **Synchronization messages**   For example: "Outlook is preparing a local copy of your Exchange mailbox. This one time process may take several minutes to complete. Some of your data may not be shown until the process is complete."

You can deploy default settings for these options by using the **Change Office User Settings** page of the Custom Installation Wizard. These settings cannot be locked down by policy.

To configure Outlook notification area message behavior

1. In the Custom Installation Wizard, on the **Change Office User Settings** page, click the plus sign (+) next to **Microsoft Office Outlook 2003**.

2. Click **Outlook System Tray Icon**.

3. Double-click an option (such as **Show Network Warnings**), and then click the **Apply Changes** radio button.

4. Select the check box for the option displayed (such as the **Check to Show Network Warnings** check box), and then click **OK**.

Removing the Date Navigator from the Navigation Pane

You can deploy Outlook 2003 to users with the Date Navigator displayed as it is shown in earlier versions of Outlook. By default in Calendar in Outlook 2003, the Date Navigator and TaskPad pane is turned off and the Date Navigator is in the Navigation Pane. Users can restore the Date Navigator to its original location by clicking **TaskPad** on the **View** menu or by dragging the splitter line in Calendar to the left or right.

You can set a default value for the Date Navigator location in the Custom Installation Wizard; however, you cannot lock down the option by using policy.

To configure the Date Navigator in Outlook Calendar to display in legacy location

1. In the Custom Installation Wizard, on the **Change Office User Settings** page, click the plus sign (+) next to **Microsoft Office Outlook 2003**.

2. Click **Miscellaneous**.

3. In the **Settings** list, double-click **Date Picker/Calendar behavior**.

4. Select the **Apply Changes** radio button.

5. Select the **Check to display Date Picker like legacy Outlook** check box.

6. Click **OK**.

Resources and related information

Information Rights Management (IRM), a new feature in Microsoft Office 2003, can help prevent sensitive information from being distributed to or read by people who do not have permission to access the content. To learn more about deploying IRM in your organization, see "Configuring Information Rights Management for Messaging in Outlook 2003" earlier in this chapter.

Outlook 2003 provides two new features that can help users avoid receiving and reading junk e-mail messages—the new Junk E-mail Filter and the disabling of automatic content download from external servers. To learn more about configuring these features for your users, see "Helping Users Avoid Junk E-Mail Messages in Outlook 2003" earlier in this chapter.

A Meeting Workspace is a new feature in Outlook 2003 that includes a Web site for centralizing all the information and materials for an upcoming meeting. To learn more about deploying customizations for Meeting Workspaces, see "Configuring Meeting Workspace Options in Outlook 2003" later in this chapter.

Configuring Exchange Server Send/Receive Settings in Outlook 2003

As part of your Microsoft Office Outlook 2003 deployment, you can define Send/Receive groups for Microsoft Exchange Server accounts and folders and specify the tasks that are performed on each group during a Send/Receive action in Outlook.

Send/Receive groups contain one or more user e-mail accounts or folders in Microsoft Outlook. (The Send/Receive group All Accounts is preconfigured and included with Outlook by default.) Users can specify different behaviors for each group, such as the frequency with which Outlook connects to the server to send and receive messages for it, or how messages are processed when Outlook is online or offline.

New to Outlook 2003 is the ability for administrators to configure Send/Receive settings for Exchange accounts. Administrators can configure the types of synchronization that will be performed on specific folders or the Offline Address Book (OAB) when a Send/Receive operation is executed. They can also specify when a Send/Receive action for each Send/Receive group will be performed normally and when users are offline. For example, a Send/Receive group can be configured to be synchronized every 10 minutes normally and every 30 minutes when users are offline.

You can also configure download options for the OAB, such as whether to download only updates to the OAB since the last OAB download.

Defining custom Send/Receive groups

You can define one or more custom Send/Receive groups for your organization that include the accounts and folders you want to be synchronized for users under different circumstances.

For example, you might define a new Send/Receive group to deploy to your users for offline synchronization and modify the default All Accounts group to not be scheduled for automatic synchronization when users are offline. The new offline Send/Receive group would include a subset of users' accounts and folders configured to be automatically updated at certain intervals when users are working offline. By configuring only critical accounts and folders to update when users are working remotely, users can still access current data that is important to their work but spend less time waiting for large downloads over slow dial-up lines.

Note   Using Cached Exchange Mode in Outlook 2003 improves the user experience when working remotely over a low-bandwidth connection. For more information about deploying this new feature, see "Setting Up Outlook 2003 Cached Exchange Mode Accounts" earlier in this chapter.

To create a new Send/Receive group for Exchange accounts and folders

1. In the Custom Installation Wizard, on the **Outlook: Specify Send/Receive Groups (Exchange Only)** page, click **New**.

2. In the **New Group Name** box, enter a name for the group and click **OK**.

3. Click **Modify**.

4. In the **Modify Group** dialog box, select options for the group, such as synchronizing forms during a Send/Receive action.

5. In the **Change folder options** section, select a folder, and then select **Include this folder in Send/Receive**.

6. Choose download options for the folder:

   ■ **Download only headers**

   ■ **Download complete item including attachments**

   ■ **Download only headers for items larger than *n* KB**
   Enter a size limit in kilobytes (KB).

7. Click another folder to include the folder in this Send/Receive group, and choose a download option.

8. When you have added all the folders that you want to include in this group, click **OK**.

Configuring Send/Receive settings for a Send/Receive group

After creating a custom Send/Receive group, you might want to specify certain Send/Receive behavior for the group—for example, to execute a Send/Receive action for this group every 10 minutes. You can also specify separate settings for how Send/Receive works when users are offline.

To specify Send/Receive settings for a Send/Receive group

1. In the Custom Installation Wizard, on the **Outlook: Specify Send/Receive Groups (Exchange Only)** page, click a group in the **Group Name** list.

2. Specify any of the options available in this dialog box.

Configuring Offline Address Book download options

In addition to configuring Send/Receive behavior for each Send/Receive group, you can also specify Offline Address Book (OAB) options for each group. If you have a Send/Receive group designed for users who work offline and connect periodically over slow connections, for example, you might choose to configure the OAB to synchronize only updates since the last download.

When deciding whether to download the Full Details OAB or a No Details OAB, consider factors such as the following:

■ If you plan to deploy Cached Exchange Mode, a Full Details OAB will be required. If a No Details OAB is already on a user's computer, it is not removed when Outlook creates a Full Details OAB for Cached Exchange Mode. For more information, see "Setting Up Outlook 2003 Cached Exchange Mode Accounts" earlier in this chapter.

■ You cannot configure the information that is included in a No Details OAB.

To specify Offline Address Book download options for a Send/Receive group

1. In the Custom Installation Wizard, on the **Outlook: Specify Send/Receive Groups (Exchange Only)** page, click a group in the **Group Name** list.

2. In the **Exchange Address Book** section, select **Download offline address book** to synchronize the OAB when this Send/Receive group is synchronized.

3. Click **Address Book Settings**.

4. Specify any of the options available in **Modify Address Book Settings** dialog box.

5. Click **OK**.

Configuring Meeting Workspace Options in Outlook 2003

A Meeting Workspace is a Web site for centralizing all the information and materials for an upcoming meeting. Before the meeting, you use a workspace to publish the agenda, attendee list, and documents you plan to discuss. After the meeting, you use the workspace to publish the meeting results and track tasks. You send a Microsoft Outlook meeting request to invite people to the meeting, and in the message, include a hyperlink that goes to the workspace where invitees can learn the details and see the materials.

You can configure a number of options to set up and manage your Meeting Workspace deployment with Microsoft Office Outlook 2003. You can manage how users choose Meeting Workspace servers and other options when creating workspaces to include in Outlook meeting requests. You can configure Meeting Workspaces to work when you use a POP server as your messaging server, and you can also view Meeting Workspace error messages in a log file to help troubleshoot problems with Meeting Workspace configurations.

Note   By default, when you use Meeting Workspaces with Outlook, you must have a Microsoft Exchange server configured as your messaging server.

A Meeting Workspace is a special type of Microsoft Windows SharePoint™ Services 2.0 Web site created under a top-level SharePoint site. Help for the Meeting Workspace as well as general SharePoint Help is available from the workspace.

Note   If you have Windows SharePoint™ Services installed on your network, users within your company can invite anyone to a workspace who is in the same Microsoft Windows NT® forest as the original user. For more information about domains and forests, see information on Active Directory in Windows Help.

Using policies to define server lists and other user options

When you use policies to enforce Meeting Workspace settings for groups of users in your organization, you can configure options such as defining the list of Meeting Workspace servers users can choose from. Or, if you do not want users to use this feature, you can disable Meeting Workspace access entirely.

In a server list, you can specify how to prepopulate the drop-down lists that users see when working with Meeting Workspaces in Outlook. You access the Meeting Workspace feature by clicking **Meeting Workspace** on an Outlook meeting request. On the Meeting Workspace task pane that is presented, click **Change settings**. On this next Meeting Workspace task pane, choose a server from the **Select a location:** drop-down list. On the same pane, you can create a new workspace, choosing a template language and a template type from drop-down lists. Or, you can link to an existing workspace by choosing one from the **Select a workspace** drop-down list.

You use Group Policy to configure the lists and settings you want for Meeting Workspace. When you load the Microsoft Office 2003 ADM files into Group Policy, policies related to Meeting Workspace are located under User Configuration\Administrative Templates\Microsoft Office Outlook 2003\Meeting Workspace. This is also the location where you create a new policy to list Meeting Workspace servers and other items in Meeting Workspace task pane drop-down lists.

Configuring server list behavior for meeting organizers

You can configure how Meeting Workspace server lists are presented to meeting organizers in Outlook—for example, server lists can show a most recently used (MRU) list, or the list of servers and templates can be repopulated from the default list each time a workspace is being created. You can also help to prevent Meeting Workspace access by disabling the Meeting Workspace option for Outlook meeting requests.

When you specify the list of servers, you can ensure that the server list is repopulated with default servers and default templates. You can also help to control whether users can access servers other than those specified. You remove the Meeting Workspace button from Outlook meeting requests with the **Disable Meeting Workspace button** policy. Double-click the policy to open the **Properties** dialog, then select Enabled to enable the policy itself. Then select **Check to disable Meeting Workspace button**.

You configure options for the Meeting Workspace **Select a location** drop-down list with the **Disable user entries to server list** policy. Double-click the policy to open the **Properties** dialog, then select **Enabled** to enable setting the policy itself. In the **Check to disable users from adding entries to server list** drop-down list, select one of the following:

■ **Publish default, allow others**—You specify a list of default servers that appears in the drop-down list, but users can specify other servers by using the **Other workspace server** pop-out dialog. In addition, other Windows Share-Point Services sites and document workspace sites that users visit appear on the server list. With this setting, no user MRU list is created.

■ **Publish default, disallow others**—The default server list you specify is locked down for users. Users cannot access the **Other workspace server** pop-out dialog to specify servers that are not on the provided list. With this setting, no user MRU list is created.

Specifying a list of servers and default templates

You can configure the list of servers and corresponding Meeting Workspace templates that will appear in a drop-down list when a user clicks **Meeting Workspace** in a meeting request. A single registry key or policy stores all the Meeting Workspace server list entries.

On the Resource Kit CD   You can deploy the registry key that specifies the list of Meeting Workspace servers to your users by using the Custom Installation Wizard (for an initial deployment) or the Custom Maintenance Wizard (to update an existing installation). These tools are installed together with other Office 2003 tools when you run the Office Resource Kit Setup program. For more information, see Appendix A, "Toolbox."

The server list policy has a specific format that must be followed. Server names are separated from each other by vertical pipes ("|") without any carriage returns (CRs) or line feeds (LFs). There are six fields per record as described below. There can be from one to five records in the policy. This is a MRU list, so the first server record (for example, Server1) is the most recently used server and the fifth server record (for example, Server5) is the oldest server reference.

The **OrganizerName** field is ignored when you use a policy to specify the server list, but the other fields should always have valid content.

Note   You can see the current server list settings on any computer that has been used to create Meeting Workspaces by examining this registry key:
HKEY_CURRENT_USER\Software\Microsoft\Office\11.0\Meetings \Profile\MRUInternal

You specify the server list for the Meeting Workspace with the **Default servers and data for Meeting Workspaces** policy. However, because the policy string is complex, you should first type the entries into a text editor (such as Notepad), then paste the entire string into the policy. When you have created the server list string following the syntax described below, double-click the policy to open the

Properties dialog, then select **Enabled** to enable setting the policy itself. In the **Default** field, paste the server list string you have created.

The syntax for the server list string is outlined below:

```
http://Server1 |Friendly name for server 1|TemplateLCID|TemplateID|Template-
Name|OrganizerName|http://Server2 |Friendly name for server 2|TemplateLCID|Tem-
plateID|TemplateName|OrganizerName|http://Server3 |Friendly name for server|
```

The list continues with the same structure, with an entry for each server you want to include.

There are six fields in each record:

- Field 1: URL of server

- Field 2: Friendly name for server

- Field 3: TemplateLCID

- Field 4: TemplateID

- Field 5: TemplateName

- Field 6: OrganizerName

Each field is separated from the next field with a vertical pipe ("|"), and each complete record is separated from the next record with a vertical pipe ("|") after the last field (OrganizerName). Thus there are a total of six vertical pipes in each record that is included in the setting.

For the field TemplateLCID, specify a decimal value that identifies the language for the template, such as 1033 (representing English).

For the other template fields, you can use a custom template or choose a template name and the corresponding TemplateID from the following table of default templates.

TemplateName	TemplateID
Basic Meeting Workspace	Mps#0
Blank Meeting Workspace	Mps#1
Decision Meeting Workspace	Mps#2
Social Meeting Workspace	Mps#3
Multipage Meeting Workspace	Mps#4

Note   You can specify a custom template name and TemplateID instead of using a default template. For more information about creating custom templates, see "Working with Templates" in the Customization section of the Administrator's Guide for Windows SharePoint Services on the Windows SharePoint Services Web site at *http://www.microsoft.com/sharepoint/assistance.*

The following is an example of a server list entry (note that OrganizerName is blank):

```
http://server1/sites/design_team|The Juniper Project|1033|MPS#4|Multipage Meeting
Workspace||
```

Configuring Meeting Workspace integration when using a POP Server

You can configure Meeting Workspace integration for Outlook when you use a POP server as your messaging server. The following configuration enables Outlook to be able to transport and persist Meeting Workspace properties for meeting organizers and meeting attendees who use a POP server.

> **Note**   Using Outlook delegates with Meeting Workspace is not supported in POP server configurations.

To use Meeting Workspaces with a POP server, the following is required:

1. The POP server must be configured to support Transport-Neutral Encapsulation Format (TNEF).

2. Outlook meeting requests must be sent by using rich transport.

This section provides a pointer to reference information that can help you configure your POP server to use TNEF, along with steps that meeting organizers must take to help ensure that meeting requests are sent by using rich transport.

The following scenario describes the user experience when Meeting Workspaces are included in meeting requests and Outlook is used with a POP server.

- The meeting organizer initiates a meeting request in Outlook and creates or links to a Meeting Workspace in the request.

- The attendee receives the meeting request and sees a Meeting Workspace table in the message body, properly formatted, that includes a link to the Meeting Workspace.

- The Meeting Workspace properties are persisted to the attendee's calendar.

- Attendee's response is sent to the Meeting Workspace server.

More about TNEF support

For Meeting Workspaces to work properly in Outlook meeting requests when a POP server is used as the messaging server, the POP server must have TNEF enabled. The Meeting Workspace properties are stored in a MAPI property associated with the meeting request form. TNEF is required to transport the properties from the meeting organizer to the meeting attendee. When the meeting attendee receives the Meeting Workspace properties (after the properties are transported by using TNEF), Outlook stores the properties in the attendee's client meeting request.

TNEF is a format for converting a set of MAPI properties—a MAPI message—into a serial data stream. The TNEF functions are primarily used by transport providers that need to encode MAPI message properties for transmission through a messaging system that does not support those properties directly. For example, an SMTP-based transport uses TNEF to encode properties like PR_SENT_REPRESENTING, which do not have direct representations in the structure of an SMTP message.

For more information about using TNEF, see the Transport-Neutral Encapsulation Format (TNEF) appendix in the Messaging API SDK on Technet at *http://msdn. microsoft.com/library/default.asp?url=/library/en-us/mapi/html/_mapi1book_transport _neutral_encapsulation_format_tnef_.asp.*

Ensuring that rich transport is used

Meeting organizers who want to use Meeting Workspace with POP messaging servers must ensure that rich transport—rather than plain text transport—is used to send the meeting request to recipients. Rich transport means ensuring that Rich Text Format attributes and iCalendar information are included together in the transport. This ensures that the Meeting Workspace properties attached to the meeting request persist in the e-mail transport from organizer to attendee. The meeting organizer must take the following steps to help ensure that rich transport is used for the meeting request:

1. Use Rich Text Format (RTF) when sending the meeting request.

2. Do not attach an iCalendar (iCal) to the meeting request. (The iCalendar format is a common format for Internet calendars.)

Note that these are only requirements if POP is the messaging server. If the organizer is running against an Exchange server, these options are not needed.

Set Rich Text Format

Rich Text Format for meeting requests in Outlook can be set per meeting request or as the default for all Outlook messages (including meeting requests).

To set Rich Text Format for one meeting request

1. In the meeting request, in the **To** box, double-click the user name.

2. In the **E-mail properties** dialog, under **Internet** format, click **Send using Outlook Rich Text format**.

You can instead configure Outlook to use RTF for all Internet messages (including meeting requests).

To set Rich Text Format as the default for all Internet messages

1. In Outlook, on the **Tools** menu, click **Options**, click the **Mail format** tab.

2. Click **Internet Format**.

3. Then in the drop-down list in the **Outlook Rich Text** options section, select **Send using Outlook Rich Text format**.

Do not send an iCalendar attachment

To specify that an iCalendar attachment is not sent with a meeting request, clear **Send as iCalendar** on the **Tools** menu in the individual meeting request. This forces the iCalendar properties to be transported in the MIME message header. (Note that this option is not available if Outlook is running against Exchange server.)

Viewing error message logs

Some Meeting Workspace errors are suppressed by default to help avoid user confusion. However, Meeting Workspace errors are written to the Windows Event Log, which can help you track down problems when troubleshooting.

Meeting Workspace users are alerted with an error message when there is a problem when creating a workspace or when a problem with the workspace arises later (for example, when a meeting workspace server fails). When problems occur separately from the process of initiating a meeting and creating a workspace, users might not understand what went wrong and what, if anything, they can do about the problem. Because these errors occur asynchronously, in some cases it may not be obvious that the error was triggered by a meeting update action.

When there are steps users can take to fix the problem, error messages about the problem are always shown to users. Error messages that will merely confuse users are suppressed by default. However, if you need to debug certain Meeting Workspace issues, it might be helpful to examine the error content in the Windows event log.

You can view the log files by using the Windows Event Viewer. To open Event Viewer, in Control Panel, double-click **Administrative Tools**, and then double-click **Event Viewer**. You can see logging information related to Outlook by clicking **Application Log** in the left pane.

Resources and related information

For more information about customizing SharePoint features, see the Administrator's Guide for Windows SharePoint Services on the Windows SharePoint Services Web site at *http://www.microsoft.com/sharepoint/assistance*.

Chapter 8

Special Deployment Scenarios for Outlook 2003

Microsoft® Office 2003 gives you considerable flexibility when you are installing in unique environments or with special configurations. You can ensure that Microsoft Office Outlook® 2003 installs quietly and does not prompt the user when it starts for the first time. You can configure Outlook for Terminal Server environments or roaming scenarios. In addition, you can control whether Outlook is deployed before, with, or after your Office deployment. A new feature, RPC over HTTP, can be enabled in conjunction with a specific Microsoft Exchange Server configuration.

Ensuring a Quiet Installation and Startup for Outlook

Like the other Microsoft Office 2003 applications, Microsoft Office Outlook 2003 prompts users for information during installation—such as the installation location—and for information when a user first starts the application—such as Outlook profile information, account migration, and so on.

If you prefer to install Outlook 2003 without any user prompts, you can use Setup options to ensure a quiet installation, just as you can with any other Office 2003 application. In addition, you can use settings in the Custom Installation Wizard to configure your installation to prevent most user prompts when Outlook 2003 first runs.

Avoiding user prompts for profile creation

You can ensure that users are not prompted to enter profile information themselves when Outlook 2003 first starts by giving them a default Outlook profile. To configure a default profile for users, choose one of the following options on the **Outlook: Customize Default Profile** page of the Custom Installation Wizard:

- **New Profile**   Existing profiles are saved, but the new profile that you have defined becomes the default profile for all users.

- **Modify Profile**   Outlook uses the customizations you specify to create default profiles for users who do not have a profile.

On the Resource Kit CD   The Office 2003 Editions Resource Kit core tool set includes the Custom Installation Wizard. This tool is installed by default when you run the Office Resource Kit Setup program. For more information, see "Custom Installation Wizard" in Appendix A, "Toolbox."

Avoiding user prompts to resolve similar Exchange Server user names

In the Custom Installation Wizard, you can configure user names for Microsoft Exchange Server mailboxes in Outlook profiles. You identify the user with a specific value or replaceable parameter. If you use the default **%USERNAME%**, then Outlook uses the user's logon name.

You can specify **=%USERNAME%** to use the exact logon name provided, rather than prompting users with possible variations when Outlook starts. This will limit—but not eliminate—user prompts for name resolution.

To avoid user prompts for name resolution altogether, you configure an exact alias matching set. For more information about how to define an Active Directory® directory service setting to always match user names exactly, see documentation for Active Directory.

Avoiding user prompts due to Personal Address Book conversions and Send Receipts options

Most required Outlook migration happens automatically when a user starts Outlook 2003 for the first time. Users typically see progress indicators as their account information and user data are migrated, but they are not prompted to enter any information. However, unless you customize your Outlook deployment, users might be prompted to choose options for Personal Address Book migration and Send Receipts options.

Controlling Personal Address Book conversions

If you want to prevent user prompts regarding Personal Address Book conversion for users starting Outlook 2003 for the first time, specify how the conversion will be managed by setting an option in the Custom Installation Wizard.

To prevent user prompting for Personal Address Book account conversion

1. In the Custom Installation Wizard, go to the **Outlook: Customize Default Settings** page.

2. Clear the check box next to **Convert Personal Address Book (PAB file) to an Outlook Address Book**.

    When you clear this option, Outlook does not import an existing PAB file into a Contacts folder at Outlook startup, and the user is not asked to import the file.

Controlling Read Receipt settings

With Outlook 2003, users can now specify a default response to e-mail messages that arrive with a return receipt request. Users can set an option to always send a return receipt (when one is requested), to never send a return receipt, or to be prompted about sending a response when a return receipt is requested. When Outlook 2003 is first started, users are prompted to choose one of these options as a default setting.

Administrators may need to implement a default setting for read receipts, depending upon the policies of their organization. An organization may want to enforce the sending of read receipts as a way of ensuring accountability, for example, or they may want to turn off the option as a way of managing privacy. Either option can be set at the initial deployment of Outlook 2003.

If you want to avoid user prompts for specifying read receipt options when Outlook starts for the first time, specify a default read receipt response option for users in the Custom Installation Wizard.

To prevent user prompting to specify a default read receipt response

1. In the Custom Installation Wizard, on the **Change Office User Settings** page, click **Microsoft Office Outlook 2003**.

2. Click on the plus (+) sign to expand the node, then expand the node next to **Tools | Options**.

3. Expand the node next to **Preferences**, then expand the node next to **E-mail Options.**

4. Click **Tracking Options**.

5. Double-click **Options** in the right pane to open the **Option Properties** dialog.

6. Click **Apply Changes**, then choose an option in the **When Outlook is asked to respond to a read request** drop-down menu.

7. Click **OK**.

User prompts caused by other messaging clients

If a messaging client other than Outlook—such as Outlook Express or a third-party client—is defined as the default client on the user's computer, there are special circumstances in which a user might be prompted for input when Outlook 2003 starts, such as the following:

■ A user has a non-Outlook client installed that is defined as the default messaging client after Outlook 2003 is installed, but before Outlook 2003 is run for the first time.

  In this case, when Outlook starts, the user is asked if Outlook 2003 should be the default client.

■ A user has a non-Outlook client installed that is defined as the default messaging client with multiple accounts defined.

  When Outlook starts, the user is prompted to choose one of the accounts to import to Outlook 2003.

Resources and related information

The Custom Installation Wizard offers a wide range of configuration options for defining and modifying user profiles. For more information about your options for configuring Outlook profiles, see "Customizing Outlook Features and Installation with the Custom Installation Wizard" in Chapter 7, "Deploying Outlook 2003."

  Outlook 2003 supports the same Setup command-line options that the other Office 2003 applications support. These options can be set to prevent any prompts from appearing during installation. For more information about ensuring a quiet installation of Office applications, including Outlook, see "Customizing How Setup Runs" in Chapter 4, "Customizing Office 2003."

Installing Outlook in a Terminal Services Environment

By using Microsoft Windows® Terminal Services, you can use Microsoft Office Outlook 2003 without having to upgrade every computer in your organization. Users can work in the latest Microsoft Office 2003 environment even when their computers have limited hard disk space, memory, or processing speed.

Windows Terminal Services allows you to run Microsoft Windows–based programs on a server and display them remotely on client computers. For example, you can install a single copy of Outlook 2003 on a Windows Terminal Services computer. Then, instead of running Outlook locally, multiple users can connect to the server and run Outlook from there.

However, there are some limitations to be aware of. For example, you cannot use Outlook with Cached Exchange Mode when you run Outlook on Windows Terminal Services. Also, to help provide the best supported Outlook experience for your users in a Terminal Services environment, pay special attention to managing Outlook features that might adversely affect performance.

Outlook features that are disabled with Terminal Services

The following Outlook features cannot be used when you are running Outlook in a Terminal Services environment:

- Offline store (OST) files.
   Features that rely on the OST (for example, Cached Exchange Mode and Offline) are not supported with Terminal Services.

- Forms Designer and the Microsoft Visual Basic® Scripting Edition (VBScript) editor.
   You can view a custom form, but you cannot design a new form or revise an existing form.

- Changing the Time Zone from within Outlook.
   Changing this setting in Outlook updates a system setting.

- Changing Zone security settings from within Outlook.
   Changing this setting in Outlook updates a system setting.

- Changing the status of a Microsoft Exchange Client Extension.
   You cannot change the status; however, if the Exchange Client Extension is already on, it should work correctly.

- Adding stationery that was not included with Outlook as part of the Terminal Services installation.

- Outlook animations are disabled.
   Examples of Outlook animations include Send/Receive animation and the timer in Journal items.

Using WordMail with Terminal Services

Outlook 2003 and Microsoft Office Word 2003 can both use a large amount of memory on the Terminal Services computer. If Outlook users use WordMail as their e-mail editor, this option takes more memory and, as a result, can affect the number of users that you can serve simultaneously in a Terminal Services environment. Although the default editor for Outlook 2003 is WordMail, you can set a different default editor as part of your customized Outlook deployment.

Note   Another option is to disable WordMail by using Group Policy. In Group Policy, load the Outlook 2003 template (Outlk11.adm). Under **User Configuration\Administrative Templates\Microsoft Office Outlook 2003\Tools | Options\Mail Format**, click **Message Format**. Double-click **Message format/editor**. In the **Use the following Format/Editor for e-mail messages** drop-down list, select an option that does not include Microsoft Word. Clear the **Use Microsoft Word to read rich text e-mail messages** check box. Then click **OK**.

To set the default Outlook 2003 editor

1. On the **Tools** menu in Outlook, click **Options**.

2. Click the **Mail Format** tab.

3. In the **Message format** section, set the option **Use Microsoft Word to edit e-mail messages**.

You can customize this setting in a test installation of Office, then capture your settings by using the Office Profile Wizard. The settings will be saved in an Office profile settings file (OPS file) that you can include with a transform (MST file) or configuration maintenance file (CMW file).

Or, you can use the **Outlook: Customize Default Settings** page in the Custom Installation Wizard or the Custom Maintenance Wizard to set the default e-mail editor.

After configuring the default editor for Outlook, install Outlook with the customization file (MST file or CMW file) that includes this new setting.

On the Resource Kit CD   The Office 2003 Editions Resource Kit core tool set includes the Custom Installation Wizard, Office Profile Wizard, and Custom Maintenance Wizard. You use these tools to customize Office application deployments. These tools are installed by default when you run the Office Resource Kit Setup program. For more information, see Appendix A, "Toolbox."

Unlocking registry settings

By default, Windows Terminal Services clients do not have write access to the registry on the Windows Terminal Services computer. To run some Outlook features, you might need to give users write access to some keys and subkeys. For example:

- To allow users the use of custom MAPI forms for Outlook 2003, unlock the subkey HKEY_CLASSES_ROOT\CLSID.

- To allow users the use of Microsoft Schedule+ resources, unlock the subkey HKEY_LOCAL_MACHINE\Software\Microsoft\Schedule+\Application.

Resources and related information

The Office Custom Installation Wizard provides a straightforward way to configure and install Outlook 2003. For more information about Outlook configuration choices, see "Customizing Outlook Features and Installation with the Custom Installation Wizard" in Chapter 7, "Deploying Outlook 2003."

Detailed information about using the Office Profile Wizard to save user options is available. For more information about the Office Profile Wizard and OPS files, see Customizing Outlook Features and Installation in the Custom Installation Wizard on the companion CD.

Configuring Outlook for Roaming Users

Roaming users move between different computers on a network. With Microsoft Office 2003, these users can move between computers without changing the way that they work. Their documents and their application settings for Microsoft Office Outlook 2003 and other Office applications travel with them, along with any system preferences.

You can help ensure a smooth roaming experience for Outlook users in your organization by following several recommended strategies and configuration options.

> **Note**   To use Outlook with roaming users, you must set up roaming user profiles on your Microsoft Windows network. For more information about configuring Windows servers to support roaming users, see the Windows documentation.

Recommended strategies for Outlook roaming

Roaming with Outlook 2003 works only between computers that are set up with the same operating system and the same versions of the software. The following recommendations will help ensure a smooth roaming experience for users:

- Roam between platforms on the same version of the same operating system.
  For example, Microsoft Windows 2000 to Microsoft Windows 2000. Supported platforms are Windows 2000 Service Pack 3 and later, and Windows XP and later.

- Ensure that the same operating system language version is installed on all computers that users roam between.

- Ensure that the same language version and release version of Outlook are installed on all computers that users roam between.

- Install Outlook on all computers for roaming users as per-computer.
  Installing as per-user is also possible but is not recommended.

- Install Outlook in the same location on all computers that will be used for roaming users.

Upgrading roaming users to Outlook 2003

If your organization already has roaming configured for Outlook users, you can help ensure a smooth transition when you upgrade to Outlook 2003 by making sure that users only roam between computers running the same version of Outlook. If you have roaming users on an older version of Outlook, be sure to upgrade all users and computers in a single area (such as a domain) at the same time.

If users roam between computers that have different versions of Outlook installed, compatibility issues may arise. For example, new features in Outlook 2003 are not available to users with Outlook 2002 profiles, which can create confusion for users roaming in an environment with a mix of Outlook versions.

Setting up roaming users with Outlook 2003

To set up roaming for users in Outlook 2003, you first decide how to manage users' data so the information they need is available to them as they roam. Then you configure user profiles for roaming by using the network Primary Domain Controller (PDC) computer.

Managing folder locations

To help ensure that a user's e-mail messages and other Outlook information roam with the user, you might need to take special steps to configure Outlook folder locations.

For example, suppose the users in your organization receive mail in an Inbox located on their Microsoft Exchange server. They can view new mail when they roam without taking special steps. However, perhaps users also need access to a personal file folder (for example, to read mail that has been transferred off of the messaging server). In this case, you can put the files that contain this data on a network share.

When you enable roaming and specify a network share for roaming files, certain files and folders are automatically available for users when they roam to different computers. Files and folders in the location defined by the environment variable %UserProfile% (on the local computer) roam with users, with the exception of one folder.

The one folder that does not roam with users in the default roaming scenario is the Local Settings folder in the %UserProfile% folder. This exception affects Outlook users because, by default, the file folders for some Outlook services—listed in the following table—are created in this non-roaming folder.

Service name	File extension
Offline Folders (OST)	.ost
Personal Folders (PST)	.pst
Personal Address Book (PAB)	.pab

Because the files reside in a non-roaming directory, Outlook can see and open them only on the computer on which they were created. To allow users to use PST or PAB files while roaming, you can place the files on a network share. Note, however, that using OST files on a network share is not a supported configuration.

There are several ways to place files on a network share. For example:

- You can set the file location to a network share for new services that you create in the Custom Installation Wizard or Custom Maintenance Wizard.

    You do this when you create a custom transform for deploying or updating Outlook. For example, you can add a PST file for all Outlook users and specify a network share where they will be stored. This allows users to move e-mail messages to the PST file, and those messages will be available to them when they roam.

- You can notify roaming users to relocate local folders to a network share.

    Users can move folders by using the Outlook user interface. This is a good choice for users who have existing Outlook files that must be accessible to them on other computers.

On the Resource Kit CD   The Office 2003 Editions Resource Kit core tool set includes the Custom Installation Wizard and Custom Maintenance Wizard, among other Office deployment tools. You use these tools to customize Office application deployments. These tools are installed by default when you run the Office Resource Kit Setup program. For more information, see Appendix A, "Toolbox."

Another option is to relocate the files into a roaming folder on the user's local computer. However, these personal files can become large. The advisability of relocating the files depends on network speed and traffic, as well as the number of users who roam in your organization. Typically, placing PST and PAB files in folders that roam with users is not recommended.

Resources and related information

You have considerable flexibility in configuring and deploying Outlook 2003. For more information about using the Custom Installation Wizard to create a custom transform for deploying Outlook 2003, see "Customizing Outlook Features and Installation with the Custom Installation Wizard" in Chapter 7, "Deploying Outlook 2003."

Integrating Outlook 2003 with Windows SharePoint Services

If groups in your organization collaborate by using Microsoft Windows SharePoint™ Services sites, a new feature in Microsoft Office Outlook 2003 and Windows SharePoint Services 2.0 allows users to share data between the two resources. This allows users to see information stored on Windows SharePoint Services team sites—such as names and phone numbers—by using Outlook folders.

You can change Outlook behavior when synchronizing information with group Web sites. Or, you can choose to help prevent users from linking information between Outlook and Windows SharePoint Services sites.

Linking to Windows SharePoint Services from Outlook

Users can use a new button in Windows SharePoint Services Contacts and Events pages—**Link to Outlook**—to link information to folders that are created in Outlook. Once the link between Outlook and a Windows SharePoint Services site is established and the user has the folder open that is linked to the site, information is refreshed every 20 minutes, by default. Only items that have changed are synchronized to the Outlook client.

Using Group Policy to change synchronization behavior or disable linking

You can use Group Policy to set policies that manage how Outlook and Windows SharePoint Services interact for users in your organization. You can set a policy to specify the time interval between information synchronizations or you can disallow linking altogether.

You can change the synchronization interval to make it longer, if, for example, users are linked from Outlook to a large group of Contacts which would trigger a time-consuming synchronization; or shorter, if users need access to updated information at all times. You can even turn off automatic synchronization. However, regardless of how the synchronization interval setting is configured, linked folders are automatically synchronized when users switch to one of these folders.

To set the synchronization interval for updating Outlook folders

1. In Group Policy, load the Outlook 2003 template (Outlk11.adm).

2. Under User Configuration\Administrative Templates\Microsoft Office Outlook 2003\SharePoint Integration, double-click **Sharepoint folder sync interval**.

3. Select **Enabled** to enable configuring the policy.

4. In the **Select interval to sync Sharepoint folders: (minutes)** box, enter a decimal value (or use the up and down arrows to select a value), then click **OK**.

Another option is to use a policy to disallow any linking between Outlook and Windows SharePoint Services for your users.

To disable linking between Outlook and Windows SharePoint Services

1. In the Group Policy snap-in, load the Outlook 2003 template (Outlk11.adm).

2. Under User Configuration\Administrative Templates\Microsoft Office Outlook 2003\SharePoint Integration, double-click **Disable Sharepoint integration in Outlook**.

3. Select **Enabled** to enable configuring the policy.

4. Select **Check to disable Sharepoint integration in Outlook**, then click **OK**.

> **Note**   To link Outlook and Windows SharePoint Services site pages, Outlook must be able to create Unicode® PST files on the user's computer. If a policy (or registry key) is set that requires ANSI (rather than Unicode) PST files for Outlook, linking cannot be established. The option to configure PST file types is in Group Policy under User Configuration\Administrative Templates\Microsoft Office Outlook 2003\Miscellaneous\PST Settings. Double-click **Preferred PST Mode (Unicode/ANSI)**, and make sure that **Enforce Unicode PST** is not the option selected in the **Choose a default format for new PSTs** drop-down list.

Installing Outlook 2003 Before Office 2003

Microsoft Office Outlook 2003 is designed to provide the best supported experience when it is installed together with Microsoft Office 2003. However, in some cases your organization might benefit from deploying Outlook and Office in stages—for example, deploying Outlook first, then deploying Office later.

This section of the chapter discusses several options for installing Outlook before Office and includes specific procedures for doing so.

Note   Installing Outlook before Office is one example of staging the deployment of an Office application; the methods described here can be used to install any Office application before installing the rest of Office. You can also install any Office application after an installation of the rest of Office. For more information about staging your deployment in this way, see "Installing Outlook 2003 After Office 2003" later in this chapter.

When you install Outlook 2003 over the network by using an administrative installation point, you can use one of the following methods to install Outlook before you install Office 2003:

- Install the stand-alone version of Outlook 2003 from the same or a different administrative installation point from which you plan to install Office.

- Run Office Setup from an Office CD to install only Outlook 2003, then use the Custom Maintenance Wizard to install the rest of Office when you are ready.

Note   Outlook 2003 cannot coexist with previous versions of Outlook. If you choose to keep previous versions, do not install Outlook 2003.

Installing a stand-alone version of Outlook before Office

One way to install Outlook 2003 before Office 2003 is to first install the stand-alone version of Outlook from a CD, then use the Office 2003 CD to install the rest of Office. With this method, you can also select whether to use one administrative installation point for both Outlook and Office, or separate installation points for each package.

Choose whether to use one or more administrative installation points

When you deploy the stand-alone version of Outlook, you can create two administrative installation points—one for Outlook, and one for the rest of Office—or you can use one administrative installation point for both packages. Each scenario has its benefits, depending on your deployment needs.

You might choose to use separate installation points, for example, if two different groups in your organization will be deploying Office and Outlook, respectively. In this scenario, you use the Office 2003 CD plus a stand-alone copy of Outlook 2003.

The separate administrative installation points can be in different folders on one network server, or they can be on separate servers. Users install Outlook from one administrative installation point, and install the rest of Office later from the second administrative installation point. In this scenario, files that are common among all Office applications are duplicated on each administrative installation point.

Another method for deploying Outlook before Office is to create a single administrative installation point that includes both Outlook and Office. You create the initial administrative installation point by running Setup with the /a command-line option from the stand-alone Outlook version. Then you install the rest of Office from the Office 2003 CD into the same folder structure.

Using one administrative installation point for both packages saves hard disk space because files that are common among all Office applications are shared on the single administrative installation point. Because Outlook and Office use the same names for their respective Setup files (Setup.exe and Setup.ini), however, you must rename the files to avoid overwriting the unique Outlook and Office versions.

Install the stand-alone version of Outlook

The process for installing Outlook from a stand-alone version includes these steps:

- Creating an administrative installation point for the stand-alone version of Outlook.

- Customizing your Outlook deployment.

- Saving your Outlook customizations in a transform.

- Installing the customized version of Outlook on users' computers.

> **Note**   As part of an initial Outlook customization, you can capture and include settings in an Office profile settings file (OPS file). To do this, you first install Outlook on a test computer and make your changes to the Outlook settings and environment. You then capture your customizations in an OPS file by running the Office Profile Wizard. Finally, you include the OPS file in the Custom Installation Wizard when you create the transform for installing Outlook.

To install the stand-alone Outlook 2003 version

1. Using the stand-alone Outlook 2003 version, run Setup.exe with the /a command-line option.

2. When prompted for the server location, enter a unique folder for Outlook on a network server. For example:

    \\server1\software\outlook

    or

    Enter the same folder that you will use for your Office deployment. For example:

    \\server1\software\office

3. Use the Custom Installation Wizard to create a transform that references the Outlook MSI file in the root of the administrative installation point used in step 2, and that specifies the appropriate Outlook configuration for your users.

    For example, you can include an OPS file for Outlook (if you created one), specify Outlook settings, and configure user profiles in the Custom Installation Wizard. Save the transform in the same folder as the Setup settings file.

4. If you are using the same administrative installation point that you will use for your Office deployment, rename the Setup files (Setup.exe and Setup.ini).

    Use consistent file names and the appropriate file name extensions; for example, OlkSetup.exe and OlkSetup.ini. (If you created the administrative image from the Microsoft Select CD subscription, the files have already been renamed for you on the CD.)

5. Edit the Outlook Setup settings file (INI file) to specify the transform that you created.

    For example, you might add the following line under the [MST] section:

    ```
    MST1=Outlook.mst
    ```

    You must remove the comment marker (;) from the [MST] header line so that the transform is read correctly.

6. Instruct users to install Outlook by using Outlook Setup from this administrative installation point.

Install Office after installing Outlook

After you have deployed the stand-alone version of Outlook, you can deploy the rest of Office by using the same or a different administrative installation point. If you use the same administrative installation point as Outlook, then you must make sure that the Outlook Setup files have been renamed so the Office Setup files do not overwrite them. Then you customize your Office deployment, save the customizations in a transform, and instruct users to install the rest of Office 2003 from the Office administrative installation point. For more information about customizing and deploying Office, see Chapter 4, "Customizing Office 2003."

Note   As part of an initial Office customization, you can capture and include settings in an OPS file. To do this, install Office on a test computer and make your changes to the Office settings and environment. When you capture your customizations by running the Office Profile Wizard and creating an OPS file, be sure to exclude Outlook settings. Then include the OPS file in the Custom Installation Wizard when you create the transform for installing Office.

To install Office after installing stand-alone Outlook

1. Using an Office 2003 CD, run Setup.exe with the **/a** command-line option.

2. When prompted for the server location, enter a folder on the network server. For example:

    \\server1\software\office

3. Use the Custom Installation Wizard to create a transform to customize Office.
    As part of your customization, on the **Set Feature Installation States** page, set **Microsoft Outlook for Windows** to **Not Available, Hidden, Locked**. In addition to customizing options for other Office applications, you can optionally fine-tune your Outlook customizations in this transform as well. When you are finished, save the transform in the same folder as the Setup settings file.

4. To specify this transform when you install Office, edit the Office Setup.ini in a standard text editor (such as Notepad) to add an entry for the Office transform in the [MST1] section. For example:

    ```
    [MST1]

    MST1=Office.mst
    ```

    Be sure to remove the comment marker (;) from the [MST] header line so that the transform is read correctly.

5. Instruct users to install Office from the administrative installation point.

Installing Outlook before Office using the Office CD

Another way to stage your deployment of Outlook 2003 and Office 2003 is to install Outlook first from an Office 2003 CD that includes Outlook. Then you use the Custom Maintenance Wizard to configure the rest of Office to be installed after Outlook by changing the installation options configured in the original Office transform. In this case, you use a single administrative installation point for both installations.

Upgrading from an earlier version of Office

If you are upgrading from an earlier version of Office, there are several issues to consider when you install Outlook before Office by using an Office CD. First, if you plan to use the Office Profile Wizard to capture Office settings, you must configure these settings and include the OPS file when creating the Custom Installation Wizard transform to deploy Outlook. (The Custom Maintenance Wizard does not allow you to include an OPS file.)

Also, when you deploy Office 2003 by using the Custom Maintenance Wizard, you limit your options for easily removing earlier versions of other Office applications. When you deploy Outlook 2003 by using the Custom Installation Wizard, you can choose to remove earlier versions of Outlook while leaving other existing Office applications. However, when you deploy Office by using the Custom Maintenance Wizard, you cannot specify to remove older versions of Office applications. However, you can use the Office Removal Wizard to remove files instead. For more information about using the Office Removal Wizard, see "Customizing Removal Behavior" in Chapter 4, "Customizing Office 2003."

Start by running Setup with the **/a** option to copy Office files to your administrative installation point. When prompted for the server location, enter a folder on a network server. For example:

\\server1\software\office

Then follow these steps to install Outlook and other Office applications in stages:

- Use the Custom Installation Wizard to create a transform that includes your Outlook and Office customizations.

- Install Outlook using the transform.

- When you want to install the rest of Office, you use the Custom Maintenance Wizard. You can include both Office and Outlook customizations in the second installation.

Using the Office Profile Wizard to capture Outlook settings

As part of an initial Outlook customization, you can capture and include settings in an OPS file. To do this, install Outlook on a test computer, and then make your changes to the Outlook settings and environment. When you capture your customizations in an OPS file by running the Office Profile Wizard, be sure to include only Outlook settings.

Optionally, you can install all of Office on the test computer and capture settings for other Office 2003 applications as well as for Outlook. In this case, capture all customizations when you run the Office Profile Wizard to create an OPS file.

Then include the OPS file in the Custom Installation Wizard when you create the transform for installing Outlook.

To install Outlook by using the Office 2003 CD

1. Start the Custom Installation Wizard and open the Office 2003 package (MSI file).

2. On the **Remove Previous Versions** page, click **Remove the following versions of Microsoft Office applications**.

3. In the table of applications, for each Office application except Microsoft Outlook, click the application name, then click **Details**.

4. Clear all the check boxes to retain the current versions of the application on users' computers, then click **OK**.
   Repeat for each application.

5. On the **Set Feature Installation States** page, set all Microsoft Office applications in the feature tree to **Not Available**.

6. Set the **Microsoft Outlook for Windows** feature to **Run from My Computer**.
   You can also install shared Office tools, converters, or other features that support your Outlook installation.

7. Configure any other installation options, then complete the transform.
   For example, you can specify Outlook profile information.

8. To specify this transform when you install Outlook, edit the Office Setup.ini in a standard text editor (such as Notepad) to add an entry for the Office transform in the [MST1] section. For example:

```
[MST1]

MST1=Office.mst
```

Be sure to remove the comment marker (;) from the [MST] header line so that the transform is read correctly.

9. Instruct users to install Outlook by running Setup from this administrative installation point.

10. Later, use the Custom Maintenance Wizard to install additional Office applications and to modify existing Office installations (including your Outlook installation) throughout your organization after your initial deployment.

Similar to the Custom Installation Wizard, the Custom Maintenance Wizard reads the Office 2003 package (MSI file) and records your changes in a configuration maintenance file (CMW file).

On the Resource Kit CD   The Office 2003 Editions Resource Kit includes the Custom Maintenance Wizard, which is installed by default when you run the Office Resource Kit Setup program. For more information, see "Custom Maintenance Wizard" in Appendix A, "Toolbox."

Resources and related information

There are a number of considerations when you choose the timing of your Outlook deployment. For more information about the advantages and disadvantages of staging an Outlook installation, see "Determining When to Install Outlook" in Chapter 6, "Planning an Outlook 2003 Deployment."

The Office Custom Installation Wizard provides a straightforward way to configure and install Outlook 2003. For more information about Outlook configuration choices, see "Customizing Outlook Features and Installation with the Custom Installation Wizard" in Chapter 7, "Deploying Outlook 2003."

Installing Outlook 2003 After Office 2003

Although it is usually simpler to deploy all of Microsoft Office 2003 at once, your organization might benefit from deploying Office and Microsoft Office Outlook 2003 in stages. For example, you might choose to wait to upgrade to Outlook 2003 until after you have installed Office 2003 and have upgraded your messaging server to a new version of Microsoft Exchange Server.

This section of the chapter discusses several options for installing Outlook after Office, and includes specific procedures for doing so.

> **Note**   Installing Outlook after Office is one example of staging the deployment of an Office application; the methods described here can be used to install any Office application after installing the rest of Office. You can also install any Office application before you install the rest of Office. For more information about staging your deployment in this way, see "Installing Outlook 2003 Before Office 2003" earlier in this chapter.

When you install Outlook 2003 over the network by using an administrative installation point, you can use one of the following methods to install Outlook after you install Office:

- Run Office Setup (on the Office 2003 CD) to install Office applications except for Outlook, then use the Custom Maintenance Wizard to install Outlook when you are ready.

   In this case, you use the same administrative installation point for both Office and Outlook.

- Install Office applications by using the Office CD, excluding Outlook. Then install the stand-alone version of Outlook.

   In this case, you can choose to install Outlook from its own administrative installation point or from the same administrative installation point used for the Office files.

There are advantages to each of these approaches. Using a stand-alone version of Outlook to install Outlook separately from Office has the advantage of allowing you to remove the previous version of Outlook (for example, Outlook 2002) at deployment. Since you are installing two separate software packages, you can use the Custom Installation Wizard to create two transforms, one for each deployment. In each transform, you specify to remove earlier versions of the applications you are installing.

By contrast, if you deploy Office and then Outlook from the Office CD, you can use a customized transform with only your Office deployment. When you deploy Outlook by using the Custom Maintenance Wizard, you cannot specify to remove older versions of Outlook. You must use the Office Removal Wizard to remove previous versions of Office applications.

> **Note**   Outlook 2003 cannot coexist with previous versions of Outlook. If you choose to keep previous versions, do not install Outlook 2003.

Installing Outlook after Office using the Office CD

One way to stage your deployment of Outlook 2003 and Office 2003 is to install Office first from an Office 2003 CD and customize your installation to exclude Outlook. Then, later, you change the installation options in the Custom Maintenance Wizard to configure Outlook to be installed as its own package. In this case, you use a single administrative installation point for both installations.

Upgrading from an earlier version of Office

If you are upgrading from an earlier version of Office, there are several issues to consider when you install Office 2003 without Outlook 2003 from the Office 2003 CD. First, if you plan to use the Office Profile Wizard to capture Outlook settings, you must configure these settings and include the Office profile settings file (OPS file) when creating the Custom Installation Wizard transform to deploy Office. The Custom Maintenance Wizard does not allow you to include an OPS file.

Also, when you add Outlook 2003 to your Office 2003 installation by using the Custom Maintenance Wizard, you cannot specify in the wizard to remove earlier versions of Outlook. When you deploy Office 2003 by using the Custom Installation Wizard, you can choose to remove earlier versions of the applications you are installing; however, when you deploy Outlook by using the Custom Maintenance Wizard, you must use the Office Removal Wizard separately to remove the previous version.

Start by using Setup with the **/a** option to copy Office files to your administrative installation point. When prompted for the server location, enter a folder on a network server. For example:

\\server1\software\office

Then follow these steps to stage an installation of Office 2003 and Outlook 2003:

- Use the Custom Installation Wizard to create a transform that is used to install Office but excludes Outlook. You include Office customizations in the transform (and, optionally, customizations for Outlook). You then install Office 2003 using the transform.

- Use the Custom Maintenance Wizard to install Outlook 2003. You can include both Outlook and Office customizations in the second installation.

> **Note**   As part of an initial Outlook customization, you can capture and include settings in an OPS file. To do this, first install Outlook on a test computer and make your changes to the Outlook settings and environment. Then capture the settings with the Office Profile Wizard.

To install Office from the Office 2003 CD while excluding Outlook 2003

1. Start the Custom Installation Wizard and open the Office 2003 package (MSI file).

2. On the **Remove Previous Versions** page, click **Remove the following versions of Microsoft Office applications**.

3. In the table of applications, click on **Microsoft Outlook**, then click the **Details...** button to open a dialog box.

   Clear the check box next to the version of Outlook you want to retain on users' computers, then click **OK**.

4. On the **Set Feature Installation States** page, set the **Microsoft Outlook for Windows** feature to **Not Available, Hidden, Locked**.

5. Set all other Microsoft Office applications in the feature tree (that you want to be installed) to **Run from My Computer**.

6. Configure any other installation options, then complete the transform.

7. To specify this transform for your installation, edit the Office Setup.ini in a standard text editor (such as Notepad) to add an entry for the Office transform in the [MST1] section. For example:

   ```
   [MST1]

   MST1=Office.mst
   ```

   Be sure to remove the comment marker (;) from the [MST] header line so that the transform is read correctly.

8. Instruct users to install Office by running Setup from the administrative installation point.

9. Later, use the Custom Maintenance Wizard to install Outlook and to modify any existing Office installations throughout your organization.

Similar to the Custom Installation Wizard, the Custom Maintenance Wizard reads the Office 2003 package (MSI file) and records your changes in a configuration maintenance file (CMW file). To add Outlook 2003 to your initial Office 2003 installation, you create a CMW file with the appropriate configuration and then run the Custom Maintenance Wizard on users' computers. For more information about using the Custom Maintenance Wizard to update your installation to include Outlook, see "Updating Feature Installation States and Application Settings" in Chapter 18, "Updating Users' Office 2003 Configurations."

On the Resource Kit CD   The Office 2003 Editions Resource Kit includes the Custom Maintenance Wizard, which is installed by default when you run the Office Resource Kit Setup program. For more information, see "Custom Maintenance Wizard" in Appendix A, "Toolbox."

Installing a stand-alone version of Outlook after Office

Another way to install Outlook 2003 after Office 2003 is to use an Office 2003 CD along with a stand-alone version of Outlook. With this option, you can choose to use one administrative installation point for Outlook and Office, or separate installation points.

Choose whether to use one or more administrative installation points

When you deploy the stand-alone version of Outlook, you can create two administrative installation points—one for Office, the other for Outlook—or you can use the same administrative installation point for both packages. Each scenario has its benefits, depending on your deployment needs.

You might choose to use separate installation points, for example, if two different groups in your organization will be installing Office and Outlook, respectively. These administrative installation points can be in different folders on one network server, or they can be on separate servers. Users install Office from one administrative installation point, and then install Outlook later from the second administrative installation point. In this scenario, files that are common among all Office applications are duplicated on each administrative installation point.

Another method for deploying Outlook after Office is to create a single administrative installation point that includes both Outlook and Office. You create the initial administrative installation point by running Setup with the **/a** command-line option from the Office 2003 CD. Then you install the stand-alone version of Outlook into the same folder structure.

This method saves disk space because files that are common among all Office applications are shared on the single administrative installation point. Because Outlook and Office use the same names for Setup files (Setup.exe and Setup.ini), however, you must rename these Setup files to avoid overwriting the unique Outlook and Office versions.

> **Important**   When users set Outlook and another Office application to **Run from Network** from separate administrative installation points, Windows loads two copies of the shared Mso.dll file if both Outlook and another Office application are being used. Mso.dll uses approximately 5 megabytes (MB) of memory each time it is loaded. Having the administrative images in the same location avoids this additional memory requirement.

Exclude Outlook when installing Office from the Office CD

The process for excluding Outlook when installing Office applications from the Office CD includes these steps:

- Copying Office files to an administrative installation point.

- Customizing your Office installation to exclude Outlook.

- Saving your customizations in a transform.

- Installing Office with the custom transform on users' computers.

> **Note**   As part of an initial Office customization, you can capture and include custom settings in an OPS file. To do this, install Office on a test computer, and then make your changes to the Office settings and environment. When you capture your customizations by running the Office Profile Wizard and creating an OPS file, be sure to exclude Outlook settings. Then include the OPS file in the Custom Installation Wizard when you create the transform for installing Office.

To install Office from the Office 2003 CD while excluding Outlook 2003

1. Using an Office 2003 CD, run Setup.exe with the **/a** command-line option.

2. When prompted for the server location, enter a folder on the network server. For example:
   \\server1\software\office

3. If you are using the same administrative installation point that you will use for your Outlook deployment, rename the Setup files (Setup.exe and Setup.ini) to prevent these files from being overwritten when you install Outlook.

Use consistent file names and the appropriate file name extensions; for example, OffSetup.exe and OffSetup.ini. (If you created the administrative image from the Microsoft Select CD subscription, the files have already been renamed for you.)

4. Start the Custom Installation Wizard and open the Office 2003 package (MSI file).

5. On the **Remove Previous Versions** page, click **Remove the following versions of Microsoft Office applications**.

6. In the table of applications, click **Microsoft Outlook**, then click **Details** to open a dialog box.

    Clear the check box next to the version of Outlook you want to retain on users' computers, then click **OK**.

7. On the **Set Feature Installation States** page, set the **Microsoft Outlook for Windows** feature to **Not Available, Hidden, Locked**.

8. Set all other Microsoft Office applications in the feature tree (that you want to be installed) to **Run from My Computer**.

9. Configure any other installation options, then complete the transform.

10. To specify this transform for your installation, edit the Office Setup.ini in a standard text editor (such as Notepad) to add an entry for the Office transform in the [MST1] section. For example:

```
[MST1]

MST1=Office.mst
```

    Be sure to remove the comment marker (;) from the [MST] header line so that the transform is read correctly.

11. Instruct users to install Office by running Setup from the administrative installation point.

Install the stand-alone version of Outlook after installing Office

When you deploy Outlook from a stand-alone version, you can use the same administrative installation point as Office or create a new location for your Outlook files. If you use the same administrative installation point as Office, then you must make sure that the Office Setup files have been renamed so the Outlook Setup files do not overwrite them. Then you customize your Outlook deployment, save the customizations in a transform, and direct users to install Outlook from the Office administrative installation point.

Note As part of an initial Outlook customization, you can capture and include settings in an OPS file. To do this, install Outlook on a test computer, and then make your changes to the Outlook settings and environment. When you capture your customizations by running the Office Profile Wizard and creating an OPS file, be sure to configure only Outlook settings, not other Office settings. Then include the OPS file in the Custom Installation Wizard when you create the transform for installing Outlook.

To install Outlook after Office by using a stand-alone version of Outlook 2003

1. Using the stand-alone version of Outlook 2003, run Setup.exe with the **/a** command-line option.

2. When prompted for the server location, enter a unique folder for Outlook on a network server. For example:

   \\server1\software\outlook

   or

   Enter the same folder that you used for your Office deployment. For example:

   \\server1\software\office

   If you use the same folder as you used for your Office deployment, make sure that the Office Setup files (Setup.exe and Setup.ini) have been renamed before you copy the files for Outlook. For example, you might rename the Office Setup files to OffSetup.exe and OffSetup.ini. Otherwise, the Outlook Setup files will overwrite the existing Office Setup files.

3. Use the Custom Installation Wizard to create a transform in which you specify the appropriate Outlook configuration for your users.

   For example, you can include an OPS file for Outlook (if you created one), specify Outlook settings, and configure user profiles. Save the transform in the same folder as the Setup settings file.

4. If you are using the same administrative installation point that you used for your Office deployment, optionally rename the Outlook Setup files to make it clearer which Setup files belong to which installation.

   To do this, in the root folder of the administrative installation point, rename Setup.exe and Setup.ini. Use consistent file names and the appropriate file name extensions; for example, OlkSetup.exe and OlkSetup.ini. (If you created the administrative image from the Microsoft Select CD subscription, files have already been renamed for you.)

5. Edit the Outlook Setup settings file (INI file) to specify the transform that you created.

   For example, you might add the following line under the [MST] section:

```
MST1=Outlook.mst
```

   You must remove the comment marker (;) from the [MST] header line so that the transform is read correctly.

6. Direct users to install Outlook from the administrative installation point using the Outlook Setup.exe file.

Resources and related information

There are a number of considerations when choosing the timing of your Outlook deployment. For more information about the advantages and disadvantages of staging an Outlook installation, see "Determining When to Install Outlook" in Chapter 6, "Planning an Outlook 2003 Deployment."

The Customization Installation Wizard provides a straightforward way to configure and install Outlook 2003. For more information about Outlook configuration choices, see "Customizing Outlook Features and Installation with the Custom Installation Wizard" in Chapter 7, "Deploying Outlook 2003."

You can use the Office Removal Wizard to remove applications after completing your initial Office installation. For more information about using the Removal Wizard, see "Customizing Removal Behavior" in Chapter 4, "Customizing Office 2003."

Configuring Outlook 2003 for RPC over HTTP

You can configure user accounts in Microsoft Office Outlook 2003 to connect to Microsoft Exchange Server 2003 over the Internet without the need to use virtual private network (VPN) connections. This feature—connecting to an Exchange account by using Remote Procedure Call (RPC) over HTTP—allows Outlook users to access their Exchange Server accounts from the Internet when they are traveling or are working outside their organization's firewall.

This section of the chapter describes the requirements and options for configuring Outlook 2003 to use RPC over HTTP, including steps for customizing options for this feature in the Custom Installation Wizard.

On the Resource Kit CD The Office 2003 Editions Resource Kit core tool set includes the Custom Installation Wizard, which you use to customize Office application deployments. These tools are installed by default when you run the Office Resource Kit Setup program. For more information, see Appendix A, "Toolbox."

There are several requirements for this feature. These include:

- Microsoft Windows XP with Service Pack 1 and the Q331320 hotfix (or later) installed on users' computers

- Outlook 2003

- Microsoft Exchange Server 2003 e-mail accounts

- Microsoft Windows Server™ 2003 (required for server components only)

> **Note**   It is highly recommended that this feature be used with Outlook user profiles configured to use Cached Exchange Mode.

About RPC over HTTP

In a local area network (LAN), Outlook communicates with Exchange servers using direct network (TCP/IP) access, also known as RPC over TCP/IP. This method provides quick, efficient access to a corporate network.

However, remote users accessing Exchange need a VPN connection, which gets them past the corporate firewall onto the corporate network. A VPN is more complex and enables access to more network services than are required for just e-mail access.

Outlook 2003 now offers a better alternative to VPN connections—RPC over HTTP. With this feature, users can have security-enhanced access to their Exchange Server accounts from the Internet when they are working outside your organization's firewall. Users do not need any special connections or hardware, such as smart cards and security tokens, and they can still get to their Exchange accounts even if the Exchange server and client computer behind the firewall are on different networks.

RPC over HTTP works by having an Exchange Server front-end computer configured as an RPC proxy server. This RPC proxy server then specifies which ports to use to communicate with the network's domain controller, global catalog (GC) servers, and all Exchange servers that the client user requires. The Exchange group in your organization must first deploy RPC over HTTP for the Exchange servers you use, and then you can configure user accounts that access those Exchange servers to use RPC over HTTP.

Understanding RPC over HTTP configuration settings

Before you configure RPC over HTTP for Outlook, you need the URL for the Exchange proxy server that is configured for RPC over HTTP. This URL should be available from your organization's Exchange administrator.

There are additional settings for RPC over HTTP in the Custom Installation Wizard. However, Outlook uses default values for these options that are likely to provide a good experience for your users and to help provide secure connections to your network. It is recommended that you not change the default options by configuring these settings. However, if necessary, you can change these settings to fit special circumstances in your organization.

Overriding the default connection type choice behavior

By default on a fast network, Outlook attempts to connect by using the LAN connection first. On a slow network, Outlook attempts to connect by using HTTP first. You can override default behavior in either case by changing the following settings:

On a fast network, connect using HTTP first, then by using the TCP/IP   To change the default behavior for fast networks, select this check box.

On a slow network, connect using HTTP first, then by using the TCP/IP   To change the default behavior for slow networks, clear this check box.

> Note   By default, these options are disabled in the Outlook user interface.

Specifying authentication and connection methods

The default authentication method is **Password Authentication (NTLM)**. If you use **Basic Password Authentication**, you will be prompted for a password each time a connection is made to the Exchange server. In addition, if you are not using Secure Sockets Layer (SSL), the password is sent in clear text, which can pose a security risk.

For increased security, it is recommended that you specify **Password Authentication (NTLM)**, together with **Connect with SSL only** and **Mutually authenticate the session when connecting with SSL**. These are the default settings in the Custom Installation Wizard where you configure RPC over HTTP. You can also ensure that these settings in the user interface are disabled (which is the default) to help prevent users from using less secure choices for RPC over HTTP communications.

> Note   If users in your organization need to configure RPC over HTTP settings in the user interface, you can configure a policy to allow them to do so. In Group Policy, under **User Configuration\Administrative Templates\Microsoft Office Outlook 2003\Tools | E-Mail Accounts**, double-click **Exchange over the Internet User Interface**. Click **Enabled** to enable configuring the policy, then click **Check to enable UI**.

Configuring RPC over HTTP to deploy with Outlook 2003

To configure Outlook 2003 with RPC over HTTP as part of your Outlook 2003 deployment, you enable the option in the Custom Installation Wizard and (optionally) specify additional settings—such as security level requirements for the communication with the Exchange server. After you specify these options, you save the settings with other configurations in the transform you use to deploy Outlook 2003 to your users.

> **Note**   It is recommended that the user accounts that you are configuring for RPC over HTTP use Cached Exchange Mode. For more information about defining Outlook profiles with Cached Exchange Mode, see "Setting Up Outlook 2003 Cached Exchange Mode Accounts" in Chapter 7, "Deploying Outlook 2003."

To configure RPC over HTTP

1. In the Custom Installation Wizard, on the **Specify Exchange Settings** page, select **Configure settings for a new Exchange Server connection or replace the settings in an existing Exchange Server connection**.

2. If you are defining a new Exchange server for users, enter a value or replaceable parameter in **User name**.

    For instance, you might specify **=%UserName%** to use the exact logon name for each user. This helps prevent user prompts when Outlook starts asking users to choose between several variations.

3. If you are defining a new Exchange server, for **Exchange Server**, enter the name of the Exchange server.

    You can skip steps 2 and 3 if you are configuring RPC over HTTP for existing Exchange users who are not moving to a new Exchange server.

4. Click **More Settings**.

5. Select the **Connect to Exchange Mailbox using HTTP** check box.

6. Type the server name for the RPC over HTTP proxy server.

    Do not enter http:// or https:// as part of the name. The appropriate entry (http:// or https://) will be included automatically in the box after you enter the name, based on the authentication settings you choose.

7. Choose whether or not to reverse default behavior for how Outlook chooses which connection type to try to use first, LAN or RPC over HTTP.

8. Select an authentication method.

    The default method is **Password Authentication (NTLM)**.

9. Click **OK** to return to the **Specify Exchange Settings** page.

10. Complete any other Outlook or Office configurations, then click **Finish** to create the transform that you can deploy to your users.

Configuring RPC over HTTP user interface options

You can configure your Outlook deployment to enable all RPC over HTTP options or disable all RPC over HTTP options. You deploy a registry key to configure these options (for example, by using the **Add/Remove Registry Entries** page in the Custom Installation Wizard). To enforce the setting, deploy the registry key in the **Policies** hive (as shown below).

By default, the RPC over HTTP options are enabled, if the user's computer has the required operating system version.

You add the value entry in the following subkey:

HKEY_CURRENT_USER\Software\Policies\Microsoft\Office\11.0\Outlook\RPC

Value name: **EnableRPCTunnelingUI**

Value data: **DWORD**

Set the value to **1** to enable RPC over HTTP user interface options. Set the value to **0** to disable the options.

Note that even if you enforce enabling the RPC over HTTP user interface options, the options will be dimmed if the user's computer does not have the required operating system version.

Deploying RPC over HTTP after deploying Outlook 2003

You can update an Outlook 2003 installation to configure RPC over HTTP or make changes to an existing RPC over HTTP installation by using the Custom Maintenance Wizard. The settings available for configuring RPC over HTTP in the Custom Maintenance Wizard are the same as those provided in the Custom Installation Wizard.

After you run the Custom Maintenance Wizard and configure the changes you want to make to your Outlook installation, you save the maintenance file and deploy it to your users.

Resources and related information

You have considerable flexibility in configuring and deploying Outlook 2003. For more information about using the Custom Installation Wizard to create a custom transform for deploying Outlook 2003, see "Customizing Outlook Features and Installation with the Custom Installation Wizard" in Chapter 7, "Deploying Outlook 2003."

You can make changes to existing Outlook deployments by using the Custom Maintenance Wizard. For more information, see "Updating Outlook 2003 by Using the Custom Maintenance Wizard" in Chapter 10, "Maintaining Outlook 2003."

Deploying Project 2003 with Outlook 2003

The Microsoft Project 2003 Outlook Integration add-in works with Microsoft Project Server 2003 to make it easier for users to use Microsoft Outlook 2003 to keep track of Microsoft Project Web Access 2003 tasks that have been assigned to them, and to update Project Server data with the time worked on a task without having to duplicate information in two applications.

The Outlook Integration add-in is included with Project Server. You can deploy this add-in to users with or after a deployment of Outlook 2003. How you deploy the add-in depends on your organization's deployment practices and whether Outlook 2003 is already installed.

> **Note**   The Microsoft Office Project 2003 Outlook Integration add-in can be used with Microsoft Outlook 2000 or later. The procedures in this section of the chapter, however, focus on deploying the add-in with Outlook 2003 or Microsoft Office 2003.

You follow these steps if you are deploying the add-in with an installation of Outlook:

- Install Outlook on an administrative installation point.

    For more information on creating an administrative installation point, see "Creating an Administrative Installation Point" in Chapter 3, "Preparing to Deploy Office 2003."

- In a transform (MST file) to be used with your Outlook deployment, include the registry keys for the required add-in information.

- Chain the add-in with an Outlook 2003 installation by using a modified Outlook Setup.ini file together with the customized Outlook transform.

The same process used to deploy the add-in with Outlook can be used to deploy the add-in with Office, except you use the Office package when creating an administrative installation point and transform, and the Office Setup.ini file when specifying the add-in to chain.

To update an existing Outlook installation to include the Outlook Integration add-in, you distribute the add-in installation file (Mpsaddin.exe) separately to run on users' computers, along with a configuration maintenance file (CMW file) that includes the required Project Server registry keys. The CMW file is created by using the Custom Maintenance Wizard.

> **Note**   As with a standard Office installation, you must have administrative rights to the computer or run Office or Outlook Setup with elevated privileges to install the Outlook Integration add-in. For more information about installing with elevated privileges, see "Installing Office with Elevated Privileges" in Chapter 5, "Installing Office 2003."

This section of the chapter describes how the Outlook Integration add-in works with Project Server 2003, and provides step-by-step deployment procedures for installing the Outlook Integration add-in by using the Custom Installation Wizard or the Custom Maintenance Wizard.

Features of the Outlook Integration add-in

The Outlook Integration add-in helps team members create and update tasks for their projects without needing to update information in both Outlook and Project Web Access. Thus, the add-in reduces the effort required to track information in two places. Users can view and update project tasks in Outlook, integrating deadlines and task descriptions with the calendaring functions in Outlook.

The Outlook Integration feature can also simplify task tracking for project managers, team leads, or team members—anyone who uses Project Web Access to monitor assignments and to enter time worked on a task in a timesheet as assignments are completed. By using the Outlook Integration feature, tasks in Project Web Access can be tracked in Outlook or—with more limited functionality—by using Outlook Web Access (OWA). Users can import new and updated tasks from Project Server manually or automatically according to a schedule that they define. Users can also send updates to Project Server, including the actual time that they worked on a task.

Users of Project Server 2003—including administrators, executives, resource managers, project managers, and team members—should still use Project Web Access and Microsoft Office Project Professional 2003 for planning projects and reviewing the time that team members report for their assignments. By placing project assignments inside a commonly used application, the Outlook Integration add-in complements the project management capabilities of Project Server by making tracking assignments more visible within an organization.

Requirements for the Outlook Integration add-in

There are a few requirements and issues you should know about before deploying the add-in to your users:

- Users must have a valid user account in Project Web Access.
- Users must use Outlook 2000 or later with the add-in.

- Installing the Outlook Integration add-in requires installing a Microsoft COM add-in, which enables users to view Project Server tasks in their Outlook calendars.

Deploying Outlook with the Outlook Integration add-in

To deploy the Outlook Integration add-in together with Outlook 2003 requires two configuration steps:

- Using the Custom Installation Wizard to configure an Outlook transform that includes the registry keys that contain required Project Server information.

- Chaining the add-in to your Outlook installation by customizing the Outlook Setup.ini file to include the add-in MSI package.

> **Note**   The same process used to deploy the add-in with Outlook can be used to deploy the add-in with Office, except you use the Office package when creating an administrative installation point and transform, and the Office Setup.ini file when specifying the add-in to chain.

When you customize a transform to include the registry keys required for the Outlook Integration add-in, you can also configure other Outlook settings for your deployment, such as adding user accounts or specifying Exchange server options. The following procedure simply describes how to configure the Project Server registry keys in the transform.

> **Note**   For more information about customizing your Outlook deployment, see "Customizing Outlook Features and Installation with the Custom Installation Wizard" in Chapter 7, "Deploying Outlook 2003."

To create an Outlook transform with the required Outlook Integration registry keys

1. Start the Custom Installation Wizard.

2. On the **Open MSI File** page, enter (or browse to) the path and file name of your Outlook MSI file. For example:
   \\server1\share\office\Outl11.msi

3. On the **Select the MST File to Save** page, enter the name of the Outlook MST file you are creating. For example:

   \\server1\share\office\OutlookWithProj.mst

4. On the Add/Remove Registry Entries page, click Add.

5. On the **Add/Modify Registry Entry** dialog, specify the Project Server URL by entering the following values:

   Root: **HKEY_CURRENT_USER**
   Data type: **REG_SZ**
   Key: **Software\Microsoft\Office\Outlook\Addins\ProjectServer**
   Value name: **ServerURL**

   For **Value data**, type the URL for the Project Server. For example, http://mycompany/projectserver/

6. Click **OK**.

7. On the Add/Remove Registry Entries page, click Add.

8. On the **Add/Modify Registry Entry** dialog, specify whether to use Microsoft Windows authentication or Project Server authentication for communicating with Project Server by selecting or entering the following values:

   Root: **HKEY_CURRENT_USER**
   Data type: **REG_DWORD**
   Key: **Software\Microsoft\Office\Outlook\Addins\ProjectServer**
   Value name: **UseWindowsUserAccount**

   For **Value data**, enter **1** to use the Windows user account or **0** to use a Project Server account.

   Note: If you do not specify Windows authentication and you have not specified a Project Server account in a registry key on each user's computer, users will be prompted to login to Project Server when Project Server data is first required when using the add-in. The registry key for Project Server accounts is described later in this chapter.

9. Click **OK**.

10. When you have completed all of your customizations, click **Finish** to save the transform.

Before you can chain the Outlook Integration add-in MSI file to your Office installation, you must extract the MSI file from the Outlook Integration add-in package (Mpsaddin.exe).

To extract the Outlook Integration add-in MSI file

1. Locate the Outlook Integration add-in package file (Mpsaddin.exe) on your Project Server CD. For example, the file may be included in the Project Server cabinet file: \\Prjsvr\Prjsvr1.cab.

If you need to extract the file from a cabinet file, double-click the file to extract the files it contains.

2. Locate the Outlook Integration add-in package. The exact file name depends on the language version of Project Server on the CD. For example, the add-in package file for English Project Server is Mpsaddin.exe_1033.

3. To extract the MSI file from the add-in package, use a program such as WinZip. For example, in WinZip, enter the file name of the package and choose to extract the files. The add-in MSI file is Prjoutlook.msi.

After configuring the Outlook transform to include the required Project Server registry key values, you chain the Outlook Integration add-in to your Outlook installation.

> **Note**   For detailed information about chaining packages with Office applications, see "Deploying Office and Other Products Together" in Chapter 5, "Installing Office 2003."

Chain an Outlook deployment to include the Outlook Integration add-in

1. Open the Outlook Setup settings file (Setup.ini) in a text editor such as Notepad.

2. Create a section called [ChainedInstall_1], and in this section, specify the name and path of the Outlook Integration add-in. For example:
   PATH=\\server\share\office Prjoutlook.msi

3. Specify the task type for this section:
   TASKTYPE=msi

4. Specify a unique display setting to apply to the add-in installation by setting the **Display** property.
   For example, you can ensure that the add-in installs quietly with the following setting:
   DISPLAY=None

The completed section in the Setup.ini file looks like this:

```
[ChainedInstall_1]
PATH=\\server\share\office\Prjoutlook.msi
TASKTYPE=msi
DISPLAY=None
```

If you use Project Server user accounts for authentication instead of Windows authentication for Project Server access, you can specify the Project Server user account in a registry key on individual users' computers. If you do not use Windows authentication and this registry key is blank, users will be prompted to login to Project Server the first time Project Server data is required by the add-in.

To set a registry key for a Project Server user name

1. Click **Start** in Windows XP or **Start Programs** in Windows 2000, then click **Run**.

2. Type **Regedit**, then press enter.

3. In the **HKEY_CURRENT_USER** tree, enter the following registry information;
    Data type: **REG_SZ**
    Key: **Software\Microsoft\Office\Outlook\Addins\ProjectServer**
    Value name: **ProjectServerUserName**
    For **Value data**, type the user's Project Server account.

Distributing the Outlook Integration add-in with Outlook 2003

You can deploy your customized version of Outlook 2003 that includes the Outlook Integration add-in to your users by using one of several methods. For example, you can have users run a command line from the administrative installation point or you can create a custom CD and provide it to your users.

As an example, suppose you choose to have users install Outlook 2003 with the Outlook Integration add-in from the administrative installation point. One option in this scenario is to create a batch file that runs Setup.exe with your command-line options. A second option is to create a Windows shortcut and add options to the command-line box. Users double-click the batch file or shortcut to run the Setup command line that you have defined. You can distribute the batch file or shortcut to users in an e-mail message or by other means used in your organization.

For instance, if your Outlook transform was named OutlookwithProject.mst, then the Setup.exe command line you include might look like this:

```
Setup.exe /qb TRANSFORMS=\\server\share\OfficeAdmin\OutlookWithProject.mst
```

The **/qb** option specifies a quiet installation (no user interaction).

Update an Outlook installation to include the Outlook Integration add-in

If you have already deployed Outlook 2003, you can deploy the Outlook Integration add-in in two steps:

-   Use the Custom Maintenance Wizard to configure the registry keys that specify the Project Server server name and Project Server client account, just as you did in the Custom Installation Wizard, then save the configuration in a CMW file.

-   Distribute the maintenance file and the Outlook Integration add-in file (for example, Mpsaddin.exe_1033) to your users as described below. You may choose to rename the file to Mpsaddin.exe so users can double-click the file to run the program.

Configuring the Project Server name and user account registry keys

Before users can work with the Outlook Integration add-in, they must login through the user interface or registry keys must be configured on their computers that specify the location of the Project Server and Project client user account information. You can define the registry keys by using the Custom Maintenance Wizard and update the registry at the same time that you deploy the Outlook Integration add-in.

To include required registry key information in a configuration maintenance file

1. In the Custom Maintenance Wizard, follow the steps to specify your Office or Outlook MSI file.

2. On the **Add/Remove Registry Entries** page, enter the Outlook Integration add-in registry keys along with the appropriate values for your organization's Project Server.

    The registry keys and values are listed earlier in this chapter in the procedure entitled "To create an Outlook transform with the required Outlook Integration registry keys."

3. Make any other customizations for your overall Office or Outlook deployment, then click **Finish** to save the CMW file.

Distributing the configuration maintenance file and add-in to users

You can deploy the Outlook Integration Setup program (for example, Mpsaddin.exe) to your users in several ways. For example, you can have users run a command line from the administrative installation point, or you can create a custom CD and provide it to your users. Because Mpsaddin.exe is a Windows Installer program (as is Office Setup.exe), you can use similar scenarios for distributing the Outlook Integration Setup program.

Next, deploy the CMW file to your users with a specific command line. One option in this scenario is to create a batch file that runs Mpsaddin.exe with your command-line options. A second option is to create a Windows shortcut and add options to the command-line box. Users double-click the batch file or shortcut to run the Setup command line that you have defined. You can distribute the batch file or shortcut to users in an e-mail message or by other means used by your organization.

Use the following syntax for your command line:

```
Maintwiz.exe /c Mycmwfile.cmw /q
```

The **/c** option specifies the configuration maintenance file to be applied to users' computers. The **/q** option prevents dialogs from being presented to the users during the update.

For simplicity, you might also include the Setup command line to install the Outlook Integration add-in in the same batch file. For instance, the Outlook Integration Setup command line might look like this:

```
Mpsaddin.exe /qn
```

The **/qn** option specifies a quiet installation (no user interaction).

Resources and related information

The Custom Installation Wizard offers a wide range of configuration options for defining and modifying user profiles. For more information about your options for configuring Outlook 2003, see "Customizing Outlook Features and Installation with the Custom Installation Wizard" in Chapter 7, "Deploying Outlook 2003."

Deploying Outlook 2003 by Using Microsoft Technologies for Software Distribution

You can use Microsoft technologies for software distribution—such as Microsoft Systems Management Server (SMS) or Group Policy software installation—to deploy Microsoft Office Outlook 2003. These technologies can be used with Microsoft Office deployment tools, or separately. If your organization uses these tools for deploying other applications, you may want to use them when deploying Outlook.

SMS is designed to be used by large organizations that manage a large number of client computers in an environment that changes quickly. Group Policy software installation, in contrast, is appropriate for smaller organizations that are more stable and require fewer changes to software configurations.

In order to use Group Policy, you must have already deployed the Active Directory directory service. In contrast, SMS can deploy software to a mixture of Microsoft Windows client computers. In addition, customized SMS packages may be available for certain Outlook features or add-ins that can help you easily deploy those items.

Resources and related information

For more information about deploying Office applications with SMS, see "Using Microsoft Systems Management Server to Deploy Office" in Chapter 5, "Installing Office 2003."

For more information about deploying Office applications with Group Policy, see "Using Group Policy to Deploy Office" in Chapter 5, "Installing Office 2003."

Chapter 9

Upgrading to Outlook 2003

Microsoft® Office Outlook® 2003 users can exchange e-mail messages and scheduling data with users of previous versions of Microsoft e-mail and calendar applications, as well as interact with users of other applications. However, previous versions of Outlook or other applications do not support all Outlook 2003 features. As you plan your upgrading strategy, consider when and how you will take advantage of new features—and also consider the differences between Microsoft Office 2003 and earlier versions of Office applications.

Planning an Upgrade to Outlook 2003

Because Microsoft Office Outlook 2003 is compatible with earlier versions of Outlook, upgrading to a new version of Outlook typically involves no more than preparing for, and distributing, the client. If you are upgrading from other Microsoft e-mail and scheduling clients, the process is simplified with the use of the import feature in Outlook.

Note   If you are upgrading from earlier Microsoft mail and calendaring programs, you can no longer import MS Mail files to Outlook 2003 and you cannot share information between Outlook 2003 and Schedule+.

To prepare for an upgrade, you must decide on the following issues:

- Which cryptographic and security settings you want for your users.

  For more information, see Chapter 11, "Administering Cryptography in Outlook 2003" and Chapter 12, "Customizing Outlook 2003 to Help Prevent Viruses."

- Which e-mail editor to use for composing Outlook e-mail messages.

- If you use Microsoft Exchange 5.5 as your messaging server, whether to upgrade to Exchange 2000 or a later version before deploying Outlook 2003.

  For more information, see "Microsoft Exchange Server Support for Outlook 2003" in Chapter 6, "Planning an Outlook 2003 Deployment."

- Whether to upgrade all users in your organization at once or in stages. If you plan to upgrade in stages, keep in mind that Outlook users might need to exchange e-mail messages and scheduling data with users of other Microsoft e-mail and calendar applications, which can complicate support issues.

- If you plan to install Microsoft Office 2003, whether to upgrade to Outlook 2003 with or after an Office 2003 deployment. If users upgrade to Outlook 2003 before upgrading to other Office applications, they will not be able to use Microsoft WordMail as their e-mail editor. The version of Microsoft Word must match the version of Outlook in order for WordMail to be available as the editor in Outlook.

  For more information about choices in staging your Outlook deployment—by upgrading groups of users in stages, or by separating the Outlook 2003 installation from the Office 2003 installation—see "Determining When to Install Outlook" in Chapter 6, "Planning an Outlook 2003Deployment."

- Whether to make changes to Outlook user profiles as part of your upgrade; for example, defining a new Exchange server or enabling new features of Outlook such as Cached Exchange Mode.

  For more information, see Chapter 7, "Deploying Outlook 2003."

- Whether your organization currently uses fax features or Outlook forms provided in an earlier version of Outlook.

  For more information, see "Upgrading to Outlook 2003 from Previous Versions" later in this chapter.

- How to manage creating and storing a backup of your existing installation. Before upgrading to any new release, it is wise to back up your existing data in case data is lost during the upgrade process.

Upgrading from an earlier version of Outlook

You can install Outlook 2003 over a Microsoft Outlook 97, Outlook 98, Outlook 2000, or Outlook 2002 installation. Like other Office 2003 applications, Outlook 2003 migrates user settings stored in the registry. In addition, if a MAPI profile already exists on a user's computer, your Outlook 2003 deployment can typically be configured to continue to use the profile. However, if you are upgrading from an Internet-only installation of Outlook 2000 or earlier, you may need to take additional steps, including recreating user profiles.

> **Note**   Outlook 2003 cannot coexist with previous versions of Outlook. If you choose to keep previous versions, do not install Outlook 2003.

Upgrading from other mail and scheduling programs

You can upgrade to Outlook 2003 from mail and scheduling programs other than earlier versions of Outlook. The table below lists migration paths supported by Outlook 2003.

Software program	Version	Comment
Schedule+	7.x, SC2	
Microsoft Exchange Client		
Outlook Express	4.x, 5.x, 6.x	
MSN® Explorer	8	New in Outlook 2003
Eudora Pro, Eudora Light	2.x, 3.x, 4.x, 5.x	New in Outlook 2003 (Eudora 5.x)

Resources and related information

The Office Custom Installation Wizard provides a straightforward way to configure and install Outlook 2003. For more information about Outlook configuration choices, see "Customizing Outlook Features and Installation with the Custom Installation Wizards" in Chapter 7, "Deploying Outlook 2003."

You can learn more about the steps for upgrading from Internet-only installations of Outlook by reviewing "Upgrading to Outlook 2003 from Previous Versions" in the next section.

You can deploy Outlook separately from the rest of Office 2003. For more information, see "Determining When to Install Outlook" in Chapter 6, "Planning an Outlook 2003 Deployment."

Upgrading to Outlook 2003 from Previous Versions

When you upgrade to Microsoft Office Outlook 2003 from an earlier version of Outlook, you must make choices about configuring Outlook user profiles, and you must be aware of fax and forms changes.

Configuring user profiles in Outlook 2003

You can configure a variety of Outlook 2003 e-mail services by using the Custom Installation Wizard to define Outlook user profiles, then saving your customizations in a transform (MST file). For example, you can define Microsoft Exchange Server connections, add POP3 accounts, or specify other e-mail support.

When you create a transform for Outlook, you have several choices for keeping, creating, or modifying user profiles. For example, you can choose to create new default profiles for new Outlook users and keep existing profiles for current Outlook users.

If you choose to modify Outlook user profiles during an upgrade, you can also configure a number of user options and other features for your users, including configuring Cached Exchange Mode, setting options to help users avoid junk e-mail messages, and defining Send/Receive groups and settings.

Upgrading with Cached Exchange Mode enabled

Cached Exchange Mode is a new feature in Outlook 2003 that can help to provide an improved experience for users who work offline or for times when a connection to the Microsoft Exchange server is slow or unavailable. Cached Exchange Mode works by downloading copies of users' Exchange mailboxes to a local file (the user's OST file). If you have users who have large Exchange mailboxes and have OST files already configured for Outlook, be aware that you may need to take special steps to help avoid errors when those users upgrade to Outlook 2003 with Cached Exchange Mode enabled.

When Cached Exchange Mode is deployed or enabled for users without an existing OST file, Outlook creates a new OST file. The new Outlook 2003 OST files are Unicode® (by default) and do not have a 2 gigabyte (GB) storage limit, unlike Outlook files created with Outlook 2002 or earlier. This means that large Exchange mailboxes can typically be successfully downloaded into an Outlook 2003 OST file.

However, when Outlook—in Cached Exchange Mode—attempts to synchronize Exchange mailboxes for users with existing OST files from earlier versions of Outlook, the attempt to update the OST may fail. To learn more about helping to prevent this problem, see "Setting Up Outlook 2003 Cached Exchange Mode Accounts" in Chapter 7, "Deploying Outlook 2003."

Upgrading from an Outlook 2000 IMO installation

When you upgrade to Outlook 2003 from an Internet Mail Only (IMO) installation of an earlier version of Outlook, you may need to recreate Outlook profiles for your users in some cases. Users may also encounter the following issues; a workaround is provided, if available.

Address book may need to be imported manually

After you upgrade from Outlook 2000 IMO to Outlook 2003, members of Windows Address Book distribution lists from your Outlook 2000 Address Book might be absent from Outlook 2003.

To work around this behavior, manually import the Windows Address Book data.

To manually import Windows Address Book data

1. On the **File** menu in Outlook 2003, click **Import and Export**.

2. Click **Import Internet Mail and Addresses**, and then click **Next**.

3. Click **Outlook Express 4.x, 5.x, 6.x**, and then click **Next**.

4. Choose how you wish to handle entries that would duplicate any current Outlook contacts, and then click **Finish**.

Rules might not work properly

After you upgrade to Outlook 2003 from Outlook 2000 IMO with multiple POP accounts, rules that are based on the **through the specified account** option might not work.

To work around this problem, recreate the rules in Outlook 2003.

To create a rule for POP accounts in Outlook 2003

1. On the **Tools** menu in Outlook 2003, click **Rules and Alerts**.

2. Click **New Rule**.

3. Click **Start from a blank rule**, and then click **Next**.

4. Under **Which condition(s) do you want to check?**, select the **through the specified account** check box, and then click the underlined value to enter the specified POP account.

5. Click **Next**.

6. Under **What do you want to do with the message?**, click **Move it to the specified folder**, and then click the underlined value to enter the specified folder.

7. Click **Next**.

8. Click **Next**.

9. Click **Finish**.

Error for unsupported fax software may not appear

When you upgrade from Microsoft Outlook 2000 in IMO mode with the Symantec Winfax Starter Edition installed and configured to Outlook 2003, the following error message should appear but might not:

"Setup has detected that you have one or more of the following features installed:

–cc:Mail

–Microsoft Mail

–Net Folders

–Microsoft Fax

–WinFax Starter Edition (SE)

These features are no longer supported in Outlook. If you continue the upgrade, you will no longer be able to use them. Would you like to continue the upgrade to Outlook?"

This error message should appear and Symantec Winfax Starter Edition should be included as one of the features that is no longer supported.

Choosing a default e-mail editor in Outlook 2003

If you are upgrading to Outlook 2003 before upgrading to Microsoft Office Word 2003, your users will not be able to use WordMail as their Outlook e-mail editor. Because WordMail is the default e-mail editor in Outlook 2003, you will need to specify the standard Outlook editor as the default when you customize your deployment. On the **Outlook: Customize Default Settings** page of the Custom Installation Wizard, under **Customize Outlook e-mail defaults**, choose **Outlook** in the **Default e-mail editor** drop-down list.

Choosing fax support in Outlook 2003

Integrated fax support is not provided in Outlook 2003. However, you can use third-party MAPI fax providers or Microsoft Windows® fax support.

WinFax—an earlier faxing program that was integrated with Outlook—is uninstalled by Outlook 2003. If the viewer is currently on a user's computer, it is uninstalled as part of the upgrade process.

Supporting forms in Outlook 2003

If you have custom solutions that depend on Electronic Forms Designer, note that Electronic Forms Designer is no longer supported in Outlook 2003.

Resources and related information

The Office Custom Installation Wizard provides a straightforward way to configure and install Outlook 2003. For more information about Outlook configuration choices, see "Customizing Outlook Features and Installation with the Custom Installation Wizard" in Chapter 7, "Deploying Outlook 2003."

Upgrading from Microsoft Exchange Client

Microsoft Office Outlook 2003 provides a straightforward upgrade path from Microsoft Exchange Client. By upgrading to Outlook, you can help to provide improved features and better integration with other Microsoft Office applications for your users.

Because both Outlook 2003 and Microsoft Exchange Client are MAPI-compatible applications, Outlook can completely replace Exchange Client. Outlook 2003 uses the same profile and other configuration information, and Outlook 2003 should be able to use all Exchange Client extensions and custom forms. Because of this compatibility, Outlook users should be able to exchange e-mail messages and share public folders with Exchange Client users. Some known exceptions are described below.

Unless you specify a particular profile when Outlook starts up for the first time, Outlook will choose the default e-mail profile to open your Personal Address Book (PAB) and personal folders. Outlook connects to the Exchange server and any other services that you specify in that profile.

Whether the profile is configured to deliver e-mail messages to the Inbox on the Exchange Server or to the Inbox in personal folders, Outlook 2003 continues to accept new e-mail messages in the same Inbox folder. After you install Outlook, you work with the same Inbox, Outbox, Sent Items, Deleted Items, and any other personal folders used by the Microsoft Exchange Client profile.

Outlook 2003 starts with the same profile configuration as Exchange Client, except that a new information service is added to the Outlook 2003 default profile. This allows Outlook and any other MAPI applications to use the Outlook Contacts folder as an e-mail address book. Outlook 2003 can also do the following:

- Recognize any folder views you define.

- Maintain the read or unread message status.

Note   The Microsoft Office Resource Kit for Office 97/98 provides additional upgrading and file-sharing information for Microsoft Exchange Client, including information about Exchange Client folders and views, client forms, and extensions. For more information, see the Microsoft Office 97/98 Resource Kit Web site at *http://www.microsoft.com/office/ork/home.htm*.

Resources and related information

You have a wide range of options for customizing Outlook 2003 installation for your users. For more information about Outlook customization features, see "Customizing Outlook Features and Installation with the Custom Installation Wizard" in Chapter 7, "Deploying Outlook 2003."

You can install Outlook 2003 separately from the rest of Office 2003. For more information, see "Determining When to Install Outlook" in Chapter 6, "Planning an Outlook 2003 Deployment."

Upgrading from Schedule+

Upgrading to Microsoft Office Outlook 2003 from Schedule+ provides enhanced functionality for users. Outlook 2003 includes all the features of Microsoft Schedule+ 7.x and Microsoft Schedule+ 1.0, including appointments, events, contacts, tasks, and additional features that are not available in Schedule+. These additional features include:

- Integrated e-mail messaging functions with journal and note items

- Additional views for calendar, contact, and task information, including side-by-side calendars and color options

- Integration with Microsoft Windows SharePoint™ Services (read-only access from Outlook)

- Advanced custom view and saved search folder capabilities

- Task delegation

Note   You cannot exchange free/busy information between Outlook and Schedule+ users.

Importing a Schedule+ data file

To upgrade to Outlook 2003 from Schedule+, install Outlook 2003, and then import the Schedule+ data file. (Schedule+ is not removed from your computer.)

> **Note**   Outlook uses the Schedule 7.x application to import the Schedule+ 1.0 CAL file. If Schedule+ 7.x is not installed on your computer, Outlook does not give you the option to import a Schedule+ 1.0 CAL file.

To import a Schedule+ 7.x SCD file or a Schedule+ 1.0 CAL file

1. On the Outlook **File** menu, click **Import and Export**.

2. In the **Choose an action to perform** list, click **Import from another program or file**, then click **Next**.

3. In the **Select file type to import from** list, click **Schedule+ 7.x** or **Schedule+ 1.0**, then click **Next**.

4. In the **File to import** box, enter the SCD or CAL file name, or click **Browse** to find the file.

   This dialog box also includes several options for dealing with entries in the data file that duplicate entries you already have in your Outlook Calendar, Contacts, or Tasks folders.

5. To replace duplicate entries in your Outlook folder with Schedule+ entries, click **Replace duplicates with items imported.**

   or

   To allow duplicate entries to be imported, click **Allow duplicates to be created.**

   or

   To avoid importing duplicate entries, click **Do not import duplicate items.**

6. If requested, enter the password for the schedule file.

7. In **The following actions will be performed** box, select the items you want to import and their destination folders.

   To change the destination folder for an item type, click **Change Destination**. To alter the way Schedule+ fields are imported into Outlook, click **Map Custom Fields**.

By default, Outlook imports Schedule+ information into the following Outlook folders:

- Appointments and events are imported into the Calendar folder.

- Contact data is imported into the Contacts folder.

- Task data is imported into the Tasks folder.

The Schedule+ data file is not modified or deleted during the import process. You can import schedule files at any time after Outlook is installed using the **Import and Export** command (**File** menu).

Note   The Covey Seven Habits tool in Schedule+ 7.x is not included in Outlook. Furthermore, because its object model is different, Outlook does not recognize Automation (formerly OLE Automation) interfaces in Schedule+ 7.x.

Upgrading to Outlook 2003 Security

If you are upgrading to Microsoft Office Outlook 2003 from a version earlier than Outlook 2000, Outlook 2003 triggers a security upgrade feature the first time a user attempts to read or send cryptographic e-mail messages. To upgrade from Outlook 97 or Microsoft Exchange Client to Outlook 2003 security, the user's security file (EPF file) must exist on the computer, and the user must know the password. To upgrade from Outlook 98 security, the user must know the digital ID password. (Users upgrading from Outlook 2000 already have the updated security features.)

Note   Users create a security file by making a backup copy of their digital IDs. Backup files for Microsoft Exchange digital IDs have an .epf extension. Backup files for Internet e-mail digital IDs have a .pfx extension.

During the upgrade process, a digital ID name is generated for the security keys of each user, which includes one signing key and one encryption key. The user must select a password to associate with the digital ID name.

The Outlook 2003 upgrade feature attempts to save the security information in a secure-enhanced store. If the EPF file cannot be found, or the user cannot remember the password, the upgrade feature can be canceled.

If you are using Microsoft Exchange Advanced Security, you can recover the security keys (that is, enroll again in Exchange Advanced Security) by asking for a new security token from the administrator. The upgrade process must occur before you are enabled to send and receive cryptographic e-mail messages.

If you are using Microsoft Certificate Server, or a public certification authority such as VeriSign™, Inc., and you forget your password, the following restrictions occur:

- You cannot gain access to your keys.

- You cannot read encrypted e-mail messages previously sent to you.

- You must re-enroll to get new digital IDs.

The following procedure describes how Outlook 2003 users can enroll in security by using Microsoft Exchange Key Management Server (KMS). Before you begin this procedure, contact the system administrator for a security token. The request for security enrollment uses this token.

To enroll in security or obtain a certificate using Microsoft Exchange KMS

1. On the **Tools** menu, click **Options**, and then click the **Security** tab.

2. Click **Get a Digital ID**, select **Set up Security for me on the Exchange Server**, and then click **OK**.

3. In the **Digital ID name** box, type the name you want to use; in the **Token** box, type your security token, and then click **OK**.

   A message is sent to Microsoft Exchange KMS. After you receive a reply, Outlook 2003 attempts to store your security keys in the security-enhanced store.

4. Select a password for your digital ID.

   You are prompted for the password every time you gain access to the keys. However, you can choose to have Outlook 2003 remember the password for a limited period of time.

5. Click **OK** to save your changes.

6. To add the certificate to the Root Store, click **Yes**.

   The dialog box provides the required information about the certificate. If you click **No**, you experience problems when you attempt to read and send security-enhanced messages, and you must repeat the entire enrollment process.

The following procedure describes how Outlook 2003 users can enroll in security by using public certification authorities.

To enroll in security or obtain a certificate by using external certification authorities

1. On the **Tools** menu, click **Options**, and then click the **Security** tab.

2. Click **Get a Digital ID**, select **Get a S/MIME certificate from an external Certification Authority**, and then click **OK**.

   A Microsoft Web page provides information about obtaining a certificate. The page lists a number of certification authorities.

3. Select the link to the certification authority that you want to use to obtain a certificate.

   While your Web browser is storing your certificate and keys on your computer, you might be prompted to select the security level to associate with your keys.

4. When prompted, select a password for your digital ID.

   You are prompted for the password every time you gain access to the keys. However, you can choose to have Outlook 2003 remember the password for a limited period of time.

5. To add this certificate to the Root Store, click **Yes**.

   While storing the certificates, you might be prompted to save the root certificate. The dialog box provides the required information about the certificate. If you click **No**, you will experience problems when you attempt to read and send secure-enhanced messages. When you experience such problems, contact your certification authority to install another copy of the root certificate.

   After the certificate and keys are installed, Outlook can access and use them.

Resources and related information

There are several options to choose from when you set up security for your Outlook 2003 users. For more information about Outlook security, see Chapter 11, "Administering Cryptography in Outlook 2003."

You can configure security options to reduce the likelihood that your users will encounter viruses. For more information, see Chapter 12, "Customizing Outlook 2003 to Help Prevent Viruses."

Sharing Information with Earlier Versions of Outlook

In general, you can separately upgrade groups of users to Microsoft Office Outlook 2003 from earlier versions of Outlook and not lose e-mail and other message functionality between users of different versions. Outlook 2003 uses the same MAPI profiles as previous versions of Outlook. However, there are a few format changes introduced in versions of Outlook that might cause backward compatibility or interoperability issues. These few exceptions are described in the following sections.

New PST and OST file format in Outlook 2003

Outlook 2003 introduces a new Unicode file format for personal folder files (PST files) and offline folder files (OST files). The new format permits larger file sizes (the previous limit of 2 gigabytes (GBs) is eliminated) and allows for storing Unicode-format information. These file format changes might introduce problems if you upgrade to Outlook 2003 and create files with the new format, and then try to share files with someone using an earlier version of Outlook.

Upgrading the Outlook 97 OST file format

The OST file in Outlook 97 version 8.03 is different in later versions of Outlook, including Outlook 2003. When you upgrade to Outlook 2003 from versions of Outlook 97 prior to version 8.03, you must recreate the OST file.

HTML-based e-mail messages

In addition to Rich Text Format (RTF) and plain text (ASCII) format, Outlook 2003, Outlook 2002, Outlook 2000, and Outlook 98 support HTML-based e-mail messages. This format allows users to send messages in HTML format.

Outlook 97 supports only RTF and plain text format, but Outlook 2003 converts and stores HTML in RTF so that Outlook 97 users can read the messages. However, the original HTML might not be displayed correctly in RTF.

Online meetings

Outlook 2003 includes enhanced support for online meetings compared to earlier releases of Outlook. If you have an environment in which users on different versions of Outlook exchange meeting requests, be aware of the limitations outlined below.

Meeting requests with Meeting Workspace

In Outlook 2003, you can link a meeting request to a Meeting Workspace. A Meeting Workspace is a Web site that serves as a central point for information and materials relating to an upcoming meeting. There are some limitations when working with Meeting Workspace if some users are on older versions of Outlook. These include the following:

- When viewing the meeting invitation as an attendee in an earlier version of Outlook, a user can click on the link in the message body to navigate to the Meeting Workspace. The user's meeting response (for example, Accept or Decline) is not recorded in the workspace when the user responds from an earlier version of Outlook. Users can optionally navigate to the workspace and manually record their responses in the workspace.

- When viewing a Meeting Workspace meeting request as an organizer of the meeting in an earlier version of Outlook, any changes you make will not be reflected in the workspace. You will need to reopen the meeting request in Outlook 2003 and resend it to the meeting attendees to update the workspace.

Other types of online meeting requests

Outlook 2003 also supports other types of online meetings, hosted by using Microsoft NetMeeting® conferencing software, Exchange Conferencing Services, or Microsoft Windows NT® Server NetShow™ Services. (NetShow Services could be hosted by a Windows® Media 9 server instead.) Online meeting requests made by using the Outlook 2003 NetMeeting or NetShow Services features may appear as in-person meeting requests to Outlook 97, Outlook 98, or Outlook 2000 users.

If your organization includes Outlook 97, Outlook 98, or Outlook 2000 users, and you schedule an online meeting by using Outlook 2003, it is best to identify the meeting format in the content of the message: NetMeeting, Exchange Conferencing Services, or NetShow Services. Otherwise, users may not be aware that the meeting is an online meeting or may be unable to tell which type of online meeting it is.

In addition, if recipients of a meeting request set or activate reminders, this action might not work with online meeting requests in environments involving different versions of Outlook. For example, recipients of meeting requests may see the following message if they attempt to activate a reminder after receiving an online meeting invitation:

"The Reminder for <Subject> cannot be set because its time has passed. Is this OK?"

Stationery and custom signatures

When you upgrade to Outlook 2003, the Outlook 98 Stationery files are moved to a new location. Outlook 98, Outlook 2000, and Outlook 2002 user signatures are preserved in Outlook 2003.

Sharing Information with Microsoft Exchange Client

Microsoft Office Outlook 2003 recognizes all Microsoft Exchange Client message properties. However, although Outlook users can share information with Microsoft Exchange Client users, Microsoft Exchange Client users might not be able to view or use portions of Outlook 2003 messaging information.

When you install and run Outlook for the first time, it recognizes and opens all the Exchange Client e-mail folders defined in the mail profile. Outlook 2003 also creates the Outlook-specific folders—Calendar, Contacts, Journal, Notes, and Tasks.

Outlook 2003 can recognize and maintain folder views in Exchange Client, including custom views. While Outlook can create more advanced custom views than Exchange Client, Outlook and Exchange Client can share public folders that might include custom views.

Limitations when exchanging messages

In a mixed environment, Outlook users should be aware that their coworkers who use Microsoft Exchange Client cannot take full advantage of many Outlook 2003 messaging features. The following items are examples of these features:

- **Enhanced standard message form**   Advanced features such as Information Rights Management message protection and message expiration might not be viewable to Microsoft Exchange Client users.

- **Voting buttons and other extended message properties**   When a Microsoft Exchange Client user opens an Outlook 2003 message, extended Outlook message properties, such as voting buttons, are ignored because they are not recognized by Microsoft Exchange Client. In this scenario, Microsoft Exchange Client users receive only the text of the Subject line and the body of the voting message. No voting buttons are displayed.

- **Private items**   Microsoft Exchange Client users can view e-mail messages or calendar items marked private if they have been granted folder access privileges for the folder where the item is stored.

- **Non-table views**   Microsoft Exchange Client cannot display Outlook non-table views (such as the day, week, and month views in the calendar), or card, icon, and timeline views.

- **Preview pane**   Outlook 2003 has a built-in preview pane called the Reading Pane. The Microsoft Exchange Client preview pane is not compatible with Outlook.

- **Saved views**   Outlook 2003 and Microsoft Exchange Client use different formats to create saved views. Outlook supports both formats, so Outlook users can use any Microsoft Exchange Client view. By contrast, Microsoft Exchange Client does not support the Outlook format, so Microsoft Exchange Client cannot use Outlook views.

- **Attachments**   Outlook users can attach Outlook items that are not messages (such as a contact) to a message. However, Microsoft Exchange Client users receive these items as text-only attachments.

Limitations with other collaboration features

There are other interoperability differences between Outlook 2003 and Microsoft Exchange Client features in addition to those relating to exchanging e-mail messages and using public folders. The following items are examples of these limitations:

- **Rules**   Microsoft Exchange Client users use the Inbox Assistant to manage rules. By contrast, Outlook 2003 includes a Rules and Alerts feature that allows users to manage Inbox Assistant rules (server-side rules) in addition to their Outlook rules (client-side rules).

- **Forms**   Forms created by using the Outlook 2003 forms design environment can be used only by Outlook users. However, if you have custom solutions that depend on Electronic Forms Designer, note that Electronic Forms Designer is no longer supported in Outlook 2003.

- **Task delegation**   When an Outlook 2003 user delegates a task to a user who is running Microsoft Exchange Client, the recipient receives only an e-mail message that lists the description of the task, start and end dates, and other information as text in the body of the message.

On the Resource Kit CD   The Microsoft Office Resource Kit for Office 97/98 provides additional file sharing information for Microsoft Exchange Client, including information about using public folders, converting rules to use with the Rules Wizard, and exchanging forms. For more information, see Microsoft Office Resource Kit for Office 97/98 at *http://microsoft.com /office/ork/home.htm*.

Reverting to a Previous Installation of Outlook

In some circumstances, you may need to go back to a previous installation of Microsoft Outlook after upgrading to Microsoft Office Outlook 2003. To do this, you first remove Outlook 2003, then reinstall your previous version of Outlook. You might also need to recreate your Outlook profile.

You remove Outlook from your deployment by changing your Office installation using the Custom Maintenance Wizard. If you installed Outlook 2003 from an Office CD, you can select Outlook from the list of components and set its feature installation state to **Not Available** to uninstall it. If you installed Outlook from a stand-alone CD, Outlook 2003 is listed as a separate product that you can remove.

To remove Outlook 2003 by using the Custom Maintenance Wizard

1. In the Custom Maintenance Wizard, enter the MSI file for Office 2003 or Outlook 2003 (depending on whether you installed from the Office CD or from the Outlook stand-alone CD).

2. On the **Set Feature Installation States** page, click the down arrow next to **Microsoft Outlook for Windows**.

3. Select **Not Available** or **Not Available, Hidden, Locked**.

4. Click **Finish** to create the CMW file.

5. Distribute the CMW file to your users.

When you have removed Outlook 2003, reinstall your previous version of Outlook following the process for your organization.

Outlook 2003 creates a backup copy of existing profiles when it first runs. After you reinstall your previous version of Outlook, the backup profile works with Outlook just as it did before you upgraded to Outlook 2003.

However, under some circumstances, you must recreate your Outlook profile. For example, POP3 and IMAP e-mail services cannot be used after reverting to a previous Outlook installation. In this case, create a new profile and add these services.

To recreate your Outlook profile after reinstalling a previous version of Outlook

■ On the **Start** menu, click **Run**, and then enter **Outlook /cleanprofile**.

When Outlook starts up, it prompts you for the required information to create a new profile.

Chapter 10

Maintaining Outlook 2003

Maintaining and reconfiguring Microsoft® Office Outlook® 2003 after your initial deployment is made easier by using the Office 2003 tools. You may want to change information in the Outlook profile or update your deployment to implement new organizational policies, for instance by configuring auto-archiving options or setting up new group mailboxes. You have several choices for how to make updates, including using the Custom Maintenance Wizard or an Outlook profile file (PRF file) to change Outlook settings.

Updating Outlook 2003 by Using the Custom Maintenance Wizard

If you need to update your Microsoft Office Outlook 2003 installation, you have two main methods of doing so:

- Use the Custom Maintenance Wizard to reconfigure Outlook settings, save those settings in a configuration maintenance file (CMW file), and apply this file to your users' installations.

- Update profile information in an Outlook profile file (PRF file), and distribute the file to your users. When Outlook imports the PRF file, user profile settings are updated.

Using the Custom Maintenance Wizard to update users' profiles might be the best choice if you are doing one or more of the following:

- Making other changes to Microsoft Office settings at the same time that you want to modify Outlook profile information.

- Making changes to other aspects of your Outlook deployment in addition to Outlook profile modifications (for example, changing an Outlook setting).

- Making substantial or complicated changes to Outlook profiles.

This section of the chapter describes how to update Outlook 2003—including updates to Outlook profiles—by using the Custom Maintenance Wizard.

> **Note**   Updating Outlook profiles by distributing a new PRF file might be the simplest strategy if you saved a PRF file with your users' Outlook profile configurations when you installed Outlook, and if you are making minor changes. For more information about updating profiles by using a PRF file, see "Updating Outlook Profiles by Using PRF Files" later in this chapter.

The Custom Maintenance Wizard offers the same Outlook settings and profile configuration options that are available in the Custom Installation Wizard. You can, for example, specify features to install or uninstall, change Outlook options to a new default value, deploy registry key settings, choose to modify existing profiles (for example, to move users to a new Microsoft Exchange server) or add new profiles (for all users).

> **On the Resource Kit CD**   The Office 2003 Resource Kit core tool set includes the Custom Maintenance Wizard, along with other Office deployment tools to customize Office application deployments. These tools are installed by default when you run the Office Resource Kit Setup program. For more information, see Appendix A, "Toolbox."

The Custom Maintenance Wizard is run from users' computers, and when it runs, it applies a customized CMW file to the client computer. Note that this behavior is different from the Custom Installation Wizard, which uses a transform to apply customizations during Setup.

Updating an Outlook installation in the Custom Maintenance Wizard

You can use the Custom Maintenance Wizard to update an Outlook installation after you have deployed Outlook. The Outlook customization pages in the Custom Maintenance Wizard are identical to those in the Custom Installation Wizard. (Note, however, that you cannot include an Office profile settings file (OPS file) in the Custom Maintenance Wizard to define Office settings.)

The following procedure shows how you might use the Custom Maintenance Wizard to change users' default delivery location for messages from a PST file to an Exchange server.

To change the default message delivery location to users' Exchange server

1. In the Custom Maintenance Wizard, on the **Outlook: Customize Default Profile** page, click **Modify Profile**, then click **Next**.

2. On the **Outlook: Specify Exchange Settings** page, specify **Configure an Exchange Server Connection**.

3. Specify an Exchange server name.

    This should be an Exchange server which is likely to be available to users when they start Outlook for the first time after they update their Outlook installation. The correct Exchange server for each user will be located and updated in each profile when Outlook starts.

    This step will ensure that new Outlook users have the appropriate configuration as well as existing users.

4. On the **Outlook: Add Accounts** page, choose **Customize additional Outlook profile and account information**.

5. From the drop-down list, choose **Exchange Server**.

6. Save the CMW file and deploy it to your users.

Deploying the updated Outlook installation to users

After you create the CMW file, you deploy it to your users to update their installation of Outlook.

First, ensure that the Custom Maintenance Wizard executable files and the configuration maintenance file you are deploying are available to users on the administrative installation point (or any file server to which users can gain access).

Then provide a command line such as the following:

```
Maintwiz.exe /c UpdateOutlook.cmw /q
```

The **/c** option specifies the maintenance file to be applied to users' computers. The **/q** option prevents dialogs from being presented to the users during the update.

Resources and related information

The Custom Installation Wizard offers a wide range of configuration options for defining and modifying user profiles. For more information about your options for configuring Outlook profiles, see "Customizing Outlook Features and Installation with the Custom Installation Wizard" in Chapter 7, "Deploying Outlook 2003."

Complete details on modifying user profile information by editing and distributing a PRF file are provided in "Customizing Outlook Profiles by Using PRF Files," also in Chapter 7.

Updating Outlook Profiles by Using PRF Files

If you need to update Microsoft Outlook profile information after installing Microsoft Office Outlook 2003, you have two main methods to choose from:

- Update profile information in an Outlook profile file (PRF file), and distribute the file to your users. When Outlook imports the PRF file, user profile settings are updated.

- Use the Custom Maintenance Wizard to reconfigure profile settings, save those settings in a configuration maintenance file, and apply that file to your users' installations.

Using a PRF file to update users' profiles might be the best choice if one or more of the following circumstances apply:

- You saved a PRF file with your users' Outlook profile configurations when you installed Outlook.

- You are making minor changes to the profiles.

- You wish to keep from inadvertently modifying other Office settings, which cannot be done by using a PRF file.

■ You want to add a service that cannot be configured by using the Custom Maintenance Wizard.

This section of the chapter describes how to update Outlook profiles by using a PRF file.

> **Note** Using the Custom Maintenance Wizard to update profiles might be the best choice if you are making other changes to Microsoft Office settings at the same time that you want to modify Outlook profile information, or you are making substantial or complicated changes to Outlook profiles. For more information about updating profiles by using the Custom Maintenance Wizard, see "Updating Outlook 2003 by Using the Custom Maintenance Wizard" earlier in this chapter.

You can update an existing PRF file by editing it in a simple text editor, such as Notepad. The PRF file contains detailed comments to guide you in making appropriate changes. All of the customizations that are available through pages in the Custom Maintenance Wizard can be made manually by editing the file.

For instance, a simple change would be to update the Microsoft Exchange server name for a group of users, following these steps:

1. In Section 1, in the [General] section, set the value for **OverwriteProfile** to **Append** as follows:

    ```
    OverwriteProfile=Append
    ```

2. In Section 4, in the [Service 1] section, set the value of **OverwriteExistingService** to **Yes** as follows:

    ```
    OverwriteExistingService=Yes
    ```

3. In Section 4, in the [Service 1] section, set a new string value for the **HomeServer** field. For example:

    ```
    HomeServer=New-Exchange-Server-Name
    ```

After you have made changes to the PRF file, you can use it to update Outlook profiles in several ways. For example, you can provide it to users by making it available on a network share or you can distribute the file by using Microsoft Systems Management Server. Because the PRF file is an executable file, users can update their profiles by simply double-clicking the file name. When users double-click the PRF file, Outlook starts and uses the PRF file information to update the users' profiles.

In addition, you can add custom features to users' Outlook profiles by editing the file. For example, if you need to add a new messaging service for your users that is not provided in the Custom Maintenance Wizard, you can make manual changes to the PRF file to add the service.

> **Note** A fast way to create a PRF file for use in your deployment is to create your preliminary configuration by specifying Outlook options in the Custom Installation Wizard, then export the settings. After saving the file, open it with a text editor and make any additional changes you choose. For more information about working with PRF files, see "Customizing Outlook Profiles by Using PRF Files" in Chapter 7, "Deploying Outlook 2003."

Resources and related information

The Custom Installation Wizard offers a wide range of configuration options for defining and modifying user profiles. For more information about your options for configuring Outlook profiles, see "Customizing Outlook Features and Installation with the Custom Installation Wizard" in Chapter 7, "Deploying Outlook 2003."

Complete details on modifying user profile information by editing and distributing a PRF file are provided in "Customizing Outlook Profiles by Using PRF Files," also in Chapter 7.

Locating and Configuring Outlook Settings

The administration tools provided with Microsoft Office Outlook 2003 help you install Microsoft Outlook with the best supported configuration for your organization, and help you update and maintain your Outlook installation to meet changing needs.

Most Outlook 2003 settings can be configured by using the Custom Installation Wizard and changed by using the Custom Maintenance Wizard. You can also install Outlook on a test computer, customize the Outlook environment, and capture the settings by using the Office Profile Wizard. Those settings can then be distributed to users' computers. You can also set system policies to enforce specific settings to maintain a more uniform environment.

There are some exceptions to how settings are normally specified and maintained. For example, some options cannot be captured by the Office Profile Wizard.

Most common settings to configure

The following table shows common Outlook 2003 settings that you might specify, and when and how you can set them. In general, the tools or templates to use for these settings include the following:

- **At initial deployment**—Custom Installation Wizard and Office Profile Wizard

- **After initial deployment**—Custom Maintenance Wizard and Office Profile Wizard

- **Lock down settings**—Policy template files (.adm), Group Policy software distribution and the Group Policy editor.

Settings	At deployment	After deployment	Lock down setting
Location of Outlook binary files	Custom Installation Wizard feature tree	Custom Maintenance Wizard feature tree	N/A
Tools | Options For example: Specify Word-Mail as Outlook editor	■ OPS file in Custom Installation Wizard ■ **Change Office User Settings** page in Custom Installation Wizard ■ **Outlook: Customize Default Settings** page in Custom Installation Wizard	■ OPS file (for standalone) in Custom Maintenance Wizard ■ **Change Office User Settings** page in Custom Maintenance Wizard ■ **Outlook: Customize Default Settings** page in Custom Maintenance Wizard	Outlk11.adm—includes most of these options. Office11.adm—includes settings common to all of Office 2003
MAPI profile For example: Microsoft Exchange connection, define PST files, and so on	Custom Installation Wizard Outlook profile configuration pages	Custom Maintenance Wizard Outlook profile configuration pages	Outlk11.adm

Settings not captured by the Office Profile Wizard

Most Outlook settings are captured in an Office profile settings file (OPS file) when you use the Office Profile Wizard to customize an Outlook installation. By design, the Profile Wizard excludes some settings, including user-specific information such as the user name and Most Recently Used file list (**File** menu).

For example, the Profile Wizard does not capture the following groups of Outlook 2003 settings:

- Profile settings, including mail server configuration

- Storage settings, such as default delivery location and personal folder files (PST files)

- E-mail accounts and directories (**Tools**|**Options**|**Mail Setup**|**E-mail Accounts**)

- Send/Receive groups (**Tools**|**Options**|**Mail Setup**|**Send/Receive**)

- Customized views; for example, the fields displayed in the Inbox or another folder

- Navigation Pane shortcuts, including Search Folders

- Auto-archive options set for a particular folder, which you set by right-clicking the folder, clicking **Properties**, and choosing options in the **AutoArchive** tab

- Delegate options (**Tools | Options | Delegates**)

In addition, the Profile Wizard does not capture the following specific Outlook 2003 settings:

- **Send Immediately when connected** check box (**Tools | Options | Mail Setup**)

- **When forwarding a message** option (**Tools | Options | Preferences | E-mail Options**)

- **Mark my comments with** option (**Tools | Options | Preferences | E-mail Options**)

- **Request S/MIME receipt for all S/MIME signed messages** check box (**Tools | Options | Security**)

- **Show an additional time zone** check box (**Tools | Options | Preferences | Calendar Options | Time Zone**)

- **Automatically decline recurring meeting requests** check box (**Tools | Options | Preferences | Calendar Options | Resource Scheduling**)

- **Automatically decline conflicting meeting requests** check box (**Tools | Options | Preferences | Calendar Options | Resource Scheduling**)

- **Automatically accept meeting requests and process cancellations** check box (**Tools | Options | Preferences | Calendar Options | Resource Scheduling**)

Settings that cannot be centrally administered

Most Outlook 2003 options are customizable by using Office tools or the Microsoft Windows® registry. The Outlook settings that cannot be configured using these methods include:

- Other Outlook settings that are stored in user-specific locations such as:

  - Navigation Pane shortcuts, including Search Folders

  - Most Recently Used (MRU) lists

  - View information, such as specific columns that are displayed for a user's Inbox or PST file

  - Delegate information specified in the **Tools | Options**, **Delegates** tab

- The options specified in **E-mail Accounts** in the **Tools | Options**, **Mail Setup** tab

- Settings for **Send/Receive Groups** for non-Exchange server accounts

Setting Up Retention Settings in Outlook 2003

Microsoft Office Outlook 2003 helps users maintain their mailboxes by providing the AutoArchive feature, which can automatically clean out expired items and archive older items from users mailboxes. If your organization uses AutoArchive, you can also configure Outlook Retention Settings that run as part of AutoArchive. These settings can help users comply with policies your company may have about how long to keep documents and items in user mailboxes.

How AutoArchive works in Outlook

Outlook mailboxes grow as users create and receive items. To keep mailboxes manageable, users need another place to store—or archive—older items that are important but not frequently used. It is typically most convenient to automatically move these older items to the archive folder and to discard items whose content has expired and is no longer valid. AutoArchive manages this process automatically for users.

AutoArchive is on by default and runs automatically at scheduled intervals, removing older and expired items from folders. Older items are those that reach the archiving age a user specifies (the default archiving age varies by the type of Outlook item). Expired items are mail and meeting items whose content is no longer valid after a certain date, such as a mail item set to expire two months ago that still appears in a user's Inbox. Users can specify an expiration date on items in Outlook at the time they create or send the item or at a later date. When the item expires, it is unavailable and shows in a folder list with a strike-out mark through it.

When AutoArchive runs, it can delete items or move items to an archive folder, depending on the settings you specify.

The archive file is a special type of Outlook data file. The first time AutoArchive runs, Outlook creates the archive file automatically in the following location:

%UserProfile%\Local Settings\Application Data\Microsoft\Outlook\Archive.pst

There are two groups of AutoArchive settings: global settings and per-folder settings. Global settings—or default settings—determine whether AutoArchive runs at all and how it handles the items in any Outlook folder (except Contacts, which is not affected by AutoArchive). Per-folder settings override the default settings so users can AutoArchive individual folders differently. If users do not specify AutoArchive settings for a specific folder, the folder automatically uses the default settings. Default settings and per-folder settings apply to the current mailbox only. Users can also choose to manually archive items.

By using Group Policy with the Outlook policy file (Outlk11.adm), you can lock down AutoArchive settings for users. In Group Policy, AutoArchive policies are located under **\User Configuration\Administrative Templates\Microsoft Office Outlook 2003\Tools | Options\Other\AutoArchive**. You have a number of options for AutoArchive settings, including how frequently to run AutoArchive and whether to prompt users before running AutoArchive.

Configuring retention policy settings

In addition to the AutoArchive settings, you can also enable retention policy settings for items in users' mailboxes. Retention policy settings can help users to follow retention policy guidelines that your company establishes for document retention.

> **Note**   Because retention policies settings are part of Outlook's AutoArchive functionality, Retention Settings only run when AutoArchive is run. Running an archive manually does not trigger Retention Settings enforcement.

Retention policy settings in Outlook can be configured to follow company policies and encourage users to retain documents and items for only a fixed period of time. Retention Settings implementation requires AutoArchive to be enabled, but Retention Settings take precedence over AutoArchive settings.

By using Group Policy with the Outlook .adm file, you can lock down Retention Settings for users. In the Group Policy snap-in, retention setting policies are located under **\User Configuration\Administrative Templates\Microsoft Office Outlook 2003\Tools | Options\Other\AutoArchive**. To set retention policies, double-click **Retention Policies**, then click **Enabled** to enable policies for these settings.

You can disable Retention Settings by clearing the **Turn Retention Policies On** check box.

The settings you can configure for Retention Settings include:

- **Maximum number of days to retain items**   You can specify a different number of days for items in the user's Inbox, Calendar, and (as a group) all other folders that are AutoArchived.

- **For items not being retained**   Choose from the drop-down list whether to move to the Deleted Items folder items that are affected by Retention Settings, or to permanently delete the items.

- **URL with corporate retention policy information**   Specify a link to a page providing more information about your organization's document retention policies.

Chapter 11

Administering Cryptography in Outlook 2003

Microsoft® Office Outlook® 2003 provides features for sending and receiving security-enhanced e-mail messages over the Internet or intranet. You can define security labels and security-enhanced receipts to help ensure secure e-mail messaging. Users can also obtain and use certificates for digital signatures or for encrypting messages.

Overview of Cryptography in Outlook 2003

Microsoft Office Outlook 2003 provides several features to help users send and receive cryptographic e-mail messages. Cryptographic features in Outlook—which include digital signing and message encryption—can be combined to help provide different levels and types of security. This section of the chapter provides an overview of Outlook 2003 features that support cryptographic messaging and an explanation of how cryptographic messaging is implemented in Outlook 2003.

> **Note**   To get full security functionality in Outlook 2003, you must install Outlook 2003 with local administrative rights or with elevated privileges. If you are installing Outlook 2003 on client computers for users who do not have local administrative rights, you can give them elevated privileges for the installation. For more information about using elevated privileges in Office installations, see "Installing Office with Elevated Privileges" in Chapter 5, "Installing Office 2003."

Cryptographic messaging features in Outlook 2003

Outlook 2003 supports the following features for cryptographic messaging:

- **Digitally sign an e-mail message.**   Digital signing provides nonrepudiation and verification of contents (the message contains what the person sent, with no changes).

- **Encrypt an e-mail message.**   Encryption helps to ensure privacy by making the message unreadable to anyone other than the intended recipient.

There are additional features that can be configured for Outlook 2003 for security-enhanced messaging, if your organization chooses to provide support for them, including:

- **Sending an e-mail message with an S/MIME receipt request.**   This helps to verify that the recipient is validating your digital signature (the certificate you applied to a message).

- **Adding a security label to an e-mail message.**   Your organization can create a customized S/MIME V3 security policy which can add labels to messages. An S/MIME V3 security policy is code that you add to Outlook that runs automatically to add information to the message header about the sensitivity of the message content. For example, an Internal Use Only label might be applied to mail that should not be sent or forwarded outside of your company.

How Outlook 2003 implements cryptographic messaging

The Outlook 2003 cryptography model uses public key encryption to send and receive signed and encrypted e-mail messages. Outlook 2003 supports S/MIME V3 security, which allows users to exchange security-enhanced e-mail messages with other S/MIME e-mail clients over the Internet or intranet.

Users can exchange signed and encrypted e-mail messages with other e-mail clients that support S/MIME. Following the S/MIME model, e-mail messages encrypted by the user's public key can be decrypted using only the associated private key. This means that when a user sends an encrypted e-mail message, the recipient's certificate (public key) is used to encrypt it; likewise, when a user reads an encrypted e-mail message, Outlook 2003 uses the user's private key to decrypt it.

In Outlook 2003, users are required to have a security profile to use cryptographic features. A security profile is a group of settings that describe the certificates and algorithms that will be used when a user sends messages that use cryptographic features. Security profiles are configured automatically (if the profile is not already present) when:

- A user has certificates for cryptography on his or her computer; and

- The user begins to use a cryptographic feature.

However, Outlook 2003 also includes flexibility for customizing these security settings for users ahead of time. You can use registry settings or Group Policy settings to customize Outlook to meet your organization's cryptographic policies and to configure (and enforce, with Group Policy) the settings you want in the security profiles. These settings are described in the table in "Setting Consistent Outlook Cryptography Options for an Organization" later in this chapter.

Digital IDs: a combination of public/private keys and certificates

S/MIME features rely on digital IDs, which associate a user's identity with a public and private key pair. The combination of a certificate and private/public key pair is called a digital ID. The private key can be saved in a security-enhanced store such as the Microsoft Windows® certificate store on the user's computer or on a Smart Card. Outlook 2003 fully supports the X.509v3 standard, which requires that public and private keys be created by a certificate authority such as VeriSign™, Inc.

Users can obtain digital IDs by using public World Wide Web–based certificate authorities such as VeriSign and Microsoft Certificate Server. Or, an administrator can provide digital IDs to a group of users. Outlook 2003 also continues to support working with Microsoft Exchange Key Management Server to obtain or provide digital IDs.

When certificates for digital IDs expire or are updated, Outlook manages updates automatically (for example, by working with the issuing certificate authority). Users do not have to change their settings.

Outlook support for security labels and signed receipts

Outlook 2003 includes support for S/MIME V3 ESS extensions about security labels and signed receipts. These extensions help you to provide security-enhanced e-mail communications within your organization and to customize security to your requirements.

If your organization develops and provides S/MIME V3 security policies to add custom security labels, the code in the security policies can enforce attaching a security label to an e-mail message. You define one or more security policies for your organization and implement them programmatically. A security label is flexible in the features it provides, depending on how it is coded—for example:

■ An Internal Use Only label might be implemented as a security label to apply to mail that should not be sent or forwarded outside of your company.

■ A label can specify that certain recipients cannot forward or print the message (if the recipient also has the security policy installed).

Users can also send security-enhanced receipt requests with messages to verify that the recipients recognize the user's digital signature. When the message is received and saved (even if it is not yet read) and the signature has been verified, a receipt is returned to the user's Inbox. This implies that the message was read. If the user's signature is not verified, no receipt is sent. When the receipt is returned, because the receipt is also signed, you have verification that the user has received and verified the message.

Classes of encryption strengths

There are two classes of encryption key strengths available from Microsoft: High (128-bit) and Low (40-bit). Microsoft provides 128-bit encryption capabilities in Windows 2000 and Windows XP, the operating systems required for Office 2003. Ensuring that users have versions of software that support high encryption will help provide our highest level of security-enhanced e-mail messaging.

Resources and related information

You can use the Outlook Security Labels application programming interface (API) to create security label policy modules to define the sensitivity of message content in your organization. For a detailed description of creating policy modules and code samples, see the MSDN article "Creating Security Label Policy Modules" at *http://msdn.microsoft.com/library/default.asp?url=/library/en-us/dnout2k2/html /odc_olseclabelapi.asp?frame=true.*

Public key cryptography can help you maintain security-enhanced e-mail systems. For more information about the use of public key cryptography in Outlook, search for "Outlook 98 Security White Paper" on the Knowledge Base Search page of the Microsoft Product Support Services Web site at *http://search.support.microsoft.com /kb/c.asp.*

Microsoft Exchange Key Management Server version 5.5 issues keys for Microsoft Exchange Server security only. Microsoft Exchange Key Management Server 5.5 Service Pack 1 supports both Exchange security and S/MIME security. For more information, see the *Microsoft Exchange Server version 5.5 Resource Guide* in the *Microsoft BackOffice Resource Kit, Second Edition*.

How Users Manage Cryptographic Digital IDs in Outlook

Microsoft Office Outlook 2003 provides ways for users to manage their digital IDs—the combination of a user's certificate and public and private encryption key set. Digital IDs help to keep users' e-mail messages secure by letting them exchange cryptographic messages. Managing digital IDs can include:

- Making a digital ID available to others.
- Exporting a digital ID to a file. This is useful when creating a backup or when migrating to a new computer.
- Importing a digital ID from a file into Outlook. A digital ID file might be a user's backup copy or might contain a digital ID from another user.
- Renewing a digital ID. This happens automatically when a digital ID is issued by a certificate authority (CA), unless the certificate has expired.

If you use more than one computer, you must copy your digital ID to each computer that you use for cryptographic messaging.

Providing your digital ID to other users

In order to exchange cryptographic e-mail messages with another user, you must have each other's public keys. You provide access to your public key through a certificate. There are several ways to provide your digital ID to others. For example, you can:

- Digitally sign an e-mail message.
- Use a directory service, such as the Microsoft Exchange Global Address Book.

Provide a certificate in a digitally signed e-mail message

To provide your public key to another user by using an e-mail message, compose an e-mail message and digitally sign it by using your certificate. When Outlook users receive the signed message, they can right-click on your name on the **To** line and then click **Add to Contacts**. The address information is saved in Contacts, and your certificate is saved in the registry.

> **Note**   If you export a Contacts list, the corresponding certificates are not included. You must add the certificates from a received e-mail message on each computer that you use.

Provide a certificate to a directory service

Another alternative might be for users to automatically retrieve your certificate from an LDAP directory (on a standard LDAP server) when they send an encrypted e-mail message. To gain access to a certificate this way, users must be enrolled in S/MIME security with digital IDs for their e-mail accounts.

Or users can obtain certificates from the Global Address Book. To do this, users must be enrolled in Microsoft Exchange Server Advanced Security.

Exporting your digital IDs

Digital IDs can be stored in three locations:

- The Microsoft Exchange Global Address Book.
- A Lightweight Directory Access Protocol (LDAP) directory service.
- A Windows file.

Microsoft Exchange Global Address Book

Users who enroll in Exchange Advanced Security have their certificates stored in their organization's Global Address Book. Alternatively, users can open the Global Address Book by using their LDAP provider.

Only certificates generated by Microsoft Exchange Server Advanced Security or by Microsoft Exchange Key Management Server are automatically published in the Global Address Book. However, externally generated certificates can be manually published to the Global Address Book (by using the **Publish to GAL** button in **Tools | Options | Security**).

Internet directory service (LDAP)

External directory services, certificate authorities, or other certificate providers can publish their users' certificates through an LDAP directory service. Outlook 2003 allows access to these certificates through LDAP directories.

Windows file

Components for your digital ID can be stored on your computer. You export your digital ID to a file by using **Import/Export** in **Tools | Options | Security**. You can encrypt the file when you create it by providing a password.

Importing digital IDs

You can import a digital ID from a file. This is useful, for example, if you want to send cryptographic e-mail messages from a new computer you have just begun using. Each computer from which you send cryptographic e-mail messages must have your certificates installed. You import digital IDs from a file by using **Import/Export** in **Tools | Options | Security**.

Renewing keys and certificates

A time limit is associated with each certificate and private key. When the keys given by the Microsoft Exchange Key Management Server or another certificate authority approach the end of the designated time period, Outlook displays a warning message and offers to renew the keys. Outlook prompts the user, offering to send the renewal message to the server or to the CA on each user's behalf.

If users do not choose to renew a certificate before it expires, they must contact the certificate authority to renew the certificate.

Setting Consistent Outlook Cryptography Options for an Organization

You can control many aspects of Microsoft Office Outlook 2003 cryptography features to help configure more secure messaging and message encryption for your organization's needs. To help control these features, you specify settings in the Windows registry or through policies. For example, you can set a policy to require a security label on all outgoing mail or a policy to disable publishing to the Global Address List.

> **Note**   A number of Outlook cryptography registry settings have an equivalent setting on the **Security** tab in the **Options** dialog box (**Tools** menu) or other user setting. However, setting the value in the user interface does not create or set the equivalent setting in the Windows registry. You can use the Windows registry to change these settings.

The settings described in this chapter are not related to virus prevention. Virus prevention settings include options for trusted code or changes to the default list of e-mail attachment types that cannot be received or opened by your users. To find out more about configuring virus prevention features, see Chapter 12, "Customizing Outlook 2003 to Help Prevent Viruses."

> **Tip**   You can use group policies to set security levels in Outlook. In Group Policy, set the **Required Certificate Authority**, **Minimum encryption settings**, **S/MIME interoperability with external clients**, and **Outlook Rich Text in S/MIME messages** policies under **Microsoft Office Outlook 2003\Tools | Options\Security\Cryptography**. For more information about using Group Policy to lock down Microsoft Office 2003 settings, see "Managing Users' Configurations by Policy" in Chapter 18, "Updating Users' Office 2003 Configurations."

Corresponding user interface options for Outlook security policies

Some of the security policies listed in this chapter correspond to user interface buttons or settings on user interface dialogs. This section lists the policies that correspond to these buttons or to options on one or more of these dialogs, grouped by the user interface button or dialog. Some policies affect settings in more than one area and appear on multiple lists.

For information about setting the policies, see the sections that follow this one. The specific setting that is affected by a policy is included for many policies in the "Corresponding UI option" column of the tables of policy settings.

Policies that affect settings on the **Tools | Options | Security** dialog:

- AlwaysEncrypt
- AlwaysSign
- ClearSign
- RequestSecurityEnhancedReceipt
- PublishtoGalDisabled
- EnrollPageURL

   Policies that affect settings on the **Tools | Options | Security | Settings** dialog:

- FIPSMode
- MinEncKey (restricts encryption algorithms available to users)

   Policies that affect settings on the **Tools | Options | Security | Settings | Security labels** dialog:

- ForceSecurityLabel
- ForceSecurityLabelX

Policies that affect settings on the **Options | Security | Settings** dialog in a new e-mail message:

- AlwaysEncrypt
- AlwaysSign
- ClearSign
- RequestSecureReceipt
- ForceSecurityLabel
- ForceSecurityLabelX

Policies that affect the toolbar buttons for encrypting and signing e-mail messages:

- AlwaysEncrypt
- AlwaysSign

Outlook security policies

The following table lists the Windows registry settings in the Policies tree that you can configure for your custom installation. You add these value entries in the following subkey:

HKEY_CURRENT_USER\Software\Policies\Microsoft\Office\10.0\Outlook\Security

Value name	Value data (Data type)	Description	Corresponding UI option
AlwaysEncrypt	0, 1 (DWORD)	When you set the value to **1**, all outgoing messages are encrypted. Default is **0**.	**Encrypt contents** check box
AlwaysSign	0, 1 (DWORD)	When you set the value to **1**, all outgoing messages are signed. Default is **0**.	**Add digital signature** check box
ClearSign	0, 1 (DWORD)	When you set the value to **1**, Clear Signed is used for all outgoing messages. Default is **0**.	**Send clear text signed message** check box
RequestSecureReceipt	0, 1 (DWORD)	When you set the value to **1**, security-enhanced receipts are requested for all outgoing messages. Default is **0**.	**Request S/MIME receipt** check box
ForceSecurityLabel	0, 1 (DWORD)	When you set this value to **1**, a label is required on all outgoing messages. (Note that the registry setting does not specify which label.) Default is **0**.	None

Value name	Value data (Data type)	Description	Corresponding UI option
ForceSecurityLabelX	ASN encoded BLOB (Binary)	This value entry specifies whether a user-defined security label must be present on all outgoing signed messages. String can optionally include label, classification, and category. Default is no security label required.	None
SigStatusNoCRL	0, 1 (DWORD)	Set to **0** means a missing CRL during signature validation is a warning. Set to **1** means a missing CRL is an error. Default is **0**.	None
SigStatusNoTrust-Decision	0, 1, 2 (DWORD)	Set to **0** means that a No Trust decision is allowed. Set to **1** means that a No Trust decision is a warning. Set to **2** means that a No Trust decision is an error. Default is **0**.	None
PromoteErrors-AsWarnings	0, 1 (DWORD)	Set to **0** to promote Error Level 2 errors as errors. Set to **1** to promote Error Level 2 errors as warnings. Default is **0**.	None
PublishtoGalDisabled	0, 1 (DWORD)	Set to **1** to disable the **Publish to GAL** button. Default is **0**.	**Publish to GAL** button
FIPSMode	0, 1 (DWORD)	Set to **1** to put Outlook into FIPS 140-1 mode. Default is **0**.	None
WarnAboutInvalid	0, 1, 2 (DWORD)	Set to **0** to display the **Show and Ask** check box (**Secure E-mail Problem** pont dialog box). Set to **1** to always show the dialog box. Set to **2** to never show the dialog box. Default is **2**.	**Secure E-mail Problem** pont dialog box

Value name	Value data (Data type)	Description	Corresponding UI option
DisableContinue-Encryption	0, 1 (DWORD)	Set to **0** to show the **Continue Encrypting** button on the final **Encryption Errors** dialog box. Set to **1** to hide the button. Default is **0**.	**Continue Encrypting** button on final **Encryption Errors** dialog box. This dialog box appears when a user tries to send a message to someone who cannot receive encrypted messages. This policy disables the button that allows users to send the message regardless. (The recipient cannot open encrypted mail messages sent by overriding the error.)
Respondto-ReceiptRequest	0, 1, 2, 3 (DWORD)	Set to **0** to always send a receipt response and prompt for a password, if needed. Set to **1** to prompt for a password when sending a receipt response. Set to **2** to never send a receipt response. Set to **3** to enforce sending a receipt response. Default is **0**.	None
NeedEncryptionString	String	Displays the specified string when the user tries unsuccessfully to open an encrypted message. Can provide information about where to enroll in security. Default string is used unless the value is set to another string.	Default string

Value name	Value data (Data type)	Description	Corresponding UI option
Options	0, 1 (DWORD)	Set to **0** to show a warning dialog box when a user attempts to read a signed message with an invalid signature. Set to **1** to never show the warning. Default is **0**.	None
MinEncKey	40, 64, 128, 168 (DWORD)	Set to the minimum key length for an encrypted e-mail message.	None
RequiredCA	String	Set to the name of the required certificate authority. When a value is set, Outlook disallows users from signing mail using a certificate from a different CA.	None
EnrollPageURL	String	URL for the default certificate authority (internal or external) from which you wish your users to obtain new digital IDs. Note: Set in HKEY_CURRENT_USER\Software\Microsoft\Office\9.0\Outlook\Security subkey if you do not have administrator privileges on the user's computer.	**Get Digital ID** button

When you specify a value for **PromoteErrorsAsWarnings**, note that potential Error Level 2 conditions include the following:

- Unknown Signature Algorithm
- No Signing Certification Found
- Bad Attribute Sets
- No Issuer Certificate Found
- No CRL Found
- Out of Date CRL
- Root Trust Problem
- Out of Date CTL

When you specify a value for **EnrollPageURL**, use the following parameters to send information about the user to the enrollment Web page.

Parameter	Placeholder in URL string
User display name	%1
SMTP e-mail name	%2
User interface language ID	%3

For example, to send user information to the Microsoft enrollment Web page, set the **EnrollPageURL** entry to the following value, including the parameters:

www.microsoft.com/ie/certpage.htm?name=%1&email=%2&help lcid=%3

If the user's name is Jeff Smith, his e-mail address is someone@example.com, and his user interface language ID is 1033, then the placeholders are resolved as follows:

www.microsoft.com/ie/certpage.htm?name=Jeff%20Smith&email=some one@example.com&helplcid=1033

Security policies for general cryptography

The following table lists additional Windows registry settings that you can use for your custom configuration. These settings are contained in the following subkey:

HKEY_CURRENT_USER\Software\Microsoft\Cryptography\SMIME\Security-Policies\Default

Value name	Value data (Data type)	Description	Corresponding UI option
ShowWithMulti-Labels	0, 1, (DWORD)	Set to **0** to attempt to display a message when the signature layer has different labels set in different signatures. Set to **1** to prevent display of message. Default is **0**.	None
CertErrorWith-Label	0, 1, 2 (DWORD)	Set to **0** to process a message with a certificate error when the message has a label. Set to **1** to deny access to a message with a certificate error. Set to **2** to ignore the message label and grant access to the message. (The user still sees a certificate error.) Default is **0**.	None

Security policies for KMS-issued certificates

The values below only apply to KMS-issued certificates. The following table lists additional Windows registry settings that you can use for your custom configuration. These settings are contained in the following subkey:

HKEY_CURRENT_USER\Software\Microsoft\Cryptography\Defaults\Provider

Value name	Value data (Data type)	Description	Corresponding UI option
MaxPWDTime	0, number (DWORD)	Set to **0** to remove user's ability to save a password (user is required to enter a password each time a key set is required). Set to a positive number to specify a maximum password time in minutes. Default is **999**.	None
DefPWDTime	Number (DWORD)	Set to the default value for the amount of time a password is saved.	None

Outlook Folder Home Pages and Security

Microsoft Office Outlook 2003 includes a Web browser feature so you can view Web pages without leaving Outlook. You do this by assigning a Web page as a home page for a folder. You can associate a Web page with any personal or public folder. Whenever you click the folder, Outlook displays the folder home page assigned to it. Although this feature provides the opportunity to create powerful public folder applications, scripts can be included on the Web page that access the Outlook object model, which exposes users to security risks.

These Folder home pages do not follow the Outlook security model. They can run script just as any other Web page can. Access to the Outlook object model allows scripts to manipulate all of the user's Outlook information on the computer.

From a security perspective, this means that anyone who can create a public folder and set that folder with a home page can include scripts that can manipulate data in users' mailboxes when the users go to that public folder. Because of this, be cautious about granting permissions for users to set public folders as home pages.

> **Tip**   You can tighten security by using a group policy to disable Folder home pages for all of your users. In Group Policy, in the **Microsoft Office Outlook 2003\Miscellaneous\Folder Home Pages for Outlook special folders** category, select the **Disable Folder Home Pages** policy and then select **Disable Folder Home Pages for all folders** in the **Settings for Disable Folder Home Pages** area. For more information about using Group Policy to lock down Office settings, see "Managing Users' Configurations by Policy" in Chapter 18, "Updating Users' Office 2003 Configurations."

Chapter 12

Customizing Outlook 2003 to Help Prevent Viruses

Microsoft® Office Outlook® 2003 includes security-related features that help guard against viruses that are spread via attachments to e-mail messages, as well as from worm viruses that replicate through Microsoft Outlook. These security-related features are installed by default with Outlook 2003, which means that a standard installation will contain the locked-down settings established by the Outlook security template. However, you can customize these settings to meet the needs of your organization.

Configuring Outlook Security Features to Help Prevent Viruses

The Microsoft Outlook security model includes a number of features to help protect users against viruses and worms that can be propagated through e-mail messages. The security-related features include object model blocks (such as limiting automated address book access), access to attachments, and so on. Security-related features are included in the product, but they can be customized. Most of the features relating to security can be customized by using the Outlook security template.

> **Note** Several features are customized by using the registry instead of the Outlook security template. These features are as follows: read as plain text, automatic picture download, and HTML mail zones. You can also lock down the settings by using policies. For more information about modifying these settings, see "Helping Users Avoid Junk E-Mail Messages in Outlook 2003" in Chapter 7, "Deploying Outlook 2003."

You customize options in the Outlook security template, then publish a form in a special public folder on your Microsoft Exchange server. The form creates items in the public folder to represent the settings. When you publish the form, the items are updated with the new security settings. Then Outlook can be directed (by a registry key setting) to reference the settings stored there. The settings can only be updated by an authorized administrator.

The settings that can be configured by the template can help to provide a high level of security. However, the higher the level of security, the more limitations there are to functionality in Outlook. Restrictions enforced by the Outlook security form include limits to specific types of attachments, heightened default security settings, and controlled access to the Outlook automation code.

Requirements for customized security settings

As an administrator, you can use the template to customize the Outlook security settings to help meet your organization's needs. For example, you can help to control the types of attached files blocked by Outlook, modify the Outlook object model security and warning levels, and specify user or group security levels. However, to customize these settings, your users must have the appropriate Outlook configuration.

To enable custom security settings, your users must be using Outlook with Microsoft Exchange Server and have their mail delivered by default to either their Exchange mailbox or an Offline Folder file (OST file). You cannot modify most of these settings if a user is using a local Personal Folders file (PST file) for a mailbox, or if your organization is using Outlook with a third-party e-mail service. (The exception is for attachment-blocking settings, which can be configured with a local PST file or when using a third-party e-mail service.)

> **Caution**   Lowering any default security settings may increase your risk of virus execution or propagation. Use caution and read the documentation before you modify these settings.

Enabling customized security settings for users

When you create custom security settings for Outlook by using the Outlook security template, the settings are stored in messages in a top-level folder in the Public Folders tree. Users who need these settings must have a special registry key set on their computers for the settings to apply.

When the key is present, Outlook will look on the Exchange server for custom security settings to apply to a user. If these settings are found, they are applied. Otherwise, the default security settings in Outlook are used.

Users without the special key will have the default Outlook security settings that are in the product.

Note that in some cases, administrator-defined security settings may interact with security settings defined by the user. Specifically, users can customize attachment-blocking behavior, if their administrator has given permission.

Installing the files required to customize security settings

The files you need to configure the security settings and publish the form to enforce the settings are included in a self-extracting executable available from the Office 2003 Resource Kit. This executable, Admpack.exe, is included in the Office Resource Kit tools available from the Toolbox of the Office 2003 Resource Kit Web site at *http://www.microsoft.com/office/ork/2003*. It is not installed by default from the Office Resource Kit Setup program. The four administrative files are as follows:

- OutlookSecurity.oft

    An Outlook template that enables you to customize Outlook client security settings that are saved in a public folder on the Microsoft Exchange server. The OFT is the form that you publish into the special public folder that Outlook can be directed to reference for client security settings.

- Hashctl.dll and Comdlg32.ocx

    Two controls used by the form.

- Readme.doc

    A document that provides information on the values and settings available in the template and describes how to deploy the new settings on the Exchange server.

Customized security settings caveats

There are a couple caveats to keep in mind when deploying customized security settings for Microsoft Office Outlook 2003:

- Outlook must be restarted to get the customized settings.

    The first time a user starts Outlook after the customized security settings have been applied, the user will see default administrative settings and not the exception or default form that has been set. The user needs to close Outlook and then restart Outlook again to get the correct security settings and permissions.

- No customized settings are applied in PIM-only mode.

    In PIM (Personal Information Manager) mode, Outlook uses the default security settings. No administrator settings are looked for or used in this mode.

Resources and related information

For more information about how administrator settings work with user settings, see "Administrator-Controlled Settings vs. User-Controlled Settings" later in this chapter.

Installing the Outlook Trusted Code Control

In Microsoft Office Outlook 2003, administrators can specify COM add-ins that are trusted by Outlook's security features and can be run without encountering the Outlook Object Model security blocks. In order to specify a COM add-in, administrators must first install the Trusted Code Control on the computer they are using to modify the security settings. The control does not need to be installed on client computers.

To install and register the Trusted Code Control

1. Copy Hashctl.dll from your working directory to the Windows® System32 folder on your administrative computer. For example, \Windows\system32.

2. From the **Start** menu, click **Run**, then type the following command line in the box to register the control:

    regsvr32 hashctl.dll

3. Copy the file Comdlg32.ocx from your working directory to the Windows System32 folder on your administrative computer.

4. From the **Start** menu, choose **Run**, then type the following command line in the box to register the control:

    regsvr32 comdlg32.ocx

Resources and related information

You can customize the list of file types that are not allowed as e-mail attachments and other security settings. For more information about configuring these settings, see "Customizing Security Settings by Using the Outlook Security Template" in the next section.

Customizing Security Settings by Using the Outlook Security Template

You can modify default security settings for the Microsoft Office Outlook 2003 client by using the Outlook Security template, which you install as a form in Outlook. The template contains three tabs:

- Outlook Security Settings
- Programmatic Settings
- Trusted Code

Note   You specify a COM add-in as trusted by Outlook's security features by using the Trusted Code tab in the Outlook Security template. Before you can use the Trusted Code tab, you must first install the Trusted Code Control on the computer you are using to modify the security settings. For more information, see "Installing the Outlook Trusted Code Control" earlier in this chapter.

When you first load the template, the settings are configured to enforce default security settings on the client.

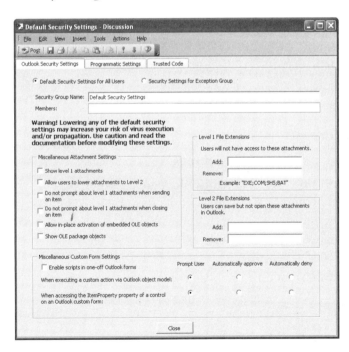

Creating a public folder for the security settings

Before you begin to modify the security settings, you must create a public folder named "Outlook Security Settings" or "Outlook 10 Security Settings" on the public folder Microsoft Exchange Server. You create this folder by using one of those names exactly, in the root folder of the Public Folder tree. You must set the folder access control lists (ACLs) so all users can read all items in the folder. However, only those users for whom you want to create or change security settings should have permission to create, edit, or delete items in the folder.

If you want multiple users to be able to edit or create items, and if the list of users can change at any time, then you must create a security group that includes all users for whom you want to give permission to create or change security settings. This security group should have Owner permissions on the security folder.

After you create the folder, you can install the security settings template, then make the changes you need.

Installing the Outlook Security template

Before you can modify security settings by using the Outlook Security template, you must publish the template as a form in the special public folder you created.

To install the Outlook Security template

1. On a computer running Outlook, open OutlookSecurity.oft from the working directory where you installed the Outlook security tools.

2. When asked to select a folder, select the **Outlook Security Settings** or **Outlook 10 Security Settings** public folder that you created on the Exchange server, and then click the **Open** button.

   The template will open in Compose mode.

3. On the **Tools** menu of the template, point to **Forms**, and then click **Publish Form**.

   The folder selected should be your current folder: **Outlook Security Settings** or **Outlook 10 Security Settings**.

4. In the **Form Name** box, type **Outlook Security Form**.

   If you are currently using the security form from the e-mail security patch, and if you are publishing the form to the Outlook Security Settings folder, then in the **Form Name** box, type the same name as the previous security form (that is, you overwrite the previous security form).

5. Click the **Publish** button to publish the security template in the Security Settings folder.

   You can now close the Outlook Security template. Do **not** save when prompted to save while closing the template.

Publishing a new security form over a previous version

There are two versions of the Outlook security form. The first version was released with the Outlook 2000 SR-1 security patch. The second version is the Outlook security form that is shipped with later versions of Outlook, starting with Outlook 2002.

If you installed the security update for Outlook 2000, you may have an earlier version of the security form already published to the security folder. In this scenario, you should overwrite the older form with the new copy, using the same name and message class. This will install the new form in place of the old one in the security folder.

If there are other forms in the security folder, you will need to open the other forms in the security folder and close them by using the **Close** button to correctly register any changes.

Modifying the default security settings

You use one of the following procedures to modify the default security settings in Outlook and store the new settings configuration in the special public folder you created for saving the settings. You can choose to create a configuration for all Outlook users, or you can set up a configuration for a specific set of users.

To specify a default Outlook security setting for all users by using the Outlook Security template

1. In Microsoft Outlook, click the drop-down arrow next to **New** on the toolbar, and select the **Choose Form** command from the list.

2. Navigate to the template you created earlier (in the "Installing the Outlook Security template" section), then select the template by name and click **Open**.

3. Click **Default Security Settings for All Users**, and specify the security settings you want.

4. Scroll to the bottom of the template and click **Close**.

Alternatively, you may choose to create a group of customized security settings for a specific set of Outlook users.

To specify a group of custom security settings for a set of Outlook users by using the Outlook Security template

1. In Microsoft Outlook, click the drop-down arrow next to **New** on the toolbar, and select the **Choose Form** command from the list.

2. Navigate to the template you created earlier (in the "Installing the Outlook Security template" section), then select the template by name and click **Open**.

3. Click **Security Settings for Exception Group**, and then type a name in the **Security Group Name** box that describes the group.

4. In the **Members** box, type the name of each user who must have custom security settings.

If the Exchange server you are running against is an Exchange 2000 or
later server, then you can use distribution lists (only server-created security
groups, not Outlook Contacts distribution lists) in the **Members** box. Otherwise, you cannot use distribution lists, and adding users from the Contacts
Address Book is not supported.

5. Specify the settings you need and then click **Close**.

> **Note**   For a security setting to apply to a user who is an administrator of
> the security settings public folder, the user (administrator) must be added
> to the member list of the security setting. It is not sufficient to have the
> administrator be a member of a distribution list that is listed in the mem-
> ber's box of the setting. You must add each administrator's name to the
> security setting. If you are using only a single default security group, then
> you do not need to add administrators' names.

If a user's name is entered as a member of more than one security group, the
settings of the most recently created group will apply. Outlook looks for the first
item that has the user's name in the **To** field.

Details on all fields, values, and settings for the template can be found in "Outlook Security Template Settings" later in this chapter.

Ensuring that security settings are properly created

Every time a security setting is created or saved, the administrator will be prompted
twice for credentials (when running on Exchange 2000 or later).

If no credentials are entered or if the wrong credentials are entered, an "Operation Failed" error message will appear. At this point, the security setting has been
created but will not work correctly. The administrator must delete the security item
and recreate it. If the item created is not deleted, then the item will be applied to
everybody, including users to whom you did not intend to apply the item.

Editing security settings

If the administrator adds a user to the Members field of an existing security form, the
administrator should make sure that all aliases already present in the form are current and active.

> **Note**   If you add the alias of a new member to an existing security form, the change may not be correctly registered unless you make other changes to the form as well. For example, you might toggle another setting on and off, or otherwise activate the form through some interaction. After you have added the new alias and activated the form, you can choose **Save** from the **File** menu of the form to save your changes.

Outlook Security Template Settings

The Microsoft Outlook Security template has three tabs: **Outlook Security Settings**, **Outlook Programmatic Settings**, and **Trusted Code**. The following sections describe the configurations you can specify on each of these tabs.

Outlook Security Settings tab

The **Outlook Security Settings** tab enables you to configure settings related to attachments, the types of files to which users can gain access, and scripting.

General settings

You can specify one or more groups of users whose members will have the same security settings. The following table describes the settings that specify security groups and members in the **Outlook Security Settings** tab.

Item	Description
Default Security Settings for All Users	Applies the default Outlook security settings to everyone.
Security Settings for Exception Group	Enables you to create custom Outlook security settings for some users.
Security Group Name	Specifies a name for the security group to which these customizations will apply. For example: "Object model access approved."
Members	Lists the names of members in this security group. If you are using an Exchange 2000 or later server, then you can use distribution lists (that is, server-based security groups). You must type names individually, separating each name by a semicolon. If a user's name is entered as a member of more than one security group, the settings of the most recently created group will apply, because Outlook looks for the first item that has the user's name in the **To** field. Administrators should not use the address book to enter an alias into the **Members** field when creating a security form. The only way to enter an alias into the **Members** field is by directly entering it into the field.

Miscellaneous attachment settings

You can specify how users will experience access to restricted (Level 1 and Level 2) e-mail message attachments. For example, you might allow users to change an attachment they receive that is specified as Level 1 (cannot be viewed by the user) to Level 2 (users can open the file after saving it to disk).

The following table describes the security options for e-mail attachments.

Item	Description
Show Level 1 attachments	Enables users to gain access to attachments with Level 1 file types.
Allow users to lower attachments to Level 2	Enables the end user to demote a Level 1 attachment to Level 2.
Do not prompt about Level 1 attachments when sending an item	Prevents users from receiving a warning when they send an item containing a Level 1 attachment. This option affects only the warning. Once the item is sent, the user will not be able to see or gain access to the attachment. If you want users to be able to post items to a public folder without receiving this prompt, you must select both this check box and the **Do not prompt about Level 1 attachments when closing an item** check box.
Do not prompt about Level 1 attachments when closing an item	Prevents users from receiving a warning when they close an e-mail message, appointment, or other item containing a Level 1 attachment. This option affects only the warning. Once the item is closed, the user will not be able to see or gain access to the attachment. If you want users to be able to post items to a public folder without receiving this prompt, you must select both this check box and the **Do not prompt about Level 1 attachments when sending an item** check box.
Allow in-place activation of embedded OLE objects	Allows users to double-click an embedded object, such as a Microsoft Excel spreadsheet, and open it in the program. However, if you are using Microsoft Word as your e-mail editor, clearing this check box will still allow OLE objects to be opened when the embedded object is double-clicked.
Show OLE package objects	Displays OLE objects that have been packaged. A package is an icon that represents an embedded or linked OLE object. When you double-click the package, the program used to create the object either plays the object (for example, if it's a sound file) or opens and displays the object. Caution should be used in displaying OLE package objects, because the icon can easily be changed and used to disguise malicious files.

Modifying the list of Level 1 file extensions

Level 1 files are hidden from the user in all items. The user cannot open, save, or print a Level 1 attachment. (If you specify that users can demote a Level 1 attachment to a Level 2 attachment, then Level 2 restrictions apply to the file.) The InfoBar at the top of the item will display a list of the blocked files. The InfoBar does not appear on a custom form. For information on a default list of Level 1 file types, see "Attachment File Types Restricted by Outlook 2003" later in this chapter.

When you remove a file extension from the Level 1 list, attachments with that file extension will no longer be blocked.

The following table describes how to add or remove Level 1 file extensions from the default list.

Action	Description
Add	Specifies the file extensions (usually three letters) of the file types you want to add to the Level 1 file list. Do not enter a period before each file extension. If you enter multiple extensions, separate them with semicolons.
Remove	Specifies the file extensions (usually three letters) of file types you want to remove from the Level 1 file list. Do not enter a period before each file extension. If you enter multiple extensions, separate them with semicolons.

Modifying the list of Level 2 file extensions

With a Level 2 file, the user is required to save the file to the hard disk before opening it. A Level 2 file cannot be opened directly from an item in an e-mail message. The following table describes how to add or remove Level 2 file extensions from the default list.

When you remove a file extension from the Level 2 list, it becomes a normal file type. You can open it, print it, and so on in Outlook; there are no restrictions on the file.

Action	Description
Add	Specifies the file extensions (usually three letters) of the file types you want to add to the Level 2 file list. Do not enter a period before each file extension. If you enter multiple extensions, separate them with semicolons.
Remove	Specifies the file extensions (usually three letters) of file types you want to remove from the Level 2 file list. Do not enter a period before each file extension. If you enter multiple extensions, separate them with semicolons.

Miscellaneous custom template settings

You can specify security settings for scripts, custom controls, and custom actions. For example, you can specify that when a program tries to run a custom action, users can decide whether to allow programmatic access for sending an e-mail message.

The following table describes the security settings for scripts, custom controls, and custom actions. (Scroll down in the Outlook Security template to see the full set of options.)

Item	Description
Enable scripts in one-off Outlook forms	Select this check box to run scripts in forms where the script and the layout are contained in the message itself. If users receive a one-off form that contains script, users will be prompted to ask if they want to run the script.
When executing a custom action via the Outlook object model	Specifies what happens when a program attempts to run a custom action using the Outlook object model. A custom action can be created to reply to a message and circumvent the programmatic send protections described above. Select one of the following: **Prompt user** enables the user to receive a message and decide whether to allow programmatic send access. **Automatically approve** always allows programmatic send access without displaying a message. **Automatically deny** always denies programmatic send access without displaying a message.
When accessing the ItemProperty property of a control on an Outlook custom form	Specifies what happens when a user adds a control to a custom Outlook form and then binds that control directly to any of the Address Information fields. By doing this, code can be used to indirectly retrieve the value of the Address Information field by getting the **Value** property of the control. Select one of the following: **Prompt user** enables the user to receive a message and decide whether to allow access to Address Information fields. **Automatically approve** always allows access to Address Information fields without displaying a message. **Automatically deny** always denies access to Address Information fields without displaying a message.

Programmatic Settings tab

The **Programmatic Settings** tab enables you to configure settings related to your use of the Outlook object model, Collaboration Data Objects (CDO), and Simple MAPI. These technologies are defined as follows:

- **Outlook object model**—The Outlook object model allows you to programmatically manipulate data stored in Outlook folders.

- **CDO**—Collaboration Data Object (CDO) libraries are used to implement messaging and collaboration functionality in a custom application. CDO is a COM wrapper of the MAPI library and can be called from any development language that supports Automation. CDO implements most but not all MAPI functionality (but more than Simple MAPI).

- **Simple MAPI**—Simple MAPI enables developers to add basic messaging functionality, such as sending and receiving messages, to their Windows-based applications. It is a subset of MAPI, which provides complete access to messaging and information exchange systems.

The following table lists descriptions for each option on the **Programmatic Settings** tab. For each item, you can choose one of the following settings:

- **Prompt user**—Users receive a message allowing them to choose whether to allow or deny the operation. For some prompts, users can choose to allow or deny the operation without prompts for up to 10 minutes.

- **Automatically approve**—The operation will be allowed and the user will not receive a prompt.

- **Automatically deny**—The operation will not be allowed and the user will not receive a prompt.

The following table describes the available options. You will need to scroll down in the template to see the full set of options.

Item	Description
When sending items via Outlook object model	Specifies what happens when a program attempts to send mail programmatically by using the Outlook object model.
When sending items via CDO	Specifies what happens when a program attempts to send mail programmatically by using CDO.
When sending items via Simple MAPI	Specifies what happens when a program attempts to send mail programmatically by using Simple MAPI.
When accessing the address book via Outlook object model	Specifies what happens when a program attempts to gain access to an address book by using the Outlook object model.
When accessing the address book via CDO	Specifies what happens when a program attempts to gain access to an address book by using CDO.
When resolving names via Simple MAPI	Specifies what happens when a program attempts to gain access to an address book by using Simple MAPI.
When accessing address information via Outlook object model	Specifies what happens when a program attempts to gain access to a recipient field, such as **To**, by using the Outlook object model.
When accessing address information via CDO	Specifies what happens when a program attempts to gain access to a recipient field, such as **To**, by using CDO.
When opening messages via Simple MAPI	Specifies what happens when a program attempts to gain access to a recipient field, such as **To**, by using Simple MAPI.
When responding to meeting and task requests via Outlook object model	Specifies what happens when a program attempts to send mail programmatically by using the **Respond** method on task requests and meeting requests. This method is similar to the **Send** method on mail messages.
When executing Save As via the Outlook object model	Specifies what happens when a program attempts to programmatically use the **Save As** command on the **File** menu to save an item. Once an item has been saved, a malicious program could search the file for e-mail addresses.

Continued

Item	Description
When accessing the Formula property of a UserProperty object in the Outlook object model	Specifies what happens when a user adds a Combination or Formula custom field to a custom form and binds it to an Address Information field. By doing this, code can be used to indirectly retrieve the value of the Address Information field by getting the **Value** property of the field.
When accessing address information via UserProperties.Find in the Outlook object model	Specifies what happens when a program attempts to search mail folders for address information using the Outlook object model.

Trusted Code tab

The **Trusted Code** tab is used to specify which COM add-ins are trusted and can be run without encountering the Outlook object model blocks. The following procedure describes how to use this feature.

To specify a trusted add-in

1. Copy the dynamic-link library (DLL) or other file that is used to load the COM add-in to a location where the administrator creating the security setting has access to it.

   This file must be the same file used on the client computers that will run the COM add-in.

2. On the **Trusted Code** tab, click **Add** and select the name of the DLL you want to add.

3. Click **Close** on the form when you have finished.

The COM add-in can now run without prompts for Microsoft Office Outlook 2003 users who use this security setting. To remove a file from the **Trusted Code** list on the **Trusted Code** tab, select the file name and click **Remove**.

> **Note**   The COM add-in must be coded to take advantage of the Outlook trust model in order for the add-in to run without prompts after being included in the **Trusted Code** list. If an add-in shows security prompts to users after being added to the **Trusted Code** list, you must work with the COM add-in developer to resolve the problem.

Deploying Customized Outlook Security Settings to Client Computers

After you configure customized Microsoft Outlook client security features by using the Microsoft Outlook security template and saving the settings in the special Microsoft Exchange public folder, you must enable the customized settings for your users. To enable the changed settings, you might need to deploy a new registry key to the client computers.

To enable the customized security settings, you create the following registry subkey, which is of type **DWORD**:

HKEY_CURRENT_USER\Software\Policies\Microsoft\Security\CheckAdmin-Settings

The following table describes the subkey values.

Key value	Description
No key	Outlook uses default security settings.
Set to **0**	Outlook uses default security settings.
Set to **1**	Outlook looks for custom administrative settings in the Outlook Security Settings folder.
Set to **2**	Outlook looks for custom administrative settings in the Outlook 10 Security Settings folder.
Set to anything else	Outlook uses default administrative settings. ·

To create a new registry subkey for distribution to client computers

1. Start the registry editor and expand the following key:
   HKEY_CURRENT_USER\Software\Policies\Microsoft\Security

2. From the **Edit** menu, choose **New**, then click **DWORD value** to add a new registry key.
   The value name for the key must be **CheckAdminSettings**.

3. Select the new key name, and then from the **Registry** menu, choose **Export Registry File**.

4. In the **Export Registry File** dialog box, type a name for the registry file and select the option for **Selected Branch** under the **Export Range** group, then click **Save** to create the registry file.
   Registry files have an .reg extension.

Administrator-Controlled Settings vs. User-Controlled Settings

In general, security settings defined by the user through the Microsoft Office Outlook 2003 user interface work as if they were added to the settings defined by the administrator. When there is a conflict between the two, the settings with a higher security level will override settings with a lower level of security.

Interactions between administrator settings and user settings

The following list describes some specific interactions between administrator security settings defined by using the Outlook Security template and security settings that a user defines in Outlook.

- **Show Level 1 attachments**. When this option is set on the **Outlook Security Settings** tab in the Outlook Security template, all file types that were set to Level 1 security are set to Level 2 security. If a user wants to block a file type, the user can customize the list to block access to specific types of attachments.

- **Level 1 file extensions — Add**. When set by the administrator, this list overrides the user's settings. Even if users are allowed to remove extensions from the default Level 1 group of excluded extensions, they cannot remove any extensions that were added to the list by using the Security template. For example, if the user wants to remove EXE, REG, and COM from the Level 1 group, but the administrator explicitly adds EXE into the Level 1 **Add** box, then the user would only be able to remove REG and COM files from the Level 1 group.

- **Level 1 file extensions — Remove**. The user's list is combined with the list set by the administrator to determine which Level 1 items are set to Level 2.

- **Level 2 file extensions — Add**. If a user turns Level 1 files into Level 2 files, and those file types are listed in the **Add** box, the files are treated as Level 2 attachments.

- **Level 2 file extensions — Remove**. There is no interaction with this setting.

- **Allow users to lower attachments to Level 2**. This setting allows a user to demote a Level 1 attachment to Level 2. If this option is unchecked, the user's list is ignored and the administrative settings help to control the security.

How security settings are controlled within the registry

The option to help prevent users from customizing their security settings is controlled either by a policy or by an option in the security template.

If the following registry key and value name are present, users cannot customize their security settings:

HKCU\Software\Policies\Microsoft\Office\11.0\Outlook
Value name: DisallowAttachmentCustomization

If the policy is present, end-user customization is disallowed. If the policy is not set on the computer, end-user customization is allowed only if it's not prohibited by an option in the Outlook Security template. The value of the key has no effect.

The registry key to set the exception list contains a semicolon-delimited list of file extensions. The value of the key is as follows:

HKCU\Software\Policies\Microsoft\Office\11.0\Outlook\Security

Value name: Level1Remove

If the value of the key is formatted incorrectly, the restrictions are ignored.

Resources and related information

A complete list of the Level 1 file extensions (for blocked e-mail attachment files) is included in the next section, "Attachment File Types Restricted by Outlook 2003."

Attachment File Types Restricted by Outlook 2003

By default, access is restricted to certain e-mail message attachments in Microsoft Outlook. In determining which attachments are blocked, Outlook checks the file type of the attachment. Files with certain file types can be completely blocked (Level 1) or the user may be required to save a file to disk before opening the file (Level 2).

By default, Outlook classifies a number of file type extensions as Level 1 and blocks files with those extensions from being received the users. There are no Level 2 file types by default, but you can create a list of Level 2 file types by using the Outlook Security template. You can demote file types from being categorized as Level 1 to being Level 2, or you can add other file types to create a Level 2 list.

Level 1 file types blocked by Outlook

The following table lists the Level 1 file types that are blocked under a default installation of Microsoft Office Outlook 2003. You can add or remove items from the default list through the **Outlook Security Settings** tab of the Outlook Security template.

File extension	File type
.ade	Microsoft Access project extension
.adp	Microsoft Access project
.app	FoxPro generated application
.bas	Microsoft Visual Basic® class module
.bat	Batch file
.chm	Compiled HTML Help file
.cmd	Microsoft Windows NT® command script
.com	Microsoft MS-DOS® program

Continued

File extension	File type
.cpl	Control Panel extension
.crt	Security certificate
.csh	Unix shell script
.exe	Executable file or program
.fxp	Microsoft FoxPro® file
.hlp	Help file
.hta	HTML program
.inf	Setup information
.ins	Internet naming service
.isp	Internet communication settings
.js	Jscript® file
.jse	Jscript-encoded script file
.ksh	Unix shell script
.lnk	Shortcut
.mda	Microsoft Access add-in program
.mdb	Microsoft Access program
.mde	Microsoft Access MDE database
.mdt	Microsoft Access file
.mdw	Microsoft Access file
.mdz	Microsoft Access wizard program
.msc	Microsoft Common Console document
.msi	Windows Installer package
.msp	Windows Installer patch
.mst	Visual Test source files
.ops	FoxPro file
.pcd	Photo CD image or Microsoft Visual Test compiled script
.pif	Shortcut to MS-DOS program
.prf	Microsoft Outlook Profile Settings
.prg	FoxPro program source file
.reg	Registration entries
.scf	Windows Explorer Command file
.scr	Screen saver
.sct	Windows script component
.shb	Shortcut into a document
.shs	Shell scrap object
.url	Internet shortcut

File extension	File type
.vb	VBScript file
.vbe	VBScript-encoded script file
.vbs	VBScript file
.wsc	Windows script component
.wsf	Windows script file
.wsh	Windows script host settings file
.xsl	XML file that can contain script

Level 2 file types restricted by Outlook

There are no Level 2 file types by default, but you can create a list of Level 2 file types for your deployment. Level 2 file types are restricted (under a default installation of Outlook 2003) and you must first save a Level 2 file to disk before you can open it—Level 2 file types cannot be opened directly from an item in an e-mail message.

As an administrator, you can add or remove attachment types from the list of Level 2 file types through the **Outlook Security Settings** tab of the Outlook Security form. Also, you can demote attachment file types from Level 1 to Level 2 by using the **Level1Remove** registry key. For more information about setting the **Level1Remove** registry key, see "Administrator-Controlled Settings vs. User-Controlled Settings" earlier in this chapter.

Part 4

Worldwide Deployment

Chapter 13

Preparing for an Office Multilingual Deployment

You can install, customize, and maintain a single version of Microsoft® Office 2003 that meets your organization's multilingual needs. The plug-in language features in Office 2003 and Office multilingual resources (such as the Multilingual User Interface Pack) allow users in international locales to work in their own languages. Users can also use a localized version of Office for the language needs of a select locale.

Overview of Office 2003 Multilingual Resources

Microsoft Office 2003 provides tools that simplify deploying and supporting Office across language boundaries—including the Microsoft Office 2003 Multilingual User Interface Pack (MUI Pack), which gives organizations the option to configure the Office user interface in multiple languages.

You have several options for installing Office language versions and language-specific tools, based on your organization's needs. These options include:

- Microsoft Office 2003 Multilingual User Interface Pack, which enables you to view the Office 2003 user interface and Help in a variety of languages.

- Microsoft Office 2003 Proofing Tools, which enables you to create and edit Office documents in other languages.

- Microsoft Office 2003 in a localized version.

For information on deploying a combination of these resources, see the sections "Combinations of multilingual options" and "Typical multilingual configurations" in this chapter.

Multilingual User Interface Pack

The Multilingual User Interface Pack (MUI Pack) includes files for displaying the Office user interface and Help in several languages. With MUI Packs, users worldwide can run the Office user interface and online Help in one or more languages, or create and edit documents in other languages. For administrators, the core functionality of Office 2003 allows them to deploy a single version of Office—regardless of what language is primarily used at their users' location—along with the necessary language resources.

Although Office is localized into specific language versions, Office with the MUI Pack provides combined support for those languages in a single product because it is built on core code that you can run internationally. (Localized versions provide additional language-specific functionality in minor areas such as right-click menus.) Language-specific user interface and Help text are stored separately. These language features "plug in" to the core Office 2003 code, and your users can install and run these features when they need them.

The plug-in language capabilities of the MUI Pack allow you to install English Office 2003 on your computer and view the Office 2003 user interface and Help in another language—for example, German. You can even view Help in one language and the user interface in another.

> **Note**   Although the MUI Pack lets you change the user interface and Help
> to any of dozens of languages, and provides proofing tools for more than 50
> languages, using Office 2003 with the MUI Pack is not the same as using a
> localized version of Office 2003. For more information on localized ver-
> sions, see "Localized versions of Office 2003" later in this chapter.

You can customize your Office installation to add MUI Pack files for several languages. You can then specify different user interface and Help text languages for different groups of users in your organization, or allow users to set their own language.

The MUI Pack is designed to enhance the English version of Office 2003; it is
not supported with localized versions of Office. (The Multilingual User Interface
Pack Setup program is available in English only; it is not localized into other languages.) In addition, the MUI Pack works only with editions Office obtained
through a Volume License agreement or similar channel; it does not work with retail
editions of Office.

Hard disk space requirements for the MUI Packs vary per MUI Pack language.
For example, the German MUI Pack requires 231 megabytes (MB) of hard disk
space. In addition, if users install from a compressed image and choose to keep the
local installation source, the German MUI Pack requires an additional 91 MB of hard
disk space for the local installation source. By contrast, the Chinese (Simplified) MUI
Pack requires 578 MB of hard disk space plus an additional 320 MB for the local
installation source.

Advantages to deploying the MUI Pack with a standard Office configuration

Deploying Office 2003 together with multilingual resources such as MUI Packs or
Proofing Tools has several advantages. The main advantage is that you can customize a standard configuration of Office for your whole organization—by using the
Custom Installation Wizard, for example—and then allow individual sites to include
language features appropriate for their areas. For more information on strategies to
use in deploying language resources, see "Office 2003 Multilingual Deployment
Strategies" later in this chapter.

If you choose to use the Custom Installation Wizard to modify the Office package (MSI file) when you configure Office for an international deployment, you
would set language settings such as the default Help language and the languages
enabled for editing. During installation, these settings will be applied to Office applications by means of a transform. In contrast, if you modify the MSI file for a MUI
Pack with the Custom Installation Wizard, these language configuration options are
not available.

To effectively install a MUI Pack with Office, the MUI Pack installation should be chained to the Office installation. By chaining the MUI Pack installation, you can ensure that the Office settings will be applied first, and that the MUI Pack will be installed before Office is started for the first time. (Starting Office without a MUI Pack installed will cause the language settings to revert to their default state.) For information on chaining installations through Setup, see "Deploying Office and Other Products Together" in Chapter 5, "Installing Office 2003."

Proofing Tools

Office 2003 Proofing Tools includes spelling and grammar checkers, thesauruses, AutoCorrect lists, and Input Method Editors—all the tools users need to create and edit Office documents in more than 50 languages. You install Proofing Tools when your users need to work in other languages but use a standard language for the user interface and Help in Office applications.

While some proofing tools are included in the MUI Pack, Office 2003 Proofing Tools is a separate product. Unlike the MUI Pack, Office 2003 Proofing Tools works with localized versions of Office 2003.

You can install Proofing Tools for one or more languages on users' computers. Each language set that you install allows a user to create and edit documents in that language.

After you have installed Office, you can install Proofing Tools separately. By developing an integrated deployment plan, however, you can install Proofing Tools (together with MUI Packs, if you choose) at the same time that you install Office 2003—by chaining Proofing Tools to the Office installation.

> **Note**   The Setup program for Office 2003 Proofing Tools is available in these languages: Dutch, Swedish, Brazilian Portuguese, English, French, German, Italian, and Spanish. (The MUI Pack Setup program is available in English only.)

Hard disk space requirements for Office 2003 Proofing Tools vary by language. For instance, Proofing Tools for German requires 48 MB of hard disk space; Proofing Tools for Chinese (Simplified) requires 365 MB. Asian languages require as much as 120 MB of hard disk space to include the necessary fonts and Input Method Editors (IMEs).

Localized versions of Office 2003

Localized versions of Office 2003 are available for users who want all Office features in their own language. Although deploying Office with the MUI Pack gives you the advantage of having a single installation of Office for your entire international organization, there are limitations to some plug-in language features in the MUI Pack. As a result, these features are only offered in localized versions.

Although MUI Packs are used only with the English version of Office 2003 and not with localized versions, users of a localized version of Office can easily share documents created by users running Office with a MUI Pack. In this way, localized versions of Office 2003 are compatible with Office 2003 with the MUI Pack.

To install a localized version of Office 2003, you follow the same procedures as when you install the English version. For example, you can customize your installation by creating a transform with the Custom Installation Wizard.

There are some advantages, and some disadvantages, to installing a localized version.

Advantages to installing a localized version of Office

Installing a localized version of Office 2003 has its advantages. For instance, the user interface of some of the features in Office 2003 with the Multilingual User Interface Pack cannot be changed. If it is important that users run these features in the users' own language, you can deploy a localized version of Office to these users. Localized versions of Office 2003 are based on the same international core as Office 2003 with the Multilingual User Interface Pack, so users can exchange documents between language versions of Office 2003 with no loss of data.

There are some differences between running Office 2003 with the Multilingual User Interface Pack and running a localized version of Office. For example:

- Office 2003 with the MUI Pack cannot switch the user interface language of Microsoft Office Excel 2003 add-ins and some ActiveX® controls.

- In Office 2003 with the MUI Pack, shortcuts on the **Start** menu are not localized.

- Localized versions of Office include localized right-click menus.

> **Note**   Although the Multilingual User Interface Pack lets you change the user interface and Help to any of dozens of languages, and provides proofing tools for more than 50 languages, using Office with the MUI Pack is not the same as using a localized version of Office 2003. For more information on localized versions, see "Localized versions of Office 2003" earlier in this chapter.

Disadvantages to installing a localized version of Office

There are some drawbacks to deploying localized versions of Office rather than building around a standard version. With separate versions, you need to customize and manage each localized version separately, including developing separate procedures for deployment, support, and administration. Also, localized versions do not usually support the ability to switch the language of the user interface.

However, some localized versions of Office 2003 provide limited ability to switch the language of the user interface to English as follows:

- Arabic
- Hebrew
- Hindi
- Japanese
- Korean
- Pan-Chinese
- Simplified Chinese
- Thai
- Traditional Chinese

In the Arabic version of Office 2003, you can also switch the user interface to French. In the Pan-Chinese (Hong Kong) version, you can switch most Office 2003 applications to Simplified Chinese (except for Microsoft Office Outlook® 2003 and Microsoft Office FrontPage® 2003).

Depending on your needs, you can deploy a localized version of Office 2003 in selected geographical areas. For example, you might deploy Office 2003 with the Multilingual User Interface Pack everywhere except Japan, where you deploy the Japanese version of Office 2003.

Combinations of multilingual options

You can install different combinations of Microsoft Office 2003 and language offerings, based on your organization's requirements. Some of these combinations are described in the following table.

If you want to...	Install the following language version and tools
Deploy a single version of Office internationally for your organization and allow users to work with a user interface and Help in one non-English language (regardless of the language used in their documents).	English Office 2003 with one MUI Pack
Deploy a single version of Office and allow users in different parts of your organization (perhaps in different countries) to work in different user interface and Help languages.	English Office 2003 with several MUI Packs

If you want to...	Install the following language version and tools
Standardize on an English user interface for your organization, and allow users to view documents in other languages.	English Office 2003 only
Standardize on an English user interface, and enable users to create and edit documents in other languages.	English Office 2003 and Office 2003 Proofing Tools
Provide users with fully localized functionality and content (such as templates and add-ins) in all Office applications in a single language, and allow them to view documents in other languages.	Localized versions of Office 2003 for one language
Provide users with fully localized functionality in all Office applications in a single language, and allow them to create and edit documents in other languages.	Localized versions of Office 2003 for one language and Office 2003 Proofing Tools

Typical multilingual configurations

Some common scenarios for deploying multilingual configurations for Office 2003 include the following:

- Mimic a localized version.

  Deploy English Office 2003 along with a MUI Pack MSI file for an additional language.

- Use English as a standard user interface, but provide Help text in native languages.

  Deploy English Office 2003 along with the MUI Pack that adds additional Help files in another language.

- Provide a multilingual version of Office on one computer.

  For example, set up a computer to be used by traveling users from different countries. Deploy English Office 2003 along with MUI Packs for each required language.

- Allow users to read and edit text in another language.

  Deploy Office 2003 (an English or localized version) along with the proofing tools for the required language or languages.

- Use a fully localized version of Office with no English text.

  Install a localized version of Office 2003. Localized versions provide a limited number of additional localized features, such as language-specific right-click menus.

Resources and related information

There are issues and limitations to be aware of when configuring users' computers. You may also want to set up browsers, fonts, and printers to take better advantage of international features. For more information about these options, see "Preparing Users' Computers for Multilingual Capabilities in Office" later in this chapter.

You can provide multilingual user interface and Help text to Office users by installing one or more MUI Packs. For more information about configuring an Office 2003 Multilingual User Interface Pack to meet the needs of your organization, see "Customizing and Installing Office 2003 MUI Packs" in Chapter 14, "Deploying Office 2003 Multilingual Resources."

You can allow users to edit and proof documents by installing Office 2003 Proofing Tools. For more information about making Proofing Tools available to users in your organization, see "Installing Proofing Tools," also in Chapter 14.

Office 2003 Multilingual Deployment Strategies

Once you select the Microsoft Office 2003 multilingual resources to use for your organization, you need to choose an appropriate deployment strategy. Your strategy will depend on the structure of your organization and the languages your users need, and will likely consider whether you:

- Deploy from a centralized administrative location.

  Customize an installation of Office with the language resources required by a specific area in your company—for example, add the German Multilingual User Interface Pack for a division located in Germany. Then deploy the custom installation from a centralized administrative location—for example, a server at the central office in London.

- Distribute Office to subsidiaries to deploy from there.

  Deploy to your international administrative departments and allow the administrative department in each subsidiary to customize the installation to meet its language needs.

- Choose one or several administrative installation points in your Office deployment.

  Using one administrative installation point might enable a more centralized deployment strategy, while using several might provide flexibility for several local customizations.

- Time your multilingual customizations to fall before, with, or after an Office deployment, and choose whether to use deployment tools such as Group Policy software installation or Microsoft Systems Management Server.

If you have chosen to deploy a localized version of Office 2003, you customize and deploy that version just as you do an English version.

Deploying multilingual features from a central administrative location

If your organization uses one administrative group to deploy Office to the entire organization, you can make all the customizations at your headquarters and deploy directly to users internationally. In this scenario, you customize the Microsoft Office 2003 Multilingual User Interface Pack (MUI Pack) and create a custom installation of Office for the language needs in each area. Users in each area then install the custom configuration for that area. (If you deploy more than one custom configuration, you can choose to use one or more administrative installation points.)

For example, if you are deploying Microsoft Office 2003 with the Multilingual User Interface Pack (MUI Pack) to users in the United States and Canada, you might create four separate customized Office deployments as follows:

- For English-speaking users in the United States, customize the installation to install only proofing tools from the MUI Pack and enable languages for editing as needed.

- For Spanish-speaking users in the United States, customize the MUI Pack to install Spanish language features from the MUI Pack, leave the installation language set at U.S. English, set the user interface and Help language to Spanish, and enable Spanish for editing (English is automatically enabled for editing if the installation language is English).

- For users in English-speaking Canadian provinces, set the installation language to Canadian English, and enable Canadian French and Canadian English for editing.

- For users in Québec, install the French MUI Pack, set the installation language to Canadian French, set the user interface and Help language to French, and enable Canadian French and Canadian English for editing.

Deploying Office from a subsidiary

If your organization's administrative resources are distributed internationally, each local subsidiary can modify the standard installation for local users.

In this case, a central corporate administrative group supplies each local office with a standard Windows Installer transform (MST file) for Office 2003 with the installation language set to English. The transform might include certain Office customizations (standardized for the whole corporation). Then local administrators customize the MUI Pack (creating a MUI Pack transform), select language settings, and modify the Office 2003 transform for the language needs in their area.

For example, if you are a site administrator in Hong Kong, you might customize the corporate deployment as follows:

- Customize the Traditional Chinese and Simplified Chinese MUI Packs to install Traditional and Simplified Chinese language features on users' computers.

- Customize the language settings to set English or Traditional Chinese as the language for the user interface and online Help; set the installation language to Traditional Chinese; and enable Simplified Chinese, Traditional Chinese, and U.K. English for editing.

- Modify the Office 2003 transform (before deploying Office 2003) to customize Office applications for Hong Kong users.

  For example, add a button to the toolbar in Microsoft Office Word 2003 for converting between Simplified Chinese and Traditional Chinese.

Choosing one or multiple administrative installation points

You can use a single centralized administrative installation point for Office 2003, the Multilingual User Interface Pack, or Microsoft Office 2003 Proofing Tools. Or you can deploy Office from one installation point, and deploy one or more MUI Packs (or proofing tools) from additional installation points. It can be easier to manage deployment from a single administrative installation point. However, there are scenarios in which using multiple installation points is a preferred method.

For example, suppose you are deploying several different sets of languages to groups in different parts of your organization. In this scenario, you might choose to use different installation points for these groups to avoid using large amounts of hard disk space when you replicate a single administrative installation point image to multiple locations around the world.

Timing your installation of multilingual features

You can chain installations of the Multilingual User Interface Pack or Proofing Tools with your Office 2003 installation. Or you can deploy Office first, and deploy other multilingual features later.

For example, if you are ready to deploy Office 2003 right away but the MUI Pack for a particular language is not yet available, you might still proceed with your Office deployment and then deploy the additional MUI Pack when it becomes available.

To learn more about options for coordinating your installation of language resources with your Office deployment, see "Customizing and Installing Office 2003 MUI Packs" in Chapter 14, "Deploying Office 2003 Multilingual Resources."

Use Systems Management Server to deploy Office with multilingual options

Systems Management Server (SMS) provides a flexible and powerful tool for deploying software. You can deploy Office with the Multilingual User Interface Pack or Proofing Tools with Systems Management Server. First, you customize your Office installation by using the Custom Installation Wizard to create transforms for Office and the multilingual features you are deploying. Then you deploy Office by creating SMS packages and distributing them to selected clients.

You cannot control the order in which components are deployed with Systems Management Server. Because of this, you must set the **CHECKINSTALLORDER** property to **FALSE** when configuring your MUI Pack or Office Proofing Tools deployment. This allows the MUI Pack or Proofing Tools to be installed even if Office is not.

For more information on using SMS to deploy Office, see "Using SMS 2.0 to Deploy Microsoft Office XP" on the Microsoft TechNet Web site at *http://www.microsoft.com/technet/prodtechnol/sms/deploy/depopt/smsoffxp.asp.*

Use Windows software installation to deploy Office with multilingual options

In Microsoft Windows® 2000 and Microsoft Windows XP or later, Group Policy provides a software installation and management solution designed to support Windows 2000 or Windows XP clients.

By default, Office must be installed before MUI Pack files are installed. However, when you deploy using Group Policy or using Microsoft Systems Management Server, you cannot specify the order in which components are installed. To help prevent installation errors, you set a property (**CHECKINSTALLORDER**) when you configure your Office installation. This property allows Office files, MUI Pack files, and proofing tools files to be installed in any order.

For more information about using Group Policy software installation, see "Using Group Policy to Deploy Office" in Chapter 5, "Installing Office 2003."

Overview of Deploying Office 2003 with the MUI Pack

Including the Microsoft Office 2003 Multilingual User Interface Pack (MUI Pack) in a Microsoft Office 2003 deployment is a two-step process that requires some decisions ahead of time, including whether to allow users to install their own languages, or whether to install MUI Packs with Microsoft Office 2003 or after Office 2003. After you decide when and how to install MUI Packs, you customize your deployment (for example, you configure the language settings and deploy the MUI Packs to your organization.

MUI Pack components

Office 2003 with MUI Pack is English Office 2003 with a MUI pack for each available non-English language of Office. The MUI Pack for Office 2003 has the following components you use to deploy a customized multilingual installation:

- **MUI Packs (Mui.msi files)**   Each language has its own package (MSI file) and can be customized individually. By default behavior, the features of a MUI Pack use the same installation state as the corresponding features in Office unless you want them to be different. For example, suppose Microsoft Office Outlook 2003 is configured not to be installed with Office, and Microsoft Office Word 2003 is configured to be installed on users' local disks. When the MUI Pack is installed, the corresponding language files for Outlook will be set to install on demand while all Word language files will be installed locally.

- **MUI wizard Setup (Muisetup.exe)**   You use this program with the **/a** option to create an administrative installation point for the languages you select. Users can also deploy MUI Packs by running this program to call the MUI Pack Wizard.

- **MUI Pack Wizard (Muiwiz.msi)**   Used by MUI Pack Setup, this wizard enables users to choose which languages to install and configures the user interface, Help, and installation language settings to be set during Setup.

Overview of the MUI Pack deployment process

A MUI Pack deployment generally follows these steps:

1. Create an administrative installation point for Office 2003.

2. Create an administrative installation point for the MUI Pack files you want to deploy (you can use the Office administrative installation point or a separate server share).

3. Customize your MUI Pack installation.

    Use the Custom Installation Wizard to create a transform for Office, for individual MUI Packs, or for both. For an Office transform, you can store language settings with other Office settings in an Office profile settings file (OPS file), or set language settings in the Custom Installation Wizard. For a MUI Pack transform, you can customize feature states and Setup properties in the Custom Installation Wizard.

    Note that language settings—such as the Help language and installed version of Microsoft Office—cannot be set when you customize individual MUI Pack installations. Instead, customize these settings when you deploy Office.

4. Configure Setup.ini to chain the installation of one or more languages packs with your Office deployment. (If you use Microsoft Systems Management Server deployment, this step is not needed.)

5. Deploy Office with selected MUI Packs to your users.

    Typically Office is installed on users' computers before the MUI Pack files, but you can circumvent this default process by using the Setup property **CHECKINSTALLORDER**. You set this option when you cannot ensure the deployment order for the components being installed—for example, if you are deploying by using Group Policy technologies for software installation or Systems Management Server.

6. Install one or more MUI Packs (possibly in addition to MUI Packs you have already installed with Office) by using a separate customized Setup settings file (Setup.ini) or by allowing users to choose MUI Packs with the MUI Pack Wizard.

Note When you install Office 2003 with the Multilingual User Interface Pack, or when you install individual MUI Packs, all corresponding Office 2000 or Office XP language pack files on users' computers are deleted by default. If you plan to keep some Office 2000 or Office XP applications, however, you can retain the Office 2000 or Office XP language packs. Specify **KEEPLPK9=1** in the [Options] section of Setup.ini or in a transform for each Office 2003 MUI pack that you install, or specify **KEEPLPK=1** on the Setup command line. Similarly, to retain Office 2000 or XP Proofing Tools, specify **KEEPPTK9=1**.

Resources and related information

In some deployment scenarios, you must know the locale identifier (LCID) for a language in order to install the correct MUI Pack. A table with this information is included in "Office 2003 MUI Pack Languages and Corresponding Locale Identifiers" in Chapter 14, "Deploying Office 2003 Multilingual Resources."

Preparing Users' Computers for Multilingual Capabilities in Office

The international features of Microsoft Office 2003 work on Microsoft Windows 2000 Service Pack 3 and later and Microsoft Windows XP, the supported operating system platforms for Office 2003. However, in preparing users' computers to take advantage of this multilingual support—including setting up browsers, fonts, and printers—there are some issues and limitations to consider.

Operating system considerations for a multilingual installation of Office

The Microsoft Windows 2000 and Microsoft Windows XP operating systems both support international features of Microsoft Office 2003. In some cases, you may need to set a specific system locale for Office to support the desired language.

Office 2003 automatically enables languages for editing when the languages are enabled in Windows 2000 and Windows XP. However, Windows XP enables some languages in groups—complex script languages and East Asian languages—that Office 2003 does not enable as groups automatically. If you want to enable complex script or East Asian languages for editing with Office on Windows XP, you must enable them manually in Office.

On the Resource Kit CD Information about limitations for language support is included in the Microsoft Office Excel 2003 workbook Wwsuppt.xls, which is installed by default when you run the Microsoft Office Resource Kit Setup program. For more information, see "International Information" in Appendix A, "Toolbox."

Displaying the user interface in other languages

Windows 2000 and Windows XP provide support for all possible Office user interface languages. You need to ensure a user's system locale (which governs the code page of the user's computer) is set to a locale that supports the primary language the user needs.

The system locale that you set depends on the primary language your users need. This is because some code pages provide support for groups of languages; other code pages provide support for only a single language. For example, if your users work primarily in Japanese, set their system locale to Japanese. If your users work primarily in French, their system locale can be any Western European system locale.

For some applications and features in Office 2003, the native code page of the operating system must support the user interface language. For these applications and features, text in the user interface—such as file names in Microsoft Office FrontPage 2003—must be supported by the operating system's system code page.

When you use FrontPage 2003 and some features (such as Microsoft Visual Basic® for Applications) you can change the user interface language to any language that is supported by the system code page of your operating system. When you change the user interface to a language that does not have code page support, FrontPage displays the user interface in English.

On the Resource Kit CD Some Office features do not change when you change the language of the user interface or Help. Information about those features is available in the Microsoft Excel workbook Intlimit.xls, which is installed by default when you run the Office Resource Kit Setup program. For more information, see "International Information" in Appendix A, "Toolbox."

Displaying Help and Microsoft Office Online assistance in other languages

Microsoft Office Online, the site on the World Wide Web for end users of the Microsoft Office System, consists of a number of international sites containing appropriate content for the local language, country, or region. These international sites represent the majority of languages in which Office 2003 and the Microsoft Office 2003 Multilingual User Interface Packs are available.

Initially, the language of the Microsoft Office Online Web site is determined by Microsoft Internet Explorer language settings. Users can view different language-specific and region-specific content on Microsoft Office Online, however, by clicking **Office Worldwide** and choosing a different international site. If their Web browser settings allow persistent cookies, the new international site persists the next time they visit Microsoft Office Online.

The Help language setting in Office applications is handled separately. When a user enters a query in an Office application, both online and offline query results are always displayed in the language set for Help (for users with Microsoft Office 2003 Multilingual User Interface Packs) or the installation language of the product (for localized versions of Office). For some languages, including English, French, and Chinese, the regional settings in Windows also result in content specific to that region.

Because users can change the international site of Microsoft Office Online independently of their Help or user interface language settings, application language settings are not synchronized with the Microsoft Office Online international site. In some cases, users may find themselves viewing Web pages with a mixture of languages and region-specific content.

Users can ensure that Help queries are returned in the appropriate language by following these guidelines:

- To display query results on Microsoft Office Online in a language other than the Office installation language or Help language setting, enter the query directly on the Microsoft Office Online language-specific or region-specific Web site.

- To ensure that query results on Microsoft Office Online are displayed in the same language as the client, choose the site that matches the language settings on the local computer.

Editing documents in other languages

All language versions of Windows 2000 and Windows XP support displaying documents in all languages. However, in the case of Asian documents, even though users can display documents, they might not be able to edit the files to include Asian characters without a special editing interface.

Input of Asian characters requires an Input Method Editor (IME). The Microsoft Office 2003 Multilingual User Interface Pack provides IMEs for Japanese, Korean, Simplified Chinese, and Traditional Chinese. The IMEs allow users to input Asian text in Office applications, regardless of the language version of their operating system. Microsoft Office 2003 Proofing Tools also includes Input Method Editors.

Using the Windows keyboard layout program

Windows 2000 and Windows XP include a keyboard layout program—On-Screen Keyboard—that makes it easier for users to type languages not represented on the physical keyboard. Be sure that the language that users want to use in the On-Screen Keyboard has been enabled for editing.

To access the Windows keyboard layout program

1. On the taskbar, click **Start**, and then click **All Programs** (Windows XP) or **Start Programs** (Windows 2000).

2. Click **Accessories**.

3. Click **Accessibility**.

4. Click **On-Screen Keyboard**.
    The **On-Screen Keyboard** dialog box is shown, and you can click the keys displayed to perform keyboard functions.

Limitations to entering multilingual content in Outlook in ANSI mode

Microsoft Office Outlook 2003 provides Unicode® support in most scenarios. When Outlook is running in Unicode mode, there are no limitations for entering content in other languages. There are, however, some scenarios in which Outlook will run in ANSI mode instead of Unicode mode. In these situations, there are limitations to be aware of.

When Outlook will be in ANSI mode

In certain scenarios, Outlook will run in ANSI mode. Note that Outlook Unicode mode only applies for Microsoft Exchange Server configurations.

The scenarios when Outlook does not support Unicode include:

■ For POP accounts when the delivery store is an ANSI PST.

■ For Microsoft Hotmail®, IMAP, and LDAP accounts.

Language limitations when Outlook is in ANSI mode

There are two main types of content that users can type in Outlook when in ANSI mode: plain text and rich text. Text typed in a plain text area cannot be saved and retrieved in a language that is not supported by the default code page set on the user's computer. For example, text entered in most fields in a Contact entry (such as the contact name or telephone number) is plain text. It cannot have special formatting (for instance, bold or italics), and it cannot be saved and retrieved in a language that is not supported by the default code page.

Other text-entry areas support rich text—for example, the message body of an e-mail message. Rich text support is provided in several ways (for instance, by using

RTF or HTML), and supports formatting, links, and similar elements. Rich text areas also support text entry and retrieval for languages that are not supported by the default code page on the user's computer.

Choosing a Web browser

The Web browser installed on users' computers can affect how well Microsoft Office 2003 supports switching to different user interface languages—and can also be a factor in whether users can create multilingual Web pages.

Supporting multilingual dialog boxes

Microsoft Internet Explorer 5 or later allows Microsoft Office 2003 applications to display certain dialog boxes in any user interface language that the operating system supports. Dialog boxes such as **New** and **Open** from the **File** menu depend on the code page of the operating system to display text.

Using Unicode in multilingual Web pages

Unicode allows users to create multilingual Web pages that not only use multiple scripts but also produce smaller files that are easy to parse on your intranet or the Internet. You need Internet Explorer 5 or later, or Netscape Navigator 4.07 or later, for your browser to interpret Unicode Web pages. If you want to maintain compatibility with earlier browsers, avoid using Unicode.

> **Note**   The Unicode format commonly used on the Internet is called Universal Character Set Transformation Format 8-bit (UTF-8). UTF-8 is the only Unicode format that is commonly supported by Web browsers and by FrontPage Server Extensions from Microsoft.

You can set Office 2003 applications to save the current HTML document in Unicode.

To save an HTML document in Unicode in Office 2003

1. In an Office application that supports this feature (such as Microsoft Office Word 2003), on the **Tools** menu, click **Options**.

2. On the **General** tab, click **Web Options**.

3. On the **Encoding** tab, in the **Save this document as** list, select **Unicode (UTF-8)**.

> **Note**   To save HTML documents in the Unicode format by default, select the **Always save Web pages in the default encoding** check box in the **Web Options** dialog box.

Using Unicode in multilingual URLs

In addition to allowing users to create HTML documents in UTF-8 encoding, Office 2003 and Internet Explorer 5 or later can send UTF-8–encoded URLs to Web servers.

UTF-8 encoding allows users to use URLs that include non-ASCII characters, regardless of the language of the user's operating system and browser, or the language version of Office. Without UTF-8 encoding, a user's Web server must be based on the same code page as that of the user's operating system in order for the Web server to interpret non-ASCII URLs. However, for a Web server to interpret UTF-8 encoded URLs, the Web server must have UTF-8 support.

> **Note**   To use UTF-8 encoded URLs, you must have Microsoft Internet Information Services (IIS) 4.0 or later or another Web server that supports UTF-8.

If your organization has code page–based Web servers that do not support UTF-8, and you have non-ASCII URLs, you should turn off UTF-8 URL encoding in Internet Explorer 5. Otherwise, when users try to use a UTF-8–encoded URL that includes non-ASCII characters, the code page based Web server that does not support UTF-8 cannot interpret the URL.

To prevent sending URLs in UTF-8 encoding

1. In Internet Explorer 5 (or later), on the **Tools** menu, click **Internet Options**.
2. In the **Internet Options** dialog box, click the **Advanced** tab.
3. Under **Browsing**, clear the **Always send URLs as UTF-8** check box.

Managing fonts for multilingual installations

Microsoft Windows 2000 and Windows XP provide fonts that allow users to view and edit documents in different languages and across different scripts. These fonts allow users to:

- Display the user interface and Help in various languages.
- Display text in various languages—in an existing document or text that you enter—including languages that require Input Method Editors (IMEs).

When users enable a language in the operating system, the fonts for that language are typically installed for them. Big fonts—such as Tahoma®—that were previously supplied by Office are now included in Windows.

However, because some fonts provided in Windows XP are not included in Windows 2000, Office 2003 also includes several fonts, such as Arial, Unicode, and Syriac. To install fonts from Office for your users, you configure the feature installation state in the Custom Installation Wizard to install the Additional Fonts feature. Note that fonts installed from Office do not update any existing Windows fonts.

Choosing the Unicode font

Some documents, such as Microsoft Access data tables, can display only one font at a time. But these documents can display multilingual text in more than one script if you use the Unicode font. The Unicode font provided by Office 2003 allows users to input and display characters across scripts and across code pages that support the various scripts.

Installing a Unicode font on users' computers has some disadvantages. First, the Unicode font file is much larger than font files based on code pages. Second, some characters might look different from their character equivalents in code pages. For these reasons, do not use the Unicode font as your default font. However, if your users share documents across many different scripts, the Unicode font might be your best choice.

Printing documents

Using the international features of Office 2003 in documents creates some special requirements for printing. You must ensure that your printers are configured for the correct paper size and for font substitution.

Specifying the correct paper size

Many printers allow you to load both A4 and letter-size paper. If users in Europe exchange documents with users in the United States, having both A4 and letter-size paper in your printers accommodates everyone's documents.

Even if your printers are stocked only with the paper commonly used in your part of the world, most Office documents are printed with no loss of text. Microsoft Word documents and Microsoft Office PowerPoint® 2003 presentations are automatically scaled to fit the printer's default paper size. Microsoft Outlook messages are printed according to locally defined default print parameters. Microsoft FrontPage documents are printed according to the browser's page layout settings.

> **Note**   For Microsoft Office Publisher 2003 documents, users must open documents and manually change the paper size. For Microsoft Office Access 2003 reports, users must open a report, manually change the paper size, close the report, reopen the report, and then print.

In some circumstances, you might not want documents scaled to fit the printer's default paper size. For example, if your printer has A4 set as its default paper size but the printer also has letter-size paper, Word cannot detect that both sizes are available. Because the printer can supply the correct size paper, you might want to turn off the resizing option that is available in Word.

> **Tip**   You can use a policy to turn off the **Allow A4/Letter paper resizing** option on the **Print** tab (**Options** menu) in Word. Using Group Policy, in the Word 2003 policy template (Word11.adm), under **Microsoft Word11\Tools | Options\Print\Printing options**, double-click **Allow A4/Letter paper resizing**. Click the **Enabled** option button to set the policy, then to turn off resizing, clear the check box in the policy. For more information about Group Policy, see "Managing Users' Configurations by Policy" in Chapter 18, "Updating Users' Office 2003 Configurations."

Setting TrueType fonts to print correctly

To display characters in multiple scripts, Office uses big fonts. In addition to being bold or italic, big fonts can also be Cyrillic, Greek, or one of several other scripts.

However, big fonts are also TrueType fonts, and many laser printers substitute built-in printer fonts when printing documents that use TrueType fonts. Built-in printer fonts cannot render text in multiple scripts, so characters in other scripts do not print properly.

For example, your laser printer might substitute its own internal version of Arial, which accommodates only Western European characters. Word uses the big font version of Arial to display Greek and Russian characters in documents, but if users print those documents, the Greek and Russian characters are printed as unintelligible Western European character strings.

To work around the problem, set the option in your printer driver to send TrueType fonts as graphics.

> **Tip** Some non-Asian printers cannot properly print Asian documents because the size of the Asian font is too large for the printer's memory. You might need to install additional memory in these printers.

Resources and related information

Documents that use Unicode are easier to share among users who work in different languages. For more information about Unicode, see "Unicode Support and Multilingual Office Documents" in Chapter 17, "Unicode Support in Office 2003."

To display localized server messages, you must install a localized version of FrontPage Server Extensions from Microsoft. For information about the latest release of FrontPage Server Extensions in a particular language, see the Microsoft FrontPage Web site at *http://www.microsoft.com/frontpage/*.

To display localized messages for servers running Windows SharePoint™ Services, you must install a localized version of Windows SharePoint Services. For information about the latest release of Windows SharePoint Services in a particular language, see the Microsoft SharePoint Products and Technologies Web site at *http://www.microsoft.com/sharepoint/assistance/*.

You can install a utility that adds code-page information to the properties shown when you right-click a font file in Windows 2000 or Windows XP. For more information about the font properties extension utility, see the Microsoft Typography Web site at *http://www.microsoft.com/typography/*.

Customizing Office Language Settings

The first time a Microsoft Office 2003 application starts up, Office 2003 applies default language settings that match the language version of Office that you have installed on the computer and the language of the operating system.

Administrators can configure these language settings in advance rather than using the default settings. If you specify custom language settings when you install Office (for example, in a transform), then Office detects that language settings are already defined and does not overwrite your settings with the default settings when users start the applications.

Four primary language settings affect the way users work with Office:

- **Installation language** Default language for Office applications and documents

- **User interface language** Language used to display menus and dialog boxes

- **Help language** Language used in Help

- **Editing languages** Functionality required to edit documents in various languages

> **Note** If you plan to use a default language for Office that differs from the system locale of the operating system, specify this setting in a transform during the Office installation. If you switch installation languages after Office is installed, customizations—such as macros added to Normal.dot in Microsoft Office Word 2003—are lost.

Language settings in the Windows registry

The first time any Office application runs after Office 2003 is installed, Office creates the following subkey in the Microsoft Windows registry:

HKEY_CURRENT_USER\Software\Microsoft\Office\11.0\Common\LanguageResources

In the LanguageResources subkey, Office creates the entry **InstallLanguage** and sets its value to the locale ID (LCID) of the installation language of Office, which is based on the system locale of the operating system. **InstallLanguage** and the other value entries in the LanguageResources subkey determine default language-related behavior in all Office 2003 applications.

For example:

- Microsoft Word looks for LCID entries and turns on language auto-detection features for all languages that are enabled for editing.

- Word checks the **InstallLanguage** value entry to determine what language to use for the initial Normal.dot file. Microsoft Office Outlook 2003 checks the same setting to set the default spelling checker.

- Word checks the **UILanguage** value entry to determine what language of user interface to display.

Methods of customizing language settings

You can configure language settings on users' computer by using one of the following methods:

- Use the Custom Installation Wizard to set language setting defaults in a transform (MST file), which is applied when you install the Office package (MSI file).

- Use the Microsoft Office Language Settings utility to specify settings on a test computer and then capture those settings in an Office profile settings file (OPS file) by using the Office Profile Wizard. You can add the OPS file to the transform or run the Office Profile Wizard separately on users' computers after Office is installed.

- Use the Group Policy snap-in to set policies that manage language settings on users' computers.

Specify settings in a transform

You customize most language settings on the **Change Office User Settings** page of the Custom Installation Wizard. These settings are applied when Office is installed and before users start up any applications.

To customize language settings in a transform

1. Start the Custom Installation Wizard

2. On the **Change Office User Settings** page, expand the tree under **Microsoft Office (user)**.

3. Under **Language Settings**, configure the settings you want to customize.

    For example, to specify a different installation language, click **Enabled Languages**, double-click **Installed version of Microsoft Office**, and select a new language from the list.

> **Note**   You cannot customize language settings in a transform applied to a Microsoft Office 2003 Multilingual User Interface Pack (MUI Pack) package (Mui.msi). Customizations in a transform applied to a MUI Pack are limited to installation location, feature installation states, shortcuts, backup installation servers, and Setup properties.

For more information about creating a transform, see "Methods of Customizing Office" in Chapter 4, "Customizing Office 2003." For more information about options on each page of the Custom Installation Wizard, see the Custom Installation Wizard Help on the companion CD.

Capture settings in an OPS file

You use the Office Profile Wizard to capture user-defined settings in an OPS file. If you add the OPS file to a transform, the settings are applied when Office is installed. You can also run the Profile Wizard separately and apply the settings after Office is installed on users' computers.

Before you create an OPS file, you must install Office 2003 and MUI Packs on the test computer. Then start each Office application and set all the language options you want to customize. You can set most language options by using the Microsoft Office Language Settings tool, which is installed with Office 2003.

To set language options on the test computer

1. On the **Start** menu, point to **Programs**, point to **Microsoft Office**, and then point to **Microsoft Office Tools**.

2. Click **Microsoft Office Language Settings**.

3. On the **Enabled Languages** tab, click the **Add** button to specify the languages that you want to be available for editing documents.

4. In the **Default version of Microsoft Office** box, select the Office installation language.

    This setting is optional. If the installation language of Office is English, French, German, Norwegian, or Serbian, however, then selecting the local variety of the language makes utilities such as spelling checkers more useful.

5. Click the **User Interface** tab.

    Note that the **User Interface** tab is available only if you have installed a MUI Pack.

6. In the **Display menus and dialogs in** box, select the user interface language.

7. In the **Display Help** box, select a language for online Help.

    If you do not specify a language for Help, the online Help language defaults to the user interface language you selected.

    After you have customized the language settings you want, run the Profile Wizard to capture the configuration in an OPS file.

To capture language settings in an OPS file

1. Start the Office Profile Wizard.

2. On the **Save or Restore Settings** page, select **Save the settings from this machine**, and enter the name and path for the OPS file.

3. Select the check boxes next to the Office 2003 applications you want to include in your OPS file.

    Make sure to select the **Microsoft Office Shared Settings** check box.

4. Click **Finish**.

    The Profile Wizard saves the Office application settings on your computer to the OPS file.

    For more information about running the Profile Wizard or adding an OPS file to a transform, see "Customizing User-defined Settings" in Chapter 4, "Customizing Office 2003."

Enabling languages without installing MUI Packs

The options on the **User Interface** tab in the Microsoft Office Language Settings dialog box include all the languages installed from MUI Packs. However, the options on the **Enabled Languages** tab include all the languages that Office can enable for editing, regardless of whether the user has installed any MUI Packs.

As a result, you can enable functionality for working with certain languages even if you do not install the MUI Packs for those languages. For example, if you select Korean as an editing language, you enable Asian and Korean features in Word even though the Korean proofing tools from the MUI Pack might not be available. If, however, you install proofing tools from a MUI Pack or from Microsoft Office 2003 Proofing Tools, then Office uses those proofing tools for the languages you enable for editing.

Note   Before a language can be enabled for editing, support for that language must be enabled in the operating system. You can enable support for languages in the appropriate Control Panel dialog (**Regional and Language Options** in Windows XP or **Regional Options** in Windows 2000).

Use policies to manage language settings

You can use policies to enforce default language settings for groups of users or computers in your organization. Unlike default settings distributed in a transform or an OPS file, users cannot modify settings enforced by policy.

When you load the Office 2003 administrative templates (ADM files) into the Group Policy snap-in, policies related to language settings are located under User Configuration\Administrative Templates\Microsoft Office 2003\Language Settings.

The following policies help manage default language settings in Office 2003:

- **Display menus and dialog boxes in** policy
  Located in the User Interface folder. Determine the language of the user interface.

- **Display help in** policy
  Located in the User Interface folder. Determine the language of online Help.

- **Installed version of Microsoft Office**
  Located in the Enabled Languages folder. Specify an installation language. By default, Office uses the system locale of the operating system.

- **Show controls and enable editing for** policies
  Located in the Enabled Languages folder. Enable editing languages from the list of languages supported by Office.

- **Do not adjust defaults to user's locale** policy
  Located in the Other folder. Prevent Office from adjusting default settings based on the user locale by setting this policy to **Never run language tune-up**. To run application-specific tune-up when an application starts (for example, to check for new IMEs and language scripts), set the policy to **Only run language tune-up for new scripts**.

  For more information about using Group Policy to set policies, see "Managing Users' Configurations by Policy" in Chapter 18, "Updating Users' Office 2003 Configurations."

Customizing language-specific settings related to user locale

In addition to using the installation language setting, Office 2003 also configures language-related settings, such as number format, to match the user locale of the operating system. This behavior is controlled by the **LangTuneUp** value entry in the LanguageResources subkey. If you do not want user locale to affect default settings, you can reset the value of **LangTuneUp** when you install Office.

LangTuneUp can have one of two values:

- **OfficeCompleted (default)**   Settings based on user locale are not applied to Office as a whole; however, individual applications still check for new input method editors (IMEs) and language scripts, and still apply application settings specific to the user locale. For example, applications ensure that newly installed keyboards have the appropriate editing languages enabled, and Word sets up fonts in Normal.dot based on user locale.

- **Prohibited**   No tuning of settings related to user locale is performed by Office as a whole or by individual Office applications.

If the **LangTuneUp** entry does not exist, Office creates it the first time an application starts and sets its value to **OfficeCompleted**.

In some scenarios, ignoring the user locale setting can help maintain a standard deployment across a multilingual organization. Setting the **LangTuneUp** value entry to **Prohibited** ensures that language settings remain consistent and macros are more compatible internationally.

For example, if your organization is based in the United States and you want to standardize settings internationally, you can deploy Office with **InstallLanguage** set to **1033** (U.S. English) and **LangTuneUp** set to **Prohibited**. Users get the same default settings regardless of their user locale.

Ignoring user locale is not always the best option. When **LangTuneUp** is set to **Prohibited**, users upgrading from a previous localized version of Office cannot migrate user settings from a language version that differs from the Office 2003 installation language.

In addition, users who read and enter Asian characters in Office documents might not always have the Asian fonts they need to display characters properly. If the installation language on the user's computer does not match the language used in the document, and **LangTuneUp** is set to **Prohibited**, then Office does not display fonts in the non-default language. If your Office installations need to support multiple Asian language user locales, make sure **LangTuneUp** remains set to **OfficeCompleted**. To help ensure that users do not change the default value, set the corresponding policy.

> **Note**   Administrators can elect to disable the Taiwanese date format in Office 2003 by customizing the **Disable Taiwan Calendar** setting. In the Custom Installation Wizard or Custom Maintenance Wizard, change this setting on the **Change Office User Settings** page. In the Group Policy snap-in, the **Disallow Taiwanese Calendar** policy is located under User Configuration\Administrative Templates\Microsoft Office 2003\Language Settings\Other.

Resources and related information

You customize most language settings when you deploy Office 2003, whether you chain MUI Packs to the core Office installation or whether you plan to deploy MUI Packs at a later time. You can modify language settings later on by setting policies in the Group Policy snap-in or by distributing new settings through the Custom Maintenance Wizard. For more information about modifying language settings after Office is deployed, see "Updating Language Settings in Office" in Chapter 16, "Maintaining an Office 2003 Multilingual Installation."

Each Office application uses language settings differently for making changes in user interfaces and other language-specific areas of the application. For more information, see "Effects of Customizing Language Settings on Office Applications" in the next section.

Effects of Customizing Language Settings on Office Applications

Applications in the Microsoft Office System have six main elements that are affected by language settings.

- **Installation language** Default language for Office applications and documents.

- **User interface language**   Language used to display menus and dialog boxes.

- **Help language**   Language used in Help.

- **Enabled languages**   Functionality required to edit documents in various languages.

- **SKU language (localized language)**   Default language version of Office purchased by the end user.

- **System locale**   Base language the operating system was installed to use.

Each of these six language elements serves various functions—how each application responds to user input, how files are formatted for display on the screen, which languages have precedence over others when used in a mixed-language file, how the overall interface will respond to user commands, what languages are used in the user interface, and so forth.

In some cases, language settings only affect the user interface, but in others it can also change what is installed as part of the application—including Help files, supporting programs, and reference files such as the dictionary, thesaurus, and grammar checker. Generally, each of these can be set independently of the others. For example, it is possible to have the installation language set to English, the user interface set to Russian, the Help language set to Chinese, and the editing language set to French, German, Japanese, and Arabic.

How language settings affect Office applications

Microsoft Office 2003 uses language elements during installation to set a base configuration of Office application language settings. Four of the six language elements in Office applications react to settings controlled by the Language Settings tool that is installed with Office. This section of the chapter attempts to document how language elements affect Office applications based on the settings the operating system is set to use during installation, and the changes a user or administrator can make by using the Language Settings tool after Office applications are installed.

The following four language elements are controlled by the Language Settings tool after Office is installed.

- **Installation language**   The installation language is set initially by the SKU language of the product. It can be changed by the **Choose the language that defines default behavior in Microsoft Office applications** option in the Language Settings tool, which changes the InstallLanguage registry entry and sets the default language for the user interface of the application and the files it creates. If a language that is not supported by the application, or has not been added from a Microsoft Office 2003 Multilingual User Interface Pack (MUI

Pack), is encountered in a received file, by default the application will use the installation language when it attempts to display the file.

- **User interface language**   When the product is installed, the user interface language is set to the same value as the SKU language. The user interface language sets the language used in menus, dialog boxes, toolbars, task panes, and error messages. Changes to this value update the registry entry UILanguage. The user interface language is controlled by the **Display Office 2003 in** combo box in the Language Settings tool.

- **Help language**   When the product is installed, the Help language is set to the same value as the SKU language. This sets the Help Language Control Identifier (HLCID) used to determine which language to display Help in. Changes to this value update the registry entry HelpLanguage. The Help language is controlled by the **Display Help in** combo box in the Language Settings tool.

- **Enabled languages (editing languages)**   When the product is installed, this is set to the same value as the SKU language. This setting is directly controlled by the **Enabled languages** list box in the Language Settings tool. It exposes functionality for editing documents in the selected language. In cases where multilingual files need to display more than one language or character set, it is necessary to use a Unicode font to support this feature.

When a MUI Pack is installed and the Language Settings tool is used to change to a different language, the user interface and Help languages are automatically set to the same settings as the installation language. However, this is only if the user interface language and Help language are each set to **(same as the system)** on the **User Interface and Help** tab.

The following two language elements are controlled by the operating system and the SKU language of the purchased product (the localized language of the Office application).

- **SKU language**   This is the default language version of Office purchased by the end user. This registry entry is set to the LCID for the fully localized version of the application being installed.

> **Note**   To use a MUI Pack you must use the 1033 (English) SKU language of Office.

- **System locale**   The base language the operating system was installed to use. This is controlled by the Regional and Language Options tool in Microsoft Windows XP and by the Regional Options tool in Windows 2000.

These language elements may be changed based on the settings in either the Windows Installer package used to install Office (for example, Pro11.msi), or a custom transform (if provided). It is also possible for these settings to be changed during installation of a MUI Pack or when an Office profile is applied to the target computer. For more information about changing language settings, see "Customizing Office Language Settings" in the previous section.

It is possible that the SKU language setting will not allow for changes to some of the language settings. In the case of a localized version of Office it is possible that some language and regional settings cannot be changed. However, the English version with MUI Packs is fully customizable for all languages supported in the various MUI Packs. There are a few languages that are not fully supported in the MUI Packs (do not provide complete dictionaries, grammar checkers, etc.).

Related operating system dependencies

Office 2003 must be installed on a computer running either Windows 2000 Service Pack 3 (SP3) or Windows XP. Because the operating system is a crucial element in how data is input into the computer and is also dependent on regionally configured language settings, it affects how Office applications function. The operating system determines the keyboard layout to use, how currency, dates, and time are formatted, and possibly how the mouse responds to user input. Though the regionally configured language settings are not set by Office applications directly, the applications do inherit these settings from the operating system. Users must take into consideration the keyboard regional setting as well as the selected languages they want to use. In some cases, characters from the selected language cannot be input until the keyboard input layout is changed to support the selected language. Use the Regional and Language Options tool in Windows XP or the Regional Options tool in Windows 2000 to create new keyboard input locales for use with the languages you add to your Office applications. If you will only need to view text, but never edit or create new text for a specific language, you do not need to load a specific keyboard regional input setting to support that language. Font support for complex script, right-to-left languages, and East Asian languages is also provided by the operating system (see the **Supplemental language support** section of the **Languages** tab in the Regional and Language Options tool—Windows XP only—to set these options).

How Office applications use language settings

Each Office application uses language settings differently based on the specific default behavior programmed for the selected language. The following lists describe the basic changes in behavior of each application as language settings are changed.

Microsoft Office Word 2003

Installation language

- Sets the Normal.dot template default template language during installation.

  The language settings in the Normal.dot template determine how Microsoft Visual Basic for Applications (VBA) functions when creating and running macros. It also sets the specific language-related default settings for Microsoft Word when it starts and loads the template. If you have a customized Normal.dot template created for use with a specific language and you choose to copy it to a computer configured with a different language, the customized Normal.dot template may or may not be compatible with the language you intend to use it with. In this case, it is usually best to allow the installation process to create a new Normal.dot and then use the template organizing utility to migrate styles, macros, autotext, and toolbar configurations to the new template. Or, if you prefer, rename your customized Normal.dot template and load it as a global template.

- Sets the default toolbar graphics and text to display.

- Sets the default language and regional preferences to use.

- Sets which preset gallery to use for bullets and numbering.

User interface language

- Sets the language of the menu options, dialog boxes, toolbars, and task panes.

- If a MUI Pack is installed, enables or disables various language-related options based on the default language specified in the Regional and Language Settings utility in Control Panel. Specifically, right-to-left language options, East Asian language options in the **Options** dialog box, and special options related to the **Find** dialog box.

Help language

- Changes the Help Language Control Identifier (HLCID). This is used to determine which localized Help files are displayed either from the application Help or from the Microsoft Office Online Web site assistance center. It also determines which language is respected by the natural language Help interface in Office applications (**Type a question for help**).

Enabled languages

- Exposes additional user interface elements. For example, Input Method Editors (IMEs), spelling and grammar checkers, or unique elements for localized fonts.

- Used by Language AutoDetect to help determine the possible languages it should check for.

- Set by users from the **Set Languages** subcommand (**Tools** menu, **Language** command).

- Inherits the language and regional settings of the operating system but can automatically switch between languages depending on the location of the insertion point within the document.

SKU language

- Only used for the initial installation. Superseded by the **Choose the language that defines default behavior in Microsoft Office applications** option in the Language Settings utility after installation.

Microsoft Office Excel 2003

Installation language

- If an installation of a localized East Asian version of Office is performed, it may offer support for additional features such as localized templates or localized add-ins.

  It also provides more country-specific fallbacks for font handling, different default number formats, and VBA backward compatibility for localized versions of Microsoft Excel.

  Installation of a localized East Asian version of Office should be chosen only if the majority of work in an organization is performed in an East Asian language.

  Excel supports Input Method Editors (IMEs) and East Asian fonts. However, an installation of a localized version is set to install fonts and defaults that more closely match the locale.

  Because of the amount of memory required to support East Asian fonts, support for Asian languages generally is limited to a smaller set of East Asian fonts. Typically, it is recommended that you install no more than four Unicode or double-byte character set–enabled fonts at any one time. If there is sufficient RAM, it is possible to support more without serious system performance degradation.

User interface language

- Sets the language of the menu options, dialog boxes, toolbars, and task panes.

Help language

- Changes the Help Language Control Identifier (HLCID). This is used to determine which localized Help files are displayed either from the application Help or from the Microsoft Office Online Web site assistance center. It also determines which language is respected by the natural language Help interface in Office applications (**Type a question for help**).

Enabled languages

■ Excel inherits the language and regional settings of the operating system.

SKU language

■ Only used for the initial installation. Superseded by the **Choose the language that defines default behavior in Microsoft Office applications** option in the Language Settings utility after installation.

Microsoft Office PowerPoint 2003

Installation language

When set to East Asian values:

■ Sets the default state of the IME to "on."

■ Adds "composite" font structure to the **Font** dialog box (**Format** menu) and default East Asian font values.

■ Adds locale-specific toolbar buttons.

■ Enables and sets linguistic feature defaults.

■ For example, setting the installation language to Japanese causes Microsoft PowerPoint to use Asian rules for controlling first and last characters.

■ Affects sorting order in the font lists—in the font toolbar control on the formatting toolbar as well as in the **Font** dialog box (**Format** menu).

■ Converts the backslash character to a Yen symbol when the installation language is Japanese.

When set to a language with right-to-left values:

■ Adds "composite" font structure to the **Font** dialog box (**Format** menu) and default right-to-left fonts.

■ Sets the default text direction from left-to-right to right-to-left behavior.

■ Sets the default state of the Auto-Keyboard switching option to "on"; otherwise, the default state is "off."

All languages:

■ Sets the Design Template behavior.

- You can create Design Templates with a single set of defaults (a "global" template). Based on the installation language, PowerPoint uses plug-in user interface support to insert the correct text defaults in the template.

- Sets the default behavior of the document.

- For example, if the language is set to an East Asian language, a presentation will have East Asian defaults. This includes fonts, East Asian typography rules, and so on.

- Used as the tie-breaker in certain cases to manage font conversion for East Asian (except Japanese) text in PowerPoint 4.0 files.

- Sets vertical underline behavior for East Asian languages.

- For example, with Chinese (either Traditional or Simplified), the vertical underline is on the left, and for Korean or Japanese, the vertical underline is on the right.

- Sets the default language used for date formats and the types of calendars available.

- Sets the default language tag for text when converting presentations from PowerPoint 3.0, 4.0, and PowerPoint 95 files that did not have a language tag saved with the file.

- Sets the rule by which font names for East Asian fonts are handled, whether they are managed by using their English name or their localized name.

- When the installation language is set to an East Asian language, PowerPoint expects East Asian font names to be localized. When the installation language is set to a non-East Asian language, PowerPoint expects East Asian font names to be in English.

- Sets how non-ANSI characters are displayed during file sharing operations with earlier versions of PowerPoint.

- For example, setting the installation language to Greek allows Greek characters written on the slide master to be saved in PowerPoint 95 format. The Greek PowerPoint 95 user can then view and edit the Greek characters correctly. The presentation can later be opened again in PowerPoint 2003 with the Greek characters included properly on the slide master.

- Corrects language variation conflicts (for example, French vs. French/Canadian) in Content Templates when those templates are opened by using the **New** command (**File** menu) or by the AutoContent Wizard.

- Sets the default text language for new text objects on new presentations if the user has not set the default language by using the **Language** command (**Tools** menu).

- Sets the text language identifier (LID) for Language AutoDetect integration with plain-text pasting.

- Sets the locale bullet schemes in the **Bullets and Numbering** dialog box (**Format** menu).

- Causes Blank.pot (if it exists) to be renamed to Oldblank.pot when the installation language changes.

- If the installation language or the system locale is set to Japanese, lists the JIS paper sizes in the **Page Setup** dialog box (**File** menu).

- Determines the order of font slots displayed in the **Font** dialog box (**Format** menu).

- If the installation language is set to an East Asian language, the font list displays East Asian fonts first.

- Determines the correct defaults for Style Checker options for East Asian and some European languages.

  The defaults are set as follows:

- The correct value for **Slide Title Style** is **Sentence case** (**0x01**) instead of "**Title case**" (**0x04**).

- Languages affected: Brazilian Portuguese, Czech, Danish, Dutch, Finnish, French, French/Canadian, Greek, Hungarian, Iberian Portuguese, Italian, Norwegian, Polish, Russian, Spanish (Modern Sort), Swedish.

- The correct value for **Number of fonts should not exceed:** is **0x04** instead of **0x03**.

- Languages affected: Japanese, Korean, Traditional Chinese, Simplified Chinese.

- The correct value for **Body punctuation** is **0x00** instead of **0x01; 0** turns the setting off and **1** turns the setting on.
  Languages affected: Korean, Traditional Chinese, Simplified Chinese (but not Japanese).

User interface language

- Changes the language of the user interface.

Help language

- Changes the Help Language Control Identifier (HLCID). This is used to determine which localized Help files are displayed either from the application Help or from the Microsoft Office Online Web site assistance center. It also determines which language is respected by the natural language Help interface in Office applications (**Type a question for help**).

Enabled languages

- If enabled, may expose an additional user interface in PowerPoint.
  For example, these languages add extra controls to the user interface:

- East Asian (Traditional Chinese, Simplified Chinese, Japanese, and Korean)

- Complex scripts (including bidirectional languages, such as Arabic and Hebrew, and other complex script languages, such as Thai and Hindi)

- Influences font association conversions if Traditional Chinese, Simplified Chinese, and Korean editing languages are set.

- If you enable editing languages other than code page 1252 languages (that is, code pages for languages that are not in the Western European code page) and you are creating Presentation Broadcast lobby pages, the lobby pages will use Numeric Character References (NCRs) for the text.
  For example, if you enable Greek (code page 1253) and you create lobby pages, the lobby pages will use NCRs for the text.

- If enabled, causes date formats for those languages to appear in the **Date and Time** dialog box (**Insert** menu).

> **Note**   Setting East Asian editing languages does not influence the Input Method Editor default startup behavior and does not change document defaults.

SKU language

- Only used for the initial installation. Superseded by the **Choose the language that defines default behavior in Microsoft Office applications** option in the Language Settings utility after installation.

System locale—Language and Regional Options

- Used as a tie-breaker in determining text language identifiers for Language AutoDetect integration with plain-text pasting.

- If the **Embed characters in use only** option is selected (Tools menu, **Options** command, **Save** tab), examines a preset list of fonts for the current system locale and determines which fonts should not be embedded, preventing the default fonts typically used in that locale from being embedded in the file.

Microsoft Office Access 2003

Installation language

- Used to expose Japanese-specific properties and enable wizards specific to East Asian languages.

- Sets the default spelling dictionary language according to the installation language setting.

User interface language

- When using MUI Packs for East Asian languages, allows East Asian wizards to function when the user interface language and the operating system language are set to the same corresponding East Asian language.

- Sets the language of the menu options, dialog boxes, toolbars, and task panes.

Help language

- Changes the Help Language Control Identifier (HLCID). This is used to determine which localized Help files are displayed either from the application Help or from the Microsoft Office Online Web site assistance center. It also determines which language is respected by the natural language Help interface in Office applications (**Type a question for help**).

Enabled languages

- Not used.

SKU language

- Only used for the initial installation. Superseded by the **Choose the language that defines default behavior in Microsoft Office applications** option in Language Settings utility after installation.

System locale—Language and Regional Options

- Used to determine default datasheet fonts and default sort order for the database.

Microsoft Office Outlook 2003

Installation language

- Determines default spelling options (**Tools** menu, **Options** command, **Spelling** tab).

User interface language

- Sets the language of the menu options, dialog boxes, toolbars, and task panes.

Help language

- Changes the Help Language Control Identifier (HLCID). This is used to determine which localized Help files are displayed either from the application Help or from the Microsoft Office Online Web site assistance center. It also determines which language is respected by the natural language Help interface in Office applications (**Type a question for help**).

Editing Languages

- Makes additional mail encodings available.

- Makes an additional property page available in the **Options** dialog box (**Tools** menu) with miscellaneous right-to-left calendar settings (for Arabic and Hebrew).

SKU language

- Only used for the initial installation. Superseded by the **Choose the language that defines default behavior in Microsoft Office applications** option in the Language Settings utility after installation.

Microsoft Office FrontPage 2003

Installation language

- Not used by FrontPage 2003.

User interface language

- Sets the language of the menu options, dialog boxes, toolbars, and task panes.

- Determines the language of the templates FrontPage loads for a new page or Web site.

- Sets the default Language Control Identifier (LCID) for any new page not tied to a specific template.

Help language

- Changes the Help Language Control Identifier (HLCID). This is used to determine which localized Help files are displayed either from the application Help or from the Microsoft Office Online Web site assistance center. It also determines which language is respected by the natural language Help interface in Office applications (**Type a question for help**).

Enabled languages

■ Exposes additional user interface elements.

For example, Arabic and Hebrew have extra options in the **Find** dialog box (**Edit** menu); right-to-left paragraph buttons are added to a toolbar; and the **Right-to-left direction in all new pages** option is added.

If the East Asian MUI Packs are installed, **Revise Hangul ending**, **Hangul Hanja Conversion**, and **TCSC converter** options are enabled.

SKU language

■ Not used.

System locale—Language and Regional Options

■ Sets the default speller.

■ Uses the default system code page to determine which character set to support when opening and saving files, since FrontPage does not support Unicode file names.

■ Used to determine the language and encoding of a page.

Microsoft Office Publisher 2003

Installation language

■ Sets language for helpful pointers (cursors).

■ If set to Japanese, prints Japanese crop marks.

■ Changes the default justification options that appear in Publisher 2003 menus and on the **Formatting** toolbar.

■ Changes the Input Method Editor (IME) status to text flow.

■ If set to an East Asian language, controls whether an IME is enabled.

■ Sets date and time format for print marks.

■ Sets default business card size.

■ Sets default font size, paragraph alignment, tab stop, bullet font, and bullet characters.

■ Used as the Language Control Identifier (LCID) applied to text in some cases where the text file format does not contain language information.

■ Set as the default language for some features when multiple East Asian languages are installed.

Determines the defaults for some text formatting preferences, including East Asian hanging punctuation default and character-spacing control (CSC) default.

■ Controls the exposure of Simplified Chinese–named font sizes.

User interface language

■ Sets language for Publisher wizards, font schemes, and color schemes. Japanese-specific wizards are only available with a Japanese user interface.

Enabled languages

■ If East Asian languages are enabled, exposes the East Asian formatting features (such as Ruby and Text Direction).

■ If East Asian languages are enabled, exposes the East Asian proofing tools.

■ If East Asian languages are enabled, exposes the East Asian font and formatting properties in the **Font** dialog box (**Format** menu).

■ If complex script languages are enabled, exposes the complex script features and options.

Help language

■ Changes the Help Language Control Identifier (HLCID). This is used to determine which localized Help files are displayed either from the application Help or from the Microsoft Office Online Web site assistance center. It also determines which language is respected by the natural language Help interface in Office applications (**Type a question for help**).

SKU language

■ Not used.

System locale—Language and Regional Options

■ Changes the calendar format.

■ Default input locale determines the default text language for new text frames.

■ As the user types, current input locale/keyboard setting is used to assign language to text.

Microsoft Office InfoPath 2003

Installation language

- The document and template language settings for XML are dependent on this setting. Users can change the document and template language through the **Set Language** dialog box (**Tools** menu).

   Document language: This is the default language for the XML document. It controls the proofing tools for all of the XML data.

   Template language: This is the language for the XML template. This value sets the default font, font size, text direction, text justification, and paragraph alignment.

User interface language

- Sets the language of the menu options, dialog boxes, toolbars, and task panes.

Help language

- Changes the Help Language Control Identifier (HLCID). This is used to determine which localized Help files are displayed either from the application Help or from the Microsoft Office Online Web site assistance center. It also determines which language is respected by the natural language Help interface in Office applications (**Type a question for help**).

Enabled languages

- Exposes additional East Asian user interface features, such as:

   Asian Typography Pane
   Line breaking in **Options** dialog box (**Tools** menu)
   Grid Pane
   Japanese **Find** and **Replace** check boxes
   Japanese **Find** and **Replace** dialog **Options** button
   Korean **Find** and **Replace** check boxes

- If the default language for Microsoft Office InfoPath™ 2003 is Turkish, the Turkish find and replace feature is used (a user interface for this is not available).

SKU language

- Not used.

Where language settings are stored

Microsoft Office 2003 stores the majority of language settings in the registry. Those settings not stored in the registry might be in templates, a language-specific folder—usually identified by a locale identifier (LCID) number, for example, \Program Files\Microsoft Office\Office 2003\1033—or within special language-specific wizards and support files.

Language settings that determine how specific Office applications respond to the user are generally stored in the registry and can be found in both the HKLM and HKCU nodes under \Software\Microsoft\Office\11.0\Common\LanguageResources. The registry values in this key relate to the various language settings mentioned in this chapter. Language settings are configured initially by the current operating system regional and language settings. Any changes to the operating system language settings using the Regional and Language Options tool in Windows XP or the Regional Options tool in Windows 2000 can also affect how Office reacts to language settings in the registry. After installation of Office, most language settings are controlled by the Microsoft Office 2003 Language Settings tool. Various options within some applications, such as the **Set language** option in Word, also affect language settings.

When a specific language is added to the installation of Office by using a Microsoft Office Multilingual User Interface Pack (MUI Pack), usually a new folder is added to the folder locations \Program Files\Microsoft Office\Office 2003 and \Program Files\Common Files\Microsoft Shared\Office 2003 and is designated by the LCID for that language. For example, the path to the Greek folder would be \Program Files\Microsoft Office\Office 2003\1032. The language-specific elements of each application—such as Help files, user interface dynamic-link libraries (DLLs), and dictionaries—are stored in the 1032 folder.

Creating an Administrative Installation Point for the Office MUI Pack

The first step to deploying a multilingual installation is to create an administrative installation point for the Microsoft Office 2003 Multilingual User Interface Pack (MUI Pack). To do this, you run the MUI Pack Setup program (Muisetup.exe) in administrative mode to install the MUI Pack in a folder on a network server.

The MUI Pack consists of language files on multiple CDs. If you want to use languages on different CDs, you must run Muisetup.exe separately for each CD you need. You can add language files to an existing administrative installation point by specifying the same location each time.

The following procedure assumes that you are creating an administrative installation point on a computer using Microsoft Windows 2000 Service Pack 3 or later or Microsoft Windows XP or later.

To create an administrative installation point for the MUI Pack

1. Create a share on a network server for the administrative installation point.

   The folder must be at least one level below the top level: for example, \\server\share\office. Also, the share must be large enough to store the resources for the languages that you need. MUI Pack hard disk-space requirements are approximately 65 MB to 290 MB per MUI Pack.

2. On a computer running Windows 2000 or Windows XP, connect to the server share.

   You must have write access to the share on which you are creating the administrative installation point.

3. On the **Start** menu, click **Run**, and then click **Browse** to locate the MUI Pack CD. (Insert the MUI Pack CD with the language you want to install.)

4. On the MUI Pack CD, select **Muisetup.exe** and click **Open**.

5. On the command line, following **Muisetup.exe**, type **/a** and then click **OK**.

6. When prompted by Muisetup.exe, accept the end-user license agreement (EULA), and then click **Next**.

7. Enter the server and the share that you created and click **Next**.

8. On the **Available Languages** page, choose the languages you want to include on this installation point.

   Note that languages not available on the current CD will appear dimmed on this page. You can add languages from other CDs to the same administrative installation point by running **Muisetup.exe /a** with additional MUI Pack CDs and specifying the same network server location.

   Also note that MUI Packs that include only proofing tools do not appear here. For more information about installing proofing tools from these MUI Packs, see "Installing Proofing Tools" in Chapter 14, "Deploying Office 2003 Multilingual Resources."

Resources and related information

More information about creating administrative installation points as part of an Office deployment is in the previous section "Creating an Administrative Installation Point for the Office MUI Pack."

Another option for deploying Office products is to use local caching. To learn more about the benefits and drawbacks of using a local cache for Office deployment see "Taking Advantage of a Local Installation Source" in Chapter 3, "Preparing to Deploy Office 2003."

Chapter 14

Deploying Office 2003 Multilingual Resources

Deploying Microsoft® Office 2003 with the Microsoft Office 2003 Multilingual User Interface Pack (MUI Pack) is typically a straightforward process. You can easily include one or more MUI Packs with your Office deployment by using several methods, including chaining packages to the installation. The topics in this chapter describe the basic customization and installation procedures for different kinds of multilingual installations.

Customizing and Installing Office 2003 MUI Packs

When you customize and install Microsoft Office 2003 Multilingual User Interface Packs (MUI Packs) together with your Office installation, you can include language options in your Office deployment to configure your users' installations appropriately for the MUI Packs you deploy. You can also chain your MUI Packs together with Office to deploy them together, simplifying the process.

Another option is to install MUI Packs after your Office installation. This scenario may be more appropriate if your language needs change after you have installed Office, or if you want to stage your Office and MUI Pack deployments.

Customization options for a MUI Pack deployment

There are several types of settings you might customize to properly configure your users' computers to use the MUI Packs you deploy, and to help ensure that a deployment with Office proceeds smoothly.

- Language settings, which include the Install Language, User Interface Language, Help Language, and Editing Languages.

- Feature installation states to help provide additional support for certain languages. For example, you could choose to install the Bidirectional Support feature on users' computers if you are deploying MUI Packs for languages that read right to left.

- Setup properties to allow deployment technologies such as Microsoft Systems Management Server (SMS) to work properly with your Office and MUI Pack installation.

For step-by-step information on configuring all of these options, see the section "Customization Methods for a MUI Pack Deployment" later in this chapter.

Language settings you can customize

You can customize the following language settings when you deploy MUI Packs with Office:

- **Installation language**   Sets defaults for Office applications and documents. Also called the default version of Office or the installed version of Office.

- **User interface language**   Determines language used by menus and dialogs.

- **Help language**   Determines language used for user Help.

- **Editing languages**   Determines functionality for editing documents in selected languages.

You can only configure these language settings when you use an Office transform; you cannot configure these settings in a MUI Pack transform.

> **Note**   If you want to help prevent your users from changing language settings, you can specify settings for users with Group Policy. In the Office policy template (Office11.adm), specify policies under Language Settings. For more information about using Group Policy with Office 2003, see "Managing Users' Configurations by Policy" in Chapter 18, "Updating Users' Office 2003 Configurations."

For more information about how language settings work and when to configure them, see "Customizing Language Settings" in Chapter 13, "Preparing for an Office Multilingual Deployment." For details about how language settings affect the behavior of each Office application, see "Effects of Customizing Language Settings on Office Applications" in Chapter 13, "Preparing for an Office Multilingual Deployment."

Feature installation states you can customize

You can customize feature installation states to help ensure that the required language features are installed for the MUI Packs you are deploying.

You select these language-specific features on the **Set Feature Installation States** page in the Custom Installation Wizard. For more information about customizing options in the Custom Installation Wizard for deploying Office with MUI Packs, see the section "Use the Office transform to customize your MUI Packs" later in this chapter.

When you customize these features, keep in mind the following:

- If your users work with Asian, Georgian, Armenian, Hindi, or Tamil text and they are not running a matching language version of Microsoft Windows®, you may need to install the Japanese or Syriac fonts on users' computers. These features are included under **Office Shared Features | International Support** on the **Set Feature Installation States** page.

- If your users need a full Unicode® font—for example, if they are working with Microsoft Office Access 2003 datasheets that include languages that use more than one code page—install the Universal font on users' computers.

Setup properties you can customize

There are three Setup properties you may want to customize when you are deploying MUI Packs: **CHECKINSTALLORDER**, **NOFEATURESTATEMIGRATION**, and **SKIPLANGCHECK**. For more information about how to use these properties with Office 2003 Setup, see "Setup Properties" in Appendix B, "Office 2003 Resource Kit Reference."

Setting the CHECKINSTALLORDER property

The **CHECKINSTALLORDER** property allows the MUI Pack files to be installed before Office is installed. Set this property to **False** when the installation order for a chained deployment cannot be determined in advance; for example, with deployments using SMS or Windows Group Policy software installation.

If you use Group Policy software installation or SMS, you cannot guarantee the order in which components are installed. This means that MUI Packs might be installed before Office, which is usually disallowed. However, by setting the **CHECKINSTALLORDER** property, MUI Packs can be installed on a user's computer even if Office is not yet installed.

If you are deploying Office with the MUI Packs by using Group Policy software installation, you must include a separate transform for each MUI Pack, in which you set the **CHECKINSTALLORDER** Setup property to **False**.

If instead you deploy Office 2003 and MUI Packs with SMS, you can specify the **CHECKINSTALLORDER** Setup property in a MUI Pack transform. You can customize the property in the Custom Installation Wizard on the **Modify Setup Properties** page. Alternatively, you can set the property in the Setup.ini file in the [Options] section or specify the property on the Setup command line.

Setting the NOFEATURESTATEMIGRATION property

Office 2003 MUI Pack Setup (Muisetup.exe) automatically matches MUI Pack feature installation states to the corresponding features in the core English version of Office. If you specify different installation states for MUI Pack features in a transform, you must set the **NOFEATURESTATEMIGRATION** property in the transform to **Do not match feature states during installation** to override the default matching behavior.

You can customize the **NOFEATURESTATEMIGRATION** property in the Custom Installation Wizard on the **Modify Setup Properties** page. Alternatively, you can set the property in the Setup.ini file in the [Options] section or specify the property on the Setup command line.

Setting the SKIPLANGCHECK property

Office 2003 MUI Pack Setup does not install a language version of a MUI Pack on computers where Windows support for the language is not installed. Language groups that require explicit support for a language on the user's computer include complex script languages, right-to-left languages, and East Asian languages. You can bypass the system language check by setting **SKIPLANGCHECK** to **1**.

Setting **SKIPLANGCHECK** does not enable language versions of Office to function properly without the necessary operating system support. Bypassing the system language check merely allows you to install Office products and language support in any order.

You can include this option as a property on the Setup command line, or you can set the property in the Setup.ini file by the setting **SKIPLANGCHECK=1** in the [Product] section. This option cannot be specified in a transform (MST file).

Customization methods for a MUI Pack deployment

There are several methods you can use to customize a MUI Pack deployment. You can include customized options for MUI Packs (such as language settings) in your Office transform, or you can customize a separate transform for MUI Packs. If you use a separate transform, you can apply that transform to multiple MUI Pack packages (MSI files).

When you customize settings for MUI Pack deployment by using the Office transform, you can specify the language settings in two ways—by specifying language settings in the Custom Installation Wizard directly when customizing Office, or by specifying an Office profile settings file (OPS file) created with the Office Profile Wizard.

If you need to customize only feature installation states or Setup properties, you can include these in a MUI Pack transform.

Use the Office transform to customize your MUI Packs

You can customize language options in the Custom Installation Wizard and save the customizations in a transform (MST file). This method can be used alone or in combination with specifying settings in an OPS file.

> **Note**   You can use the Custom Installation Wizard to configure Setup properties in addition to configuring language settings and feature installation states. However, in a MUI Pack deployment, you only change MUI Pack Setup properties when you create a separate MUI Pack transform. For more information, see the section "Use a MUI Pack transform to customize your MUI Packs" later in this chapter.

To specify language options in the Custom Installation Wizard

1. In the Custom Installation Wizard, specify the MSI file for Office.
    For example: \\server\share\Pro11.msi

2. On the **Set Feature Installation States** page, open **Office Shared Features**.
    By opening **International Support**, you can choose installation states for fonts (for example, for **Japanese Font**).
    By opening **Proofing Tools**, you can choose installation states for proofing tools available in the MUI Pack.

3. On the **Change Office User Settings** page, click the plus sign (+) next to **Microsoft Office 2003 (user)** to expand the tree.

4. Click the plus sign next to **Language Settings** and select the language options that you want for your deployment.

For example, to set the User Interface Language, click **User Interface**, then double-click **Display menus and dialog boxes in Properties**. In the **Display menus and dialog boxes in Properties** dialog, choose **Apply Changes**, and then choose a language from the drop-down menu.

5. To include an OPS file in the same transform, on the **Customize Default Application Settings** page, browse to the OPS file you have created.

  Note that the settings you specify in the **Change Office User Settings** page take precedence over settings in an OPS file included in the same transform.

6. Make any other customizations required for your deployment, then click **Finish** to create the transform.

Capture settings in an OPS file

When you run Office to specify language settings and user preferences, you can capture these settings by using the Office Profile Wizard. Then, using the Custom Installation Wizard, you add the OPS file to your transform. Because the choice of editing languages affects the functionality of certain applications, you can create unique OPS files for different groups of users based on the languages they need.

  In general, follow these steps to configure and capture language settings by using the Office Profile Wizard.

1. Install Office on the test computer, and then install any Multilingual User Interface Pack files.

2. Customize the Office environment and language settings.

3. Save the settings in an OPS file by using the Office Profile Wizard.

> **Note**   The Office Profile Wizard stores and retrieves Office 2003 customizations. By using the Profile Wizard, you can create and deploy a standard user profile when you deploy Office 2003 so that all of your users start off with the same settings. For more information about the Profile Wizard and OPS files, see "Updating Feature Installation States and Application Settings" in Chapter 18, "Updating Users' Office 2003 Configurations."

Install Office and the MUI Pack on a test computer

You install Microsoft Office on a test computer by using Office Setup (Setup.exe) on the Office CD. Then install the MUI Pack files that you want to customize by using the MUI Pack Setup program (Muisetup.exe). The MUI Pack Setup program starts the Multilingual User Interface Pack Setup Wizard, which will step you through installing MUI Pack files.

Configure Office and language settings on your computer

Once you have installed Office and the MUI Pack files, you start the Office applications you want to configure and customize toolbars, settings, templates, custom dictionaries, and any other options you choose. Then you run the Language Settings tool and specify any of the following language settings:

- Installation Language (also called the default version of Office)
- Enabled Languages (also called Editing Languages)
- User Interface Language
- Help Language

To update language settings by using the Language Settings tool

1. On the taskbar, click Start, then point to **All Programs** (for Windows XP) or **Start Programs** (for Windows 2000).

2. Point to **Microsoft Office**, point to **Microsoft Office Tools**, and then click **Microsoft Office 2003 Language Settings**.

3. On the **User Interface and Help** tab, choose a language in the **Display Office 2003 in** drop-down list.

    Only languages for which you have installed a MUI Pack are displayed; therefore, the **User Interface and Help** tab is displayed in the Language Settings tools only when you have at least one MUI Pack installed on your computer.

4. Choose a language in the **Display Help in** drop-down list.

    Only languages for which you have installed a MUI Pack are displayed.

5. On the **Enabled Languages** tab, select a language in the scroll list, then click **Add** to enable the language for editing.

6. Change the Installation Language by choosing a language in the **Choose the language that defines default behavior in Microsoft Office applications** drop-down list.

    For instance, you might add a few languages to the list of enabled languages for your users. Typically, most users creating multilingual documents rarely work with more than three languages. Limiting the number of enabled languages results in a user interface that is less cluttered and allows Office applications to run efficiently for particular languages.

Capture settings in an OPS file

Once you have customized Office and the language settings, you save these settings by using the Office Profile Wizard. These settings will be used to customize users' installations of Office and MUI Pack files. You then include the OPS file in the Custom Installation Wizard when you create a transform that is applied when Office 2003 is installed.

Office profiles and multiple languages

Office user profiles generated by the Profile Wizard are independent of the operating system—including operating systems in other languages. For example, a profile settings file created on Microsoft Windows 2000 (U.S. English version) can be restored to a computer with Windows XP (Japanese version).

However, Office user profiles are specific to a particular Office language version. For example, if you create an OPS file in the U.S. English version of Office 2003, it cannot be restored to a computer with the German version of Office 2003 installed. There is some overlap between language families. For example, you can restore a U.S. English Office profile to an English or Australian version of Office 2003.

This Office language limitation exists because the different Office versions include localized folder names for the folders that contain the Office user profile information. You can find out more information about Office language limitations in Intlimit.xls in "International Information" in Appendix A, "Toolbox."

Use a MUI Pack transform to customize your MUI Packs

You create a MUI Pack transform when you want to customize the way that MUI Packs are installed—for instance, after Office is installed. Or you may need to customize individual MUI Packs so that they can be deployed with Office by using SMS or Group Policy software installation.

An advantage of deploying MUI Packs with Office is that you can customize language settings in your Office transform, which you cannot do with a MUI Pack transform. You might use the MUI Pack transform to do the following:

- Customize feature states, such as choosing to install the Optical Character Recognition Modules for a MUI pack under Office Shared Features.

- Customize Setup properties, such as specifying the **NOFEATURESTATEMIGRATION** property.

- Specify an additional (replicated) server for downloading the MUI Pack.

Note You customize default language settings in your Office deployment. If you have already deployed Office, you can modify language settings by using the Custom Maintenance Wizard. For more information, see "Updating Feature Installation States and Application Settings" in Chapter 18, "Updating Users' Office 2003 Configurations."

This procedure provides an example of settings you might customize in a MUI Pack transform.

To customize options in a transform for a MUI Pack

1. In the Custom Installation Wizard, on the **Open MSI File** page, enter (or browse to) the name of the MSI file for the MUI Pack you want to customize.

2. On the **Set Feature Installation States** page, open **Office Shared Features**.
   By opening **International Support**, you can choose installation states for fonts (for example, for **Japanese Font**).
   By opening **Proofing Tools**, you can choose installation states for proofing tools available in the MUI Pack.

3. On the **Identify Additional Servers** page, click **Add**, then type in or browse to a network share with a replicated copy of the administrative installation point.

4. On the **Modify Setup Properties** page, choose or add Setup properties that you want to include in the MUI Pack transform.
   To modify an existing property, click the property, then click **Modify**. For example, click **NOFEATURESTATEMIGRATION**, then click **Modify**. Select **Do not match feature states during installation** from the drop-down menu, then click **OK**.

5. Click **Finish** to create the transform.

Install MUI Packs with an Office installation

If you know the language requirements of your organization at the time that you deploy Office, you might choose to install Office and the MUI Packs at the same time—a straightforward process that uses chaining.

> **Note**   For detailed information about chaining packages with Office, see "Deploying Office and Other Products Together" in Chapter 5, "Installing Office 2003."

Typically, when you chain MUI Packs to an Office installation, you follow these steps:

1. Install the MUI Packs on your administrative installation point.

2. Customize an Office transform to include language settings and other options for MUI Pack deployment, as described earlier in this chapter.

You can also create separate MUI Pack transforms, but this limits your customization options.

3. Edit the Office Setup.ini file to add a section for each MUI Pack that you want to chain with your Office installation.

To customize Setup.ini to chain MUI Pack packages to your Office installation

1. Open the Office Setup settings file (Setup.ini) in a text editor such as Notepad.

2. Create a section called [ChainedInstall_1], and in this section specify the name and path of the MUI Pack you want to chain. For example:

   PATH=\\server1\share\office\1041\Mui.msi

3. Add the following entry to this section:

   TASKTYPE=msi

4. Specify other options in this section, such as **IgnoreReturnValue** or **Reboot**.

5. Specify a unique display setting or transform to apply to the MUI Pack installation by setting the **Display** or **MST** property.

   For example, you can ensure that the MUI Pack installation installs quietly:

   DISPLAY=None

6. Specify additional options by using the **Cmdline** property. For example, set the **NOFEATURESTATEMIGRATION** property to **True** to cancel the custom action that matches installation states for MUI Pack feature states to corresponding Office feature installation states:

   CMDLINE=NOFEATURESTATEMIGRATION=TRUE

   The completed section in the Setup.ini file looks like this:

```
[ChainedInstall_1]
PATH=\\server\share\Office\1041\Mui.msi
TASKTYPE=msi
DISPLAY=None
CMDLINE=NOFEATURESTATEMIGRATION=True
```

Install MUI Packs after an Office installation

You can install MUI Pack packages after your Office installation, rather than chaining them to an Office installation. As with a combined Office and MUI Pack deployment, you can configure language settings in your Office transform when you deploy MUI Packs after Office. If you want to change the language settings after you install the MUI Packs, you use the Custom Maintenance Wizard.

> **Note** You can have users configure their own language settings. Users might choose to do this, for example, if they run the MUI Pack Wizard to install the languages they need from the MUI Pack administrative installation point.

Even if you choose to deploy MUI Packs after Office, you may want to create an Office administrative installation point that includes the MUI Pack files. This helps you simplify and control the deployment process. For example, you can standardize installation of language resources for all the users in your organization.

While you install Office first and later deploy MUI Packs, you can still use the process of chaining MUI Pack packages (if you want to install more than one MUI Pack). However, to install MUI Packs separately from Office, you customize the Setup.ini file in the first MUI Pack folder instead of customizing the Office Setup.ini file. You add a Chained Install section to the Setup.ini file for each additional MUI Pack you are installing. Then you install the MUI Packs by running Setup in the first MUI Pack folder.

The following procedure uses the example of deploying the French, Spanish, and Vietnamese MUI Packs by using a MUI Pack chained installation after your initial deployment of Office.

> **Note**   For detailed information about chaining packages with Office, see "Deploying Office and Other Products Together" in Chapter 5, "Installing Office 2003."

To use a chained installation to install multiple MUI Packs after an Office deployment

1. Using a text editor such as Notepad, open the Setup.ini file in the first MUI Pack folder. For example, open the following Setup.ini file in the French MUI Pack folder:

   \\server1\share\office\1036\Setup.ini

2. Create a section called [ChainedInstall_1], and in this section specify the name and path of the first MUI Pack you want to chain with the French MUI Pack. For example, to add the Spanish MUI Pack:

   PATH=\\server1\share\office\3082\Mui.msi

3. Add the following entry to this section:

   TASKTYPE=msi

4. Optionally, specify other options in this section, such as a **Display** property.

5. Create a section called [ChainedInstall_2], and in this section specify the name and path of the next MUI Pack you want to chain. For example, to add the Vietnamese MUI Pack:

   PATH=\\server1\share\office\1066\Mui.msi

6. Add the following entry to this section:

   TASKTYPE=msi

7. Optionally, specify other options in this section, such as a **Display** property.

Users can now install this group of MUI Packs by running the Setup command line in the French MUI Pack folder. For example:

```
\\server1\share\office\1036\setup.exe /qb-
```

Resources and related information

Some MUI Packs contain only proofing tools. For more information about installing proofing tools from those MUI Packs, see "Installing Proofing Tools" in the next section.

In addition to specifying language features and providing support for international users, you can customize many other aspects of your Office installation by using the Custom Installation Wizard. You can also use the Office Profile Wizard to save language-related settings to a file you distribute as part of a custom installation of Office. For more information about customizing deployments by using these wizards, see "Customizing Office Features and Shortcuts" in Chapter 4, "Customizing Office 2003."

After Microsoft Office has been deployed, you might want to change the language settings you originally deployed with Office. In this case, you can modify language settings for your Office installation by using the Custom Maintenance Wizard. The Custom Maintenance Wizard is installed by default when you run the Office Resource Kit Setup program. For more information, see "Updating Feature Installation States and Application Settings" in Chapter 18, "Updating Users' Office 2003 Configurations."

Installing Proofing Tools

Microsoft Office 2003 Proofing Tools includes spelling and grammar checkers, thesauruses, AutoCorrect lists, Hyphenator, and other editing tools that help users create and edit Office documents in more than 50 languages. Proofing tools for all languages are included on a single CD, but you can install the tools for only the languages that users need.

Proofing tools are also included in the Microsoft Office 2003 Multilingual User Interface Pack (MUI Pack). The same proofing tools that come with localized versions of Office 2003 are included in the corresponding MUI Pack for each language.

Hard disk space requirements for Office 2003 Proofing Tools vary by language. For instance, Proofing Tools for German requires 48 MB of hard disk space; Proofing Tools for Chinese (Simplified) requires 365 MB. Asian languages require as much as 120 MB of hard disk space to include the necessary fonts and Input Method Editors (IMEs).

Whether you install tools from the Proofing Tools CD or from a MUI Pack, you can choose to install proofing tools with, or separately from, a deployment of Office. As part of your installation, you can customize which tools to install by creating a transform using the Custom Installation Wizard.

Customizing a proofing tools installation

You may want to omit a language feature from a proofing tools installation or make other customizations when you install proofing tools with Office. Using the Custom Installation Wizard to create a transform (MST file), you can customize an installation that includes settings for the language features you want users to install. Users will receive these customizations when they install proofing tools using this transform.

Using a transform, you can omit a language feature from the installation by setting the feature to **Not Available, Hidden, Locked** on the **Set Feature Installation States** page of the wizard. Users cannot change the installation state of a feature marked as **Not Available, Hidden, Locked** during Setup, nor can they add or remove the feature later by using **Add/Remove Programs** in Control Panel.

> **On the Resource Kit CD**   The Microsoft Office 2003 Editions Resource Kit includes the Custom Installation Wizard, which is installed by default when you run the Office Resource Kit Setup program. For more information about using the Custom Installation Wizard, see the Custom Installation Wizard Help on the companion CD. To install the tool, see "Custom Installation Wizard," also on the companion CD.

You can customize an Office 2003 Proofing Tools installation, or you can customize a MUI Pack transform to install the proofing tools you need.

To create a transform to customize an Office 2003 Proofing Tools installation

1. Start the Custom Installation Wizard.

2. When prompted for an MSI file, enter (or browse to) the Ptk.msi file from the administrative installation point, if you are installing tools from Office 2003 Proofing Tools.

3. On the **Set Feature Installation States** page, select the languages you want to install and set the appropriate installation states.

> **Tip**   To install only a few languages, set the installation state of the entire **Microsoft Office 2003 Proofing Tools** feature in the transform to **Not Available**. Then expand the feature tree, select the languages you want, and set them to another installation state.

If Office is already installed, the installation states for proofing tools that you install will match the installation states of the Office installation (unless you specify the **NOFEATURESTATEMIGRATION** property).

If you are installing proofing tools from a MUI Pack, customize your installation using the steps that follow.

To create a transform to customize an installation of proofing tools from a MUI Pack

1. Start the Custom Installation Wizard.

2. When prompted for an MSI file, enter (or browse to) the MSI file for the MUI Pack from which you are installing proofing tools. For example, if you are installing from the Japanese MUI Pack, you browse to:
   \\server1\share\office\1041\Mui.msi

3. On the **Select Feature Installation States** page, click on the **Microsoft Office** drop-down arrow and select **Not Available** for all features.
   (You can alternately specify **Not Available, Hidden, Locked**.)

4. Click on the **Office Shared Features** node (plus (+) sign), then click on the **Proofing Tools** node.

5. Click on the drop-down arrows to set the appropriate installation state for the language features you want to install (for example, **Run from My Computer**).

For your customizations to be applied when users run Setup from the administrative installation point, Setup must be instructed to use your custom transform. You can use the **TRANSFORMS=** command-line option to specify this transform, or you can specify the transform in Setup.ini.

For example, users might use the following command line to install proofing tools from Office 2003 Proofing Tools:

```
\\server1\Proof\ptksetup.exe /q TRANSFORMS=\\server1\Proof\Proof.mst
```

Or you could add the following entry to your Setup.ini file:

```
[MST1]
MST1=Proof.mst
```

Installing proofing tools from Office 2003 Proofing Tools

The Office 2003 Proofing Tools CD provides a single resource from which you can install any of the proofing tools. You can install proofing tools on a local computer or deploy tools to a group of users.

When you deploy to a large group of users, you can install proofing tools separately from Office or together with Office. When you install proofing tools separately from Office, you can customize and install the tools for one user or all users in your organization.

For example, you may want to customize a proofing tools installation to omit a language feature. When you customize for all users at once, you can deploy proofing tools customized in a standard way for everyone. This simplifies your deployment and helps you to control the deployment process.

Creating an administration installation point for Office 2003 Proofing Tools

Whether you choose to install proofing tools from the Office 2003 Proofing Tools CD during an Office deployment or allow users to run Ptksetup.exe themselves, you first install the tools on an administrative installation point. When you install the tools on the administrative installation point, you can choose which languages to make available to your users. The administrative installation point serves as a location from which the tools are installed.

To install Office 2003 Proofing Tools on an administrative installation point

1. On a server, run **Ptksetup.exe** with the **/a** command-line option from the Office 2003 Proofing Tools CD.

2. When prompted, enter the installation location and product key, and then click **Next**.

3. Accept the end-user license agreement (EULA), and then click **Next**.

4. Click **Install**.

This loads proofing tools files to the location you have specified as the administrative installation point, from which users can install the tools.

Installing Office 2003 Proofing Tools on a computer

If you have one or two users who need proofing tools, you can install proofing tools from the Proofing Tools CD to individual computers.

To install Office 2003 Proofing Tools on a single computer

1. On the Office 2003 Proofing Tools CD, run Ptksetup.exe.

2. When prompted, enter the product key, and then click **Next**.

3. Enter the user name, initials, and organization, and then click **Next**.

4. Accept the end-user license agreement (EULA), and then click **Next**.

5. On the **Type of Installation** page, choose **Custom Install**.

6. On the **Advanced Customization** page, click the node (plus (+) sign) for the languages you want to install and use the drop-down arrows to set the appropriate installation states.

7. Click **Install**.

Installing Office 2003 Proofing Tools with an installation of Office

If you deploy tools from Office 2003 Proofing Tools at the same time that you deploy Office 2003, you can chain the installation of Proofing Tools so it is installed on a user's computer during the same operation.

To chain Proofing Tools to an Office installation, you customize the Office Setup.ini file to include the MSI packages you want to install.

> **Note**   For more information about the many options available to you when creating chained install sections in Setup settings files, see "Deploying Office and Other Products·Together" in Chapter 5, "Installing Office 2003."

To chain Proofing Tools with your Office deployment

1. Open the Office Setup settings file (Setup.ini) in a text editor such as Notepad.

2. Create a new section called [ChainedInstall_1].

3. In the [ChainedInstall_1] section, specify the name and path of the Office 2003 Proofing Tools MSI file. For example:
   PATH=\\server1\share\office\ptk.msi

4. Add the following entry to the [ChainedInstall_1] section:
   TaskType=msi

5. Specify other options in this section, such as **IgnoreReturnValue** or **Reboot**.

6. Specify a unique display setting or transform to apply to the Proofing Tools installation by setting the **Display** or **MST** property in the [ChainedInstall_1] section.

For example, you can ensure that the Proofing Tools installation installs quietly with the following setting:

DISPLAY=None

Using the settings in the above procedure, the completed section looks like this:

```
[ChainedInstall_1]
PATH=\\server1\share\office\ptk.msi
DISPLAY=None
TRANSFORMS=\\server1\share\office\Proof.mst
TASKTYPE=msi
IGNORERETURNVALUE=0
REBOOT=0
```

This example assumes that your proofing tools files are in the same folder as your Office files on an administrative installation point.

Tip   If your proofing tools are located in the same folder as your Office administrative installation point, you can specify all paths as relative paths instead of as absolute paths (as in the above example). Using a relative path will allow you to copy the files to new servers later, if necessary, without updating the INI file to use the new server name. If your proofing tools files are located in a different folder (and possibly on a different server) than your Office administrative files, you should specify paths as absolute paths (for example, \\server1\proof\ptk.msi).

Now users can install Office and proofing tools together by running Office Setup.

Note   This chaining technique does not work when deploying by using Group Policy software installation.

Installing Office 2003 Proofing Tools separately from an Office installation

You can install Proofing Tools separately from an Office installation. One way to do this is to have users install the tools for themselves from the administrative installation point, or from a command line that you distribute to them in a batch file, an e-mail message, or some other means used by your organization. In either installation, you can use a transform that applies customizations when Proofing Tools Setup.exe is run. For example, the Setup command line might look like this:

```
\\server1\share\proof\Ptksetup.exe /qb TRANSFORMS=Proof.mst
```

Installing proofing tools from a MUI Pack

You may already have MUI Packs available that include the proofing tools your organization needs. In this scenario, you do not need to purchase the Proofing Tools CD. You can customize a MUI Pack deployment to install the proofing tools you need along with any other language resources from the MUI Pack.

If just a few users need proofing tools for a language, you can install proofing tools from a MUI Pack CD on their local computers. When you deploy to a large group of users, you can install proofing tools from a MUI Pack together with your Office deployment, or the tools can be installed separately from an Office installation.

Creating an administration installation point for proofing tools from a MUI Pack

Whether you choose to install proofing tools from a MUI Pack together with an Office installation or separately, you first install the proofing tools you want to make available to your users on an administrative installation point. Users can run Muisetup.exe from this location and choose languages they wish to install on their computers.

To install proofing tools from a MUI Pack on an administrative installation point

1. On a server, run **Muisetup.exe** with the **/a** command-line option on the Office 2003 MUI Pack CD that includes proofing tools for the languages you want.

2. Enter the installation location and product key, and then click **Next**.

3. Accept the end-user license agreement (EULA), and then click **Next**.

4. On the **Select Feature Installation States** page, select the proofing tools you want users to be able to install and set the appropriate installation states.

5. Click **Install**.

Users can run Muisetup.exe at this location to install the proofing tools they need, or you can customize a deployment of Office to include proofing tools from this folder.

Installing proofing tools from a MUI Pack on an individual computer

If you have one or two users who need proofing tools, you can install proofing tools from a MUI Pack to individual computers.

To install proofing tools from a MUI Pack on a single computer

1. On the Office 2003 MUI Pack CD, navigate to the folder for one language, identified by an LCID. For example, the LCID for German is 1031.

2. In that language folder, run Setup.exe.

3. Accept the end-user license agreement (EULA), and then click **Next**.

4. On the **Type of Installation** page, choose **Proofing Tools Only**.

5. Click **Install**.

Installing proofing tools from a MUI Pack with an installation of Office

If you deploy proofing tools from an Office 2003 MUI Pack at the same time that you deploy Office 2003, you can chain the installations together so that they are installed on a user's computer during the same operation.

To do this, you customize the Office Setup settings file (Setup.ini) to include the MSI package for the Office 2003 MUI Pack. The following example assumes that you have customized a MUI Pack transform called German.MST that selects the German proofing tools and contains any other customizations you need for the MUI Pack.

To include proofing tools from a MUI Pack in your Office installation

1. Open the Office Setup settings file (Setup.ini) in a text editor such as Notepad.

2. Create a new section called [ChainedInstall_1].

3. In the [ChainedInstall_1] section, specify the name and path of the MUI Pack MSI file. For example:

    PATH=\\server1\share\office\1031\Mui.msi

4. Add the following entry to the [ChainedInstall_1] section:

    TASKTYPE=msi

5. Specify other options in this section, such as **IgnoreReturnValue** or **Reboot**.

6. Specify a unique display setting or transform to apply to the proofing tools installation by setting the **Display** or **MST** property in the [ChainedInstall_1] section. For example:

    MST=\\server1\share\office\1031\German.MST

Using the above examples, the completed section in the Setup.ini file looks like this:

```
[ChainedInstall_1]
PATH=\\server1\share\office\1031\Mui.msi
MST=\\server1\share\office\1031\German.MST
TASKTYPE=msi
```

> **Tip** If your MUI Pack files and folders are located in the same folder as your Office administrative installation point, you can specify all paths as relative paths instead of as absolute paths (as in the above example). Using a relative path will allow you to copy the files to new servers later, if necessary, without updating the INI file to use the new server name. If your MUI Pack files are located in a different folder (and possibly on a different server) than your Office administrative files, you should specify paths as absolute paths (for example, \\server1\muipacks\mui.msi).

Now users can install Office and proofing tools from a MUI Pack together by running Office Setup.

> **Note** This chaining technique does not work when deploying by using Group Policy software installation. For information on deploying Office with Group Policy, see "Using Group Policy to Deploy Office" in Chapter 5, "Installing Office 2003."

Installing proofing tools from a MUI Pack separately from Office

You can provide proofing tools from a MUI Pack for users to install separately from your Office installation. One option is for users to install tools for themselves from the MUI Pack administrative installation point, as described in the section "Creating an administration installation point for proofing tools from a MUI Pack" earlier in this chapter.

Another option is to provide a customized deployment by giving users a MUI Pack Setup command line (for example, in a batch file) that includes a transform file with the options you choose. Specify the Setup.exe program in one of the MUI Pack folders on the administrative installation point.

For example, the Setup command line to install proofing tools from a German MUI Pack might be:

```
\\server1\share\office\1031\Setup.exe /qb TRANSFORMS=Mui.mst
```

Resources and related information

You may need to provide proofing tools in one language while including MUI Pack support in another language for a group of users. For more information about customizing your Office deployment with different combinations of language resources for different users, see "Deploy Different Language Configurations to Different Groups of Office Users" in Chapter 15, "Sample Office 2003 Multilingual Deployments."

You have customization options when you install proofing tools together with Office. For more information about chained deployments, see "Deploying Office and Other Products Together" in Chapter 5, "Installing Office 2003."

For more information about using the Custom Installation Wizard to create transforms, see the Custom Installation Wizard Help on the companion CD.

Installing Localized Versions of Office 2003

Localized versions of Microsoft Office 2003 are available for users who want all Office features in their own language. Although deploying Office with the Multilingual User Interface Pack (MUI Pack) gives you the advantage of having a single installation of Office for your entire international organization, there are limitations to some plug-in language features in the MUI Pack. As a result, these features are offered only in localized versions.

Although MUI Packs work only with the English version of Office 2003 and not with localized versions, users of a localized version of Office can easily share documents created by users running Office with a MUI Pack. In this way, localized versions of Office 2003 are compatible with Office 2003 with MUI Packs.

To install a localized version of Office 2003, you follow the same procedure as installing any other Office 2003 package (MSI file). For example, you can customize your installation by creating a transform with the Custom Installation Wizard.

> **On the Resource Kit CD**   The Office Resource Kit tools, which include the Custom Installation Wizard, are contained in a self-extracting executable file (Ork.exe) that can be downloaded from the Office Resource Kit Toolbox at *http://www.microsoft.com/office/ork/2003*. The tools are available only in English.

Although the deployment process is the same for localized versions of Office as for other Office 2003 products, there are certain deployment settings you should be aware of when deploying the new language version of Office for Hindi. These settings can help users have a better experience when using Hindi Office.

First, when you install the Hindi localized version of Office 2003, you should set the user locale to one of the Indic languages—such as Gujarati, Hindi, Kannada, Konkani, Marathi, Punjabi, Sanskrit, Tamil, or Telugu. Setting the user locale to an Indic language will ensure that the language settings for Office (for example, the installation language) are set appropriately for Hindi users.

Second, when working in Hindi Office, Window title bars may display with very small fonts. The small fonts also appear in Setup dialogs when users install Hindi Office from a stand-alone CD. To have a better reading experience, users can change the font size and format in Windows.

To change the font size and format to make Hindi dialogs more readable

1. In Windows XP, on Control Panel, click **Appearance and Themes**, then click **Display**. In Windows 2000, on Control Panel (or in Classic View in Control Panel in Windows XP), click **Display**.

2. On the **Appearance** tab, click **Advanced**.

3. In the **Advanced Appearance** dialog, in the **Item** drop-down list, choose **Active Title Bar**.

    This lets you change format settings for the Active Window title bar.

4. In the **Size** drop-down box next to the **Font** drop-down box, choose **11**.

    or

    Keep the same font size but click the **Bold (B)** button to change the font from **Bold** to regular text.

or

Change the font size to 11 and change the font from **Bold** to regular text.

5. Click **OK** twice to save the settings.

Resources and related information

The advantages and disadvantages of deploying a localized version or deploying MUI Packs are discussed in "Overview of Office 2003 Multilingual Resources" in Chapter 13, "Preparing for an Office Multilingual Deployment."

Detailed information about deploying Office—which can be applied to deploying a localized version—is included in Chapter 4, "Customizing Office 2003" and Chapter 5, "Installing Office 2003."

Installing Office Language Resources that Upgrade or Coexist with Existing Language Resources

It is straightforward to upgrade to the Microsoft Office 2003 Multilingual User Interface Pack (MUI Pack) from earlier language packs—such as the Office 2000 Multi-Language Pack (LPK) or the Office XP MUI Pack—but it is also possible to have MUI Packs coexist with MultiLanguage Packs on the same computer. The same is true for Microsoft Office 2003 Proofing Tools, which can be installed on a computer with an existing installation of earlier proofing tools.

The need for language resources to coexist on the same computer typically arises when different versions of Office or Office applications—for example, Microsoft Word 2002 and Word 2000—coexist on that computer. If you are upgrading to Office 2003 and not keeping any applications from earlier versions of Office, you can upgrade to Office 2003 MUI Packs or proofing tools and remove the existing multilingual files from users' computers. Deleting the files avoids using extra hard disk space or potentially confusing users with unneeded software on their computers.

> **Note** If you must install Office 2003 to coexist with an earlier version of Office, be aware that each version must be installed in version-specific folders on users' computers. Microsoft Office Outlook® 2003 cannot coexist with any earlier versions of Outlook.

In both scenarios—upgrading to a new version of Office 2003 and having Office 2003 coexist with earlier versions of Office—user settings are migrated automatically.

Upgrading an earlier language pack installation

When you upgrade a language pack installation as part of your Office 2003 deployment, you need to decide whether to keep existing language pack files or remove them from users' computers.

By default, when Office 2003 MUI Packs are installed, all previous MultiLanguage Pack and MUI Pack files are deleted. However, if you are upgrading an existing Multi-Language Pack or MUI Pack installation after you have deployed Office 2003, you must use a method other than the Custom Installation Wizard—such as using the Office Removal Wizard —to remove existing language pack files from users' computers.

You may want to keep earlier versions of language packs on users' computers if you plan to have Office 2003 applications coexist with earlier versions of Office applications.

To customize your deployment of Office to retain earlier language pack support

1. In the Custom Installation Wizard, on the **Remove Previous Versions** page, click **Remove the following versions of Microsoft Office applications**.

2. Double-click **Microsoft Multi-Language Packs**, and clear the box next to **Microsoft Multi-Language Packs**.

Upgrading a Proofing Tools installation

When you upgrade an Office 2003 Proofing Tools installation, there are several issues to consider.

When you install Office 2003 Proofing Tools, older proofing tools files are removed by default. However, you may want to retain those older versions on users' computers if you plan to have Office 2003 applications coexist with earlier versions of Office applications. To keep all proofing tools files from earlier releases, specify **KEEPPTK9=1** in the Setup settings file (Setup.ini) or on the Setup command line.

In addition, custom dictionaries have been improved. Dictionaries included in older versions of Office Proofing Tools were in ANSI format. These dictionaries have been upgraded to support custom dictionaries created and written in Unicode. This allows organizations to have multiple languages from different code pages in the same dictionary file. Existing dictionaries will migrate to the new format when you install Office 2003 Proofing Tools.

Upgrading an Input Method Editor installation

The Microsoft Office 2003 MUI Pack includes Input Method Editors (IMEs) for the languages that you choose to install. If your organization uses IMEs, you can install and use any of the updated IMEs supplied with the Office 2003 MUI Pack.

Upgrading to Office 2003 with the MUI Pack could result in multiple Input Method Editors on your users' computers. Existing IMEs may not be uninstalled by the Office installation process, but instead could be unregistered from the Active keyboard when Office 2003 Setup runs.

To migrate with language-specific IMEs, install the MUI Pack languages that your organization needs. The corresponding IMEs will be installed automatically with the languages.

Note   If your users have Microsoft Windows 2000 and Windows XP, they must enable the language for the IME before installing the IME. To do this, go to **Regional Options** (**Regional and Language Options** in Windows XP) in Control Panel. Under the **Language settings for the system** area in the **General** tab, choose the language of the IME. This process will install the appropriate language support files.

Resources and related information

Procedures for various MUI Pack deployment scenarios are included in Chapter 15, "Sample Office 2003 Multilingual Deployments."

Patching an existing MUI Pack installation is straightforward. For more information, see "Distributing Multilingual User Interface Pack Updates" in Chapter 16, "Maintaining an Office 2003 Multilingual Installation."

You can use the Office Removal Wizard to remove applications or files after completing your initial Office installation. For more information about using the Removal Wizard, see "Customizing Removal Behavior" in Chapter 4, "Customizing Office 2003."

Office 2003 MUI Pack Languages and Corresponding Locale Identifiers

In some deployment scenarios, you must know the locale identifier (LCID) for a language in order to install the correct MUI Pack. Microsoft Office 2003 Multilingual User Interface Packs (MUI Packs) are installed on the administrative installation point under folder names by their corresponding locale identifier.

For example, when you include MUI Packs as part of an Office deployment, you specify the Mui.msi file in the LCID folder for a language—such as \1031\Mui.msi for the German MUI Pack MSI file.

The following table lists Office 2003 MUI Pack languages and corresponding locale identifiers.

Language	Locale identifier (LCID)
Arabic	1025
Basque	1069
Bulgarian	1026
Catalan	1027
Chinese (Simplified)	2052
Chinese (Traditional)	1028
Croatian	1050
Czech	1029
Danish	1030
Dutch	1043
English (U.S.)	1033
Estonian	1061
Finnish	1035
French	1036
Gaelic (Ireland)	2108
Galician	1110
German	1031
Greek	1032
Gujarati	1095
Hebrew	1037
Hindi	1081
Hungarian	1038
Icelandic	1039
Indonesian	1057
Italian	1040
Japanese	1041
Kannada	1099
Korean	1042
Latvian	1062
Lithuanian	1063
Marathi	1102
Norwegian (Bokmal)	1044
Polish	1045

continued

Language	Locale identifier (LCID)
Portuguese (Brazil)	1046
Portuguese (Portugal)	2070
Punjabi	1094
Romanian	1048
Russian	1049
Serbian	2074
Slovak	1051
Slovenian	1060
Spanish	3082
Swedish	1053
Tamil	1097
Telugu	1098
Thai	1054
Turkish	1055
Ukrainian	1058
Urdu	1056
Vietnamese	1066
Welsh	1106

Chapter 15

Sample Office 2003 Multilingual Deployments

There are a variety of ways to deploy Microsoft® Office 2003 in a multilingual environment. This chapter describes several deployment scenarios, with step-by-step examples of how to customize and install Office in those situations. If your organization's deployment needs do not follow one of these examples exactly, you can often adapt aspects of these examples to help you customize your own multilingual deployment.

Deploy Office with One MUI Pack

The multilingual needs of your users might only require you to install one Microsoft Office 2003 Multilingual User Interface Pack on their computers. Customizing and deploying Office 2003 with one MUI Pack is a straightforward process:

- Install Office on an administrative installation point.

- Specify the customized language settings for your users (as well as any other Office configurations) in a transform.

- Chain the MUI Pack to the Office installation in the Setup.ini file.

> **Note**   For more information about creating an administrative installation point for Office, see "Creating an Administrative Installation Point" in Chapter 3, "Preparing to Deploy Office 2003."

After you create an administrative installation point for Office, add the MUI Pack file that you plan to deploy. The following example shows how to add the Japanese MUI Pack, but the process can be applied to any MUI Pack you need to deploy.

To add the Japanese MUI Pack to an administrative installation point

1. Insert the CD that contains the Japanese MUI Pack.

2. On the **Start** menu, click **Run**, and then click **Browse** to locate the MUI Pack CD.

3. On the MUI Pack CD, select **Muisetup.exe** and click **Open**.

4. On the command line, following **Muisetup.exe**, type **/a** and click **OK**.

5. When prompted by Muisetup.exe, accept the end-user license agreement (EULA) and click **Next**.

6. Enter the server and the share for your Office administrative installation point and click **Next**.

    Or, if you have decided to store your MUI Pack administrative images in a different location, enter that location here.

    A share must be large enough to store the resources for the language that you need in addition to the Office 2003 files. Hard disk space requirements for the MUI Packs vary per MUI Pack language. For example, the German MUI Pack requires 231 megabytes (MB) of hard disk space. In addition, if users install from a compressed image and choose to keep the local installation source, the German MUI Pack requires an additional 91 MB of hard disk space for the local installation source. By contrast, the Chinese (Simplified) MUI Pack requires 578 MB of hard disk space plus an additional 320 MB for the local installation source.

7.   On the **Available Languages** page, choose **Japanese**.

> **Note**   Languages that are not available on the current CD will appear dimmed on this page. You can add languages from other CDs to the same administrative installation point by running **Muisetup.exe /a** with additional MUI Pack CDs and specifying the same network server location.

You can include language feature customizations for the MUI Pack in your Office transform. The following example shows how you would set the installation language to Japanese, but this process can be applied to the other languages, as well.

To create an Office transform with language settings for Japanese

1.   Start the Custom Installation Wizard.

2.   On the **Open MSI File** page, enter (or browse to) the MSI file name for your Office installation (for example, Pro11.msi) from the administrative installation point for Office:

   \\server1\share\office\Pro11.msi

3.   On the **Select the MST File to Save** page, enter the name of the Japanese MST file you are creating; for example:

   \\server1\share\office\OfficeWithJapanese.mst

4.   On the **Set Feature Installation States** page, click on the **Microsoft Office** node (plus (+) sign), click on the **Office Shared Features** node, and then click on the **International Support** node.

5.   Click on **Japanese fonts** and select an installation state (only if the computer you are installing Office on is not running the Japanese version of Microsoft Windows®).

6.   On the **Change Office User Settings** page, click **Microsoft Office 2003 (User)**.

7.   Navigate the tree under **Language Settings** to **Enabled Languages**.

8.   Double-click **Installed version of Microsoft Office** to open the **Properties** page for this setting.

9.   Click **Apply changes**, then select **Japanese** from the **Installed version of Microsoft Office** drop-down menu.

10.   Click **OK**.

Now you chain the Japanese MUI Pack to your Office installation. As shown by the following example, to chain packages, you customize the Office Setup.ini to include the MSI packages you want to install.

> **Note**   For detailed information about chaining packages with Office, see "Deploying Office and Other Products Together" in Chapter 5, "Installing Office 2003."

To chain the Japanese MUI Pack with your Office deployment

1. Open the Office Setup settings file (Setup.ini) in a text editor, such as Notepad.

2. Create a section called [ChainedInstall_1], and in this section specify the name and path of the Japanese MUI Pack. For example:
   PATH=\\server1\share\office\1041\Mui.msi

3. Specify the task type for this section:
   TASKTYPE=msi

4. Specify other options for this section, such as **IgnoreReturnValue** or **Reboot**.

5. Specify a unique display setting or MUI Pack transform to apply to the MUI Pack installation by setting the **Display** or **MST** property.

   For example, you can ensure that the MUI Pack installation installs quietly with the following setting:
   DISPLAY=None

6. Specify additional options by using the **Cmdline** property.

   For example, set the **NOFEATURESTATEMIGRATION** property to **True** to cancel the custom action that matches installation states for MUI Pack feature states to corresponding Office feature installation states:
   CMDLINE=NOFEATURESTATEMIGRATION=TRUE
   The completed section in the Setup.ini file looks like this:

```
[ChainedInstall_1]
PATH=\\server1\share\office\1041\Mui.msi
TASKTYPE=msi
DISPLAY=None
CMDLINE=NOFEATURESTATEMIGRATION=True
```

After completing the above procedures, you can provide users with a command line to install Office with the Japanese MUI Pack:

```
\\server1\share\office\setup.exe /qb TRANSFORMS=\\server1\share\office\OfficeWith-
Japanese.mst
```

Deploy Office with Multiple MUI Packs

The users in your organization might need to use multiple Microsoft Office 2003 Multilingual User Interface Packs in their daily work. In this scenario, you might choose to deploy more than one MUI Pack with your Microsoft Office deployment. The process for doing this is as straightforward as it is when you deploy one MUI Pack.

For example, suppose you want to install French and Polish language features on the user's computer at the same time that you deploy Office. French language features are installed from one CD disk, and Polish language features from another CD. The sequence of tasks in this situation is as follows:

1. Create an administrative installation point for the core Office product (English).

2. Use Muisetup.exe to create the French and Polish MUI Packs administrative image to the same administrative installation point.

3. Use the Custom Installation Wizard with the Office package (MSI file) to customize language settings for French and Polish, and then save the transform with a name (for example, OfficeFrPo.mst).

4. Edit the Setup.ini file to chain the French and Polish MUI Packs MSI files to the Office installation.

After you have created your administrative installation point for Office, add the MUI Pack files that you plan to deploy.

> **Note**   For more information about creating an administrative installation point for Office, see "Creating an Administrative Installation Point" in Chapter 3, "Preparing to Deploy Office 2003."

The following examples make use of the French and Polish MUI Packs, but the processes can be applied to any languages that you are deploying.

To add MUI Packs to an administrative installation point

1. Insert the CD that contains the French MUI Pack.

2. On the **Start** menu, click **Run**, and then click **Browse** to locate the MUI Pack CD.

3. On the MUI Pack CD, select **Muisetup.exe** and click **Open**.

4. On the command line, following **Muisetup.exe**, type **/a** and click **OK**.

5. Enter the server and the share for your Office administrative installation point and click **Next**.

A share must be large enough to store the resources for the languages that you need, in addition to the Office 2003 files. Hard disk space requirements for the MUI Packs vary per MUI Pack language. For example, the German MUI Pack requires 231 megabytes (MB) of hard disk space. In addition, if users install from a compressed image and choose to keep the local installation source, the German MUI Pack requires an additional 91 MB of hard disk space for the local installation source. By contrast, the Chinese (Simplified) MUI Pack requires 578 MB of hard disk space plus an additional 320 MB for the local installation source.

6. On the **Available Languages** page, choose **French** and click **Install**.

    Note that languages that are not available on the current CD will appear dimmed on this page.

7. Insert the CD that contains the Polish MUI Pack.

8. Run **Muisetup.exe** with the **/a** option again.

9. On the **Available Languages** page, choose **Polish** and click **Install**.

Now customize your Office transform to include language settings for French and Polish.

To create an Office transform with language settings for French and Polish

1. Start the Custom Installation Wizard.

2. On the **Open MSI File** page, enter (or browse to) the MSI file name for your Office installation (for example, Pro11.msi) from the administrative installation point for Office:

    \\server1\share\office\Pro11.msi

3. On the **Select the MST File to Save** page, enter the name of the MST file you are creating, for example:

    \\server1\share\office\OfficeWithFrPo.mst

4. On the **Change Office User Settings** page, click **Microsoft Office 2003 (User)**.

5. Navigate the tree under **Language Settings**, and set the language features you want for this deployment.

    For example, you might choose to enable editing for both languages. Open **Enabled Languages**, and click **Show controls and enable editing for**. In the languages shown in the right-hand pane, open **French**, click **Apply changes**, then click **Check to turn setting on**. Click **OK**. Follow the same steps for enabling **Polish**.

Now you chain the French and Polish MUI Packs to your Office installation. To chain packages, you customize the Office Setup.ini file by using a text editor, such as Notepad, to include the MSI files you want to install.

> **Note**   For detailed information about chaining packages with Office, see "Deploying Office and Other Products Together" in Chapter 5, "Installing Office 2003."

To chain the French and Polish MUI Packs with your Office deployment

1. Open the Office Setup settings file (Setup.ini) in a text editor, such as Notepad.

2. Create a section called [ChainedInstall_1], and in this section specify the name and path of the MUI Pack you want to chain.

   1036 is the LCID for French and 1045 is the LCID for Polish. So to add the French MUI Pack, you might enter:

   PATH=\\server1\share\office\1036\mui.msi

3. Create a section called [ChainedInstall_2], and in this section specify the name and path of the second MUI Pack you want to chain. For example, to add the Polish MUI Pack, you might enter:

   PATH=\\server1\share\office\1045\mui.msi

4. Specify the task type for this section:

   TASKTYPE=msi

5. Specify other options for this section, such as **IgnoreReturnValue** or **Reboot**.

6. Specify a unique display setting or MUI Pack transform in each section to apply to that MUI Pack installation by setting the **Display** or **MST** property. (You can, instead, specify these options on the command line.)

   For example, you can ensure that the MUI Pack installation installs quietly by setting the following:

   DISPLAY=None

7. Specify additional options in each section by using the **Cmdline** property. For example, set the **NOFEATURESTATEMIGRATION** property to **True** to cancel the custom action that matches installation states for MUI Pack feature states to corresponding Office feature installation states:

   CMDLINE=NOFEATURESTATEMIGRATION=TRUE

   Using the above examples, the completed sections in the Setup.ini file look like this:

```
[ChainedInstall_1]
PATH=\\server1\share\office\1036\mui.msi
TASKTYPE=msi
DISPLAY=None
CMDLINE=NOFEATURESTATEMIGRATION=True
[ChainedInstall_2]
PATH=\\server1\share\office\1045\mui.msi
TASKTYPE=msi
DISPLAY=None
CMDLINE=NOFEATURESTATEMIGRATION=True
```

After completing the above procedures, you can provide a command line such as the following for your users to install Office with these MUI Packs. (In this example, the Office transform is specified in the Setup command line but you could instead include the transform in Setup.ini by using the **MST** option in the main section of the file—not in the chained installation sections.)

```
\\server1\share\office\setup.exe /qb TRANSFORMS=\\server1\share\office\Office-
FrPo.mst
```

From a user's perspective, installation works like this:

1. Office Setup installs Office, as specified in the OfficeFrPo.mst transform.

2. When Office installation is complete, Office Setup runs MUI Pack Setup to install the French MUI Pack, as specified in the Setup.ini file.

3. When the French MUI Pack installation is complete, Office Setup runs MUI Pack Setup to install the Polish MUI Pack, as specified in the Setup.ini file.

At the end of the process, the user has English Office installed with French and Polish language features enabled. By running the Microsoft Office Language Settings utility from the **Start** menu, users can switch the user interface and Help language of Office to English, French, or Polish.

Deploy Different Language Configurations to Different Groups of Office Users

In many organizations, you must install different language resources for different groups of users. In this case, you create separate Microsoft Office transforms, separate Microsoft Office 2003 Multilingual User Interface Pack transforms, and a customized Setup.ini for each group. First, you decide whether to use one or separate administrative installation points for your deployment. Then, typically, you follow these steps:

- In each Office transform, specify the customized language settings for a group of users.

- In each MUI Pack transform, define customizations, such as setting Setup properties.

- In the Setup.ini file, chain the languages to the Office installation.

For example, you might have one group of users that speaks French but needs to edit documents in German. You might have a second group of users that speaks Russian but needs to edit in Hungarian. In this scenario, you customize two sets of

Office and MUI Pack transforms, along with the corresponding Setup.ini files, one set for each group of users.

First, you create one or more administrative installation points on the server to deploy the following Office configurations:

- Core Office (English) plus the French MUI Pack and German proofing tools from the German MUI Pack

- Core Office (English) plus the Russian MUI Pack and Hungarian proofing tools from the Hungarian MUI Pack

Choose the number of installation points to use

You can use the same administrative installation point, or two separate installation points, to deploy Office with multiple multilingual configurations.

If you choose to use the same administrative installation point for two Office installations, you must take steps to ensure that the correct Setup.ini file is used for each installation. (This is not a problem if you use different administrative installation points because the file names will not need to be different.) First, you specify two different Setup.ini files to use, one for each deployment. Then you have two options for using the appropriate Setup.ini file for an installation: the **/settings** option for Setup.exe, or two copies of Setup.exe with names that correspond to the correct Setup.ini file.

For example, suppose you have two Setup.ini files, SetupFra.ini, and SetupRus.ini. In this situation, choose one of these two methods for installation:

- Use **/settings** to specify which Setup.ini file to use on the Setup.exe command line you provide to your users. For example:
    Setup.exe /settings \\server\share\Office\SetupFra.ini
    and
    Setup.exe /settings \\server\share\Office\SetupRus.ini

- Copy Setup.exe for each language, and rename the Setup.exe files to match corresponding Setup.ini file names. Then direct users to run the appropriate Setup program file. For example:
    SetupFra.exe will by default use SetupFra.ini.
    SetupRus.exe will by default use SetupRus.ini.

Create a transform for different groups of users

Once you have decided whether to use one or more administrative installation points, you customize Office for each group by using separate transforms. You also create separate MUI Pack transforms to include proofing tools that provide additional language-editing capabilities.

Choices for installing proofing tools

You can install proofing tools from Microsoft Office 2003 Proofing Tools instead of using the proofing tools included in the Multilingual User Interface Pack. To do this, you chain Office 2003 Proofing Tools to your Office installation as you would a MUI Pack. However, your installation is not as scalable if you choose to use Office 2003 Proofing Tools instead of installing the proofing tools included in the Multilingual User Interface Pack.

For example, suppose you install proofing tools for a language from Office 2003 Proofing Tools and then decide to include proofing tools for another language later. Proofing Tools includes all languages in a single MSI file. When you install the proofing tools for the first language, you might have disabled installation for all the other proofing tools in the MSI file. In this case, if you want to later deploy proofing tools for another language, you must use the Custom Maintenance Wizard to change the feature state for the additional proofing tools.

For example, you create the Office transform for the French-speaking group as described in this procedure.

To create an Office transform with language settings for French and German

1. Start the Custom Installation Wizard.

2. On the **Open MSI File** page, enter (or browse to) the MSI file name for your Office installation (for example, Pro11.msi) from the administrative installation point for Office:

   \\server1\share\office\Pro11.msi

3. On the **Select the MST File to Save** page, enter the name of the MST file you are creating; for example:

   \\server1\share\office\OfficeWithFrGr.mst

4. On the **Change Office User Settings** page, click **Microsoft Office 2003 (User)**.

5. Navigate the tree under **Language Settings** to **Enabled Languages**.

6. Double-click **Installed version of Microsoft Office** to open the **Properties** page for this setting.

7. Click **Apply changes**, then select **French** from the **Installed version of Microsoft Office** drop-down menu.

8. Click **OK**.

9. Click **Show controls and enable editing for**.

10. In the languages shown in the right-hand pane, open **French**, click **Apply changes**, then click **Check to turn setting on**.

11. Click **OK**.

12. Follow steps 9 through 11 again with German.

13. Make any other customizations to Office settings, then click **Finish**.

Next, you customize a transform to select the proofing tools from the German MUI Pack.

To create a transform for German proofing tools from the German MUI Pack

1. Start the Custom Installation Wizard.

2. On the **Open MSI File** page, enter (or browse to) the German MUI Pack MSI file:
   \\server1\share\office\1031\Mui.msi

3. On the **Select the MST File to Save** page, enter the name of the MST file you are creating; for example:
   \\server1\share\office\1031\MUIGermanPT.mst

4. On the **Select Feature Installation States** page, click on the **Microsoft Office** drop-down arrow and select **Not Available** for all features.
   (You can alternately specify **Not Available, Hidden, Locked**.)

5. Click on the **Office Shared Features** node (plus (+) sign), click on the **Proofing Tools** node, then choose an installation state (for example, **Run from My Computer**).

6. Click **Finish**.

Modify Setup.ini to chain the MUI Packs

After you create the custom transforms, you modify Setup.ini to chain the French MUI Pack with the Office installation and apply the transform to install the German proofing tools. To chain packages, you customize the Office Setup.ini file by using a text editor, such as Notepad, to include the MSI packages you want to install.

The following procedures describes how to chain the French and German MUI Packs to an Office deployment, including the transform created earlier to install the German proofing tools from the German MUI Pack. You would follow a similar procedure to chain the Russian and Hungarian MUI Packs, creating a Setup file called (for example) SetupRus.ini.

> **Note** For detailed information about chaining packages with Office, see "Deploying Office and Other Products Together" in Chapter 5, "Installing Office 2003."

To chain the French MUI Pack with your Office deployment

1. Open the Office Setup settings file for the French and German installation (SetupFra.ini) in a text editor, such as Notepad.

2. Create a section called [ChainedInstall_1], and in this section specify the name and path of the MUI Pack you want to chain.

   1036 is the LCID for French, and 1031 is the LCID for German. To add the French MUI Pack, for this example, you might enter:

   PATH=\\server1\share\office\1036\Mui.msi

3. Create a section called [ChainedInstall_2], and in this section specify the name and path of the second MUI Pack you want to chain. To add the German MUI Pack, you might enter:

   PATH=\\server1\share\office\1031\mui.msi

4. Specify the task type for this section:

   TASKTYPE=msi

5. Specify other options for this section, such as **IgnoreReturnValue** or **Reboot**.

6. Specify a unique display setting or MUI Pack transform in each section to apply to that MUI Pack installation by setting the **Display** or **MST** property. (You can, instead, specify these options on the command line.)

   In this example, specify the MST file for the German MUI Pack:

   MST=\\server1\share\office\1031\MUIGermanPT.mst

7. Specify additional options to each ChainedInstall section by using the **Cmdline** property. For example, set the **NOFEATURESTATEMIGRATION** property to **True** to cancel the custom action that matches installation states for MUI Pack feature states to corresponding Office feature installation states:

   CMDLINE=NOFEATURESTATEMIGRATION=TRUE

   The completed sections in the Setup.ini file look like this:

```
[ChainedInstall_1]
PATH=\\server1\share\office\1036\Mui.msi
TASKTYPE=msi
CMDLINE=NOFEATURESTATEMIGRATION=True
[ChainedInstall_2]
PATH=\\server1\share\office\1031\Mui.msi
TASKTYPE=msi
MST=\\server1\share\office\1031\MUIGermanPT.mst
CMDLINE=NOFEATURESTATEMIGRATION=True
```

Deploying to your users

Now that you have completed the steps to configure Office and to configure and chain the MUI Packs and proofing tools you want, you next provide a command line to users that installs Office with the language features you have chosen.

The French-speaking group installs Office by using the following command line (for example):

```
\\server1\share\office\SetupFra.exe /qb TRANSFORMS=\\server1\share\office\Office-
WithFrench.mst
```

The French-speaking group ends up with a French user interface and Help system with both French and German editing tools enabled.

The basic procedures for deploying to Russian-speaking users are identical, substituting the appropriate languages. Then the Russian-speaking group installs Office by using the following command line (for example):

```
\\server1\share\office\SetupRus.exe /qb TRANSFORMS=\\server1\share\office\Office-
WithRussian.mst
```

This group ends up with a Russian user interface and Help system with both Russian and Hungarian editing tools enabled.

Chapter 16

Maintaining an Office 2003 Multilingual Installation

Once you have deployed Microsoft® Office 2003 multilingual resources in your organization, Office 2003 allows you to further customize and maintain that installation.

In this chapter:

Updating Language Settings in Office

After you have deployed Microsoft Office 2003 to users, you can modify many language settings without reinstalling the product. For example, if you install Microsoft Office 2003 Multilingual User Packs (MUI Packs) after your initial Office deployment, you can enable those languages. You can modify users' language settings by using one of the following methods:

■ Use the Custom Maintenance Wizard to create a configuration maintenance file (CMW file) containing new language settings.

   For more information about using the Custom Maintenance Wizard to modify user-defined settings after Office is installed, see "Updating Feature Installation States and Application Settings" in Chapter 18, "Updating Users' Office 2003 Configurations."

■ Set policies using the Group Policy snap-in. Settings enforced by policy cannot be altered by users.

   For more information about using the Group Policy snap-in to set Office-related policies, see "Managing Users' Configurations by Policy," in Chapter 18, "Updating Users' Office 2003 Configurations."

Changing the installation language

All Microsoft Office 2003 applications use the default installation language to determine language-related default behavior. The installation language is determined by the locale ID (LCID) assigned to the **InstallLanguage** value entry in the Microsoft Windows® registry.

For example, if the value of **InstallLanguage** is **1041** (Japanese), then Microsoft Office Word 2003 creates its initial Normal.dot file based on Japanese settings and automatically enables commands for Asian text layout.

By default, Office creates the **InstallLanguage** value entry in the HKEY_CURRENT_USER\Software\Microsoft\Office\11.0\Common\LanguageResources subkey and sets its value to match the system locale of the operating system.

You can change the default Office installation language for your organization's needs. However, you do not need to switch installation languages merely to enable other languages for editing in Office applications. In fact, some custom settings are lost when you switch installation languages after Office is installed. For example, users' Normal.dot file is replaced and any customizations saved in the template are lost.

Other language-specific settings are also affected when you switch the installation language. For example, Word, Microsoft Office PowerPoint® 2003, and Microsoft Office Outlook® 2003 automatically update default settings (such as the default paper size) to correspond with the new installation language.

All of the language settings that you can set in a transform (MST file) using the Custom Installation Wizard can also be set in a configuration maintenance file (CMW file) using the Custom Maintenance Wizard. The **Change Office User Settings** page is identical in both wizards; and in both cases, the options in the tree correspond to options that you can set by policy in the Office policy templates.

To specify a new default installation language in a CMW file

1. Start the Custom Maintenance Wizard.

2. On the **Change Office User Settings** page, expand the tree under **Microsoft Office (user)**.

3. Under **Language Settings**, click **Enabled Languages**, double-click **Installed version of Microsoft Office**, and select a new language from the list.

4. Save the CMW file.

You can also use the Group Policy snap-in to specify a new default installation language by policy. Unlike default settings distributed in a transform, Office profile settings file (OPS file), or CMW file, users cannot modify settings enforced by policy. When you load the Office 2003 policy templates (ADM files) into the Group Policy Editor, policies related to language settings are located under User Configuration\Administrative Templates\Microsoft Office 2003\Language Settings.

To specify a default installation language policy

1. Open the Group Policy Object (GPO) for which you want to set policy.

2. Double-click **User Configuration** and then expand the tree to the Administrative Templates\Microsoft Office 2003\Language Settings\Enabled Languages folder.

3. Double-click **Installed version of Microsoft Office**.

4. Click **Enabled** and then select the language you want.

5. Save the Group Policy Object.

> **Note** If you change any language setting, including the installation language, you must restart your applications before the updated language is available.

Enabling additional editing languages

Rather than changing the default installation language of Office, you can modify language-specific features in Office 2003 applications by enabling additional languages for editing.

For example, Word automatically detects the language a user is typing based on the languages that are enabled for editing. If proofing tools are installed, Word uses the spelling checker, AutoCorrect list, and other editing tools for the languages it detects.

> **Note**   Before East Asian, right-to-left, or complex script languages can be enabled for editing, support for these languages must be enabled in the operating system. You can enable support for languages in the appropriate Control Panel dialog box (**Regional and Language Options** in Windows XP, or **Regional Options** in Windows 2000).

Some Office 2003 applications also display commands and dialog box options based on enabled languages. For example, if you enable an Asian language in Word, you can configure Asian text layout in the **Format** menu.

To enable additional editing languages in a CMW file

1. Start the Custom Maintenance Wizard.

2. On the **Change Office User Settings** page, expand the tree under **Microsoft Office (user)**.

3. Under **Language Settings**, click **Enabled Languages**, and then click **Show controls and enable editing for**.

4. Double-click the languages you want to enable for editing.

5. Save the CMW file.

In the Group Policy Editor, the corresponding policies are located in the following location:

User Configuration\Administrative Templates\Microsoft Office 2003\Language Settings\Enabled Languages\Show controls and enable editing for

Resources and related information

For more information about configuring language-related settings for your international deployment, see "Customizing Language Settings" in Chapter 13, "Preparing for an Office Multilingual Deployment."

You can deploy Office 2003 so that its default settings are based on a particular language. For more information about customizing language features when deploying Office 2003 with the Multilingual User Interface Pack, see "Customizing Language Settings" in Chapter 13, "Preparing for an Office Multilingual Deployment."

For a complete list of how language settings are used by Office applications, see "Effects of Customizing Language Settings on Office Applications" in Chapter 13, "Preparing for an Office Multilingual Deployment."

Removing Office Multilingual Resource Files

In a busy international organization, a user might need a set of Microsoft Office 2003 Multilingual User Interface Pack (MUI Pack) features or proofing tools for a particular language installed on a computer for short-term use. When a user no longer needs to work with files in that language, or if a roaming user (one who moves between different computers) moves on, these files remain on the computer, taking up hard disk space. You can remove the files when they are no longer needed, if you prefer.

To remove Office 2003 Multilingual User Interface Pack files

1. In Control Panel, double-click the **Add/Remove Programs** icon.

2. Click the language name of the Multilingual User Interface Pack file that you want to remove, and then click **Remove**.

   If you have installed proofing tools separately from Microsoft Office 2003 Proofing Tools, use the following steps to remove those files.

To remove Office 2003 Proofing Tools files

1. In Control Panel, double-click the **Add/Remove Programs** icon, and then double-click **Office 2003 Proofing Tools**.

2. Click **Add or Remove Features**, select **Proofing Tools for Office 2003**, and then click **Not Available**.

3. Click **Update Now**.

Sharing Multilingual Files Between Different Versions of Office

File compatibility affects how users share files between different versions of Microsoft Office applications. Language compatibility also affects how users share different language versions of Office files—for example, there are complications when sharing files from the Japanese version of Microsoft Office 95 with files from Microsoft Office 2003 when using the Multilingual User Interface Pack (MUI Pack). Several options can help you share files across language versions of Office when used correctly.

Sharing Office files across language versions

When all users in an international organization are using Microsoft Office 2003, there are relatively few complications—whether the files are from Microsoft Office 2003 with the Microsoft Office 2003 Multilingual User Interface Pack (MUI Pack) or from localized versions of Office 2003. Even during a staged deployment of applications within the Microsoft Office System, you can still share files with older localized versions of Office.

If you are using a staged deployment to install Office 2003, you can save files created in Office 2003 applications to file formats for use with previous localized versions of Office applications. This allows the earlier versions of Office applications to open the file, yet it also preserves the Office 2003 multilingual features. However, these file formats vary by Office application and are not the same as the exact file formats used by previous localized versions. Thus, if you save Office 2003 files in the exact format of the previous localized version, multilingual features of Office 2003 are lost. In other words, earlier releases of Office may or may not support the multiple language handling abilities of the current version of the application.

For example, Microsoft Office Word 2003, Microsoft Office Excel 2003, and Microsoft Office PowerPoint 2003 can display multiple Asian languages in the same file. When these files are saved in the file format of versions of Office earlier than Office 2000, the multi-Asian language feature is lost and only one of the languages is displayed correctly.

Unicode® allows you to share multilingual files between Office 2003, Office XP, Office 2000, and Office 97 without any loss of text. Versions of Office previous to Office 97 might not properly display multilingual text from an Office 2003 file, because they are based on code pages, not Unicode. For more information about Unicode and how it supports multilingual documents in Office, see "Unicode Support and Multilingual Office Documents" in Chapter 17, "Unicode Support in Office 2003."

Your operating system can determine whether you can display Asian or right-to-left text (such as Arabic, Hebrew, Farsi, or Urdu) between different versions of Office.

To display a right-to-left language, you must set the regional and language options of the operating system to the right-to-left language you want to use. To display Asian languages, note the following:

- Office 2003, Office XP, and Office 2000 provide files—including fonts—that extend an operating system's ability to support Asian languages.

- The Office 97 Asian support files—including fonts—extend an operating system's ability to support Asian languages.

- To display or edit Asian text in an older version of Office (earlier than Office 97), you must configure the regional and language options of the operating system to match the Asian language you want to use.

Sharing Access database files across language versions

Microsoft Office Access 2003 can open databases created in any previous localized version of Access.

Note   Users of previous localized versions of Access cannot open Access 2003 databases.

Opening Access databases prior to Access 2003

Because the default file format in Access 2003 is the same as in Access 2000, all Access 2000 database users can share databases with Access 2003 users. However, if you are using Access 97 or earlier and only part of your organization is upgrading to Access 2002, you might want to leave existing databases in the format of your previous version of Access so all users can open the databases.

If you are using Access 2003 and want to open databases in Access 97 or earlier, you might not be able to open the older databases if the language version of your operating system differs from the operating system on the computer used to create the database. Access databases are saved in a particular sort order, and the default sort order matches the sort order used by the operating system on the computer used to create the database.

For example, a database created in Access 95 on a computer running the Arabic version of Microsoft Windows 95 uses the Arabic sort order by default and cannot be opened on a computer running the English version of Microsoft Windows 95/98 or the English version of Windows NT® 4.0. The file can only be opened on an operating system that can support the language and regional settings of the application and the operating system together.

> **Note**   Microsoft Windows 2000 Service Pack 3 (SP3) and Microsoft Windows XP include international sort order support for multiple languages. Users running Access 2003 on either of these operating systems can open databases from previous versions of Access in the native sort order.

Opening forms and reports from previous localized versions

Access 2003 can open and read the English and European-language content of forms and reports from any previous localized version of Access. However, if the database is based on a code page other than Latin 1 (code page 1252) some text might be rendered incorrectly.

For example, a database created in Access 95 on the Greek version of Windows 95 is based on the Greek code page. When an Access 2003 user running the English version of Windows 98 opens the database, the operating system maps code points to the new code page, so some Greek characters might appear as accented European characters, question marks, open boxes, or other unintelligible characters.

Converting databases from previous localized versions of Access

If Access 2003 users do not need to share a database from a previous localized version of Access with users of the older version, convert the database to the Access 2000 file format. If the database was saved in the default sort order on a computer running a non-English version of the operating system, convert it by using the **Convert database** option in Access 2003 and saving it in the Access 2000 file format. Access converts the data to Unicode during the conversion process.

Using the original language sort order

When you convert an older database to the Access 2000 file format, Access uses the sort order to determine which code page to use for converting the data to Unicode. Access 2003 associates the General sort order with the Western European code page, so if non–Western European data is stored in the General sort order, the data corrupts when Access 2003 converts it.

Therefore, if the older database is based on a non-English version of the operating system, and it is saved in the General sort order, you must compact it again in the original language sort order before converting it to the Access 2000 file format. Otherwise, Access 2003 cannot properly convert the data to Unicode.

To convert a localized database to the Access 2000 file format

1. Open the database in the original, localized version of Access.

    You must open the database on a computer running the same language version of the operating system as that used to create the database, or you can open the database on a computer running Windows 2000 SP3 or Windows XP with regional and language options set to support the original sort order.

2. Change the sort order to match the regional and language options of the operating system, and then compact the database again.

    The steps for changing sort order and compacting a database vary with each version of Access. For more information, see Access Help.

3. Start Access 2003, but do not open the database.

4. On the **Tools** menu, point to **Database Utilities**, point to **Convert Database**, and then click **To Access 2002–Access 2003 File Format**.

5. In the **Database to Convert From** dialog box, select the database you want to convert, and click **Convert**.

Specifying the code page for the General sort order

If the older database is in a language that had no sort order in earlier versions of Access, you can still convert the database to the Access 2000 file format.

For example, databases in earlier versions of Access based on Vietnamese, Farsi, or a Baltic version of the operating system (Estonian, Latvian, or Lithuanian) use the General sort order by default because previous versions of Access did not support sort orders for those languages. To convert these databases, you must create a registry entry to prevent Access 2003 from corrupting the non–Western European data.

To convert non–Western European databases that use the General sort order

1. If you are converting an Access version 1.*x* or 2.0 database, go to the following registry subkey:

   HKEY_LOCAL_MACHINE\Software\Microsoft\Jet\4.0\Engines\Jet 2.*x*

   or

   If you are converting an Access 95 or 97 database, go to the following registry subkey:

   HKEY_LOCAL_MACHINE\Software\Microsoft\Jet\4.0\Engines\Jet 3.*x*

2. In the Jet 2.*x* or Jet 3.*x* subkey, create a new value entry named **ForceCp** and set the value to **ANSI** to use the computer's default code page.

   You can specify a different code page by setting the value to the code page number, such as **1257** for Windows Baltic Rim.

3. Convert the database to the Access 2000 file format.

4. Delete the **ForceCP** value entry from the registry so that Access 2003 reverts to using the sort order of a database to determine the code page.

Removing conflicting data to solve indexing problems

Access 2003 upgrades some sort orders so that they differ from previous versions of Access. In the new sorting, characters that were considered different in older databases might be considered the same in Access 2003. As a result, the converted database might contain conflicting data, making it impossible to create a unique index for some tables. To create a unique index on the affected tables, you must remove the conflicting data.

A similar problem might occur when changing the sort order of a database. Characters might be different in one language but equivalent in another language. For example, the Western European lowercase *i* and uppercase *I* are considered equivalent when sorting alphabetically. But in Turkish a lowercase *i* might be dotted or not dotted, and the two *i* characters are not considered equivalent when sorting alphabetically. Because they are considered equivalent in the General sort order, however, these characters can create conflicting data when you upgrade a Turkish database to the Access 2000 file format.

Sharing Excel workbooks across language versions

In Excel 2003 you can open and edit any workbook created in a previous localized version of Excel, regardless of the language, provided the operating system supports the language of the file. For example, you can use Excel 2003 to open and edit a Korean Excel 2000 file on an operating system configured for Korean. If you need to share files across languages (for example, opening a Korean Excel workbook on a Spanish system), it is recommended that you use Windows 2000 SP3 or Windows XP; each supports multiple languages, keyboard locales, and other regional settings.

Users of Excel 2003 and previous localized versions can share workbooks as follows. In Excel 2003, you can open and save:

- Localized Excel 5/95 files only on a same-language operating system (since these files do not use Unicode).

  On Windows 2000 SP3, this requires that the regional options be set to the same language of the operating system used to create the Excel file.

- Any Excel 97 or Excel 2000 file without language limitations, providing the operating system is set to the same language and regional support options as the operating system the file was created on.

- European, Asian, and complex script (Hebrew, Arabic, Thai, and Vietnamese) files in the Excel 97/2000 format, providing the operating system is set to the same language and regional support options as the operating system the file was created on.

Platform support for multilingual file sharing

Windows XP provides our best support for organizations with requirements for multilingual file sharing. In Windows XP, you can enable support for multiple languages or even change your code page using the Regional and Language Options utility in Control Panel. If you must open and edit Excel workbooks in multiple languages on the same computer, it is recommended that you use the Windows XP operating system.

To view an Excel file in a language other than the default language on Windows XP, check to be sure that the other language is enabled in the Regional and Language Options utility. The correct characters will be displayed when you open, edit, and save the file when the correct settings are used. This works for all Unicode Excel versions (Excel 97 and later, including Excel 2003).

Multilingual file sharing with non-Unicode files

Sharing multilingual files that cannot support Unicode can be a problem. Files that do not support Unicode include Excel files created in versions earlier than Excel 97 (including Excel 5 and Excel 95), converted files saved from another application using any file format previous to Excel 97, or Lotus files. Opening these files on a computer that does not support the localized version of these files will not work properly.

With Windows XP, you can change the code page to the correct language by using the Regional and Language Options tool. Now you can view and edit the non-Unicode file that was created in the other language.

Sharing FrontPage files across language versions

Microsoft Office FrontPage® 2003 allows you to work with more languages and characters than you can with previous versions. FrontPage now has full Unicode support and recognizes more HTML 4.0 character entity references than do previous versions. However, file names and URLs are still dependent on regional and language options of the operating system. To help ensure that all users can access files on a FrontPage server, it is recommended that you use ASCII file names (characters from the numeric 32 to 255 range of the ASCII character set).

Character entity references make up a set of HTML characters that are represented by easy-to-remember mnemonic names. For example, the character entity reference **å** specifies a lowercase *a* topped by a ring (å). It's easier to remember **å** than it is to remember **&229;**.

In FrontPage 2003, you can open and edit any document created in FrontPage 2002, FrontPage 2000, FrontPage 98, or FrontPage 97, regardless of the language used in the document, provided the operating system supports the language of the file.

Note   FrontPage 2003 and Microsoft Internet Explorer 5 encode URLs in UTF-8, a Unicode format. To use FrontPage 2003 to edit FrontPage-based Web sites that include non-ASCII URLs, you must either have a Web server that supports UTF-8 or turn off UTF-8 encoding.

The enhanced language features in FrontPage 2003 affect file sharing between FrontPage 2003 and previous versions in the following ways:

- In a folder list or view in FrontPage 2003, folder and file names are displayed correctly regardless of your default language.

  However, to open or save files, the code page of the file name must be supported by the operating system. This does not affect the content of the document, just the file name.

- If you use FrontPage 2003 to create a file in some languages, such as Thai, you cannot open or edit that file in FrontPage 97 or FrontPage 98.

  If you try to open the file, both FrontPage 97 and FrontPage 98 will display an error message.

- If you use FrontPage 2003 to create a document that contains a Unicode character, such as **Β** for the Greek capital letter beta (Â), you cannot display that character in FrontPage 2000 or earlier versions.

  If you save the document in a version of FrontPage earlier than FrontPage 2002, the Unicode character is deleted.

- If you use FrontPage 2003 to create a document that contains an HTML 4.0 character entity reference, you cannot edit that character in FrontPage 2000 or earlier versions.

The character entity reference appears as **δ** and is not deleted if you save the document in a version earlier than FrontPage 2002.

Exchanging Outlook messages across language versions

Enhancements in Microsoft Office Outlook 2003 make it easier to exchange Outlook messages across language versions. You can enable multilingual display support for Outlook, and you can specify Auto-Select Outbound Encoding for all mail messages. As in Outlook 2000, Outlook 2003 supports Unicode in the body of mail messages.

Enabling multilingual display support for Outlook

There are two ways to enable Outlook to display content in multiple languages—through Office Setup or the Regional and Language Options tool in Control Panel. Please note that multilingual support must be installed on both the sending and receiving sides of an e-mail exchange to help ensure full functionality.

The first way to install multilingual support is through Office Setup. Font support may have to be added manually by following these steps:

1. Rerun Setup, and then select **Add/Remove components**.

2. Expand the **Office Shared Features** section, and then under **International Support**, make sure the font corresponding to the desired language is installed locally.

3. Select **OK** to apply the changes.

The second way to install multilingual support is through the operating system.

Installing multilingual support for Windows 2000 users

1. In Control Panel, double-click **Regional Options**.

2. Click the **General** tab.

3. In the list shown under **Language settings for the system**, select the check boxes next to the languages you want to use for sending and receiving messages.

4. Click **OK**.

> **Note**   A system restart is required after installing the support files.

Installing multilingual support for Windows XP users

1. In Control Panel, double-click **Regional and Language Options**.

2. Click the **Regional Options** tab.

3. In the **Standards and formats** section, select the default language you want to use.

4. Click the **Languages** tab.

5. Click the **Details** button in the **Text services and input languages** section.

6. Set the **Default input language** to the language you want to use.

7. Add any keyboard support you need to support the alternate languages you may switch between in the **Installed services** section.

8. Select the appropriate language support options for the selected languages in the **Supplemental Language support** section.

9. Click the **Advanced** tab.

10. Choose the appropriate settings in the **Language for non-Unicode programs** section as needed.

11. Adjust the **Code page conversion tables** as needed.

Outlook data that is not in the body of the message—such as Contacts, Tasks, and the To and Subject lines of messages—are limited to characters defined by the system code page. Such characters might be unintelligible for a recipient whose operating system uses a different code page.

Specifying character encoding

In addition to enabling multilingual display support for Outlook, you can specify the character encoding (also known as the code page) of the message being sent.

It is recommended that you rely on the new Auto-Select Outbound Encoding feature, which was introduced with Outlook 2002. This feature is automatically switched on when you have Internet Explorer 5.5 or later installed. Auto-Select Outbound Encoding scans the entire text of outgoing messages to determine a minimal popular encoding capable of representing all characters and is optimized so the majority of the receiving e-mail programs can interpret and render the content.

You can also manually select an encoding that supports the characters being sent and that the recipient's e-mail application can interpret. For example, if all users' e-mail applications support multilingual Unicode data, Unicode (UTF-8) encoding is an excellent choice, since it supports one of the largest ranges of characters for different scripts.

> **Note** An Outlook 2002 user's default **Preferred encoding for outgoing messages** is the Internet encoding that corresponds to the user's Windows code page. For example, **Japanese (JIS)** encoding for a Japanese Windows code page, **Western European (ISO)** encoding for a Western European Latin1 code page, or **Cyrillic (KOI8-R)** encoding for a Cyrillic code page.
>
> The active Windows code page of your operating system is defined by your system locale. On Windows 2000 SP3 it can be set in **Regional Options** in Control Panel by selecting the **Set Default** button, which opens the **Select System Locale** dialog box.

To enable Auto-Select Outbound Encoding in Outlook 2003

1. On the **Tools** menu, click **Options**, and then click the **Mail Format** tab.

2. Click **International Options**, and select the **Auto-Select encoding for outgoing messages** check box.

3. Select a character encoding in the **Preferred encoding for outgoing messages** box.

   This encoding is used by Auto-Select Outbound Encoding in cases where more than one minimal popular encoding can represent all the text. If you prefer, you can manually specify the character encoding.

To manually specify character encoding in Outlook 2003

1. On the **Tools** menu, click **Options**, and then click the **Mail Format** tab.

2. Click **International Options**, and clear the **Auto-Select encoding for outgoing messages** check box.

3. Select a character encoding in the **Preferred encoding for outgoing messages** box.

   This encoding is now used for all messages you create, regardless of the text (characters) you type into them. Note that the **Auto-Select encoding for outgoing messages** check box is only available if you have Internet Explorer 5.5 or later installed.

4. If you want message flags and Forward and Reply headers to be in English, select the **Use English for message flags** and **Use English for message headers on replies and forwards** check boxes.

   If you clear these check boxes, message flags and headers match the language of the Outlook user interface, and e-mail applications that run in another language might not display the text properly.

> **Tip**   You can use a policy to set character encoding for Outlook 2003 messages. You set these policies in **Microsoft Office Outlook 2003\Tools | Options\Mail Format\International Options**. For more information about using policies with Office applications, see "How Policies Work" in Chapter 26, "Using Security-related Policies."

When you click **Send To** on the **File** menu in Office applications to create e-mail messages, the content of the message is saved in HTML format. The **Preferred encoding for outgoing messages** setting in Outlook determines the character encoding for the message, or if Auto-Select Outbound Encoding is activated, Outlook automatically selects an appropriate encoding.

When you do not want to rely on Auto-Select Outbound Encoding, you can manually set the encoding of mail messages by picking an appropriate encoding from the Format.Encoding list. If you do rely on the Auto-Select Encoding feature, Outlook will always show **Auto-Select** in the Format.Encoding menu and will not allow users to manually overwrite the option.

Sharing PowerPoint presentations across language versions

Localized Microsoft PowerPoint 2000 can open and read PowerPoint 2003 presentations directly, but localized PowerPoint 95 must have the PowerPoint 97 converter for PowerPoint 95 installed, or PowerPoint 2003 presentations must be saved in PowerPoint 97-2002 & 95 format.

PowerPoint 4.0 users can open PowerPoint 2003 presentations if they install the PowerPoint 97 converter for PowerPoint 4.0.

Users of PowerPoint 2000 and previous localized versions can share presentations as follows:

- In PowerPoint 2000, you can open and edit any presentation created in a previous localized version of PowerPoint, regardless of the language, provided the operating system supports the language of the file.

- In localized PowerPoint 97, you can open and edit PowerPoint 2003 presentations, regardless of the language, provided the operating system supports the language of the file.

- In localized PowerPoint 95, in addition to an operating system that supports the language of the file, you need the following to open PowerPoint 2003 presentations:

  You must have the PowerPoint 97 converter for PowerPoint 95 installed.
  or
  The file must be in PowerPoint 97-2002 & 95 format.

■   In localized PowerPoint 4.0, in addition to an operating system that supports the language of the file, you must have the PowerPoint 97 converter for PowerPoint 4.0 installed to open PowerPoint 2003 presentations.

Opening presentations from previous localized versions in PowerPoint 2003

When you open PowerPoint 95 or PowerPoint 4.0 presentations in PowerPoint 2003, PowerPoint 2003 converts the text to Unicode. Because PowerPoint 2000 and PowerPoint 97 both support Unicode, PowerPoint 2003 does not need to convert PowerPoint 97, PowerPoint 2000, or PowerPoint 2002 text.

PowerPoint 2003 can display English and European text in presentations from any language version of PowerPoint 2002, PowerPoint 2000, PowerPoint 97, PowerPoint 95, and PowerPoint 4.0. If PowerPoint 2003 users have enabled the appropriate language in Microsoft Office Language Settings, PowerPoint 2003 can display text in any language provided the operating system supports the language of the file.

> **Note**   Some unknown characters might appear when you open an English or European-language version of PowerPoint 95 or PowerPoint 4.0 presentation in the Korean, Simplified Chinese, or Traditional Chinese version of PowerPoint 2003. To correct this problem, click **Options** on the PowerPoint 2003 **Tools** menu, and then click the **Asian** tab. Clear the **Convert font-associated text for** check box.

Opening PowerPoint 2003 presentations in localized PowerPoint 2003, PowerPoint 2002, PowerPoint 2000, and PowerPoint 97

PowerPoint 2003 files containing Unicode surrogate pairs will in most cases be displayed correctly if you have the appropriate language support installed on your computer. Editing these characters, however, will not work correctly. PowerPoint 2003 files containing Hindi characters will in most cases display individual characters correctly if you have the appropriate language support installed on your computer. Layout for the Hindi text in PowerPoint 2002 might be different than it is in PowerPoint 2003, and editing may not work correctly.

Localized versions of PowerPoint 2000 and PowerPoint 2002 can display PowerPoint 2003 text as shown in the following table.

This language version of PowerPoint 2003...	...can display text in these languages
U.S./European, Asian, right-to-left language (Arabic, Hebrew)	English, European, Asian, right-to-left language (Arabic, Hebrew)
Thai	Thai, English, European, Asian, right-to-left language (Arabic, Hebrew)
Vietnamese	Vietnamese, English, European, Asian, right-to-left language (Arabic, Hebrew)

Opening PowerPoint 2003 presentations in localized PowerPoint 97

Localized PowerPoint 97 can directly open and read PowerPoint 2003 presentations. However, to display Asian or right-to-left (Arabic, Hebrew, Farsi, or Urdu) text that doesn't match the language version of PowerPoint 97, you must have the appropriate language support installed on your computer.

For Asian text, you can install the Office 97 Asian support files, but for right-to-left text, you must use a compatible right-to-left language version of PowerPoint 97.

The layout for the Hindi text in PowerPoint 97 might be different than it is in PowerPoint 2003, and editing will not work correctly.

Localized versions of PowerPoint 97 can display PowerPoint 2003 text as shown in the following table.

This language version of PowerPoint 97...	...can display text in these languages
U.S./European	English, European, Asian (Asian requires the Office 97 Asian support files)
Asian	English, European, matching Asian and nonmatching Asian (nonmatching Asian requires Office 97 Asian support files)
Right-to-left language (Arabic, Hebrew)	English, European, and a compatible right-to-left language

> **Note**   The layout for Asian text in PowerPoint 97, PowerPoint 2000, and PowerPoint 2002 might be different than it is in PowerPoint 2003.

Opening PowerPoint 2003 presentations in localized PowerPoint 95 and PowerPoint 4.0

Depending on the language, localized PowerPoint 95 can open and read Power-Point 2003 presentations by using the PowerPoint 97 converter for PowerPoint 95 or if the presentations are saved in the PowerPoint 97-2002 & 95 format. Similarly, localized PowerPoint 4.0 can open and read PowerPoint 97, PowerPoint 2000, PowerPoint 2002, and PowerPoint 2003 presentations by using the PowerPoint 97 converter for PowerPoint 4.0, depending on the language.

Note   The PowerPoint 97 converter for PowerPoint 4.0 cannot be used with Asian versions of PowerPoint 4.0. Therefore, users of Asian versions of PowerPoint 4.0 cannot open PowerPoint 2003 presentations.

Localized versions of PowerPoint 95 and PowerPoint 4.0 can display Power-Point 2003 text as shown in the following table.

This language version of PowerPoint 4.0/95...	...can display text in these languages
U.S./European	English, European
Asian (PowerPoint 95 only)	English, European, and the matching Asian language
Right-to-left language (Arabic, Hebrew) (PowerPoint 95 only)	English, European, and a compatible right-to-left language

Sharing Publisher files across language versions

Microsoft Office Publisher 2003 can open and read publications created in any localized version of Publisher. However, previous localized versions of Publisher cannot open Publisher 2003 publications.

Publisher 2003 supports editing right-to-left text (for languages such as Arabic, Hebrew, Farsi, and Urdu) on versions of Windows that support right-to-left display and processing. Some right-to-left text as well as some formatting may not be preserved when saving a publication in an earlier version of Publisher if the version does not support editing right-to-left text.

When you use Publisher 2003 to open documents composed in Publisher 97 or earlier, Publisher converts the text to Unicode. Because Publisher 2003, Publisher 2002, Publisher 2000, and Publisher 98 all support Unicode, Publisher 2003 does not need to convert the text for documents created in those later versions.

Sharing Word documents across language versions

Each new version of Word can successfully open more language versions from older releases of Word. For example, English Word 2000 can open Asian Word 6.0-95 files correctly—something that English Word 97 cannot do. English Word 2003 correctly opens and handles all legacy documents, including Thai Word 6.0-2000 documents, as well as Hindi/Tamil documents created in South Asian Word 2000.

Users of previous versions of Word can also share documents with Word 2003 users. Just as with non-localized versions, localized Word 97 can open and read

Word 2003 documents directly, but localized Word 95 or Word 6.0 must have the Word 97-2002 converter installed, or the Word 2003 documents must be saved in Rich Text Format (RTF).

RTF allows you to exchange multilingual documents between Microsoft Office versions. In Office XP (as well as Office 2000 and Office 97), RTF files support Unicode and also allow Word 95 and Word 6.0 to use all Unicode characters that occur in single-byte code pages. As long as the Word 95 or Word 6.0 user does not save the file, the complete Unicode content of the document is preserved when the RTF file is reopened in Word 2003 (as well as in Word 2002, Word 2000, and Word 97).

On the Resource Kit CD   The *Microsoft Office 2003 Editions Resource Kit* includes a spreadsheet that shows how Word manages documents created in different versions of Word or when the original file was created using localized instances or MUI packs. The file Multimui.xls is installed by default when you run the Office Resource Kit Setup program. For more information, see "International Information" in Appendix A, "Toolbox."

Opening documents from previous localized versions in Word 2003

When you open Microsoft Word 95 or 6.0 documents in Word 2003, Word converts the text to Unicode. Because Word 2003, Word 2002, Word 2000, and Word 97 all support Unicode, these versions do not need to convert text when documents are opened in another version.

Word 2003 can display English and European-language text in documents from any language version of Word 97, Word 95, and Word 6.0. Word 2003 can display text in any language provided the operating system supports the language of the file, except for Unicode-only languages, such as Hindi, Georgian, and Armenian.

Opening Word 2003 documents in localized Word 2000

Word 2000 can directly open and read Word 2003 documents. The file format is essentially unchanged. However, there are a few new features in Word 2003 that are not accessible in Word 2000 (for example, new table styles).

Opening Word 2003 documents in localized Word 97

Word 97 can directly open and read Word 2003 documents. However, to display Asian or right-to-left (Arabic, Hebrew, Farsi, or Urdu) text that doesn't match the language version of Word 97, you must have the appropriate language support installed on your system.

For Asian text, you can install the Office 97 Asian support files, but for right-to-left text, you must use a compatible right-to-left language version of Word 97.

Localized versions of Word 97 can display Word 2003 text as shown in the following table.

This language version of Word 97...	...can display text in these languages
U.S./European	English, European, and Asian (Asian requires the Office 97 Asian support files)
Asian	English, European, matching Asian, and non-matching Asian (non-matching Asian requires the Office 97 Asian support files)
Right-to-left language (Arabic, Hebrew)	English, European, and a compatible right-to-left language

Note   The layout for Asian text in Word 97 might be different than it is in Word 2003.

Opening Word 2003 documents in localized Word 95 and Word 6.0

Depending on the language, localized Word 95 and Word 6.0 can open and read Word 2003 documents by using the Word 97-2002 converter, or Word 95 and Word 6.0 can open and read Word 2003 documents that are saved in RTF.

Localized versions of Word 95 and Word 6.0 can display Word 2003 text as shown in the following table.

This language version of Word 6.0/95...	...can display text in these languages
U.S./European	English, European
Asian	English, European, and the matching Asian language
Right-to-left language (Arabic, Hebrew)	English, European, and a compatible right-to-left language

Running macros from previous localized versions of Word

When Word 2003 opens older localized documents, it converts WordBasic to Visual Basic® for Applications (VBA) and translates the commands to English. Converted macros use the form WordBasic.732. However, strings—including user-created strings and WordBasic strings—are not translated. If a command is a WordBasic command, the language of the arguments accepted by that command can be either English or the localized language.

In Word 2003, Word 2002, Word 2000, and Word 97, you can write macros that work in all language versions of Word 2003, Word 2002, Word 2000, and Word 97. Be sure to use enumerations in your VBA code, and do not refer to objects by the names used in the user interface, because these names are different in each language version.

Resources and related information

The Unicode standard provides unique character values for every language that Office supports and makes it even easier to share multilingual documents. For more information, see "Unicode Support and Multilingual Office Documents" in Chapter 17, "Unicode Support in Office 2003."

You can use the Microsoft Office Language Settings tool to enable languages for editing. For more information, see "Customizing Language Settings" in Chapter 13, "Preparing for an Office Multilingual Deployment."

For some languages, you need to have an operating system and fonts that allow you to display and edit the text. For more information, see "Preparing Users' Computers for Multilingual Capabilities in Office" in Chapter 13, "Preparing for an Office Multilingual Deployment."

Distributing Multilingual User Interface Pack Updates

Microsoft Office 2003 Multilingual User Interface Pack (MUI Pack) service packs and product updates are designed to help improve the security, performance, and reliability of Office MUI Packs. A service pack, such as Office 2003 MUI Pack Service Pack 1 (SP1), typically updates the entire MUI Pack package and represents a new baseline version of the product.

Between service packs, Microsoft may also offer product updates developed in response to emerging issues such as virus attacks or bug fixes. These interim product updates, which typically update specific features, require the most recent baseline version of the product.

MUI Pack service packs and product updates are typically released shortly after a corresponding core Office service pack or product update. You can apply Office and MUI Pack updates at the same time or at different times, and in any order.

The strategies for applying updates to MUI Pack installations are the same as the strategies for updating core installations of Office 2003:

- If you deployed Office and the MUI Packs from a compressed CD image and took advantage of the local installation source, you can distribute MUI Pack client updates directly to users.

  When you install Office from a compressed CD image, you can chain MUI Packs to the core installation. In this case, chained MUI Pack packages inherit the same local installation source properties as Office 2003.

- If you deployed Office and the MUI Packs from an administrative installation point, you apply the MUI Pack administrative update (MSP file) to the administrative image and then recache and reinstall the MUI Pack on users' computers.

When you install Office from an administrative installation point, you can include MUI Packs in the same image and apply administrative updates to them in the same way.

> **Note** If a particular service pack has language dependencies, separate versions of the update are made available for each language in which Office 2003 is released.

For more information about updating users' installations, see "Distributing Office 2003 Product Updates" in Chapter 18, "Updating Users' Office 2003 Configurations."

Chapter 17

Unicode Support in Office 2003 Editions

Microsoft® Office 2003 Editions provide broad support for Unicode®, making it straightforward to share files across language versions of Office 2003 Editions. There are a few limitations to full Unicode support that may be important to note, such as the inability to print scripts or special characters on some printers. In general, however, Unicode helps you easily share documents across languages and different versions of Office.

Unicode Support and Multilingual Office Documents

Sharing documents in a multilingual environment can be challenging when the languages involved span multiple Microsoft Windows® code pages. However, using the Unicode character encoding standard overcomes many of these challenges, and in Microsoft Office 2003 Editions, all applications are capable of using Unicode.

Office 2003 Editions provide the conversion tables necessary to convert code page–based data to Unicode and back again for interaction with previous applications. Because Office 2003 Editions provide fonts to support many languages, users can create multilingual documents with text from multiple scripts.

Unicode support in Office 2003 Editions also means that users can copy multilingual text from Office 97 documents and paste it into any Office 2003 Editions document, and the text is displayed correctly. Conversely, multilingual text copied from any Office 2003 Editions document can be pasted into a document created in any Office 97 application (except Microsoft Access).

In addition to document text, Office 2003 Editions support Unicode in other areas, including document properties, bookmarks, style names, footnotes, and user information. Unicode support in Office 2003 Editions also means that you can edit and display multilingual text in dialog boxes. For example, you can search for a file by a Greek author's name in the **Open** dialog box. In addition, Microsoft Office Outlook® 2003 now supports Unicode throughout the product.

> **Note**   For more information about Unicode support in Outlook 2003, see "Unicode Enhancements in Outlook 2003" in Chapter 6, "Planning an Outlook 2003 Deployment."

Understanding Unicode

Without Unicode, systems typically use a code page–based environment, in which each script has its own table of characters. Documents based on the code page of one Windows operating system rarely travel well to a Windows operating system that uses another code page. In some cases, the documents cannot contain text that uses characters from more than one script.

For example, if a user running the English version of the Microsoft Windows® 98 operating system with the Latin code page opens a plain text file created on a computer running the Japanese version of Windows 98, the code points of the Japanese code page are mapped to unexpected or nonexistent characters in the Western script, and the resulting text is unintelligible.

The universal character set provided by Unicode overcomes this problem.

The following sections describe how scripts and code pages are used in representing characters in different languages. Understanding scripts and code pages helps provide a foundation for understanding how Unicode facilitates a straightforward way of providing language support.

Scripts

Multilingual documents can contain text in languages that require different scripts. However, a single script can be used to represent many languages.

For example, the Latin or Roman script has character shapes—glyphs—for the 26 letters (both uppercase and lowercase) of the English alphabet, as well as accented (extended) characters used to represent sounds in other Western European languages.

The Latin script also has glyphs to represent all of the characters in most European languages and some non-European languages. Some European languages, such as Greek or Russian, have characters for which there are no glyphs in the Latin script; these languages have their own scripts.

Some Asian languages use ideographic scripts that have glyphs based on Chinese characters. Other languages, such as Thai and Arabic, use scripts that have glyphs that are composed of several smaller glyphs, or glyphs that must be shaped differently depending on adjacent characters. These scripts are referred to as complex scripts in this documentation.

Code pages

A common way to store plain text is to represent each character by using a single byte. The value of each byte is a numeric index—or code point—in a table of characters called a code page. Each code point corresponds to a character in the default code page of the computer on which the text document is created. For example, a byte with a code point whose value is decimal 65 represents the capital letter 'A' on a computer with Microsoft Code Page 1252 (or Latin 1).

For single-byte code pages, each code page contains a maximum of 256 byte values because each character in the code page is represented by a single byte.

A code page with a limit of 256 characters cannot accommodate all languages because all languages together use far more than 256 characters. Therefore, different scripts use separate code pages. There is one code page for Greek, another for Cyrillic, and so on.

In addition, single-byte code pages cannot accommodate Asian languages, which commonly use more than 5,000 Chinese-based characters. Double-byte code pages—in which each character is represented by one or two bytes—were developed to support these languages. (The first 128 characters of double-byte code pages are single-byte code points, to help ensure that English characters—which use only these first 128 characters—are mapped by virtually all code pages, include double-byte code pages.)

One drawback of the code page system is that the character represented by a particular code point depends on the specific code page on which it was entered. If you do not know which code page a code point is from, you cannot determine how to interpret the code point accurately. This can cause problems when a text document is shared between users on different computers.

For example, unless you know which code page it comes from, the code point 230 might be the Greek lowercase zeta (æ), the Cyrillic lowercase zhe (æ), or the Western European diphthong (æ). All three characters have the same code point (230), but the code point is from three different code pages (1253, 1251, and 1252, respectively). Users exchanging documents between these languages are likely to see incorrect characters.

Unicode: a worldwide character set

Unicode is a character encoding standard developed by the Unicode Consortium to create a universal character set that can accommodate all known scripts. Unicode can use more than one byte for every character; so in contrast to code pages, every character has its own unique code point. For example, the Unicode code point of lowercase zeta (X) is the hexadecimal value 03B6, lowercase zhe (X) is 0436, and the diphthong (æ) is 00E6. The Unicode encoding standard enables almost all written languages in the world to be represented by using a single-character set.

Currently in the Microsoft Windows operating systems, the two systems of storing text—code pages and Unicode—coexist. However, Unicode-based systems are replacing code page–based systems. For example, Microsoft Windows NT® 4, Microsoft Windows 2000, Microsoft Windows XP, Microsoft Office 97 and later, Microsoft Internet Explorer 4.0 and later, and Microsoft SQL Server 7.0 and later all support Unicode.

> **Note**   The Microsoft Visual Basic® for Applications environment does not support Unicode. Only characters supported by the active Windows code page can be used in the Visual Basic Editor or displayed in custom dialog boxes or message boxes.
>
> You can use the **ChrW()** function to manipulate text outside the code page. The **ChrW()** function accepts a number that represents the Unicode value of a character and returns that character string.

Unicode Support in Outlook 2003

Microsoft Office Outlook 2003 supports Unicode and provides full support for multilingual data. If you work in a multinational organization or share messages and items with people who use Outlook on systems that run in other languages, you can take advantage of Unicode support in Outlook. Running Outlook in Unicode mode enables you to work with messages and items that are composed in different languages.

Previous versions of Outlook provided support for multilingual Unicode data in the body of e-mail messages. However, Outlook data—such as the To and Subject lines of messages and the **ContactName** and **BusinessTelephoneNumber** properties of contact items—was limited to characters defined by your system code page.

Outlook 2003 no longer has this limitation, provided Outlook is running in Unicode mode with Microsoft Exchange Server as the messaging server. (Unicode mode is also supported with POP3 accounts, as long as items are delivered to a Personal Folders file (PST file) that supports Unicode data.

Non-Unicode systems typically use a code page–based environment, in which each script has its own table of characters. Items based on the code page of one operating system rarely map well to the code page of another operating system. In some cases, the items cannot contain text that uses characters from more than one script.

In Outlook 2003, the two systems of storing text code pages and Unicode coexist. However, Unicode mode is recommended and is the default mode, if the configurations of a user's profile, Exchange server, and administrator settings allow it. The mode is automatically determined by Outlook based on these settings and cannot be changed manually by users.

Running Outlook in Unicode mode on the Exchange server can also ensure that by default, the Offline Folder files (OST files) and PST files used in Outlook profiles can store multilingual Unicode data and also offer greater storage capacity for items and folders than non-Unicode Outlook files.

Resources and related information

You can learn about additional Unicode support improvements in Outlook 2003. For more information about these features, see "Unicode Enhancements in Outlook 2003" in Chapter 6, "Planning an Outlook 2003 Deployment."

Printing and Displaying Unicode Text in Office

Not all printers can print characters from more than one code page. In particular, printers that have built-in fonts might not have characters for other scripts in those fonts. Also, new characters such as the euro currency symbol might be missing from a particular font.

Although the Microsoft Office System contains many workarounds to enable printing on such printers, it is not possible in all cases. If text is not printing correctly, updating the printer driver might fix the problem. If the latest driver does not fix the problem, you can look for an option in the printer driver options called "download soft fonts," or "print TrueType as graphic." Change this setting and try printing again.

If the text still does not print correctly, you can create a registry entry that works around the printing problems of most printers; the printing quality, however, might be lowered.

To set the registry so that extended characters are printed correctly

1. Go to the following registry subkey:
    HKEY_CURRENT_USER\Software\Microsoft\Office\11.0\Word\Options

2. Add a new value entry named **NoWideTextPrinting** and set its value to **1**.

Compressing Office Files That Contain Unicode Text

Because Unicode uses more bytes to store information, Microsoft Office 2003 Editions files may be larger when stored in Unicode than they would be if stored in earlier, non-Unicode versions of Office. However, Microsoft Office Word 2003 can automatically compress portions of files to reduce the size.

Office 2003 Editions store text in a form of Unicode called UTF-16, just as Office XP does. Unicode characters are encoded in two bytes (or very rarely, four bytes) rather than what is used in non-Unicode systems—for example, a single byte, or a mixture of one and two bytes in some Asian languages. Generally, Office 2003 Editions files with multilingual text are similar in size to Office 97, Office 2000, or Office XP files. However, Office 2003 Editions files may be 30 to 50 percent larger than files created in previous, non-Unicode versions of Office (Office 95 and earlier).

Note   If a file contains text from only English or Western European languages, there is little or no increase in file size because Office 2003 Editions applications can compress the text.

When Word 2003 users open and save an English or Western European file from a previous, non-Unicode version of Word (a version earlier than Office 2000), Word converts the contents to Unicode. The first time the file is saved, Word analyzes the file and notes regions that can be compressed, but the resulting file is temporarily twice the size of the original file. The next time the file is saved, Word performs the compression, and the file size returns to normal.

For Microsoft Office PowerPoint® 2003 files, text is typically a small percentage of file size, so Unicode does not significantly increase file size.

Copying Multilingual Text in Different Formats in Office

You can use the Clipboard to copy multilingual text from one Microsoft Office 2003 Editions application to another. Text from the Clipboard that is formatted as RTF, HTML, or Unicode can successfully be pasted into Office applications.

Multilingual text formatted as RTF, HTML, or Unicode

When you copy text from a Microsoft Office 2003 Editions document, the RTF or HTML formatting data, as well as the Unicode text data, is stored on the Clipboard. This allows applications that do not support Unicode but do support data in multiple code pages to accept RTF text from the Clipboard, which retains some of the multilingual content. For example, both Microsoft Word 95 and Microsoft Word 6.0 accept multilingual text from the Clipboard as RTF format from later versions of Word.

All language versions of Word 95 and Word 6.0 can display text in most European languages. However, Asian and right-to-left language versions cannot display other Asian or right-to-left languages. Also, English and European versions of Word 6.0 and Word 95 cannot display any Asian or right-to-left text properly.

Word 97 can accept RTF and Unicode text from the Clipboard and display content in all European and most Asian languages. Word 2000 (and later) accepts HTML as well and properly handles all Asian and right-to-left content.

Microsoft Access 2000 (and later) and Microsoft Excel 2000 (and later) all support copying multilingual Unicode, RTF, or HTML text to the Clipboard. However, Access and Excel cannot accept RTF content. They can accept HTML-formatted text or Unicode text from the Clipboard instead.

Multilingual code page–based single-byte text

In some rare conditions, users may paste single-byte (ANSI) text into an Office 2003 Editions item (such as a Word document or an Excel worksheet) that is encoded in a code page that is different from the one their operating system uses. If this occurs, they may get unintelligible characters in that item, depending on the application into which they are pasting. This problem occurs because Office cannot determine which code page to use to interpret the single-byte text.

For example, you might paste text from a non-Unicode text editor that uses fonts to indicate which code page to use. If the text editor supplies only RTF and single-byte text, the font (and code page) information is lost when the text is pasted in an application that does not accept RTF (for example, Excel). Instead, the application uses the operating system's code page, which maps some characters' code points to unexpected or nonexistent characters.

Troubleshooting Corrupt Office Text Results with Older Multilingual Files

There may be occasions when a user cannot successfully use Microsoft Office 2003 Editions to open a file created in an older system. There are several possible scenarios that can create this problem, and for each situation there are steps you can take to work around the issues, including the following:

- The document is a pre-Office 97 document that was created using some incorrectly made TrueType fonts.

    For example, a document that looked fine in Microsoft Word 95 can be opened in Microsoft Word 2002, and the document text is converted to a mixture of characters from Western Europe. This situation occurs because the fonts used in the Word 95 document were marked internally as Western European, and the text data was therefore converted to Unicode Western European text. There are a few other variations on this problem involving symbol fonts; but in all cases you can try one of the following solutions to correct the problem:

- Change the fonts that display the incorrect characters.

- Use the "broken fonts add-in" that ships with Office 2003 Editions. In Word, install the add-in. Then, on the **Tools** menu, click **Repair Broken Text**.

- The document is a pre-Office 97 document created under a "shell" program designed to enable English Microsoft Windows to support Chinese or other Asian language (for example, Chinese Star, RichWin, and TwinBridge).

    In this case, try one of the following solutions:

    - If you open the document in Word, ensure that the correct Chinese language is enabled by checking the setting in the Microsoft Office Language Settings tool (in Windows XP, click **Start**, then point to **All Programs**, then point to **Microsoft Office Tools**, then click **Microsoft Office 2003 Language Settings**). Then set options in Word for the document so that the correct Far Asian features are used.

To set Word features appropriate for Far Asian language documents

1. In Word, on the **Tools** menu, click **Options**.

2. On the **Compatibility** tab, set the value of the **Recommend options for** option to the appropriate setting—for example, **English Word 6/95 documents.**

3. In the **Options** section, select the features that are appropriate for a Far Asian document. (By default in this scenario, Word selects the options that are compatible with an English document.)

    - If characters are not displayed correctly in Word, try changing the following setting. On the **Tools** menu, click **Options**, then click the **General** tab (if it is not already selected). Under **English Word 6.0/95 documents**, in the drop-down list, choose **Automatically detect Asian text**.

    - If you open the document in Microsoft PowerPoint, on the **Tools** menu, click **Options**, then click **Asian**. Locate the option **convert from font-associated text**, and set the language correctly.

- The document is HTML, and the encoding of the file is not marked correctly in the file.

    In this case, with the document currently open, on the **Tools** menu, click **Options**, then click the **General** tab, and click **Web Options**. Click the **Encoding** tab, then change the encoding to open the file with different values until the characters in the file are shown correctly.

Part 5

Maintenance

Chapter 18

Updating Users' Office 2003 Configurations

After Microsoft® Office 2003 is deployed to users, you can modify users' configurations, lock down a particular configuration, or deploy service packs and product updates by using the tools provided in the *Microsoft Office 2003 Editions Resource Kit* and the Microsoft Windows® operating system.

Updating Feature Installation States and Application Settings

After you have deployed the Microsoft Office 2003 client to users, you can modify many aspects of the installation without reinstalling the product. For example, you can install applications or features that were excluded from the initial installation. You can also modify application settings on users' computers to apply a standard Office configuration throughout the organization.

If you used internal tools or other management software to distribute Office, or if you deployed Office and other business-critical products together, Office tools still provide the most efficient means to update users' Office 2003 configurations. Using tools such as the Custom Maintenance Wizard and Office Profile Wizard, you can make the following modifications to users' configurations:

- Change the organization name that appears in Office applications.

- Update the list of servers that Windows Installer uses as an installation source.

- Change feature installation states to install or remove applications or features.

- Add or remove files.

- Add or remove registry entries.

- Modify user settings, including security levels and Microsoft Office Outlook® 2003 profile information.

The method you choose to update user-defined settings depends on the following:

- **How extensively you want to reconfigure Office 2003**   You can distribute a standard configuration for all of Office 2003 and overwrite settings that were migrated from previous versions or set by users after the installation. Or you can update just a few key options.

- **How and when you deploy Office 2003 applications**   If you are staging your deployment of Office 2003, you can install and customize a subset of applications and features.

- **Whether you want to enforce your custom settings**   Settings that you distribute through a configuration maintenance file (CMW file) or Office profile settings file (OPS file) appear to users as the default settings—but users can choose different options for themselves. By contrast, using system policies ensures that your settings are always applied.

The following table lists typical scenarios for updating users' configurations and the recommended methods and tools to use in each case.

Scenario	Method	Tool
Stage deployment of applications or features that were omitted from the initial installation	Change the deployed installation state of selected features	Custom Maintenance Wizard (**Set Feature Installation States** page)
Set options for new features or adjust an existing configuration	Add user settings to a CMW file	Custom Maintenance Wizard (**Change Office User Settings** page)
Change default security levels or the trusted sources list	Specify security settings in a CMW file	Custom Maintenance Wizard (**Specify Office Security Settings** page)
Change migration and e-mail options for Outlook	Specify Outlook settings in a CMW file	Custom Maintenance Wizard (**Outlook: Customize Default Settings** page)
Modify or replace users' Outlook profile	Change Outlook profile settings in a CMW file	Custom Maintenance Wizard (**Outlook: Customize Default Profile** page)
Update settings that are not captured in an OPS file	Add registry values to a CMW file	Custom Maintenance Wizard (**Add/Remove Registry Entries** page)
Distribute a standard configuration that overwrites individual users' settings, including migrated settings	Capture settings in an OPS file and distribute them to client computers	Office Profile Wizard
Prevent users from modifying the options you set	Set Office system policies	Group Policy snap-in with Office policy template files (ADM files)

On the Resource Kit CD The Office 2003 Editions Resource Kit includes the Custom Maintenance Wizard and the Office Profile Wizard, both of which are installed by default when you run the Office Resource Kit Setup program. For more information, see "Custom Maintenance Wizard" or "Office Profile Wizard" in Appendix A, "Toolbox."

Changing feature installation states

The Custom Maintenance Wizard helps you make changes to the deployed installation state of any Office 2003 applications or features that are part of the original Office package. Similar to the way the Custom Installation Wizard reads the Office 2003 package (MSI file) and records changes in a transform (MST file), the Custom

Maintenance Wizard reads the MSI file and records changes in a configuration maintenance file (CMW file). When you run the Custom Maintenance Wizard on a user's computer, the changes in the CMW file are applied.

> **Note**   You cannot use the Office Profile Wizard to modify feature installation states.

Create a configuration maintenance file

The **Set Feature Installation States** page of the Custom Maintenance Wizard displays the same feature tree that appears in the Custom Installation Wizard, and you select from among the same installation states for each feature:

- **Run from My Computer**   Windows Installer copies files and writes registry entries and shortcuts associated with the feature to the user's hard disk, and the application or feature runs locally.

- **Run all from My Computer**   Same as **Run from My Computer**, except that all child features belonging to the feature are also set to this state.

- **Run from Network**   Windows Installer leaves components for the feature on the administrative installation point, and the feature is run from there.
   Note that some child features do not support **Run from Network**; these child features are installed on the local computer.

- **Run all from Network**   Same as **Run from Network**, except that all child features belonging to the feature are also set to this state.

- **Installed on First Use**   Windows Installer leaves components for the feature and all its child features on the administrative installation point until the user first attempts to use the feature, at which time the components are automatically copied to the local hard disk. If a child feature does not support **Installed on First Use**, it is set to **Not Available**.

- **Not Available**   The components for the feature, and all of the child features belonging to the feature, are not installed on the computer.

- **Not Available, Hidden, Locked**   The components for the feature are not installed and the feature does not appear in the feature tree when users run Setup in maintenance mode—nor can users install it by changing the state of the parent feature or by calling Windows Installer directly from the command line.

Tip   To run the Custom Maintenance Wizard with the feature tree fully expanded, use the **/x** command-line option. Note that you cannot use **/x** with **/c**, which runs the wizard to apply a CMW file to the local computer.

Although the Custom Maintenance Wizard and Custom Installation Wizard are very similar, you cannot use the Custom Maintenance Wizard to set or reverse all the customizations that you can apply through a transform. For example:

- **Hidden features**   In the Custom Installation Wizard, right-click a feature and select **Hide** to conceal it from users in the Setup user interface. There is no corresponding **Hide** or **Unhide** setting in the Custom Maintenance Wizard—hidden features remain hidden.

  However, if you set a feature to **Not Available, Hidden, Locked** in the transform, you can reverse the setting in a CMW file.

- **Installation states that depend on network connections**   Unlike the Custom Installation Wizard, the Custom Maintenance Wizard does not allow you to disable the **Run from Network** and **Installed on First Use** installation states for a particular feature.

  Moreover, if you selected the options in the Custom Installation Wizard that disable these settings for a feature when you installed Office, you cannot set that feature to **Run from Network** or **Installed on First Use** in a CMW file.

- **Parent and child features**   If you update the feature installation state of a child feature to **Run from My Computer**, **Run from Network**, or **Installed on First Use**, the Custom Installation Wizard automatically updates the parent feature to the same state. The Custom Maintenance Wizard, by contrast, does not install a child feature unless the parent feature is also installed.

  For example, if you apply a CMW file that installs Microsoft Excel add-ins, only users who have Excel installed get the add-ins. If a user does not have Excel installed, then the wizard ignores this setting in the CMW file.

Note   When you run the Custom Maintenance Wizard to create a CMW file, you must use the same Office 2003 package (MSI file) that you used to install Office initially.

Apply the CMW file to users' computers

After you create the CMW file, store it on the administrative installation point in the same folder as Maintwiz.exe. To apply updates to Office features, you run the Custom Maintenance Wizard on users' computers. You can create a shortcut that includes the appropriate command line and distribute it to users through e-mail. In the command line, you must include the **/c** option and specify the CMW file, as shown in the following example:

```
<path>\maintwiz.exe /c "MyConfig.cmw"
```

The wizard calls Windows Installer to apply the changes in the CMW file to the user's computer. By default, the Custom Maintenance Wizard runs with a minimal user interface, displaying only progress indicators and error messages. To run the wizard silently, add the **/q** option to the command line.

If you installed Office from an administrative installation point, the Windows Installer searches for a valid source from which to apply a CMW file when users run the Custom Maintenance Wizard. If you installed Office from a compressed CD image and created a local installation source, however, then you must store the CMW file on the original compressed image. Unlike Windows Installer, the Office Source Engine does not search for any valid source; it checks only the source from which the user originally installed Office and passes that information to the Custom Maintenance Wizard. Unless users are administrators of their computers, they can only apply a CMW file from the compressed image from which they installed Office in the first place.

If Office 2003 was installed per-computer, the new feature installation states are applied per-computer and affect all users the same way. However, if Office 2003 was installed per-user, then Windows Installer makes the changes only for the user who applies the CMW file.

For example, if a user applies a CMW file that sets Microsoft Excel to **Not Available**, Windows Installer removes all Excel files, shortcuts, and registry information from the computer. When a second user logs on, however, the Excel shortcut is still available. If that user clicks the shortcut, Windows Installer repairs the installation and reinstalls Excel. When the first user logs on again, Excel is present on the computer, but no Excel shortcut is displayed for that user.

Note For security reasons, only administrators can apply CMW files from any location to a user's computer. To allow non-administrator users to apply the updates to their computers, you must store the wizard (Maintwiz.exe) and CMW file in a subfolder on the administrative installation point. Alternatively, you can set the Windows Installer policy **Allow CMW files at any location to be applied**. However, setting this policy leaves the computer highly vulnerable, potentially allowing an attacker to run malicious code on the computer.

For detailed information about each page of the Custom Maintenance Wizard, see the Office 2003 Editions Resource Kit Reference on the companion CD.

Staging application deployment

Many organizations stage their deployment of Office applications. For example, when the structure of an organization changes, an administrator might need to add or remove Office applications to match users' new responsibilities. Or, a company might delay installation of Microsoft Outlook to coordinate with an upgrade of their e-mail servers.

During your initial deployment of Office, you can set any application or feature to **Not Available** or **Not Available, Hidden, Locked** in a transform (MST file). When Setup runs on users' computers, that application or feature is not installed. Later, you can use the Custom Maintenance Wizard to create a CMW file that changes the feature state to **Installed on My Computer**. The next time the user logs on, Windows Installer installs the application or feature on the local computer. (For details about creating a CMW file and distributing it to users, see the previous section.)

Note, however, that some Setup functionality works only during the initial deployment of Office:

- **Applying a transform**   You cannot use the Custom Maintenance Wizard to apply a transform. Many of the customizations you make in a transform can also be set in a CMW file. However, if you need to include a transform, deploy the stand-alone version of the application—for example, Word.msi and not Pro11.msi.

- **Removing a previous version**   The Removal Wizard automatically removes previous versions of the applications you are installing during Setup. However, the Removal Wizard does not run automatically when you apply a CMW file. If you are deploying a new application and you want to remove its previous version, run the stand-alone Removal Wizard before you distribute the CMW file.

For more information about staging your Outlook deployment, see "Installing Outlook 2003 Before Office 2003" or "Installing Outlook 2003 After Office 2003" in Chapter 8, "Special Deployment Scenarios for Outlook 2003."

Changing user-defined application settings

After Office is installed, users can customize many options in Office applications—everything from the screen resolution to the default file format for saving documents. Most of these user-defined settings are recorded as values in the Windows registry. You can specify default application settings after Office is installed by using one of the following tools:

■ **Custom Maintenance Wizard** Use the Custom Maintenance Wizard to modify settings applied in a transform (MST file) or to distribute new settings with other customizations that can be made only in a CMW file—such as an updated organization name, additional installation sources, or new applications and features.

■ **Office Profile Wizard** Use the Office Profile Wizard to apply a standard Office configuration to a group of users or to restore a saved configuration to a new computer.

Update settings with the Custom Maintenance Wizard

All of the user-defined settings that you can set in a transform (MST file) can also be set in a CMW file. The **Change Office User Settings** page is identical in both wizards; and in both cases, the options in the tree correspond to options that you can set by policy in the Office policy templates.

The Custom Maintenance Wizard also includes pages for setting security levels, customizing Outlook settings and profile information, adding or modifying registry entries, and adding files such as custom templates or dictionaries. These pages correspond to identical pages in the Custom Installation Wizard. For more information about setting options on these pages, see "Customizing User-defined Settings" in Chapter 4, "Customizing Office 2003."

For detailed information about each page of the Custom Maintenance Wizard, see the Office 2003 Editions Resource Kit Reference on the companion CD.

Distribute new settings with the Profile Wizard

The Profile Wizard captures a broad range of Office application settings by recording entire sections of the Windows registry in an Office profile settings file (OPS file). When you apply settings from the OPS file to users' computers, the wizard overwrites existing Office application settings with the settings stored in the OPS file. For these reasons, the Profile Wizard is the right tool for capturing and distributing a complete Office user configuration. (If you need to update only a few settings, use the Custom Maintenance Wizard instead.)

When you distribute updated user settings in an OPS file, you must run Proflwiz.exe separately on users' computers. Unlike the Custom Installation Wizard, the Custom Maintenance Wizard does not allow you to add an OPS file to the CMW file, nor can you use the Custom Maintenance Wizard to run the Profile Wizard.

Running the Profile Wizard separately also allows you to customize the process more precisely. For example, you can include only the settings you want to manage, and you can exclude applications that you want to leave untouched. This approach is helpful when you deploy Office in stages and you need to customize applications separately at each stage of the process.

Note   Although the interfaces differ, the Profile Wizard and Save My Settings Wizard use the same executable file: Proflwiz.exe. The Save My Settings Wizard ships with Office and is designed to help users back up and restore settings on their own computers. The Profile Wizard, which is included in the Office Resource Kit, is intended for administrators who manage configurations throughout an organization.

Create an OPS file

Before you create the OPS file, you must install Office on a test computer, and then start each Office application and set all the options you want to capture. You can set most options by using the **Options** command (**Tools** menu). To customize toolbars and menus, use the **Customize** command (**Tools** menu). After you have customized the Office applications, run the Profile Wizard to create the OPS file.

To save settings to an OPS file

1. Start the Profile Wizard.

2. On the **Save or Restore Settings** page, select **Save the settings from this machine**, and enter the name and path for the OPS file.

3. Select the check boxes next to the Office 2003 applications you want to include in your OPS file.

4. Click **Finish**.

    The Profile Wizard saves the Office application settings on your computer to the OPS file.

Note   By design, Profile Wizard does not capture all user-specific Outlook 2003 settings. For more information, see "Office Profile Wizard" in Appendix B, "Office 2003 Resource Kit Reference."

Reset settings to default values

When you run the Profile Wizard to apply an OPS file, you can select the **Reset to defaults before restoring settings** check box. This option returns Office application settings on the local computer to their default settings before applying customized settings from the OPS file. If a user has customized settings that are not included in the OPS file, reapplying default values ensures that you are distributing a consistent Office configuration throughout the organization.

If you want to reset only certain settings to their default values, you must edit one of the Profile Wizard text files (ResetO11.ops) to determine more precisely which settings are restored and which are ignored.

> **Note**   The **Reset to defaults before restoring settings** option returns all existing Office application settings to their default values, including settings in applications that you have excluded from the OPS file.

Customize the Profile Wizard to include or exclude settings

When you create an OPS file, you can customize the Profile Wizard to include or exclude particular settings or files by modifying one of the following files:

- **Opw11adm.ini**   Use this file as a template for creating custom INI files to use with the Profile Wizard; available in the Office Resource Kit. To preserve the original INI file as a backup, save the customized INI file with a new name.

- **Opw11usr.ini**   Use this file as a template to create custom INI files to use with the Save My Settings Wizard; comes with Office 2003.

- **ResetO11.ops**   Use this file to reset specified user-defined settings to their default values; available in the Office Resource Kit.

For more information about customizing the Profile Wizard INI files, see "Office Profile Wizard" in Appendix B, "Office 2003 Editions Resource Kit Reference."

Distribute the OPS file to users

You may use any of the following methods to distribute custom settings to users:

- Send the OPS file to users and have them apply it by running the Save My Settings Wizard.

- Use a software distribution management tool, such as Microsoft Systems Management Server, to push the Profile Wizard and OPS file to client computers.

- Save the Profile Wizard, OPS file, and any custom INI file on the Office 2003 administrative installation point, and create a shortcut that includes appropriate command-line options.
  For example, the following shortcut runs the wizard quietly and restores settings from MyConfig.ops:

```
<path>\Proflwiz.exe /r MyConfig.ops /q
```

For a complete list of command-line options that you can use with the Profile Wizard, see "Office Profile Wizard" in Appendix B, "Office 2003 Resource Kit Reference."

Preserving customized settings during a staged deployment

When Office is deployed in stages, it is easy to overwrite settings in previous user profiles. It is even easier to overwrite settings when you are not the only administrator installing Office applications. One way to help control which settings are affected in a given deployment is to customize the Profile Wizard.

For example, you might invest time customizing Office 2003 in the lab. You run the Profile Wizard to capture your user profile settings. You do not configure Outlook because someone else is installing Outlook next month, but you do deploy Microsoft Office Excel 2003, Microsoft Office Word 2003, and Microsoft Office PowerPoint® 2003 with a default user profile.

One month later, your colleague deploys Outlook. Like you, he customizes Office 2003 in the lab and uses the Profile Wizard to capture his user profile settings. But he does not exclude settings for any of the other applications—the customized settings that you deployed and the customized settings that users have been working with for a month.

When your colleague installs Outlook, he inadvertently changes your settings for Excel, Word, and PowerPoint. And, if he happens to select the **Reset to defaults before restoring settings** option, all of your OPS file settings are gone—along with any later user configurations—even if he did not explicitly change them in his profile.

You can avoid this scenario by selecting only the applications for which you want to save or restore settings when you run the Profile Wizard. On the **Save or Restore Settings** page of the wizard, select only the Office applications that you are deploying at any given time.

Using Office policies to change settings

After Office has been deployed throughout your organization, you can set policies that define and maintain a standard Office 2003 configuration on users' computers. Unlike other customizations, including settings distributed in a CMW or OPS file, policies are reapplied each time a user logs on to the network, and users cannot change them.

For more information about setting Office policies, see "Managing Users' Configurations by Policy" later in this chapter.

Distributing Office 2003 Product Updates

Microsoft Office 2003 service packs and product updates are designed to help improve the security, performance, and reliability of Office applications. A service pack, such as Office 2003 Service Pack 1 (SP1), typically updates the entire Office package and represents a new baseline version of the product.

Between service packs, Microsoft may also offer product updates developed in response to emerging issues such as virus attacks or bug fixes. These interim product updates, which typically update specific applications or features, require the most recent baseline version of the product. Interim updates are also cumulative; for example, you can apply the fifth Microsoft Office Word 2003 patch without applying Word 2003 patches one through four.

> **Note**   Although interim product updates must be installed on the most recent baseline version of Office (for example, Office 2003 Service Pack 2), service packs themselves do not have this requirement. You can apply a service pack to any previous baseline version, including the initial release version of Office 2003.

New functionality in Office 2003 Setup has made deploying service packs and product updates more efficient. Administrators now have the option of installing Office from a compressed CD image on the network—which creates a local installation source on users' computers—and distributing binary client patches to users. Because users always have access to the local installation source, they can apply the smaller client patches. And because the original source on the network remains at a baseline level, clients never become out of sync with an updated version.

For organizations that choose to install Office from an uncompressed administrative installation point, Microsoft will continue to release full-file administrative versions of each update. As in past versions, administrative updates (MSP files) are applied to the administrative image on the network, and users recache and reinstall Office from there.

The strategy you choose for updating Office on users' computers depends on several factors:

- **Deployment method**   The method you use to deploy Office 2003 in the first place determines your options for updating clients later on. If you want to be able to distribute binary patches throughout your organization, for example, deploy Office from a compressed CD image and take advantage of the local installation source, which Setup creates by default on users' computers.

- **Management practices** If your organization maintains strong centralized control over software deployment—for example, if you use Microsoft Systems Management Server to help control software distribution—you can more reliably keep clients synchronized with an updated administrative installation point.

- **Network capacity** Recaching and reinstalling Office from an updated administrative image requires considerably more network bandwidth than distributing binary updates.

- **Client hard disk capacity** Caching all installation files on the local computer requires approximately 240 MB of hard disk space in addition to the space required by a typical installation of Office 2003.

> **Important**   To help ensure that the update process works correctly over time, settle on one method of updating Office clients.

Caching installation files locally and distributing client updates

Client updates, or binary patches, are applied directly to the client computer and update, rather than replace, Office files. When you maintain a baseline installation image on the network and distribute binary patches, client computers never get out of sync with the image because the MSI file version remains the same on both the source and the client. Even during such operations as detect and repair or install on demand, client computers updated with binary patches work correctly with the original source.

To apply client patches, however, users almost always need access to the installation source. If you plan to keep Office 2003 up to date by distributing client patches to users, you should deploy Office from a compressed image of the CD on the network and take advantage of the local installation source.

Typically, client patches are smaller than administrative patches and, when compared to updating from an administrative image, easier to distribute to clients. When new users install Office from the baseline compressed CD image, however, you must chain any previously distributed binary patches to the Office installation—and that can increase the time it takes to install Office for the first time.

Microsoft recommends this updating strategy if you:

- Have experienced synchronization problems between client computers and administrative installation points in the past.

- Distribute software updates to different groups of users or at different times.

Because the original installation image remains at the same level, it can support clients with a variety of patches applied. You do not need to maintain different installation images for different clients.

■ Have network bandwidth limitations.
   Binary patches are smaller than full-file patches.

■ Support users who have limited or unreliable network access—for example, traveling users.

This method requires the following:

■ An edition of Office 2003 that is compatible with the Custom Installation Wizard and other administrative tools (retail editions of Office 2003 do not support these tools).

■ A compressed installation source—such as a copy of the Office 2003 CD on a read-only share—with creation of a local installation source enabled.

■ Users who are administrators of their computers or who can easily be granted elevated privileges for the installation (for example, through a deployment tool such as Microsoft Systems Management Server).

Installing from a CD image

When users install Office 2003 from the CD or a compressed CD image, Setup copies installation files to a hidden folder on the local computer. Windows Installer uses this local installation source both to install Office initially and to repair and update Office later on. You can distribute the client patches reliably because users have the necessary access to the source on their own computers when applying a client patch requires it, even when they do not have access to the network.

To create a compressed CD image, you copy the contents of the Office 2003 CD (including all hidden folders) to a network share; you do not run Setup to create the image. After that, the process of customizing a compressed CD image is similar to the process of customizing an administrative installation point. Creation of the local installation source is enabled by default, and you do not need to set any additional local installation source options.

Unlike when deploying from an administrative installation point, however, you must accept the EULA and enter a valid Volume License Key before users can install Office from the compressed CD image. New functionality has been added to the Custom Installation Wizard to handle these settings by means of a transform (MST file) applied during the client installation. For more information, see the Help for the **Configure Local Installation Source** page in the Custom Installation Wizard.

When you create an administrative installation point, Setup extracts compressed cabinet (CAB) files from the Office 2003 CD. Once the files are extracted,

Setup can no longer create a local installation source, and users must rely on the administrative image as a source from that point forward.

For more information about deploying from a compressed CD image, see "Taking Advantage of a Local Installation Source" in Chapter 3, "Preparing to Deploy Office 2003."

Updating existing installations

The compressed CD image on the network represents the Office 2003 baseline for your organization. Once you have established a baseline, you can deploy client updates to individual computers as needed. You can use a variety of methods to distribute the patches to users:

- Use a tool such as Microsoft Systems Management Server (SMS) or Tivoli to deploy the update.

- Post the EXE file that contains the patch on a network share and direct all users to run it.

- Use the stand-alone version of the OHotFix utility to extract the patch (MSP file) from the EXE file and apply it to users' computers.

The OHotFix utility is packaged in a self-extracting executable file and is available on the Office Resource Kit Web site. Download OHotFix (Offinst.exe) from the Office XP Resource Kit Toolbox at *http://www.microsoft.com/office/ork/xp/appndx/appc00.htm#Offinst*.

Creating new installations

When a new client computer installs Office from this image, you must include all current patches to help ensure that the new client has all the latest updates. You can chain as many client patches as necessary to the core Office installation. However, Office 2003 patches are cumulative; you only need to install the latest patches related to a particular application to get all the fixes included in earlier patches. You can apply a service pack to any previous baseline; for example, the client version of Office 2003 SP2 can be applied to either Office 2003 SP1 or the initial release version of Office 2003.

You can chain client updates to the core Office 2003 installation by adding the appropriate files to the [ChainedInstall_*n*] sections of the Setup settings file (Setup.ini). Use either the OHotFix utility or Windows Installer to accomplish this.

To use the OHotFix utility to chain client patches

1. Extract each binary patch (MSP file) from the corresponding client update (EXE file).

2. Modify the OHotFix INI file to run in quiet mode and to apply the patches.

3. In the Setup.ini file, chain OHotFix.exe to the core Office installation.

For example:

```
[ChainedInstall_1]
TASKTYPE=exe
PATH=\\server\share\admin_install_point\1234\OHotFix.exe
```

For more information about OHotFix, see Installing Client Update Files with OHotFix on the Office XP Resource Kit Web site at *http://www.microsoft.com/office /ork/xp/journ/Ohotfix.htm*.

To use Windows Installer to chain client patches

1. Extract each binary patch (MSP file) from the corresponding client update (EXE file).

2. In the Setup.ini file, chain Msiexec.exe to the core Office installation.
   You must create a separate [ChainedInstall_*n*] section for each patch.
   For example:

```
[ChainedInstall_1]
TASKTYPE=exe
PATH=C:\Windows\System32\MSIExec.exe
CmdLine=\\server\share\admin_install_point\1234\[MSP file] /qb /lpiwaeo
[path\name of log file]
```

Microsoft Windows correctly finds and starts Msiexec.exe even if the Windows folder is not in the same location on all computers in your organization.

For more information about chaining, see "Deploying Office and Other Products Together" in Chapter 5, "Installing Office 2003."

Updating Office from a patched administrative installation point

Office administrative updates provide full-file replacement of files changed by a service pack or product update. They are typically applied to an administrative installation point on the network from which Windows Installer performs a recache and reinstallation of Office on users' computers. By installing complete files, as opposed to patched files, the administrative update can correctly replace any files on the server that have been modified with previous updates.

Recaching and reinstalling replaces the previously cached MSI file on users' computers and overwrites any old files with the newer versions. In an ideal computing environment, Office is recached and reinstalled promptly each time an administrative installation point is patched. If you can impose a consistent update process throughout your organization, this is still a good method of keeping existing clients up to date with the latest patches. In addition, new clients that install from the administrative image automatically get the updated version—you do not need to chain patches to the core installation.

When there is a delay between updating the administrative image and recaching Office on clients, however, client computers can become out of sync with the administrative image. Operations that rely on the source—such as install on demand or detect and repair—fail because the client does not recognize the updated administrative image, which has a new version of the Office MSI file. Relying on this method of updating clients may require you to set up two administrative images: the patched image for updated clients, and an unpatched baseline image for everyone else.

Microsoft recommends this updating strategy if you:

- Maintain strong centralized control over software deployment and lock down user configurations.

    For example, if you use SMS or Group Policy software installation to deploy and maintain Office, creating and maintaining an administrative image may be the most efficient method of keeping clients up to date.

- Support users who have consistent and reliable network access.

- Support users who are not administrators of their computers and to whom you cannot easily grant elevated privileges for the patching process.

- Run any Office applications from the source.

    You cannot use the **Run from Network** feature installation setting from a compressed source.

This method requires the following:

- An edition of Office 2003 that is compatible with the Custom Installation Wizard and other administrative tools (retail editions of Office 2003 do not support these tools).

- Sufficient network capacity to handle recaching and reinstalling Office throughout an organization.

For more information about deploying Office from an administrative image, see "Running Setup from an Installation Image" in Chapter 5, "Installing Office 2003."

Patching an administrative installation point

You must install administrative updates (MSP files) from the command line. On the command line, you run Windows Installer with options to specify the path to the MSI file and the name and path of the MSP file.

- The MSI file is the Windows Installer package file from your original administrative image.

- The MSP file is the Office administrative update file that contains information about the changes in the upgrade. The update instructs Windows Installer to add, update, or remove files in the administrative image.

Before you update an administrative installation point, make sure that no clients are using the share. If a file on the share is in use during the upgrade process, a newer version of that file is not copied to the administrative installation point.

To apply an update to an Office administrative installation point

1. Download the self-extracting executable file for the update and double-click the file name to extract the MSP file.

   Administrative updates for Office 2003 are made available on the Office Resource Kit Web site at *http://www.microsoft.com/office/ork/2003*.

2. Connect to the server share for your administrative installation point.

   You must have write access to the administrative installation point on the server and the appropriate privileges to carry out the task, including the Change privilege.

3. On the **Start** menu, click **Run** and then type the Windows Installer command line with the appropriate options for your installation. Use the following syntax:

   ```
   msiexec.exe /p [path\name of update MSP file]/a [path\name of MSI file] /qb /
   lv* [path\name of log file]
   ```

If an update contains multiple MSP files, you must run the command line separately for each MSP file that you apply to the administrative installation point—you cannot reference multiple MSP files on the same command line. The following table describes the command-line options.

Command-line option	Description
Msiexec.exe	Executable file name for Windows Installer.
/p	Directs Windows Installer to apply an update to an existing installation.
[path\name of update MSP file]	Path and file name of the MSP file for the update.
/a	Directs Windows Installer to perform an administrative installation of a product on a network share.
[path\name of MSI file]	Path and file name of the Windows Installer package for your original administrative image.
/qb	Sets the user interface to the basic level (simple progress and error handling).
/lpiwaeo	Turns on logging and sets a path for the log file. The default setting **/lpiwaeo** logs a subset of information, such as error messages and warnings. Use **/lv*** to log all information.
[path\name of log file]	Path and file name of the Windows Installer log file.

Updating client computers

After you update your administrative installation point, you need to perform a recache and reinstallation on all client computers that use the administrative image as a source. Any new client installations from the administrative installation point automatically include the updated version of Office.

To update an existing client installation from an administrative installation point, users need only rerun Setup.exe on the administrative installation point. If the administrative image has been patched, Setup automatically triggers the recache and reinstallation of all Office 2003 applications and features. Unless Setup is set to run in quiet mode, users are prompted to update.

Alternatively, you can distribute the following command line to the clients:

```
setup.exe REINSTALL=[list of features modified by the update] /qb
```

In this case, Setup.exe calls Windows Installer to perform the installation and automatically generates log files. You can run this command line by creating a logon script, distributing it as a batch file, deploying it by using SMS, or using other means according to your practice. The options for this command line are described in the following table.

Command-line option	Description
Setup.exe	Executable file name for Office Setup program.
REINSTALL=[*value*]	Specifies whether to reinstall all applications or only the features affected by the patch. The default **REINSTALL=all** reinstalls all applications and features in the updated package.
/qb	Directs Setup to run in quiet mode.

Each update that Microsoft releases includes documentation listing all the features affected by the update. You can minimize the time and network bandwidth needed to update users' computers by setting the **REINSTALL** property to reinstall only the features modified by the update. Note that the values for **REINSTALL** shown in the feature list are case sensitive.

Synchronizing independently updated client computers

If you originally installed Office 2003 on a client computer from an administrative installation point, you must follow the recache and reinstallation procedure described above to update that client. If you update the client directly by applying a binary patch, the client and administrative images become out of sync, which can cause future updates to fail. To synchronize an independently updated client computer to recognize an updated administrative image, users must uninstall Office and reinstall from the updated administrative image.

Resources and related information

If you have the Active Directory® directory service and Group Policy set up in your organization, you can set a policy that prevents users from downloading client patches directly from the Microsoft Office Online Downloads site. In the Group Policy snap-in, under User Configuration\Administrative Templates\Microsoft Office 2003\Miscellaneous, set the **Block updates** policy. For more information about setting policies for Office 2003, see "Managing Users' Configurations by Policy" in the next section.

The strategies for applying updates to Multilingual User Interface Packs are identical to those for updating the core Office installation. For more information, see "Distributing Multilingual User Interface Pack Updates" in Chapter 16, "Maintaining an Office 2003 Multilingual Installation."

Transforms can only be applied when Office is initially installed. You cannot apply transforms when you patch Office. For more information about updating users' configurations after Office is installed, see "Updating Feature Installation States and Application Settings" earlier in this chapter.

Managing Users' Configurations by Policy

In a Microsoft Windows–based network, Group Policy settings help administrators control how users work with Microsoft Office 2003. By setting policies, you can define and maintain a particular Office 2003 configuration on users' computers. Unlike other customizations—for example, default settings distributed in a transform (MST file)—policies are reapplied each time a user logs on to the network (or at some other interval set by the administrator), and users cannot edit the Windows registry to change them.

You can use Office policies to:

- Control entry points to the Internet.

- Manage security settings in Office applications.

- Hide or disable new behavior that might confuse users and result in unnecessary calls for support.

- Hide settings and options that are not needed and might distract users.

- Lock down a standard configuration on users' computers.

You can set policies that apply to the local computer (and every user of that computer) or that apply only to individual users. Per-computer policies are set under **Computer Configuration** in the Group Policy snap-in and are applied the first time any user logs on to the network from that computer. Per-user policies are set under **User Configuration** and are applied when the specified user logs on to the network from any computer.

Active Directory and Group Policy

In Office 2003, Group Policy has replaced the System Policy Editor as the recommended mechanism for setting and maintaining policies throughout an organization. The Active Directory™ directory service provides the framework for centralized administration of users and computers. Active Directory stores information about objects on the network and makes this information easy for administrators and users to find and use.

Network objects in this context include users, computers, and printers, as well as domains, sites, and organizational units. A structured data store provides the basis for a logical, hierarchical organization of all directory information.

Active Directory makes it possible to manage all users, computers, and software on the network through administrator-defined policies, known as Group Policy in Windows 2000 or later. A collection of Group Policy settings is contained in a Group Policy object (GPO), and the GPO is associated with an Active Directory container. You can set policies that apply to an entire site, a domain, or an individual organizational unit.

Group Policy encompasses a wide range of options, including registry-based policy settings, security settings, software installation scripts, folder redirection, remote installation services, and Internet Explorer maintenance. The policies contained in the Office policy templates are registry-based policies.

Office 2003 policies

Office policies allow administrators to manage most options that configure the Office 2003 user interface, including:

- Disabling or enabling menu commands and their corresponding toolbar buttons.

- Disabling or enabling shortcut keys.

- Specifying settings for most options in the **Options** dialog box (**Tools** menu).

The Office policy templates (ADM files) also include policies that help you control the way Windows Installer functions.

Each Office 2003 policy represents an option or feature in an Office application. Each policy also corresponds to one or more value entries in the Windows registry. All policy information is stored in the same area of the registry.

For example, all user-specific policy settings are stored in the HKEY_CURRENT_USER\Software\Policies\Microsoft\Office\11.0 subkey, which mirrors most of the HKEY_CURRENT_USER\Software\Microsoft\Office\11.0 subkey. Computer-specific policies are stored in the HKEY_LOCAL_MACHINE\Software\Policies\Microsoft\Office\11.0 subkey. By default, both Policy subkeys are locked, making them inaccessible to users.

Office 2003 policy template files

When you use the Group Policy snap-in to set policy, you first load the Office policy templates (ADM files) and then configure the settings you want to manage. You can add several ADM files and set the entire configuration of a computer at one time.

The Office 2003 Editions Resource Kit includes the following policy template files (ADM files), which list the options you can control for each application.

ADM file	Application
Office11.adm	Shared Office 2003 components
Access11.adm	Microsoft Office Access 2003
Excel11.adm	Microsoft Office Excel 2003
Gal11.adm	Clip Organizer
Instlr11.adm	Windows Installer 2.0
Outlk11.adm	Microsoft Office Outlook 2003
Ppt11.adm	Microsoft Office PowerPoint 2003
Pub11.adm	Microsoft Office Publisher 2003
Rm11.adm	Relationship Manager
Scrib11.adm	Microsoft Office OneNote™ 2003
Word11.adm	Microsoft Office Word 2003
Inf11.adm	Microsoft Office InfoPath™ 2003

When you install the Office policy template files, they are automatically saved to the %SystemRoot%\Inf folder on your computer. To download the templates, see the Office 2003 Editions Resource Kit Toolbox on the companion CD.

Policies in the templates are organized in a hierarchy that, in general, follows the user interface. Settings found in the **Options** dialog box (**Tools** menu) are listed under **Tools | Options** in the template for each application. However, the policies for some settings that appear in multiple applications are consolidated in the Office11.adm template.

For example, several Office applications allow users to customize the way the application works with the Web through the **Web Options** button on the **General** tab of the **Options** dialog box. You set policies to manage users' interaction with the Web in all Office applications in the Office11.adm template under **Tools | Options\General\Web options**.

Because policy settings are stored in a different area of the registry for each release of Office, you cannot use the policy templates from a previous version. To configure policies for Office 2003, you must use the policy templates for Office 2003.

Using the Group Policy snap-in

After you set up an Active Directory™ and Group Policy infrastructure in your organization, you use the Group Policy Microsoft Management Console (MMC) snap-in to set Office 2003 policies from the Office policy templates (ADM files). Once you set policies for a particular Group Policy object, Windows automatically implements the policies on users' computers.

To set policy using the Group Policy snap-in

1. Open the Group Policy object (GPO) for which you want to set policy.

2. Right-click **Administrative Templates** and select **Add/Remove Templates**.
    A list of ADM files already added to the GPO appears.

3. To add another ADM file, click **Add**.
    A list of all the ADM files in the %SystemRoot%\Inf folder of the local computer appears. (You can also select an ADM file from another location.)

4. Select an ADM file and click **Open** to add it to the GPO.

5. Double-click **Computer Configuration** or **User Configuration** and then expand the tree under **Administrative Templates** to find the Office 2003 policies.

6. Under **Settings** in the right pane, set the policies you want.

7. Save the Group Policy object.
    Windows automatically enforces the policies the next time each user logs on. Policies remain in effect until the administrator clears them.

Policies in the Group Policy snap-in can have one of three states:

- **Not configured**   The policy is not enforced. If the policy was previously enforced, those settings are removed from the registry and the option returns to either the default setting or the last setting specified by the user.

- **Enabled**   The policy is enforced. For most policies, additional settings appear in the box. These settings determine what happens when the policy is enforced. Note that clearing a particular setting only changes the behavior enforced by the policy; to reverse the policy altogether, choose **Not Configured**.

- **Disabled**   The policy is not configured or is ignored.

For most Office 2003 policies, the effect of setting a policy to **Disabled** is the same as setting it to **Not configured**. Settings return to their default values, and users can change settings to which they have access through the user interface or the Windows registry.

For more information about setting Group Policy, see the "Step-by-Step Guide to Understanding the Group Policy Feature Set" at *http://www.microsoft.com /windows2000/techinfo/planning/management/groupsteps.asp.*

Using the Group Policy Management Console (Windows Server 2003 only)

Microsoft Windows Server™ 2003 includes the new Group Policy Management Console (GPMC), a single solution for managing all Group Policy–related tasks. By using GPMC, administrators can manage Group Policy for multiple domains and sites within a given forest.

The simplified user interface supports drag-and-drop functionality and also allows administrators to back up, restore, import, copy, and create reports for Group Policy objects (GPOs). These operations are fully scriptable, which lets administrators customize and automate management.

More information about GPMC is available on the Microsoft Windows Server 2003 Web site at *http://www.microsoft.com/windows.netserver/gpmc/default.mspx*.

Disabling user interface elements

You can set policies that disable menu commands, toolbar buttons, and shortcut keys. By setting these policies, you can help prevent users from changing or gaining access to particular features or options. A menu item or command bar button that has been disabled by policy appears grayed out in the user interface and is unavailable to users.

Disabling menu items and command bar buttons

A number of menu items and command bar buttons are listed by name in the policy templates in the **Disable items in user interface | Predefined | Disable command bar buttons and menu items** policy. These items include commands that administrators frequently choose to disable, such as the **Hyperlink** command (**Insert** menu) and the **Macro** command (**Tools** menu).

To disable any other command in an Office 2003 application, you set the **Custom | Disable command bar buttons and menu items** policy and add the control ID for the command you want to disable.

To disable a menu item and the corresponding command bar button

1. Select the check box to set the **Custom | Disable command bar buttons and menu items** policy for the appropriate Office 2003 application.

2. Click the **Show** button.

3. Click **Add** and enter the control ID for the item you want to disable.

Menu items and their corresponding command bar buttons share the same control ID. For example, in Microsoft Word the control ID for both the **Save** command (**File** menu) and **Save** button (**Standard** toolbar) is **3**.

Finding control IDs in Visual Basic for Applications

You can look up control IDs for any item on a menu or toolbar in Office 2003 applications by using Microsoft Visual Basic® for Applications (VBA). You can either look up a single control ID or use a macro to find a series of control IDs. Then you enter the control ID into the Group Policy snap-in to disable that menu command and toolbar button.

Menu commands and their corresponding toolbar buttons share the same control ID. For example, the control ID for both the **Save** command (**File** menu) and the **Save** button (**Standard** toolbar) in Microsoft Word is **3**.

Finding a single control ID

You use the Immediate window in VBA to look up the control ID for a single item on a menu. For example, the following command returns the value **748**, which is the control ID for the **Save As** command on the **File** menu in Microsoft Word:

```
? commandbars("menu bar").controls("file").controls("save as...").id
```

For Microsoft Excel, use `worksheet menu bar` instead of `menu bar` in the previous example.

You use the same command to find the control ID for a toolbar button. For example, the following command displays the control ID for the **Document Map** button (**Standard** toolbar) in Word:

```
? commandbars ("standard").controls ("document map").id
```

Finding all the control IDs for a menu or toolbar

If you want to find the control IDs for all the items on a menu or toolbar, you can create a macro in VBA. For example, the following macro opens a series of message boxes to display the commands and corresponding control IDs for each item on the **File** menu for any Office 2003 application:

```
Sub EnumerateControls()
    Dim icbc As Integer
    Dim cbcs As CommandBarControls
    Set cbcs = Application.CommandBars("Menu Bar").Controls("File").Controls
    For icbc = 1 To cbcs.Count
        MsgBox cbcs(icbc).Caption & " = " & cbcs(icbc).ID
    Next icbc
End Sub
```

To disable all of the items on a menu, you can enter each item individually in the Group Policy snap-in. Or, you can disable the entire menu by entering the control ID for the menu itself.

For more information about using Visual Basic for Applications, see the Language Center for Visual Basic at *http://msdn.microsoft.com/vbasic/vblang/default.asp*.

Disabling shortcut keys

Several built-in shortcut keys are listed by name in the policy templates in the **Disable items in user interface | Predefined | Disable shortcut keys** policy. For example, you can disable **CTRL+K**, the shortcut for the **Hyperlink** command (**Insert** menu).

To disable any other shortcut key in an Office 2003 application, you set the **Custom | Disable shortcut keys** policy and add the virtual key code for the shortcut. (A virtual key code is a hardware-independent number that uniquely identifies a key on the keyboard.)

To disable a shortcut key

1. Select the check box to set the **Custom | Disable shortcut keys** policy for the appropriate Office 2003 application.

2. Click **Show**.

3. Click **Add** and enter the shortcut key and modifier for the item you want to disable by using the following syntax:

    key,modifier

    where *key* is the value of a key (for example, **G**) in Windows, and *modifier* is the value of either a modifier key (for example, **ALT** or **SHIFT**) or a combination of modifier keys in Windows.

    Use the following values to refer to keys in the Group Policy snap-in:

Modifier or key	Value
ALT	16
CONTROL	8
SHIFT	4
A-Z	A sequential number between 65 and 90, where A = 65, and Z = 90

For example, to disable the shortcut key **ALT+K**, enter **75,16** (*key* = **75**; *modifier* = **16**).

If you have multiple modifier keys for the shortcut key, you add the values of the modifier keys together to determine the actual modifier key value you enter. For example, for **ALT+SHIFT**, enter **20** (16+4).

Locking down an Office configuration

Many administrators use policies to lock down users' Office configurations as one part of their overall security strategy. In addition, maintaining a standard Office configuration throughout an organization can help reduce support costs, create a consistent user environment for users who share computers, and limit access to the Internet by disabling entry points in Office applications.

Using environment variables in policies

Environment variables—which use the **REG_EXPAND_SZ** data type—expand in the Windows registry to replace file names, paths, or other changeable values. You can use environment variables in policies. For example, the **Default file location** policy for Excel 2003 specifies the default location for saving Excel files. If you want users to store their Excel files on the network under their user names, you can specify a network drive and the following environment variable:

```
drive:\%Username%\
```

When you distribute the policy, the environment variable is written to each user's registry. Office 2003 recognizes **%Username%** as an environment variable and expands it to whatever the **%Username%** variable is set to on the user's computer. For example, Office expands the environment variable in the preceding example to *drive*:\UserA\ for User A, *drive*:\UserB\ for User B, and so on.

You can also use any other appropriately defined environment variable to set **Default file location** to a particular path or folder. Because Office recognizes the **REG_EXPAND_SZ** data type, you can use environment variables that exist by default in the operating system or variables you set on your own.

Chapter 19

Maintaining Office 2003 Installations

Microsoft® Office 2003 has features to help repair installations and report problems when they occur. The automatic and manual Detect and Repair feature, which was included in Office XP, helps reduce the number of required manual reinstallation tasks for administrators when users encounter problems. Microsoft Application Error Reporting—which helped Microsoft learn about the most commonly encountered problems in Office XP—has been enhanced in Office 2003.

Repairing Office 2003 Installations

Microsoft Office 2003 allows users to manually repair an installation if there is any concern that the current installation is not functioning properly. Office can also automatically repair itself if it detects a corrupt component or application, and if the core files of each application have not been deleted or damaged. A library of file names maintained in the registry helps the detection system determine what files should be replaced when a specific application or component cannot be started. If required, Office calls Windows Installer and reinstalls only the affected files and registry entries.

Repairing Office installations manually

Users and administrators have the option of repairing an installation of Office 2003 to its original installation configuration by using the Detect and Repair feature.

To repair Office by using Detect and Repair

1. In the application you are repairing, click the **Help** menu.

2. Click **Detect and Repair**.

    Selecting the **Discard my customized settings and restore default settings** check box is not encouraged unless the user who initiates this action is sure she or he wants to remove all custom settings they may have for Office applications. The effects of the two options in this dialog are explained in the sidebar just below this procedure.

3. Click **Start**.

Options in the Detect and Repair dialog box

The **Detect and Repair** dialog box has two options to consider:

- Restore my shortcuts while repairing
- Discard my customized settings and restore default settings

Restoring shortcuts may not be a valid option depending on the configuration established by the administrator. Restoring shortcuts while repairing re-enables the use of shortcuts that were deleted or corrupted. But if the user who initiates the repair is not the administrator of the system, or does not have permissions to perform an update of software, then this task will not complete.

The most sensitive option is the **Discard my customized settings and restore default settings**. When detect and repair runs with this option selected, the configuration for the user currently logged on is destroyed; the configuration settings of other users, however, are not deleted. Deleting a configuration when a user is not expecting it can cause troubles; therefore, it is suggested that the profile of the affected user be saved prior to running detect and repair. (You can save a user's profile by using either the Office Profile Wizard or the Save My Settings Wizard.) Selecting the **Discard my customized settings and restore default settings** option is only suggested if the user wishes to restore his or her configuration settings to those when Office was originally installed.

Administrators also have the option of using remote desktop administration to force a repair of a user's installation, if required.

Note   For installations of Office 2003 on Terminal Services–enabled servers, users with administrative privileges are the only individuals who have the option to perform a repair.

For a repair to function properly, the installation source from which Office was installed must be available. If this installation source is not available, Office can use an alternate source specified in the transform used to install Office. Alternate installation sources can be specified in the **Identify Additional Servers** page of the Custom Installation Wizard or Custom Maintenance Wizard.

Running the Reset011.ops file

In order to discard all settings for all users, it is necessary for all users to run the **Detect and Repair** command with the **Discard my customized settings and restore default settings** check box selected. However, in many cases this is not possible or not feasible. The recommended way to accomplish this task without running this feature is to have all users delete all custom user settings in the registry, which can be accomplished by running the Reset011.ops file. This file is included with Office 2003 and is not part of the Office Resource Kit. Each user runs the Office Profile Wizard or Save My Settings Wizard and provides the following command line option:

```
proflwiz.exe /d RESET011.OPS
```

All custom settings for the user running this program will be removed when this command is issued. The path to ResetO11.ops must be provided if this file is not in the same folder as Proflwiz.exe.

Removing and reinstalling Office is not a way to discard user settings. When Office is removed and reinstalled on a computer, the previous user settings—whether they were customized by the user themselves or by a transform or configuration maintenance file—are still present in the registry. By default, user settings are not removed when Office is removed. To remove these settings, each user must run the Office Profile Wizard or Save My Settings Wizard with the above command line.

Forcing a global repair of Office installations

If required, you can force Setup to repair Office 2003. You use the **/f** command-line option with Setup and save the command line in a batch file. You then distribute the batch file by using a logon script, Microsoft Systems Management Server (SMS), or some other method employed by your organization. It is recommended that users understand, before the repair commences, that their installation of Office 2003 is being repaired, and that their personal settings will not be lost.

For more information, look up **/f** in "Setup Command-line Options" in Appendix B, "Office 2003 Resource Kit Reference."

Reporting Office 2003 Application Crashes

Microsoft Office 2003 includes the Application Error Reporting client (Dw20.exe), a tool that collects information automatically whenever an Office application crashes and allows users to send a report directly to Microsoft. Microsoft uses the data to address problems and enhance future versions of the applications.

In large organizations, administrators can redirect error reports to an internal server, analyze the reports for themselves, and filter the data sent to Microsoft. They do this by setting policies for the Corporate Error Reporting tool (Cer.exe), which manages the error-reporting process. A new Microsoft Windows Corporate Error Reporting tool replaces the version of Cer.exe that shipped with Microsoft Office XP. Although the two versions are very similar, the new one works with both the Application Error Reporting client and the Windows Error Reporting client.

Note For more information about Corporate Error Reporting or to download the tool, see the Windows Online Crash Analysis Web site at *http://oca.microsoft.com/en/Cerintro.asp.*

Installing the Corporate Error Reporting tool

You use the Corporate Error Reporting tool (CER) to configure the CER file server, set the CER reporting options, manage users' error reports, and send error reports to

Microsoft for further analysis. Because the CER program can manage remote CER file servers, you can install it on any CER file server or on an administrator's computer.

The computer on which you install and run Corporate Error Reporting must meet the following system requirements:

- Microsoft Windows® 2000 operating system; Windows XP; or Microsoft Windows Server™ 2003 Standard, Enterprise, Datacenter, or Web Edition

- Microsoft Internet Explorer 4.01 Service Pack 1 or later with access to the Internet (for error reporting)

- Windows Installer version 2.0 or later

- 200 megahertz (MHz) processor (recommended)

- 64 megabytes (MB) of RAM (recommended)

To install the Corporate Error Reporting program

1. Double-click the Cer.msi file to start Windows Installer.

2. Follow the instructions in the Corporate Error Reporting Setup Wizard to complete the installation process.

    To start the Corporate Error Reporting tool after installation, click **Start**, point to **Programs**, and then click **Corporate Error Reporting**.

    For more information about using the Corporate Error Reporting tool, including creating the file folder tree in which to store error data, see the Corporate Error Reporting Help file (Cerhlp.chm).

Configuring application error reporting

In order for Corporate Error Reporting to collect error data from Office application crashes, the Application Error Reporting client (Dw20.exe) must be configured to report errors to the CER file folder tree instead of directly to Microsoft over the Internet. You can accomplish this by using Group Policy, if you have an Active Directory® directory service infrastructure set up in your organization.

> **Note**   Corporate Error Reporting policies for the core English version of Office 2003 are included in the Aer_1033.adm policy template file. When you install Office 2003, this template is automatically saved to the %SystemRoot%\Inf folder on your computer, and the policies are available in the Group Policy snap-in.

To redirect Office application error reporting to an internal server

1. Start the Group Policy snap-in and open the Group Policy object for which you want to set policy.

2. Right-click **Administrative Templates** and load the Aer_1033.adm template.

3. Click **Computer Configuration** or **User Configuration** and expand the tree.
    Error reporting policies are located under Administrative Templates \Application Error Reporting.

4. Click **Corporate Error Reporting**.

5. In the right pane, double-click **Local error reporting file path**.

6. Click **Enabled**.
    Setting this policy enables Corporate Error Reporting, which allows you to send all error reports to a local file server. When you select **Disable** or **Not Configured**, error reports are sent to Microsoft, unless error reporting is disabled.

7. In the **Local error reporting file path** box, enter the path to the CER File Folder tree, and then click **OK**.

You can achieve the same results by specifying values in the Windows registry. Dw.exe looks for value entries in the following subkeys, listed in order from highest to lowest precedence:

- HKEY_CURRENT_USER\Software\Policies\Microsoft\PCHealth\ErrorReporting \DW

- HKEY_LOCAL_MACHINE\Software\Policies\Microsoft\PCHealth\ErrorReporting \DW

- HKEY_CURRENT_USER\Software\Microsoft\PCHealth\ErrorReporting\DW

- HKEY_LOCAL_MACHINE\Software\Microsoft\PCHealth\ErrorReporting\DW

For example, setting the value entry **DWFileTreeRoot** to a drive letter or UNC path activates corporate error reporting and redirects it to a local file server.

Additional error reporting policies that you can set for Office applications include the following:

- Replace Microsoft with your company name
    Located in the Corporate Error Reporting folder. Enabling this policy allows you to substitute the name of your company in place of Microsoft in the error reporting dialog box. If you choose **Disabled** or **Not Configured**, users are prompted to send error reports to Microsoft. This policy is equivalent to setting the **DWReportee** value entry to the name of your organization.

- Hide Don't Send button
    Located in the Corporate Error Reporting folder. Enabling this policy hides the **Don't Send** button in the error reporting dialog box; users see only the **Send Error Report** button. When this policy is enabled, a user can still click **Cancel** if prompted to send additional data, such as documents. This policy is equivalent to setting the **DWAlwaysReport** value entry to **1**.

- Disable error reporting

  Located in the General Reporting folder. Enabling this policy disables application error reporting entirely. If you choose **Disabled** or **Not Configured**, then users might be prompted to send error reports. This policy is equivalent to setting the **DWReportee** value entry to **1**.

- Do not upload user documents

  Located in the General Reporting folder. Enabling this policy excludes documents and other files from error reports. If you choose **Disabled** or **Not Configured**, then users might be prompted to include documents or other files in error reports. This policy is equivalent to setting the **DWNoFileCollection** value entry to **1**.

- Bypass queue and send all reports

  Located in the Queued Reporting folder. Enabling this policy disables error report queuing and ensures that all error reports are sent at the time the error occurs. If you choose **Disabled** or **Not Configured**, error reports might be queued. This policy is equivalent to setting the **DWBypassQueue** value entry to **1**.

- Send all queued reports silently

  Located in the Queued Reporting folder. Enabling this policy sends all queued error reports without prompting the user. If you also set the **Local error reporting file path** policy, reports are sent to a local file server. This policy is equivalent to setting the **DWAllQueuesHeadless** value entry to **1**.

> **Tip**   In Windows XP or later, you can view additional information about these and other error reporting policies by opening the policy and then clicking the **Explain** tab.

For more information about using the Group Policy snap-in to set Group Policy, see "Managing Users' Configurations by Policy" in Chapter 18, "Updating Users' Office 2003 Configurations."

Customer Experience Improvement Program

A new feature of Microsoft Office 2003 is the Customer Experience Improvement Program. Microsoft uses this optional method to identify the usefulness of product features installed on a user's computer by collecting data at specified checkpoints (determined by Microsoft and driven by received data). All data collected by the Customer Experience Improvement Program reporting process is anonymously gathered and reported to Microsoft.

This program helps determine which Office 2003 features are used—how often, how much, and by what percentage compared with other Office applications installed on the user's computer. The resulting data helps Microsoft prioritize bug fixes by feature and product and determine whether a feature is used enough to be included in future releases of a product.

> **Note**   By default, the Customer Experience Improvement Program prompts users to participate after two days of using any Office application. Administrators can disable the prompt by setting a policy. If the policy is not enabled, users can still choose not to participate when prompted.

Some features of Office are dependent on the data collection features of the Customer Experience Improvement Program. For example, users who choose to participate automatically receive updates of the new extended error messages. These error messages provide explanatory text about errors users encounter, as well as helpful links to further information on the Web that might suggest how to correct or avoid the error. Without participating in the Customer Experience Improvement Program, users do not receive these updates.

The Customer Experience Improvement Program (**Help | Customer Feedback Options**) is included with Office 2003 and is turned off by default. The following Windows registry setting controls whether it is enabled:

Subkey: HKEY_CURRENT_USER\Software\Microsoft\Office\Common

Value entry: **QMEnable**

Value type: **DWORD**

Possible value data settings: **[0 | 1]**

Setting the **QMEnable** data value to **1** enables the program; setting it to **0** disables it. This setting is available as a policy in the Office 2003.adm policy template under **Office 2003 | Help | Privacy Settings | Enable Customer Experience Improvement Program**.

Even though the Customer Experience Improvement Program may be disabled in the registry, this setting only turns off the reporting feature; the program still records data to a log file. If a crash occurs and a user decides to allow the Microsoft Application Error Reporting process to submit a crash report to Microsoft, the last data collected by the Customer Experience Improvement Program is submitted as part of the report to help isolate where the problem occurred.

> **Note**   A user who chooses to participate in the Customer Experience Improvement Program is not prompted before the data is sent to a Microsoft data collection server; the data is automatically submitted when a sufficient quantity of data is collected.

Part 6

Collaboration Resources

Chapter 20

Information Rights Management

Information Rights Management (IRM) is a feature of Microsoft® Office 2003 Editions designed to enhance collaboration methods and restrict unauthorized access to the content of Microsoft Office Word 2003, Microsoft Office Excel 2003, Microsoft Office PowerPoint® 2003, and Microsoft Office Outlook® 2003 files. IRM uses encryption, permissions, licenses, Microsoft Active Directory® directory service, license revocation, and Microsoft Windows Rights Management Services for Microsoft Windows Server™ 2003 or Passport to help provide a rights-managed method of content collaboration among a well-defined and carefully managed group of individuals.

Overview of Information Rights Management

Information Rights Management (IRM) technology in Microsoft Office 2003 helps to give organizations and information workers greater control of their sensitive information. IRM is a persistent file-level technology from Microsoft that allows the user to specify permission for who can access and use documents or e-mail messages, and it helps to prevent sensitive information from being printed, forwarded, or copied by unauthorized individuals. Once permission for a document or message has been restricted with this technology, the usage restrictions travel with the document or e-mail message as part of the contents of the file.

Note   The ability to create content or e-mail messages with restricted permission using Information Rights Management is available only with the Microsoft Office Professional Edition 2003 version of the following applications—Microsoft Office Word 2003, Microsoft Office Excel 2003, Microsoft Office PowerPoint® 2003, and Microsoft Office Outlook 2003. IRM is also available in the stand-alone versions of those applications.

IRM support in Office 2003 helps corporations and knowledge workers address two fundamental needs:

- Restricted permission for sensitive information

    Most corporations today rely on firewalls, logon security-related measures, and other network technologies in an effort to help protect their sensitive intellectual property. The fundamental limitation of these technologies is that, once legitimate users have access to the information, they can share it with unauthorized people, potentially breaching security policies. IRM helps prevent the sensitive information itself from unauthorized access and reuse.

- Information privacy, control, and integrity

    Information workers often deal with confidential or sensitive information, relying on the discretion of others to keep sensitive materials in-house. IRM eliminates any temptation to forward, copy, or print confidential information by helping to disable those functions in documents and messages with restricted permission.

For information technology (IT) managers, IRM helps enable the enforcement of existing corporate policies regarding document confidentiality, workflow, and e-mail retention. For CEOs and security officers, it significantly reduces today's risk of having key company information in the hands of the wrong people, whether by accident, thoughtlessness, or through malicious intent.

When enabled by the organization by using Microsoft Windows Rights Management Services (RMS) for Windows Server 2003, users of Office 2003 can easily take advantage of this technology. A simple user interface based on customizable "permission policies" (available from the **File** menu) makes IRM convenient and approachable. Integration with Active Directory directory service provides a level of convenience not seen on today's document-specific passwords. Finally, the Rights Management Add-in for Microsoft Internet Explorer allows the users of Microsoft Windows®—if they have the proper permission—to read e-mail messages and some documents with restricted permission whether or not they have Office 2003.

Organizational policy

Using IRM technology, Office 2003 allows companies to create "permission policies" that appear in Office applications. For example, a company might define a policy called "Company Confidential," which specifies that documents or e-mail messages using that policy can be opened by users inside the company domain only. There is no limit to the number of policies that can be created.

Rights Management Add-in for Internet Explorer

Since permissions are granted at the application level, Office documents with restricted permission can only be opened by Office 2003 or later. However, the Rights Management Add-in for Internet Explorer allows users without Office 2003 to read content with restricted permission.

Additional server requirements for IRM

Windows Server 2003 with Windows Rights Management Services is required to enable IRM with Office 2003. This service enables users to share documents and messages with restricted permission using Microsoft .NET Passport as the authentication mechanism, as opposed to Active Directory.

Passport

If an RMS server is not in place on the domain, but use of the IRM feature is required, access to the Internet from each client workstation must be provided to allow users access to the Microsoft Passport servers. Passport accounts can be used when assigning permissions to the various users who will need access to the contents of the file. However, this does not allow for groups of users to gain access to a file. Each user must be specifically granted permission to the file when using Passport accounts.

Usage and enforcement of permissions

IRM uses various levels of permissions to restrict access to the content of a file.

The following rights are enforced by the Office applications. These rights are grouped into a list of custom settings in the Office applications and three levels of permission.

Office bases all of its permission enforcement on these rights defined in the Microsoft Windows Rights Management Services for Windows Server 2003.

- **Full Control**   Gives the user every right listed below, and the right to make changes to the permissions associated with the content. Expiration does not apply to users with Full Control.

- **View**   Allows the user to open IRM content. This maps to the "Read" Access in the Office user interface.

- **Edit**   Allows the user to edit the IRM content.

- **Save**   Allows the user to save the file.

- **Extract**   Allows the user to make a copy of any portion of the file and paste it into the work area of another application.

- **Export**   Allows the user to save the content in another location or format that may or may not support IRM.

- **Print**   Allows the user to print the contents of the file.

- **Allow Macros**   Allows the user to run macros against the contents of the file.

- **Forward**   Allows e-mail recipients to forward an IRM e-mail message.

- **Reply**   Allows e-mail recipients to reply to an IRM e-mail message.

- **Reply All**   Allows e-mail recipients to reply to all users on the To: and CC: lines of an IRM e-mail message.

- **View Rights**   Allows users permission to view the rights associated with the file. Office ignores this right.

A user can specify one of several predefined groups of rights when creating IRM content:

- **Read**   User with Read permission has only the View right.

- **Do Not Forward**   In Outlook, the author of an IRM e-mail message can apply Do Not Forward permission to the users in the To:, Cc:, and Bcc: lines.
  This permission includes the View, Reply, and Reply All rights.

- **Change**   Users with Change permission have View, Edit, Extract, Export, and Save rights.

Additional permissions in Office documents

In addition to the permission groups mentioned previously, specific rights can be specified in the advanced user interface of Word, Excel, and PowerPoint. Outlook always enables messages to be viewed by a browser that supports Rights Management.

The following options are available on the **Permission** dialog for Word, Excel, and PowerPoint:

- **This document expires on**   This option allows the author to specify a date after which the IRM content becomes unreadable for everyone but users with Full Control.

- **View content in trusted browsers**   This option allows the author to specify whether users without Office 2003 can view the content in the Rights Management Add-in for Internet Explorer.

- **Require a connection to verify a user's permission**   This option gives the author the ability to force users to connect to the Windows Rights Management server every time content is opened. This is useful if permissions to a shared document change over time and the author wants to make sure every user is verified prior to opening the document.

Customizing Information Rights Management and Installing Client Software

Information Rights Management (IRM) is a new feature in Microsoft Office 2003 for managing access to content in files or messages created within Office.

Installing the Rights Management client software

Even though IRM is an integral part of the Microsoft Office System, the necessary client software to interact with the RMS server or the Passport service on the Internet requires separate installation and configuration.

For more information about the RM Update for Windows clients, see the Windows Rights Management documentation on the Windows Server 2003 Web site at *http://www.microsoft.com/windowsserver2003/rm*.

Permission policies

For corporations, administrators can create a custom permission policy that configures various people and groups with customized IRM permissions. In some cases, this can greatly simplify the process of setting permissions, because a single custom permission policy can replace the user's need to select multiple permission settings.

For instructions on how to create, edit, and post custom rights policy templates, see the Windows Rights Management documentation on the Microsoft Windows Server 2003 Web site at *http://www.microsoft.com/windowsserver2003/rm*.

How to deploy permission policies

When the permission policies are ready, they should be posted to a server share where all users can have access to them or they should be copied to a local folder on the user's computer. The IRM policy settings available in the Office11.adm template can then be used to point to the location where these permission policies are stored (either locally or on an available server share). Once the permission policies are available and the necessary Group Policy settings are implemented and propagated to users, the IRM **Permissions** menu option displays the available custom permission policies in a submenu.

For more information about how to use Group Policy with Office applications, see "How Policies Work" in Chapter 26, "Using Security-related Policies."

Using Group Policy to access custom permission policies

It is possible to enable and distribute the configured policies provided in the **Manage Restricted Permissions** section of the Office11.adm policy template. When the IRM policy **Specify Permission Policy Path** is implemented and propagated through Active Directory directory service, IRM will automatically locate any available templates stored in the location specified. The IRM-enabled Office applications will then display the custom permission policies.

These are the core registry entries associated with IRM. Most of these have parallel policy entries.

The following two registry entries are under HKLM\Software\Microsoft\Office\11.0\Common\DRM:

Value name:	**CorpLicenseServer**
Value type:	**REG_SZ**
Value data:	\<URL\>

IRM registry entries

This setting allows the administrator to override the location of the Windows Rights Management server specified in Active Directory.

Value name:	**CorpCertificationServer**
Value type:	**REG_SZ**
Value data:	\<URL\>

This setting allows the administrator to override the location of the Windows Rights Management server specified in Active Directory for certification.

The remaining registry entries are under HKCU\Software\Microsoft\Office\11.0 \Common\DRM:

Value name: **Disable**

Value type: **DWORD**

Value data: **[0 | 1]**

If this key is set to **1**, the Rights Management–related options within the user interface of all Office applications are disabled. This is identical to the **Disable Information Rights Management User Interface** policy.

Value name: **DisablePassportCertification**

Value type: **DWORD**

Value data: **[0 | 1]**

If this key is set to **1**, users cannot open content created by a Passport-authenticated account. This is identical to the **Disable Microsoft Passport service for content with restricted permissions** policy.

Value name: **IncludeHTML**

Value type: **DWORD**

Value data: **[0 | 1]**

If this key is set to **1**, users without Office 2003 can view the content in the Rights Management Add-in for Internet Explorer. This is identical to the **Allow users with earlier versions of Office to read with browsers** policy.

Value name: **RequestPermissionURL**

Value type: **REG_SZ**

Value data: URL or e-mail address

This setting allows the administrator to specify a location where a user can obtain more information about getting access to IRM content. It can be either a URL or an e-mail address. This is identical to the **Additional permissions request URL** policy.

Value name: **RequireConnection**

Value type: **DWORD**

Value data: **[0 | 1]**

If this key is set to **1**, any users attempting to open an Office document having IRM permissions enabled will be forced to connect to the Internet or local area network to have their license confirmed by either Passport or RMS. This is identical to the **Always require users to connect to verify permission** policy.

Value name:	**AutoExpandDLsEnable**
Value type:	**DWORD**
Value data:	**[0	1]**

If this key is set to **1**, any user who attempts to apply permissions to a file will encounter different behavior when they select a group name in the **Permissions** dialog box. When a group is selected, the dialog box automatically expands to display all the members of the group. This is identical to the **Always expand groups in Office when restricting permission for documents** policy.

Value name:	**AdminTemplatePath**
Value type:	**REG_SZ**
Value data:	<UNC or aliased drive>

If this key is present, Office applications using IRM scans the path provided in this registry entry to see if any permission policy templates exist. If they are there, the title for each is displayed in the **Permission** dialog box (**File** menu). This is identical to the **Specify Permission Policy Path** policy.

Resources and related information

More up-to-date information regarding Information Rights Management will be available from the Office 2003 Resource Kit Web site at *http://www.microsoft.com/office/ork/2003*.

Chapter 21

SharePoint Products and Technologies

Microsoft® Windows® SharePoint™ Services 2.0 and Microsoft Office SharePoint Portal Server 2003 are designed to help you share information both within your organization and over the Internet. When used with Microsoft Office, Microsoft SharePoint Products and Technologies can provide such services as a central repository for documents, an interactive work environment for collaboration, and an architecture that allows you to separate the Web-hosting processes from the site data–retrieval processes.

SharePoint Products and Technologies have been developed to meet the needs of different sizes of teams and organizations:

- Windows SharePoint Services is focused on the needs of small or ad hoc workgroups that need an informal means to collaborate and share status on a common group of documents.

- Office SharePoint Portal Server is designed for large workgroups with structured processes that need greater management control over their information. Features include formal publishing processes, as well as the ability to search for and aggregate content from multiple data stores and file formats.

The subjects in this chapter summarize the new features in Windows SharePoint Services and SharePoint Portal Server 2003.

What's New in Windows SharePoint Services

Microsoft Windows SharePoint Services helps users work together and share information. SharePoint sites provide a central repository for documents, information, and ideas, and allow users to work interactively with these items and with each other.

Windows SharePoint Services is an update and revision to SharePoint Team Services v1.0 from Microsoft, and offers many improvements over SharePoint Team Services v1.0.

What's new for administrators of Windows SharePoint Services

The architecture for Windows SharePoint Services has been revised from that of SharePoint Team Services v1.0. The new architecture allows you to separate the Web hosting processes from the site data retrieval processes. All documents, metadata, and site data are stored in a Microsoft SQL Server or Microsoft SQL Server Desktop Engine 2000 (MSDE) database, rather than split between a database and the Web server metadata. This improves reliability by ensuring complete transactional integrity of the data, and enables larger scale scenarios.

You can have multiple, stateless front-end Web servers, and one or more back-end database servers, so you can create a load-balanced server farm for large organizations or Internet service providers (ISPs). Of course, Windows SharePoint Services can still be installed quickly to a single server if your organization's needs are simpler.

The following new features have been added for administrators of Windows SharePoint Services:

- **Easy installation for small deployments**   If you want to set up Windows SharePoint Services on a single server with MSDE, you can run Setup with the default settings and have a working site within minutes.

- **Support for server farm deployments**   With Windows SharePoint Services, you can set up a server farm configuration, which includes multiple front-end Web servers and multiple back-end databases.

- **Site migration**   SharePoint Team Services v1.0 sites can be migrated to Windows SharePoint Services by using the command-line migration tool (Smigrate.exe).

- **Site level backup and restore**   Each site in a server farm can be individually backed up and restored. This feature can be used for archiving inactive sites prior to their deletion.

- **Support for multiple language sites**   Multiple language sites can be hosted on a single server or server farm running Windows SharePoint Services. Each site can also have its own regional settings, such as time zone.

- **Site quotas and notifications**   Server administrators can set quotas for site storage size and generate automatic notifications for the site owner when a site reaches its size limit.

For more information about any of these features, or for information about installing and managing Windows SharePoint Services, see the *Administrator's Guide for Windows SharePoint Services* on the Window SharePoint Services Web site at *http://www.microsoft.com/sharepoint/assistance*.

Using Office 2003 and Windows SharePoint Services together

When you use both Microsoft Office 2003 and Windows SharePoint Services in your organization, your users can take advantage of several Office 2003 features that interact with Windows SharePoint Services. For example, when using Office 2003 and Windows SharePoint Services together, users get:

- **Integrated file open and save**   Users of Microsoft Office Excel 2003, Microsoft Office Word 2003, Microsoft Office PowerPoint® 2003, Microsoft Office InfoPath™ 2003, Microsoft Office FrontPage® 2003, and Microsoft Office Outlook® 2003 can open files from and save files directly to SharePoint sites from within the client application.

- **Document check-in and check-out from the client application**   Users can check out or check in a file from within Word, Excel, PowerPoint, and FrontPage. Checking a file out locks the file while it is being edited, thus preventing others from overwriting or editing it inadvertently.

- **Automatic metadata promotion**   File properties and metadata from Excel, Word, PowerPoint, and InfoPath documents are automatically copied and updated in SharePoint document libraries.

- **Synchronized Events and Contacts lists**   With Outlook 2003, users can view Events and Contacts lists on a SharePoint site or in Outlook, and items hosted on a Windows SharePoint Services site can be dragged onto a user's personal calendar in Outlook.

- **Datasheet viewing and editing**   With Office 2003 installed on the user's computer, list views are enhanced with the **Edit in Datasheet** option. This option offers a rich client-side editor for lists, which allows fast spreadsheet-style editing with add row, copy and paste, and "fill-down" as well as richer view filtering and sorting options.

- **List data editing with Excel and Microsoft Office Access 2003**   Users can edit, analyze, and synchronize data with SharePoint lists from within Excel and Access.

- **Picture editing**   Users can view and edit pictures in a SharePoint picture library by using a new image-editing tool from Office 2003.

- **Shared Attachments**   Users can send documents that are hosted in a SharePoint site as attachments. Local copies of Shared Attachments can be updated with the updated copy on the SharePoint site.

- **Quick access to tasks with the Windows SharePoint Services Task Pane** A task pane in Excel, Word, and PowerPoint shows information about the status of documents stored in SharePoint document libraries. The task pane displays data from the SharePoint site, such as presence of team members, document status and properties, related links, related documents, and tasks.

- **Quick collaboration with Document Workspaces** Users can use Word 2003 to create a Document Workspace on a Windows SharePoint Services server for collaboration on a document. Document Workspaces can also be created from the browser from within a SharePoint document library.

- **Enhanced coordination with Meeting Workspaces** Users can create Meeting Workspaces when they create a meeting invitation in Outlook. Meeting Workspaces provide a place for managing meetings and their collateral information such as attendees, agendas, documents, decisions, and action items. Attendee tracking is propagated to the SharePoint site automatically. Meeting Workspaces can also be created from SharePoint event lists.

- **Solution package creation in FrontPage 2003** Sites can be packaged for deployment in every location in an organization by using FrontPage 2003 solution packages. Web log, News and Reviews, and Issue tracking solution packages are available out of the box.

- **Web Parts and Web Part previewing in FrontPage 2003** Users can browse and search Web Part galleries to locate Web Parts for use in a Web Part Page. They can preview Web Parts in FrontPage 2003 before publishing them, and they can build new user interfaces by creating Web Part connections between Web Parts on the same page and across pages by using FrontPage 2003.

- **Integration with Microsoft Business Solutions** Users with Office 2003 can take advantage of the templates for Great Plains and Web Parts for data (such as DataCalc or Web Clipper). These are available as the Microsoft Office Web Parts and Components package to enhance Windows SharePoint Services.

- **Integration between InfoPath 2003 and SharePoint form libraries** Users with InfoPath 2003 can publish a solution package into a SharePoint form library. Key properties from the InfoPath documents are promoted into the form library so that they can be sorted and filtered, enabling the creation of custom views and editing through a SharePoint list.

- **Document editing in InfoPath 2003** Users can start InfoPath 2003 from a SharePoint form library to autoaggregate a number of InfoPath files in that library and create a single report. For example, a user could create a rollup status report that combines the information from many individual status reports.

For more information about any of these features, see the Help system for Office 2003.

What's New in Office SharePoint Portal Server 2003

Microsoft Office SharePoint Portal Server 2003, using the combined collaboration features of SharePoint Products and Technologies, facilitates easy, connected collaboration across an enterprise organization. SharePoint Portal Server enables people to work together on documents, projects, and tasks; helps to provide secure access to relevant information across multiple systems; and presents specific applications and customized content based on a user's functional group and organizational role.

SharePoint Portal Server 2003 is an update to Microsoft SharePoint Portal Server 2001 and offers a number of improvements, several of which are described in the following sections.

What's new for administrators of SharePoint Portal Server

Microsoft Office SharePoint Portal Server 2003 provides an architecture that addresses the most demanding performance needs. By using the latest technologies, SharePoint Portal Server 2003 provides a centralized, unified interface for enterprise users and highly flexible deployment options.

The following new features have been included to help administrators.

Architecture

- **Scalable, distributed architecture** SharePoint Portal Server 2003 scales from a single server to a server farm with multiple front-end Web servers and back-end database servers. Front-end Web servers are stateless, so the load can be balanced across them to support the largest of organizations. You can deploy up to a hundred portal sites per server farm when using a shared services topology.

- **Shared services** Deliver shared services to multiple portal sites from a centrally managed and configured server farm. Shared services can include indexing and search, user profiles, audiences, alerts, and personal sites.

- **Communication with external partners by using an extranet** If you work with external partners, or if you have users who need to access data from outside of your organization's firewall, you can use SharePoint Portal Server 2003 in an intranet/extranet environment. In this configuration, internal and external users can view and interact with the same content and data. You can also employ the antivirus protection and blocked file extension features to help protect your server integrity.

International

- **Support for multiple language sites** Multiple language sites can be hosted on a single server or server farm running SharePoint Portal Server 2003. Note that site language is independent from server language.

- **Regional settings for each site** Each site can have its own regional settings, such as time zone.

- **New word breakers** Word breakers for Czech, Finnish, Hungarian, and Portuguese are available, as well as the original set of SharePoint Portal Server 2001 word breakers for English, French, Spanish, Japanese, Thai, Korean, Chinese Traditional, and Chinese Simplified.

Management

- **Alerts** The portal site now automatically identifies and optimizes alerts that have the potential for generating large numbers of results; it will deactivate any alert that generates an excessive number of results. Administrators can deactivate or delete any user's alerts and alert results. Misdirected e-mail messages can be prevented by locking e-mail address fields to use only user profile data. You can also customize the format of the alert results e-mail messages by using an .xsl file.

- **Single sign-on** Single sign-on allows you to store and map account credentials so that users don't have to sign on again when portal-based applications retrieve information from enterprise applications.

- **Security-enhanced integration of enterprise applications** Tight integration with Microsoft BizTalk® Server 2002 helps to enable rich and secure enterprise application integration using single sign-on. Connectors from Actional enable integration with PeopleSoft, SAP, and Siebel.

- **Full-text searching** The portal site delivers a scalable, high-performance indexing and query handling infrastructure. By using a multiserver topology, you can manage your resources by propagating content indexes from the index management server to multiple dedicated search servers. HTTPS indexing enables crawling of security-enhanced Web sites over Secure Sockets Layer (SSL). In addition, protocol handlers for Microsoft Windows SharePoint Services 2.0 sites enable the portal site to crawl information in site pages, document libraries, lists, and list items. IFilters now provide the ability to full-text search files created by Microsoft Publisher and Microsoft Visio® in addition to the existing capability to search files in Microsoft Word, Microsoft Excel, Microsoft PowerPoint, MIME, XML, and HTML formats.

- **Audiences** Audiences allow organizations to target content—such as Web Parts, news, lists, and list items—to one or more specific audiences based on job role or task. You can leverage your investment in Microsoft Active Directory® directory service to easily create audiences from existing distribution lists and security groups.

- **Backup and restore** Improved backup and restore helps to enable flexible site recovery. Each site in a server farm can be individually backed up and restored. This feature can also be used for archiving inactive sites prior to their deletion.

■ **User profiles** Easily create user profiles by importing properties and user data from Active Directory. User profiles make it easy to find people and enable content managers to target information by using audiences. Add properties to the flexible user profile for use by integrated applications or to enable portal users to find people more easily.

■ **Inactive site management** Site owners are periodically asked to confirm that the sites are in use or delete them. If multiple notices are sent to the site owner without any response, the administrator can specify that the site be automatically deleted.

Security

■ **Works with standard Windows authentication and security methods** Use SharePoint Portal Server 2003 with any Microsoft Internet Information Services 6.0 authentication method, connect to the database by using Windows authentication or SQL Server authentication, and integrate SharePoint Portal Server 2003 with Active Directory.

■ **SharePoint administrators group** Allow members of a domain group to perform central administration tasks without granting them administrator rights to the local server computer.

■ **Manage users from SharePoint Central Administration** Use the SharePoint Central Administration pages to add or delete users on all sites and assign site owners.

■ **Domain group support** Use domain groups to help control access to your site.

■ **Blocked file extensions** Server administrators can block the upload of specific file types (for example, MP3 or EXE files).

For a complete list of new administrator features, and information about using these features, see the Administrator's guide for SharePoint Portal Server 2003 on the Assistance Center for Microsoft SharePoint Products and Technologies Web site at *http://www.microsoft.com/sharepoint/assistance*.

Using Office 2003 and Office SharePoint Portal Server 2003 together

When you use both Office 2003 and SharePoint Portal Server in your organization, your users can take advantage of several Office 2003 features that interact with SharePoint Portal Server. For example, when using Office 2003 and SharePoint Portal Server together, users get:

■ **Integrated file open and save** Users of Microsoft Office Excel 2003, Microsoft Office Word 2003, Microsoft Office PowerPoint 2003, Microsoft Office InfoPath 2003, Microsoft Office FrontPage 2003, and Microsoft Office

Outlook 2003 can open files from and save files directly to SharePoint sites from within the client application.

- **Document check-in and check-out from the client application**   Users can check out or check in a file from within Word, Excel, PowerPoint, and FrontPage. Checking a file out locks the file while it is being edited, thus preventing others from overwriting or editing it inadvertently.

- **Synchronized Events and Contacts lists**   With Outlook 2003, users can view Events and Contacts lists on a SharePoint site or in Outlook, and items can be dragged onto a user's personal calendar in Outlook.

- **Datasheet viewing and editing**   With Office 2003 installed on the user's computer, list views are enhanced with the **Edit in Datasheet** option. This option offers a rich client-side editor for lists, which allows fast spreadsheet-style editing with add row, copy and paste, and "fill-down" as well as richer view filtering and sorting options.

- **List data editing with Excel and Access**   Users can edit, analyze, and synchronize data with SharePoint lists from within Excel and Access.

- **Picture editing**   Users can view and edit pictures in a picture library by using a new image-editing tool from Office 2003.

- **Shared attachments**   Users can send documents that are hosted in a SharePoint site as attachments. Local copies of shared attachments can be updated with the updated copy on the SharePoint site.

For more information about any of these features, see the Help system for Office 2003.

What's new for site users of SharePoint Portal Server

Microsoft Office SharePoint Portal Server 2003 creates a portal site that remembers who you are and what information you care about and work with. Based on Web Part Page technology, SharePoint Portal Server helps to deliver customization and personalization that is flexible, secure, and reliable. SharePoint Portal Server provides a rich set of features focused on ensuring that portal site users have easy access to relevant information from a variety of entry points.

The following are a just few of the new features for users of SharePoint Portal Server 2003:

- **Areas**   You can organize information on the portal site by using areas. If you find a useful link missing from an area, add a link and see if the content manager approves it. You can add an item to more than one area on the portal site.

- **News**   Microsoft Office SharePoint Portal Server 2003 enables you to highlight information, such as announcements and other key company information, by adding items to the News area. A news item can be either text-based content or a link to an existing news item, such as a press release or an article on a news service.

- **Personal sites**   My Site is a personal SharePoint site that provides personalized and customized information for you. In addition, My Site provides quick access to things you need to do your work, such as links to documents, people, or Web sites as well as alerts to track changes to content within the portal and your organization. From My Site, you can also update your user profile and share links with other portal users.

- **User profiles**   Easily find information about people, their documents, and their shared links.

- **Alerts**   Get alert results in e-mail messages immediately or in daily or weekly summaries for portal site content. You can now add alerts for people, lists, list items, and the Site Directory in addition to news, areas, topics, search queries, documents, and backward-compatible document libraries. Alert results are shown in an easy-to-read HTML format and now identify whether the alert result is sent because content changed or was added. You can manage all of your alerts from the My Alerts page.

- **Lists and views**   From Microsoft Windows SharePoint Services 2.0, SharePoint Portal Server adds both predesigned and custom lists to all SharePoint sites. For example, you can create a picture library to share a collection of digital pictures or create an issue-tracking list to maintain a history on a specific issue. You can also use calendar views for any SharePoint list that has a date and time column. In addition, you can add attachments to list items, including HTML pages, documents, and images.

- **Simple site creation and page customization**   By using Self-Service Site Creation, you can create SharePoint sites, such as team sites or Meeting Workspace sites, on demand without involving the information technology (IT) department. In addition, you can customize a page by changing or adding Web Parts. Each list and library on a site is a Web Part, enabling easy customization and personalization using the browser.

- **Search**   Faster results and improved relevancy ranking enable you to find the information you need easily. Search results now include people, picture libraries, list items, and user profiles. If you search for an image, you'll see a thumbnail view of the image; if you search for a person, you will see her personal profile. You can also group search results in different ways, such as by author, site, date, or area. From the search results page, you now can save a useful search to the My Links Web Part on your personal site.

- **Site Directory**   The Site Directory provides a central location from which to view and access all Web sites associated with a specific portal site. You can also create sites based on Microsoft Windows SharePoint Services 2.0 or add links to existing sites. In addition, adding a site to the Site Directory is a quick and easy way to include content in search results.

What's new for content managers of SharePoint Portal Server

SharePoint Portal Server 2003 helps to enable you to easily share information, use best practices, and work together with others on documents, projects, and other efforts. SharePoint Portal Server offers a number of features that make it easy to find, organize, and work together on documents. Content managers have the option to approve content before it is displayed on the portal site, establish expiration dates for temporary content, and control who has access to the content they manage.

The following are a just few of the new features for content managers:

- **Lists and views** From Microsoft Windows SharePoint Services 2.0, SharePoint Portal Server adds predesigned and custom lists to all SharePoint sites. List managers can approve or reject items that are submitted to the list and add comments. List managers can also apply permissions to a list, allowing only specific users to make changes to the list.

- **Support for list and site templates** Users can save SharePoint lists as templates, and reuse them or distribute them to other sites. Administrators and Web designers can save sites as templates to capture best practices or to define a consistent look and feel.

- **Areas** The portal site is a hierarchy of rich subsites that enable content managers to add lists, images, and documents to one or more areas. Content managers can approve or reject items that are submitted to the area. In addition, security can be managed at the area level, allowing only specific users to make contributions or changes to the area.

- **Portal site map** Manage portal areas and topics using drag-and-drop functionality in a browser. Create, move, rename, and delete categories by using the portal site map.

- **Topic Assistant** The portal site suggests items to list under an area that the content manager can approve or reject. As areas are added to the portal site, and items are added to areas, the Topic Assistant continues to learn and suggest items for each area.

- **Site Directory** To organize and display the sites in meaningful ways, you can create views that sort, filter, and group the sites. The Site Directory also offers Web Parts for "Newest sites," "Sites I added," and "Spotlight Sites." The Site Directory can be configured to automatically approve sites for searching or to require approval for each site.

- **News** To make managing news items easier, you can specify start and end dates for content display and automatically hide expired news items. As a content manager, you can vary the display of news items—from headlines to summaries to expanded views—by modifying the properties of the Web Part.

Chapter 22

Accessing Information on the Web

Microsoft® Office enables users to access Web services as they work and to share information with other users by storing information on the Web. Several features in Office provide ways to store information to an Internet or intranet location, whether that information consists of Office documents, Microsoft Office Internet Free/Busy Service information, or published HTML documents. Users can even back up their Office settings to a World Wide Web location and retrieve those settings from wherever the users happen to be. As an Office administrator, you can determine the extent to which your users can take advantage of Web access or other Web-related features.

Managing Web Access from Office Applications

While the Web access and connectivity features built into Microsoft Office 2003 offer a wealth of services, some organizations may need to limit the access of Office applications to the Web. An organization's policies may restrict Web access for certain workgroups, for example, or confidential projects may drive a strict security policy.

At the highest level, Web access can be managed through the proxy servers that control the Web gateway to your organization. Within Office 2003, however, you can also help to control the Web access capabilities of individual applications or features.

The following list provides a survey of many of the features you can configure to enable or take advantage of Web access in Office 2003 applications. The settings are listed as they appear in the Custom Installation Wizard and Custom Maintenance Wizard. Although the list does not represent a comprehensive view of Web connectivity or security, it does offer a guide to the range of control you can enforce in your installations.

Settings on the Change Office User Settings page

The largest collection of Web access settings is coordinated through the **Microsoft Office 2003 (user)** node of the **Change Office User Settings** page of the Custom Installation Wizard or the Custom Maintenance Wizard. Individual applications may also provide settings that can affect Web interaction with the product.

Microsoft Office Access 2003

No explicit Web access control is offered through this node.

Microsoft Office Excel 2003

- **Tools | Options**
  Web Options
  General
  Save any additional data necessary to maintain formulas
  Load pictures from Web pages not created in Excel

- **Tools | Macro**
  Security
  Trust access to Visual Basic® Project

- **Tools | Autocorrect Options**
  Internet and network paths as hyperlinks

Microsoft Office FrontPage® 2003

No explicit Web access control is offered through this node.

Microsoft Office Outlook® 2003

- **Tools | Options**
  Preferences
  Calendar Options
  Free/Busy Options
  Disable the Microsoft Office Internet Free/Busy Service
  Options
  Internet Free/Busy Options
  Mail Format
  Internet Formatting
  HTML Options
  Security
  HTML Mail External Content Settings
  Block download of content from unsafe zones
  Block all external content
  Block Trusted Zones
  Block Internet
  Block Intranet

- **Tools | Macro**
  Security
  Outlook: Trust all installed add-ins and templates

- **Tools | E-Mail Accounts**
  Exchange over the Internet
  Enable Exchange Over Internet User Interface

- **Outlook Today Settings**
  URL for custom Outlook Today

The Security node also provides a number of settings related to cryptography and other security options. For detailed information about configuring Microsoft Office Outlook 2003 security, see Chapter 12, "Customizing Outlook 2003 to Help Prevent Viruses."

Microsoft Office PowerPoint® 2003

- **Slide Show | Online Broadcast | Set Up and Schedule**
  Broadcast Settings
  Other Broadcast Settings
  Settings related to Web access for chat services, media downloads, and event URL listing
  Server Options
  Other NetShow Settings
  Settings related to admin URL's and the location of audio/video ASD files

Microsoft Office Word 2003

- **Tools | Options**
  General
  E-mail Options
  Filter HTML before sending
  Save smart tags in e-mail
  Spelling & Grammar
  Ignore Internet and file addresses

Microsoft Office 2003 (machine)

- **Security Settings**
  While no explicit Web access control is offered through this node, the section does provide a collected view of security settings available through the individual application settings. Examples include macro security level, trust access to Microsoft Visual Basic development system projects, and trust relationships with installed add-ins and templates.

- **Help | Check for Updates**
  Check for Updates

Microsoft Office 2003 (user)

- **Tools | AutoCorrect Options (Excel, PowerPoint, and Access)**
  Smart Tags
  More Smart Tags URL
  Check for new actions URL
  Recognize smart tags in Word
  Recognize smart tags in Excel

- **Tools | Options | General | Web Options**
  Files
  Check if Office is the default editor for Web pages created in Office
  Browsers
  Rely on VML for displaying graphics in browsers
  Allow PNG as an output format
  Target Monitor
  Encoding
  Default or specific encoding

- **Tools | Options | General | Service Options**
  Completely disable Template Taskpane

- **Online Content**
  Online content options
  Never show online content or entry points
  Use only offline content whenever available
  Use online content whenever available

- **Help**
    Microsoft Office Online
    Help | Privacy Settings
    Enable Customer Experience Improvement Program

- **Security Settings**
    Specify Trusted Alert Sources
    Check to enable all sites as safe subscription sources
    Check to enable all intranet sites as safe subscription sources
    Check for trusted zone sites to be safe for subscription sources

- **Collaboration Settings**
    Default message text for a review request
    Contains settings for enabling Web discussions
    Default message text for a reply
    Contains settings for enabling Web discussions

- **Web Archives**
    Allow Web Archives to be saved in HTML encoding
    Web Archive encoding
    Save new Web pages as Web archives
    Default format for "Publish"
    PowerPoint: Web page format compatibility

- **Smart Documents (Word, Excel)**
    Disable Smart Document's use of manifests
    Completely disable the Smart Documents feature in Word and Excel

- **Services**
    Disable Fax over Internet feature

- **Instant Messaging Integration**
    A collection of settings related to the configuration of and user information contained in instant messages

- **Manage Restricted Permissions**
    Disable Information Rights Management User Interface
    Additional permissions request URL
    Make documents with restricted documents viewable in trusted browsers
    Always require users to connect to verify permission
    Disable Microsoft Passport service for content with restricted permission

- **Miscellaneous**
    Prevent access to Web-based file storage
    Disable hyperlinks to web templates in File | New and task panes
    Do not upload media files
    Do not display paths in alerts
    Web Folders: Managing pairs of Web pages and folders
    Disable Web view in the Office file dialogs
    Block updates from the Office Update Site from applying

Microsoft Clip Organizer

No explicit Web access control is offered through this node.

Microsoft Office InfoPath™ 2003

- **Security**
    Disable opening of solutions from the Internet security zone
    Disable installed solutions full access to machine

Microsoft Office Publisher 2003

- **Miscellaneous**
    Disable Tools | Tools on the Web
    Prevent web pages displayed in Publisher from accessing the Office object model

Microsoft Office OneNote™ 2003

No explicit Web access control is offered through this node

Settings on the Set Feature Installation States page

You can control the installation of some Web-related services through the following settings on the **Set Feature Installation States** page of the Custom Installation Wizard or Custom Maintenance Wizard.

Office Shared Features

- Office 2003 Web Components
- Microsoft Office Download Control
- Office SOAP Toolkit

Office Tools

- Smart Tag .NET Programmability Support
- HTML Source Editing
- Microsoft Windows SharePoint™ Services Support
- Save My Settings Wizard
- Smart Tag Plugins
- Hosted Web

Managing Internet Free/Busy Information

With the Microsoft Office Internet Free/Busy Service, users can publish their free/busy times to a shared Internet location or an Exchange server. Members of the service can view each other's free/busy information and can help to control which members have access to their information.

To turn on the Microsoft Office Internet Free/Busy Service

1. In Microsoft Office Outlook 2003, on the **Tools** menu, click **Options**.

2. Click **Calendar Options**, and then click **Free/Busy Options**.

3. Select **Publish and search using Microsoft Office Internet Free /Busy Service**.

To publish their information, users enter their preferences in the **Free/Busy Options** dialog box, such as how many months' worth of information to publish, how often to update the information, and whether to publish the data to the free/busy service or to a specific location.

When users join the Microsoft Office Internet Free/Busy Service, they can select which other members can view their free/busy information. Members can also send invitations to other users to view their data. The free/busy service relies on Passport to help provide secure transactions between Outlook and the Internet.

As an administrator, if you are concerned about users accessing free/busy information over the Internet, you can help to prevent your users from having access to the free/busy service by changing a setting in the Custom Installation Wizard or Custom Maintenance Wizard, or by setting a policy.

To change the free/busy service setting through the Custom Installation Wizard or Custom Maintenance Wizard

1. Open the **Change Office User Settings** page.

2. Expand the **Microsoft Office Outlook 2003** node down to **Calendar Options**, and then click **Free/Busy Options** to display the settings.

3. Double-click the setting for **Disable the Microsoft Office Internet Free/Busy Service**, and then select the **Apply Change** button to configure the option.

To disable or enable the Microsoft Office Internet Free/Busy Service by using the Group Policy snap-in, set the following policy in the Office11.adm administrative template:

Microsoft Office Outlook 2003\Instant Messaging Integration\Display Free/Busy item in Name menu

For more information about using policies to help control user options, see "Using Group Policy to Deploy Office" in Chapter 5, "Installing Office 2003."

Managing the Save My Settings Wizard

The Save My Settings Wizard allows users to back up their Microsoft Office settings to a file or to the World Wide Web. If the user saves to the World Wide Web, the wizard saves the settings to the Microsoft Web site and uses a Passport account to help secure the settings. The settings are not accessible by Microsoft and are not used for any purpose other than allowing users to restore their settings.

> **Note**   The Save My Settings Wizard is the end-user name for the Office Profile Wizard, an administrator tool. For more information about what settings are preserved when you run these wizards, see "Customizing User-defined Settings" in Chapter 4, "Customizing Office 2003."

The Save My Settings Wizard is installed with the default installation of Microsoft Office 2003. If you do not want users to be able to use the Save My Settings Wizard, you can disable it during Setup. If you just want to disable the ability to upload the settings file to servers on the World Wide Web, you can do so by using a policy.

Disabling the Save My Settings Wizard

To use the Custom Installation Wizard to disable the Save My Settings Wizard in the Office installation, go to the **Set Feature Installation States** page and set the following feature to **Not Available**:

Office Tools\Save My Settings Wizard

When you deploy Office with this setting, the Save My Settings Wizard will not be available to your users. If you later want to make the wizard available, you can use the Custom Maintenance Wizard to add the Save My Settings Wizard again.

Controlling Save My Settings Wizard options

If you want to allow users to use the wizard but not to save their settings to a Web site, you can disable the Web functionality only by using a policy. To stop users from saving their settings to the World Wide Web, open the Office11.adm administrative template in the Group Policy snap-in and set the following policy:

Microsoft Office 2003\Save My Settings Wizard\Prevent users from uploading settings to the Internet

You can also set a default location (such as a specific location on your corporate network) to store users' settings files. To set the default storage location, open the Office11.adm administrative template in the Group Policy snap-in and select the following policy:

Microsoft Office 2003\Save My Settings Wizard\Default location to store settings file (OPS)

For more information about using policies to help control user options, see "Using Group Policy to Deploy Office" in Chapter 5, "Installing Office 2003."

Part 7

Security

Chapter 23

Office 2003 Security Environment

Security was a major focus in the development of Microsoft® Office 2003. More emphasis was placed on eliminating security flaws than in any previous release of the Microsoft Office System, which helped to produce our most robust level of security to date. However, administrative and user-level security vulnerabilities can still be exposed by improper configuration of settings and by user methods. This chapter addresses specific security issues an administrator should take into consideration when deploying or maintaining an Office configuration in a corporate setting. Along with this information are suggestions and recommendations for how to limit exposure to attacks and how to manage the security of a deployed installation through security-related policies.

Overview of Office Security

Establishing the most secure computing environment possible requires limiting the vulnerability of applications and data to malicious attacks. Unfortunately, closing all the possible holes in an organization's security is difficult, maybe impossible. Therefore, one of the best methods of establishing a more security-enhanced environment is to limit the number of possible avenues of attack.

The methods discussed in this chapter of the *Microsoft Office 2003 Editions Resource Kit* should help the administrator implement procedures to help limit direct assaults on data from external and internal attacks. Part of implementing these methods is training users on how to protect themselves and the company from attack. This training usually builds user awareness of the issue of security and ownership of the data they are trying to protect.

Knowledgeable users who know how to implement security and are aware of the possible threats are the first line of defense against unauthorized access to content; by the same token, untrained users can expose an organization to unauthorized or malicious use of its data. Establishing a corporate policy for how files are distributed and handled helps mitigate security vulnerabilities caused by untrained users.

Microsoft Office 2003 provides new methods and features for helping to manage application and document security. Understanding how to use and set the following security-related features in Microsoft Office can help establish a more secure environment:

- Macro security

- Certificate revocation

- Trusted sources

- Microsoft ActiveX® controls

- Password and encryption protection

- Privacy options

- Rights Management (Information Rights Management)

Microsoft Visual Basic® for Applications (VBA) is also an aspect of security that administrators should be aware of. VBA can be used for malicious use and therefore can be disabled if need be. However, disabling VBA has a number of effects on Office functionality that should be understood before it is disabled.

Each of the areas above is discussed in subsequent sections of this chapter or is addressed in other referenced content. It is highly recommended that you review these components and features prior to deploying Office to determine whether you need to make changes to suit your business needs.

The majority of these security-related settings are controlled through the Custom Installation Wizard or Custom Maintenance Wizard, or by using policies. At deployment, the **Specify Office Security Settings** page of the Custom Installation Wizard is used to set the various security options for macro and ActiveX controls. Security settings for macros (and almost any executable program or file run within an Office application) can be changed to High, Medium, or Low by using this page. The default level for macro security in Office is High. Changing Office feature installation states does not affect the macro security settings unless an administrator specifically sets the security settings to a level other than High using this page. However, it is also possible to control these settings by using a policy or by copying an Office configuration from one computer to another using the Office Profile Wizard.

Macro Security Levels in Office 2003

Macro security is used to help control the activation of executable code embedded within a template, document, workbook, presentation, and in most cases objects connected to these storage files through an OLE link or Dynamic Data Exchange (DDE) connection. Depending on the setting of macro security, the following startup options for files loaded into Microsoft Office 2003 applications are available:

- Run executables automatically when trusted (achieved through High and Medium macro security levels)

- Block executables because they are not trusted (High macro security level)

- Prompt to enable and run an executable because it is currently not trusted (High macro security level)

- Run executables only after user approval (Medium macro security level)

- Run all executables without any security precautions (Low macro security level)

Each of these security levels can be set by administrators and distributed to some or all users in an organization by using the Custom Installation Wizard, Custom Maintenance Wizard, Office Profile Wizard, or the Group Policy snap-in (requires the use of the Active Directory® directory service).

Setting macro security levels in Office applications

Macro security for Microsoft Office Word 2003, Microsoft Office Excel 2003, Microsoft Office Outlook® 2003, Microsoft Office Publisher 2003, Microsoft Office Access 2003, and Microsoft Office PowerPoint® 2003 can be set to High, Medium, or Low through the **Security** dialog box of the user interface. This dialog box can be found by clicking on the **Tools** menu, pointing to **Macro**, and then clicking **Security**.

It is highly recommended that you select **High** and only select **Medium** if absolutely necessary. Setting the security level to Low allows a macro, Microsoft Visual Basic for Applications (VBA) program, or other executable file or program to run without the knowledge or approval of the user.

When you set security levels to High, Medium, or Low, the following conditions apply:

- **High security**   Executables must be signed by an acknowledged trusted source (certificate of trust) in order to run. Otherwise, all executables associated with, or embedded in, documents are automatically disabled without warning the user when the documents are opened. All Office applications are installed with macro security set to High by default.

- **Medium security**   Users are prompted to enable or disable executables in documents when the documents are opened. This level requires the acceptance of a certificate of trust for each executable, which is accepted by adding the certificate to a segment of the registry. Later requests by a macro to run from a trusted source which is accepted and available from the registry are automatically accepted (the executable runs without prompting the user).

- **Low security**   Executables are run without restrictions. This security level does not protect against malicious programs, does not allow for acceptance of certificates of trust, is considered generally insecure and, therefore, is not recommended.

Administrators can set the macro security level by using the **Specify Office Security Settings** page of either the Custom Installation Wizard or the Custom Maintenance Wizard. These settings will be applied when Office is either installed or a maintenance update is applied.

Users can set the macro security level within Word, Access, Excel, Outlook, or PowerPoint by clicking on **Tools**, pointing to **Macro**, and then clicking **Security**. They can also gain access to the security features of each application by clicking **Tools**, clicking **Options**, and then clicking the **Security** tab.

> **Note**   New to this release of Office is a component that checks all XML files with references to XSLs (XML transforms) for possible script. If script is found, it is disabled if the macro security is set to High. If the macro security level is set to Medium, the user is prompted as to whether to run the script. If macro security is set to Low, the script is run without any prompting.

Digitally signing a macro

You can use the program Selfcert.exe to sign macros or templates you create for your own personal use. Certificates created for use on your own computer are accepted only for the computer the certificate was created on.

Selfcert.exe calls Makecert.exe; both programs are available with Office in the Office 2003 folder and are not available with the *Microsoft Office 2003 Editions Resource Kit*. However, signing a macro, template, or file with Selfcert.exe does not provide a high enough level of authentication to provide reliable tracking of the source of the file back to its developer. Therefore, if a file you sign with a signature created from Selfcert is distributed to other users, they will not be able to accept your certificate if they are running High security, because the certificate does not have a high enough security level to authenticate who you are. Only a certificate issued by a certificate authority can be used to provide a distributable certificate and signature to others and still pass through Medium and High security levels in Office.

There are limitations to the deployment of Selfcert.exe certificates applied to a macro when macro security is set to High:

- Setting security to Low and then running the macro does not register the certificate in the trusted sources list.

  Security must be set to Medium or High before any certificates are posted to the trusted Trust Publishers list. In cases where security is set to High on all computers, a Selfcert.exe-signed macro can be deployed, but it does not have a secure enough certificate for use by other users who are running with the High security level. Only a certificate issued by a certificate authority can be used to provide a distributable certificate and signature to others and still pass through Medium and High security levels in Office.

- Selfcert.exe-issued certificates are not managed by a certificate authority and do not provide for certificate revocation checking.

- Selfcert.exe does not provide a certificate of trust with a traceable signature.

How Office Performs Certificate Revocation

Microsoft Office uses some of the security settings set by Microsoft Internet Explorer when it attempts to authenticate certificates of trust prior to use, even if the certificate is already accepted and present on a user's computer. Each time an Office application attempts to run an executable signed with an attached certificate, one of the following events occurs if the **Check for publisher's certificate revocation** check box is checked in the Internet Explorer **Advanced settings** dialog: either the server maintained by the certificate authority who issued the certificate is checked for a revocation status, or a cached file downloaded from that same certificate authority is examined (dependent on the update cycle of revocation information by the certificate authority). The only exception to this behavior is with a Microsoft ActiveX control that was already installed if the certificate of trust associated with the control was already accepted and is present in the Trusted Publishers Store.

The **Check for publisher's certificate revocation** setting of Microsoft Internet Explorer is set to enabled by default during a non-customized installation of Internet Explorer. (In previous versions, certificate revocation was set to install in a disabled state.) Because Office inherits this setting from Internet Explorer, Office will automatically check for certificate revocation when installed. Administrators can turn off certificate revocation, but it is recommended that they keep this feature enabled.

This feature adds a slight amount of time to the handling of executables, because each application attempting to load and run a program with an associated certificate must determine whether a certificate has been listed as revoked. The certificate revocation check process can take even longer if the certificate revocation list is being downloaded for the first time from the certificate authority, or is being updated. However, once this list is cached to the user's local drive, the revocation check is relatively short. This entire process is dependent on access to the Internet.

To check whether certificate revocation is enabled

1. Start Internet Explorer.

2. Click **Tools**, click **Internet Options**, and then click the **Advanced** tab.

3. Under the **Security** section of the tree view control, set the **Check for publisher's certificate revocation** check box to checked.

> **Note**   If your company has chosen not to allow access to the Internet, or has closed off access to much of the Internet through a proxy server (firewall), it is recommended that you allow access to the various companies that provide certificate revocation checking so users can validate certificates of trust on a regular basis. Check with your network administrator or proxy server administrator for possible options you can explore to allow access to certificate revocation servers available from certificate authorities.

Working with Trusted Trust Publishers

The development and use of certificates of trust through Microsoft Authenticode® technology helps to provide a secure method of assuring the viability of programs written by third-party vendors. Trusted Trust Publishers (previously known as Trusted Sources) provides a means of cataloging and tracking back to the source who wrote a program and assures that rigorous methods were employed to identify the program as safe for use. The use of trusted Trust Publishers allows users to choose whether to allow executables to run from identifiable vendors.

Administrators have the option of turning off the trusted Trust Publishers feature by setting security to Low, which is not recommended; or by enabling a list of trusted Trust Publishers as a default. When trusted Trust Publishers evaluation is enabled, any executables (add-ins, applets, macros, EXE programs, and so forth) are automatically run from the user's computer, providing the certificate of trust was accepted and stored in the trusted Trust Publishers segment of a user's registry.

How trusted Trust Publishers works

The trusted Trust Publishers feature requires the use of a special embedded digital signature that is applied to an executable. This digital signature includes a certificate, which identifies the source of the executable.

A digital signature is like a seal of approval. A signature provides some degree of assurance to the user that the code is safe to execute because of the cost and rigorous process required to obtain the signature and apply it to an executable. The signature also provides assurance in other ways: it ensures the code is from the source listed in the certificate that was used to sign the code, and it ensures the code has not been tampered with after the creators of the certificate signed it.

A digital signature requires the owners of the signature to identify themselves to a certificate authority, which then issues a certificate of trust. In this way, a digital signature can be used to prove that the data or code is really from the user or source that the digital signature claims it is from, and it provides a means of tracing the data or code back to the people who developed it.

Accepting certificates of trust in Office applications

If a document contains digitally signed executables and users attempt to open the document with their security set to High or Medium, they are prompted to trust the source of the certificate if a reference to the certificate is not already present in the trusted Trust Publishers store. If they choose to trust the source, any subsequent document with an executable signed with the same certificate of trust automatically allows the executable to run, regardless of the security level set for the application.

It is possible to trust all currently installed add-ins and templates on a computer when Microsoft Office is being installed. This allows all files currently installed to the computer, those being installed along with Office, and those already present in the Office templates folder to be trusted even though the files may not be signed.

To specify trusted Trust Publishers in the following Office applications—Word, Access, Excel, Outlook, or PowerPoint

1. On the **Tools** menu, point to **Macro**, and then click **Security**.

2. To view or remove trusted Trust Publishers, click the **Trusted Publishers** tab.

3. To trust all add-ins and templates currently installed on the computer, set the **Trust all installed add-ins and templates** check box to checked.

Adding trusted Trust Publishers

Users can add trusted Trust Publishers to the local trusted Trust Publishers store by accepting the request to trust a signed executable (an applet, a program, and so forth) the first time it attempts to run. Macro security for the Office application must be set to Medium or High to force this request.

It is possible for administrators to add Microsoft or other digital certificates to the list of trusted Trust Publishers without accepting a request to trust the source. In the Custom Installation Wizard or the Custom Maintenance Wizard, administrators can add the digital certificate to the **Add the following digital certificates to the list of Trusted Publishers** list box in the **Specify Office Security Settings** page.

For administrators interested in maintaining a specific list of certificates for all users, it is possible to block users from adding to the list of trusted Trust Publishers by enforcing a policy. To block users from making any changes to the trusted Trust Publishers store, use the Office11.adm policy template to set the **Microsoft Office 2003 | Security Settings** policy of each application to checked (for example, **Word: Trust all installed add-ins and templates**). Unlike the setting of security options through the Custom Installation Wizard or Custom Maintenance Wizard, the use of a policy forces the implementation of administrative settings on a user's computer whenever the user logs on, dependent on the method used to distribute the policy file. Thus, any changes the user may have made to an application during a previous session are overwritten, if those areas that were changed are controlled by policy.

For installations of Microsoft Office 2003 on Microsoft Windows® 2000, if a list of trusted Trust Publishers is added to the HKCU node of the registry, users can add trusted Trust Publishers through the user interface of an application. However, if the list of trusted Trust Publishers is stored in the HKLM node of the registry, then users cannot add to their list of trusted Trust Publishers (local machine supersedes current user).

For installations of Office 2003 on Windows XP or later, trusted certificates of trust are stored in the Windows Trusted Publisher store. There is also a different dialog displayed for sources on this operating system.

> **Note**   The policy distribution method used (REG file, Active Directory versus NT logon) plays a significant role in the effectiveness and timeliness of policy implementation.

Distributing non-Microsoft trusted Trust Publishers

You can distribute non-Microsoft trusted Trust Publishers to users with a new process that requires the creation and use of a CER file. Office includes three CER files, which have the information for the three Microsoft certificates needed for Office applications.

On the Resource Kit CD   The Microsoft CER files are included in the Office Information documents folder that is installed with the Microsoft Office 2003 Editions Resource Kit. They can be found in the %Program-Files%\OrkTools\Ork11\Lists and Samples\Office Information folder. The Office Information documents can also be downloaded from the Toolbox on the companion CD or from the Office 2003 Resource Kit Web site at *http://www.microsoft.com/office/ork/2003*.

Office applications are installed with these certificates, but the certificates are not trusted by default. Administrators must choose to add these as part of the deployment of Office in the Custom Installation Wizard (**Specify Office Security Settings** page) if they want users to trust Microsoft certificates of trust.

For applications other than those included with Microsoft Office, the CER file can be obtained through two possible methods:

■ By exporting the certificate content from a signed DLL to a CER file.

If you do not have a test installation of Office where you have already trusted this certificate, this is the only method to obtain the certificate information. The procedure for doing this is below.

■ By exporting a trusted certificate from a Trusted Publisher store to a CER file.

If you have a test installation of Office and you have accepted a certificate from an external vendor, you can obtain the certificate information for the creation of a CER file from the **Security** dialog of any Office application. The procedure for doing this follows.

To export a certificate from a DLL to a CER file

1. Open Windows Explorer.

2. Find the signed DLL file that has the certificate you want to distribute.

3. Right-click on the DLL.

4. Click **Properties**.

5. Click the **Digital Signatures** tab and select the certificate from the **Signatures list**, and then click **Details**.

6. In the **Digital Signatures Detail** dialog, click **View certificate**.

7. In the **Certificate** dialog, click the **Details** tab.

8. Click **Copy to File**.

9. In the resulting Certificate Export Wizard, click **Next** to go to the **Export File Format** page.

10. Select the DER encoded binary X.509 (.CER) option and click **Next**.

11. In the **File to Export** page, provide a path and file name to the folder where you want to save the CER file, and click **Next**.

12. Click **Finish** on the last page to perform the export.

To export a certificate from a Trusted Publisher store to a CER file

1. Open Word, Excel, PowerPoint, Outlook, or Access, and click on the **Tools** menu.

2. Click **Macro** and then click **Security**.

3. Click the **Trusted Publishers** tab and select the certificate you want to distribute.

4. Click **View**.

5. In the **Certificate** dialog, click the **Details** tab.

6. Click the **Copy to File** button.

7. In the resulting Certificate Export Wizard, click **Next** to go to the Export File Format page.

8. Select the DER encoded binary X.509 (.CER) option and click **Next**.

9. In the **File to Export** page, provide a path and file name to the folder where you want to save the CER file, and click **Next**.

10. Click **Finish** on the last page to perform the export.

Distributing CER files

To distribute the CER files you have created, you can use:

■ Active Directory (can be used anytime)

■ The Custom Installation Wizard (only at initial deployment)

■ The Custom Maintenance Wizard (only after deployment)

To include a CER file for propagation to users who are part of Active Directory directory services, use the appropriate method for the type of Office installation you have configured for your installation of Active Directory. For information about Active Directory, search for "Active Directory" on the Windows 2000 Advanced Server Web site at *http://www.microsoft.com/windows2000/advancedserver/*.

To include a CER file in either a transform or CMW file

1. Start the Custom Installation Wizard or Custom Maintenance Wizard.

2. Load the appropriate MSI file and provide a transform or configuration maintenance file name.

3. In the **Specify Office Security Settings** page, click **Add**.

4. Browse for the CER file you created in the previous section and either double-click on it or select it, and then click **Add**.

This process imports the contents of the CER file into the transform or maintenance file, which will be included with a new or updated installation of Office. The appropriate information is then saved to the registry during either of those installations. Once the CER file is in place, the user can then run executables that were signed with this certificate of trust without being blocked or prompted to accept the certificate.

ActiveX Controls and Office Security

Microsoft ActiveX controls can pose a security risk in some situations because the controls can be used to distribute malicious code or viruses, especially on computers where appropriate security-related settings are not in place.

For instance, if an ActiveX control that is not signed is downloaded from a Web page to a computer where High or Medium security is not enabled through Microsoft Internet Explorer, the control will run without warning. If that control contains malicious code capable of introducing a virus or some other form of attack, the computer and data could be damaged.

The following information describes what an ActiveX control is and how to help defend against some of the problems that might be introduced when a control is installed or used without appropriate examination.

What is an ActiveX control?

An ActiveX control is essentially an OLE or Component Object Model (COM) object. It is a self-registering program or control; that is, it adds registry entries for itself automatically the first time it is run.

An ActiveX control can be as simple as a text box, as complex as an entire dialog, and in some cases as complex as a small application. ActiveX controls are used as controls or dialogs for Internet Web sites, as add-ins to major applications from third-party vendors, and as plug-in utilities. Therefore, ActiveX is synonymous with Java, Netscape plug-ins, and scripting. However, the advantage of ActiveX over these other programming options is that ActiveX controls can also be used in applications written in different programming languages, including all of the Microsoft programming and database languages.

ActiveX controls are not standalone solutions. They can only be run from within host applications, such as Internet Explorer, a Microsoft Visual Basic® application, Visual C++® development system, Visual Basic for Applications, and so on. ActiveX controls facilitate the distribution of specialized controls over networks and the integration of those controls within Web browsers. This includes the ability of the control to identify itself to applications that use ActiveX controls.

ActiveX controls can be scripted from Web pages. This means you can create (or buy) an ActiveX control to provide a control for a user interface or graphics device interface (GDI) element. Once created, you can use a scripting language such as Visual Basic Scripting Edition (VBScript) or JavaScript™ to use the control. Your script instructs the control how to work.

Security settings related to unsafe ActiveX initialization

Four security settings are available for use with ActiveX controls within the Custom Installation Wizard and Custom Maintenance Wizard. These settings are found on the **Specify Office Security Settings** of each wizard:

- **Do not configure**   The transform or configuration maintenance file does not modify the setting specified on the user's computer. New applications are installed with the default setting, which is **Prompt user to use persisted data**.

- **Prompt user to use control defaults**   The user is warned before an application initiates ActiveX controls that might be unsafe. If the user trusts the source of the document, the control is initialized using its default settings. This setting disables the ability of the control to use and save persisted data. It forces the control to start up using its default settings. This reduces the possibility of an errant setting or deliberate attack from causing a problem on the computer. When this setting is enabled, the user is warned when the control is started but the user has the option of ignoring the setting.

- **Prompt user to use persisted data**   The user is warned before an application initiates ActiveX controls that might be unsafe. If the user trusts the source of the document, the control is initialized using the previously stored data associated with the control. Potentially, the ActiveX control could be used to introduce a virus if this setting is used.

- **Do not prompt**   This allows the control to run in its default configuration. If this setting is used, it allows the ActiveX control to use stored information between sessions and does not present a dialog to the user prompting them for how the control should be activated.

Use of these settings in the Custom Installation Wizard or Custom Maintenance Wizard provides administrators extra control over how potentially unsafe ActiveX controls run on users' computers. More information about the registry entry for this security feature is available in "How Policies Work" in Chapter 26, "Using Security-related Policies."

Code signing

Because an ActiveX control allows access to root operating system services, it needs something to assure that it is not a malicious program. This assurance is provided by Microsoft Authenticode, which allows an ActiveX developer the option to digitally vouch for his or her code—also known as code signing. Code signing, when used, allows users the ability to identify the author of any program before allowing it to either be installed or executed on their computer.

If you have used unsigned or unmarked ActiveX controls with Internet Explorer, you may have seen dialog boxes declaring the:

- Control is not signed
- Control is not safe for initializing
- Control is not safe for scripting

ActiveX controls downloaded automatically over the Internet can do anything a regular program can do—such as deleting files or registry entries. Java addresses this problem by limiting what a Java applet can do to files and the registry. Java cannot, for instance, gain direct access to the computer's file system. ActiveX controls take a different approach: they demand positive identification of the author of the control, verification that the control was not modified since it was code signed, and confirmation that it is a safe control. Because of this approach, ActiveX controls can use the full power of the operating system but rely on the strict method of obtaining a certificate of trust from a certificate authority to assure whether the control is safe to install and use.

Installing an ActiveX control

If a user attempts to install and run an unregistered ActiveX control from the Internet, Internet Explorer checks to see if the control was digitally signed. If the ActiveX (OCX) file has a certificate of trust that is already trusted on the user's computer, it is accepted, installed, and registered. Depending on the security level set for use by Internet Explorer, if the certificate of trust is unknown to the system, the user is presented with the option to install the control. If the user accepts the option to install the control, the certificate of trust associated with the control is noted in the registry.

If the ActiveX (OCX) file is installed as part of an application from a CD or other locally opened resource, there is no examination of the certificate (if there is one) associated with the OCX file. It is assumed the file is associated with an application that has been deemed safe to install by the user, and it is installed and registered without challenge.

Once the control is installed on a user's system, the control no longer invokes code-signing dialog boxes when started. After a control is installed, it is considered safe even if it was not digitally signed originally.

Signing an ActiveX control

To digitally sign a control, you will need to obtain a certificate from a certificate authority, which can be located by using the term "certificate authority" in a search engine. Follow the directions for signing controls from the certificate authority you decide to use.

Certificate authorities provide different levels of trust certificates, ranging from individual certificates to corporate-wide certificates. Check each certificate authority's Web site to determine if they have one that is right for you.

Determining if an ActiveX control is safe

Since the digital signature of an ActiveX control stays with the file it was attached to, there is a permanent evidence of the designed intent of the control by the developers. However, this evidence does not account for all possible conditions the control may be used in but were never tested for.

ActiveX controls marked as safe are supposed to be safe in all possible conditions. So a control marked as safe for scripting (SFS) or safe for initialization (SFI) must be written to protect itself from any unpredictable results a script author might unintentionally create when scripting the control. While it is relatively easy for a programmer to create a control with adequate guards to avoid misuse, it is impossible to guarantee that the control is always safe when used with scripting created by another author or programmer.

If a control is marked safe for initializing or safe for scripting, the developers are claiming that no matter what values are used to initialize the control, it will not do anything to damage a user's system or compromise the user's security when the control is initialized in any way.

The developer of an ActiveX control should take extra care to ensure that a control is in fact safe before it is marked as safe. For example, each ActiveX control, at a minimum, should be evaluated for the following issues:

- It does not over-index arrays or otherwise manipulate memory incorrectly, thereby causing a memory leak or corrupt memory region.

- It validates and corrects all input, including initialization, method parameters, and property setting functions (implements acceptable I/O validation and defense methods).

- It does not misuse any data about, or provided by, the user.

- It was tested in a variety of circumstances.

Important Aspects of Password and Encryption Protection

Microsoft Office Excel 2003, Microsoft Office Word 2003, and Microsoft Office PowerPoint 2003 offer several features to help restrict access to files through the use of passwords or encryption. These file-level security measures are separate from any operating system–level security options.

The use of file encryption is another method of protecting a document from unauthorized changes versus saving the file in a permissions-enabled hard disk or folder. When saved, the file is scrambled with an encryption code, making the contents of the document unreadable to anyone who does not have the password and ciphers required to decrypt the document. To use encryption, users working with a file must set and remember a password.

Embedded password references

Setting encryption of documents for most Microsoft Office 2003 applications can be partially automated through the use of macros or custom programs using the application object. However, the practice of hard-coding a password into any kind of program is not recommended because programs are routinely examined by attackers for clear text use of passwords. Embedding a password into a macro or program can lead to weakened security.

For example, to set the automatic encryption of a document in Word, use the *SaveAs* method in Visual Basic® for Applications. This method has four password related arguments—*LockComments*, *Password*, *WritePassword*, or *ReadOnlyRecommended*. These arguments allow a programmer to prompt the user for a password in order to save a document and ask for a password from the user to apply to the file. If however, the password is saved as part of the macro, it is an exposed password ready to be obtained by an attacker. The password, if used programmatically, should never be stored in a macro; it should be requested by means of a dialog.

For good security, applying strong password methods and implementing encryption helps to provide additional protection against any attempted security attacks. Documentation regarding the implementation of strong password methods is available by searching the Windows NT® Server Web site at *http://www.microsoft.com/ntserver /techresources/security/* using the phrase **strong password**.

Microsoft Office Access 2003 does not provide the same method of password and file encryption methods available with Excel, Word, and PowerPoint. For encryption, password, and security-related schemes for Access 2003, see "Overview of Access Security" from the Contents pane of Access 2003 Help.

> **Note**   To use encrypted documents in collaboration, you must clear the **Encrypt document properties** check box in the **Encryption Type** dialog (**Tools | Options | Security tab | Advanced...**). Clearing this check box is required because the routing information within the document must be accessible by the routing handling programs.

Protecting Excel workbooks

Microsoft Excel supports three levels of workbook file protection when a file is saved. These three options can all be used together or separately:

- **Password to open**   Requires the user to enter a password to open a workbook. The supplied password is the cipher used by the encryption algorithm.

- **Password to modify**   Requires the user to enter a password to open the workbook with read/write permission. The user can click **Read Only** at the prompt, and Excel opens the workbook in a read-only state.

- **Read-only recommended**   Prompts the user to open the workbook in a read-only state. If the user clicks **No** at the prompt, Excel opens the workbook with read/write permission, unless the workbook has a different method of password protection enabled.

Encryption is provided by various cryptographic methods available from the **Advanced...** button on the **Security** dialog (**File | Save As | Tools | General Options...** menu option). Default encryption can also be set for users by implementing a policy. See the section "Advanced encryption options" later in this chapter.

In addition to applying protection to an entire workbook, you can help to protect segments within a workbook from unauthorized changes.

> **Note**   The **Protect Workbook** option is not as secure as using a password to encrypt the entire workbook because Excel does not use encryption when you apply protection to only specific segments.
>
> For example, hidden cells on a protected worksheet can be viewed if a user copies across a range on the protected worksheet that includes the hidden cells, opens a new workbook, pastes, and then uses the **Unhide** command to display the cells.

You can provide a modicum of protection to a workbook with the following protection options (**Tools** menu | **Protection** option):

■ **Protect Sheet**   Allows the creator of the workbook the ability to apply protection to a worksheet and the contents of locked cells. It also allows the creator of the file the option of restricting the following formatting capabilities:

- **Select locked cells**
- **Select unlocked cells**
- **Format cells**
- **Format columns**
- **Format rows**
- **Insert columns**
- **Insert rows**
- **Insert hyperlinks**
- **Delete columns**
- **Delete rows**
- **Sort**
- **Use AutoFilter**
- **Use PivotTable® reports**
- **Edit objects**
- **Edit scenarios**

■ **Allow Users to Edit Ranges**   Provides the creator of a workbook the ability to let other users make changes to specific ranges in a worksheet. This method uses network security permissions (NT Authentication) so the creator can select the UserID of an individual and provide specific access rights to data within a range of a worksheet.

■ **Protect Workbook**   Allows the creator of a workbook the option to help protect the structure or windows of the workbook with a password. Protection of these two elements of a workbook are:

- **Structure**   Worksheets and chart sheets in a workbook with protection cannot be moved, deleted, hidden, unhidden, or renamed, and new sheets cannot be inserted.

- **Windows**   Windows in a workbook with protection cannot be moved, resized, hidden, unhidden, or closed. Windows in a workbook with protection are sized and positioned the same way each time the workbook is opened.

- **Protect and Share Workbook**   Allows the owner of the workbook the ability to help protect it with a password and disable the ability of others to make changes without maintaining a history of what has changed. Protected change histories (Track Changes enabled) cannot be cleared by the user of a shared workbook or by the user of a merged copy of a workbook.

Protection methods can be implemented on other aspects of a workbook, such as the cells or formulas of a worksheet, graphic objects, or scenarios.

- Cells or formulas on a worksheet, or items on a chart sheet
    Contents of protected cells on a worksheet cannot be edited. Protected items on a chart sheet cannot be modified. Implement by right-clicking on the cell of interest, select **Format Cells...**, then click the **Protection** tab. Use of this feature on a protected cell requires the worksheet of which it is part to be protected.

> **Tip**   You can also hide a formula so only the result of the formula appears in the cell.

- Graphic objects on a worksheet or chart sheet
    Protected graphic objects can be locked. This prevents the object or chart from being moved or edited. Requires the worksheet of which it is part to be protected. Option to lock the object or chart is available in the **Properties** tab of the **Format Chart Area** dialog.

- Scenarios on a worksheet
    Definitions of protected scenarios can be set to locked (**Tools** menu, **Scenarios** option, **Add** button, **Prevent changes**).

If a user assigns password protection to a workbook and then forgets the password, it is impossible to perform the following activities:

- Open the workbook.

- Gain access to the workbook's data from another workbook through a link.

- Remove protection from the workbook.

- Recover data from the workbook.

Caution You should advise users to use strong passwords that are not based on words that can be found in a dictionary or that can be easily derived by references to familiar items, people, or places they have visited. The use of strong passwords helps to reduce the possibility of someone guessing the password used to apply encryption to the file. Only if absolutely necessary should passwords be written down. If they are, they should be stored in a secure place.

Protecting Word documents

Microsoft Word supports three levels of document protection. These protection methods are accessed by clicking **File**, clicking **Save As**, clicking **Tools**, and then clicking **Security Options**. These three options can all be used together or separately:

- **Password to open** Requires the user to enter a password to open a document. This applies an encryption algorithm by using the password as a cipher to encrypt the file. Click **Advanced** for encryption options if you wish to use an encryption algorithm other than what is supplied as a default, or if you wish to change the encryption key length.

- **Password to modify** Requires the user to enter a password to open the document with read/write permission. If the user clicks **Read Only** at the prompt, Word opens the document as read-only and does not require a password to view the contents. Setting the **Read-only recommended** check box to checked is meaningless if you have provided a File modify password.

- **Read-only recommended** Prompts viewers of the document to open it as read-only if they do not need to make any edits to the content. Even though this option appears in the same section of the **Security** dialog as **Password to open** and **Password to modify**, this is not a form of protection by itself. If a user chooses to respect the **Open as read-only** option, this option helps to protect the original document from being overwritten by an inadvertent save (or by the automatic Save AutoRecover feature). The ability of a user to ignore this protection option is as easy as selecting **No** at the **Open as read only** prompt when a document is opened. Nothing prevents the user from ignoring the read-only recommended setting unless it is combined with a more secure protection option. If **No** is selected, Word opens the document with read/write permission, unless the document has other password protection methods in place.

Encryption is provided by various cryptographic methods available from the **Advanced...** button on the **Security** dialog (**File | Save As... | Tools | Security Options...** menu option). Default encryption can also be set for users by implementing a policy. See the "Advanced encryption options" section later in this material.

In addition to encrypting an entire document, you can add a modicum of protection to specific elements of a document to restrict viewers of the document from making unauthorized changes. This method is not as secure as encrypting the entire document because Word does not use encryption when you apply protection to only selected elements. These methods are more for collaboration purposes than for security needs. Protection of this type is not meant to protect intellectual property from malicious users. For example, field codes can be viewed in a text editor such as Notepad even if forms or sections of a document are set to use the following protection methods instead of using encryption.

Specific elements you can set to a protected mode in a document are:

- **Tracked changes**   Changes made to the document cannot be accepted or rejected, and change tracking cannot be turned off.

- **Comments**   Users can insert comments into the document but cannot change the content of the document.

- **Forms**   Users can make changes only in form fields or unprotected sections of a document.

To restrict edits to tracked changes in a Word document

1. Open the document in Word.
2. Select the **Protect Document...** menu option (**Tools** menu).
3. Select **Editing restrictions**.
4. Set the **Allow only this type of editing in the document** option to checked.
5. In the drop-down combo box, select **Tracked changes**.
6. Under the **Start enforcement** section, click the **Yes, start enforcing protection** button.
7. In the resulting **Start enforcing protection** dialog, you can optionally add a password to the **Enter new password (optional)** text box.
8. Save the document.

After setting the protection status of a document, you can unprotect it at any time. To do so, select the **Unprotect** menu option (**Tools** menu) and provide the password used to set the protection.

If a user assigns password protection to a document and then forgets the password, it is impossible to perform the following activities:

- Open the document.

- Gain access to the documents data from another document with a link.

- Remove protection from the document.

- Recover data from the document.

Caution   You should advise users to use strong passwords that are not based on words that are found in a dictionary or that can be easily derived by references to familiar items, people, or places they have visited. The use of strong passwords reduces the possibility of someone guessing the password used to encrypt the file. Only if absolutely necessary should passwords be written down. If they are, they should be stored in a very secure place.

Protecting PowerPoint presentations

Microsoft PowerPoint supports two levels of presentation file protection. The user who creates a presentation has read/write permission to a presentation and controls the protection level. The two levels of presentation protection are:

- **Password to open**   Requires the user to enter a password to open a presentation. Click the **Advanced...** button on the **Security** dialog (**File | Save As... | Tools | Security Options...** menu option) for encryption options if you wish to use an encryption algorithm other than what is supplied as a default.

- **Password to modify**   Requires the user to enter a password to open the presentation with read/write permission. The user can optionally click **Read Only** at the prompt, and PowerPoint opens the presentation as read-only.

PowerPoint encrypts password-protected presentations by using encryption algorithms. Encryption is provided by various cryptographic methods available from the **Advanced...** button on the **Security** dialog (**File | Save As... | Tools | Security Options...** menu option). Default encryption can also be set for users by implementing a policy. See the "Advanced encryption options" section later in this chapter.

Optionally, you can encrypt document properties, too. To do so, click the **Advanced...** button and set the **Encrypt document properties** check box to checked. This helps to restrict unauthorized people from opening the presentation using a text editor and viewing any clear text (ASCII text) in the presentation.

If a user assigns password protection to a presentation and then forgets the password, it is impossible to perform the following activities:

■ Open the presentation.

■ Gain access to the presentation data from another presentation through a link.

■ Remove protection from the presentation.

■ Recover data from the presentation.

Caution   You should advise users to use strong passwords that are not based on words that are found in a dictionary or that can be easily derived by references to familiar items, people, or places they have visited. The use of strong passwords reduces the possibility of someone guessing the password used to encrypt the file. Only if absolutely necessary should passwords be written down. If they are, they should be stored in a very secure place.

Password and encryption options

Password and encryption options are in the **Security** tab within the **Tools | Options...** dialog. They can also be accessed from the **File | Save As... | Tools | Security Options...** option (**File | Save As... | Tools | General Options...** for Excel).

There are also hot keys for these options. The groups and controls are:

■ **File encryption options for this document**

  ■ Password to open

  ■ Advanced...

■ **File sharing options for this document**

  ■ Password to modify

  ■ Read-only recommended

  ■ Digital Signatures...

  ■ Protect Document...

Note The use of the term *digital signature* is not the same as when used with code signing or certificates attached to executable code. In this instance, a *digital signature* is the unique identifying element of an individual's mark on a document, like a legal and binding signature at the bottom of a page. When attached to a document, workbook, or presentation, it implies the user has signed the document and has validated its contents.

Search the World Wide Web for a certificate authority that issues digital signatures.

- **Privacy options**

    - Remove personal information from file properties on save

    - Warn before printing, saving, or sending a file that contains tracked changes or comments

    - Store random number to improve merge accuracy

    - Make hidden markup visible when opening or saving

- **Macro security**

    - Macro Security...

Protect Document dialog

Within the previous release of Word the **File sharing options for this document** section of the **Security** tab (**Tools | Options | Security** tab) is a button to access the **Protect Document...** dialog. This button provides the same functionality as the **Tools | Protect Document** menu option and the **File | Save As... | Tools | Security Options... | Protect Document...** button. The user interface of this feature of Word has changed significantly. A dialog no longer appears. A task pane has replaced the dialog and appears to the right of the document window with the options you can select to set the document protection.

Encryption

Encryption is a standard method of securing the content of a file. There are several encryption methods available for use with Word, Excel, and PowerPoint files; Access can use encryption as well, but implements it using a different method. Microsoft Office Outlook 2003 allows for encryption as well, but also implements it using different methods.

If you work for a government agency, contract for a government agency, or are at the corporate level where security is much more important, it is highly recommended you use the most secure form available, exercise great care in the distribution of encrypted files, and keep tight control of the passwords used to gain access to the content of encrypted files. Also, it is highly recommended that you use a different password for each and every file, and not use a password that can be found easily in a dictionary, that is the name of a current project in the company, or is any easily derived number (phone number, Social Security number, driver's license number, license number of a car) or anything that could be derived through a relatively simple search into an individual's background or family life.

Encryption types available to Office 2003 are whatever encryption types are available on the operating system when Office is installed. Only Weak Encryption (XOR) and Office 97/2000 Compatible encryption are installed by Office, and they are installed for compatibility reasons only. If you want to create a different type of encryption for your company, you will need to use a programming language that supports CSP (Cryptographic Service Provider). Information on how to create, install, and deploy a new encryption type is usually included with the CSP documentation.

Types of encryption

Encryption is a form of scrambling the content of a file to render the information within it unusable unless the correct password is used to unlock the cipher used to encrypt the file. The bit length of the cipher used to encrypt a document helps to determine the overall security of the document. The longer the bit length, the harder it should be for someone to decrypt the content. Encryption offsets the character values in a document by the value of the encryption mask. A bit mask is directly related to the bit length (40-bit, 128-bit, 256-bit, or a custom length as defined in the **Advanced** button of the **Security** dialog). For example:

Content of File A:

```
The Quick Brown Fox Jumped Over The Lazy Dog.
```

Content of File A after saved with a 16-bit encryption string (two characters) using a simple bitmask with the values "AZ":

```
_2$z_/(9*z_(.-/z59z
/,*$>a_7?3z_2$z

;;#a-.=oz
```

While some people might find this to be well scrambled, others with good encryption knowledge and a few minutes could probably decrypt this with some simple programs. As a rule, the longer the encryption bit length, the harder it is for someone to decode the content of the file.

Some of the possible encryption types you might find in the **Encryption Type** dialog are:

- **Weak Encryption (XOR)**   Not recommended, provided for legacy files only
- **Office 97/2000 Compatible**   Not recommended, provided for legacy files only
- **RC4, Microsoft Base Cryptographic Provider v1.0**
- **RC4, Microsoft Base DSS and Diffie-Hellman Cryptographic Provider**
- **RC4, Microsoft DH SChannel Cryptographic Provider**
- **RC4, Microsoft Enhanced Cryptographic Provider v1.0**
- **RC4, Microsoft Enhanced DSS and Diffie-Hellman Cryptographic Provider**
- **RC4, Microsoft Enhanced RSA and AES Cryptographic Provider (Prototype)**
- **RC4, Microsoft RSA SChannel Cryptographic Provider**
- **RC4, Microsoft Strong Cryptographic Provider**

For an in-depth discussion of security, see the Microsoft Security Web site at *http://www.microsoft.com/security.*

Updating encryption

Other than possibly changing the default encryption type, there are no issues associated with the maintenance of encryption within Office 2003, unless you choose to create your own encryption type using Cryptographic Service Provider (CSP) support from your software compiler.

Advanced encryption options

Administrators have the option of adding three values to a registry entry to each user's computer to set a default encryption type for all Office applications that can use encryption methods. The values can be included in a transform, configuration maintenance file, or Office profile settings file (OPS file), or they can be distributed by using a REG file. (The policy version can be distributed using Active Directory.) When created for use as part of a REG file, it is advisable to add them to the registry of a test computer and then export the value using the **File | Export...** option of regedit.exe.

The default encryption type for a typical Office installation is not the strongest possible encryption type available for Office; therefore, for commercial use it is advisable to set a higher level encryption type and larger key length value than provided by

the default installation. Administrators can change the default encryption type only
through the use of these registry entries:

HKCU\Software\Microsoft\Office\11.0\Common\Security

HKCU\Software\Policies\Microsoft\Office\11.0\Common\Security

Value name: **DefaultEncryption**

Value type: **MultiString**

Value data: "*<Encryption Provider>*","*<Encryption Algorithm>*","*<Encryption Key Length>*"

Example:

DefaultEncryption="Microsoft Enhanced Cryptographic Provider
v1.0","RC4","128"

To find the Encryption Provider information for this registry value

1. Start any encryption-enabled application, such as Word.

2. Select **File** | **Save as**....

3. Select the **Tools** extended menu option.

4. Select **Security Options**... from the drop-down list.

5. Click the **Advanced**... button.

6. From the **Encryption Type** dialog, copy the name of the encryption type
   name and encryption algorithm from the **Choose an encryption type** list.

7. For the selected encryption type, determine the minimum and maximum key
   length the algorithm can use by scrolling the key length entry control.

Assemble your information into the **DefaultEncryption** value data field.

Note   The larger the key length value, the more difficult it is for anyone to
discover the encryption key used to encrypt the file. It is recommended that
you use the largest value possible (128 in most cases).

To disable advanced encryption on all users' computers, administrators can set
the following registry entry:

HKCU\Software\Microsoft\Office\11.0\Common\Security

HKCU\Software\Policies\Microsoft\Office\11.0\Common\Security

Value name: **DisableCustomEncryption**

Value type: **DWORD**

Value data: **[0 | 1]**

Example:

DisableCustomEncryption=1

To disable the ability of users to create encrypted files, administrators can disable access to the password user interface in all Office applications by using the following registry entry.

HKCU\Software\Microsoft\Office\11.0\Common\Security

HKCU\Software\Policies\Microsoft\Office\11.0\Common\Security

Value name: **DisablePasswordUI**

Value type: **DWORD**

Value data: **[0 | 1]**

Example:

DisablePasswordUI=1

Privacy Options

It is recommended that all administrators read the Microsoft Office Privacy Statement, which can be found by searching for **privacy statement** in the Help task pane of any Microsoft Office System application (located by clicking the **Help** menu).

Privacy options are features within most Microsoft Office 2003 applications that allow anyone working with an Office 2003 item—such as a Microsoft Office Word 2003 document or a Microsoft Office Excel 2003 workbook—to remove user-identifiable properties attached to that file. Examples of such properties include the user's name or user's initials that are retrieved from the registry and typically attached to comments or appear in the **Properties** dialog under the **File** menu.

Administrators do not have the ability to remove all personal or hidden author and editor data from a document by using policies or privacy tools, but they can remove those references which are attached to the following Office document objects:

- Tracking changes

- Comments

- Property lists

- Footnotes

- Versions

> **Note**   Authoring references not entered by the application are not removed automatically. For instance, those references entered through the use of field codes are not removed or changed. Or, if hidden text was used to tag a line, and the author of the hidden text embedded his or her initials or name in the hidden text, this reference is not removed because it is not an identified author reference.

The privacy feature of Office can replace these known references by changing all known instances of application-inserted references to a generic user name (Author) or by deleting the reference entirely.

For example, Word uses four options to help protect access to private information. The check boxes are grouped under **Privacy options** on the **Security** tab (**Tools | Options | Security**). Not all Office applications take advantage of these four:

- **Remove personal information from file properties on save**

  Also available in Excel, Microsoft Office Access 2003, Microsoft Office Publisher 2003, Microsoft Office Visio® 2003, and Microsoft Office PowerPoint 2003. This option, which is off by default, removes all application-tagged identifiable references—who created a file, made changes to a file, or placed comments in a file—when the file is saved. A policy setting does not exist to enable or disable this setting.

- **Warn before printing, saving, or sending a file that contains tracked changes or comments**

  Available only in Word. Off by default, this option causes a dialog to appear whenever a request to save, print, or send by means of an e-mail message a document containing markup—change tracking or comments—is made. When set, this option applies to all files. This option can also be enabled or disabled using a policy available in the Word11.adm policy template.

- **Store random number to improve merge accuracy**

  Available in Word. This option, which is on by default, determines whether the file to save will receive a stamp with the RSID number for a particular editing session. The RSID number is a harmless pseudo-random number that reveals no information about a document's authorship or origin. Word uses the RSID information, if present, to enhance the results of merging two versions of a document; but the RSID information is not required for a merge to succeed. This option can also be enabled or disabled using a policy available in the Word11.adm policy template.

RSID compatibility issue between Word and Outlook

If a Word document is submitted to Microsoft Office Outlook 2003 for attachment to an e-mail message, or if you are using Word as the e-mail editor, setting the **Store random number to improve merge accuracy** option requires also setting an option in Outlook. Follow these steps to make the setting in Outlook:

1. Click **Tools**.

2. Click **Options**.

3. Click the **Preferences** tab.

4. Click **E-mail Options**.

5. Click **Advanced E-mail Options**.

6. At the bottom of the dialog, uncheck the **Add properties to attachments to enable Reply with Changes** check box.

- **Make hidden markup visible when opening or saving**

    Available only in Word. This option overrides the settings in the **Show** button (**Reviewing** toolbar). (It may be necessary to enable this button on the **Reviewing** toolbar. To do so, click the drop-down arrow to the far right on the **Reviewing** toolbar, point to **Add or Remove Buttons**, point to **Reviewing**, and then check the **Show** option.)

    Markup is considered to be anything in the file that can be hidden from view, such as comments, ink annotations, insertions or deletions, and formatting (hidden text, spaces, paragraph marks, tabs, and so forth).

    When a file is saved and this option is set to checked, regardless of the settings as selected in the **Show** button, in subsequent openings of the file the markup will be displayed.

    This option appears in the privacy options section because most markup has associated user information attached to it. When this option is set to checked, user information can be seen by other users when they open and examine the file. By default this option is set to checked.

Privacy issues posed by messaging and collaboration

Though it is not commonly thought of as a privacy issue, e-mail messaging, collaboration, and communication programs like Instant Messaging do present privacy issues. In these cases, the user is typically revealing information about who they are to others.

Generally, privacy issues are associated with revealing information of a sensitive nature to Microsoft—such as through application error reporting—or propagation of a document with information about a specific individual who either created or collaborated on a document with others. Since many companies have a corporate image they wish to maintain, it is also important for administrators to take into consideration the privacy issues of the company as well as employees when making decisions to control privacy settings. For instance, collaboration features, Instant Messaging, and Outlook 2003 e-mail settings should be reviewed to determine if they meet the privacy standards established by the company. Correctly setting access to these features and applications will help to alleviate employee and corporate privacy concerns.

Privacy-related policies

You can help to control privacy settings by using policy settings available from the various ADM policy templates that are included with the *Microsoft Office 2003 Editions Resource Kit*. Not shown in the following list are the various collaboration, Instant Messaging, and Outlook policies that can help control some of the privacy issues noted earlier. It is recommended that an administrator perform a thorough review of all the policy settings available for Office to determine if any of the policy settings will positively affect privacy concerns.

For example:

Word:

Warn before printing, saving, or sending a file that contains tracked changes or comments

Application Error Reporting:

Do not upload user documents

Do not upload any additional data

Office:

Enable Customer Experience Improvement Program

Prevent users from uploading settings to the internet

Default location to store settings file (OPS)

Feedback URL

Publisher:

Update personal information when saving

Disabling Visual Basic for Applications

Visual Basic for Applications (VBA) was at one time considered a security risk because of its ability to run macros attached to files or e-mail messages. The risk, however, is not with VBA itself—it is with the problems caused when VBA is intentionally used by attackers to disrupt or sabotage work.

Visual Basic for Applications is now an installable feature of Microsoft Office 2003. It can be left out of an installation by changing its installation state.

Note   Not installing VBA does not protect against malicious programs (such as compiled programs) created with other programming languages, nor does it remove the possibility of script-based programs from being used to accomplish the same goal.

VBA can be turned off by setting the install option for VBA to **Not Available** or **Not Available, Hidden, Locked** in the **Set Feature Installation States** page of the Custom Installation Wizard, Custom Maintenance Wizard, or the Setup.exe **Advance Customization** page; any other installation option turns VBA on (including setting Microsoft Office Access 2003 to **Run from My Computer** because VBA is required by Access to run).

Turning VBA off presents significant issues:

- Access 2003 cannot be installed to a user's computer and is removed if it is already installed.

- Some of the downloads available from Microsoft Office Online and the Microsoft Office 2003 Editions Resource Kit Toolbox will not run.

- Macros will not run.

- All programs, add-ins, and macros dependent on VBA will not run.

It is recommended that you not turn off VBA. Instead, you should use the security features of Office to limit the potential for malicious attacks to computer hardware or software.

In general, setting security options to the most restrictive settings helps defend against malicious attacks entering through scripts, add-ins, or other programs. If High security is enabled, it allows organizations to retain VBA as an installed feature.

Mitigating Potential Security Threats

Recent changes to security-related features within Microsoft Office 2003 have caused changes to how the Microsoft Office 2003 package is installed. In past versions, the default configuration provided for previous versions usually included a different means of storing and acknowledging certificates of trust as well as fewer options for administrators to restrict the startup of Microsoft ActiveX controls. Now, ActiveX controls have six possible startup configurations.

There are several other improvements that are not obvious due to changes at the source code level that reduced buffer overflow attacks and changed how attachments to e-mail messages are run. These changes in how Office applications are installed and run is an attempt to help reduce possible security threats.

But even with all these new changes, it is still up to the administrator to create and test an installation of Office that meets the security needs of the company. This may require a full evaluation of all the sections of Office applications that access the Internet; receive or send e-mail messages; receive attachments; run ActiveX controls, add-ins, or macros; and determine how passwords are created and maintained.

Ultimately, Office applications are only as secure as the network, operating system, and passwords used to help secure access to data created by the applications. This section intends to lay out general guidelines for administrators who are new to the security features of Office and show how administrators can augment the built-in security-related features with simple changes in how Office is deployed and used on users' computers.

Evaluate security-sensitive features

There are several features of Office 2003 that have security-sensitive areas. Specifically, any feature with a method for accessing the Internet or allowing access to the network is considered a possible security risk. Use of virus-checking software mitigates most problems associated with these entry points, but diligence about protecting intrusion from external communication lines should also be maintained. This can be mitigated in a few ways: by keeping virus-checking software current with updates available from the virus-checking software manufacturer, by creating a proxy server (firewall) to disable access to undesired Web sites, or by reducing the access of external TCP/IP to open ports on your local network.

Administrators may also want to disable access to some features and settings of Office 2003 applications. To do so, consult the policy templates (ADM files) for each Office application and also examine the policies for the operating system to determine if any of the settings may help provide for a more secure computing environment.

Evaluate all external software

Executables purchased from software manufacturers other than Microsoft should always have a valid digital signature as part of a certificate obtained from a certificate authority. If a product is purchased and it does not have a valid certificate of trust, it is recommended that you not install it. However, if installing the product is absolutely necessary, evaluate the product prior to distributing it to users within the company. During the evaluation, carefully examine the product to make sure it only performs as expected and does not intentionally or unintentionally distribute a virus.

> **Note**   Activation or installation of any executable added to an Office application usually forces the process of acceptance of the certificate of trust. If a request to accept a certificate of trust is not presented during the installation or startup of a new executable, it is possible the certificate of trust has been accepted previously or your macro security setting is set to Low.

Reduce access points that pose security threats

Reducing the threat of an attack is partially accomplished by minimizing entry points for attack and installing virus-checking software that is kept up to date.

Reducing the threat of an attack is based on several factors, which may force a change in business practices. Some of these changes may include:

- Installing a firewall (proxy server).

- Implementing password access to the network.

- Enforcing password and rights management to servers and shares within the corporate network.

Each of these is a critical step to reducing the threat of attack. However, it usually requires training users to help them recognize when they are not practicing safe security methods. The first line of real defense for corporations for reducing their vulnerability to attack is to train users to practice safe computing methods. Instructing users to not open suspicious e-mail messages or run unapproved programs downloaded from the Web or brought in from home will eliminate several entry points for worms, viruses, and Trojan horse programs.

There are other methods for reducing the exposure to possible attacks. They are associated with installing only the required software to get the work done and turning on only the options required for business purposes.

Remove unused features

If an application is set to install by default and you do not need it, set it to **Not Available** or **Not Available, Hidden, Locked** in either the Custom Installation Wizard or Custom Maintenance Wizard. Most of the necessary work to accomplish this task should be performed prior to deploying Office to users. A test computer should be created for evaluating the various configurations of Office you create using these tools. The necessary configuration changes you create should be identified and included in the transform that is used to install Office. Use the Custom Maintenance Wizard for any post-installation reconfiguration of Office security settings.

Secure non-secure settings

Any data access points to the Internet, network, or floppy drive are vulnerable to attack. There are several policies available in the policy templates (accessed through the Group Policy snap-in) to help reduce the threat these access points can present. Options, processes, or dialogs used to set or gain access to these ports should be evaluated and checked to be sure the settings comply with your corporate policies for safe computing. Several of these policies are available in the system.adm, conf.adm, and inetres.adm templates (%windir%\system32\grouppolicy\adm or %windir%\inf).

Apply digital signatures to documents and internally developed macros

By attaching digital signatures to documents, it is possible to increase the safety of a document, since you have a good idea of who created it. If your company uses digital signatures for documents, then you might want to intercept the **SaveAs** menu option and force the use of the **ActiveDocument.Signatures.Add** method that will display a dialog of the digital signatures the user can apply to the current document prior to saving it. Use of the **Signatures.Add** method requires the use of digital signatures supplied by a certificate authority.

Chapter 24

Locked-down Configurations

The Microsoft® Windows® 2000 and Microsoft Windows XP operating systems can help to provide a security-enhanced working environment for multiple users. This enhanced security is achieved by allowing permission-restricted access to registry branches and hard disk folders on NTFS-formatted disks connected to the same computer running these operating systems. When this restrictive access is enabled on a computer, the computer configuration is known as locked down.

With a locked-down configuration, only someone with administrative permissions to the registry and system-related folders on the hard disk where the operating system resides can make changes to the configuration of the computer. Locking down a system helps to prevent users from installing new software, removing existing software, changing currently configured application settings, updating system files to different levels, and viewing other users' files.

Locking Down an Office Configuration

Administrators can configure an installation of Microsoft Office 2003 that restricts user access to some or all menu options by using policies, the Custom Installation Wizard or—after an initial installation—the Custom Maintenance Wizard.

To further restrict access to system areas from users, administrators can lock portions of the registry and folders or drives using the security-related features of Microsoft Windows 2000 and Windows XP. Locking the registry can be accomplished safely for the following registry branches:

- HKEY_LOCAL_MACHINE (HKLM)

- HKEY_CLASSES_ROOT (HKCR)

- HKEY_CURRENT_CONFIG (HKCC)

Locking down the HKEY_USERS or HKEY_CURRENT_USER branches can present problems for some applications and should only be done by an experienced administrator after thorough testing of Office applications on a test computer.

Each customized installation of Office is unique and requires testing, especially if registry branches are going to be locked down. Users can encounter problems when applications they are using try to make changes to a locked portion of the registry.

To lock down the registry for systems running Windows 2000 and Windows XP, use the Registry Editor (regedt32.exe for Windows 2000 and regedit.exe for Windows XP). Regedit.exe and regedt32.exe are not available as shortcuts from the **Start** menu. You must run them by selecting **Start**, pointing to **Run**, then typing **regedt32** or **regedit** in the **Open** combo box.

To lock down a branch of the registry with regedt32 for Windows 2000

1. Select the registry branch or node you want to lock down.

2. Select **Security**.

3. Select **Permissions**.

4. Add permissions for administrators of the computer to **Full Control**, if those permissions are not already present.

5. Set permissions for **Everyone** to **Read**.

6. Click **OK**.

To lock down a branch of the registry with regedit for Windows XP

1. Select the registry branch or node you want to lock down.

2. Select **Edit**.

3. Select **Permissions**.

4. Add permissions for administrators of the computer to **Full Control**, if those permissions are not already present.

5. Set permissions for **Everyone** to **Read**.

6. Click **OK**.

Changes to permissions are enforced the moment you click **OK**.

You can also create an access control list (ACL) to lock the Policies subkey in the Windows registry. This option prevents users from changing a policy configuration setting by modifying security settings in the user's registry. See the Group Policy snap-in Help for further information.

To lock the Office-related nodes of the registry, set permissions to HKLM\Software\Microsoft\Office or HKCU\Software\Microsoft\Office, or both. If you don't want users to have write or edit permissions to any Microsoft applications, set permissions for the nodes HKLM\Software\Microsoft or HKCU\Software\Microsoft, or both. Locking just these nodes does not lock down all of the possible Office registry entries. However, it does cover the majority of entries available to users.

Resources and related information

Enabling Terminal Services on an operating system applies specific permissions to the HKCU and HKLM nodes of the registry. See "Locking Down the Operating System" in the next section for more information.

To restrict access to menu options, see "Managing Users' Configurations by Policy" in Chapter 18, "Updating Users' Office 2003 Configurations."

Locking Down the Operating System

The Microsoft Windows 2000 and Microsoft Windows XP operating systems allow administrators to set permissions-restricted access to the registry. Restricting access to the registry allows administrators to maintain the configuration of the computer so users won't create confusion for other users by installing, modifying, or removing applications without the knowledge or permission of other users.

Administrators can lock the registry by using the regedit.exe or regedt32.exe utilities available with Windows 2000 or Windows XP. Administrators can apply permissions-restricted access to the HKLM or HKCU nodes of the registry to block changes to these sections of the registry, thereby preventing users who do not have the correct permissions to the registry from adding or removing applications that require the writing or editing of registry entries.

Locking the registry has effects on all applications that store information in the registry, including Microsoft Office 2003 applications. Administrators who attempt to make changes to the configuration of the registry—either to registry settings, or permission changes to the various nodes or branches—should diligently test and evaluate their changes on a test computer prior to rolling them out to users. If you do not test registry changes, it is possible to encounter unexpected results when they are implemented.

If needed, it is possible to be more granular in your approach. Instead of locking down the entire node in the registry, it is possible to apply permission-restricted access to specific keys or subnodes of the registry, thereby opening some sections of the registry for writing, editing, or deletion.

If you wish to specifically lock the entire operating system (freeze a configuration), set the highest level nodes to permission-restricted access. If you want users to have the ability to add or remove specific applications, but not be able to make changes to the operating system, set permissions to the system nodes in the appropriate branches of the registry tree. For example, to lock the system-related nodes, set permissions to HKLM\System or HKCU\System, or both. Locking just these nodes does not lock down all of the possible operating system–related registry entries; however, it does cover the majority of entries available to users.

To remove any doubt of whether or not a section of the registry is locked down, lock the highest level node (HKLM and HKCU).

Because permission-restricted access to the registry is dependent on Windows NT® authorization of an existing user account, locking down the system also implies maintaining user IDs, passwords, and maintaining user accounts on a regular basis.

Terminal Services

A locked-down configuration is implemented by default when Terminal Services is enabled on either Windows 2000 or Windows XP. Terminal Services is a term applied to operating systems providing remote multiuser access. These operating systems are available for use by more than one user simultaneously. Since these operating systems allow multiple users to log on to the system at the same time through remote communication links, it creates potential configuration control issues if all users are allowed to make changes to the configuration of the computer at any time. Therefore, a locked-down configuration is implemented by default for Terminal Services–enabled systems.

A Terminal Services installation locks down the two branches of the registry named HKEY_CURRENT_USER (HKCU) and HKEY_LOCAL_MACHINE (HKLM). These two branches of the registry must be locked to help prevent all users, except administrators, from making changes to the registry. Implementing this restrictive action helps to give control of the configuration of the operating system to the administrator.

The locking of registry branches forces more frequent monitoring of the system by administrators since users are not allowed to make configuration changes to the computer on their own. Administrators should review and make necessary changes to the system on a scheduled basis. If the administrator cannot perform the necessary review and maintenance of Terminal Services, they should consider revising some of the restrictions or allow one local user administrative access so he or she can manage the addition or removal of software depending on the needs of all users.

Chapter 25

Code Development and Built-in Office Security Settings

Macro security settings are essentially the same across Microsoft® Office 2003 applications. It is recommended that you review how these security settings affect associated features in an application and how they can affect custom-built macros or programs created with the Microsoft Visual Basic® development system, since disabling a macro may limit functionality in each application to a degree that is unacceptable to users.

Understanding Built-In Office Security Features

Administrating security features of Microsoft Office 2003 can be difficult due to the myriad of possible security issues businesses encounter every day. Understanding the built-in security features of Office can help make identifying the necessary configuration changes for a specific business security requirement easier to accomplish. The following content presents information about the macro security model of Visual Basic for Applications for Office and the Microsoft Office antivirus application programming interface (API).

Understanding macro security

Macro security depends on Microsoft Authenticode® technology. Authenticode uses a digital signature as a means of identifying a data file and executable code attached to an Office item—such as a document, workbook, presentation, or e-mail message—so it can be traced back to the originator of the work. The validation of this signature requires the legitimate authentication of the author who signed the macro, and the authentication of the certificate of trust created for the author and included with the signature. Attaching a signature to a file, executable, Microsoft ActiveX® control, dynamic-link library (DLL), or other data file requires obtaining a certificate from a certificate authority.

Use of the term macro also implies any executable that can be attached and embedded into a document, worksheet, e-mail message, and so forth, for Microsoft Office Word 2003, Microsoft Office Excel 2003, or Microsoft Office PowerPoint® 2003. For Microsoft Office Outlook® 2003, Microsoft Office Publisher 2003, and Microsoft Office FrontPage® 2003, the term macro is explicitly used for macros used by Visual Basic for Applications. Macro security does not apply to ActiveX controls (OCX files) since the method of installing an ActiveX control to a user's computer requires the installation of the control to pass authentication during an installation, not each time the control is run. After installation, the ActiveX control is considered safe to run since it has passed authentication.

Office 2003 applications inherit some of the security settings of Microsoft Internet Explorer. Office applications can optionally instruct the core Internet Explorer components to use different security settings when they make calls to open a URL, if required.

Macro security levels are configurable in each product which implements macro development or use. The possible level settings are High, Medium, and Low. For a detailed overview of these settings, see "Understanding Macro Security Levels in Office" later in this chapter.

Understanding the Office antivirus API

The Office antivirus API is a library of function calls for use by developers who create virus-checking software. Virus-checking software developed exclusively for use with Office uses this specially designed API function library to scan all known Office file types for possible virus signatures. This scanning occurs regardless of the security settings of any of the Office applications. If a document is opened that contains a macro or executable, the antivirus software scans the document for known viruses and determines if the macro contains any virus-like characteristics. If the virus software detects a virus, the document is not allowed to load into the work area of the application, and a warning is displayed.

In previous releases of Office, there was occasional confusion over the two types of antivirus-checking software available to users. Virus-checking software created using the Office antivirus API can only evaluate files used by Office applications. If you have purchased virus-scanning software, you should examine the product documentation that came with the software to make sure which type of virus checking the program performs. If you have installed the software and are unsure whether or not it uses the Office antivirus API, open the **Security** dialog (**Tools** menu | **Macro** | **Security** option) and check the bottom left corner. If it is compatible, it will display a message stating the virus-checking software is installed and working.

Office, by default, does not include a specific virus-checking software program compatible with the Office antivirus API. Users or administrators must purchase this software from a third-party vendor. Only after the antivirus software is installed will a message appear in the **Security** dialog.

Understanding Macro Security Levels in Office

Different types of signed and unsigned macros react differently to the three levels of macro security settings—High, Medium, and Low. Users can change these settings through the **Security Level** tab in the **Security** dialog box (**Tools** menu, **Macro** submenu) of any Microsoft Office 2003 application that helps to enforce macro security.

In all cases Low security presents no prompt to the user, and all macros are allowed to run. When macro security is set to Low, certificates of trust attached to macros are not examined by the system and are not presented to the user for acceptance. Since the user is never prompted to accept or reject these certificates, they are not posted to the trusted Trust Publishers store for Office applications.

Only when macro security is set to Medium or High and a user agrees to trust a certificate can a certificate be added to the trusted Trust Publishers store. Certificates can also be added by the administrator in a couple of ways—when deploying Office with the certificate of trust embedded in a transform, or by using the Active Directory® directory service to deploy the certificate to all users who need it.

The following list summarizes the effect High and Medium security settings have on signed and unsigned macros. The list does not present the Low security option because Low security has the same effect in all cases.

> **Note**   New to this release of Office is a component that checks all XML files that have references to XSLs (XML transforms) for a possible script. If a script is found, it is disabled if the macro security is set to High. If the macro security level is set to Medium, the user is prompted as to whether to run the script. If macro security is set to Low, the script is run.

- Unsigned macros
    High—Macros are disabled.
    Medium—User is prompted to enable or disable macros.

- Signed macros from a trusted source with a valid certificate
    High and Medium—Macros are enabled.

- Signed macros from an unknown source with a valid certificate
    High and Medium—Information about the certificate is displayed. Users must then determine whether they should enable any macros based on the content of the certificate. To enable the macros, users must accept the certificate.

> **Note**   A network administrator can lock the list of trusted sources and prevent a user from adding a certificate of trust to the list, thereby disabling all macros.

- Signed macros from any source with an invalid certificate
    High and Medium—User is warned of a possible virus. Macros are disabled. The user cannot trust the certificate.

- Signed macros from any source where validation of the certificate is not possible because the public key is missing or an incompatible encryption method was used
    High—User is warned that certificate validation is not possible. Macros are disabled.
    Medium—User is warned that certificate validation is not possible. User is given the option to enable or disable macros.

- Signed macros from any source, in which the macro was signed after the certificate had expired or was revoked by the certificate authority

    High—User is warned that the certificate has expired or was revoked. Macros are disabled.

    Medium—User is warned that the certificate has expired or was revoked. User is given the option to enable or disable macros.

Further information about macro security levels is available in the Help for each of the respective Office applications that enforces macro security.

Programming-related security issues

Prior to Office XP, when a macro was started and attempted to run another macro by using an internal call to that macro, that macro was not challenged by macro security—regardless of whether the macro was signed or trusted. One of the assumptions behind allowing this was that a trusted macro would only make a call to run other safe macros. The primary reason this was done was so any calls to other macros in a procedural execution of chained macros would not halt execution.

Unfortunately, when macros are run unchallenged, it is the same as running them without security. If a macro marked as safe calls and executes a bad macro or an infected application, the results could be harmful.

To address this issue, a new security method was added to all Visual Basic for Application (VBA) application objects called **AutomationSecurity**. This method can be used with the **Application** object for each Office application, allowing programmers a means of controlling how security is handled when a macro calls another macro or external program.

Example:

```
Application.AutomationSecurity=msoAutomationSecurityByUI
```

The values for use with this method are:

- **msoAutomationSecurityLow**   Sets the macro security to Low for this application; macros are run without checking their certificate for authenticity; this is not recommended.

- **msoAutomationSecurityByUI**   Sets the macro security to the same level as is currently set in the user interface for the application (as found in the **Security** dialog); this is recommended.

- **msoAutomationSecurityForceDisable**   Sets the macro security level to High; all macros must be from a trusted source in order to run. This setting is recommended but may cause confusion if users expect the security to be at the same level as that set in the user interface.

It is highly recommended that prior to using any form of the **Open** method, that **Application.AutomationSecurity** be set to **msoAutomationSecurityForceDisable** or **msoAutomationSecurityByUI** unless a good reason for setting it otherwise is identified. Choosing to set **AutomationSecurity** to **msoAutomationSecurityLow** should be done only if it can be assured that the content of the file to open will not introduce a virus.

For programmers who need to instruct Office applications to open files or start applications or utilities from a command embedded within a macro or program, it is recommended to set **AutomationSecurity** to **msoAutomationSecurityByUI** prior to opening a file or starting an executable to conform to the security level set for the application by the user.

High security and Excel 4.0 macros

If you plan to use macros created using Excel 4.0 Macro Language (XLM) with Microsoft Office Excel 2003, you need to add a registry entry to enable them if macro security is set to High. All Office applications have macro security set to High by default when installed, unless a lower security level was specified in a transform (MST file) or Office profile settings file (OPS file).

This registry entry is necessary because Excel 4.0 XLM macros cannot be digitally signed and, therefore, cannot load when High macro security is enabled. (High security requires a macro to be signed with a valid certificate from a trusted source.)

Because some Excel add-ins were created using XLM, you may need to add the following registry entry to each user's computer to allow the macros to run. The same is true for add-ins created from XLM macros you want to run as exceptions under High macro security in Excel. To add this entry, you can use a transform, configuration maintenance file (CMW file), or REG file.

HKEY_LOCAL_MACHINE\SOFTWARE\Microsoft\Office\11.0\Excel\Security
Value name: **XLM**
Value type: **DWORD** (integer)
Value data: [**0** | **1**]

Creating and setting the **XLM** registry value to **1** allows users to load XLM macros. Setting this value to **0** or removing the registry entry returns Excel 2003 to its default behavior of not allowing XLM macros to run in High security.

When this registry entry is added and set to **1**, users are warned about XLM macros when they attempt to open a workbook that contains these macros, and they are given the option to open the workbook and enable the use of macros. Users should run a virus check on any XLM macro before they enable it. Even though XLM macros are allowed through the High security check, the High security feature for all forms of macros (such as VBA macros) is still enabled.

Setting this registry entry allows for automatic and silent disabling of non-signed VBA macros; however, the XLM macros are evaluated as if Excel was set to Medium security. The administrator of the computer can force the running of signed and trusted VBA macros, but also allow exceptions for Excel 4.0 macros. If you set this registry entry, users should be educated about viruses that affect Excel 4.0 and how they are enabled if a workbook is opened.

> **Note** Addition of this registry entry provides no indication to the user through the user interface that the system is running in a modified or reduced level of High security. Administrators should understand the risks of implementing this registry entry.

Addressing Security-related Programming Mistakes

The administration of Microsoft Office 2003 does not typically involve programming. However, many administrators use programming languages such as Visual Basic for Applications (VBA) to create custom solutions. Some administrators are also responsible for coding efforts and managing programmers who build programs for use within their organization.

This part of the chapter covers the core programming issues associated with using the Microsoft Office programming objects to create and run custom programs that interact with Office applications.

For more information on how to use these objects, see the MSDN Web site at *http://msdn.microsoft.com/* or the VBA Help for each application.

Security issues posed by Visual Basic for Applications

Over the past few years, security-related issues have caused several changes to Microsoft Office programming objects and how these objects are accessed by applications created in Visual Basic for Applications (VBA) and other programming languages. Since VBA is usually used to gain access to the core object of each Office application, it can also be used by attackers when VBA programmers make simple programming mistakes.

When an entry point into an Office application's core dynamic-link library (DLL) is exploited through VBA, nothing can stop an attacker from accessing every aspect of information stored in any file for any application. Therefore, careful attention should be taken to evaluate code written for any Office application object.

The following information presents some of the properties, methods, and functions used by many of the Office application programming objects which are most susceptible to incorrect usage. The most important of all objects is the **Application** object itself. This core object is the heart and soul of each Office application; if a programmer does not take proper precautions when writing code that uses this object, inadvertent mistakes can be made that will jeopardize the content of files or provide an entry point for attackers to exploit corporate systems.

Application object

The focus of the following material is centered on the Microsoft Office Word 2003 **Application** object, with references to related **Application** objects for other Office applications as needed. In many cases, the following material applies to other Office applications and their respective core object.

You can help to protect against external programs gaining access to the Visual Basic Project where all macros for a given application are stored (for example, Word stores macros in templates). By leaving the default setting of **Trust access to Visual Basic Project** unchecked, access to the core object that allows programs to modify or add macros to a macro repository is restricted and cannot be written to.

A policy is available to manage this setting. It is recommended that prior to setting this policy, an in-depth review of all custom and internal tools and utilities be performed to determine if the need exists to open access to the **VBProject** object of each application. If none of the programs needs to exploit the **VBProject** object, an administrator can safely leave access disabled.

For instances where access to the **VBProject** object of an application is required, a few precautions can be taken to reduce the possibility of attack. Beyond the recommended macro security setting of High, it is also recommended that internal applications (macros or compiled code from C or Visual Basic) should be given special attention and checked to see if the use of the **AutomationSecurity** property of the **Application** object is set at the beginning of each program and that a certificate of trust, issued from a certificate authority, was also compiled into the custom application.

By design, an **Application** object exists for each Office application that can use VBA. In the case of Microsoft Word, this object represents the Microsoft Word application. It includes properties and methods used to return other objects (child or parent objects, depending on the position in the object hierarchy). For example, the **ActiveDocument** property of the **Application** object can be used to return the **Document** object.

Example:

```
Set CurrentDocument as Application
CurrentDocument = Application.ActiveDocument
```

The **UserName** property can now be used to return an important piece of information from the **Application** object. The following example displays the user name for Word in a standard message box.

```
MsgBox CurrentDocument.UserName
```

AutomationSecurity property of the Application object

An existing issue with VBA causes several security concerns for administrators. When a trusted macro makes a call to start another application or to run another macro, it does not check the security of the called program unless the **Automation-Security** property is specifically instructed to do so.

Therefore, it is now recommended that programmers set the following statement at the beginning of each macro to circumvent this issue.

```
Application.AutomationSecurity = msoAutomationSecurityByUI
```

The **AutomationSecurity** property is automatically set to **msoAutomationSecurityLow** when Word, Microsoft Office Excel 2003, Microsoft Office PowerPoint 2003, Microsoft Office Outlook 2003, or another Office application runs a trusted macro. For security-minded administrators and programmers, this should be changed explicitly at the first line of every macro. To avoid breaking solutions that rely on the default setting, you should be careful to reset this property to **msoAutomationSecurityByUI** after programmatically opening a file or another macro or program from within a trusted macro. Also, this property should be considered for use immediately before and after starting a program if the **Shell** or **Execute** statements are used.

The **AutomationSecurity** property can be set to one of the following constants:

- **msoAutomationSecurityByUI**   Uses the security setting specified in the **Security** dialog box.

- **msoAutomationSecurityForceDisable**   Disables all macros in all files opened programmatically without showing any security alerts.

- **msoAutomationSecurityLow**   Enables all macros. This is the default value after a macro is started and is not recommended.

Application object method to avoid

Some code, when invoked, can cause actions an administrator would prefer not to see. One such property that should not be used in most user-based macros is **ShowVisualBasicEditor**.

This property can be used to turn on the Visual Basic Editor if it is currently not enabled. Example:

```
Application.ShowVisualBasicEditor = True
```

The problem with this is it allows a user to view information about the computer system that an administrator might not want users to see. Also, it is probably not a good idea for most user applications to start the Visual Basic Editor when most users do not write macros.

Common programming mistakes

One of the common problems programmers tend to fall into is embedding a password or UserID into a program. As a rule of thumb, passwords and UserIDs should never be stored in a program. A user should always be prompted for his UserID and password by using a dialog. The UserID and password should never be cached to the system permanently. Only after examining the UserID and password for correct formatting should they then be passed to the method or property they will be used by. In the following example, a dialog was created to prompt the user for his UserID and password. This dialog has two variables named **UserID** and **Password**.

Example:

```
UserIDPasswordDlg.Show
Set appOffice = Application.OfficeDataSourceObject
   appOffice.Open &
   bstrConnect:="DRIVER=SQL Server;SERVER=ServerName" &
   ";UID=" & UserIDPasswordDlg.UserID &
   ";PWD=" & UserIDPasswordDlg.Password &
   ";DATABASE=Northwind", bstrTable:="Employees"
UserIDPasswordDlg.Close
```

This method of string use limits the exposure of the UserID and password to only the time between the user entering the information and submitting it to the **bstrConnect** parameter.

Password-enabled or UserID-enabled objects, methods, or properties

The following objects and their related methods or properties are known to cause issues related to programmers possibly embedding passwords and UserIDs into macros. A search and review of all these objects and the listed methods or properties is suggested for all macros and related executable programs that can access the parent object of any Office application.

- **System.Connect**
- **Document.Protect**
- **Document.SaveAs**
- **Document.VBASigned**
- **Document.WritePassword**
- **Document.MailMerge.DataSource.ConnectString**
- **Document.OpenDataSource**
- **Document.OpenHeaderSource**

System object

If an attacker can gain access to the **Application** object of each application, he can easily take advantage of the **System** property to return the **System** object. If the operating system is Microsoft Windows®, the following example could make a network connection to a shared resource through a UNC name of \\Project\Info.

```
If System.OperatingSystem = "Windows" Then
     System.Connect Path:="\\Project\Info"
End If
```

The following example displays the current screen resolution (for example, "Resolution = 1024 x 768").

```
MsgBox "Resolution = " & System.HorizontalResolution& " x " & _
System.VerticalResolution
```

The **System** object can also access the environment variables that are automatically generated by the operating system. Critical environment variables are User-Name, UserProfile, UserDomain, and so forth.

Connect method of the System object

The **Connect** method establishes a connection to a network drive through a **System** object. It can be used by attackers to gain access to content on hard drives the logged-on user may have access to.

```
System.Connect(…, Password)
```

Password—If the network drive requires permissions for access, provide the password here. *This is the problem parameter.* If saved as part of a program, security can be compromised. The following example should *never* be used. Instead, a dialog should ask the user for the password.

Example of **Path** and **Password** parameters of the **Connect** method.

```
System.Connect Path:="\\Project\Info", Password:="A82jbkdeiJ8"
```

> Note   Embedding a password or UserID in a program is not recommended.

Document object

The **Document** object represents a document in Word.

Like other objects, it has methods or properties that can be used to compromise security if improperly used by programmers.

Protect method of the Document object

The **Protect** method sets protection options for sections of a document. When set, a user of a document with these settings enabled can only edit those sections they have permissions to, such as adding comments, making revisions, or completing a form. This setting is only secure if the document uses a password to open it (encrypted). Documents are not considered protected until the entire file is encrypted in some form. Since the document is not protected or encrypted by just setting the **Protect** method, the contents are not actually protected; access is only restricted if encryption is used.

```
Document.Protect(…, Password)
```

> **Password**—The password required to decrypt the specified document.

> **Note**   Embedding a password or UserID in a program is not recommended.

SaveAs method of the Document object

The **SaveAs** method saves the specified document with a new name or format. The arguments for this method correspond to the options in the **Save As** dialog box (**File** menu).

```
Document.SaveAs(…, Password, …, WritePassword, …)
```

> **Password**—A password string for opening the document for reading.
> **WritePassword**—A password string for saving changes to the document.
> Instead of hard-coding these entries into a program, it is suggested the user be prompted for the passwords.

VBASigned property of the Document object

The **VBASigned** property might be useful to administrators who are concerned about documents not being safe to open. By attaching digital signatures to documents, it is possible to increase the safety of the document since you have a good idea who created it. To do so, you can use the document object **ActiveDocument** along with its **VBASigned** property. If it returns a "True", it was digitally signed by someone. If your company uses digital signatures for documents, then you might want to intercept the **SaveAs** method and force the use of the **ActiveDocument.Signatures.Add** method to display a dialog of the digital signatures the user can apply to the current document prior to saving it. Use of the **Signatures.Add** method requires the use of digital signatures supplied by a certificate authority.

To identify a digital signature attached to a document, use the **SignatureSet.Item** method, assign the returned item to a **signature** object and then test the properties of that object, specifically the **IsCertificateExpired** property. Use the **Signatures.Delete** method to remove a digital signature from a **Signature** collection.

This example loads a document called "Temp.doc" and tests to see whether or not it has a digital signature. If no digital signature is found, the example displays a warning message.

```
Documents.Open FileName:="C:\My Documents\Temp.doc"
If ActiveDocument.VBASigned = False Then
   MsgBox "This document has no digital signature.", _
   vbCritical, "Digital Signature Warning"
End If
```

WritePassword property of the Document object

The **WritePassword** property sets a password for saving changes to the specified document.

This example sets the **WritePassword** property to the password provided by the user in the PSWDDlg dialog. The **ActiveDocument.WriteReserved** conditional test is used to determine if a **WritePassword** has already been applied to the document (adding another password would change the existing password and in this case is not recommended).

```
PSWDDlg.Show
If ActiveDocument.WriteReserved = False Then
ActiveDocument.WritePassword = PSWDDlg.PSWDVar1
End If
PSWDDlg.Close
```

MailMerge object

The **MailMerge** object represents the mail merge functionality in Word.

Use the **MailMerge** property to return the **MailMerge** object. The **MailMerge** object is always available regardless of whether the mail merge operation has begun. Use the **State** property to determine the status of the mail merge operation. The following example executes a mail merge if the active document is a main document with an attached data source. This object has a password or connection property that can be compromised by storing a password or UserID as part of the program.

```
If ActiveDocument.MailMerge.State = wdMainAndDataSource Then
   ActiveDocument.MailMerge.Execute
End If
```

MailMerge DataSource object

The MailMerge.DataSource object represents the mail merge data source in a mail merge operation. This object has a potential password issue.

Use the **DataSource** property of the **Document** object to return the **MailMerge.DataSource** object. The following example displays the name of the data source associated with the active document.

```
If ActiveDocument.MailMerge.DataSource.Name <> "" Then _
    MsgBox ActiveDocument.MailMerge.DataSource.Name
```

The following example displays all the field names in the data source associated with the active document.

```
For Each aField In ActiveDocument.MailMerge.DataSource.FieldNames
    MsgBox aField.Name
Next aField
```

ConnectString property of the MailMerge DataSource object

The **ConnectString** property of the **MailMerge DataSource** object sets or returns the connection string for the specified mail merge data source.

This example creates a new main document and attaches the Customers table from a Microsoft Office Access 2003 database named "Northwind.mdb." The connection string is displayed in a message box. The problem here is that the password and UserID could potentially be stored in this program and that is not a recommended method. It is suggested that the user of the program that accesses the data source be prompted for his UserID and password through a dialog and the resulting variables be submitted to the connection parameter of the **OpenDataSource** method.

```
Dim docNew As Document
Set docNew = Documents.Add
docNew.MailMerge.OpenDataSource & _
    Name:="C:\Program Files\Microsoft Office\Office" & _
    "\Samples\Northwind.mdb", _
    LinkToSource:=True, AddToRecentFiles:=False, _
    Connection:="TABLE Customers"
MsgBox docNew.DataSource.ConnectString
```

OpenDataSource method

The **OpenDataSource** method attaches a data source to the specified document, which becomes a main document if it isn't one already.

expression.OpenDataSource(…, PasswordDocument, PasswordTemplate, …, WritePassword-Document, WritePasswordTemplate, Connection, …)

PasswordDocument—The password used to open the data source.
PasswordTemplate—The password used to open the template.
WritePasswordDocument—The password used to save changes to the document.
WritePasswordTemplate—The password used to save changes to the template.
Connection—A range within which the query specified by an **SQLStatement** is to be performed. How you specify the range depends on how data is retrieved. For example:

- When retrieving data through ODBC, you specify a connection string.
- When retrieving data from Microsoft Excel using dynamic data exchange (DDE), you specify a named range.
- When retrieving data from Microsoft Access, you specify the word "Table" or "Query" followed by the name of a table or query.

OpenHeaderSource method

The **OpenHeaderSource** method attaches a mail merge header source to the specified document.

```
expression.OpenHeaderSource(…, PasswordDocument, PasswordTemplate, …, WritePassword-
Document, WritePasswordTemplate, …)
```

PasswordDocument—The password required to open the header source document.

PasswordTemplate—The password required to open the header source template.

WritePasswordDocument—The password required to save changes to the document data source.

WritePasswordTemplate—The password required to save changes to the template data source.

When a header source is attached, the first record in the header source is used in place of the header record in the data source.

Signature object

Security-enhanced digital signatures are only available from certificate authorities.

A signature object corresponds to a digital signature that can be attached to a document. **Signature** objects are contained in the **SignatureSet** collection of the **Document** object.

You can add a **Signature** object to a **SignatureSet** collection using the **Add** method, and you can return an existing member using the **Item** method. To remove a Signature from a **SignatureSet** collection, use the **Delete** method of the **Signature** object.

AttachCertificate property

True if the digital certificate that corresponds to the specified **Signature** object is attached to the document.

IsCertificateRevoked property

True if the digital certificate that corresponds to the **Signature** object was revoked by the issuer of the certificate (certificate authority). Read-only Boolean.

The following example prompts the user to select a digital signature to sign the currently active document in Word. To use this example, open a document in Word and pass this function the name of a certificate issuer and the name of a certificate signer that match the **Issued By** and **Issued To** fields of a digital certificate in the **Digital Certificates** dialog box. This example tests to make sure the digital signature the user selects meets certain criteria, such as not having expired, before the new signature is committed to the disk.

```
Function AddSignature(ByVal strIssuer As String, strSigner As String) As Boolean
    On Error GoTo Error_Handler
    Dim sig As Signature
    'Display a dialog to the user with a list of digital signatures.
    'If the user selects a signature, then add it to the Signatures
    'collection. If a selection is not made an error is returned.

    Set sig = ActiveDocument.Signatures.Add

    'Test the following properties before committing a Signature object
    'to disk.
    If sig.Issuer = strIssuer And sig.Signer = strSigner And _
        sig.IsCertificateExpired = False And _
        sig.IsCertificateRevoked = False And sig.IsValid = True Then
        MsgBox "Signed"
        AddSignature = True
    Else
    'Remove the Signature object from the SignatureSet collection.
        sig.Delete
        MsgBox "Not signed"
        AddSignature = False
    End If
    'Commit all signatures in the SignatureSet collection
    'to the disk.
    ActiveDocument.Signatures.Commit
    Exit Function
Error_Handler:
    AddSignature = False
    MsgBox "Action cancelled."
End Function
```

Chapter 26

Using Security-related Policies

The increase in malicious attacks on corporate computers and data has forced businesses worldwide to develop better methods of protecting their data and systems. To help administrators use the security-related features of Microsoft® Office 2003, policies can be enabled to turn security-related features on and off—as well as have those settings enforced at logon—for all Microsoft Windows® 2000 and Microsoft Windows XP users on a corporate network.

How Policies Work

Policies are special registry entries designed to help control the configuration of either the operating system or any applications designed to respect policy settings. Applications respecting policies are expected to have an associated ADM template that administrators use to set policy entries. The ADM template must be loadable by the Group Policy snap-in that is included with Microsoft Windows 2000 and Microsoft Windows XP.

The ADM templates for use with Microsoft Office 2003 Editions applications are included with the Office Resource Kit tools. In a typical installation of the tools on the Microsoft Windows XP or Microsoft Windows 2000 platform, the templates can be found in the INF folder of the WINDIR path—for example, C:\Windows\INF. Typically, the policies for the installed operating system are found in the system.adm policy template.

As part of the design of policies, a special node exists on both the HKLM and HKCU branches of the registry. Microsoft operating systems such as Windows 2000 and Windows XP respect policy settings specifically designed for use with these systems. Policies can be used to configure the user interface to appear with specific configuration changes specially suited for a business need—such as disabling access to software, utilities, or special features of the operating system that may be deemed unnecessary or detrimental to productivity. Or, policies can be used to enable a feature that is not normally turned on when the product is installed in a default configuration.

Structure of a policy registry entry

The two most important registry branches in the registry are HKLM and HKCU. HKLM stands for HKEY_Local_Machine and HKCU stands for HKEY_Current_User. Policy settings set in the Local Machine branch are expected to apply to all users and are generally considered the most enforceable and best protected from user changes. Policy settings set in the Current User branch are specific to only the logged-on user.

Both the HKLM and HKCU registry branches are designed to have a Policies node. This is not an absolute for all custom applications, but it is the preferred design approach and is recommended for all developers. Applications are expected to follow the order of precedence indicated in the example provided below, as do all Microsoft applications designed specifically for Windows 2000 and Windows XP.

- HKLM\Software\Policies\Microsoft\...

- HKLM\Software\Microsoft\...

- HKCU\Software\Policies\Microsoft\...

- HKCU\Software\Microsoft\...

Registry entries found in the Policies node are mirror entries to those found in the non-policy entries. For example:

HKLM\Software\Policies\Microsoft\Office\11.0\Common\Toolbars
AutoExpandMenus DWORD 1
HKLM\Software\Microsoft\Office\11.0\Common\Toolbars
AutoExpandMenus DWORD 1
HKCU\Software\Policies\Microsoft\Office\11.0\Common\Toolbars
AutoExpandMenus DWORD 1
HKCU\Software\Microsoft\Office\11.0\Common\Toolbars
AutoExpandMenus DWORD 1

Any of the above registry entries would be respected by any Office 2003 application. However, the difference is that the Policies registry entry cannot be set by the user, only by the administrator who has created a POL file by using the Office11.adm policy template. However, if the user knows where this entry is in the registry, the user could manually change the entry.

Unless the permissions for the registry are set so that only the administrator can make changes, it is possible for users to defeat policy settings. Therefore, it is common practice for administrators to apply permissions to the registry in order to block changes to the Policies node by users. For Terminal Services–enabled systems, applying registry permissions is performed automatically by the operating system when Terminal Services is enabled.

It is common for the operating system and applications to respect both the HKLM and HKCU nodes of the registry if a Policies node is found in the registry.

If you develop a custom application that you want to add policy support to, there are general guidelines available within the MSDN Web site at *http: //msdn.microsoft.com*, though there may not be support for the development of ADM templates. Examining existing ADM templates will generally provide enough information and examples for you to develop ADM templates if needed.

First-time installation policy concerns

As part of a first-time installation of Office, administrators are usually concerned about security-related policies such as:

- Trust all installed add-ins and templates

- Security Level (macro security)

- Trust access to Visual Basic Project

- Disable VBA for Office applications

- Unsafe ActiveX initialization

- Automation Security

- Prevent users from changing Office encryption settings

- Specify Trusted Alert Sources

- Prevent users from uploading settings to the Internet

- Feedback URL

- Prevent access to Web-based file storage

- Disable Information Rights Management User Interface

- Disable hyperlinks to Web templates in File | New and task panes

- Prevent users from customizing attachment security settings

- Allow access to e-mail attachments

- Outlook virus security settings

- Configure Add-in Trust level

- Task Manager security key

- Prohibit access to Control Panel

- Prevent access to the Command Prompt (DOS window)

Each of these policies is available within the various Office 2003 ADM policy templates. Their related non-policy registry entries are usually also settable through the Custom Installation Wizard and the Custom Maintenance Wizard within the **Change Office User Settings** and the **Specify Security Settings** pages. By setting non-policy registry entries in three places—in the **Specify Security Settings** page, through the **Change Office User Settings** page, and then in the Group Policy snap-in—the desired settings are enforced in all possible places. And if permissions to the registry nodes are set to only accept changes from administrators, the settings are enforced to the greatest extent possible. However, if a user gains access to the most secure and highest order of precedence settings (usually the HKLM node), the user can defeat the setting.

Administrators should guard their user accounts and review the Administrators network group account to be sure no one has forged access to permission-restricted levels of their systems.

Important policies

Following are noted the registry settings for important policies that were requested by administrators. The ActiveX® control initialization registry entry is somewhat complex in that it has six possible settings (even though only three are revealed through the Custom Installation Wizard and Custom Maintenance Wizard). Administrators who need to set ActiveX initialization to a more refined setting can review the following ActiveX initialization documentation.

Macro security level

If you use the **Specify Office Security Settings** page of either the Custom Mainte-nance Wizard or the Custom Installation Wizard, and you change the **Default Secu-rity Level** for an application, this process is the same as using the **Security** dialog box available through the application's user interface. Use of this registry entry sets the macro security level for each application specified in the **<APP>** portion of the key to the respective value data listed here.

    <APP> = Word, Excel, Access, PowerPoint, Publisher, Outlook

    HKCU\Software\Microsoft\Office\11.0\<APP>\Security

    The parallel policy key is:

    HKLM\Software\Policies\Microsoft\Office\11.0\<APP>\Security

    Value name: **Level**

    Value type: **REG_DWORD**

    Value data: **[1 | 2 | 3]**

    1. Low

    2. Medium

    3. High

    Use of the policy is recommended in situations where you never want users to have the ability to change the macro security level.

ActiveX initialization

Through the use of the common security key, you can instruct Office to set ActiveX initialization security for all Office applications. This registry entry can be set by using the **Specify Office Security Settings** page of either the Custom Installation Wizard or the Custom Maintenance Wizard.

    HKCU\Software\Microsoft\Common\Security

    The parallel policy key is:

    HKLM\Software\Policies\Microsoft\Common\Security

    HKCU\Software\Policies\Microsoft\Common\Security

    The value name **UFIControls** can be set for either of these nodes to the fol-lowing values and respective actions:

    Value name: **UFIControls**

    Value type: **REG_DWORD**

    Value Data: [**1** | **2** | **3** | **4** | **5** | **6**]

    Safe For Initialization (SFI) is a term used by ActiveX developers to mark a con-trol as being safe to open and run and not capable of causing ill effects to any sys-tems, regardless of whether it has persisted data values or not. If a control is not marked SFI, it is possible for the control to adversely affect a system—or it is merely possible the developers did not test the control in all situations and are not sure whether their control may be compromised at some future date.

The value data can be explained as follows:

1. Regardless of how the control is marked, load it and use the persisted values (if any). This setting does not prompt the user.

2. If SFI, load the control in safe mode and use persisted values (if any). If not SFI, load in un-safe mode with persisted values (if any), or use the default (first-time initialization) settings. This setting does not prompt the user.

3. If SFI, load the control in un-safe mode and use persisted values (if any). If not SFI, prompt that it is marked unsafe. If the user chooses **No** at the prompt, do not load the control. Otherwise, load it with default (first-time initialization) settings.

4. If SFI, load the control in safe mode and use persisted values (if any). If not SFI, prompt that it is marked unsafe. If the user chooses **No** at the prompt, do not load the control. Otherwise, load it with default (first-time initialization) settings.

5. If SFI, load the control in un-safe mode and use persisted values (if any). If not SFI, prompt that it is marked unsafe. If the user chooses **No** at the prompt, do not load the control. Otherwise, load it with persisted values.

6. If SFI, load the control in safe mode and use persisted values (if any). If not SFI, prompt that it is marked unsafe. If the user chooses **No** at the prompt, do not load the control. Otherwise, load it with persisted values.

If you are a programmer interested in knowing more about ActiveX controls marked as SFI, see the documentation on ActiveX control development for information about safe mode for ActiveX controls. Look for the following object and method: **IObjectSafetyImpl::SetInterfaceSafetyOptions**. The IObjectSafety interface allows a client to retrieve and set an object's safety levels. For example, a Web browser may call **IObjectSafety::SetInterfaceSafetyOptions** to set a control to safe for initialization or safe for scripting.

> **Note**   Not all ActiveX controls respect the safe mode registry setting and therefore may load persisted data even though you instructed the control to use safe mode from this registry setting.

When setting the **Unsafe ActiveX Initialization** option in the Custom Installation Wizard or Custom Maintenance Wizard, the following conditions apply:

- **Prompt user to use control defaults**   Sets the UFIControls registry entry to a data value of **4**. If the control is marked Safe For Initialization (SFI), the control is loaded in safe mode and uses any persisted values. If the control is not marked SFI, the user is prompted that the control is marked unsafe. If the user chooses **No** at the prompt, the control is *not loaded at all*. If the user chooses **Yes**, the control is *loaded with default* (first-time initialization) *settings*.

- **Prompt user to use persisted data**   Sets the UFIControls registry entry to a data value of **6**. If the control is marked Safe For Initialization (SFI), the control is loaded in safe mode and uses any persisted values. If the control is not marked SFI, the user is prompted that the control is marked unsafe. If the user chooses **No** at the prompt, the control is *not loaded at all*. If the user chooses **Yes**, the control is *loaded with persisted values*.

- **Do not prompt**   Sets the UFIControls registry entry to a data value of **1**. This setting loads the control, uses any persisted data, and runs it regardless of whether or not the control is marked as SFI.

- **<do not configure>**   Leaves the default configuration for this option set to **3—Prompt user to use control defaults**.

It is possible for an administrator to set the ActiveX initialization settings to one of the six possible values by using the **Add/Remove Registry Entries** page of either the Custom Installation Wizard or the Custom Maintenance Wizard.

Operating System Policies

The operating system policies discussed in this chapter do not directly affect macro security in Microsoft Office 2003 Editions, nor do they change the way security is handled by any of the Office applications. However, these policies can help limit the exposure of critical portions of a network, operating system, or user interface to potentially destructive changes by users. Some of these settings can even mitigate the first level of attack by most attackers.

By setting these policies, an administrator can reduce the amount of data that users are exposed to or reduce the number of choices users must make while they interact with the system. As a result, productivity can increase by not having to support some features and by streamlining the user interface of the operating system. The policies in this section are available within the listed templates.

It is highly recommended that administrators examine the policy templates for the operating systems their users are working with. Several policies provide methods to help control and enforce the configuration of the operating system and help reduce the probability of a user inadvertently creating a problem. These policies potentially limit access to features of the operating system that users do not need to use or should not use.

> **Note**   The system.adm template cannot be copied between different versions of Microsoft Windows operating systems. The Microsoft Windows 2000 and Microsoft Windows XP operating systems each have a unique system.adm template. Attempting to use a system.adm from a Windows XP system on a Windows 2000 system may cause unexpected results.

The ADM templates discussed in this chapter are not included with the Office Resource Kit and should already be installed in the INF directory of the Windows install folder. (The Windows install folder can be discovered by entering **SET** in a command prompt and looking for the returned **WINDIR** environment variable value.)

Windows 2000 and Windows XP policies

The following list of policy templates and associated policy groupings provides a sampling of the policies you can explore to limit the user environment in Microsoft Windows 2000 and Microsoft Windows XP operating systems.

The following policy templates are available for both Windows 2000 and Windows XP:

- system.adm
- conf.adm
- inetres.adm
- dw20.adm

These templates should already be installed on your computer. When you install the Office Resource Kit to any computer, the AER_1033.adm (or respective language-related instance of the application error reporting file) will be copied into the INF folder. The AER_1033.adm file replaces the dw20.adm template. When Office 2003 is installed to a system where policies are enabled and in use, the dw20.adm template used by the administrator to create a POL file should be removed from the system, and the settings that were in use should now be reset by using the AER_1033.adm version of the template and then redistributed.

For each template, the respective policy groupings (and the differences between Windows 2000 and Windows XP) are noted below.

- system.adm
        Start Menu and Taskbar
        Desktop
Active Desktop
Active Directory
        Control Panel
Add/Remove Programs
Display
Printers
Regional and Language Options
        Shared Folders—(Windows XP)
        Network
Offline Files
Network Connections—(Windows XP)
Network and Dial-up Connections—(Windows 2000)

System
User Profiles—(Windows XP)
Scripts—(Windows XP)
Ctrl + Alt + Del Options—(Windows XP)
Logon—(Windows XP)
Logon/Logoff—(Windows 2000)
Group Policy
Power Management—(Windows XP)
    Windows Components
Windows Explorer
Microsoft Management Console
Task Scheduler
Terminal Services—(Windows XP)
Windows Installer
Windows Messenger—(Windows XP)
Windows Update

- conf.adm
    Netmeeting
Application Sharing
Audio & Video
Options Page

- dw20.adm
    Application Error Reporting
General Reporting
Corporate Error Reporting
Queued Reporting

- AER_1033.adm—replacement for dw20.adm
    Application Error Reporting
General Reporting
Corporate Error Reporting
Queued Reporting

- inetres.adm
    Internet Explorer
Internet Control Panel
Offline Pages
Browser menus
Toolbars
Persistence Behavior
Administrator Approved Controls

Security-related policies

Each operating system uses templates with the same names, but depending on the operating system, there may be different sets of available policies and, as noted below, different text to describe the same policy. Windows XP has more available policies and is a superset of the Windows 2000 policies.

The following list of policies has what are considered to be some of the most beneficial policies available to an administrator in a corporate setting. However, it is recommended that an administrator examine all of the available policies that are part of the system.adm template. Many of the available policies can simplify administration of a large-scale deployment of Office and the related workstations that it is installed to.

- system.adm
  Remove Run menu from Start Menu
  Disable Control Panel—(Windows 2000)
  Prohibit access to the Control Panel—(Windows XP)
  Disable Task Manager—(Windows 2000)
  Remove Task Manager—(Windows XP)
  Disable Logoff—(Windows 2000)
  Remove Logoff—(Windows XP)
  Disable the command prompt—(Windows 2000)
  Prevent access to the command prompt—(Windows XP)
  Disable registry editing tools—(Windows 2000)
  Prevent access to registry editing tools—(Windows XP)
  Run only allowed Windows applications
  Don't run specified Windows applications
  Disable Add/Remove Programs—(Windows 2000)
  Remove Add/Remove Programs Programs—(Windows XP)
  Password protect the screen saver
  Disable and remove the Shut Down command—(Windows 2000)
  Remove and prevent access to the Shut Down command—(Windows XP)
  Disable deletion of printers—(Windows 2000)
  Prevent deletion of Printers—(Windows XP)
  Disable addition of printers—(Windows 2000)
  Prevent addition of printers—(Windows XP)
  Hide these specified drives in My Computer
  No "Entire Network" in My Network Places

- Inetres.adm
  Disable changing proxy settings
  Disable changing ratings settings
  Disable changing certificate settings
  Do not allow AutoComplete to save passwords

        Disable Internet Connection wizard

        Disable the Security Page

        Disable the Advanced Page

        File menu: Disable Save As... menu option

        Disable Save this program to disk option

- Conf.adm

        Prevent automatic acceptance of Calls

        Prevent sending files

        Prevent receiving files

        Disable Chat

        Disable application Sharing

        Prevent Sharing

        Prevent Desktop Sharing

        Prevent Sharing Command Prompts

        Prevent Sharing Explorer Windows

        Limit the Bandwidth of Audio and Video

        Disable Audio

        Disable full duplex Audio

        Prevent sending Video

        Prevent receiving Video

Unlike previous releases of the Office Resource Kit, the registry keys associated with these policies will not be presented here. Instead, if you plan to use the policy registry entries by using a means other than the Active Directory® directory service, it is recommended that you open the ADM template that the policy entry is stored in and paste the related policy from the template into a REG file. From this REG file, you can distribute the policy registry entries to anyone you want to, employing the means your organization uses to distribute such files. Another option for implementing these policies is to create a test workstation, implement the policies on that computer, and then use the Office Profile Wizard to capture the profile of that computer and distribute it to other users. This process may require customization of the INI file used by the Office Profile Wizard. Remember, though, that a computer profile captured from a Windows XP computer will not implement the Windows XP–only policies on a Windows 2000 computer. Any unsupported policies distributed to the registry of the Windows 2000 computer are ignored.

> **Note**   If you are deploying Office to both Windows 2000 and Windows XP operating systems, use of the system.adm template when creating a policy file requires special handling in the Active Directory implementation of policies on a corporate network. They cannot be used interchangeably.

If you want to propagate policy registry entries at the time of deployment, it is possible to include the registry entries in the **Add/Remove Registry Entries** page of the Custom Installation Wizard, and they will be stored in the transform. However, management of the policies after distribution in this method is much more difficult than using Active Directory or distributing the POL file from the domain controller during logon.

> **Note**   Unlike previous releases of Office, the System Policy Editor is no longer supported. Also, posting of a policy file created by the System Policy Editor is no longer supported since the Group Policy snap-in does not create a POL file that can combine both the HKLM and HKCU portions of the registry into one POL file. Only Active Directory implementations of policy files are supported for Office 2003.

Office Security-related Policies

Provided in this section are policies related to security settings of Microsoft Office 2003 Editions applications. This same information can be found by examining the various ADM policy templates that are included with the Office Resource Kit and are installed during a typical installation.

The policies presented here are listed by the respective ADM policy template, policy grouping, and then the security-related policy text name. The registry key is not documented here. However, it is possible to find the registry key in the ADM template and then copy that key information and the possible data value you may need to put into a REG file or to use with the **Add/Remove Registry Entries** page of the Custom Installation Wizard or Custom Maintenance Wizard. Copying the registry entry is not a recommended step in deploying policies; use of Active Directory is the recommended method of policy propagation to users on a corporate network.

> **Note**   If you have multiple versions of Office currently installed throughout a corporate network, the policy settings will not conflict with one another because of the method in which the registry nodes for Microsoft Office XP (Office 10.0) and Microsoft Office 2003 (Office 11.0) are stored within the registry.

■   AER_1033.adm—Automatic Error Reporting (replacement for dw20.adm)
        General Reporting
Disable error reporting
Do not upload user documents
Do not upload any additional data
        Corporate Error Reporting
Hide Don't Send button
URL to launch after reporting
URL to explain why user should report
        Queued Reporting
Bypass queue and send all reports
Send all queued reports silently

■   ACCESS11.adm—Microsoft Office Access 2003
        Tools | Macro—Security
Security Level
Trust all installed add-ins and templates
Trust access to Visual Basic Project
        Tools | Security—Workgroup Administrator
Path to shared Workgroup information file for secured MDB files
        Disable items in user interface—Custom
Disable command bar buttons and menu items
Disable shortcut keys
        Disable items in user interface—Predefined
Disable command bar buttons and menu items
Disable shortcut keys
        Miscellaneous
Do not prompt to convert older databases

■   EXCEL11.adm—Microsoft Office Excel 2003
        Tools | Macro—Security
Security Level
Trust all installed add-ins and templates
Trust access to Visual Basic Project
        Disable items in user interface—Custom
Disable command bar buttons and menu items
Disable shortcut keys
        Disable items in user interface—Predefined
Disable command bar buttons and menu items
Disable shortcut keys
        Miscellaneous
OLAP PivotTable User Defined Function (UDF) security setting

■   FP11.adm—Microsoft Office FrontPage 2003

Disable items in user interface—Custom
Disable command bar buttons and menu items
Disable items in user interface—Predefined
Disable command bar buttons and menu items

- GAL11.adm—Microsoft Clip Organizer
    Disable Clips Online access from Clip Organizer
    Clip Organizer Online URL
    Disable menu item: File | Send to Mail Recipient (as Attachment)
    Disable menu item: Tools | Tools on the Web...
    Prevent automatically importing clips
    Prevent users from importing new clips

- INF11.adm—Microsoft Office InfoPath 2003
    Disable items in user interface—Custom
Disable command bar buttons and menu items
    Disable items in user interface—Predefined
Disable command bar buttons and menu items
Disable shortcut keys
    Security
Disable opening of solutions from the Internet security zone
Disable installed solutions full access to machine

- INSTLR11.adm—Windows Installer
    Always install with elevated privileges

- OFFICE11.adm—Microsoft Office 2003
    Tools | AutoCorrect options...
Check for new actions URL
    Tools | Options | General | Service Options—Online Content
Online Content Options
    Help—Help | Privacy Settings
Enable Customer Experience Improvement Program
    Help—Help | Detect and Repair
Discard my customized settings and restore default settings
    Security Settings
Disable VBA for Office applications
Unsafe ActiveX Initialization
Automation Security
Prevent users from changing Office encryption settings
Specify Trusted Alert Sources
Prevent Word and Excel from loading managed code extensions
    Shared paths
Web Query dialog home Page

Save My Settings Wizard
Prevent users from uploading settings to the internet
Default location to store settings file (OPS)
Help on the Web
Feedback URL
Customizable Error Messages
Base URL
Disable items in user interface
Disable Information Rights Management User Interface
Services
Disable Fax Over Internet feature
Instance Messaging Integration
Allow IM to query people not on the buddy list
Manage Restricted Permissions
Additional permissions request URL
Make document with restricted documents viewable in trusted browsers
Always require users to connect to verify permissions
Never allow users to specify groups when restricting permission for document
Miscellaneous
Do not upload media files
Disable hyperlinks to web templates in File | New and task panes
Prevent access to Web-based file storage
Disable web view in the Office file dialogs

- OUTLK11.adm—Microsoft Office Outlook 2003
    Tools | Macro—Security
Security Level
Outlook: Trust all installed add-ins and templates
Disable items in user interface—Custom
Disable command bar buttons and menu items
Disable shortcut keys
Disable items in user interface—Predefined
Disable command bar buttons and menu items
Disable shortcut keys
Outlook Today settings
URL for custom Outlook Today
Miscellaneous
NetMeeting
Junk e-mail filtering
Auto-repair of MAPI32.DLL
Prevent users from adding e-mail account types
Prevent users from making changes to Outlook profiles

■ PPT11.adm—Microsoft Office PowerPoint 2003
   Tools | Options—Edit
Password protection
   Tools | Macro—Security
Security Level
Trust all installed add-ins and templates
Trust access to Visual Basic Project
   Slide Show | Online Broadcast | Setup and Schedule—Broadcast settings
Send audio
Send video
   Slide Show | Online Broadcast | Setup and Schedule—Broadcast settings—
Other Broadcast Settings
Chat server URL
Event URL
Help page URL
Video/audio test page URL
   Disable items in user interface—Custom
Disable command bar buttons and menu items
Disable shortcut keys
   Disable items in user interface—Predefined
Disable command bar buttons and menu items
Disable shortcut keys

■ PUB11.adm—Microsoft Office Publisher 2003
   Tools | Macro—Security
Security Level
Trust all installed add-ins and templates
   Miscellaneous
Disable Tools | Tools on the Web...
Prevent web pages displayed in Publisher from accessing the Office object model
Disable web view in the Office file dialogs

■ RM11.adm—Information Rights Management
   (no security-related policies)

■ SCRIB11.adm—Microsoft Office OneNote 2003
   Security
Saving personal information in OneNote files

■ WORD11.adm—Microsoft Office Word 2003
   Tools | Options—General
   Tools | Macro—Security
Allow background open of web pages
Security Level

Trust all installed add-ins and templates

Trust access to Visual Basic Project

      Disable items in user interface—Custom

Disable command bar buttons and menu items

Disable shortcut keys

      Disable items in user interface—Predefined

Disable command bar buttons and menu items

Disable shortcut keys

Part 8

Appendixes

Appendix A

Toolbox

The Microsoft® Office 2003 Editions Resource Kit tools are designed to help you customize, configure, and deploy Office 2003 within your organization. If you have the Office 2003 Resource Kit CD, you can install the core tools and support documents through one integrated Setup program. The tools are also available for download on the Office 2003 Resource Kit Web site at *http://www.microsoft.com/office/ork/2003*.

Answer Wizard Builder

The Answer Wizard Builder enables you to create your own Answer Wizard content to address questions specific to your organization. Users sometimes submit queries to the Answer Wizard (the intelligence engine behind the Office Assistant) that the Answer Wizard cannot answer because the question is unique to your situation. A user might ask for the path to a printer on your local network, for example, or ask for the location of a form on your intranet.

You can use the Answer Wizard Builder utility to add custom Help content to any application that uses the Office Assistant. The Answer Wizard Builder is supported on computers running Microsoft Office 2003 or Office XP.

Install the Answer Wizard Builder

The Answer Wizard Builder is automatically installed on your computer when you install the Office Resource Kit. To locate the tool, click the **Start** button, point to **Programs**, point to **Microsoft Office**, point to **Microsoft Office Tools**, point to **Microsoft Office Resource Kit**, and then click **Answer Wizard Builder**.

The Answer Wizard Builder can also be downloaded from the Toolbox on the Office 2003 Resource Kit Web site.

Resources and related information

The version of the Answer Wizard Builder provided with the Office 2003 Resource Kit is unchanged from the version released with Office XP. For more information about the Answer Wizard Builder, see Making Custom Help Content Accessible in the Office XP Resource Kit at *http://www.microsoft.com/office/ork/xp/two/admd02.htm*.

CMW File Viewer

The CMW File Viewer (CMWView.exe) enables you to view the changes that a configuration maintenance file (CMW file) makes to a user's computer. This viewer also provides a list of all possible changes the Custom Maintenance Wizard can make through a CMW file.

To use the CMW File Viewer, you must supply the path and file name of the CMW file you created with the Custom Maintenance Wizard. The CMW File Viewer is not a separate application—instead, it reads the CMW file and creates a plain-text file, which is displayed by the Notepad text editor.

Install the CMW File Viewer

The CMW File Viewer is automatically installed on your computer when you install the Microsoft Office 2003 Editions Resource Kit. To locate the tool, click the **Start** button, point to **Programs**, point to **Microsoft Office**, point to **Microsoft Office Tools**, point to **Microsoft Office Resource Kit**, and then click **CMW File Viewer**.

When the **CMWView** dialog box is displayed, search for the CMW file you want to view. When you have selected the file, click the **Open** button to display the text file created by the CMW File Viewer.

The CMW File Viewer can also be downloaded from the Toolbox on the Office 2003 Resource Kit Web site.

Custom Installation Wizard

The Custom Installation Wizard enables you to record changes to the master installation in a Windows Installer transform (MST file) without altering the original package (MSI file). Because the original package is never altered, you can create a different transform for every installation scenario you need. When you run Setup with both the package and the transform, Windows Installer applies the transform to the original package, and Setup uses your altered configuration to perform the installation.

By using the Custom Installation Wizard, you can also create a transform that runs additional Setup programs, such as the Office Profile Wizard, at the end of the Microsoft Office 2003 installation.

For Office 2003, the Custom Installation Wizard has been updated to include new application information, such as additional settings for Microsoft Office Outlook® 2003 and security configurations. You must use the new version of the Custom Installation Wizard to modify Office 2003 installations—previous versions of this tool cannot modify Office 2003. The Office Resource Kit installs the Custom Installation Wizard and its shortcuts to a version-specific location on your computer.

Install the Custom Installation Wizard

The Custom Installation Wizard is automatically installed on your computer when you install the Office Resource Kit. To locate the tool, click the **Start** button, point to **Programs**, point to **Microsoft Office**, point to **Microsoft Office Tools**, point to **Microsoft Office Resource Kit**, and then click **Custom Installation Wizard**.

The Custom Installation Wizard can also be downloaded from the Toolbox on the Office 2003 Resource Kit Web site.

Resources and related information

For more information about the Custom Installation Wizard, see "Methods of Customizing Office" and other topics in Chapter 4, "Customizing Office 2003."

Custom Maintenance Wizard

The updated Custom Maintenance Wizard enables you to make changes to a Microsoft Office 2003 installation after the initial deployment. Using the Custom Maintenance Wizard, you can modify almost every feature that you can set in the

Custom Installation Wizard—including default user settings, security levels, Microsoft Outlook settings, and registry keys.

The Custom Maintenance Wizard works by creating a configuration maintenance file (CMW file) based on the Windows Installer package (MSI file) used in the Office 2003 installation. To apply the changes to a client computer, you run the Custom Maintenance Wizard from a command line on the client computer, specifying the CMW file that contains the changes you want to apply.

You must use the new version of the Custom Maintenance Wizard to modify Office 2003 installations—previous versions of this tool cannot modify Office 2003. The Office Resource Kit installs the Custom Maintenance Wizard and its shortcuts to a version-specific location on your computer.

Install the Custom Maintenance Wizard

The Custom Maintenance Wizard is automatically installed on your computer when you install the Office Resource Kit. To locate the tool, click the **Start** button, point to **Programs**, point to **Microsoft Office**, point to **Microsoft Office Tools**, point to **Microsoft Office Resource Kit**, and then click **Custom Maintenance Wizard**.

The Custom Maintenance Wizard can also be downloaded from the Toolbox on the Office 2003 Resource Kit Web site.

Resources and related information

For more information about using the Custom Maintenance Wizard, see "Updating Feature Installation States and Application Settings" in Chapter 18, "Updating Users' Office 2003 Configurations."

Customizable Alerts

The Customizable Alerts folder contains the Errormsg.xls workbook, which includes information needed to work effectively with custom error messages. This workbook consists of several worksheets with lists of error messages for Microsoft Office 2003 applications.

There are worksheets for Microsoft Office Access 2003, Microsoft Office Excel 2003, Microsoft Office Outlook 2003, Microsoft Office PowerPoint® 2003, and Microsoft Office Word 2003 error messages, and another worksheet for error messages shared between two or more Office applications. Each worksheet contains two columns of information:

- Error Message Text: Provides the exact text that appears to users in each error message.

- Error ID: Provides the required error number used to identify an error message.

Install Customizable Alerts

The Customizable Alerts folder is automatically installed on your computer when you install the Office Resource Kit. To locate the folder, click the **Start** button, point to **Programs**, point to **Microsoft Office**, point to **Microsoft Office Tools**, point to **Microsoft Office Resource Kit**, and then click **Customizable Alerts**. The computer will display a folder containing the workbook.

The Customizable Alerts folder can also be downloaded from the Toolbox on the Office 2003 Resource Kit Web site.

HTML Help Workshop

Version 1.3 of Microsoft HTML Help Workshop, included with the Microsoft Office 2003 Editions Resource Kit, can be used to create Help topics that provide information and assistance specific to your organization. You can also integrate those topics with the Microsoft Office XP Help system, or combine them with custom Answer Wizard databases to create a complete assistance solution.

Also included in the Office Resource Kit are two cascading style sheets that you can use to build your own custom Help topics using Microsoft styles. The style sheets, Office10.css and Startpag.css, must be used with Internet Explorer 4.0 or later.

Install HTML Help Workshop

HTML Help Workshop is copied to your computer by the Office Resource Kit Setup program, but you must install the files separately. To install HTML Help Workshop, run Htmlhelp.exe from the \Program Files\ORKTools\ORK11\TOOLS\HTML Help Workshop folder on your computer. This executable will copy the style sheets (Office11.css and Startpag.css) and the Htmlhelp.exe application to a location you specify.

HTML Help Workshop can also be downloaded from the Toolbox on the Office 2003 Resource Kit Web site.

International Information

The International Information folder contains updated reference files (see table) that provide information on international versions of Microsoft Office 2003.

Workbook file name	Description
Intlimit.xls	Lists the limitations of plug-in language compatibility by component.
MultiMUI.xls	Lists components of the Microsoft Office 2003 Multilingual User Interface Pack (MUI Pack) and Microsoft Office 2003 Proofing Tools by language.
Wwfeatre.xls	Lists the effect of various language settings on each Office application.
Wwsuppt.xls	Lists support, by language of operating system, of different language features of Office applications.

Install International Information

The International Information documents are automatically installed on your computer when you install the Office Resource Kit. To locate the documents, click the **Start** button, point to **Programs**, point to **Microsoft Office**, point to **Microsoft Office Tools**, point to **Microsoft Office Resource Kit**, and then click **International Information**. The computer will display a folder containing the workbooks.

The International Information folder can also be downloaded from the Toolbox on the Office 2003 Resource Kit Web site.

MST File Viewer

The MST File Viewer (MSTView.exe) enables you to view the customizations that a transform (MST file) makes when Microsoft Office 2003 is installed on a user's computer. Transforms are created by using the Custom Installation Wizard.

To use the MST File Viewer, you must supply it with the path and file name of the MST file you created with the Custom Installation Wizard. The MST File Viewer is not a separate application—instead, it reads the MST file and creates a plain-text file containing readable content. The information is then displayed through the Notepad text editor.

Install the MST File Viewer

The MST File Viewer is automatically installed on your computer when you install the Microsoft Office Resource Kit. To locate the tool, click the **Start** button, point to **Programs**, point to **Microsoft Office**, point to **Microsoft Office Tools**, point to **Microsoft Office Resource Kit**, and then click **MST File Viewer**.

When you run the tool, the **Windows Installer Transform Viewer** dialog box is displayed. You need to specify both a Windows Installer base package (MSI file) and the transform (MST file) you want to view. After you select the files, click **View Transform** to display the text file created by the MST File Viewer.

The MST File Viewer can also be downloaded from the Toolbox on the Office 2003 Resource Kit Web site.

Office Converter Pack

The Microsoft Office Converter Pack bundles together a collection of file converters and filters that can be deployed to users. The Converter Pack can be useful to organizations that use Microsoft Office 2003 in a mixed environment with earlier versions of Office and other applications, including Office for the Macintosh and third-party productivity applications. While these converters and filters have been available previously, they are packaged together here for convenient deployment.

Install the Office Converter Pack

The Office Converter Pack is copied to your computer by the Office 2003 Resource Kit Setup program, but you must install the files separately. To install the Office Converter Pack, run Oconvpck.exe from the \Program Files\ORKTools\ORK11\TOOLS\Office Converter Pack folder on your computer. This executable file will copy the converter files to a predetermined location on your computer:

- Text converters are copied to \Program Files\Common Files\Microsoft Shared\TextConv\

- Graphics converters are copied to \Program Files\Common Files\Microsoft Shared\Grphflt

The Office Converter Pack can also be downloaded from the Toolbox on the Office 2003 Resource Kit Web site.

Summary of converters and filters

When you install the Microsoft Office Converter Pack, only the converters and filters that are appropriate for your version of the Microsoft Office programs are made available for installation.

Text Converters

The following text converters are installed by the Microsoft Office Converter Pack for your installed version of Microsoft Office.

For Import (Read) and Export (Save)
- AmiPro 3 (Ami332.cnv)
- Microsoft Word for DOS versions 3.x–6.0 (Doswrd32.cnv)
- Microsoft Works 3.0 (Works332.cnv)
- Microsoft Works 5.0
- RFT-DCA (Rftdca32.cnv)
- Windows Write versions 3.0 and 3.1 (Write32.cnv)
- WordPerfect 4.x (Wpft432.cnv)

For Import (Read) Only
- dBASE version 2.0, 3.0, and 4.0 (Dbase32.cnv)
- Microsoft FoxPro® (Dbase32.cnv)
- WordStar 3.3, 3.45, 4.0, 5.0, 5.5, 6.0, and 7.0 for DOS (Wrdstr32.cnv) and versions 1.0 and 2.0 for Windows (Wrdstr32.cnv)

For Export (Save) Only
- WordStar 4.0 and 7.0 for DOS (Wrdstr32.cnv)

> **Note**   The Microsoft Office Converter Pack registers its installed text converters in the following registry location:
> HKEY_LOCAL_MACHINE\Software\Microsoft\Shared Tools\Text Converters

Image Filters

The following image filters are available to install from the Microsoft Office Converter Pack, based on the version of the Microsoft Office program you have installed.

For Import (Read) and Export (Save)

- FPX (Flash Pix) (Fpx32.flt)
- GIF (Graphics Interchange Format) (Gifimp32.flt)
- JPEG File Interchange Format (Jpegimp.flt)
- PNG (Portable Network Graphics) (Png32.flt)
- WPG (WordPerfect Graphics) (Wpgexp32.flt and Wpgimp32.flt)

Import (Read) Only

- BMP (Windows Bitmap) (Bmpimp32.flt)
- CDR (CorelDRAW) versions 3.0, 4.0, 5.0, and 6.0 (Cdrimp32.flt)
- CGM (Computer Graphics Metafile) (Cgmimp32.flt)
- DRW (Micrografx Designer & Draw) (Drwimp32.flt)
- DXF (AutoCAD Format 2D) (Dxfimp32.flt)
- EMF (Windows Enhanced Metafile) (Emfimp32.flt)
- EPS (Encapsulated Postscript) (Epsimp32.flt)
- PCD (Kodak Photo CD) (Pcdimp32.flt)
- PCX (PC Paintbrush) (Pcximp32.flt)
- PICT (Macintosh PICT) (Pictim32.flt)
- TGA (Truevision Targa) (Tgaimp32.flt)
- TIFF (Tag Image File Format) (Tiffim32.flt)
- WMF (Windows Metafile) (Wmfimp32.flt)

> **Note**   The Microsoft Office Converter Pack registers its installed image converters in the following registry location:
> HKEY_LOCAL_MACHINE\Software\Microsoft\Shared Tools\Graphics Filters

Office Information

The Office Information folder contains a variety of support files for Microsoft Office 2003, including the product file list, comprehensive registry key list, and security certificates. The following table lists the documents and other files available the folder.

Document file name	Description
Cfgquiet.ini	Contains default settings for the Microsoft Office Server Extension log file.
Filelist.xls	Lists all files provided with Microsoft Office XP.
MSCert01.cer MSCert02.cer MSCert03.cer	Microsoft certificates used on the **Specify Office Security Settings** page of the Custom Installation Wizard to sign macros and add-ins.
Presbrod.xls	Describes registry entries that can be set on client computers to specify default values and restrictions for using Presentation Broadcasting.
Regkey.xls	Lists default registry key values.
Stopword.doc	Contains the list of words not indexed by the Find Fast utility.

Install Office Information

The Office Information documents are automatically installed on your computer when you install the Office Resource Kit. To locate the documents, click the **Start** button, point to **Programs**, point to **Microsoft Office**, point to **Microsoft Office Tools**, point to **Microsoft Office Resource Kit**, and then click **Office Information**. The computer will display a folder containing the files and documents.

The Office Information documents can also be downloaded from the Toolbox on the Office 2003 Resource Kit Web site.

Office Profile Wizard

The Office Profile Wizard helps you to create and distribute a default user profile that includes standard locations for files and templates. Using the Profile Wizard, you can preset options so that users do not have to customize their settings. You can also change default values to match your organization's needs or to ensure that users have access to shared templates. When you deploy a standard user profile, all of your users start with the same Office configuration.

When you save an Office user profile, you create an Office profile settings file (OPS file). You can include your OPS file in a Windows Installer transform (MST file) to distribute the settings when Microsoft Office 2003 is deployed. You can also use the Profile Wizard to help back up and restore user-defined settings from one computer to another.

Install the Office Profile Wizard

The Office Profile Wizard is automatically installed on your computer when you install the Office Resource Kit. To locate the tool, click the **Start** button, point to **Programs**, point to **Microsoft Office**, point to **Microsoft Office Tools**, point to **Microsoft Office Resource Kit**, and then click **Profile Wizard**.

The Office Profile Wizard can also be downloaded from the Toolbox on the Office 2003 Resource Kit Web site.

Resources and related information

For more information about the Office Profile Wizard, see "Customizing User-Defined Settings" in Chapter 4, "Customizing Office 2003."

Office Removal Wizard

Although version removal functionality is built into Microsoft Office 2003 Setup and the Custom Installation Wizard, a standalone version of the Office Removal Wizard is available as well. You can use this tool to exert a detailed level of control over which files to remove and which to retain. For example, if you are upgrading in stages to Office 2003, you can use the Removal Wizard to remove previously installed versions of the specific applications you choose to upgrade.

The Office Removal Wizard can detect and remove Microsoft Office 4.x, Office 95, Office 97, Office 2000, and Office XP, as well as Microsoft Office Multilingual User Interface Packs (MUI Packs) and individual Office applications. A companion file list allows you to review and edit the detailed list of files that can be removed. The Removal Wizard does not remove documents or other user files from the computer.

Install the Office Removal Wizard

The Office Removal Wizard is automatically installed on your computer when you install the Office Resource Kit. To locate the tool, click the **Start** button, point to **Programs**, point to **Microsoft Office**, point to **Microsoft Office Tools**, point to **Microsoft Office Resource Kit**, and then click **Removal Wizard**.

The Office Removal Wizard can also be downloaded from the Toolbox on the Office 2003 Resource Kit Web site.

Resources and related information

For more information about the Office Removal Wizard, see "Customizing Removal Behavior" in Chapter 4, "Customizing Office 2003."

OPS File Viewer

The OPS File Viewer (OPSView.exe) enables you to view changes that an Office profile settings file (OPS file) makes to a user's computer. This viewer also provides a list of all possible changes that the Office Profile Wizard can make to a user's computer through an OPS file.

To use the OPS File Viewer, you must supply the path and file name of an OPS file you created with the Office Profile Wizard. The viewer is not a separate application—instead, it reads the OPS file and creates a plain-text file, which is displayed by the Notepad text editor.

Install the OPS File Viewer

The OPS File Viewer is automatically installed on your computer when you install the Office Resource Kit. To locate the tool, click the **Start** button, point to **Programs**, point to **Microsoft Office**, point to **Microsoft Office Tools**, point to **Microsoft Office Resource Kit**, and then click **OPS File Viewer**.

When the **OPSView** dialog box is displayed, search for the OPS file you want to view. When you have selected the file, click **Open** to display the text file created by the OPS File Viewer.

The OPS File Viewer can also be downloaded from the Toolbox on the Microsoft Office 2003 Editions Resource Kit Web site.

Outlook Administrator Pack

If your organization is using Microsoft Outlook 98, Outlook 2000, Outlook 2002, or Microsoft Office Outlook 2003 with a server that has server-side security, such as Microsoft Exchange Server, you can customize the security features to meet your organization's needs. For example, you can control the types of attached files blocked by Outlook, modify the Outlook Object Model warning notifications, and specify user- or group-security levels.

The Outlook Administrator Pack consists of four files, packaged into one self-extracting executable file. When you run the executable file, the following files are copied to a location you specify:

- Comdlg32.ocx—A file used by the Trusted Code control that provides a user interface for selecting the trusted COM add-in.

- Hashctl.dll—A file used by the Trusted Code control to specify trusted COM add-ins.

- OutlookSecurity.oft—An Outlook template that enables you to customize the security settings on the Microsoft Exchange server.

- Readme.doc—A document that provides information about the values and settings available in the OutlookSecurity.oft template and describes how to deploy the new settings on Exchange Server.

Install the Outlook Administrator Pack

The Outlook Administrator Pack is copied to your computer by the Microsoft Office 2003 Editions Resource Kit Setup program, but you must install the files separately. To install the Outlook Administrator Pack, run Admpack.exe from the \Program Files\ORK-Tools\ORK11\TOOLS\Outlook Administrator Pack folder on your computer. This executable file will copy the four administrative files to a location you specify.

The Outlook Administrator Pack can also be downloaded from the Toolbox on the Office 2003 Resource Kit Web site.

Package Definition Files

The package definition files (SMS format) are used by Microsoft Systems Management Server to install Office remotely. For Microsoft Office 2003, the package definition files are consolidated into two core files: Office11.SMS, which covers all Office 2003 editions, and Mui11.SMS, which covers the Microsoft Office 2003 Multilingual User Interface Packs (MUI Packs). You must have Systems Management Server 2.0 with Service Pack 2 to deploy Office 2003.

Install the package definition files

The package definition files are automatically installed on your computer when you install the Office Resource Kit. To locate the files, click the **Start** button, point to **Programs**, point to **Microsoft Office**, point to **Microsoft Office Tools**, point to **Microsoft Office Resource Kit**, and then click **Package Definition Files**.

The package definition files can also be downloaded from the Toolbox on the Office 2003 Resource Kit Web site.

Resources and related information

For more information about using Systems Management Server to deploy Office 2003, see "Using Microsoft Systems Management Server to Deploy Office" in Chapter 5, "Installing Office 2003."

Policy Template Files

The policy template files provided with the Microsoft Office 2003 Editions Resource Kit enable you to set policies globally for users of Office on a network. By using policies, an administrator can quickly enforce a user configuration on users' computers when users, groups, or computers log on to the network.

The Microsoft Office policy template files (ADM files) describe all of the policy settings you can set for Office. These ADM files are used with the Group Policy snap-in included in Microsoft Windows operating systems to apply policies to users' computers.

The Office Resource Kit Setup program installs the following policy templates in the \Windows\INF folder on your computer.

File name	Template description
ACCESS11.ADM	Microsoft Office Access 2003
EXCEL11.ADM	Microsoft Office Excel 2003
FP11.ADM	Microsoft Office FrontPage® 2003
GAL11.ADM	Microsoft Clip Organizer
INF11.ADM	Microsoft Office InfoPath™ 2003
OFFICE11.ADM	Microsoft Office 2003
ONENT11.ADM	Microsoft Office OneNote™ 2003
OUTLK11.ADM	Microsoft Office Outlook 2003
PPT11.ADM	Microsoft Office PowerPoint 2003
PUB11.ADM	Microsoft Office Publisher 2003
WORD11.ADM	Microsoft Office Word 2003

The policy template files can also be downloaded from the Toolbox on the Office 2003 Resource Kit Web site.

Resources and related information

For more information about Office policies, see "Managing Users' Configurations by Policy" in Chapter 18, "Updating Users' Office 2003 Configurations."

Appendix B

Office 2003 Resource Kit Reference

The Microsoft® Office 2003 Editions Resource Kit Reference, on *http://www.microsoft.com* and on the book companion CD, provides detailed information about the mechanics of the installation and maintenance processes. Use the Reference to look up definitions for options, properties, and settings. The Reference also provides information about text files and tools used both during and after installation.

Setup Command-line Options

When you run Setup for Microsoft Office 2003, you can use command-line options to change some of the parameters that Setup uses to install Office, such as display settings and default values for Setup properties.

> **Note** In most cases, command-line options override duplicate customizations in the Setup settings file (Setup.ini) or in a transform (MST file).

Information on the following command-line options is included in this section:
/a
/autorun
/f
/i
/j
/l
/noreboot
/p
/q
/settings
/skiplangcheck
/webinstall
/x
property=value

For more information about command-line options that you can use with Microsoft Windows Installer (Msiexec.exe), see the Platform SDK on the MSDN Web site at *http://msdn.microsoft.com/library/default.asp?url=/library/en-us/msi/setup /roadmap_to_windows_installer_documentation.asp.*

/a [*msifile*]

Create an administrative installation point for the specified package (MSI file). The package must be in the same folder as Setup.exe, and both must be at the root of the administrative installation point.

Examples:

```
/a Pro11.msi
```

/autorun

Run Setup automatically when the Office CD is inserted into the CD-ROM drive; used only in the Autorun.inf file.

/f[*options*] [*msifile*]

Force repair of an application associated with the specified package (MSI file). The package must be in the same folder as Setup.exe, and both must be at the root of the administrative installation point. Alternatively, you can specify the product code for the package; the product code can be copied from the [Product] section of the Setup settings file.

> **Note**   You must specify the same package that was used to install the application originally.

Valid values for *options* include the following:

a	Force reinstallation of all files regardless of checksum or version.
c	Reinstall file if missing or corrupt.
d	Reinstall file if missing or a different version is present.
e	Reinstall file if missing or an equal or older version is present.
m	Rewrite all required HKEY_LOCAL_MACHINE registry entries.
o	Reinstall file if missing or an older version is present.
p	Reinstall file only if missing.
s	Reinstall all shortcuts and overwrite existing shortcuts.
u	Rewrite all required HKEY_CURRENT_USER registry entries.
v	Retrieve the package from the original source and recache it on the local computer.

The **Detect and Repair** command (**Help** menu) in Office applications performs the same function as **/focums**. Running Setup and selecting **Reinstall** performs the same function as **/fecums**.

> **Important**   If a user applies a client patch to a computer, you cannot use the **/f** switch to recache and reinstall Office on that computer from an updated administrative installation point. In this case, users must uninstall Office and reinstall from the updated administrative image.

Examples:

```
/fpiwae Proll.msi

/fvm {12345678-1234-1234-1234-123456789123}
```

/i [*msifile*]

Install applications using the specified package. The package must be in the same folder as Setup.exe, and both must be at the root of the administrative installation point.

> **Note**   By default, Setup.exe directs Windows Installer to perform the same function as **/i**.

Example:

```
/i Pro11.msi
```

/j*option* [*msifile*] [/t *mstfile*]

Advertise the application on the computer and install on first use; you must specify an option to advertise the application to either the computer or the user. You should use **/j** only when running Setup from an administrative installation point. If no package is specified, Setup uses the package specified in Setup.ini. To apply a transform to the advertised application, use the option **/t** and specify an MST file.

Valid values for *option* include the following:

m	Advertise to all users on the computer.
u	Advertise to the current user (not recommended for Office 2003).

> **Note**   In addition to **/t**, you can use the following three command-line options when you use **/j** to advertise Office: **/l**, **/q**, and **/settings**.

For more information about advertising Office 2003 to users or computers, see "Running Setup from an Installation Image" in Chapter 5, "Installing Office 2003."

Example:

```
/jm Pro11.msi /t Custom.mst
```

/l[*options*] *logfile*

Create a log of installation actions for Setup and a log file for each Windows Installer task. The **/l** option overrides default settings specified in the [Logging] section of Setup.ini.

Values for *options* include the following and capture the corresponding data:

a	Start of action notification
c	Initial UI parameters
e	Error messages
i	Information-only messages
m	Out-of-memory messages
o	Out-of-disk-space messages
p	Property table list in form *property=value*
r	Action data record; contains action-specific information
u	User request messages
v	Verbose; includes debug messages
w	Warning messages
*	Turn on all logging options except **v**
+	Append to existing log file

Logfile specifies the name and path of the log file to create. When you include (*) in the log file name, Setup creates a unique file name for each instance of Setup. Example:

```
/lv* "%temp%\Office Setup(*).txt"
```

This command line creates the following log files:

- Setup.exe log file

  ```
  "%temp%\OfficeSetup(0001).text"
  ```

- Windows Installer log file for core Office 2003 package

  ```
  "%temp%\OfficeSetup(0001)_Task(0001).txt"
  ```

The following example shows default logging options for Office 2003:

```
/lpiwae
```

For more information about logging, see "Customizing How Setup Runs" in Chapter 4, "Customizing Office 2003."

/noreboot

Do not restart the computer or display a restart dialog box at the end of the installation. The **/noreboot** option sets the Windows Installer **REBOOT** property to **ReallySuppress** for each package included in the Office installation except the last one.

/p [*mspfile*]

Apply an administrative update (MSP file) to a client installation of Office. You can also use **/p** to apply an update to an administrative installation by including the **/a** option and the name and path of the MSI file on the administrative installation point. To apply the patch quietly, include **/qb** on the command line; to generate a log file, include **/l**.

Examples:

```
msiexec /p [mspfile] /qb /l[options]

msiexec /p [mspfile] /a [msifile] /qb /l[options]
```

For more information about patching Office installations, see "Distributing Office 2003 Product Updates" in Chapter 18, "Updating Users' Office 2003 Configurations."

/q[*options*]

Set the Setup user interface display level.

Valid values for *options* include the following:

b	Display only simple progress indicators and error messages (**basic**).
f	Display all dialog boxes and messages; equivalent to omitting the **/q** option (**full**).
n	Display no user interface; equivalent to specifying **/q** with no options (**none**).
r	Display all progress indicators and error messages but collect no user information (**reduced**).
-	Suppress all modal dialog boxes; use only with **b**.
+	Add completion message to the **n** or **b** option.
!	Hide the **Cancel** button; use only with **/qb**.

> **Note** The completion message is displayed only when Setup does not have to restart the computer after the installation.

For more information about display settings, see "Customizing How Setup Runs" in Chapter 4, "Customizing Office 2003."

/settings file

Specify a custom Setup settings file for Setup.exe to use in place of Setup.ini. The settings file must be in the same folder as Setup.exe, or the path must be included on the command line.

Example:

```
/settings MyApp.ini
```

For more information about creating a custom Setup INI file, see "Methods of Customizing Office" in Chapter 4, "Customizing Office 2003."

/skiplangcheck

For information about this command-line option, see **SKIPLANGCHECK** later in this appendix.

/webinstall *path*

No longer supported by Setup. For security reasons, Microsoft no longer supports installing Office from an administrative installation point on a Web server (HTTP source). Installing from an HTTP source is not recommended for Office or any other Windows Installer package (MSI file).

You can still use a hyperlink on a Web page to point to an Office administrative installation point that is hosted on a file server (for example, a UNC path).

/x [*msifile*]

Remove the application associated with the specified package. The package must be in the same folder as Setup.exe, and both must be at the root of the administrative installation point.

> **Note**   You must specify the same package that was used to install the application originally.

Example:

```
/x Pro11.msi
```

property=value

Specify a property value on the command line. If the value contains spaces, enclose it in quotation marks ("). To specify two or more property-value pairs, separate them with spaces.

For more information about properties you can set for Office, see "Setup Properties" in the next section.

Example:

```
TRANSFORMS="C:\Acct Dept.mst" DISABLEROLLBACK=1 USERNAME="Manager"
```

Setup Properties

Microsoft Office 2003 Setup and Microsoft Windows Installer use properties to help control the Office installation process. The default values for Setup properties are defined in the Windows Installer package (MSI file). You can specify new property values on the command line, in the Setup settings file (Setup.ini), or on the **Modify Setup Properties** page of the Custom Installation Wizard.

Information on the following Setup properties is included in this appendix:

- **ADDDEFAULT**
- **ADDLOCAL**
- **ADDSOURCE**
- **ADVERTISE**
- **ALLUSERS**
- **ARPCOMMENTS**
- **ARPCONTACTS**
- **ARPHELPLINK**
- **ARPHELPTELEPHONE**
- **ARPNOMODIFY**
- **ARPNOREMOVE**
- **ARPNOREPAIR**
- **CHECKINSTALLORDER**
- **CIWEXTRASHORTCUTSDIRS**
- **COMPANYNAME**
- **COMPLETEINSTALLDESCRIPTION**
- **COMPLETETEXT**
- **CUSTOMINSTALLDESCRIPTION**
- **CUSTOMTEXT**
- **DEFAULTREMOVECHOICEDESCRIPTION**
- **DISABLEREMOVEPREVIOUS**
- **DISABLEROLLBACK**
- **DISABLESCMIGRATION**
- **DONOTMIGRATEUSERSETTINGS**
- **DONTUSEOCIWORGNAME**

- **ERRORSUPPORTTEXT_ADMIN_DEFAULT**

- **ERRORSUPPORTTEXT_ADMIN_DEFAULT_PERMISSION**

- **ERRORSUPPORTTEXT_ADMIN_DEFAULT_PROBLEM**

- **FATAL_ERROR_TEXT**

- **INSTALLLOCATION**

- **KEEPALLTEXT**

- **LIMITUI**

- **MINIMUMINSTALLDESCRIPTION**

- **MINIMUMTEXT**

- **MSINODISABLEMEDIA**

- **NOCANCEL**

- **NOFEATURESTATEMIGRATION**

- **NOUSERNAME**

- **OPCREMOVAL**

- **OUTLOOKASDEFAULTCALENDARAPP**

- **OUTLOOKASDEFAULTCONTACTSAPP**

- **OUTLOOKASDEFAULTMAILAPP**

- **OUTLOOKASDEFAULTNEWSAPP**

- **OWC10EXISTS**

- **PIDKEY**

- **PROOFONLYINSTALLDESCRIPTION**

- **REBOOT**

- **REINSTALL**

- **REMOVE**

- **RUNFROMSOURCEINSTALLDESCRIPTION**

- **RUNFROMSOURCETEXT**

- **SETUPDW**

- **SKIPCHECKBOXDIALOG**

- **SKIPREMOVEPREVIOUSDIALOG**

- **SOURCELIST**

- **StrContactInfo**

- **TARGETDIR**

- **TRANSFORMATSOURCE**

- **TRANSFORMS**

- **TRANSFORMSSECURE**

- **TYPICALINSTALLDESCRIPTION**

- **TYPICALTEXT**

- **UPGRADEINSTALLDESCRIPTION**

- **UPGRADETEXT**

- **USERNAME**

About properties

You use several different types of Setup properties to customize Office. Some types of properties must be set in a particular way in order to achieve the desired results.

Boolean properties

A number of properties used with Office 2003 Setup are Boolean properties. Boolean properties are either set or not set; they do not take a specific value. If a Boolean property exists, it is considered set, regardless of the property value. You set a Boolean property by assigning it any value—typically, the value **1** or **True**.

Example:

```
setup.exe DONOTMIGRATEUSERSETTINGS=1
```

On the **Modify Setup Properties** page of the Custom Installation Wizard, you can clear any Boolean property in the default list by selecting the value **Clear Property**. If you add a Boolean property, you can clear it by assigning it a null string (""); leaving its value blank does not change the existing state of the property. On the Setup command line or in Setup.ini, you clear a Boolean property by assigning it a null string ("").

Example:

```
Setup.exe DONOTMIGRATEUSERSETTINGS=""
```

Public and private properties

There are two types of Setup properties:

- Public property names are all uppercase and can be specified on the command line, in the Setup settings file, or on the **Modify Setup Properties** page of the Custom Installation Wizard.

- Private property names are a mix of uppercase and lowercase letters and can be specified only on the **Modify Setup Properties** page of the Custom Installation Wizard.

If you enter a property name on the command line or in Setup.ini, Setup assumes that it is a public property and converts the name to all uppercase letters. When you enter a property name in the Custom Installation Wizard, you must enter the name exactly as it is defined, in all uppercase or in mixed-case letters. With few exceptions, all properties that you can use for managing the installation process are public properties.

For more information about using Setup properties to customize an Office installation, see "Methods of Customizing Office" in Chapter 4, "Customizing Office 2003."

ADDDEFAULT

ADDDEFAULT=[string]

Return a set of features to their default installation states, as defined in the original Windows Installer package and transform (MST file). You can specify all, or you can specify a list of feature names separated by commas. Only the features you specify are reset to their default installation states; child features—including hidden child features—are not included unless you specify them explicitly.

You use the **ADDDEFAULT** property only during the initial installation—for example, to return all features to their default states before using the **ADDLOCAL**, **ADDSOURCE**, or **ADVERTISE** properties. Note, however, that regardless of how you list them on the command line, Windows Installer always evaluates these properties in the following order:

1. **ADDLOCAL**

2. **REMOVE**

3. **ADDSOURCE**

4. **ADDDEFAULT**

5. **REINSTALL**

6. **ADVERTISE**

For example, if the command line specifies `ADDSOURCE=all`, `ADDLOCAL=MyFeature`, then MyFeature is set to **Run from My Computer** first. Then **ADDSOURCE=all** is evaluated, and all features (including MyFeature) are set to **Run from Network**. For more information about working with Windows Installer properties, see the Platform SDK on the MSDN Web site at *http://msdn.microsoft.com/library/default.asp?url= /library/en-us/msi/setup/roadmap_to_windows_installer_documentation.asp.*

> **Note**   If a feature is advertised by default in the Windows Installer package, then the **ADDDEFAULT** property sets the feature to the same state as when the user activated the feature for the first time.

Examples:

```
ADDDEFAULT=all
```

```
ADDDEFAULT="ASSISTANTClippit,ASSISTANTDot,ASSISTANTRocky"
```

ADDLOCAL

ADDLOCAL=[string]

Install a set of features to run from the user's computer. You can specify **all**, or you can specify a list of feature names separated by commas.

You can use **ADDLOCAL** with the **ADDDEFAULT**, **ADDSOURCE**, and **ADVERTISE** properties. Note, however, that regardless of how you list them on the command line, Windows Installer always evaluates these properties in the following order:

1. **ADDLOCAL**
2. **REMOVE**
3. **ADDSOURCE**
4. **ADDDEFAULT**
5. **REINSTALL**
6. **ADVERTISE**

For example, if the command line specifies `ADDSOURCE=all`, `ADDLOCAL=MyFeature`, then MyFeature is set to **Run from My Computer** first. Then **ADDSOURCE=all** is evaluated, and all features (including MyFeature) are set to **Run from Network**. For more information about working with Windows Installer properties, see the Platform SDK on the MSDN Web site.

Examples:

```
ADDLOCAL=all
```

```
ADDLOCAL="ASSISTANTClippit,ASSISTANTDot,ASSISTANTRocky,EXCELFiles"
```

ADDSOURCE

ADDSOURCE=[string]

Install a set of features to run from the network server. You can specify **all**, or you can specify a list of feature names separated by commas.

You can use **ADDSOURCE** with the **ADDDEFAULT**, **ADDLOCAL**, and **ADVERTISE** properties. Note, however, that regardless of how you list them on the command line, Windows Installer always evaluates these properties in the following order:

1. **ADDLOCAL**
2. **REMOVE**
3. **ADDSOURCE**
4. **ADDDEFAULT**
5. **REINSTALL**
6. **ADVERTISE**

For example, if the command line specifies `ADDSOURCE=all`, `ADDLOCAL=MyFeature`, then MyFeature is set to **Run from My Computer** first. Then **ADDSOURCE=all** is evaluated, and all features (including MyFeature) are set to **Run from Network**. For more information about working with Windows Installer properties, see the Platform SDK on the MSDN Web site.

Examples:

```
ADDDEFAULT=all
```

```
ADDSOURCE="ASSISTANTClippit,ASSISTANTDot,ASSISTANTRocky,EXCELFiles"
```

ADVERTISE

ADVERTISE=[string]

Advertise a set of features on the user's computer. In this state, features are installed the first time the user attempts to use them. You can specify **all**, or you can specify a list of feature names separated by commas.

If you specify that a parent feature be advertised, then all of its child features are also advertised; if a child feature does not support the **Installed on First Use** installation state, then it is set to **Not Available**.

Examples:

```
ADVERTISE=all
```

```
ADVERTISE="ASSISTANTClippit,ASSISTANTDot,ASSISTANTRocky,EXCELFiles"
```

ALLUSERS

ALLUSERS=[string]

Install Office for all users of the computer or for only the current user. By default, Windows Installer installs Office for all users of the computer. Setting

ALLUSERS to a null value ("") overrides this default behavior and installs Office per user.

Values include the following:

1	Install Office for all users of the computer; requires administrative privileges.
2	Install Office for all users of the computer; default value for Office.
""	Install Office only for the user running Setup.

> **Note**   Because only an administrator can install Office, Setup terminates if the user does not have administrative privileges. For Office, setting **ALLUSERS** to **1** has the same effect as setting it to **2**.

Example:

```
ALLUSERS=""
```

ARPCOMMENTS

ARPCOMMENTS=[string]

Display additional text in **Add/Remove Programs** (Control Panel) when a user selects Office. Limited to 255 characters, not all of which may be displayed.

Example:

```
ARPCOMMENTS="Word processing and e-mail applications"
```

> **Note**   In Microsoft Windows® XP or later, users without administrative privileges are prevented from changing or removing programs listed in **Add/Remove Programs**.

For more information about properties related to **Add/Remove Programs**, see the Windows Installer Property Reference on the MSDN Web site at *http://msdn.microsoft.com/library/default.asp?url=/library/en-us/msi/setup/property_reference.asp.*

ARPCONTACTS

ARPCONTACTS=[string]

Display a list of support contacts in **Add/Remove Programs** (Control Panel) when a user selects Office. Limited to 255 characters.

Example:

```
ARPCONTACTS="For assistance with Office 2003, contact Help Desk."
```

> **Note**   In Microsoft Windows XP or later, users without administrative privileges are prevented from changing or removing programs listed in **Add/Remove Programs**.

For more information about properties related to **Add/Remove Programs**, see the Windows Installer Property Reference on the MSDN Web site.

ARPHELPLINK

ARPHELPLINK=[string]

Display a link to a Web site in **Add/Remove Programs** (Control Panel) when a user selects Office. Limited to 255 characters.

Example:

```
ARPHELPLINK="http://MyWebServer/LocalHelp"
```

> **Note**   In Microsoft Windows XP or later, users without administrative privileges are prevented from changing or removing programs listed in **Add/Remove Programs**.

For more information about properties related to **Add/Remove Programs**, see the Windows Installer Property Reference on the MSDN Web site.

ARPHELPTELEPHONE

ARPHELPTELEPHONE=[string]

Display a Help desk telephone number in **Add/Remove Programs** (Control Panel) when a user selects Office. Limited to 255 characters.

Example:

```
ARPHELPTELEPHONE="Ext. 1000"
```

> **Note**   In Microsoft Windows XP or later, users without administrative privileges are prevented from changing or removing programs listed in **Add/Remove Programs**.

For more information about properties related to **Add/Remove Programs**, see the Windows Installer Property Reference on the MSDN Web site.

ARPNOMODIFY

ARPNOMODIFY=[boolean]

Help prevent users from modifying the Office configuration through **Add/Remove Programs** (Control Panel); makes the **Change** button unavailable.

> **Note**   When the **ARPNOMODIFY** property is set, users can still run Office Setup in maintenance mode from the command line.

Example:

```
ARPNOMODIFY=1
```

> **Note**   In Microsoft Windows XP or later, users without administrative privileges are prevented from changing or removing programs listed in **Add/Remove Programs**.

For more information about properties related to **Add/Remove Programs**, see the Windows Installer Property Reference on the MSDN Web site.

ARPNOREMOVE

ARPNOREMOVE=[boolean]

Help prevent users from removing Office through **Add/Remove Programs** (Control Panel); makes the **Remove** button unavailable.

> **Note**   When the **ARPNOREMOVE** property is set, users can still run Office Setup in maintenance mode from the command line.

Example:

```
ARPNOREMOVE=1
```

> **Note**   In Microsoft Windows XP or later, users without administrative privileges are prevented from changing or removing programs listed in **Add/ Remove Programs**.

For more information about properties related to **Add/Remove Programs**, see the Windows Installer Property Reference on the MSDN Web site.

ARPNOREPAIR

ARPNOREPAIR=[boolean]

Help prevent users from repairing Office through **Add/Remove Programs** (Control Panel); makes the **Repair** button in the **Support Info** dialog box unavailable.

Example:

```
ARPNOREPAIR=1
```

> **Note**   In Microsoft Windows XP or later, users without administrative privileges are prevented from changing or removing programs listed in **Add/ Remove Programs**.

For more information about properties related to **Add/Remove Programs**, see the Windows Installer Property Reference on the MSDN Web site.

CHECKINSTALLORDER

CHECKINSTALLORDER=[string]

Bypass the check that prevents some Microsoft Office 2003 Multilingual User Interface Packs (MUI Packs) from being installed before Office 2003. Use this property when the installation order for packages cannot be determined in advance, as when you are using Group Policy software installation to distribute packages or when you are using Microsoft Systems Management Server without chaining. Setting the CHECKINSTALLORDER property to False allows MUI Pack packages to be installed on the computer before Office 2003 is installed.

> **Note**   If you are using Group Policy software installation to deploy Office 2003 and MUI Packs, you must create a separate transform for each MUI Pack, in which you set the **CHECKINSTALLORDER** property to **False**. If you are using SMS, you can specify a value for **CHECKINSTALLORDER** once on the command line or in Setup.ini.

Example:

```
CHECKINSTALLORDER=False
```

For more information about installing Office 2003 with MUI Packs, see "Overview of Deploying Office 2003 with the MUI Pack" in Chapter 13, "Preparing for an Office Multilingual Deployment."

CIWEXTRASHORTCUTSDIRS

CIWEXTRASHORTCUTSDIRS=[string]

Search additional locations for custom shortcuts to remove when Office is removed (in addition to the folders that Setup searches by default). Enter an absolute folder path or a subfolder relative to a predefined folder. Separate multiple entries with a semicolon (;).

Example:

```
CIWEXTRASHORTCUTDIRS="<StartMenu\Programs>\CorpApps;C:\Office\Tools"
```

For more information about removing custom shortcuts, see "Customizing Office Features and Shortcuts" in Chapter 4, "Customizing Office 2003."

COMPANYNAME

COMPANYNAME=[string]

Specify an organization name, which appears in the **About** box (**Help** menu) and on the banner page of Office applications.

> **Note**   If you enter an organization name on the **Specify Default Path and Organization** page of the Custom Installation Wizard, that setting takes precedence over the **COMPANYNAME** property set on the **Modify Setup Properties** page of the wizard, in the [Options] section of Setup.ini, or on the command line. For more information about resetting **COMPANYNAME** on the command line, see **DONTUSEOCIWORGNAME**.

Example:

```
COMPANYNAME="My Business"
```

COMPLETEINSTALLDESCRIPTION

COMPLETEINSTALLDESCRIPTION=[string]

Customize the text displayed by Setup to describe the **Complete Install** option. The following example shows the default value in the English version of Office.

Example:

```
COMPLETEINSTALLDESCRIPTION="Install all of Microsoft Office 2003 on your computer,
including all optional components and tools."
```

For more information, see "Customizing How Setup Runs" in Chapter 4, "Customizing Office 2003."

COMPLETETEXT

This property is not customizable. Unlike the radio button labels for other installation options in Setup (such as the **Custom Install** option), you cannot change the label for the **Complete Install** option. However, you can customize the description by setting the **COMPLETEINSTALLDESCRIPTION** property.

For more information, see "Customizing How Setup Runs" in Chapter 4, "Customizing Office 2003."

CUSTOMINSTALLDESCRIPTION

CUSTOMINSTALLDESCRIPTION=[string]

Customize the text displayed by Setup to describe the **Custom Install** option. The following example shows the default value in the English version of Office.

Example:

```
CUSTOMINSTALLDESCRIPTION="Customize your Microsoft Office 2003 installation by
choosing which features to install on your computer. Recommended for advanced users."
```

For more information, see "Customizing How Setup Runs" in Chapter 4, "Customizing Office 2003."

CUSTOMTEXT

CUSTOMTEXT=[string]

Customize the label displayed by Setup for the **Custom Install** installation option. The following example shows the default value in the English version of Office.

> **Note** The ampersand (&) precedes the character in the string that is to be used as the access key for the button. Pressing down both the access key and the ALT key selects the option.

Example:

```
CUSTOMTEXT="&Custom Install"
```

For more information, see "Customizing How Setup Runs" in Chapter 4, "Customizing Office 2003."

DEFAULTREMOVECHOICEDESCRIPTION

DEFAULTREMOVECHOICEDESCRIPTION=[string]

Customize the text displayed by Setup to describe the **Remove previous versions** option. The following example shows the default value in the English version of Office.

Example:

```
DEFAULTREMOVECHOICEDESCRIPTION="Choose whether to keep or remove previous versions
of Office applications."
```

For more information, see "Customizing How Setup Runs" in Chapter 4, "Customizing Office 2003."

DISABLEREMOVEPREVIOUS

DISABLEREMOVEPREVIOUS=[boolean]

Do not display the **Remove Previous Versions** page during Setup.
Example:,

```
DISABLEREMOVEPREVIOUS=1
```

DISABLEROLLBACK

DISABLEROLLBACK=[boolean]

Disable the rollback feature of Windows Installer.
Example:

```
DISABLEROLLBACK=1
```

For more information about properties related to **Add/Remove Programs**, see the Windows Installer Property Reference on the MSDN Web site.

DISABLESCMIGRATION

DISABLESCMIGRATION=[boolean]

Retain custom shortcuts created for previous versions of Office.

Example:

```
DISABLESCMIGRATION=1
```

DONOTMIGRATEUSERSETTINGS

DONOTMIGRATEUSERSETTINGS=[boolean]

Specify whether to copy the user's application settings when upgrading from a previous version of Office. If you apply a transform that includes an Office profile settings file (OPS file), the **DONOTMIGRATEUSERSETTINGS** property is set by default; otherwise, the property is not set by default.

> **Note**   Setting the **DONOTMIGRATEUSERSETTINGS** property is equivalent to clearing the **Migrate user settings** check box on the **Customize Default Application Settings** page of the Custom Installation Wizard.

Example:

```
DONOTMIGRATEUSERSETTINGS=1
```

For more information about migrating user settings, see "Customizing User-Defined Settings" in Chapter 4, "Customizing Office 2003."

DONTUSEOCIWORGNAME

DONTUSEOCIWORGNAME=[boolean]

Ignore the organization name specified on the **Specify Default Path and Organization** page of the Custom Installation Wizard. To override the organization name specified in a transform, use the **DONTUSEOCIWORGNAME** property with the **COMPANYNAME** property on the command line.

Example:

```
DONTUSEOCIWORGNAME=1 COMPANYNAME="My Business"
```

See also: **COMPANYNAME**

ERRORSUPPORTTEXT_ADMIN_DEFAULT

ERRORSUPPORTTEXT_ADMIN_DEFAULT=[string]

Customize the error message displayed by Setup during installation of Office 2003. The following example shows the default value in the English version of Office.

Example:

```
ERRORSUPPORTTEXT_ADMIN_DEFAULT="Contact your Information Technology department for
assistance."
```

ERRORSUPPORTTEXT_ADMIN_DEFAULT_PERMISSION

ERRORSUPPORTTEXT_ADMIN_DEFAULT_PERMISSION=[string]

Customize the error message displayed by Setup during installation of Office 2003. The following example shows the default value in the English version of Office.

Example:

```
ERRORSUPPORTTEXT_ADMIN_DEFAULT_PERMISSION="Verify that you have sufficient permis-
sions to access the registry or contact your Information Technology department for
assistance."
```

ERRORSUPPORTTEXT_ADMIN_DEFAULT_PROBLEM

ERRORSUPPORTTEXT_ADMIN_DEFAULT_PROBLEM=[string]

Customize the error message displayed by Setup during installation of Office 2003. The following example shows the default value in the English version of Office.

Example:

```
ERRORSUPPORTTEXT_ADMIN_DEFAULT_PROBLEM="If problem persists, contact your Informa-
tion Technology department for assistance."
```

FATAL_ERROR_TEXT

FATAL_ERROR_TEXT=[string]

Customize the text that users see when an installation fails. The following example shows the default value in the English version of Office.

Example:

```
FATAL_ERROR_TEXT="Installation ended prematurely because of an error."
```

INSTALLLOCATION

INSTALLLOCATION=[string]

Specify the installation location for Office 2003. On the **Specify Default Path and Organization** or **Modify Setup Properties** page of the Custom Installation Wizard, you can specify a path relative to a predefined folder. A value set on the command line or in Setup.ini overrides a value set in a transform.

Note   Office 2003 is installed in a version-specific folder. If you choose to keep a previous version of Office on the computer, you can specify the same location without overwriting any files.

Example:

```
INSTALLLOCATION="C:\Program Files\MyApp"
```

KEEPALLTEXT

KEEPALLTEXT=[string]

Customize the label displayed by Setup for the **Keep all previous versions** check box, which appears on the **Remove Previous Versions** page of Setup only when users are upgrading from a previous version of Office. The following example shows the default value in the English version of Office.

Note   The ampersand (&) precedes the character in the string that is to be used as the access key for the button. Pressing down both the access key and the ALT key selects the option.

Example:

```
KEEPALLTEXT="&Keep all previous versions"
```

Note   If Microsoft Office Outlook® 2003 is already installed on the computer, then the **Keep all previous versions** check box does not appear at all. Unlike other Office applications, Outlook 2003 cannot coexist on the computer with a previous version of Outlook.

For more information, see "Customizing How Setup Runs" in Chapter 4, "Customizing Office 2003."

LIMITUI

LIMITUI=[boolean]

Disable interactive Setup user interface; equivalent to using the **/qb** command-line option or setting the **Display** property to **basic** in the Setup settings file. When the **LIMITUI** property is set, Setup ignores the **/qf** and **/qr** command-line options and the **Display=full** and **Display=reduced** property settings.

Setting the **LIMITUI** property on the **Modify Setup Properties** page of the Custom Installation Wizard does not affect the initial installation; however, it disables the Setup user interface when Setup runs in maintenance mode after the initial installation.

> **Tip**   You can use the **LIMITUI** and **ARPNOMODIFY** properties together to help prevent users from running Setup after Office is installed or making any changes to the installation.

Example:

```
LIMITUI=1 ARPNOMODIFY=1
```

See also **ARPNOMODIFY**

MINIMUMINSTALLDESCRIPTION

MINIMUMINSTALLDESCRIPTION=[string]

Customize the text displayed by Setup to describe the **Minimum Install** option. The following example shows the default value in the English version of Office.

Example:

```
MINIMUMINSTALLDESCRIPTION="Install Microsoft Office 2003 with only the minimal
required components. Recommended low disk space installation."
```

For more information, see "Customizing How Setup Runs" in Chapter 4, "Customizing Office 2003."

MINIMUMTEXT

MINIMUMTEXT=[string]

Customize the label displayed by Setup for the **Minimum Install** installation option. The following example shows the default value in the English version of Office.

> **Note**   The ampersand (&) precedes the character in the string that is to be used as the access key for the button. Pressing down both the access key and the ALT key selects the option.

Example:

```
MINIMUMTEXT="&Minimal Install"
```

For more information, see "Customizing How Setup Runs" in Chapter 4, "Customizing Office 2003."

MSINODISABLEMEDIA

MSINODISABLEMEDIA=[string]

Allow users who install Office 2003 from an administrative installation point on the network to rely on physical media, such as CD, as an alternate resiliency source.

When you run Setup with the **/a** option to create an administrative installation point, Windows Installer automatically sets the **DISABLEMEDIA** property to **1**, which prevents users who install from the administrative image from using a CD as an alternate source. However, because Windows Installer 2.0 allows users to switch between compressed and uncompressed sources, this setting is no longer required.

To prevent Windows Installer from setting the **DISABLEMEDIA** property, set **MSINODISABLEMEDIA** to **1** on the command line or in Setup.ini when you create the administrative installation point. Users who install Office from this image will be able to rely on a CD—either a copy of the uncompressed administrative image or a copy of the compressed Office 2003 CD—as an alternate source.

Example:

```
setup.exe /a MSINODISABLEMEDIA=1
```

NOCANCEL

NOCANCEL=[boolean]

Remove the **Cancel** button from all dialog boxes displayed during Setup.

Example:

```
NOCANCEL=1
```

NOFEATURESTATEMIGRATION

NOFEATURESTATEMIGRATION=[boolean]

Disable default feature installation state migration for the Office package. When you upgrade to Office 2003, Setup detects and matches feature installation states from the previous version. Setting the **NOFEATURESTATEMIGRATION** property overrides this default behavior.

> **Note**   You can also override default installation state migration on a per-feature basis on the **Set Feature Installation States** page of the Custom Installation Wizard.

Example:

```
NOFEATURESTATEMIGRATION=1
```

For more information, see "Customizing Office Features and Shortcuts" in Chapter 4, "Customizing Office 2003."

NOUSERNAME

NOUSERNAME=[boolean]

Prevent Setup from defining a user name during a quiet installation. Setting the **NOUSERNAME** property allows users to enter their own user names the first time they run an Office application. Set this property when you install Office on a computer that you plan to use as a hard disk image.

Example:

```
NOUSERNAME=1
```

For more information, see "Creating a Hard Disk Image" in Chapter 5, "Installing Office 2003."

OPCREMOVAL

OPCREMOVAL=[string]

Prevent Setup from removing previous versions of Office during the installation or performing any other cleanup tasks. To turn default removal behavior back on, you must set **OPCREMOVAL** to **On**. Any other value turns the property off, as shown in the following examples.

Examples:

```
OPCREMOVAL=Off
```

```
OPCREMOVAL=0
```

> **Note**   Turning off the **OPCREMOVAL** property is not the same as selecting the option **Remove the following versions of Microsoft Office applications** on the **Remove Previous Versions** page of the Custom Installation Wizard and then clearing all the check boxes. Even with all the check boxes cleared, Setup performs some general cleanup. If this property is turned off, however, Setup does not perform any cleanup.

For more information, see "Customizing Removal Behavior" in Chapter 4, "Customizing Office 2003."

OUTLOOKASDEFAULTCALENDARAPP

OUTLOOKASDEFAULTCALENDARAPP=[string]

Specify whether Outlook is the default calendar application. Valid values include the following:

1	Set Outlook as the default calendar application.
0	Prevent Outlook from being set as the default calendar application.

Example:

```
OUTLOOKASDEFAULTCALENDARAPP=0
```

OUTLOOKASDEFAULTCONTACTSAPP

OUTLOOKASDEFAULTCONTACTSAPP=[string]

Specify whether Outlook is the default contacts application. Valid values include the following:

1	Set Outlook as the default contacts application.
0	Prevent Outlook from being set as the default contacts application.

Example:

```
OUTLOOKASDEFAULTCONTACTSAPP=0
```

OUTLOOKASDEFAULTMAILAPP

OUTLOOKASDEFAULTMAILAPP=[string]

Specify whether Outlook is the default e-mail application. Valid values include the following:

1	Set Outlook as the default mail application.
0	Prevent Outlook from being set as the default mail application.

Example:

```
OUTLOOKASDEFAULTMAILAPP=0
```

OUTLOOKASDEFAULTNEWSAPP

OUTLOOKASDEFAULTNEWSAPP=[string]

Specify whether Outlook is the default news application. Valid values include the following:

| 1 | Set Outlook as the default news application. |
| 0 | Prevent Outlook from being set as the default news application. |

Example:

```
OUTLOOKASDEFAULTNEWSAPP=0
```

OWC10EXISTS

OWC10EXISTS=[string]

Ensure that the upgraded version of Microsoft Office XP Web Components is included in the Office 2003 installation.

Microsoft Office Professional Edition 2003 includes both Office 2003 Web Components (Owc11.msi) and an upgraded version of Office XP Web Components (Owc10.msi). Both MSI files appear on the installation image, and both versions are included in the Office 2003 feature tree. Office 2003 Web Components are installed by default; however, the upgraded Office XP Web Components are installed only if a previous version of Office XP Web Components exists on the user's computer.

If your organization uses solutions that rely on Office XP Web Components and you are deploying to new clients (that is, not upgrading), then you can ensure that the upgraded Office XP Web Components are included in the Office 2003 installation by setting the **OWC10EXISTS** property.

Example:

```
OWC10EXISTS=1
```

PIDKEY

PIDKEY=[string]

Enter a 25-character Volume License Key on the Setup command line or in the Setup settings file. When you set the **PIDKEY** property, users are not required to enter a product key when they install Office.

Example:

```
PIDKEY="1234567890123456789012345"
```

PROOFONLYINSTALLDESCRIPTION

PROOFONLYINSTALLDESCRIPTION=[string]

Customize the text displayed by Setup to describe the option to install only the proofing tools when you deploy Office 2003 with MUI Packs. The following example shows the default value in the English version of Office.

Example:

```
PROOFONLYINSTALLDESCRIPTION="Install only the proofing tools and other editing tools
that come with Microsoft Office 2003 Multilingual User Interface Pack. Additional
```

features may be added or removed after installation through Add/Remove Programs in
Control Panel."

REBOOT

REBOOT=[string]

Determine whether Setup restarts the computer or prompts the user to restart during the installation of a package (MSI file). If you install Office 2003 or a MUI Pack quietly and the Windows Installer **REBOOT** property is not set to **REALLYSUP-PRESS**, then Setup automatically restarts the computer if Windows Installer detects a file in use at the end of the installation. In Windows 2000 or later, however, there is no harm in ignoring a requested reboot for a file in use. To prevent Setup from prompting the user or automatically restarting the computer, set the **REBOOT** property to **REALLYSUPPRESS**.

Example:

```
[Options]

REBOOT=REALLYSUPPRESS
```

Note   The Windows Installer **REBOOT** property—which takes the value **FORCE**, **SUPPRESS**, or **REALLYSUPPRESS**—is not the same as the Office 2003 Setup **Reboot** option, which takes the value **1** or **0**. You use the **Reboot** option to restart the computer in order to complete a chained installation. In this case, Setup manages the restart process and the installation process is not interrupted. For more information, see the **[ChainedInstall_n]** entry in "Setup Settings File" in this appendix.

REINSTALL

REINSTALL=[string]

Reinstall a set of features on the user's computer. If you specify **all**, the entire product is reinstalled. You can also specify a list of feature names separated by commas. Only the features you specify are reinstalled; no child features—including hidden child features—are included.

Examples:

```
REINSTALL=all

REINSTALL="ASSISTANTClippit,ASSISTANTDot,ASSISTANTRocky,EXCELFiles"
```

REMOVE

REMOVE=[string]

Remove a set of features from the user's computer. If you specify **all**, the entire product is removed. You can also specify a list of feature names separated by commas. If you specify that a parent feature be removed, then all of its child features are also removed.

Examples:

```
REMOVE=all

REMOVE="ASSISTANTClippit,ASSISTANTDot,ASSISTANTRocky,EXCELFiles"
```

RUNFROMSOURCEINSTALLDESCRIPTION

RUNFROMSOURCEINSTALLDESCRIPTION=[string]

Customize the text displayed by Setup to describe the Run from Network option. The following example shows the default value in the English version of Office.

Example:

```
RUNFROMSOURCEINSTALLDESCRIPTION="Install Microsoft Office 2003 to run from the net-
work source. Requires minimal space on your hard drive, and the source will be
required in order to use Office."
```

For more information, see "Customizing How Setup Runs" in Chapter 4, "Customizing Office 2003."

RUNFROMSOURCETEXT

RUNFROMSOURCETEXT=[string]

Customize the label displayed by Setup for the **Run from Network** option. The following example shows the default value in the English version of Office.

Note The ampersand (&) precedes the character in the string that is to be used as the access key for the button. Pressing down both the access key and the ALT key selects the option.

Example:

```
RUNFROMSOURCETEXT="Run From N&etwork"
```

For more information, see "Customizing How Setup Runs" in Chapter 4, "Customizing Office 2003."

SETUPDW

SETUPDW=[string]

Set or disable Setup error reporting (DW.exe). Set the **SETUPDW** property to **0** to prevent Dw.exe from reporting installation errors to Microsoft; set it to **1** to collect information about Setup failures and send the data to Microsoft. This property affects only Setup error reporting, and has no effect on application crash reporting.

> **Note**   The **SETUPDW** property is set to **0** by default when you create an administrative installation point.

Example:

```
SETUPDW=1
```

For more information, see "Customizing How Setup Runs" in Chapter 4, "Customizing Office 2003."

SKIPCHECKBOXDIALOG

SKIPCHECKBOXDIALOG=[string]

Do not display the page that appears during Setup when users select the **Custom Install** option. On this page users can select the check box next to any application to install a typical set of features. Setting the **SKIPCHECKBOXDIALOG** property to **1** hides the page and prevents users from selecting installation options for themselves.

Example:

```
SKIPCHECKBOXDIALOG=1
```

SKIPREMOVEPREVIOUSDIALOG

SKIPREMOVEPREVIOUSDIALOG=[string]

Do not display the **Remove Previous Versions** dialog box during Setup. The Custom Installation Wizard sets this property to **1** when you select the **Remove the following versions of Microsoft Office applications** option on the **Remove Previous Versions** page of the Custom Installation Wizard.

Example:

```
SKIPREMOVEPREVIOUSDIALOG=1
```

SOURCELIST

SOURCELIST=[string]

Specify additional network servers to use when the primary Office installation image is unavailable; equivalent to the list specified on the **Identify Additional Servers** page of the Custom Installation Wizard.

After Office is installed, Windows Installer continues to reference the administrative installation point for installing on demand, repairing features, or running Setup in maintenance mode. Copying the original administrative image to backup servers helps ensure that users always have access to a network source.

If you install Office from a compressed CD image with a local installation source enabled, then Windows Installer relies on the cache on the local computer for these operations. If the local installation source is corrupted or deleted, however, then the Office Source Engine goes to compressed images specified by **SOURCELIST** to recreate the local installation source.

> **Note**   Separate a list of server shares with semicolons. Use a drive letter only if the drive is part of a standard drive scheme used throughout the organization.

Example:

```
SOURCELIST="\\backup1\office11;\\backup2\office11"
```

For more information, see "Setup Sequence of Events" in Chapter 3, "Preparing to Deploy Office 2003."

StrContactInfo

StrContactInfo=[string]

Provide contact information for technical support when Setup displays an error message; applies only to errors displayed by Setup.exe.

> **Note**   You cannot set this property (or other properties shown in mixed-case letters) on the Setup command line or in the Setup settings file. You can set the **StrContactInfo** property only on the **Modify Setup Properties** page of the Custom Installation Wizard.

Example:

Enter the following value on the **Modify Setup Properties** page:

```
"For help with this error, please contact Help Desk at ext. 1000."
```

TARGETDIR

TARGETDIR= [string]

Specify the location where the Office package is copied during an administrative installation; used only when running Setup with the **/a** command-line option.

Example:

```
TARGETDIR="\\server\share\OfficeXPAIP"
```

TRANSFORMATSOURCE

TRANSFORMATSOURCE=[boolean]

Apply the transform from the root of the administrative installation point and do not cache it on the local computer. The **TRANSFORMATSOURCE** property applies to the package regardless of the user; it provides reliable transform storage for roaming users.

Example:

```
TRANSFORMATSOURCE=1
```

TRANSFORMS

TRANSFORMS=[string]

Specify a transform to apply to the installation; use only on the Setup command line. The **TRANSFORMS** property is equivalent to the **MST1** option in the [MST] section of the Setup settings file. The value can be a path relative to the folder that contains Setup.exe, an absolute path, or an environment variable.

You cannot use the **TRANSFORMS** property in the Setup settings file to specify a transform for the Office 2003 package or any chained packages.

> **Note**   If you misspell the **TRANSFORMS** option on the command line as **TRANSFORM** (singular), then Setup returns an error and your transform is not applied. Similarly, if you enter **Cmdline=TRANSFORM=** in the [ChainedInstall_*n*] section, then your transform is not applied; in this case, however, no error is displayed.

Example:

```
TRANSFORMS="\\server\share\OfficeAIP\Custom.mst"
```

For more information, see "Methods of Customizing Office" in Chapter 4, "Customizing Office 2003."

TRANSFORMSSECURE

TRANSFORMSSECURE=[boolean]

Cache the transform on the local computer in a location where the user does not have write access, and apply the transform only if the MST file is located at the root of the administrative installation point (that is, in the same folder as the MSI file). The **TRANSFORMSSECURE** property applies to the package regardless of the user; it helps to provide secure transform storage for traveling users.

Example:

```
TRANSFORMSSECURE=1
```

TYPICALINSTALLDESCRIPTION

TYPICALINSTALLDESCRIPTION=[string]

Customize the text displayed by Setup to describe the **Typical Install** option. The following example shows the default value in the English version of Office.

Example:

```
TYPICALINSTALLDESCRIPTION="Install Microsoft Office 2003 with only the most commonly
used components. Additional features may be installed on first use, or added later
through Add/Remove Programs in Control Panel."
```

For more information, see "Customizing How Setup Runs" in Chapter 4, "Customizing Office 2003."

TYPICALTEXT

TYPICALTEXT=[string]

Customize the label displayed by Setup for the **Typical Install** installation option. The following example shows the default value in the English version of Office.

> **Note** The ampersand (&) precedes the character in the string that is to be used as the access key for the button. Pressing down both the access key and the ALT key selects the option.

Example:

```
TYPICALTEXT="&Typical Install"
```

For more information, see "Customizing How Setup Runs" in Chapter 4, "Customizing Office 2003."

UPGRADEINSTALLDESCRIPTION

UPGRADEINSTALLDESCRIPTION=[string]

Customize the text displayed by Setup to describe the **Upgrade** installation option when the user is upgrading from a previous version of Office. The following example shows the default value in the English version of Office.

Example:

```
UPGRADEINSTALLDESCRIPTION="Install Microsoft Office 2003 based on your current
Office configuration, and remove previous versions of Office from your computer."
```

For more information, see "Customizing How Setup Runs" in Chapter 4, "Customizing Office 2003."

UPGRADETEXT

UPGRADETEXT=[string]

Customize the label displayed by Setup for the Upgrade installation option when the user is upgrading from a previous version of Office. The following example shows the default value in the English version of Office.

> **Note**   The ampersand (&) precedes the character in the string that is to be used as the access key for the button. Pressing down both the access key and the ALT key selects the option.

Example:

```
UPGRADETEXT="&Upgrade"
```

USERNAME

USERNAME=[string]

Specify a default user name, which appears in the **About** box (**Help** menu) and on the banner page of Office applications. The name is also used in Office documents to identify the author or the source of revision marks and comments.

Example:

```
USERNAME="Don Funk"
```

Setup Settings File

Setup.exe reads the Setup settings file (Setup.ini) and writes tasks to the registry based on the information contained in the settings file. You can customize Setup.ini or create your own custom INI files to help control many aspects of the installation process.

Information on the following Setup settings file sections is included in this section of the chapter:

> **[MSI]**
> **[Product]**
> **[MST]**
> **[Options]**
> **[Display]**
> **[Logging]**
> **[MinOSRequirement]**
> **[OfficeWebComponents]**
> **[Cache]**
> **[ChainedInstall_*n*]**

For more information about customizing Setup.ini or creating your own custom INI file, see "Methods of Customizing Office" in Chapter 4, "Customizing Office 2003."

[MSI]

Specify the name of the Windows Installer package (MSI file) to install; equivalent to the **/i** command-line option. The package must be in the same folder as Setup.exe, and both must be at the root of the installation image.

Example:

```
[MSI]
MSI=Pro11.msi
```

[Product]

Specify product information. Setup uses this information to determine whether the product is installed. Typically, you do not modify this section of the Setup settings file.

Example:

```
[Product]
ProductCode={12345678-1234-1234-1234-123456789123}
ProductName=Microsoft Office 2003
Version=11.0
```

You can add the **SKIPLANGCHECK** option to the [Product] section to bypass the default language version check.

> **SKIPLANGCHECK**=[string]

Bypass the check that prevents a particular language version of Office 2003—either a localized product or a Microsoft Office 2003 Multilingual User Interface Pack (MUI Pack)—from being installed on a computer on which the operating system does not support that language; equivalent to including the **/skiplangcheck** option on the command line. Language groups that require explicit installation on the user's computer include complex script languages, right-to-left languages, and East Asian languages.

For example, Setup performs this check and does not install a Japanese MUI Pack on the computer unless support for East Asian languages (Microsoft Windows XP or later) or Japanese (Microsoft Windows 2000) has been installed. You can bypass the language check and install the MUI Pack anyway by setting **SKIP-LANGCHECK** to **1**. You cannot set the **SKIPLANGCHECK** option on the command line or in a transform (MST file).

> **Note**   Setting **SKIPLANGCHECK** does not enable language versions of Office to function properly without the necessary operating system support; bypassing the check merely allows you to install Office products and language support in any order.

If you set **SKIPLANGCHECK** to **0** (the default), then Setup behaves as described in the following table.

Type of installation	Results
Quiet installation (/**q**)	Setup performs the language check and terminates if the MUI Pack language version is not supported by the operating system. No error message is displayed, but information is written to the log file.
Advertised installation (/**j**)	Setup performs the language check and terminates if the MUI Pack language version is not supported by the operating system. No error message is displayed, and no information is written to the log file.
Administrative installation (/**a**)	No language check is performed.

For more information about installing Office 2003 with MUI Packs, see "Overview of Deploying Office 2003 with the MUI Pack" in Chapter 13, "Preparing for an Office Multilingual Deployment."

[MST]

Specify the name and path of a transform (MST file) to apply to the installation of the package specified in the [MSI] section; equivalent to setting the **TRANSFORMS** property on the Setup command line. If the transform is in the same folder as the Windows Installer package (MSI file), you do not need to include the path.

Example:

```
[MST]
MST1=\\marketing\software\Custom1.mst
MST2=\\engineering\software\Custom2.mst
```

> **Note** You must use the key **MST1** in the [MST] section of Setup.ini; do not use **MST** or **TRANSFORMS**. You can specify multiple transforms—for example, **MST1**, **MST2**, and so on. Note, however, that Setup applies the transforms in the order in which they are listed, regardless of the numbers you assign to them.

[Options]

Define Setup properties to apply to the installation of the package specified in the [MSI] section. Use the format *property=value*.

Example:

```
[Options]
USERNAME=Customer
REBOOT=Suppress
COMPANYNAME=Northwind Traders
DONOTMIGRATEUSERSETTINGS=1
```

> **Note** You specify only public properties in the [Options] section of Setup.ini. For more information about public and private properties, see "Setup Properties" earlier in this appendix.

[Display]

Set the Setup user interface display level; equivalent to the **/q** command-line option. Settings include the following:

Display=none	Display no user interface.
Display=basic	Display only simple progress indicators and error messages.
Display=reduced	Display all progress indicators and error messages but collect no user information.
Display=full	Display all dialog boxes and messages.
Completion-Notice=yes | no	Add completion message at the end of the installation; use only when the display is set to **none** or **basic**.
-	Suppress all modal dialog boxes; use only with **basic**.
+	Add a completion message at the end of the installation; use with basic or none. For example, **basic+**.
!	Hide the **Cancel** button; use only with **basic**. For example, **basic!+**.

For more information about display settings, see "Customizing How Setup Runs" in Chapter 4, "Customizing Office 2003."
Example:

```
[Display]
Display=basic
CompletionNotice=yes
```

[Logging]

Create a log file for Setup and a log file for each Windows Installer task; equivalent to the **/l** command-line option. In this section you define the name and path of log files and specify logging options by using the following format:

- **Type=**<*options*>

- **Path=**<*path*>

- **Template=**<*file name*>.txt

Type

Specify the data to include in the Windows Installer log file. (You cannot specify options for the Setup log file.) The following options are identical to the options used with the **/l** command-line option:

a	Start of action notification
c	Initial UI parameters
e	Error messages
i	Information-only messages
m	Out-of-memory messages
o	Out-of-disk-space messages
p	Property table list in form property=value
r	Action data record; contains action-specific information
u	User request messages
v	Verbose; includes debug messages
w	Warning messages
*	Turn on all logging options except **v**
+	Append to existing log file

Example:

```
Type=piwaeo
```

Path

Specify the folder in which to create log files. The path may contain environment variables. The default setting is %Temp%.

Example:

```
Path="%Temp%\Office log files"
```

> **Note**   You must use a fully qualified path to specify the location for log files. If you use a relative path with a drive letter, no log files are created and no error message is displayed.

Template

Specify the name to use for log files. The name may contain environment variables.

You must include the .txt file name extension when you specify a Setup log file name. Appending (*) to the file name results in a unique log file for each installation performed by Setup.exe. The same log file name is used for each Windows Installer log file, with the task number from Setup.ini appended to the file name.

Examples:

```
Template=OfficeSetup(*).txt
Template=Office_%UserName%(*).txt
```

For more information about logging during the Office installation, see "Customizing How Setup Runs" in Chapter 4, "Customizing Office 2003." For more information about Windows Installer logging options, see the Platform SDK on the MSDN Web site at *http://msdn.microsoft.com/library/default.asp?url=/library/en-us/msi/ setup/roadmap_to_windows_installer_documentation.asp.*

[MinOSRequirement]

Specify the minimum supported operating system for Office 2003. Office 2003 requires Microsoft Windows 2000 Service Pack 3 or Windows XP or later; you cannot specify an earlier version. For more information, see the Platform SDK on the MSDN Web site.

Example:

```
[MinOSRequirement]
VersionNT_1=500
WindowsBuild_1=2195
ServicePackLevel_1=3
```

[OfficeWebComponents]

Used to specify the MSI file for Office Web Components. This section appears only when you create an administrative installation point for an Office product that includes an Office Web Components package.

[Cache]

Specify options that control the way Office installation files (CAB files) are cached on the local computer during Setup. Because Setup creates the local installation source before applying a transform (MST file), you must set local installation source properties such as **CDCACHE** and **LOCALCACHEDRIVE** in the Setup settings file, and not on the Modify Setup Properties page of the Custom Installation Wizard.

> **Note**   These settings are applied only when Office is installed from the CD or an image of the compressed CD on the network. Administrative installation points do not support creation of a local installation source during Setup. When you run Setup with the **/a** option, Setup extracts the compressed CAB files on the network share. Setup does not install Office Source Engine (Ose.exe) to copy source files to users' computers; instead, Windows Installer uses the original source.

To customize the local installation source, set the properties defined in the following table.

Option	Value	Description
LOCALCACHEDRIVE	*"drive"*	Override default Setup behavior and specify a drive for the local cache. After the first Office 2003 product is installed, all subsequent installations use this location for the local installation source.
PURGE	0 | 1	Set to **1** to delete the local installation source after Setup completes. Default is **0**.
CDCACHE	auto | 0 | 1 | 2	Set to **auto** to cache the entire source on the drive with the most space (the default). If insufficient space exists, cache only the features selected for installation. If space is not available for selected features, install from the CD.
		Set to **1** to cache only the features selected for installation; if space is not available, the installation fails.
		Set to **2** to force caching of entire source; if space is not available, the installation fails.
		Set to **0** to disable creation of a local installation source and run the installation directly from the source.
DELETABLECACHE	0 | 1	Set to **0** to hide the option that allows users to delete the local cache at the end of Setup. Bypass-enabled CD default is **1**.

When **CDCACHE** is set to **auto** (the default), Setup uses the following criteria to determine how and where to create the local installation source. If both an NTFS and a FAT drive meet the disk space requirement, Setup uses the NTFS drive.

- If there is no existing cache and free space is equal to or greater than 2 GB, then cache the entire source on the drive with the most space.

- If there is no existing cache and free space is less than 2 GB but greater than 1.5 GB, then cache installation files for selected features on the drive with the most space.

- If a local cache already exists and free space is less than 2 GB but greater than 1.5 GB, then cache the entire source in that location.

- If a local cache already exists and free space is less than 1.5 GB but greater than 1 GB, then cache installation files for selected features in that location.

- If free space is less than the minimum required for a particular installation, install from the CD.

> **Note**   The **PURGE** and **DELETEABLECACHE** properties behave differently then other Windows Installer properties. If you set either of these properties to **0** in Setup.ini or on the command line, then the property is not passed to Windows Installer during the installation. If you set either property to **1** in a transform and later wish to reverse the setting, you cannot do so by resetting the property to **0** on the command line or in Setup.ini. Instead, you must reset the property in the transform.

For more information about caching installation files on the local computer, see "Taking Advantage of a Local Installation Source" in Chapter 3, "Preparing to Deploy Office 2003."

Example:

```
[Cache]
CDCACHE=1
DELETABLECACHE=0
```

[ChainedInstall_*n*]

Install an additional package (MSI file) or other executable file (such as an EXE file or a BAT file) as part of the Office installation. Add a [ChainedInstall_*n*] section to Setup.ini for each chained installation; replace the placeholder *n* with a consecutive number. Chained packages are installed in order after the core Office package is successfully installed.

To customize the chained installation, set the following properties:

TaskName	Assign a friendly name to the installation (optional). Setup uses this name in the Setup log file.
Path	Specify the path and file name of the MSI file or an executable file (required).
TaskType	Identify whether the chained installation is an MSI file or EXE file (required).
MST	Specify the path and file name of a transform to apply to the chained package (for MSI files only). You can specify only one transform in this entry; to specify multiple transforms, add the **TRANSFORMS** property to the **Cmdline** entry.
Display	Specify a display setting for the chained installation; may differ from global display level set for the core Office package. If this value is not set, Setup uses the display level set for the core Office package.
CmdLine	Add other options to the command line that Setup passes for the chained package. The value of **CmdLine** is limited to 1239 characters. Setup truncates the command line after it reaches that limit.
	Note that you cannot use **CmdLine** to override the installation type (**/j** or **/i**) set for the primary package; that setting is automatically applied to all chained packages.
Reboot	To restart the computer after a chained installation completes, set this option to **1**; Setup restarts and resumes the installation process. The default setting is **0**, which suppresses computer restarts prompted by files in use.
IgnoreReturnValue	To continue to install successive chained installations even if this installation fails, set this property to **1**.

> **Note**   If you inadvertently enter an incorrect name or path for the MSI file, then Setup halts the installation process and neither the chained package nor any subsequent chained packages are installed. This occurs even if **IgnoreReturnValue** is set to **1** (this is the only case in which **IgnoreReturn-Value** is ignored). The installation failure is logged, but no error message is displayed.

Setting the **Reboot** option in this section of Setup.ini allows Setup to control the restart process by adding a task to the registry that directs Setup to restart the computer and then resume the installation process, including any additional chained installations. Set this option to restart the computer in order to complete a chained installation or when a subsequent chained installation requires the restart.

> **Note**   The **Reboot** option in this section of Setup.ini takes the value **1** or **0**. It is not the same as the Windows Installer **REBOOT** property, which takes the value **FORCE**, **SUPPRESS**, or **REALLYSUPPRESS**. For more information about the Windows Installer property, see **REBOOT** in "Setup Properties" in Appendix B.

The following example adds the French MUI Pack to the Office 2003 installation. The package is installed silently (regardless of the display setting specified for the Office installation), the customizations in the transform French.mst are applied, and an alternate source is identified for when the primary administrative installation point is unavailable:

```
[ChainedInstall_1]
TaskType=msi
Path=\\server\share\admin_install_point\1036\Mui.msi
Display=None
MST=French.mst
Cmdline=SOURCELIST=\\server2\share admin_install_point\1036
```

OPC File Syntax

The Removal Wizard (Offcln.exe) and the Microsoft Office 2003 Setup program use OPC files to remove unnecessary or obsolete components from previously installed versions of Office and related applications.

The following OPC files come with Office 2003:

- **Oclncore.opc**   Global OPC file; located in the \Files\Pfiles\MSOffice\Office 2003 folder on the administrative installation point. Specifies components associated with the core English version of Office 2003. To exclude components from removal, edit the default Oclncore.opc file.

- **Oclncust.opc**   Template file for adding additional content to be deleted by the Removal Wizard; located in the \Files\Pfiles\MSOffice\Office 2003 folder on the administrative installation point. To add components to the removal list, customize the Oclncust.opc file.

- **Oclnintl.opc**   Satellite OPC file for each language version of Office 2003; located in the LCID subfolders. Specifies language-specific components of Office 2003.

You can customize the removal process by modifying Oclncore.opc or by creating a new OPC file. For more information about customizing removal behavior during Setup or when running the standalone Removal Wizard, see "Customizing Removal Behavior" in Chapter 4, "Customizing Office 2003."

[Definitions] section

Specify the value of dependency variables. Dependency variables identify which applications or groups of files are candidates for removal. The [Definitions] section appears only in Oclncore.opc and uses the following syntax:

```
dependency variable=value
```

Values

- **KEEP**   Do not delete files. The values **FALSE** and **EXIST** are equivalent to **KEEP** and can be used in the OPC file.

- **REMOVE**   Always delete files. The values **TRUE** and **NOTEXIST** are equivalent to **REMOVE** and can be used in the OPC file.

- **DETECT**   Detect the presence of an application and determine whether Setup or the user has specified that application for removal. Files from previous versions are removed by default, unless the user has chosen to keep them.

Dependency variables

Dependency variables represent an application or set of files. Offcln.exe recognizes the following dependency variables:

Office XP applications and components

ACCESS10	ARTGALLERY10	DAO10
EQUATION10	EXCEL10	FRONTPAGE10
GRAPH10	MSDRAW10	MSINFO10
MSQUERY10	OFFICE10	OUTLOOK10
POWERPOINT10	PUBLISHER10	WORD10

Office 2000 applications and components

ACCESS9	ARTGALLERY9	BINDER9
DAO9	EQUATION9	EXCEL9
FRONTPAGE9	GRAPH9	MSINFO9
MSQUERY9	OFFICE9	OUTLOOK9
POWERPOINT9	PUBLISHER9	WORD9

Office 97 applications and components

ACCESS97	ACCESS97RT	ARTGALLERY97
BINDER97	DAO97	DMM97
EQUATION97	EXCEL97	GRAPH97
MSINFO97	MSQUERY97	OFFICE97
OUTLOOK97	PHOTOED97	POWERPOINT97
SBFM97	SCHEDULE97	WORD97

Office 95 applications and components

ACCESS95	ACCESS95RT	ARTGALLERY95
BINDER95	BOOKS95	EQUATION95
EXCEL95	GRAPH95	IMAGER95
MSINFO95	MSQUERY95	POWERPOINT95
SCHEDULE95	WORD95	WORDART95

Other applications

ARTGALLERY98	FRONTPAGE1X	FRONTPAGE97
FRONTPAGE98	HAGAKI1	HAGAKI2
HAGAKI3	HAGAKI4	HAGAKI5
MSDRAW9	MSDRAW97	MSDRAW98
ORGCHART1	ORGCHART2	PHOTODRAW1
PHOTODRAW2	PROJECT10	PROJECT9
PROJECT95	PROJECT98	PUBLISHER3
PUBLISHER4	PUBLISHER5	TEAMMANAGER97
WORDART98		

Special cleanup operations

The following keywords represent applications or files that the Removal Wizard does not detect by default; however, they can be set to **KEEP** or set to **REMOVE** to be removed in aggressive mode.

BUTTON94	CLIPART94	CLIPART95
DAO95	FONTS94	FONTS95
GRPHFLT97	GRAPHFILTER94	GRPHFLT95
OFFICEGENERIC95	OFFICEHELP95	PROOF94
PROOF95	SOUNDS95	SYSTEM94
SYSTEM95	TEXTCONV94	TEXTCONV95
	WINDOWS94	WINDOWS95

You can also change the value of the following dependency variables:

- **TEMPFOLDERCONTENTS** Default value is **KEEP**. To remove files from temporary folders, set to **REMOVE**.

- **TEMPTWIDDLEFILESONLY** Default value is **KEEP**. To remove files from temporary folders that begin with a tilde (~), set to **REMOVE**. These files are deleted by an application when it closes and are usually safe to remove.

> **Note** You cannot add new dependency variables to Oclncore.opc. Offcln.exe recognizes only the dependency variables listed in the [Definitions] section. You can only change the default values.

[Commands] section

```
[command instruction, dependency variables] "description"
```

Determine the actions to execute on specified files during the removal process. This section consists of a series of commands with the following syntax:

```
action
action
```

Command instruction

- **RISKY** In aggressive mode, execute the actions in the command; in safe mode, skip the command. Typically used for shared files and database drivers, which may affect other applications.

- **SAFE** Always execute the actions in the command.

Dependency variables

List of one or more dependency variables from the [Definitions] section of Oclncore.opc. You can customize the list of dependency variables in the command to add or exclude files. Separate multiple dependency variables with commas.

Offcln.exe uses the following logic to determine whether to perform the actions in the command:

- If all the dependency variables in the dependency list have the value **REMOVE**, then Offcln.exe executes the actions listed in the command.

- If any dependency variable has the value **KEEP**, then Offcln.exe skips the command entirely.

- If a dependency variable has the value **DETECT**, Offcln.exe changes it to either **REMOVE** in aggressive mode or **KEEP** in safe mode and then executes or skips the command accordingly.

Description

Describe the files represented by the dependency variables listed in the command. This string is displayed in the **Files You Can Remove** page of the Removal Wizard.

> **Note** You cannot begin a description with a space. You cannot use a tab character or quotation mark (") anywhere in the string.

Actions

Determine what actions to perform on the files represented by the dependency variables. You can add, modify, or remove actions.

To help ensure that an action is always performed, create a new command in Oclncust.opc and add the command instruction **SAFE** without a list of dependency variables. Actions listed in this command are executed regardless of the values specified in the [Definitions] section.

> **Note** In many actions, you can use a predefined keyword to represent a commonly used folder instead of entering an explicit path. For a list of keywords and corresponding folders, see the **Keywords** section later in this appendix.

Application INI Entry

Specify a section or line to remove from an INI file for any application. Use the following syntax:

```
INI=folder\file,section,key
```

folder	Fully qualified path or predefined folder keyword.
file	INI file name.
section	Section name from the INI file.
key	A line in the INI file that contains this key is deleted. If the key is not present, the entire section is deleted. Optional.

File

Specify files to be removed. Use the following syntax:

```
[KEYWORD][path]\file ["description"]
```

KEYWORD	Predefined folder keyword; optional. Use all uppercase letters. If you enter a partial path without specifying a keyword, the previous keyword is used.
path	A fully qualified path. Optional if the *KEYWORD* value includes the full path.
file	Name of the file to remove.
description	String that describes the file to remove; optional.

In the following example, the action deletes MyTemplate.dot and all batch and bitmap files in the Custom folder under the Microsoft Word 97 folder.

```
WORD97DIR\Custom\MyTemplate.dot
\Custom\*.bat
\Custom\*.bmp
```

Menu Item

Remove an item on the **Start** menu. Use the following syntax:

```
MENU_ITEM=group\item
```

group	Name of the Program\Start Menu group.
item	Item to remove.

Example:

```
MENU_ITEM=Microsoft FrontPage\Personal Web Server
```

Registry Entry

Remove an entry from the Microsoft Windows registry. Use the following syntax:

```
HKxx\key
```

HK*xx*	Top-level registry key, defined as follows: ■ **HKLM** for HKEY_LOCAL_MACHINE ■ **HKCR** for HKEY_CLASSES_ROOT ■ **HKCU** for HKEY_CURRENT_USER ■ **HKUR** for HKEY_USERS
key	Subkey or value entry to remove

Example:

```
HKLM\Software\Microsoft\Windows\Currentversion\Uninstall\WordView
```

> **Note** Dependency variables associated with Office XP and Office 2000 do not list all the registry keys that are removed when Office is removed. During the removal process, Offcln.exe calls Windows Installer to remove the product or application, and Windows Installer automatically deletes the appropriate registry keys.

SharedDLL File

Remove a dynamic-link library (DLL) or other shared file. This action removes the registry entry associated with the application. Use the following syntax:

```
SHAREDDLL=folder\file
```

folder	Predefined folder keyword or fully qualified path for the shared file; stored in the subkey HKEY_LOCAL_MACHINE\Software\Microsoft\Windows\CurrentVersion\SharedDLLs
file	Name of the shared file.

Examples:

```
SHAREDDLL=OFFICE97DIR\msroute.dll
```

```
SHAREDDLL=OFFICE97DIR\hlink.srg
```

```
SHAREDDLL=OFFICE97DIR\osa.exe
```

Shortcut File

Remove a shortcut to a file by deleting the LNK file. You can specify a version number so that only shortcuts to a particular version of the file are removed.

In this action, you specify the target file rather than the LNK file itself; this ensures that shortcuts are removed regardless of how they have been renamed or moved. You can also specify a new Windows Installer component for the LNK file, to update the shortcut instead of removing it.

Use the following syntax:

```
SHORTCUT=folder\target_file | feature | version | component | command line
```

folder	Predefined folder keyword or fully qualified path.
target_file	Name of the target file that the LNK file points to.
feature	Windows Installer feature associated with the file.
version	Version number of the target file. If you specify a version, shortcuts to other versions are not removed.

component	Windows Installer component to which the updated shortcut should point.
command line	Command line included in the LNK file. Offcln.exe removes the LNK file only if it contains this command line.

The following example removes any LNK file in the Start\Programs\Office folder that points to Microsoft Excel 2000:

```
SHORTCUT=SYSMENUPROGRAMSDIR\Office\Excel.exe||9
```

This example finds any LNK file in the Start\Programs\Office folder that points to Excel 2000 and updates it to point to Microsoft Excel 2002.

```
SHORTCUT-SYSMENUPROGRAMSDIR\Office\excel.exe||9|Global Excel Core
```

Special Action

Use predefined special functions to remove files. Use the following syntax:

```
SPECIAL\function
```

Function	Description
RemoveTempFiles	Remove all files from the following temporary folders: Windows\Temp Windows\Tmp %Temp% %Tmp% drive:\Temp drive:\Tmp
RemoveTwiddleTempFiles	Remove all files with a tilde (~) as the first character in the temporary folders listed above.
RemoveOffice95Shortcut LnksAndTmps	Remove LNK, TMP, and PIF files in the Office 95 Shortcut Bar folder.
RemoveDuplicate WWINTL32DLL	Remove Wwintl32.dll from the Windows\System folder if it is also present in the Word 95 folder.

User Modifiable File

Remove an Office file that can be customized by the user, such as a template or sample document. Use the following syntax:

```
USER_MODIFIABLE_FILE=folder\file
```

folder	Predefined folder keyword or fully qualified path.
file	Name of file to remove.

Example:

```
USER_MODIFIABLE_FILE=ACCESS95DIR\samples\orders.mdb
```

Win.ini Entry

Remove a section or key from the Win.ini file. Use the following syntax:

```
Win.ini, section, key
```

section	Win.ini section to remove.
key	A line in Win.ini that contains this key is deleted. If the key is not present, the entire section is removed. Optional.

Keywords

Predefined keywords represent commonly used folders. You can use a keyword instead of an explicit path. Keywords must be entered in all uppercase letters.

Keywords and their corresponding folders are listed in the following table.

Keyword	Folder
ACCESS10DIR	Access 2002 folder
ACCESS9DIR	Access 2000 folder
ACCESS97DIR	Access 97 folder
ACCESS95DIR	Access 95 folder
BOOKS95DIR	Bookshelf® 95 folder
CLIPART97DIR	Office 97 Clip art folder
DMM97DIR	Direct Mail Manager 97 folder
EXCEL10DIR	Excel 2002 folder
EXCEL9DIR	Excel 2000 folder
EXCEL97DIR	Excel 97 folder
EXCEL97VIEWERDIR	Excel 97 Viewer folder
EXCEL95DIR	Excel 95 folder
EXCEL95VIEWERDIR	Excel 95 Viewer folder
FRONTPAGE10DIR	FrontPage® 2002 folder
FRONTPAGE9DIR	FrontPage 2000 folder
FRONTPAGE98DIR	FrontPage 98 folder
FRONTPAGE97DIR	FrontPage 97 folder
FRONTPAGE1XDIR	FrontPage 1.1 folder
IMAGER95DIR	Microsoft Imager 95 folder
MSAPPS9XDIR	Shared application files folder for Office 2000
OFFICE10DIR	Office folder under Office XP folder

Keyword	Folder
OFFICE9DIR	Office folder under Office 2000 folder
OFFICE97DIR	Office folder under Office 97 folder
OFFICE95DIR	Office folder under Office 95 folder
OFFICEROOT10DIR	Office 2002 folder
OFFICEROOT9DIR	Office 2000 folder
OFFICEROOT97DIR	Office 97 folder
OFFICEROOT95DIR	Office 95 folder
OUTLOOK10DIR	Outlook 2002 folder
OUTLOOK9DIR	Outlook 2000 folder
OUTLOOK97DIR	Outlook 97 folder
OUTLOOK9798DIR	Outlook 97 or 98 folder
POWERPOINT10DIR	PowerPoint® 2002 folder
POWERPOINT9DIR	PowerPoint 2000 folder
POWERPOINT97DIR	PowerPoint 97 folder
POWERPOINT97VIEWERDIR	PowerPoint 97 Viewer folder
POWERPOINT95DIR	PowerPoint 95 folder
POWERPOINT95VIEWERDIR	PowerPoint 95 Viewer folder
PUBLISHER10DIR	Publisher 2002 folder
PUBLISHER5DIR	Publisher 5.0 folder
PUBLISHER4DIR	Publisher 4.0 folder
PUBLISHER3DIR	Publisher 3.0 folder
ROOTDIR	Root of all local hard drives.
ROOT97DIR	Root folder of the hard disk containing Office 97
ROOT95DIR	Root folder of the hard disk containing Office 95
SBFM97DIR	Small Business Financial Manager 97 folder
SCHEDULE97DIR	Schedule+ 97 folder
SCHEDULE95DIR	Schedule+ 95 folder
SOUNDS97DIR	Shared sound files folder for Office 97
SOUNDS95DIR	Shared sound files folder for Office 95
SYSAPPDATADIR	Application Data folder
SYSDESKTOPDIR	System and user-specific desktop folders
SYSDIR	Windows System folder
SYSMENUPROGRAMSDIR	Programs folder below Start Menu folder
SYSMENUROOTDIR	Windows Start Menu folder
SYSMENUSTARTUPDIR	Startup folder under Start Menu\Programs folder

Keyword	Folder
SYSPROGRAMFILESDIR	Systems Program Files folder
SYSQLAUNCHDIR	Quick Launch folder
TEMPLATES97DIR	Templates folder for Office 97
WINDIR	Windows root folder
WORD10DIR	Word 2002 folder
WORD9DIR	Word 2000 folder
WORD97DIR	Word 97 folder
WORD97VIEWERDIR	Word 97 Viewer folder
WORD95DIR	Word 95 folder
WORD95IADIR	Word 95 Internet Assistant folder
WORD95VIEWERDIR	Word 95 Viewer folder

Office Profile Wizard

Use the Office Profile Wizard to save and to restore user-defined settings in Microsoft Office 2003 applications. Most user-defined settings can be stored in an Office user profile. When you run the Office Profile Wizard to save a user profile, you create an Office profile settings file (OPS file). You can add an OPS file to a transform to apply the settings during an Office installation. Alternatively, you can run the Profile Wizard separately to restore settings to users' computers after Office is installed.

The sections of this topic include the following:

Save or Restore Settings
Profile Wizard INI files
Command-line options
Settings not captured by the Profile Wizard

Save or Restore Settings

Start the Profile Wizard and specify the mode in which to run it; specify the OPS file to use to save or restore settings. On this page, you can also limit the Profile Wizard to selected Office applications.

Save the settings from this machine

Capture settings from the local computer in an OPS file; equivalent to using **/s** on the command line.

Restore previously saved settings

Restore settings from an OPS file to the local computer; equivalent to using **/r** on the command line.

Reset to defaults before restoring settings

Restore user settings to their default values before applying an OPS file; equivalent to using **/d** on the command line. This option is available only when running the wizard to restore previously saved settings.

Settings File

Specify the OPS file to use for saving or restoring settings.

Select the applications for which you want to save/restore settings

Save or restore settings for only selected applications

Profile Wizard INI files

The Profile Wizard uses the file Opw11adm.ini file to determine which settings to include in the OPS file. The INI file contains a complete set of application settings, registry entries, folders, and files such as templates to capture in the OPS file. However, you can customize Opw11adm.ini to include or exclude particular folders, files, or registry entries in the OPS file.

Open Opw11adm.ini in Notepad or another text editor and add or remove entries in the appropriate sections. For more information about what to include in each section and what syntax to use, as well as examples, see the comments in the INI file. To preserve Opw11adm.ini as a backup, save the customized INI file with a different name.

> **Note**   When you run the Profile Wizard to create an OPS file, use the **/s** command-line option to specify your custom INI file. If you do not specify an INI file on the command line, then the wizard uses Opw11adm.ini.

File/folder sections

Section	Contents
[IncludeFolderTrees]	List of folder trees to include in the OPS file; includes all subfolders in the tree.
[IncludeIndividualFolders]	List of folders to include; does not include subfolders.
[IncludeIndividualFiles]	List of files to include.
[ExcludeFiles]	List of files to exclude from the OPS file.
[FolderTreesToRemoveToResetToDefaults]	List of folder trees to delete before restoring settings from the OPS file; includes subfolders.
[IndividualFilesToRemoveToResetToDefaults]	List of files to delete before restoring settings from the OPS file.
[ExcludeFilesToRemoveToResetToDefaults]	List of files to keep when resetting to default values, regardless of their location.

When you run the Profile Wizard to apply the OPS file to users' computers, files listed in Reset to Defaults sections of the INI file are ignored unless you also select the **Reset to defaults before restoring settings** check box.

Registry sections

Section	Contents
[SubstituteEnvironmentVariables]	List of environment variables to substitute in registry entries; values must take REG_EXPAND_SZ data type.
[IncludeRegistryTrees]	List of registry trees to include; includes all subkeys and values in the tree.
[IncludeIndividualRegistryValues]	List of registry keys to include; includes only values in the key, not subkeys.
[ExcludeRegistryTrees]	List of value entries to include; does not include subkey, but only named value.
[ExcludeIndividualRegistryKeys]	List of registry keys to exclude; excludes all subkeys and values in the tree.
[ExcludeIndividualRegistryValues]	List of value entries to exclude; excludes only values in the key, not subkeys.
[RegistryTreesToRemoveToResetToDefaults]	List of registry trees to delete before restoring settings from the OPS file; deletes subkeys.
[IndividualRegistryValuesToRemoveToReset-ToDefaults]	List of registry values to delete before restoring settings from the OPS file.
[RegistryTreesToExcludeToResetToDefaults]	List of registry trees to keep when resetting to defaults; keeps all subkeys and values in the tree.
[RegistryKeysToExcludeToResetToDefaults]	List of registry keys to keep when resetting to defaults.
[RegistryValuesToExcludeToResetToDefaults]	List of value entries to keep when resetting to defaults; keeps only values, not subkeys.

When you run the Profile Wizard to apply the OPS file to users' computers, registry keys and values listed in Reset to Defaults sections of the INI file are ignored unless you also select the **Reset to defaults before restoring settings** check box.

Command-line options

The Profile Wizard recognizes the following command-line options.

Options for Proflwiz.exe

Option	Definition
/?	Display the command-line syntax for Proflwiz.exe.
/a	Run Proflwiz.exe with the administrator interface (Profile Wizard); use Opw11adm.ini by default.
/u	Run Proflwiz.exe with the user interface (Save My Settings Wizard); use Opw11usr.ini by default.
/q	Run in quiet mode; do not display progress indicators or error messages. Can be used with /**r** or /**s**.
/e	Display error messages; suppress progress indicators. Can be combined with /**p**. Cannot be used with /**q**.
/p	Display progress indicators; suppress error messages. Can be combined with /**e**. Cannot be used with /**q**.
/f	Display completion notice. Can be combined with /**e** or /**p**. Cannot be used with /**q**.
/**i** *<INI file>*	Use specified INI file. If the path or file name contains a space, you must enclose it in quotation marks ("").
/**s** *<OPS file>*	Save settings from local computer to specified OPS file. Cannot be used with /**r**. Displays error messages and progress indicators by default. If the path or file name contains a space, you must enclose it in quotation marks ("").
/**r** *<OPS file>*	Apply settings from specified OPS file to the local computer. Cannot be used with /**s**. Displays error messages and progress indicators by default. If the path or file name contains a space, you must enclose it in quotation marks ("").

> **Important**   If you select a custom INI file in user mode, you cannot use the Save My Settings Wizard to upload an OPS file to the Web. The **Save to the Web** option is disabled for all INI files except the original, unmodified Opw11usr.ini file.

Options for Office applications

Option	Definition
/access	Capture or restore settings for Microsoft Office Access 2003.
/all	Capture or restore settings for all applications, including shared applications.
/common	Capture or restore settings for shared applications.
/d	Set user settings for specified applications to default values; equivalent to the **Reset to defaults before restoring settings** option in the Profile Wizard.
/designer	Capture or restore settings for Forms Designer.
/fp	Capture or restore settings for Microsoft Office FrontPage 2003.
/ol	Capture or restore settings for Microsoft Office Outlook 2003.
/ppt	Capture or restore settings for Microsoft Office PowerPoint 2003.
/project	Capture or restore settings for Microsoft Office Project Professional 2003.
/pub	Capture or restore settings for Microsoft Office Publisher 2003.
/rm	Capture or restore settings for Relationship Manager.
/scribbler	Capture or restore settings for Microsoft Office OneNote™ 2003.
/visio	Capture or restore settings for Microsoft Office Visio® 2003.
/word	Capture or restore settings for Microsoft Office Word 2003.
/xdocs	Capture or restore settings for Microsoft Office InfoPath™ 2003.
/xl	Capture or restore settings for Microsoft Office Excel 2003.

Sample command lines

- Start the Profile Wizard and use the default OPW10adm.ini.

  ```
  ProflWiz.exe /a
  ```

- Start the Save My Settings Wizard and use the default OPW10usr.ini.

  ```
  ProflWiz.exe
  ```

- Start the Profile Wizard, use a custom INI file named Custom.ini to determine which settings to include or exclude, and save the configuration in an OPS file named MyConfig.ops.

  ```
  ProflWiz.exe /a /i Custom.ini /s MyConfig.ops
  ```

- Start the Profile Wizard and restore settings from an OPS file named MyConfig.ops but only settings for Word and Excel. Because only some applications are specified, the user is prompted to confirm.

  ```
  ProflWiz.exe /a /r MyConfig.ops /word /xl
  ```

- Start the Profile Wizard and restore settings from an OPS file named MyConfig.ops quietly, without displaying anything to the user.

```
ProflWiz.exe /a /r MyConfig.ops /q
```

Settings not captured by the Profile Wizard

By design, the Profile Wizard excludes some user-specific settings, such as security settings in Office applications. In addition, the following Outlook settings are not captured in an OPS file:

- Profile settings, including mail server configuration

- Storage settings, such as default delivery location and personal folder files (PST files)

- E-mail accounts and directories (**Tools | Options | Mail Setup | E-mail Accounts**)

- Send/Receive groups (**Tools | Options | Mail Setup | Send/Receive**)

- Customized views; for example, the fields displayed in the Inbox or another folder

- Outlook Bar shortcuts

- Auto-archive options set for a particular folder, which you set by right-clicking the folder, clicking **Properties**, and choosing options in the **AutoArchive** tab

- Delegate options (**Tools | Options | Delegates**)

- **Send Immediately when connected** check box (**Tools | Options | Mail Setup**)

- **When forwarding a message** option (**Tools | Options | Preferences | E-mail Options**)

- **Mark my comments with** option (**Tools | Options | Preferences | E-mail Options**)

- **Request secure receipt for all S/MIME signed messages** check box (**Tools | Options | Security**)

- **Show an additional time zone** check box (**Tools | Options | Preferences | Calendar Options | Time Zone**)

- **Automatically decline recurring meeting requests** check box (**Tools | Options | Preferences | Calendar Options | Resource Scheduling**)

- **Automatically decline conflicting meeting requests** check box (**Tools | Options | Preferences | Calendar Options | Resource Scheduling**)

- **Automatically accept meeting requests and process cancellations** check box (**Tools | Options | Preferences | Calendar Options | Resource Scheduling**)

Office profiles and multiple languages

Office user profiles generated by the Profile Wizard are independent of the operating system—including operating systems in other languages. For example, an OPS file created on Microsoft Windows 2000 (U.S. English version) can be restored to a computer with Microsoft Windows XP (Japanese version).

However, Office user profiles are specific to a particular Office language version. For example, if you create an OPS file in the U.S. English version of Office 2003, it cannot be restored to a computer with the localized German version of Office 2003 installed. (You can, however, restore the OPS file to a computer with the Microsoft Office 2003 Multilingual User Interface Pack (MUI Pack) for German installed, since the MUI Pack works with the core U.S. English version of Office.) There is some overlap between language families. For example, you can restore a U.S. English Office profile to a localized English or Australian version of Office 2003.

This Office language limitation exists because the different Office versions include localized folder names for the folders that contain the Office user profile information.

Glossary

access control list (ACL)   Contains a list of UserIDs or groups and their security permissions. Identifies who can update, modify, or delete an object on a computer or resource on the network.

administrative installation point   Network share from which users install Microsoft Office. Created by running Setup with the **/a** command-line option; contains all the Office files.

administrative rights   Highest level of permissions that can be granted to an account in Microsoft Windows. An administrator can set permissions for other users and create groups and accounts within the domain.

advertise   Windows Installer method for making an application available to the user without installing it. When the user attempts to use the application for the first time, the application is installed and run. Applications can be advertised by using the **/j** command-line option or by using Group Policy software installation. *See also* assign, publish.

assign   Method of installing an application when using Windows 2000 Group Policy software installation. An administrator assigns the application to a user, group, or computer. When the application is selected for the first time, Windows Installer installs the application. Assigning places a shortcut for the assigned application in the **Start** menu. *See also* advertise, publish.

automatic recovery   *See* rollback.

Blocked Senders list   A list of domain names and e-mail addresses that users want to be blocked. E-mail addresses and domain names on this list are always treated as junk e-mail, or spam.

cache   A special memory subsystem in which frequently used data values, such as files that are made available for use offline, are duplicated for quick access.

certificate   A digital means of proving your identity. When you send a digitally signed message you are sending your certificate and public key. Certificates are issued by a certificate authority and, like a driver's license, can expire or be revoked.

certificate authority   An entity, similar to a notary public, that issues digital certificates, keeps track of who is assigned to a certificate, signs certificates to verify their validity, and tracks which certificates are revoked or expired. Before issuing a certificate, the certificate authority requires you to provide identification information. For example, VeriSign, Inc., is a recognized certificate authority.

chaining, chained package   Method used to include additional packages in an Office installation; chained packages are specified in the Setup settings file.

character entity reference   A set of HTML characters that are represented by easy-to-remember mnemonic names.

character set   A grouping of alphabetic, numeric, and other characters that have some relationship in common. For example, the standard ASCII character set includes letters, numbers, symbols, and control codes that make up the ASCII coding scheme. *See also* code page.

child feature   A subordinate feature in the Office feature tree; contained within a parent feature. Setting an installation state for a parent feature can affect the installation state of a child feature.

clear text   Unencrypted, non–machine dependent, ASCII text in readable form.

CMW file   A file created by the Custom Maintenance Wizard. *See also* configuration maintenance file.

code page   Ordered set of characters in which a numeric index (code point) is associated with each character of a particular writing system. There are separate code pages for different writing systems, such as Western European and Cyrillic. *See also* Unicode.

code point   Numeric value in Unicode encoding or in a code page; corresponds to a character. In the Western European code page, 132 is the code point for the letter ä; however, in another code page, the code point 132 might correspond to a different character.

complex script   Writing system based on characters that are composed of multiple glyphs or characters whose shapes depend on adjacent characters. Thai and Arabic use complex scripts. *See also* glyph.

configuration maintenance file   A CMW file created by the Custom Maintenance Wizard; applies changes to feature installation states and other settings after Office is installed.

decrypt   The process of converting cipher (scrambled) text back into plain, readable text. Recipients decrypt (unlock) the e-mail messages, macros, or programs sent to them by using the private key that matches the public key used for encryption.

digital ID   Contains a private key that stays on the originator's computer and a certificate (with a public key). The certificate is sent with digitally signed messages or included with macros or programs. Recipients save the certificate and use the public key to encrypt messages to the sender.

digital signature   Confirms that an e-mail message, macro, or program originated from a trusted source who signed it. Also confirms that the message, macro, or program has not been altered. Includes the signer's certificate (with the public key).

Document libraries   A folder where a collection of files is stored amid the files often using the same template. Each file in a library is associated with user-defined information that is displayed in the content listing for that library.

elevated privileges   In Windows 2000 or later, a method of granting administrator rights to an installation program to modify system areas of the Windows registry or password-secured folders of a hard disk. Can be accomplished by logging on with administrator rights, advertising the program, giving administrator rights to all Windows Installer programs, or using Microsoft Systems Management Server. *See also* advertise.

encryption   The process of encoding data to prevent unauthorized access. An encrypted message is unreadable to all but the recipient, who has a public key that will decrypt it because the key matches the private key that the sender used to encrypt it.

encryption, 128-bit   High level of encryption. Uses a 128-bit key to scramble the contents of a file or data packet to make the data unreadable without the decryption key.

encryption, 40-bit   Low level of encryption. Uses a 40-bit key to scramble the contents of a file or data packet to make the data unreadable without the decryption key.

file allocation table (FAT)   Common file format of file cataloging for Microsoft MS-DOS® and Windows operating systems; physical method of storing and accessing files from a hard disk. The FAT contains a list of all files on the physical or logical drive.

File Folder Tree   A folder tree structure where crash-reporting data from DW.exe is reported. Used as an intermediate storage area so that administrators can review the data before it is submitted to Microsoft.

FrontPage Server Extensions   A set of programs and scripts that support authoring in Microsoft FrontPage and extend the functionality of a Web server.

FTP   File Transfer Protocol. Protocol used to gain remote access to a Web server.

glyph   Shape of a character as rendered by a font. For example, the italic "a" and the roman "a" are different glyphs representing the same alphabetical character.

Group Policy   In Windows 2000 or later, allows administrators to manage users' computer configuration, including installation and maintenance of Office applications. You use Group Policy to define configurations for groups of users and computers, and you can specify settings for registry-based policies, security, software installation, scripts, folder redirection, and remote installation services.

home page   Main page of a Web site. Usually has hyperlinks to other pages, both within and outside the site. One Web site can contain many home pages. For example, the Microsoft home page contains a Products home page, which contains other home pages.

host   The main computer in a system of computers connected by communications links.

hyperlink   Colored and underlined text or a graphic that you click to go to a file, a location in a file, an HTML page on the World Wide Web, or an HTML page on an intranet. Hyperlinks can also go to newsgroups and to Gopher, Telnet, and FTP sites.

ideographic script   Writing system that is based on characters of Chinese origin, where the characters represent words or syllables that are generally used in more than one Asian language.

input locale   Sets what language is currently being entered and how to display it. Usually used in reference to the keyboard, code page, and font configuration of an operating system. *See also* user locale.

Input Method Editor (IME)   Software utility that converts keystrokes to characters in an ideographic script (Korean, Chinese, Japanese, and so on).

installation language   Locale ID (LCID) assigned to the value entry **InstallLanguage** in the Windows registry. Also called the default version of Office. This entry, along with other language settings, determines default behavior of Office applications.

installation state   The installation setting applied to an Office application or feature; determines whether a feature is installed locally, run from the network, installed on demand, not installed, or not available to users.

Internet   Refers to the worldwide collection of networks that use the TCP/IP protocols to communicate with each other. The Internet offers a number of tools, including e-mail messaging, the World Wide Web, and other communication services.

intranet   An internal Web site for an organization.

JavaScript   A cross-platform, World Wide Web scripting language. JavaScript code is inserted directly into an HTML page. JavaScript makes it possible to build Java programs.

Kerberos protocol   A network security protocol that uses cryptography to provide mutual authentication between a client computer and a server or between one server and another before a network connection is opened between them.

Key Management server   The server computer running Microsoft Exchange Server that distributes and keeps track of private keys.

keypath   A file or registry entry listed as part of a component or feature of Office. If missing, triggers a reinstall of that component.

LAN   Local area network. A computer network technology designed to connect computers separated by a short distance. A LAN can be connected to the Internet and used for intranet Web sites.

LDAP   Lightweight Directory Access Protocol. A protocol that provides access to Internet Directories.

local installation source   Installation source on the user's computer created when the user installs Office from the CD or a compressed CD image on the network. Windows Installer uses the local installation source to repair, update, and reinstall Office, minimizing the user's reliance on a network source.

locale   The set of information that corresponds to a given language and country. The code locale setting affects the language of terms, such as keywords, and defines locale-specific settings, such as the date formats and character sorting order.

locale ID (LCID)   A 32-bit value defined by Windows that consists of a language ID, sort ID, and reserved bits. Identifies a particular language. For example, the LCID for U.S. English is 1033 and the LCID for Japanese is 1041.

maintenance mode   Configuration mode of an operating system for installing, updating, or removing applications. An important consideration for Windows NT–based operating systems where users require access to security-related sections of the registry or a hard disk. *See also* elevated privileges.

Meeting Workspace   A Web site for centralizing all the information and materials for a meeting. You use a workspace to publish the agenda, attendee list, and documents you plan to discuss. After the meeting, you use the workspace to publish the meeting results and track tasks. You include a hyperlink that goes to the workspace in the message text when you send a Microsoft Outlook meeting request to invite people to the meeting.

MSDE   Microsoft Data Engine (also known as Microsoft SQL Server 2000 Desktop Engine). A data store based on Microsoft SQL Server technology, but designed and optimized for use on smaller computer systems, such as a single user computer or a small workgroup server.

MSI file   *See* package (MSI file).

MST file   *See* transform (MST file).

Navigation Pane   The column on the left side of the Outlook window that includes panes such as Shortcuts or Mail and the shortcuts or folders within each pane. Click a folder to show the items in the folder.

NetMeeting   Microsoft conferencing software that you can use to communicate by both audio and video, work as a group in Windows-based programs, exchange graphics on an electronic whiteboard, transfer files, or chat by text.

network domain name   A group of users in a network who share a common set of shared resources, such as server disk drives and printers. A large network may have several domains based upon the needs of each set of users.

network place   A folder on a network file server, Web server, or Microsoft Exchange 2000 server. Create a shortcut to a network place to work with files there. Some network places, such as document libraries, have features not available with local folders.

NLS files   National Language Support files. Files that extend the ability of the operating system to support multilingual features.

nonrepudiation   The inability of senders to deny responsibility for their e-mail message, and the inability of recipients to claim they never got the message. Both digital signatures and S/MIME receipts assist in nonrepudiation.

NTFS file system (NTFS)   Designed exclusively for use with the Windows NT operating system. NTFS helps to provide stronger security and more flexible file management methods than does FAT. *See also* file allocation table (FAT).

Office user profile   A collection of user-defined options and settings captured by the Office Profile Wizard in an Office profile settings file (OPS file) and applied to another computer.

Offline Folder file (OST file)   The file on your hard disk that contains offline folders. The offline folder file has an .ost extension. You can create it automatically when you set up Outlook or when you first make a folder available offline.

OPS file   A file created by the Office Profile Wizard. *See also* Office user profile.

package (MSI file)   In Windows Installer, a relational database that contains all the information necessary to install a product. The MSI file associates components with features and contains information that controls the installation process.

Personal Address Book (PAB)   A customizable address book used to store personal e-mail addresses you use frequently. However, Contacts offers more advanced features for this function. Personal Address Book files have a .pab extension and can be copied to the hard disk.

Personal Folders file (PST file)   Data file that stores your messages and other items on your computer. You can assign a PST file to be the default delivery location for e-mail messages. You can use a PST file to organize and back up items for safekeeping.

plug-in language features   User interface, online Help, and editing tools that users can install with Office XP to run Office in the users' own language and to create documents in many other languages.

POP   Post Office Protocol. A common protocol that is used to retrieve e-mail messages from an Internet e-mail server.

private key   The secret key kept on the sender's computer that the sender uses to digitally sign messages to recipients and to decrypt (unlock) messages from recipients. Private keys should be password protected. A message encrypted with someone's public key must be decrypted with that person's corresponding private key. Part of a digital ID.

public key   The key a sender gives to a recipient so that the recipient can verify the sender's signature and confirm that a message or file was not altered. Recipients also use the public key to encrypt (lock) e-mail messages to the sender. Part of a digital ID.

publish   A method of advertising an application by using Windows 2000 Group Policy software installation. A published application is not advertised with shortcuts or **Start** menu icons. Instead, the application is configured to be installed the first time another application requests it, such as when double-clicking a DOC file from Windows Explorer. *See also* advertise, assign.

quiet installation   Also known as unattended installation. An installation run by using the **/q** command-line option that runs without generating any user prompts.

remote procedure call (RPC)   In programming, a request by one program to a second program on a remote system. The second program generally performs a task and returns the results of that task to the first program. For example, Outlook uses remote procedure calls to communicate with Microsoft Exchange Server.

right   File- and folder-level permissions that allow access to a Web site.

roaming user   User who uses more than one computer on a regular basis. Works at multiple sites using multiple computers.

roaming user profiles   Account information established for roaming users, usually within a given domain of a network. Automatically configures the computer when the user logs on.

rollback   A method used by Windows Installer to recover from a failed install. Similar to the rollback definition used in SQL. Consists of storing files, folders, and registry settings marked for deletion in a hidden temporary folder. If a serious error is encountered during the installation of new software, the files, folders, and registry settings are returned to their previous settings (as if the attempted installation never happened).

Safe Recipients list   A list of mailing lists or other subscription domain names and e-mail addresses that users belong to and want to receive messages from. Messages sent to these addresses are not treated as junk e-mail.

Safe Senders list   A list of domain names and e-mail addresses that users want to receive messages from. E-mail addresses in Contacts and in the Global Address Book are included in this list by default.

script   In character sets, a set of characters from a particular writing system, such as Arabic, Cyrillic, Hebrew, or Latin.

scripting language   A programming language designed specifically for Web site programming. Examples include JavaScript and VBScript.

Search Folders   Virtual folders that contain views of all e-mail items matching specific search criteria. The items remain stored in one or more Outlook folders.

Secure Multipurpose Internet Mail Extensions (S/MIME)   Method of security that allows users to exchange encrypted and digitally signed messages with any S/MIME-compliant mail reader. Messages are encrypted or digitally signed by the sending client and decrypted by the recipient.

Secure Sockets Layer   A proposed open standard that was developed by Netscape Communications for establishing a secure communications channel to help prevent the interception of critical information, such as credit card numbers.

security labels   An Outlook feature that allows you to add information to a message header about the sensitivity of the message content. The label can also restrict which recipients can open, forward, or send the message.

Setup settings file   An INI file, such as Setup.ini, read by Setup.exe at the start of the installation process; contains properties that help to control the installation process.

S/MIME receipts   An e-mail security feature used to request confirmation that a message was received unaltered, and information about who opened the message and when it was opened. When you send a message with an S/MIME receipt request, this verification information is returned as a message to your Inbox.

SMTP mail server   An e-mail server that uses the Simple Mail Transfer Protocol. SMTP is available with Windows NT Server 4.0 and Windows 2000 Server.

SQL server   A network or Web server that uses the standardized query language protocol for requesting information from a database. More commonly, a computer with an installed configuration of Microsoft SQL Server with a configured database that is available from a network location.

system locale   In Windows NT and Windows 2000, the setting that determines the code page and default input locale. *See also* code page, input locale, user locale.

transform (MST file)   In Windows Installer, a relational database that contains information about components, features, and Setup properties. A transform is based on a particular package and contains the modifications to apply to that package during installation. You use the Custom Installation Wizard to create transforms for Office.

traveling user   Uses more than one computer on a regular basis, often a portable computer the user takes to different locations. Traveling users might have different language requirements or need access to different configurations of the same application (local or remote). *See also* roaming user.

Unicode   Universal character set designed to accommodate all known scripts. Unlike most code pages, Unicode uses a unique two-byte encoding for every character, also known as double byte character set (DBCS). Unicode is a registered trademark of Unicode, Inc.

URL   Uniform Resource Locator. An address that specifies a protocol (such as HTTP or FTP) and a location of an object, document, World Wide Web page, or other destination on the Internet or an intranet. Example: http://www.microsoft.com/.

user locale   Setting that determines formats and sort orders for date, time, currency, and so on. Also known as regional settings. *See also* input locale.

VBScript (Microsoft Visual Basic Scripting Edition)   A subset of the Visual Basic for Applications programming language optimized for Web-related programming. As with Java-Script, code for VBScript is embedded in HTML documents.

vCard   The Internet standard for creating and sharing virtual business cards.

virtual server   A virtual computer that resides on an HTTP server but appears to the user as a separate HTTP server. Several virtual servers can reside on one computer, each capable of running its own programs and each with individualized access to input and peripheral devices. Each virtual server has its own domain name and IP address and appears to the user as an individual Web site or FTP site.

Web query   In Microsoft Excel, a query that retrieves data stored on your intranet or the Internet.

Web server   A computer that hosts Web pages and responds to requests from browsers. Also known as an HTTP server, a Web server stores files whose URLs begin with http://.

Windows Installer shortcut   An application shortcut that supports Windows Installer install-on-demand functionality. On Windows NT 4.0, requires the Windows Desktop Update. *See also* advertise, assign, publish.

Index

Get a **Free**
e-mail newsletter, updates,
special offers, links to related books,
and more when you
register online!

Register your Microsoft Press® title on our Web site and you'll get a FREE subscription to our e-mail newsletter, *Microsoft Press Book Connections*. You'll find out about newly released and upcoming books and learning tools, online events, software downloads, special offers and coupons for Microsoft Press customers, and information about major Microsoft® product releases. You can also read useful additional information about all the titles we publish, such as detailed book descriptions, tables of contents and indexes, sample chapters, links to related books and book series, author biographies, and reviews by other customers.

Registration is easy. Just visit this Web page and fill in your information:

http://www.microsoft.com/mspress/register

Microsoft®

- -

Proof of Purchase

Use this page as proof of purchase if participating in a promotion or rebate offer on this title. Proof of purchase must be used in conjunction with other proof(s) of payment such as your dated sales receipt—see offer details.

Microsoft® Office 2003 Editions Resource Kit

0-7356-1880-1

CUSTOMER NAME

Microsoft Press, PO Box 97017, Redmond, WA 98073-9830

System Requirements

To use the *Microsoft® Office 2003 Editions Resource Kit* tools and documentation you need a computer that meets the requirements of Office 2003 Editions.

All Microsoft Office editions in the 2003 release have approximately the same minimum system requirements.

Processor	Pentium 233 MHz or higher processor; Pentium III recommended
Operating system	Microsoft Windows® 2000 Service Pack 3 or later, or Windows XP or later (recommended)
Memory	64 MB RAM (minimum); 128 MB RAM (recommended)
Monitor	Super VGA™ (800 x 600) or higher resolution with 256 colors
Disk drive	CD-ROM drive
Pointing device	Microsoft Mouse, Microsoft IntelliMouse®, or compatible pointing device

Note None of the Microsoft Office editions in the 2003 release run on the Microsoft Windows Millennium Edition, Windows 98, or Windows NT® operating systems. If any client computers are currently running one of these operating systems, you must upgrade the operating system before installing Microsoft Office.